SHOE LUST

SCHUH-LUST
DÉSIR DE CHAUSSURES

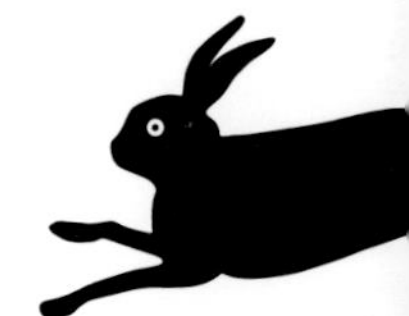

THE PEPIN PRESS

COLOPHON

The Pepin Press BV
P.O. Box 10349
1001 EH Amsterdam, The Netherlands
mail@pepinpress.com
www.pepinpress.com

ISBN 978 90 5496 170 3

Concept by
Pepin van Roojen

Collected by
María del Rosario González y Santeiro
Jorge Margolles Garrote

Edited by
Antonia Edwards

Graphic design by
Maria da Gandra
Maaike van Neck

This book is produced by The Pepin Press
in Amsterdam and Singapore.

Printed and bound in Singapore

SHOE LUST

Shoe Lust contains a beautifully presented collection of works by shoe designers from around the world. With an aim to showcase some of the best examples of extraordinary, cutting edge shoe design, we have selected thirty contemporary designers for their innovation, artistic integrity and ability to push the boundaries of traditional shoe making. Through a stunning collection of photographs alongside profiles and interviews, Shoe Lust reveals the inspiration, design philosophy and creative processes of each designer. From sculptural, conceptual and wearable art to shoes that draw on timeless, leatherwork traditions, all demonstrate an experimental and daring approach to materials and subject matter. Other titles available in this series include Exceptional Jewellery and Avant Garde Bags.

SCHUH-LUST

Schuh-Lust bietet eine faszinierend präsentierte Kollektion mit Arbeiten von Schuhdesignern aus aller Welt. Wir stellen die besten Beispiele für außergewöhnliches, avantgardistisches Schuhdesign vor und haben dafür 30 aktuelle Designer nach ihrer Innovativität, ihrer künstlerischen Authentizität und ihrer Fähigkeit ausgewählt, neue Maßstäbe in der traditionellen Schuhhandwerkskunst zu setzen. Fantastische Fotos, Künstlerprofile und Interviews geben Einblick in die Inspiration, die gestalterische Philosophie und die kreativen Prozesse jedes einzelnen Designers. Allen gemeinsam ist der experimentierfreudige, mutige Umgang mit den Materialien und Sujets - ganz gleich, ob es nun um skulpturale und konzeptuelle Kunstobjekte zum Tragen geht oder um zeitlose Schuhdesigns in der Tradition des Lederhandwerks. Weitere Bände aus dieser Reihe sind Schmuck spektakulär und Avantgarde-Taschen.

DÉSIR DE CHAUSSURES

L'ouvrage Désir de chaussures renferme une collection magnifiquement présentée d'œuvres de créateurs de chaussures à travers le monde entier. Dans le but de présenter quelques-uns des meilleurs exemples de design moderne, nous avons sélectionné trente créateurs contemporains pour leur innovation, leur intégrité artistique et leur capacité à repousser les limites de la création traditionnelle de chaussures. À travers une collection de photos étonnante, ainsi que des profils et des interviews, l'ouvrage Désir de chaussures révèle l'inspiration, la philosophie et le processus créatifs de chaque créateur. Utilisant aussi bien l'art sculptural, conceptuel et mettable que les traditions intemporelles de la maroquinerie, tous démontrent une approche expérimentale et audacieuse quant aux matériaux et aux thèmes qu'ils abordent. D'autres titres sont disponibles dans cette série : Bijoux d'exception et Sacs d'avant-garde.

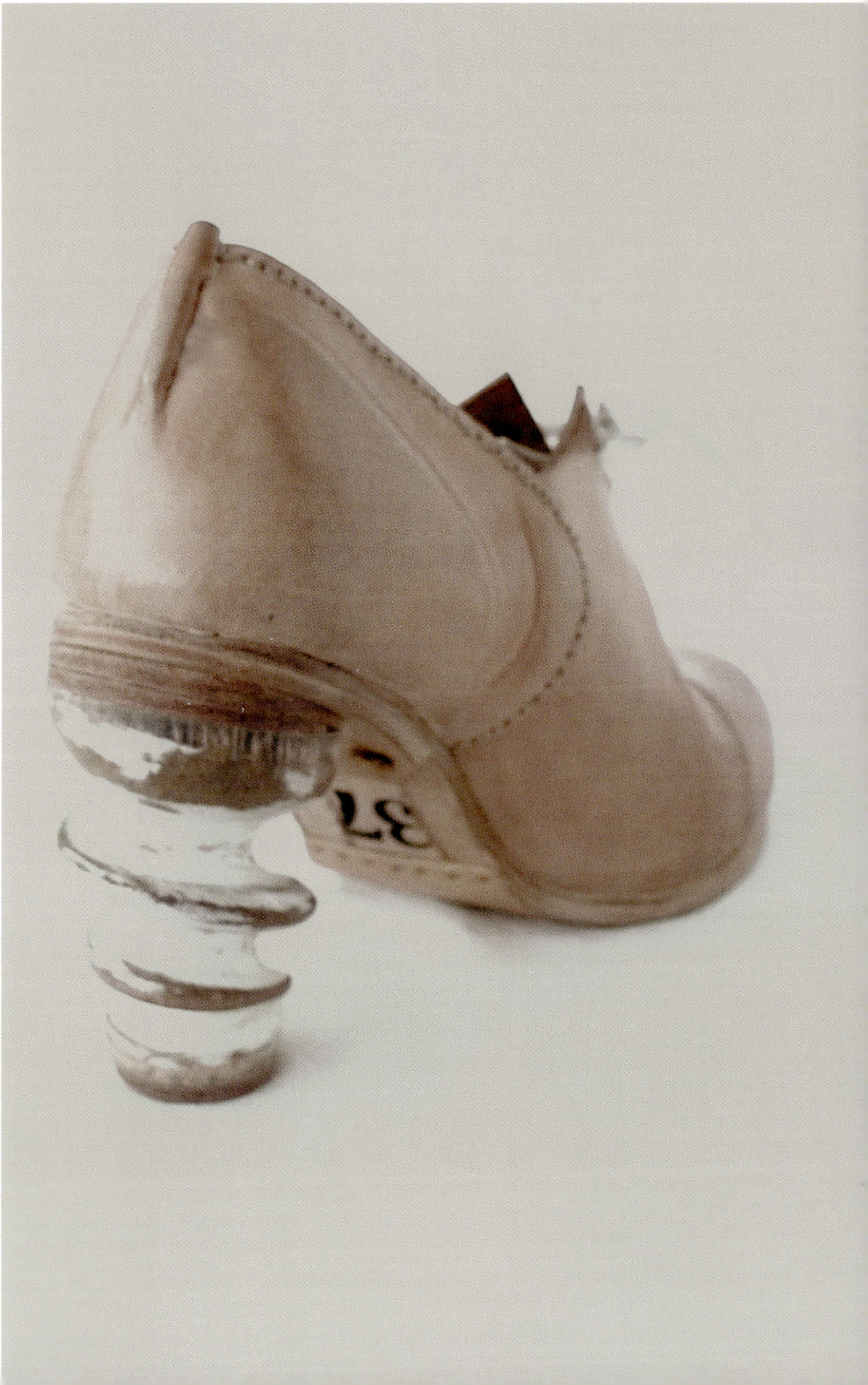

Miguel Muñoz Wilson, Munoz Vrandecic.

CONTENTS

PHOTOGRAPHY CREDITS

Product names included when provided by the designers. All images supplied by the designers.

ANTASTASIA RADEVICH Photography by Charl Marais.

ANDREIA CHAVES Not provided.

AOI KOTSUHIROI Photography © Aoi Kotsuhiroi

BEHNAZ KANANI Photography by Reza Kanani.

MDOT, BOOJI Portrait shot by Jason Bass, all product shots by Mdot.

JUNJI KOIKE, CHRISTIAN PEAU Photography by Jin Studio.

CIPHER Portrait shot by Laurent Segretier, all product shots by Henry Temple and Gareth Joe.

ELIA MAURIZI Not provided.

ERÏK BJERKESJÖ Photography by Philip Karlberg (pp.78-81).

FLUEVOG Photography by John Fluevog Shoes.

GEORGIA TURRI, GEORGIA TURRI/GETU Portrait shot by Yoshie Nishikawa (www.yoshienishikawa.com), still life photos by Lorenzo Di Nozzi (www.lorenzodinozzi.com).

GIENCHI Photography by Yuri Catania.

GIO METODIEV, GIO DIEV Portrait shot by Laurent Elie Badessi, product shots by White Honey.

HEAVY MACHINE Product shots by Steven Lin, naked shots by Matteo Cibic.

JAN JANSEN Portrait shot by Joost vanManen, product shots by Joost Guntenaar.

JEROME C. ROUSSEAU © Jerome C. Rousseau.

JOANNE STOKER S/S 2012 Collection photography and styling by Sasha Rianbow (www.sasharainbow.com). S/S and A/W 2011 Collections by Thomas Kinghts (www.thomasknights.com), styling by Sasha Rainbow.

KEI KAGAMI Portrait shot by © Kei Kagami, product shots by © Martin Kullik. Special thanks to Steinbeisser (www.steinbeisser.org).

KRON BY KRONKRON Photography by Saga Sigurdardottir.

LIAM FAHY Not provided.

MELISSA Photography by Melissa Shoes Archive.

MIGUEL MUÑOZ WILSON, MUNOZ VRANDECIC Photography by © muñozvrandecic.

ENRIQUE CORBI, N.D.C. MADE BY HAND Photography by Hendrik Boxy.

NINA HJORTH Photography by Julian Meagher.

DOMINIKA NOWAK, NUNC Photography © Nunc.

PHONG CHI LAI Photography by Peter Ryle (www.peterryle.com) (pp.236-239 and pp.242-243). Colour shots by Ren Hodgeson (pp.240-241). Photography by Freya Esders (p.244).

DAITA KIMURA, THE OLD CURIOSITY SHOP Photography by The Old Curiosity Shop.

TRACEY NEULS Photography by Uli Schade.

ANGELA SPIETH AND MICHAEL OEHLER, TRIPPEN Photography by © Juergen Holzenleuchter, Ottensoos.

REM D KOOLHAAS AND GALAHAD CLARK, UNITED NUDE Photography by United Nude.

ZJEF VAN BEZOUW, ZJEFWORKS Not provided.

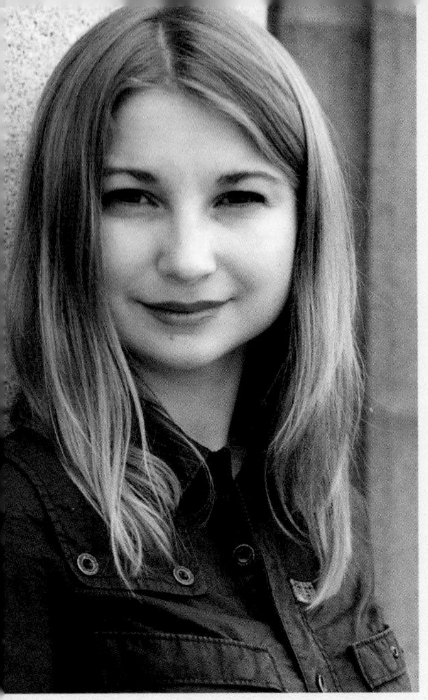

ANASTASIA RADEVICH

Please introduce yourself. **I AM A CANADIAN FOOTWEAR DESIGNER OF BELARUSIAN ORIGIN.** How did you get started? **I GREW UP IN A FAMILY OF SHOE DESIGNERS AND WAS SURROUNDED BY CREATIVITY AND THE SMELL OF LEATHER FROM CHILDHOOD.** What is your work about? **EXPRESSION OF IDEAS AND FEELINGS.** What do you consider your most innovative design so far? **THE KINETIK COLLECTION WAS A HUGE CHALLENGE. IT WAS UNREALISTIC FOR QUITE A WHILE AND I WENT THROUGH MANY BATTLES TO MAKE IT WORK.** How would you describe the design process? **SKETCHES, STORIES, DIVING INTO THE ATMOSPHERE OF THE COLLECTION FOLLOWED BY HARD WORK IN MAKING IT HAPPEN.** What are the most and least gratifying stages of the creative process? **A LOT OF EXPERIMENTATION AND CRAFTING GOES ON BEFORE GETTING BEAUTIFUL RESULTS. WHENEVER I FAIL TO ACHIEVE SOMETHING I BRAINSTORM UNTIL I FIND A SOLUTION AND THE MOST GRATIFYING MOMENT IS WHEN YOU FIND ONE. THE LEAST GRATIFYING PART IS WHEN YOU USE MATERIALS THAT ARE VERY EXPENSIVE AND END UP THROWING AWAY THE RESULTS.** Name one of your heroes. **AYRTON SENNA.** What would be your colour of choice for an important piece? **SKY BLUE.** What role does your work play in your life? **IT DRIVES ME CRAZY AND KEEPS ME FIT. MY MIND NEVER SLEEPS.** How do you view the state of your profession in general? **THE CURRENT STATE OF SHOEMAKING IS POLARISED. ON THE ONE HAND THERE ARE LESS AND LESS ARTISANS, ON THE OTHER, TECHNOLOGY IS EVOLVING AND IS PROVIDING BETTER SOLUTIONS IN SHOEMAKING.** What do you consider vulgar and what elegant? **POLITICS IS VULGAR, THE UNIVERSE IS ELEGANT.** What does beauty mean to you? **SOMETHING TRUE, UNIQUE, BALANCED AND AT PEACE WITH ITSELF.**

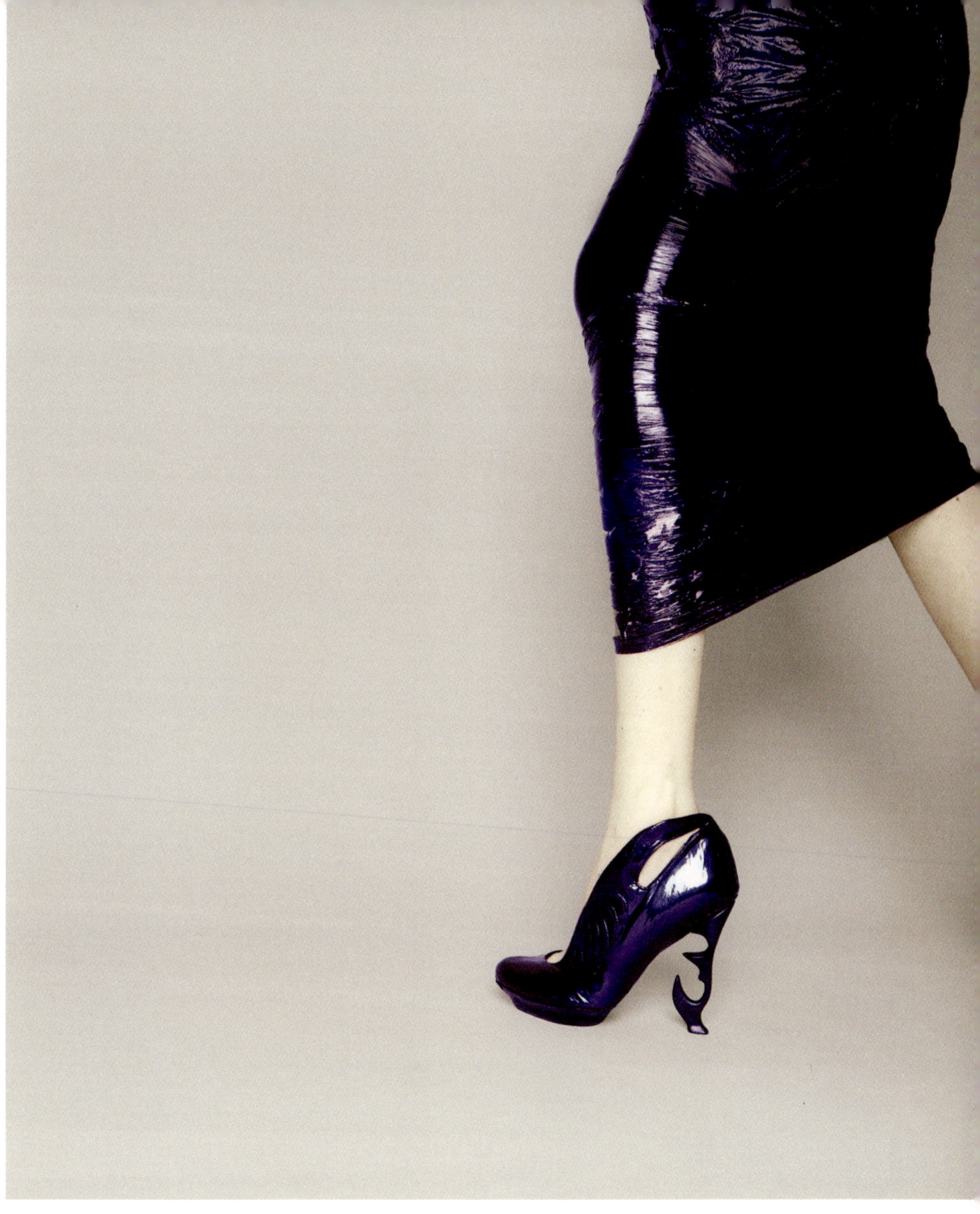

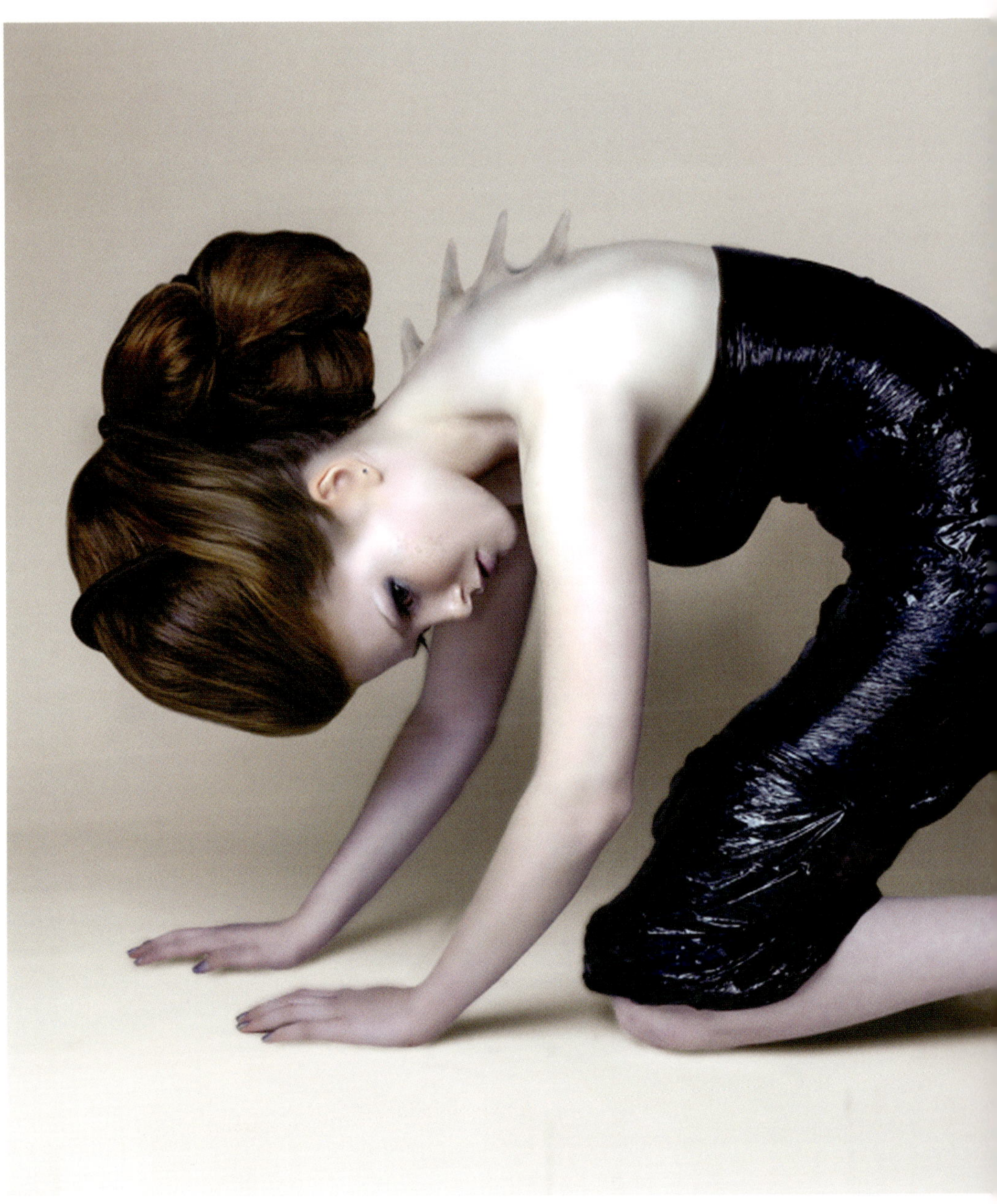

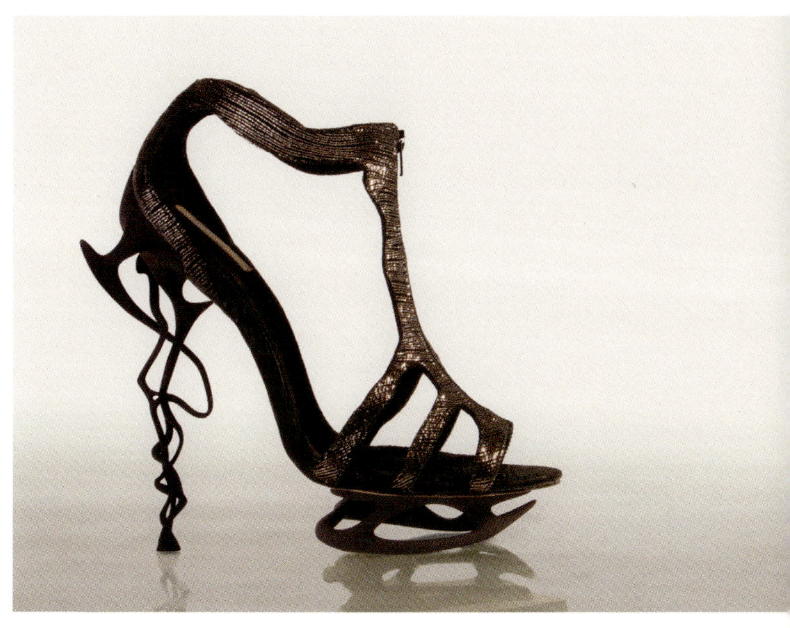

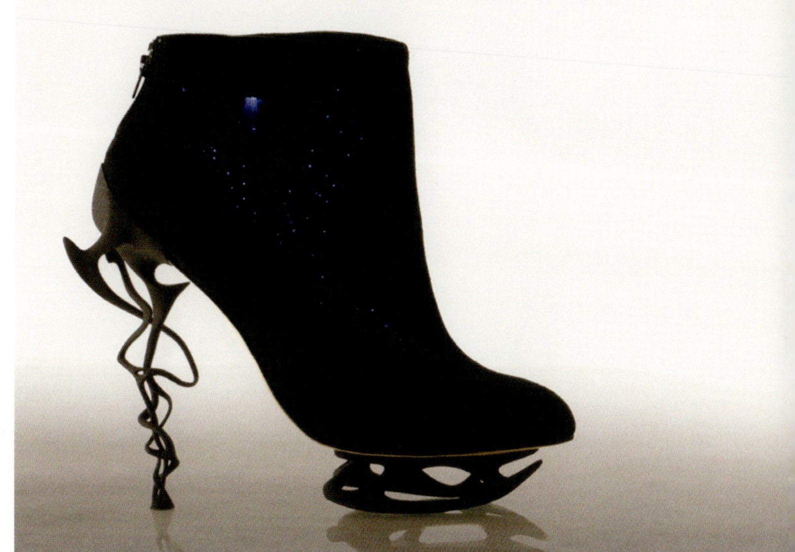

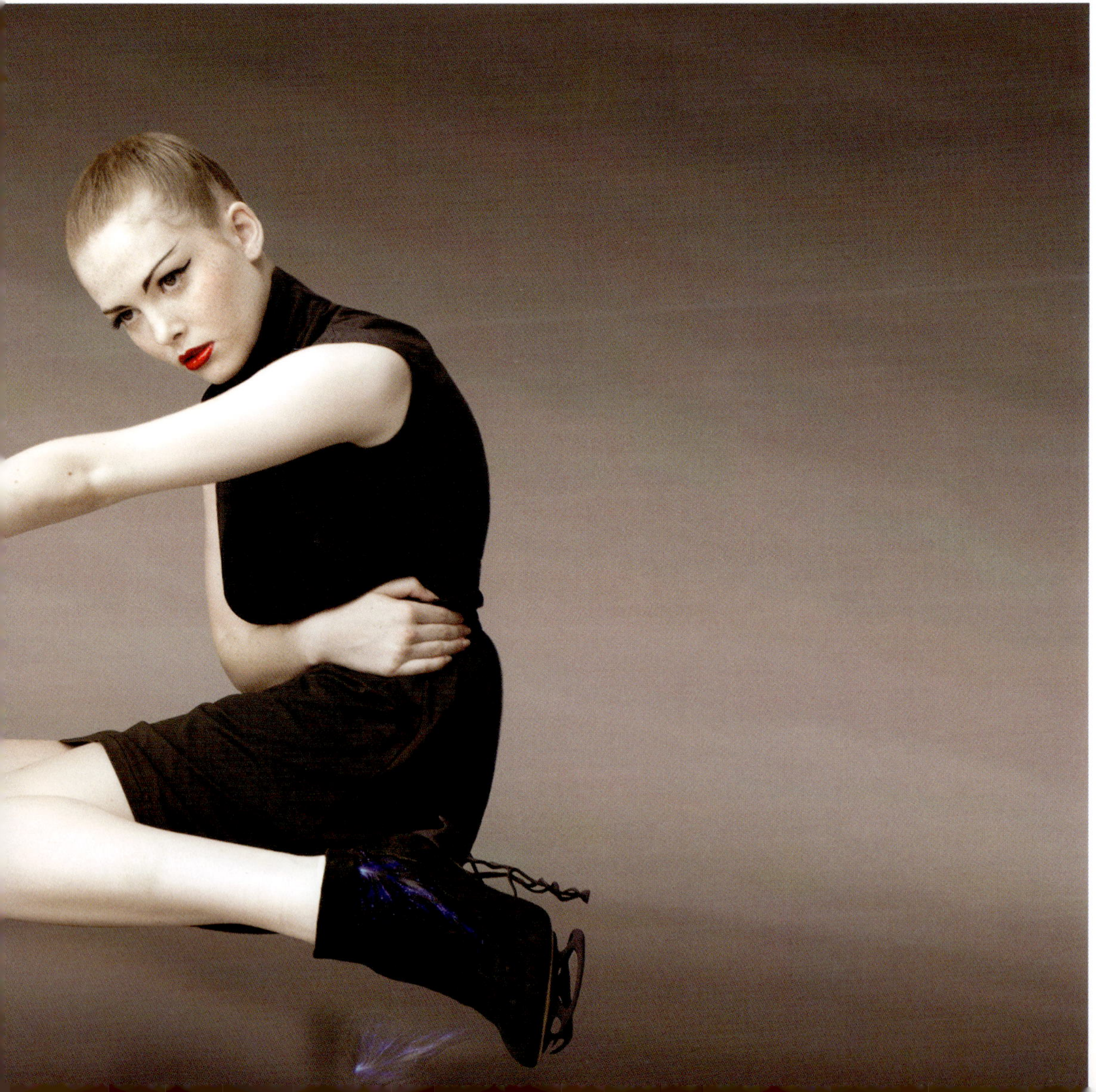

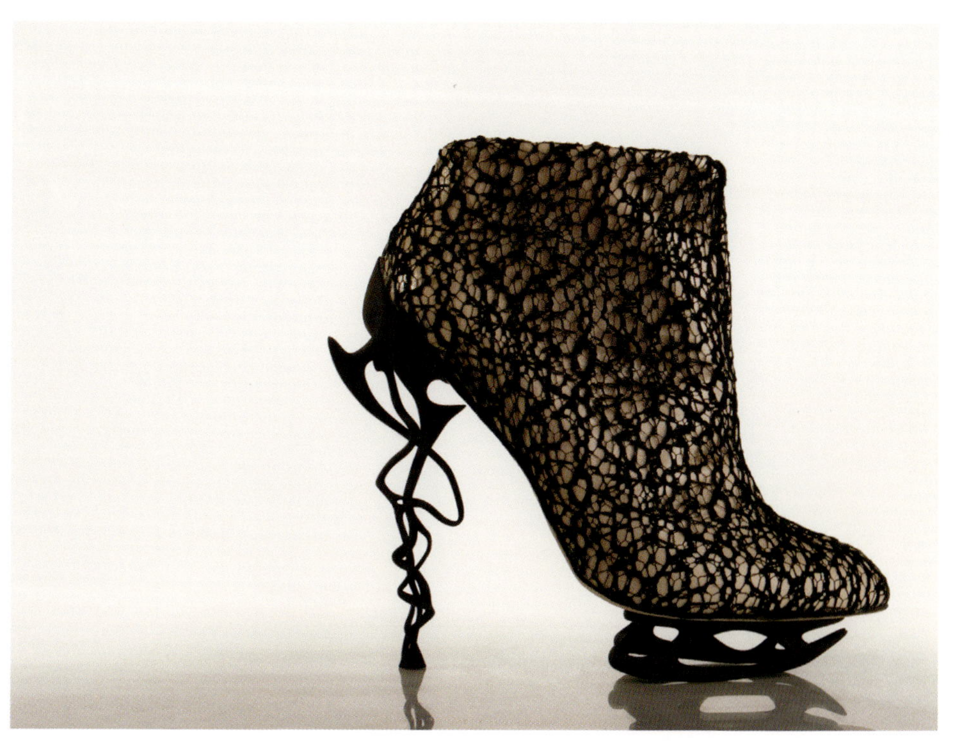

ANTASTASIA RADEVICH

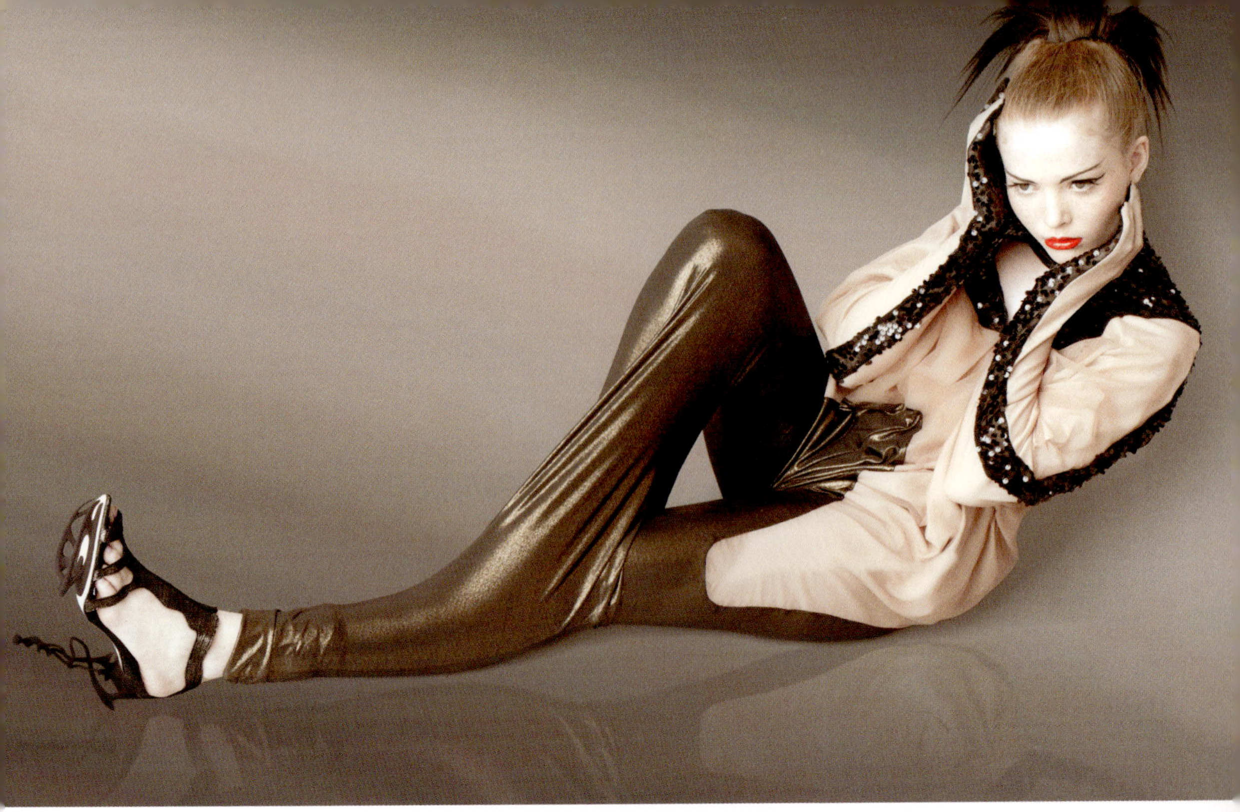

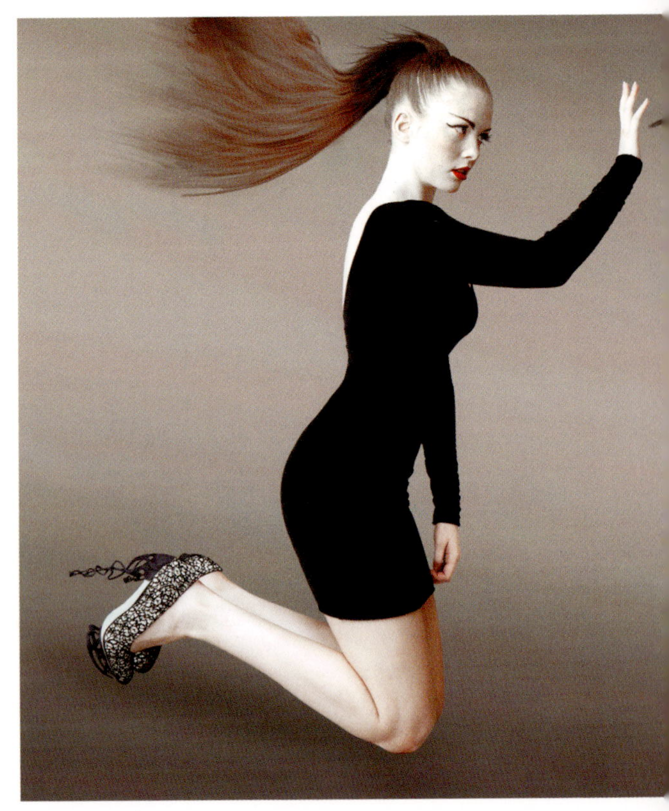

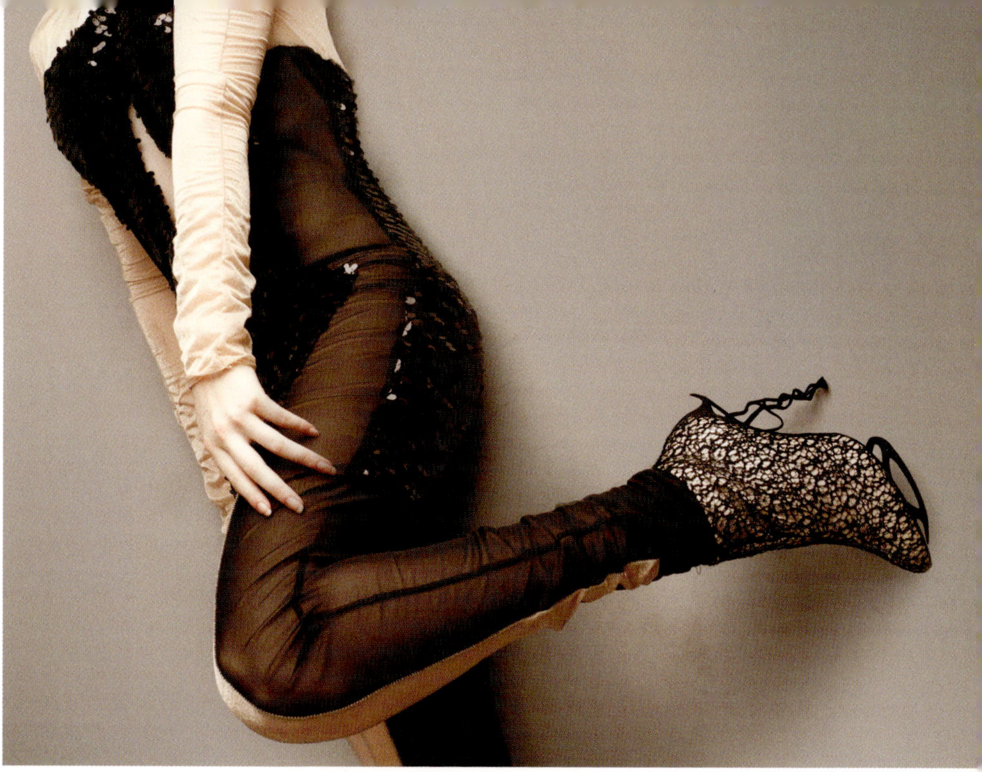

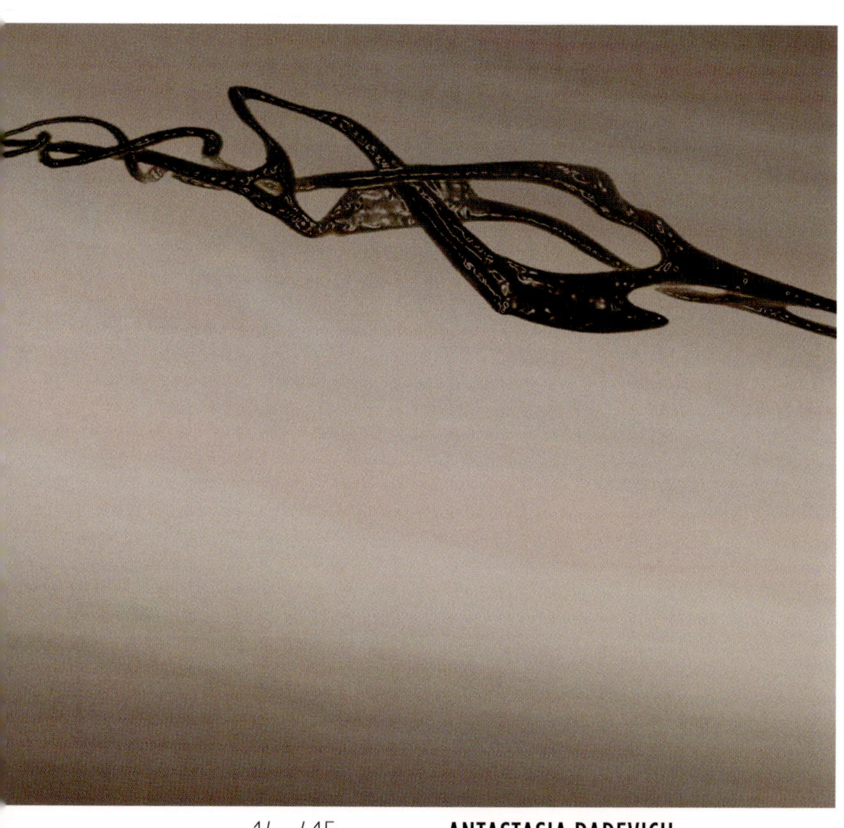

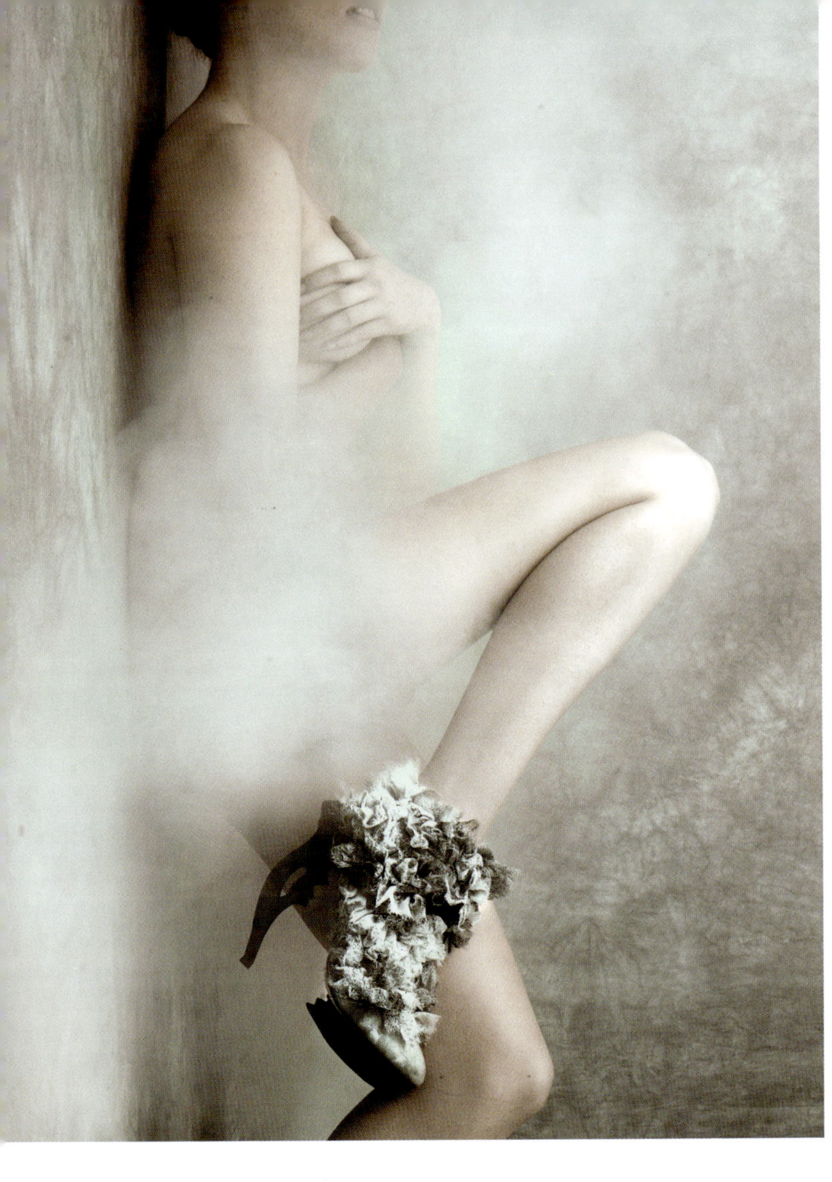

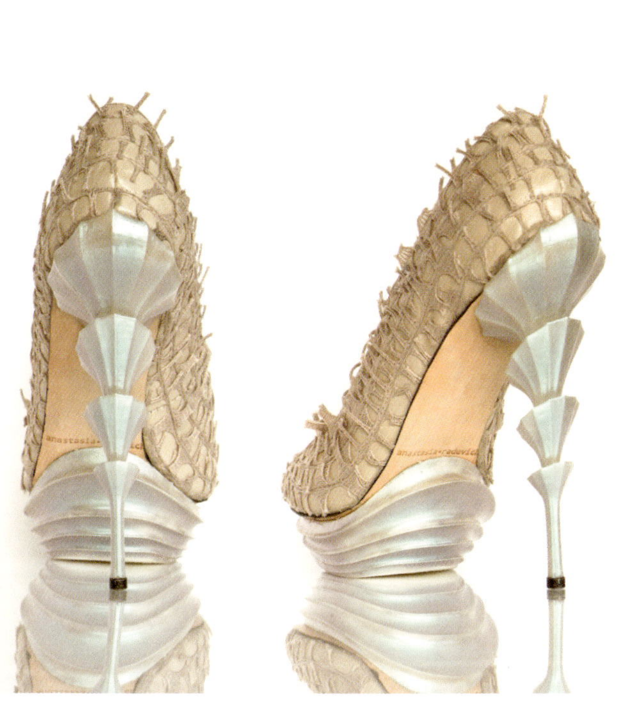

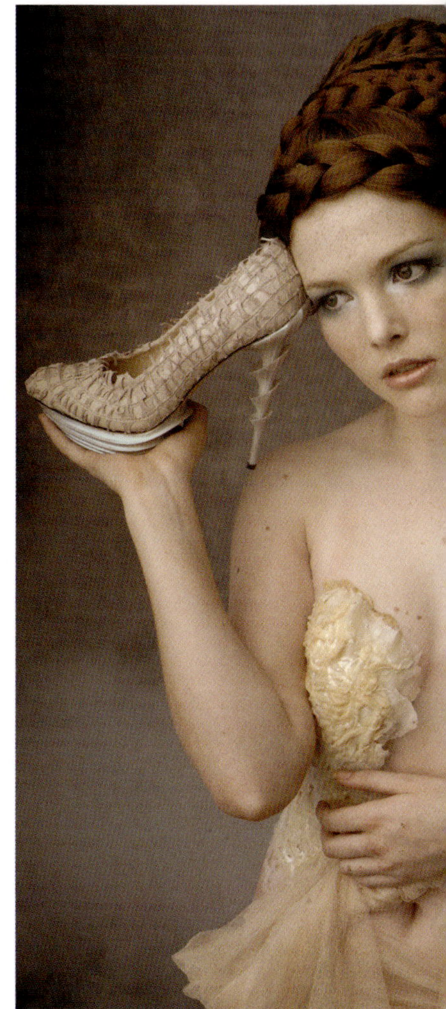

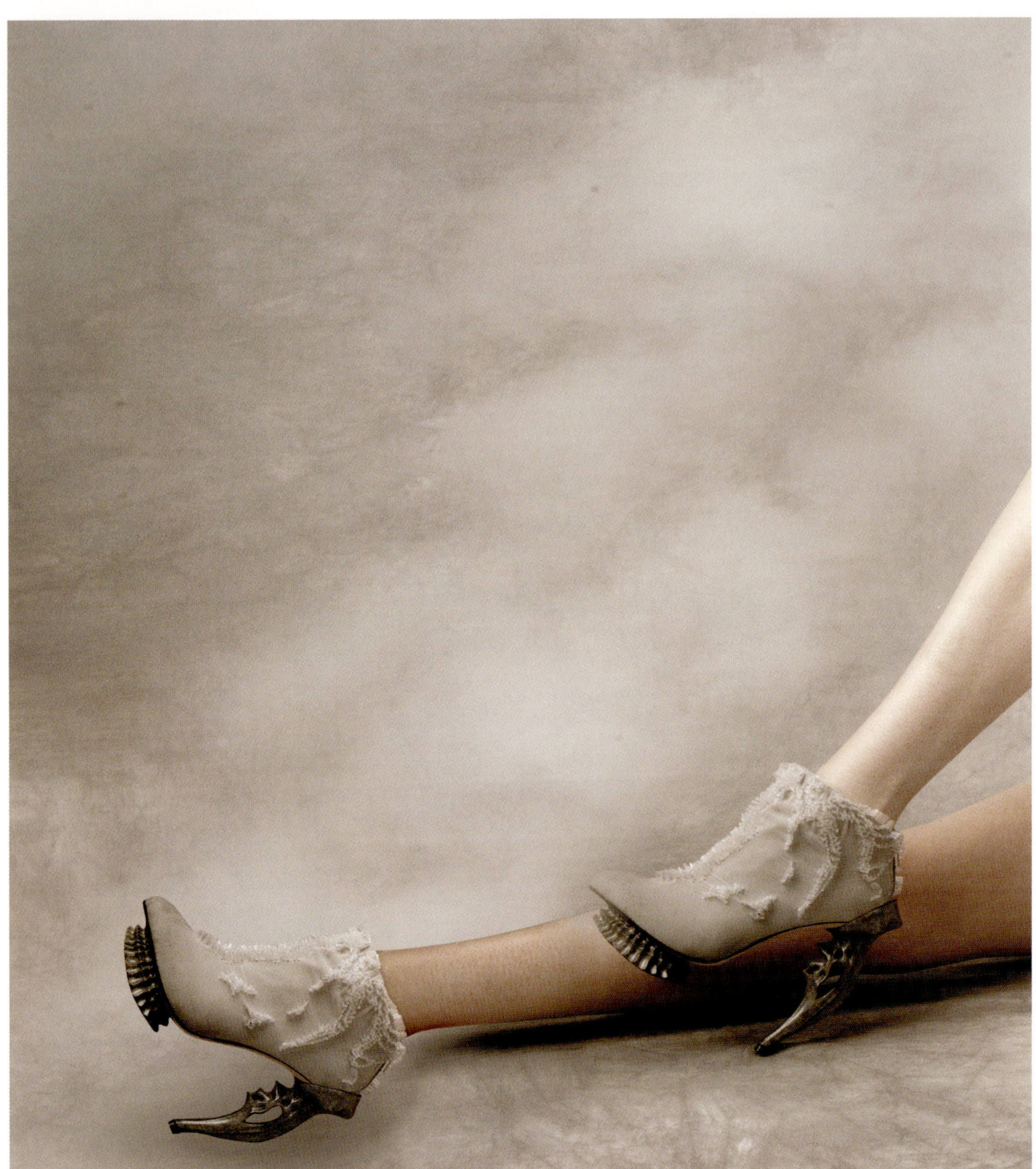

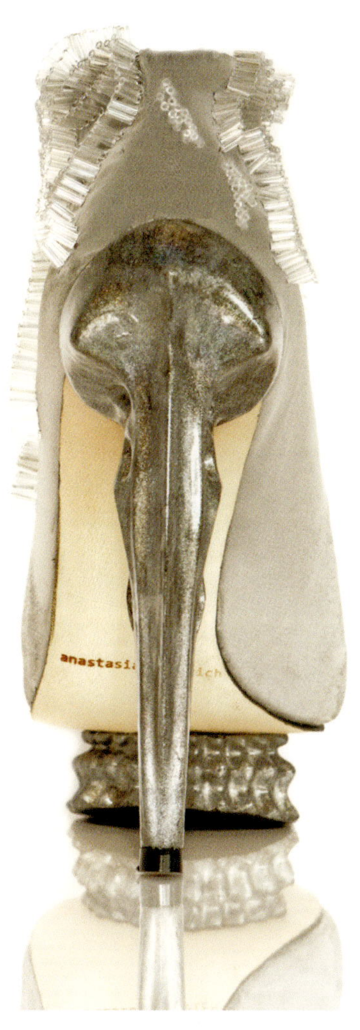
anastasia

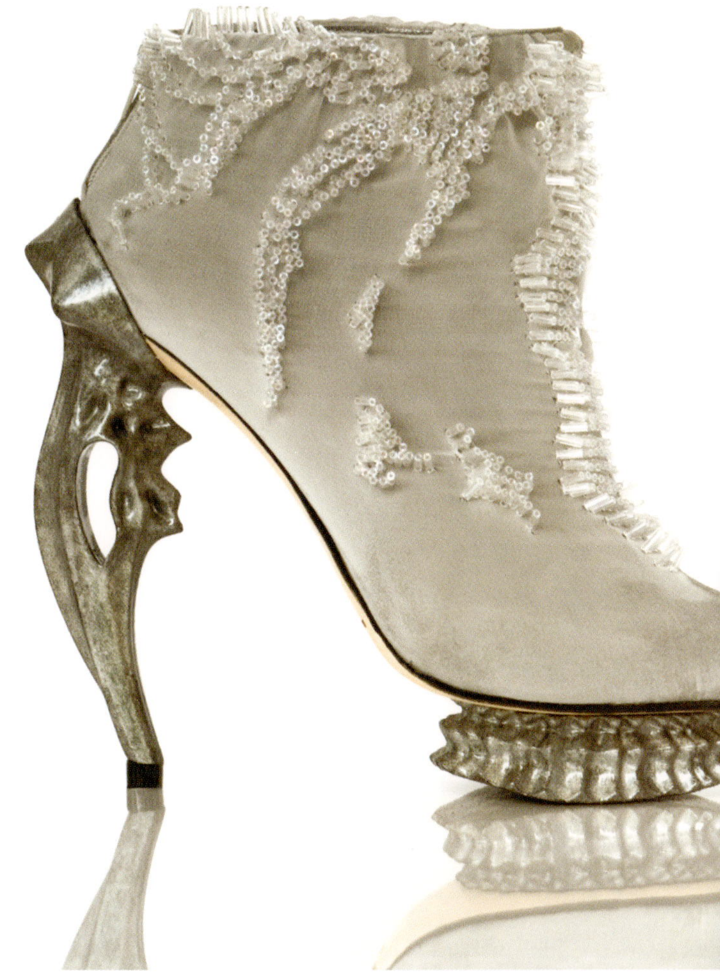

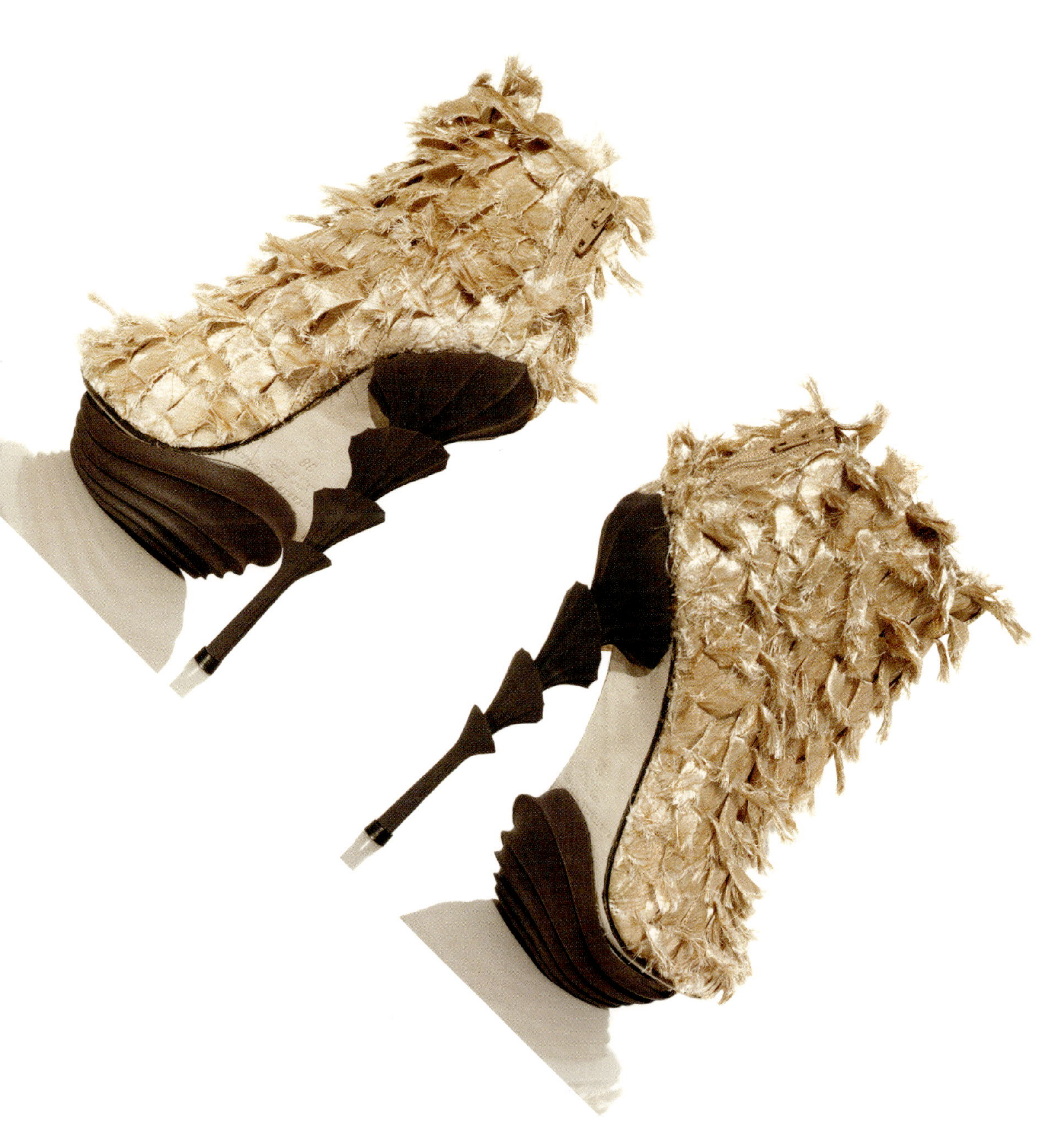

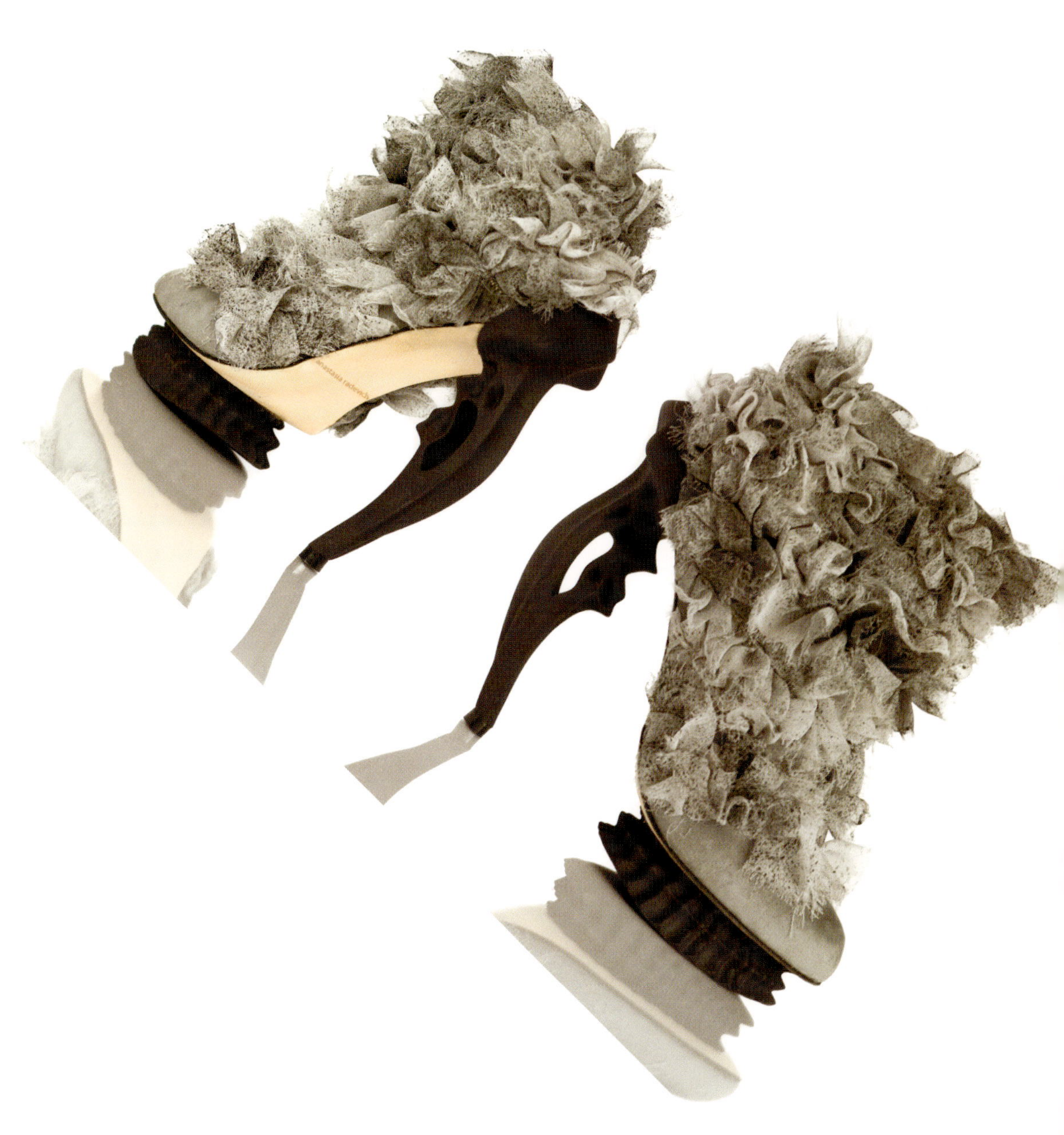

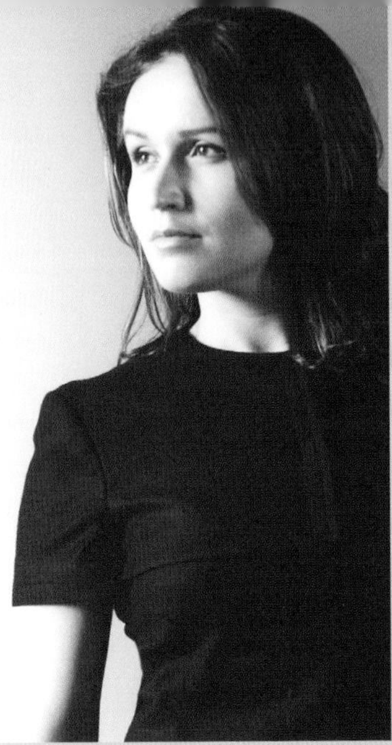

ANDREIA CHAVES

I am originally from San Paulo, Brazil and studied at Polimoda Fashion Institute in Florence, Italy. I work between Italy and Ireland. My ambition is to bring a fresh perspective to fashion by fusing the mastery and traditions of making with 21st-century technology. **MY LIMITED EDITION INVISIBLE SHOE SERIES IS HANDMADE IN ITALY USING A COMBINATION OF LEATHER MAKING TECHNIQUES AND ADVANCED 3D PRINTING TECHNOLOGY. FOR THIS PROJECT I HAVE ALSO COLLABORATED WITH THE DUTCH COMPANY FOC (FREEDOM OF CREATION).** The collection is a study of optical effects which are applied to shoe design. The series explores the concept of invisibility though the chameleon effect. The shoe's reflective finished surfaces create an obscured optical effect that changes with every step taken. Following on from the shoe's primary function of protecting the feet, this innovative design concept draws on the idea of protection through camouflage.

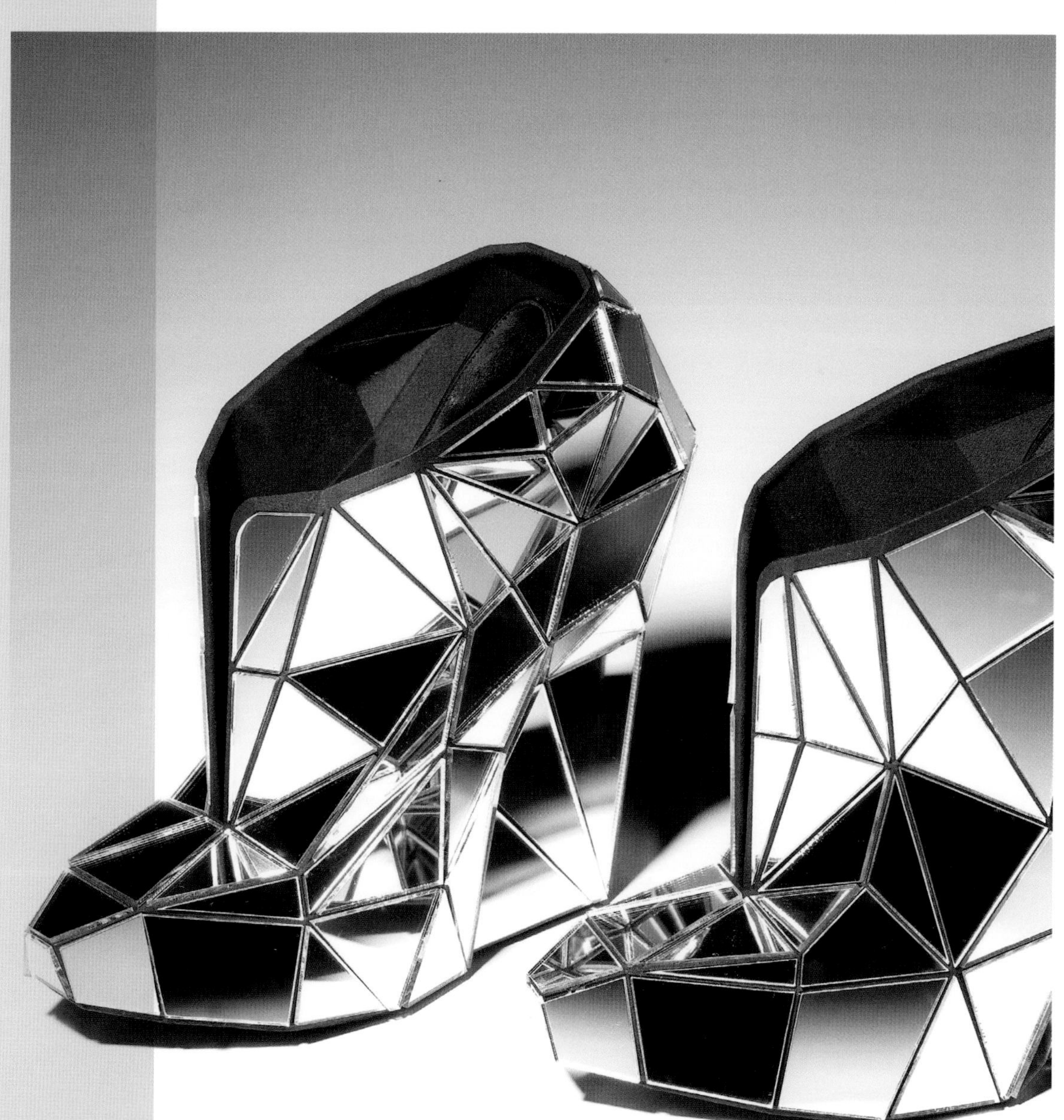

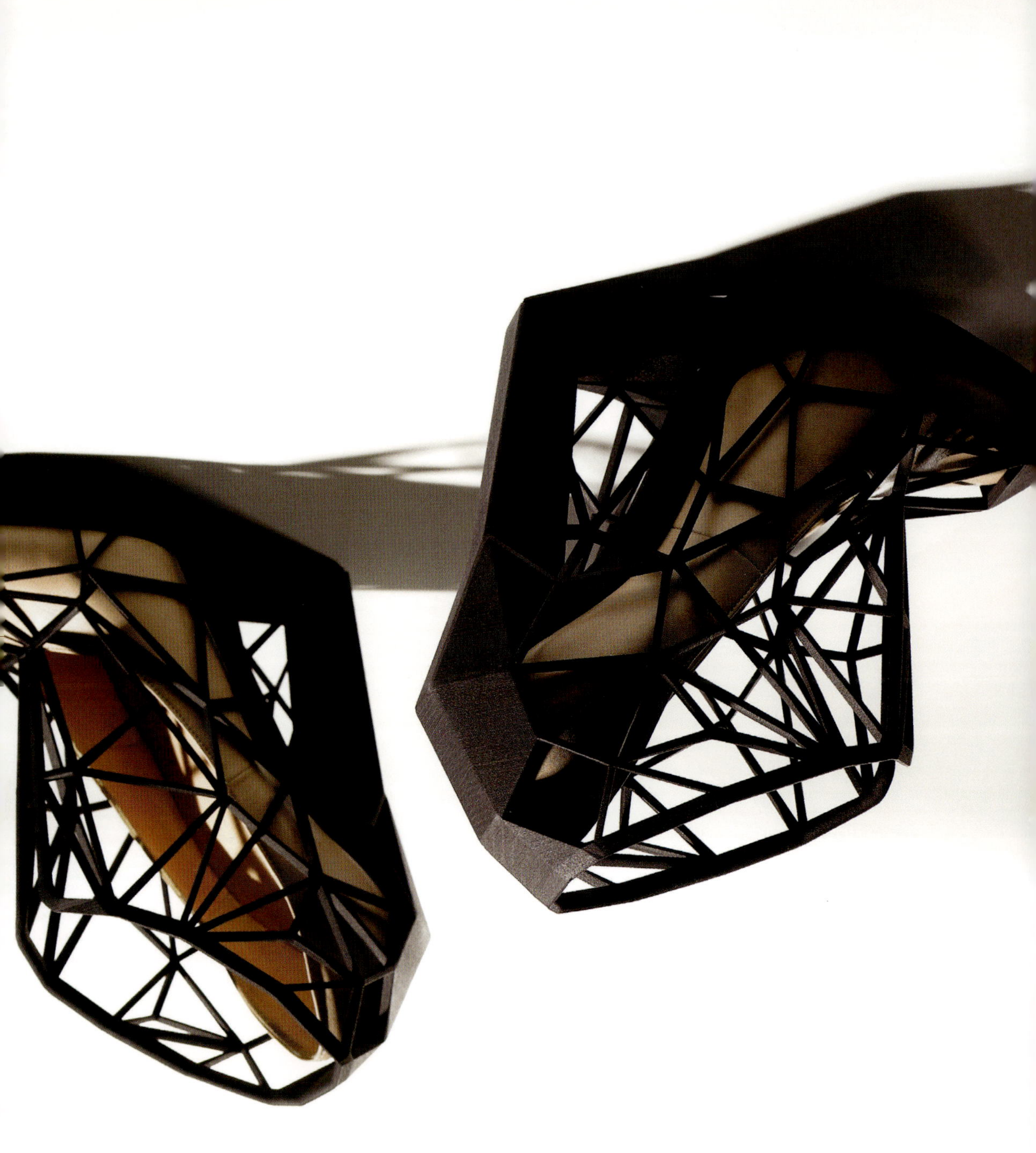

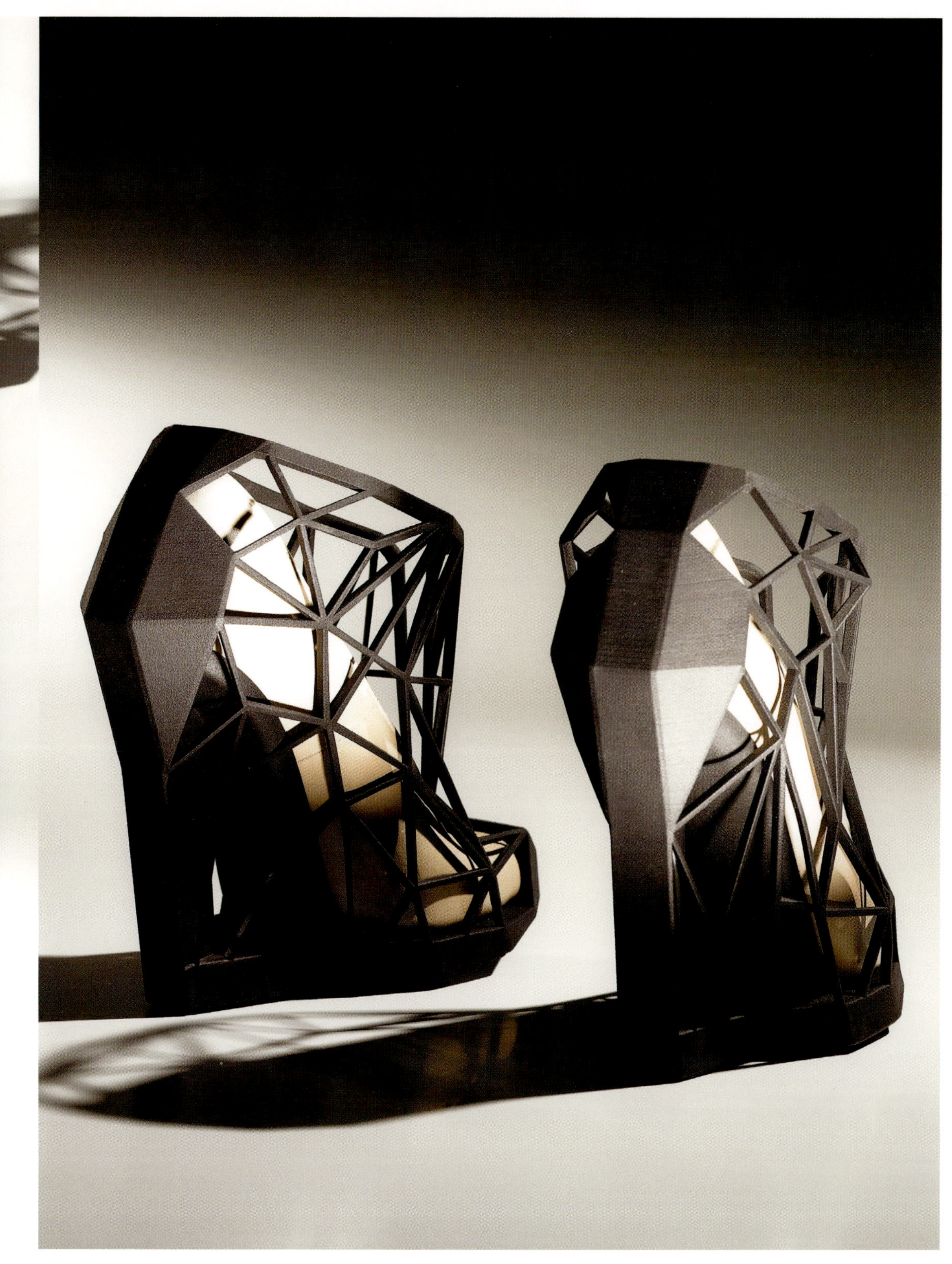

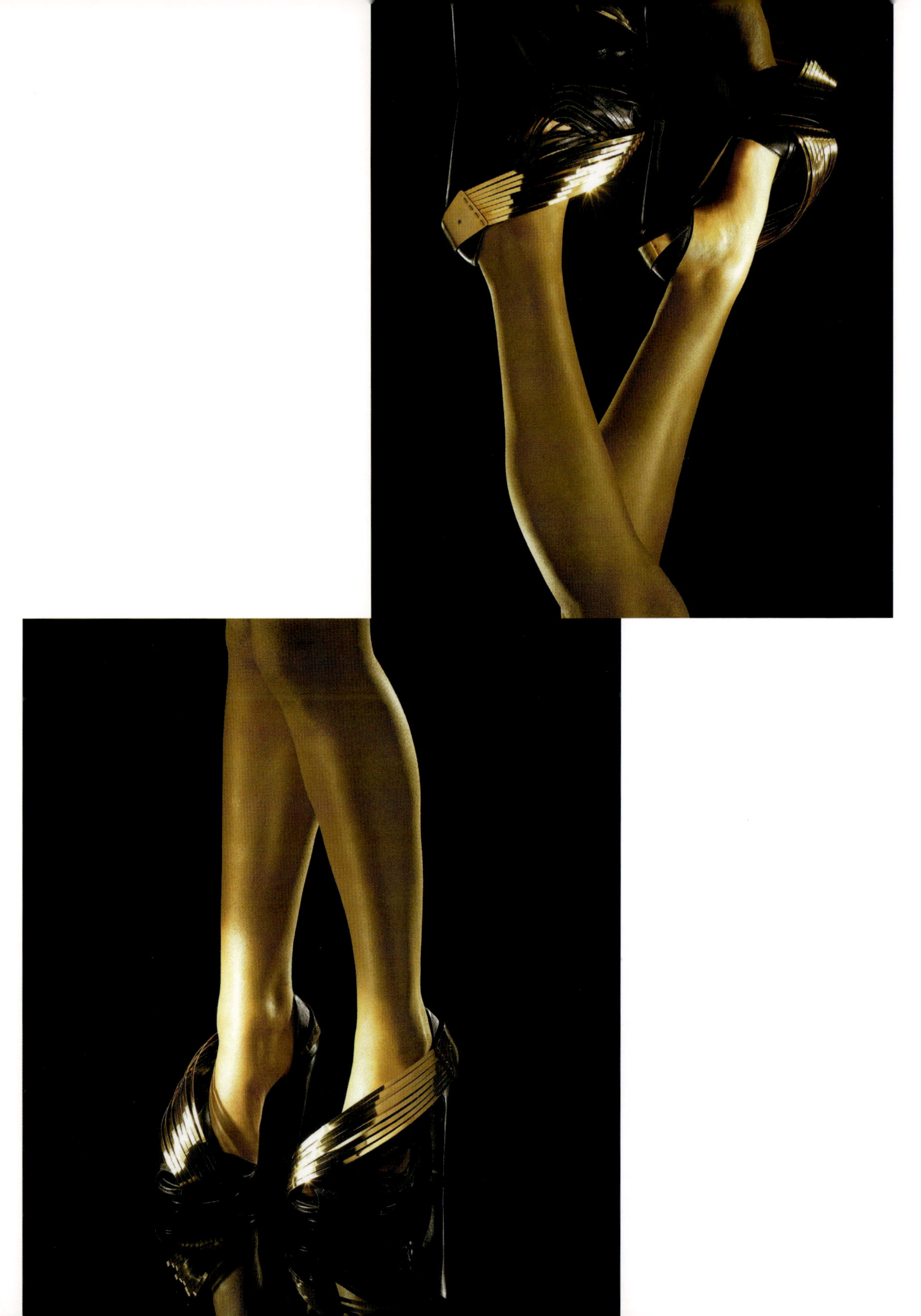

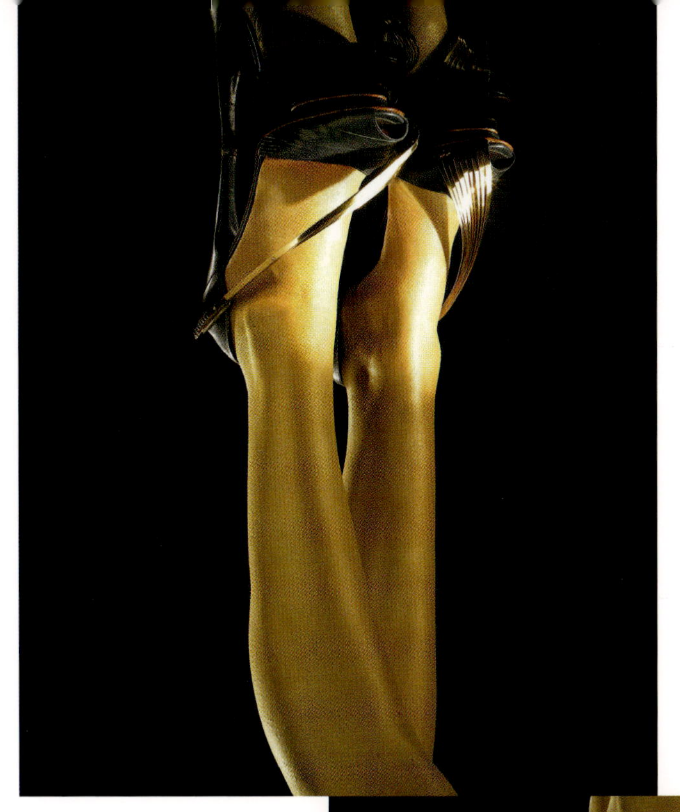

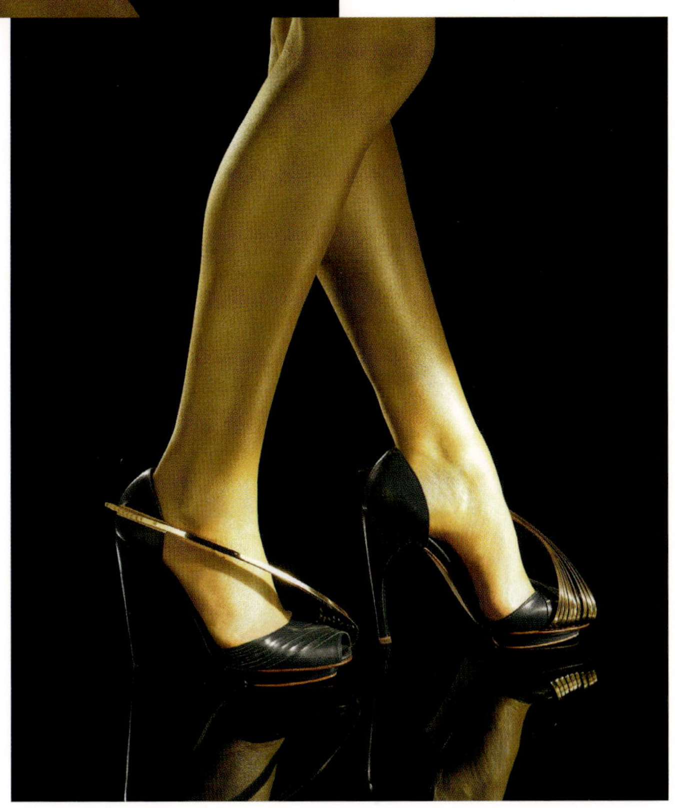

THE COLOUR OF THE DAY BY AOI KOTSUHIROI

The sky refused to tell anything anymore. Stones clung to the road seeking a tomorrow to see a little further on. **PARKED IN FRONT OF THE SUPERMARKET, I WATCHED THE SILENT COMINGS AND GOINGS OF MERCHANDISE. ROTTEN FRUITS FELL FROM THE TRUNKS OF THE CARS, THAT DULL SOUND SPREADING OVER THE GROUND AND THEN MY VISION BLURRED. I CLOSED MY EYES TO MEMORIES.** I walked in silence, my hands rubbing that worthless wall, refusal in my fingers as if by choice, I went through. **I WAS ON THE OTHER SIDE, AS IF IN BALANCE. A RAIN OF HESITATION HIT MY FACE, LIKE AN AWAKENING TO NOT GO UNDER.** I wanted to see the distance standing, strolling to the smile of the day. I slammed the door, started the car, my bare feet slipped onto the pedals, I'd left outside what I didn't want. **THE ROAD, FLOODED WITH HABITS, TURNED ITS BACK ON ME. IN THIS INDIFFERENCE, I WAITED.** Close to me, she slept in the delicacy of slumber, after this long turn, her face had changed. Lying down, she let herself be carried away. **SHE WANTED TO BREATHE FEELINGS. SHE DESCRIBED HOW BEAUTIFUL IT WAS. SHE TALKED TO ME ABOUT THE INSTINCT FOR SENSING WITH HER BODY, FORGETTING THIS FORM OF REASON, SHE CONTINUED LIKE THIS, SPEAKING OF THE INSTANT.** She wanted to fashion moments that did not exist, a sort of relationship, images that made her happy. **SHE KEPT HER OBJECTS CLOSE, THEY WERE HER PRECIOUS WRITING. SHE TALKED TO ME ABOUT HER CHANGING BODY, WHEN IN HER NAKEDNESS SHE WORE HER OBJECTS, SHE FELT HER OWN GESTURES DIFFERENTLY, SHE WAS LIGHT, HER OUTLOOK FOUND A BALANCE.** I slowed down and opened the window, I needed air and her.

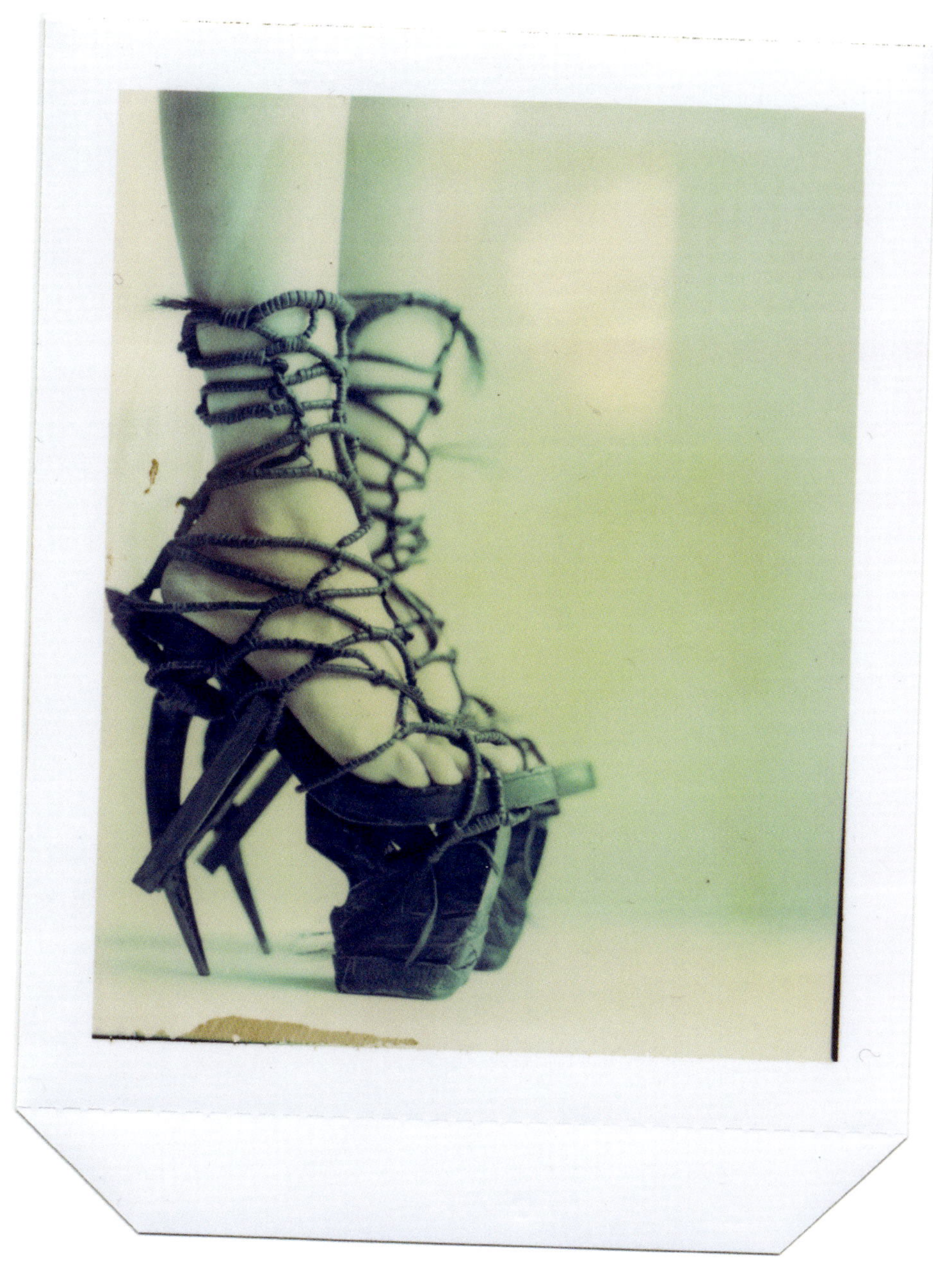

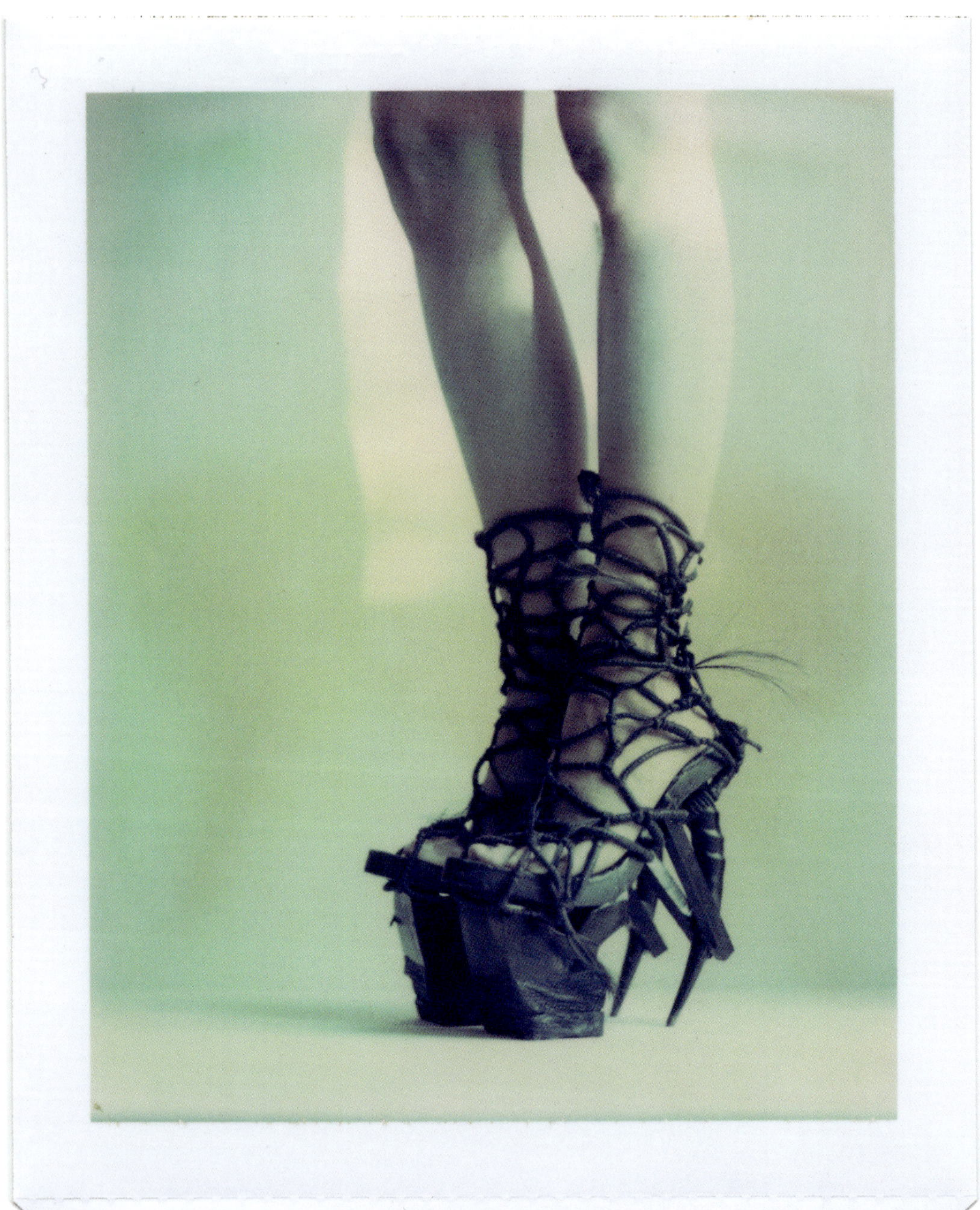

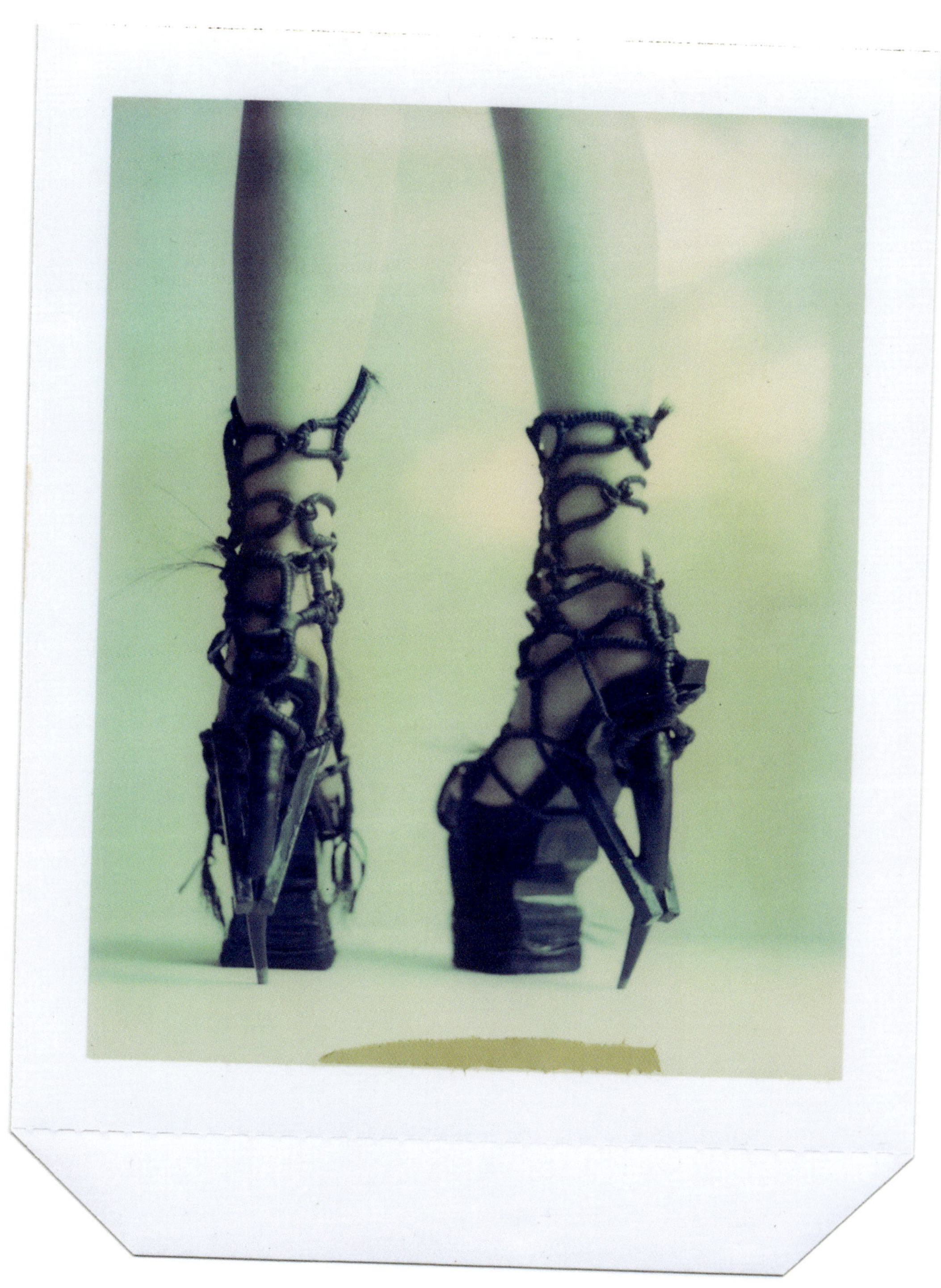

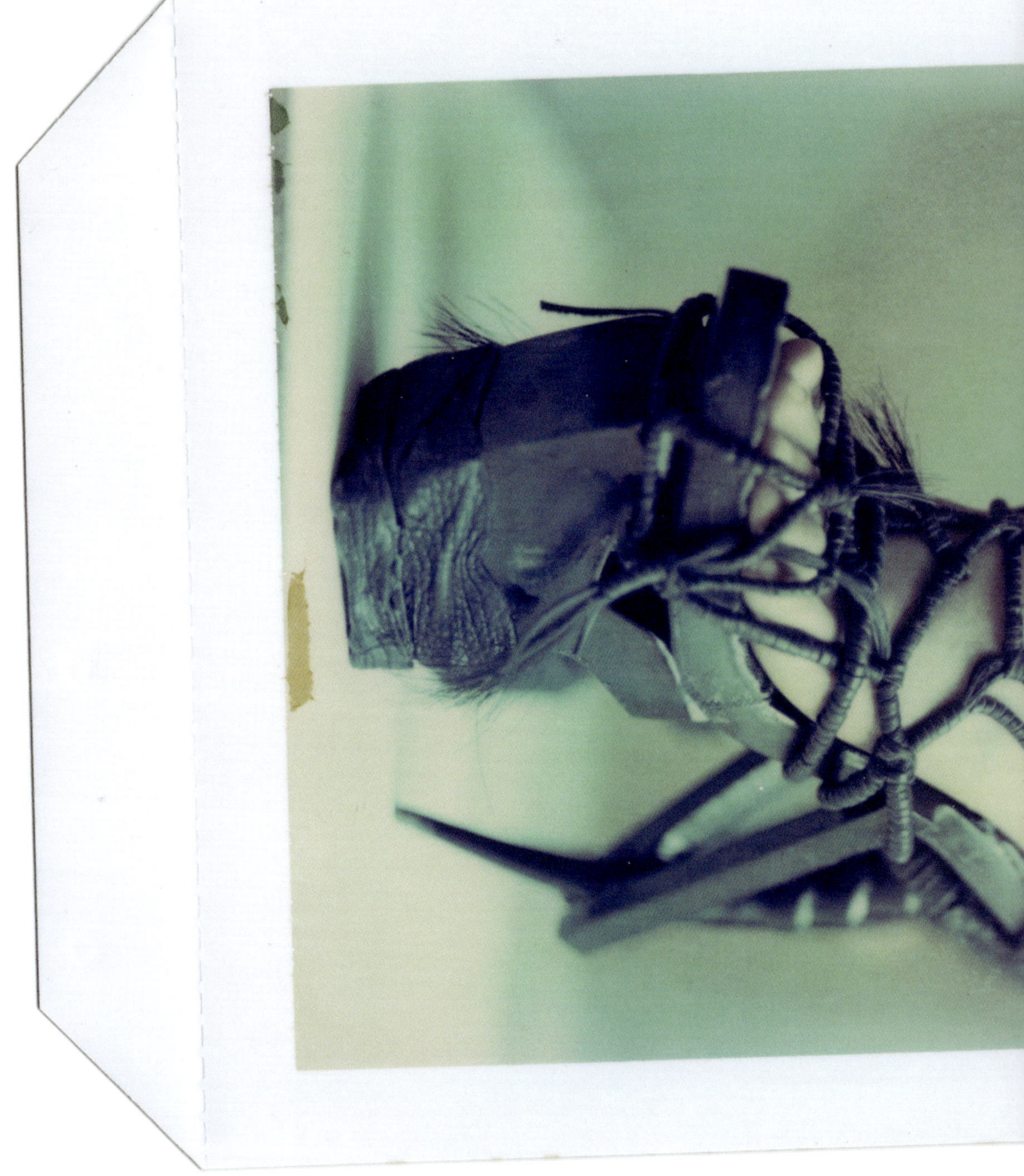

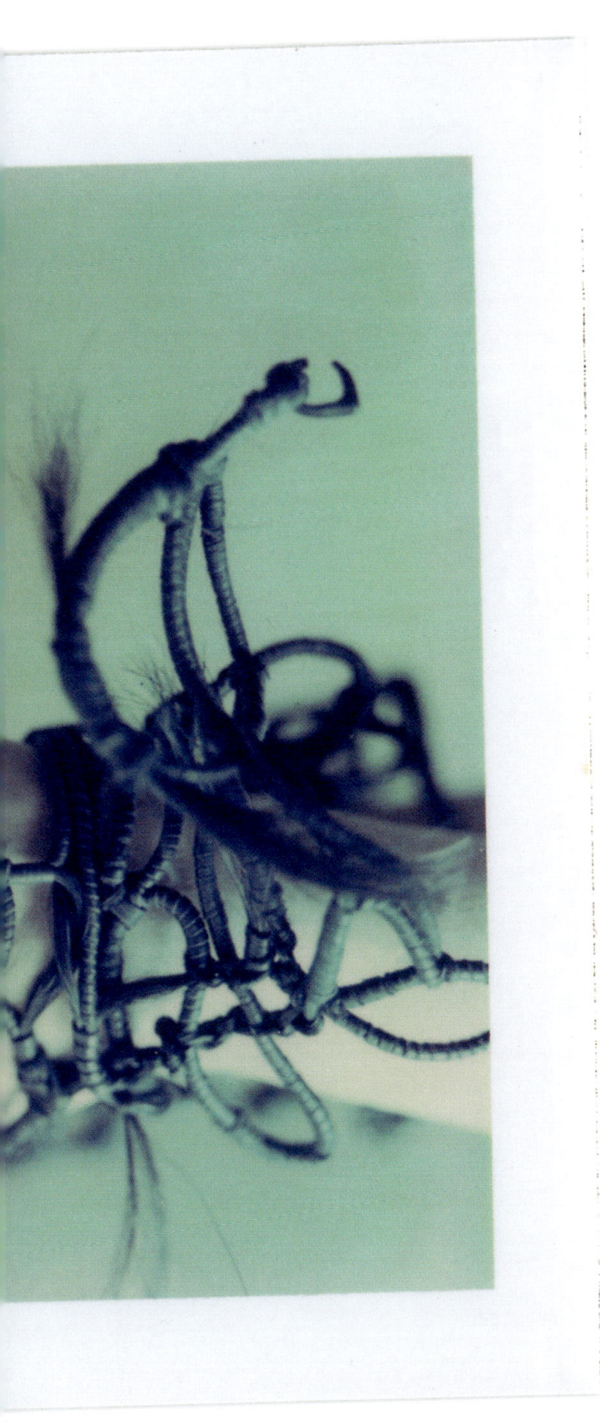

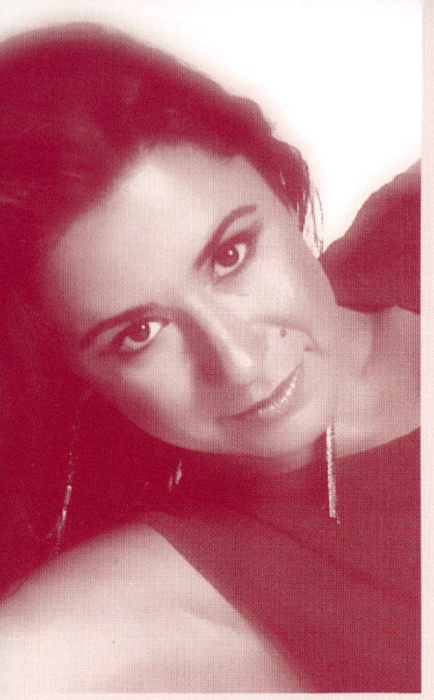

BEHNAZ KANANI

Please introduce yourself. **MY NAME IS BEHNAZ KANANI AND I AM A LONDON BASED SHOE DESIGNER OF PERSIAN DESCENT.** How did you get started? **I WENT TO CORDWAINERS COLLEGE AND AFTER FINISHING MY STUDIES IN 1997 WENT TO ITALY WHERE I STARTED MY FIRST JOB AS A DESIGNER.** What is your work about? **MY WORK IS ABOUT SELF EXPRESSION. IT IS A MIX OF MAGICAL ELEMENTS WITHOUT A FORMULA.** What made you choose shoe design? **THERE'S ALWAYS A REASON FOR CHOOSING ONE PATH OVER ANOTHER. MINE WAS AN INNATE PASSION AND DESIRE FROM CHILDHOOD THAT GREW STRONGER AND LED ME TO CHOOSE DESIGN OVER MEDICINE. AFTER MY STUDIES I LEFT LONDON TO WORK FULL TIME IN ITALY, THE PULSING HEART OF SHOEMAKERS.** What kind of person are your designs made for? **MY DESIGNS ARE BEST SUITED TO A WOMAN WITH GREAT INDIVIDUALITY. SHE IS FEMININE, WELL CENTRED WITH A STRONG CHARACTER AND GREAT TASTE. SHE ALSO HAS A COSMIC AWARENESS. I DESIGN FOR WOMEN WHO ARE HAPPY.** What makes your work different from others? **EACH ARTIST PUTS THEIR UNIQUE SOUL, LOVE AND EMOTION INTO THEIR WORK. WHETHER A CHEF, PAINTER OR SHOE DESIGNER, WE ALL HAVE AN ESSENCE THAT SEPARATES US FROM THE REST.** What do you consider your most innovative design so far? **LISA OR VENUS FROM SPRING/SUMMER 07, CAMELIA FROM SPRING/SUMMER 08 AND BATYA FROM AUTUMN/WINTER 09-10. MY SIGNATURE HEEL REPRESENTS THE FEMALE BODY AND THE PORON® CUSHIONING USED FOR THE INSOLES WAS DEVELOPED BY NASA FOR THEIR SPACE SUITS.** What are your design rituals? **I START WITH A THEME, A PAINTING OR A COLOUR PALETTE THAT EXCITES ME AND LET THE DESIGNS FLOW WHILST DESIGNING, I BEAR IN MIND THE WOMAN THAT'S GOING TO WALK WITH MY CREATIONS, AS WELL AS THE SHAPE OF THE FOOT.** What stage of the creative process do you find the most gratifying and which the least? **THE MOST GRATIFYING STAGE IS HOLDING IN MY HANDS THE PERFECTLY MADE SAMPLE OF MY IDEA. THE LEAST GRATIFYING IS WHEN MY TECHNICAL CONSULTANTS SAY IT CANNOT BE DONE. HOWEVER, THIS ALSO ENCOURAGES ME TO FIND A SOLUTION. TRYING TO WORK OUT HOW TO MAKE THE IMPOSSIBLE POSSIBLE IS EXCITING.** Are there any artists or art movements that have influenced you? **THE SURREALISM MOVEMENT. THE 1920S WAS A DECADE OF ELEGANCE, CREATIVITY, JAZZ MUSIC, AMERICAN GANGSTERS, MODERN DANGEROUS WOMEN, FAST CARS, SUCCESS AND EVERYTHING BEAUTIFUL. WOMEN CHOSE BEAUTY, INDIVIDUALITY AND FUNCTIONALITY. THEY SET THE BAR FOR CLASSIC STYLE WITH SILHOUETTES AND LINES THAT EPITOMISED QUALITY AND LUXURY. I'M ALSO INSPIRED BY THE ART DECO MOVEMENT. PERSONALITIES SUCH AS COCO CHANEL, GRETA GARBO AND LOUISE BROOKS WERE WOMEN WITH ATTITUDE AND HAD A TIMELESS CLASSIC STYLE THAT WAS ALSO SEXY AND STILL INFLUENCES WHAT WE WEAR TODAY.** What are your thoughts on the culture of quick consumption and over-commercialisation? **IT'S A PITY THAT DESIGNERS START OFF WITH GREAT CREATIVE EXPRESSION THEN AS THEIR BUSINESS TRIES TO GROW THEY COMPROMISE THEIR INNOVATIVE TALENT FOR COMMERCIAL AND CORPORATE CONFORMISM. I AM INTERESTED IN ORIGINAL BUT WEARABLE ART. MY SHOES SHOULD EXCITE BUT AT THE SAME TIME BE COMMERCIALLY VIABLE. I MUST SAY OUR WORK AS DESIGNERS IS EXTREMELY CHALLENGING, IT IS ABOUT PUSHING AN IDEA FORWARD AND FINDING THAT FINE LINE WITHOUT CROSSING IT.**

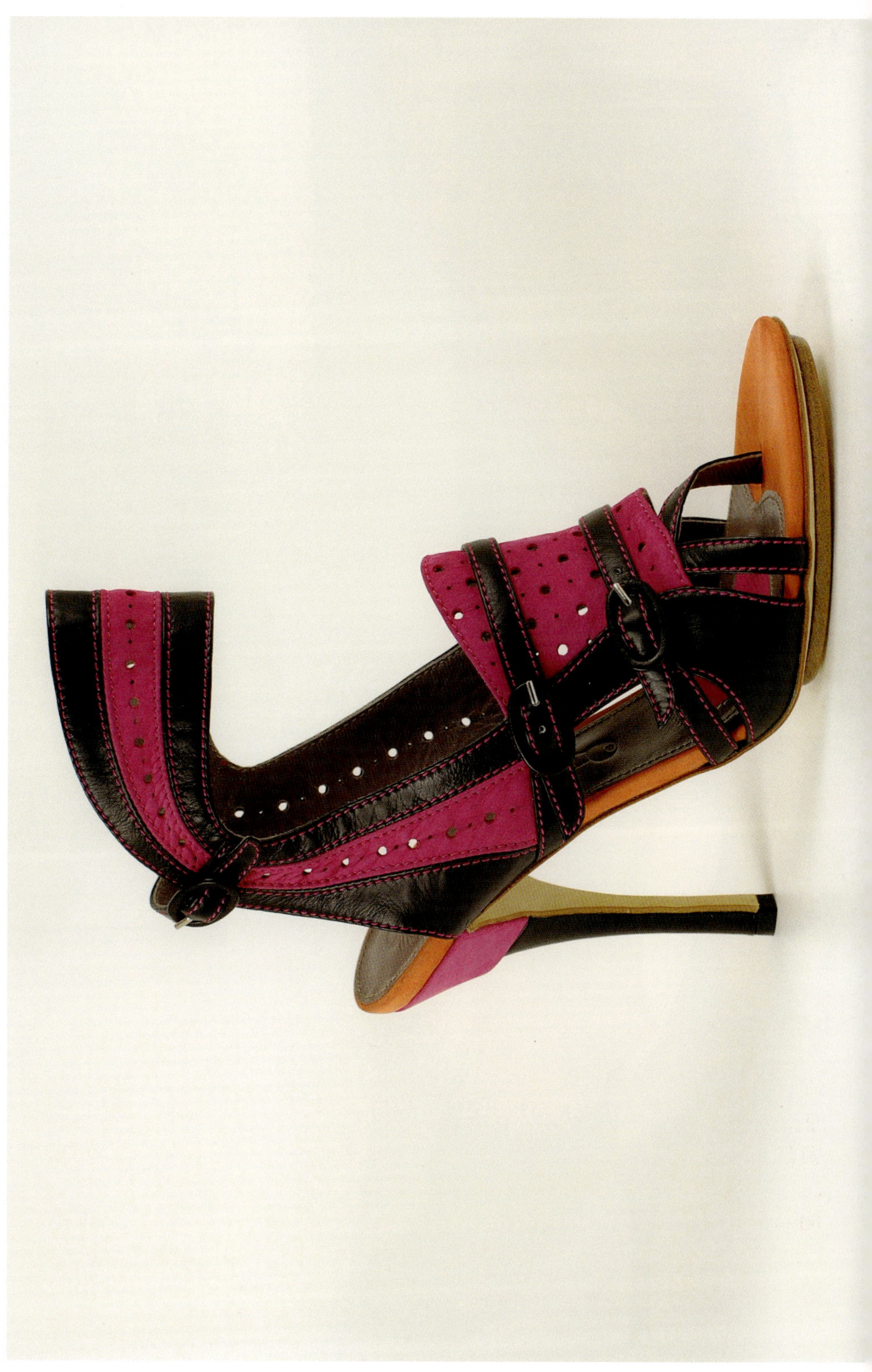

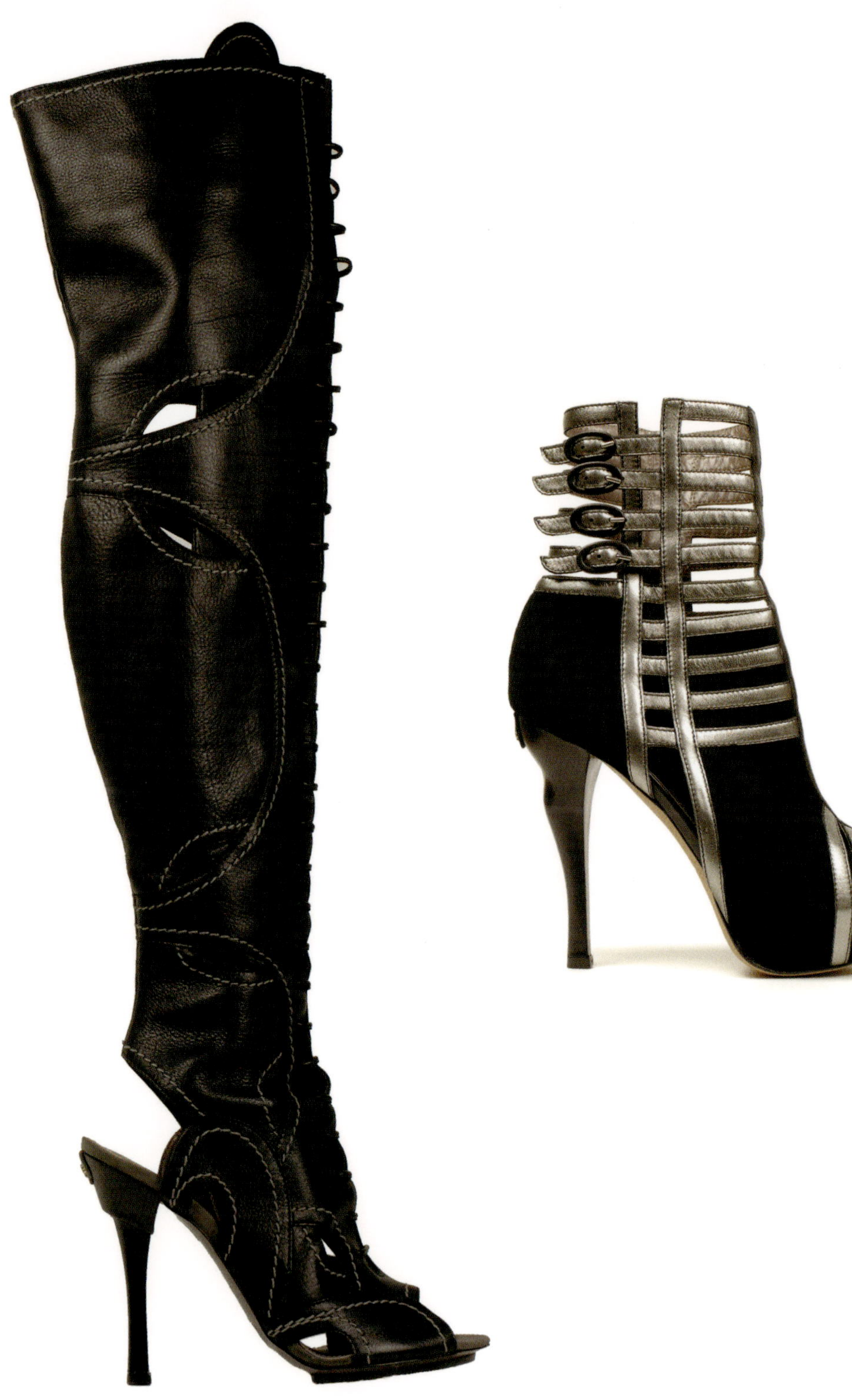

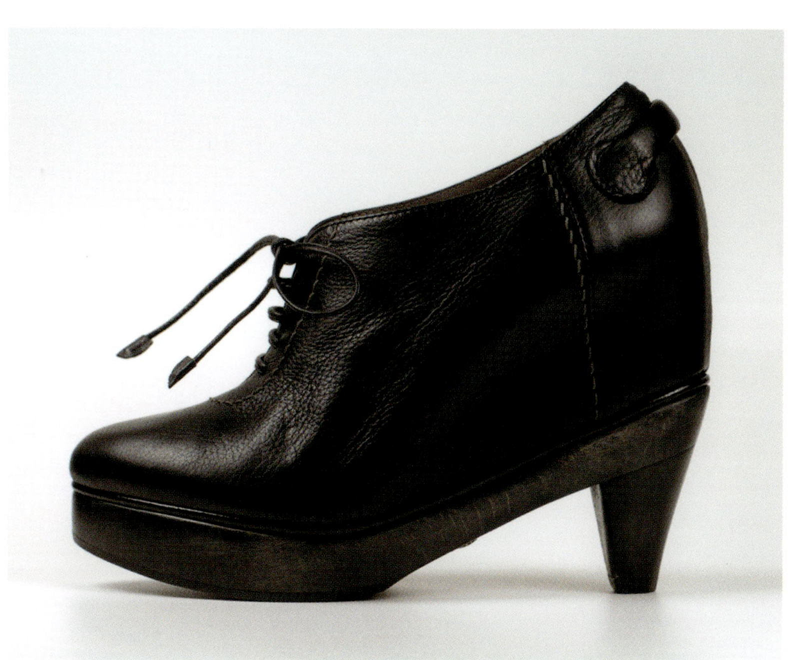

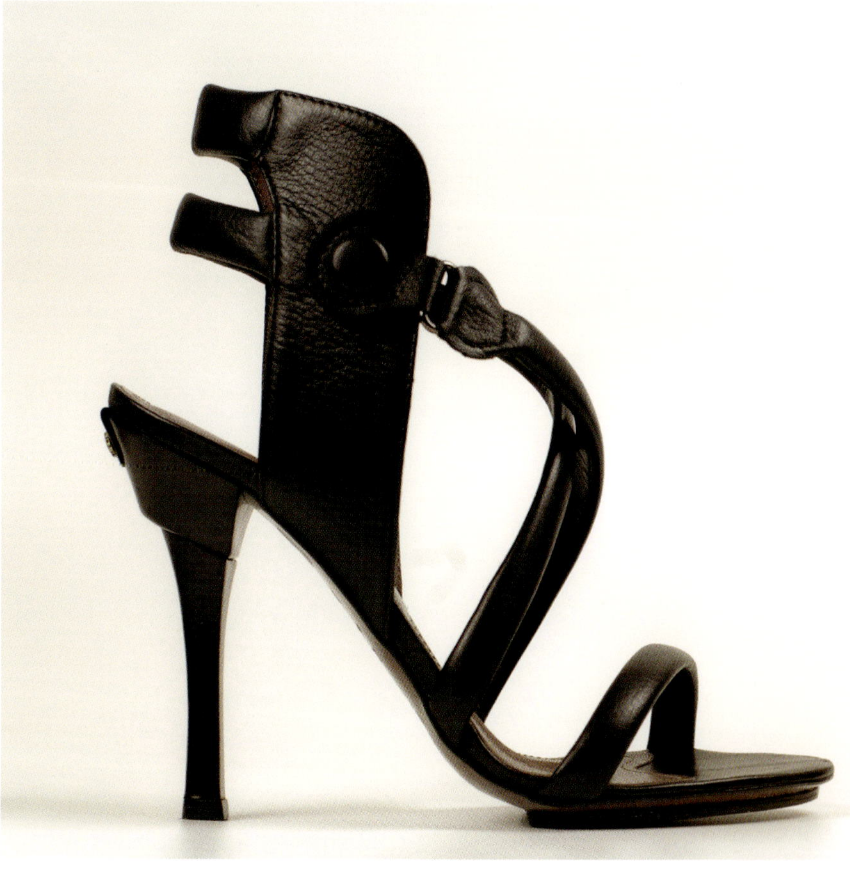

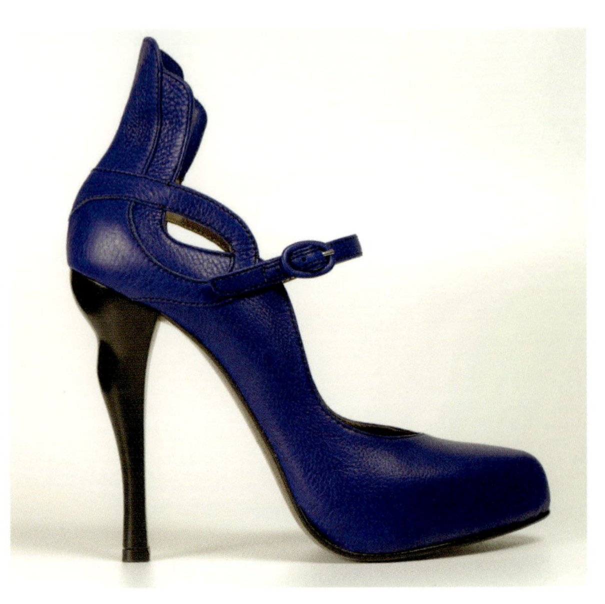

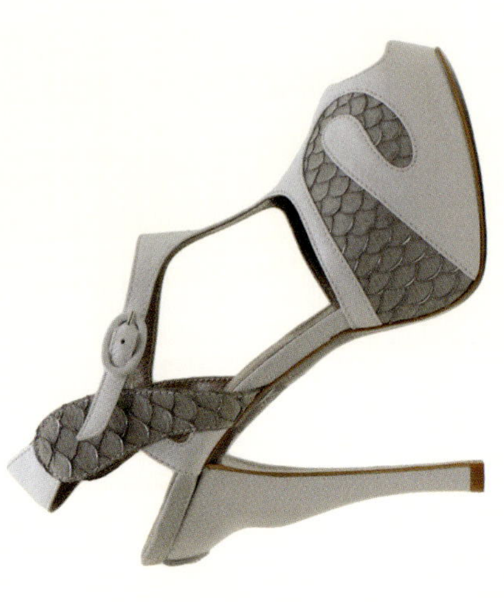

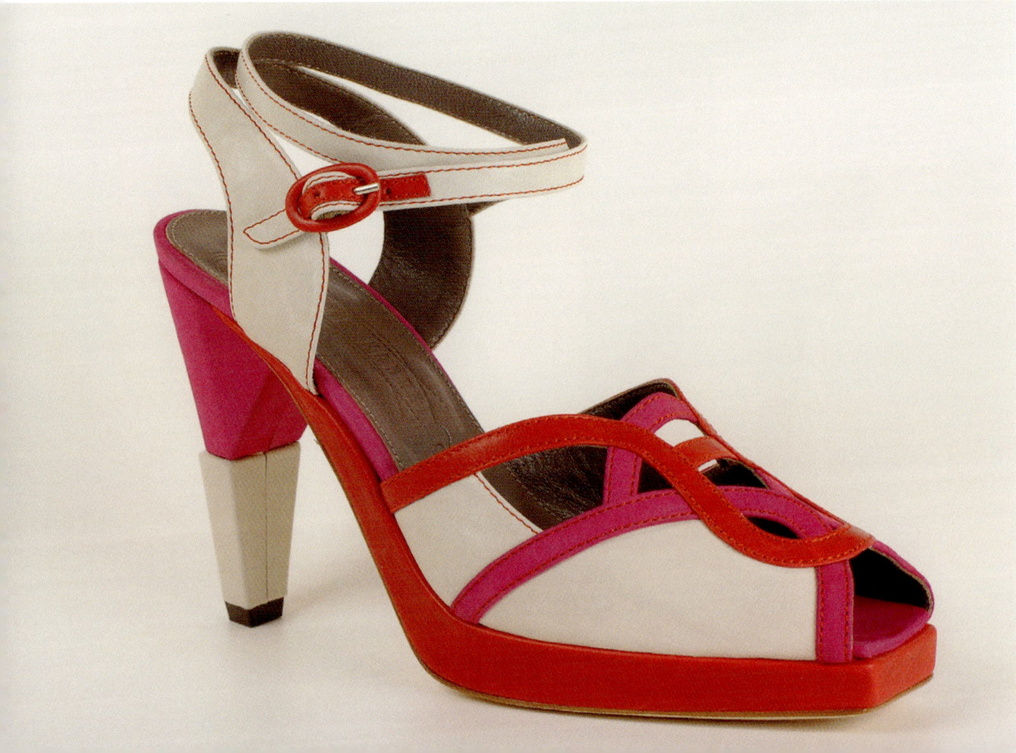

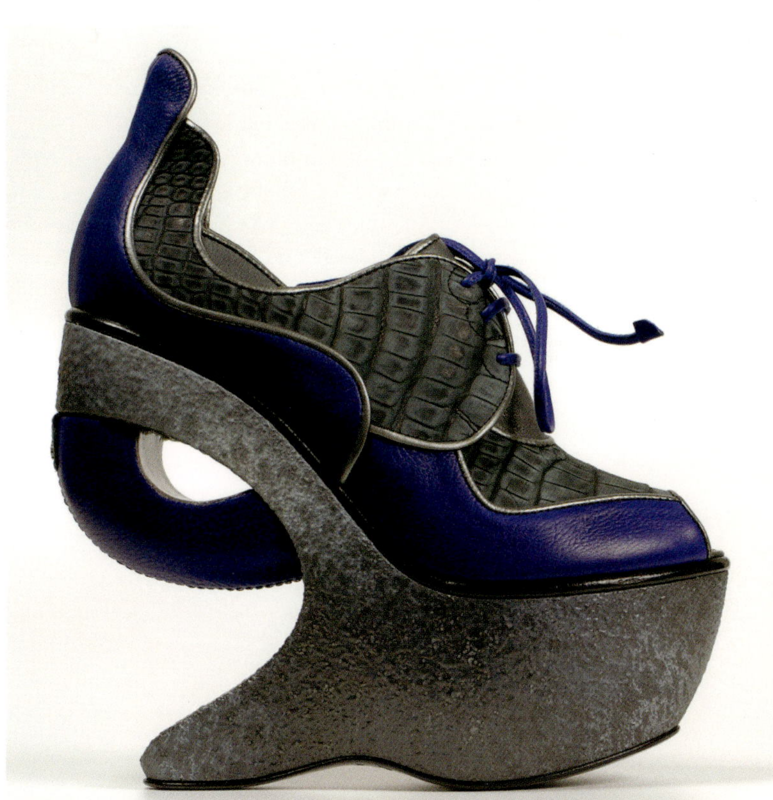

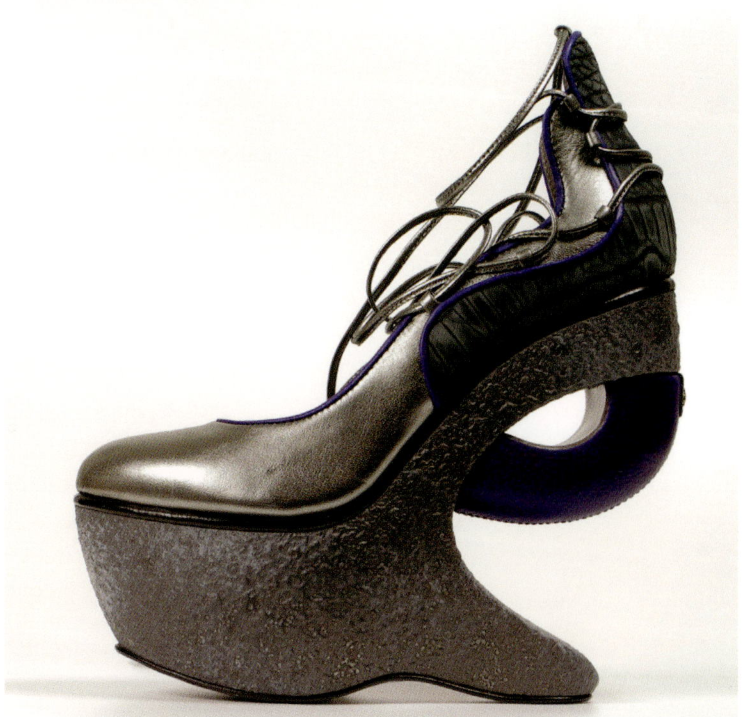

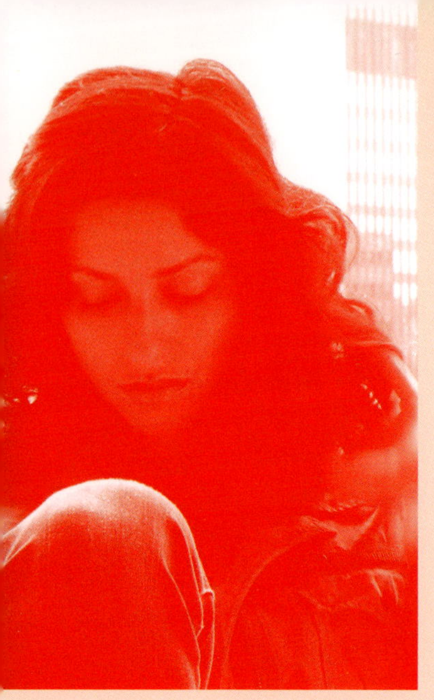

MDOT, BOOJI

Please introduce yourself. **MY NAME IS MDOT. SOME PEOPLE CALL ME M. I RUN AN INDEPENDENT FOOTWEAR AND ACCESSORIES LINE. I'M VERY FORTUNATE TO HAVE THE LIFE THAT I HAVE AND I'VE WORKED VERY HARD TO ACHIEVE IT.** How did you get started? **IT'S ALMOST TEN YEARS SINCE I FIRST STEPPED FOOT INTO THE FOOTWEAR INDUSTRY. I WAS EAGER TO LEARN AND HAVING SOMEONE BELIEVE IN ME FUELLED MY AMBITION TO MAKE PRODUCTS. LEARNING THE BUSINESS HANDS ON FROM THE BOTTOM UP WAS PRICELESS AND MADE ME WHO I AM TODAY.** What is your work about? **IT'S ABOUT FOOTWEAR AS A STATEMENT AND GOOD DESIGN THAT'S GREEN AND RESPONSIBLE. MY STYLE IS RESERVED BUT SPONTANEOUS AND THIS IS REFLECTED IN MY WORK.** Is there a specific reason why you chose shoe design? **IT CHOSE ME. I WAS ALWAYS INTERESTED IN MAKING PRODUCTS, SPECIFICALLY FURNITURE. HOWEVER AN OPPORTUNITY TO BUILD A FOOTWEAR COMPANY LED ME HERE.** What makes your work different from others? **GREEN, VEGAN SHOES WITH STYLE. I ALSO HAVE VERY LITTLE MARKETING BUDGET. OUR BRAND LOYALISTS CARRY US BY WORD OF MOUTH THROUGHOUT THE GLOBE.** What do you consider your most innovative design so far? **EVEN THOUGH IT WAS CREATED IN THE FIRST SEASON, THE INNOVATIVE AND FUNCTIONAL DETACHABLE BAG WAS OUR SIGNATURE DESIGN.** What are your design rituals? **I ALWAYS TAKE OUT A WEEK FOR INTENSIVE RESEARCH AND DEVELOPMENT TIME. I BURY MYSELF IN EVERYTHING ABOUT MAKING SHOES AND HAVE MATERIAL BOOKS SPRAWLED OUT OVER THE LAB FLOORS ALONG WITH PRINT OUTS OF SHOES AND SKETCHES. INITIAL DESIGN IDEAS ARE USUALLY PULLED FROM SOMEWHERE ALONG THE WAY.** Which parts of the job do you find the most and least gratifying? **MOST GRATIFYING IS GETTING EMAILS OR LETTERS FROM PEOPLE THAT REALLY BELIEVE IN YOUR PRODUCT AND ARE ROOTING FOR THE BRAND. IT'S AMAZING! THE LEAST GRATIFYING IS GOING TO POOR COUNTRIES TO MAKE PRODUCTS BECAUSE OF THE COMPETITIVE MARKETPLACE AND NOT BEING ABLE TO MAKE A PRODUCT IN MY OWN COUNTRY FOR EXPORT.** Who or what has played a big part in your development as an artist? **ONE FACTOR THAT HAS PLAYED A BIG PART IN MY DEVELOPMENT IS MY UPBRINGING. I WAS FORTUNATE ENOUGH TO COME TO AMERICA AND BUILD ANYTHING I WANTED FROM NOTHING, UNLIKE MY COUSINS WHO HAD TO STAY BEHIND. THIS ENCOURAGED ME TO ALWAYS SEIZE THE OPPORTUNITY. I ALSO ADMIRE VISIONARIES SUCH AS JAKE BURTON.** Is the culture of quick consumption and over-commercialisation a fact of life? **OF COURSE IT'S A FACT OF LIFE. IT IS WHAT THE WORLD HAS EVOLVED INTO, BUT EVERY COMPANY HAS THE CHOICE TO BE ALTERNATIVE OR GO WITH THE MASSES.** How do you see the current state of your profession in general? **IT IS A GREAT TIME IF YOU BUILD THE GROUND WORK WITH STRONG RELATIONSHIPS. OF COURSE I FEAR THE COMPETITIVE MARKETPLACE DUE TO GIANT MEGA BRANDS MAKING A CHEAPER PRODUCT EVERY YEAR AND MAKING IT ALMOST IMPOSSIBLE FOR INDEPENDENTS TO SURVIVE.**

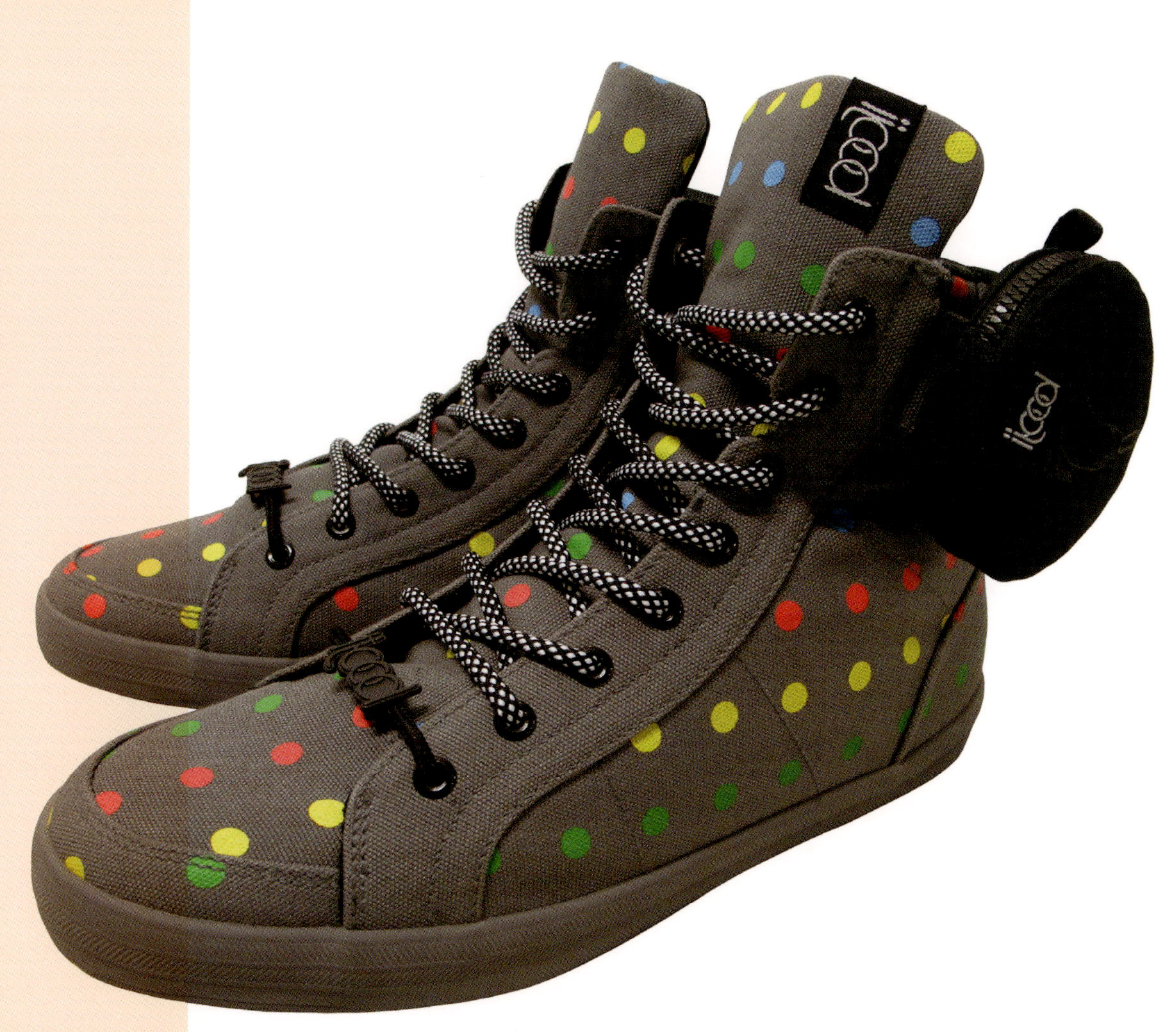

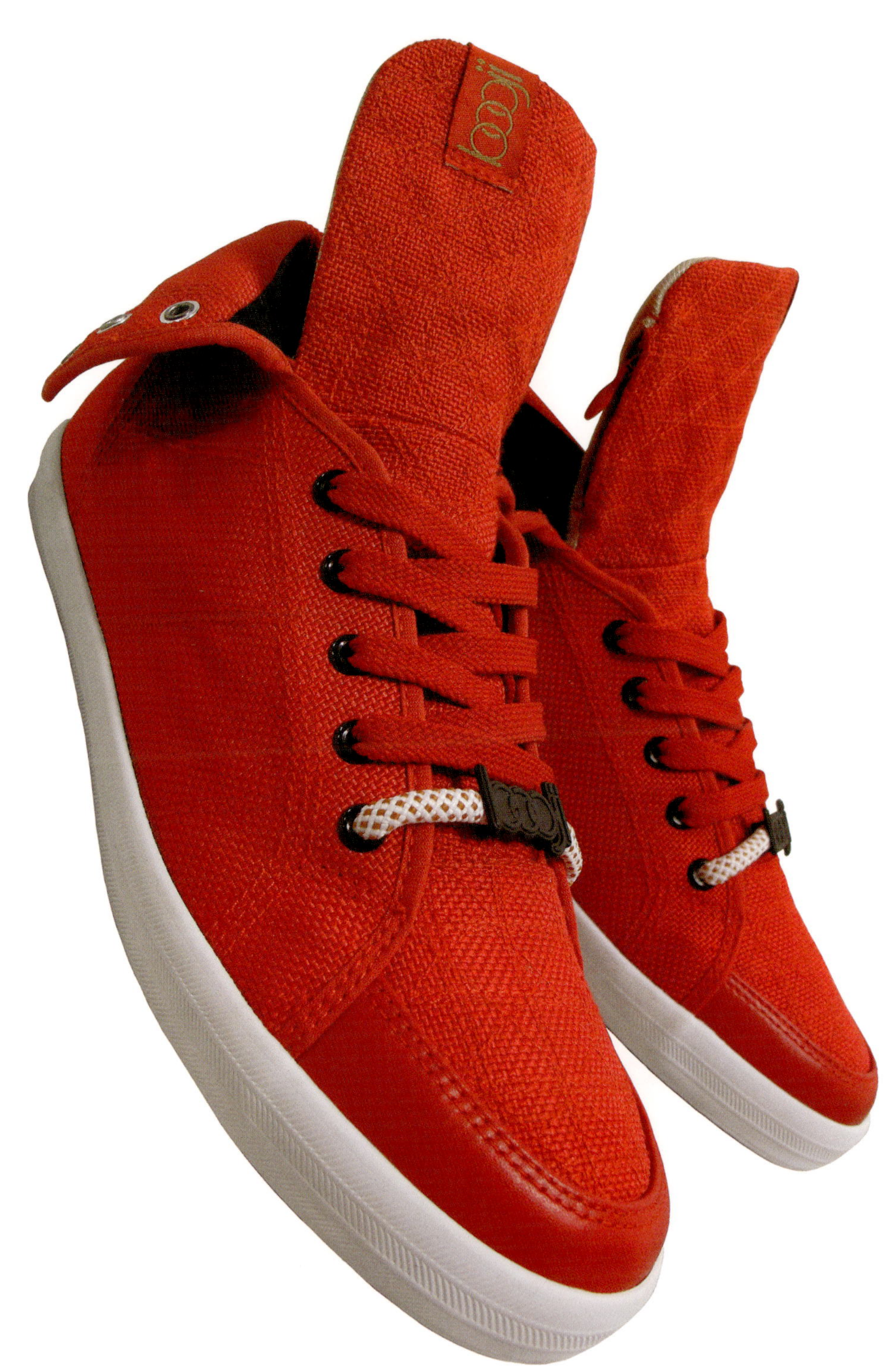
booji

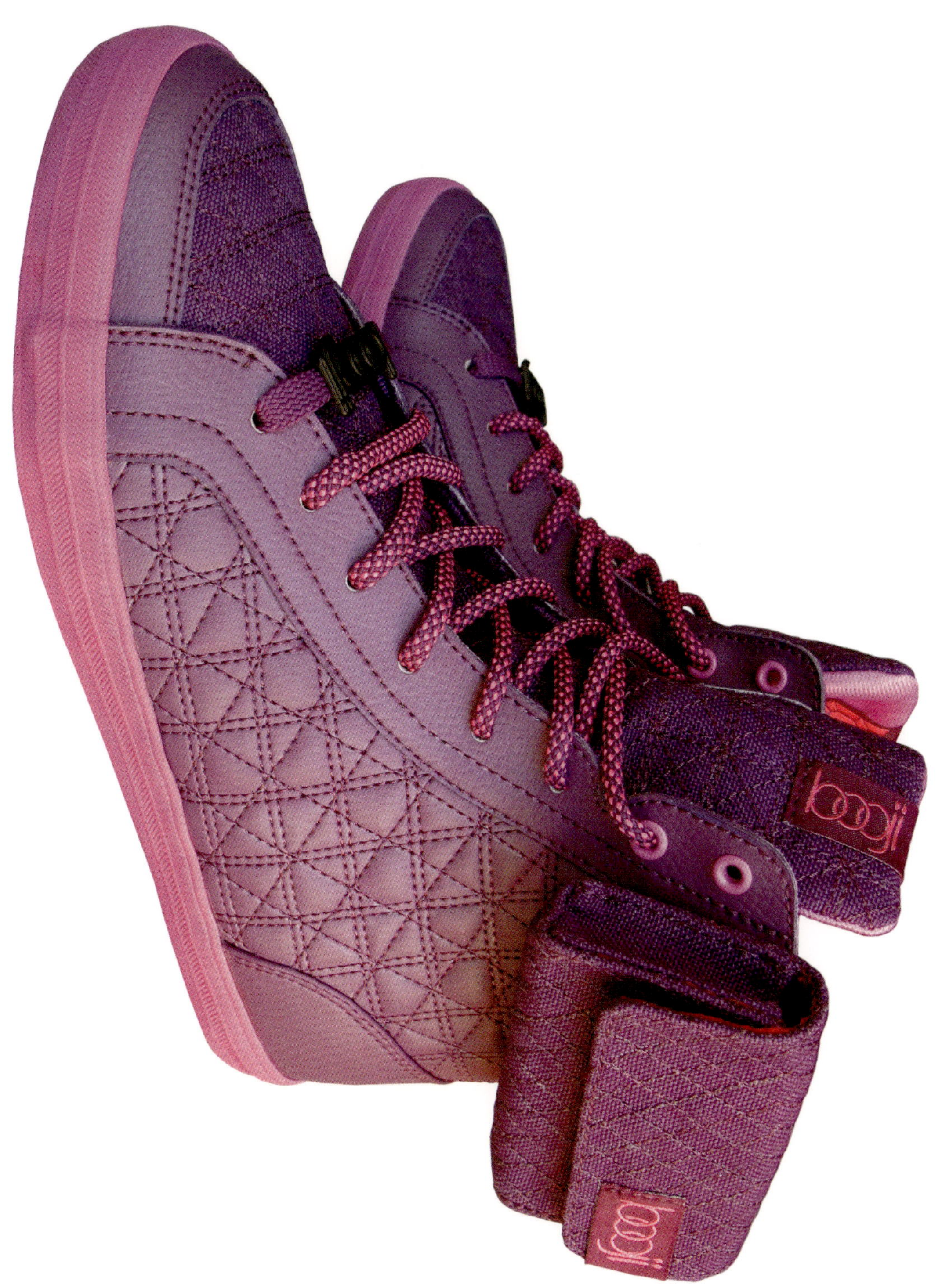
booji
booji

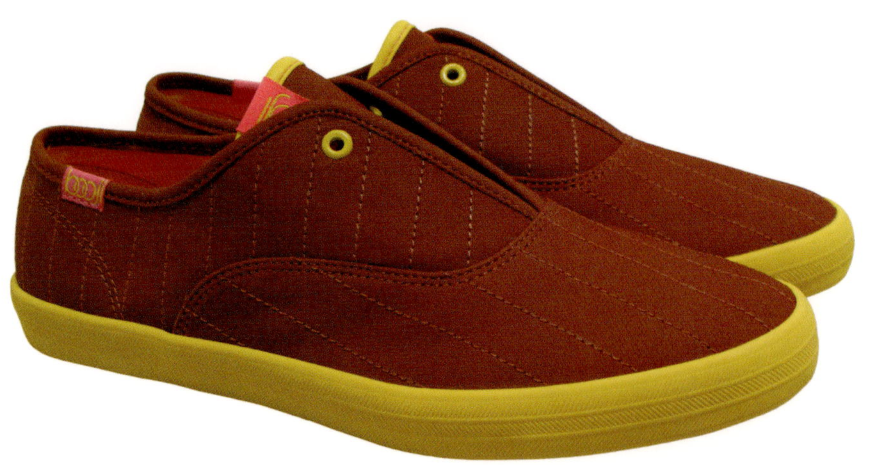

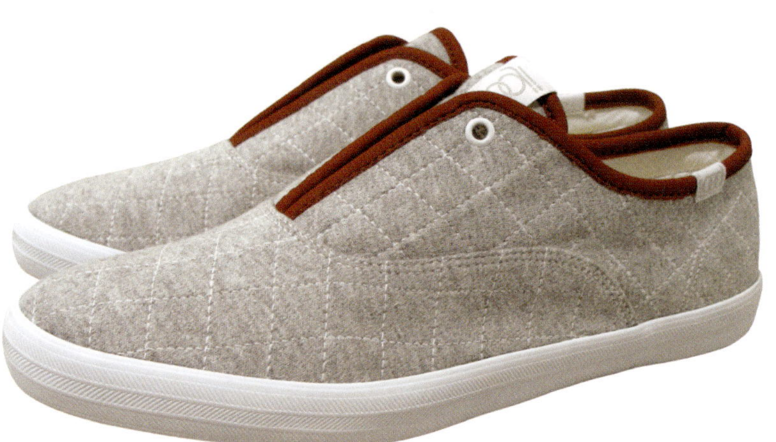

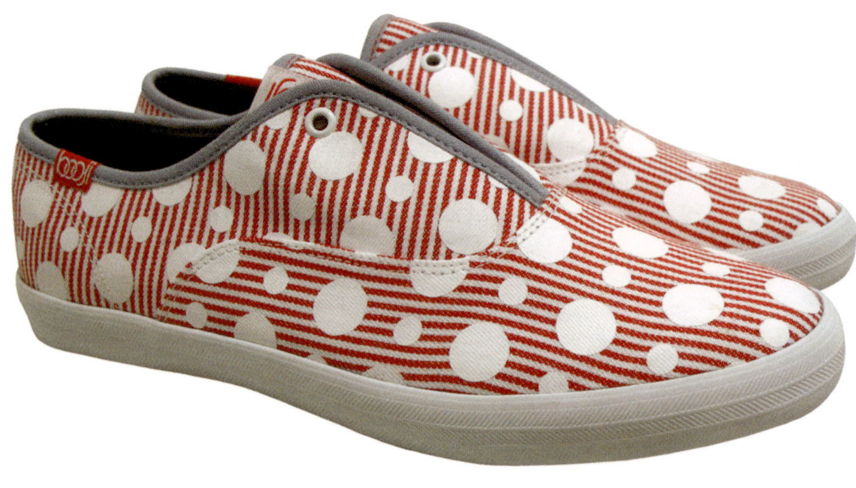

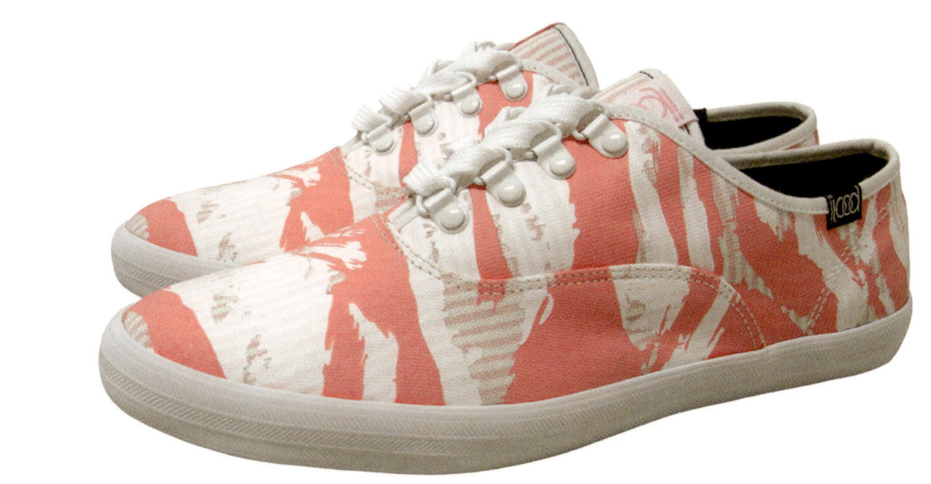

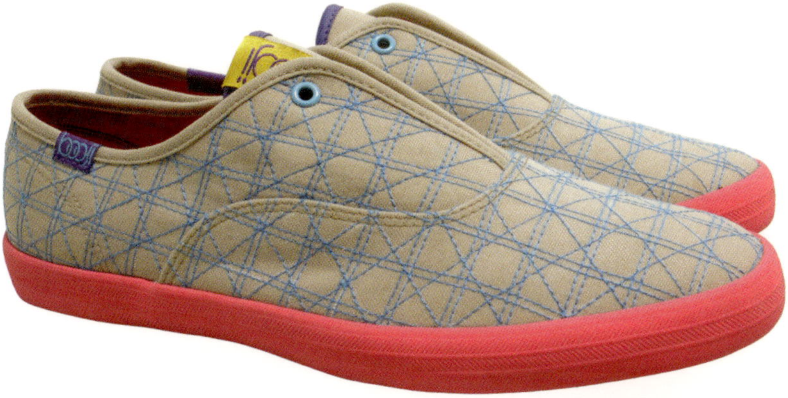

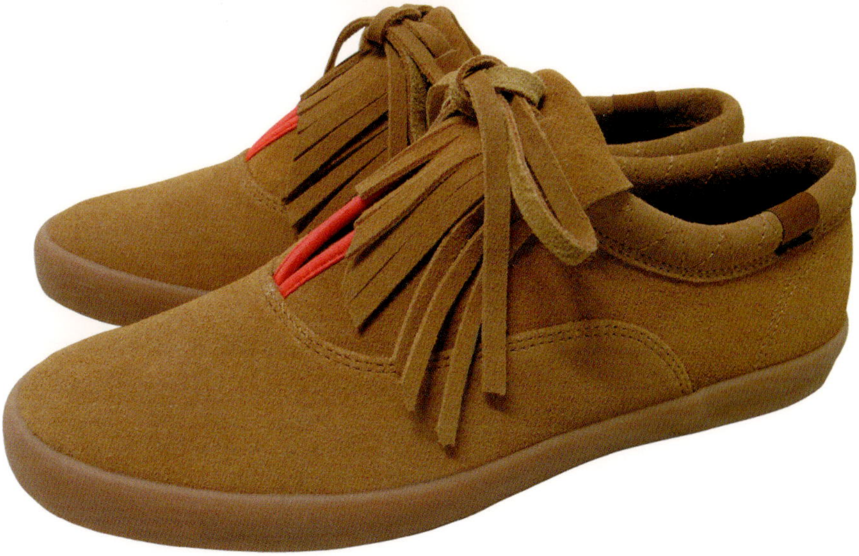

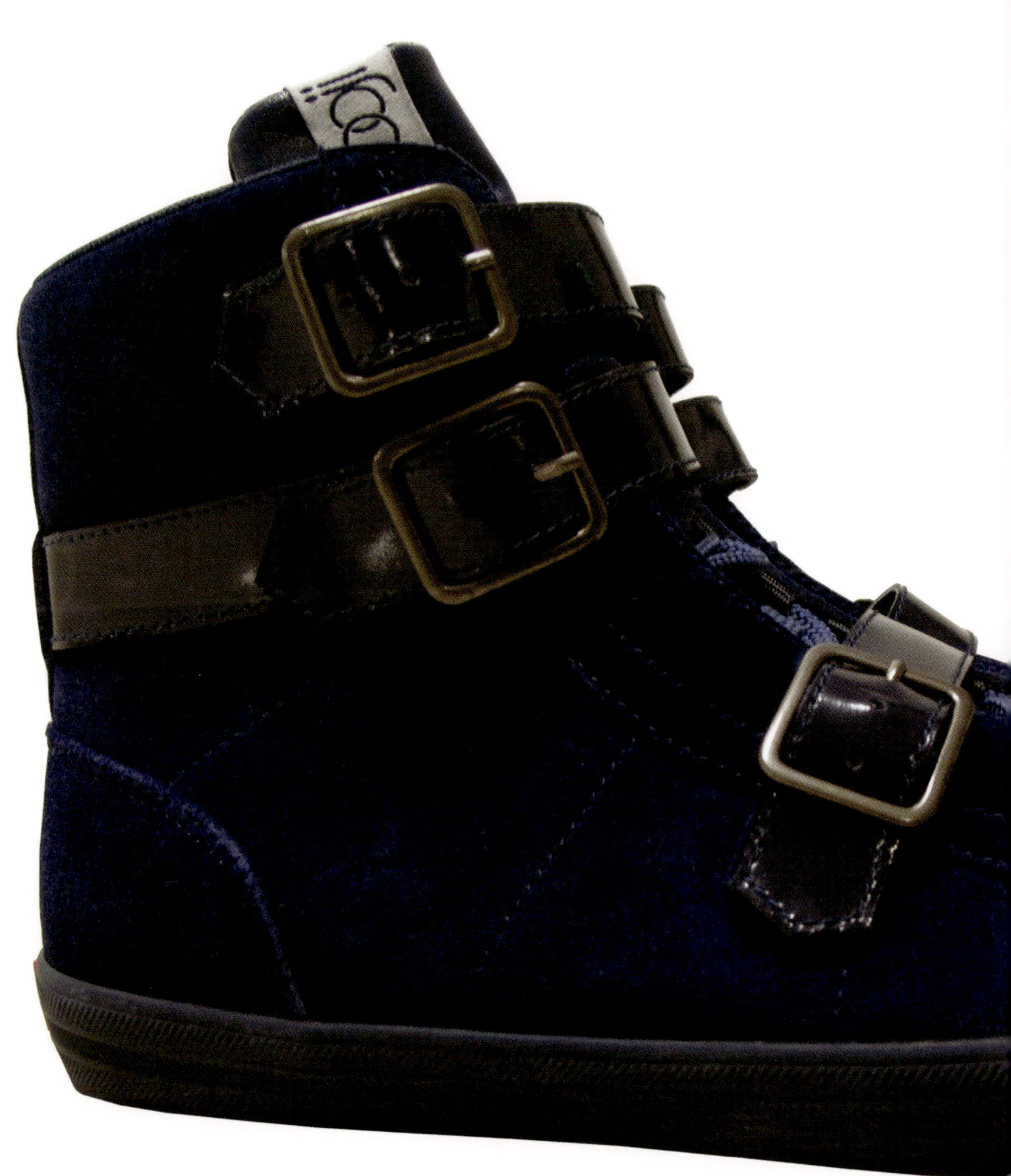

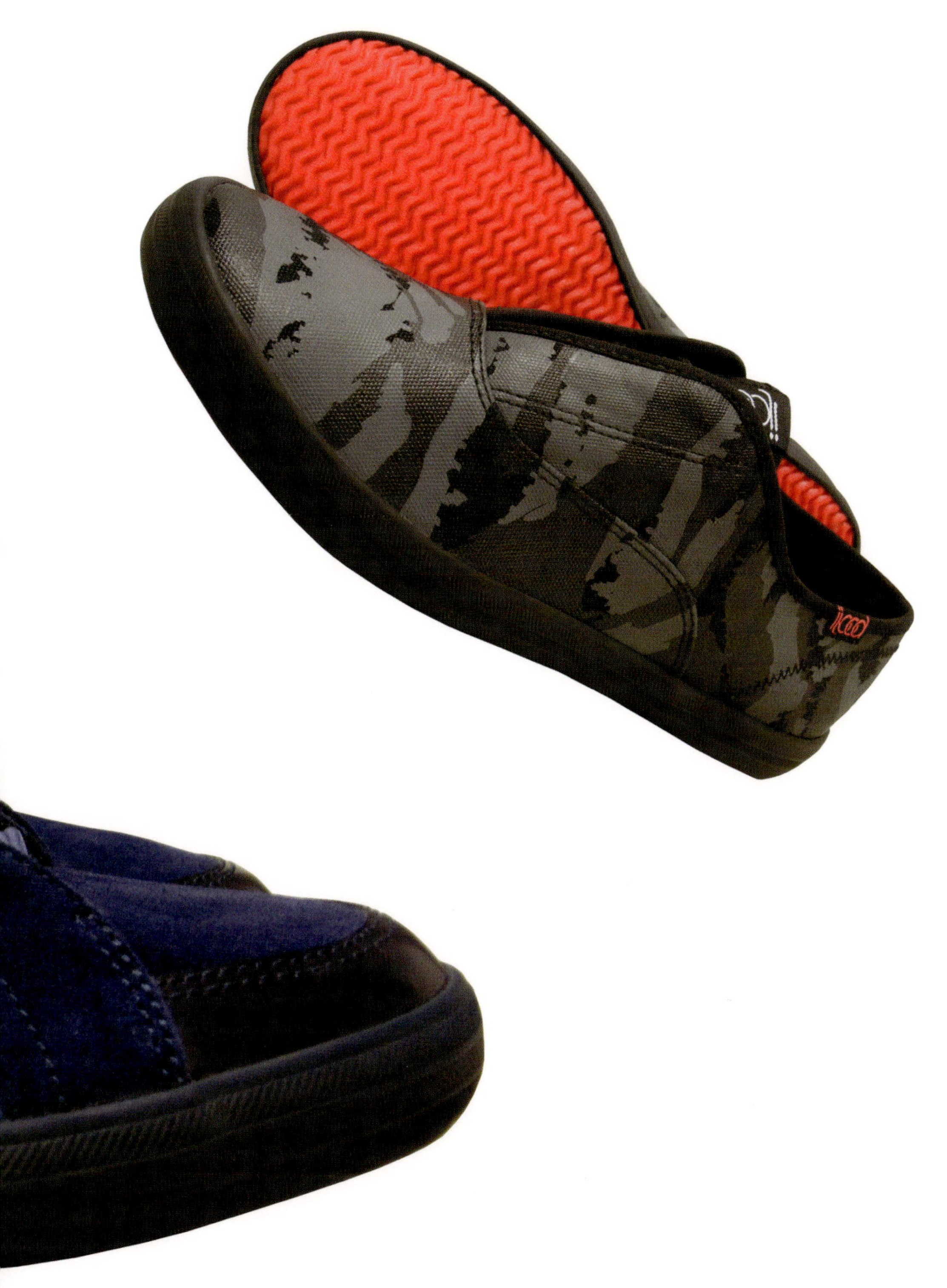

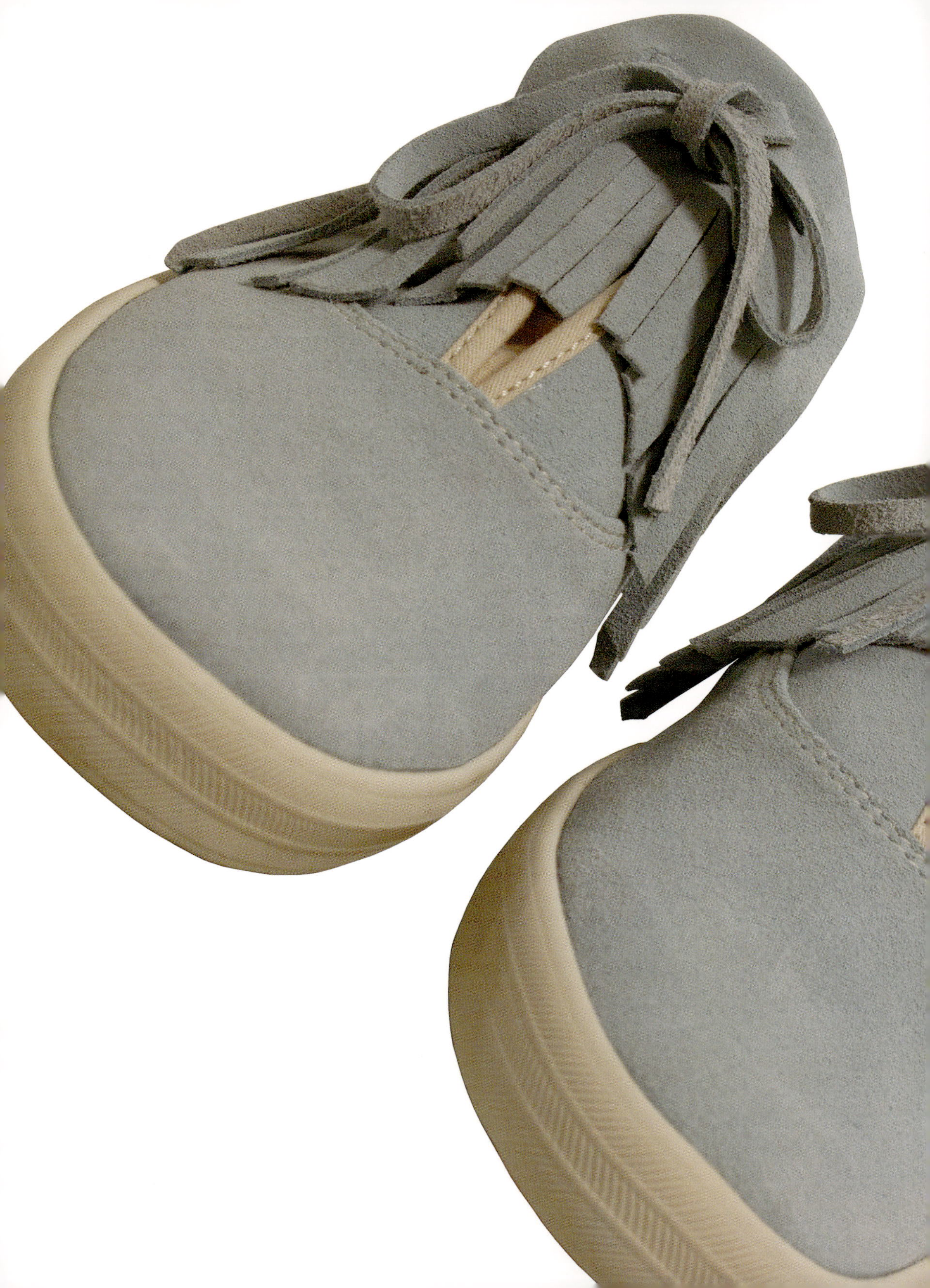

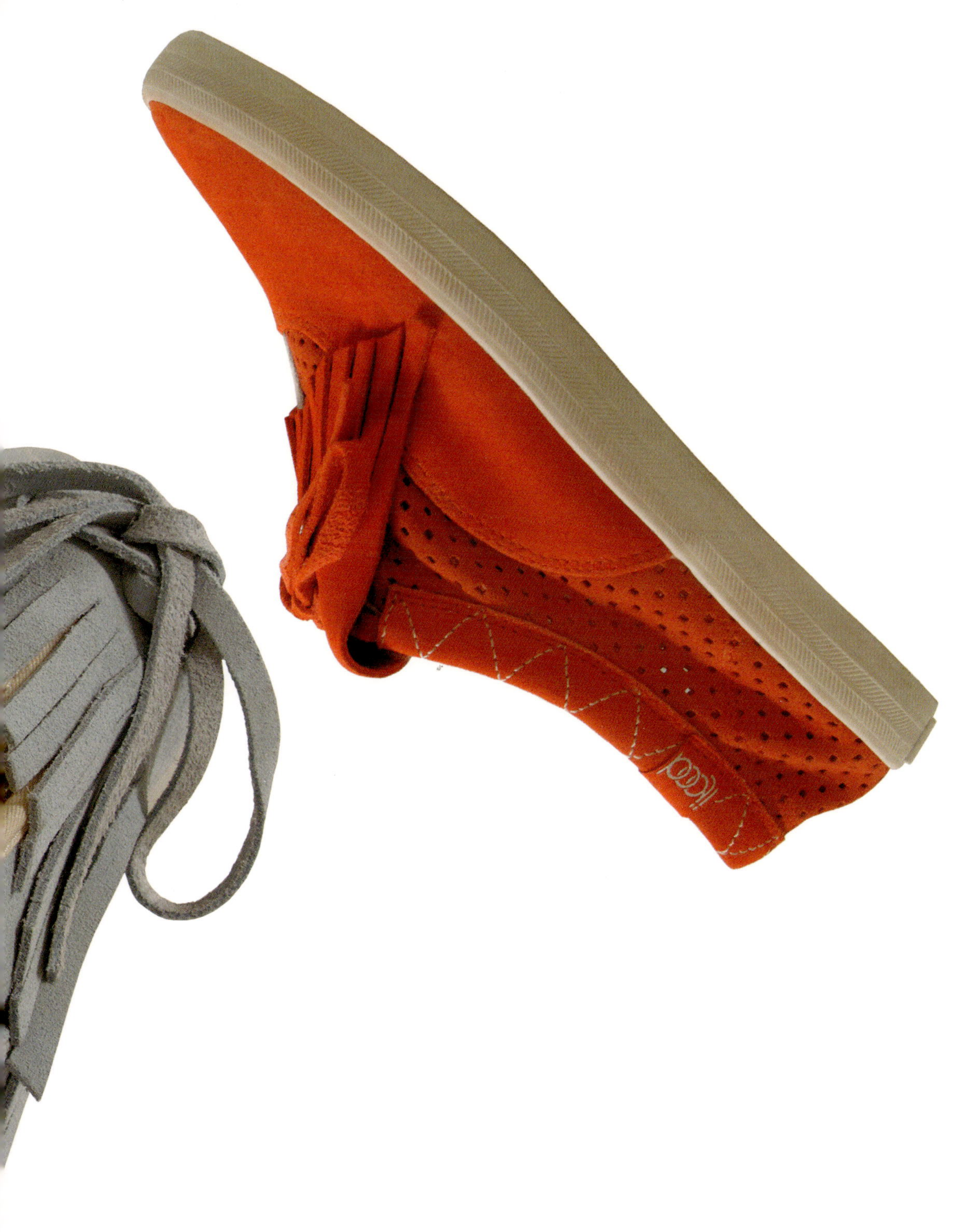

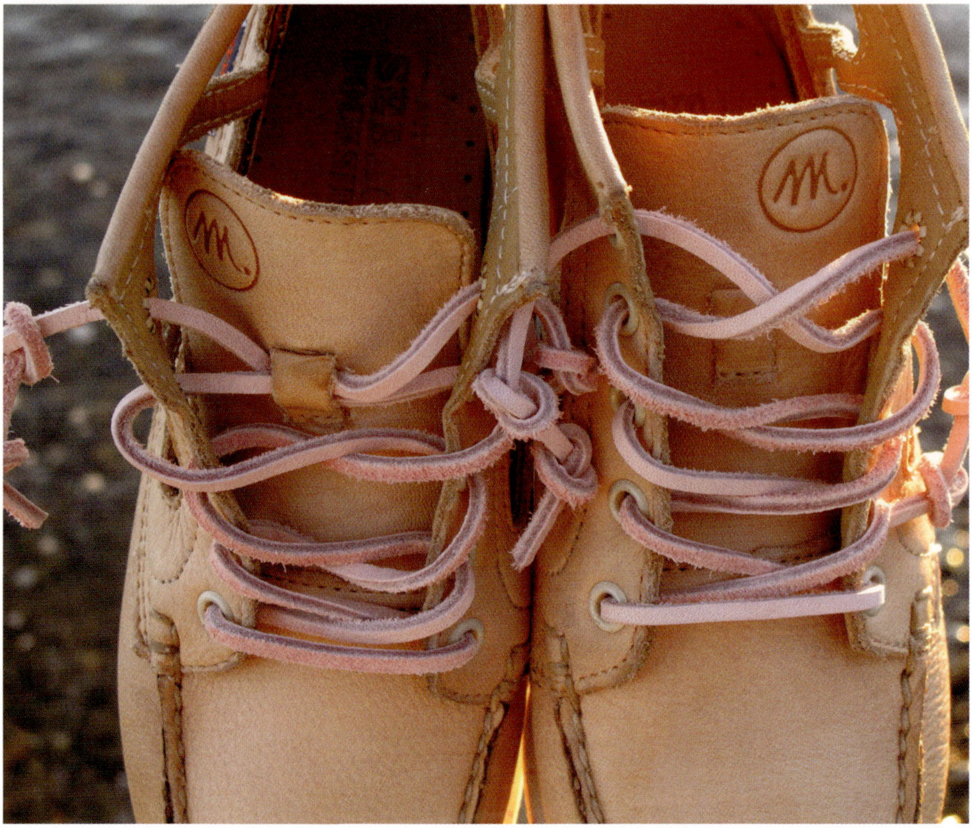

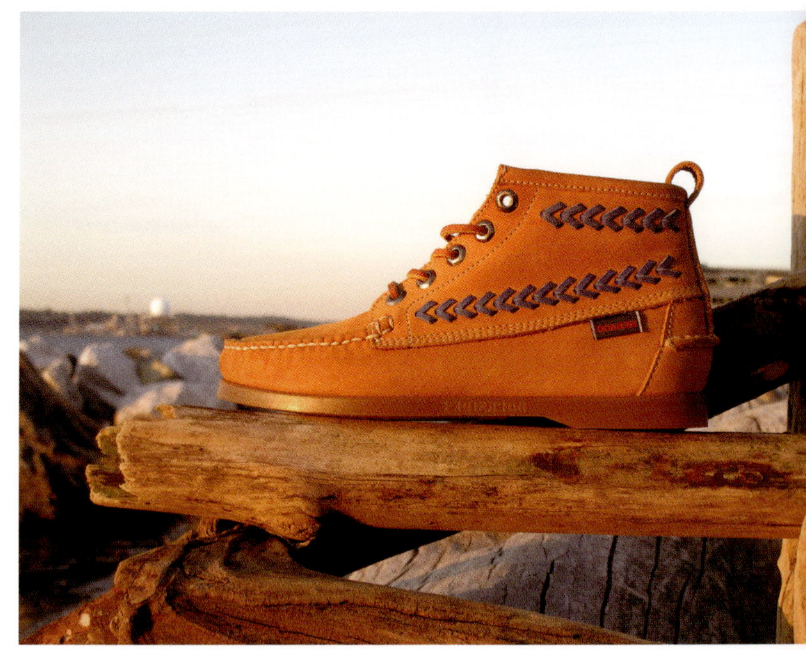

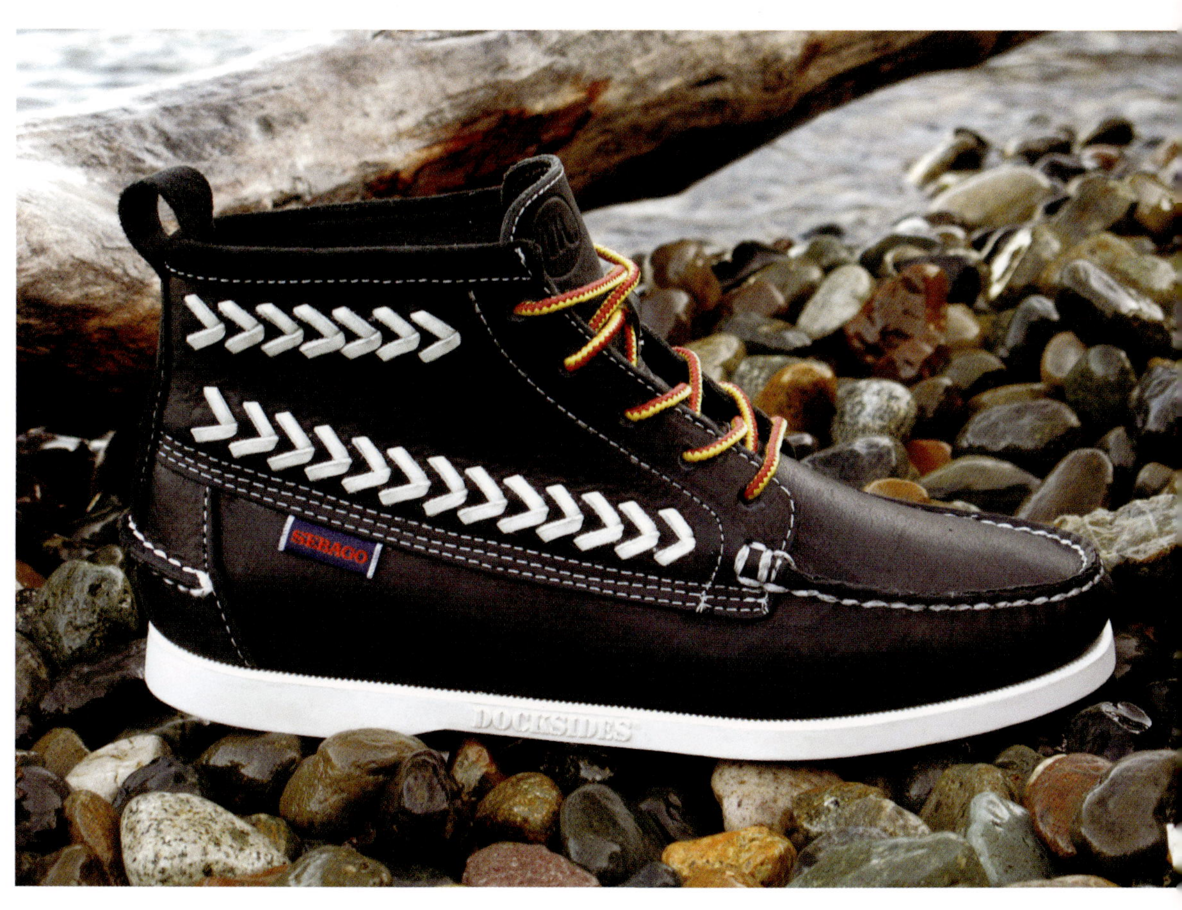
SEBAGO
DOCKSIDES

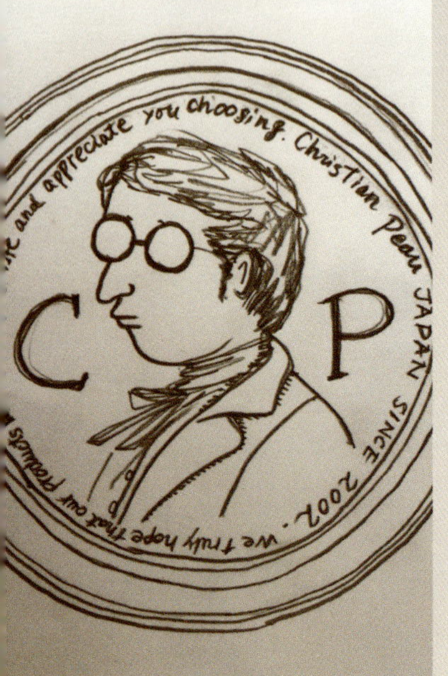

JUNJI KOIKE, CHRISTIAN PEAU

How did you get started? **AFTER EIGHT YEARS OF APPRENTICESHIP AT A CLOTHING COMPANY, I STUDIED THE LEATHER INDUSTRY BY MYSELF.** What is your work about? **MODERN CLASSICS.** Is there a specific reason why you chose shoe design? **UNLIKE BAGS AND CLOTHES, SHOES CAN HURT PEOPLE WHEN THEY ARE WORN. THIS MEANS SHOE DESIGN REQUIRES GREAT SKILL AND TECHNIQUE. SHOES CAN ALSO ALTER AND ENHANCE THE APPEARANCE OF CLOTHES. THESE TWO POINTS I AM INTERESTED IN.** Describe the most gratifying stage of the creative process. **PICKING UP THE NEW SAMPLES IS AS EXCITING AS TAKING A HOT LOAF OF BREAD OUT OF THE OVEN.** Who or what has played a part in your development as an artist? **GEN TARUMI.** What would be your material of choice for a special piece? **CORDOVAN.** What is vulgar to you and what elegant? **WAR AND THEFT IS VULGAR. PEACE IS ELEGANT.** What does beauty mean for you? **COURTSHIP BEHAVIOUR.**

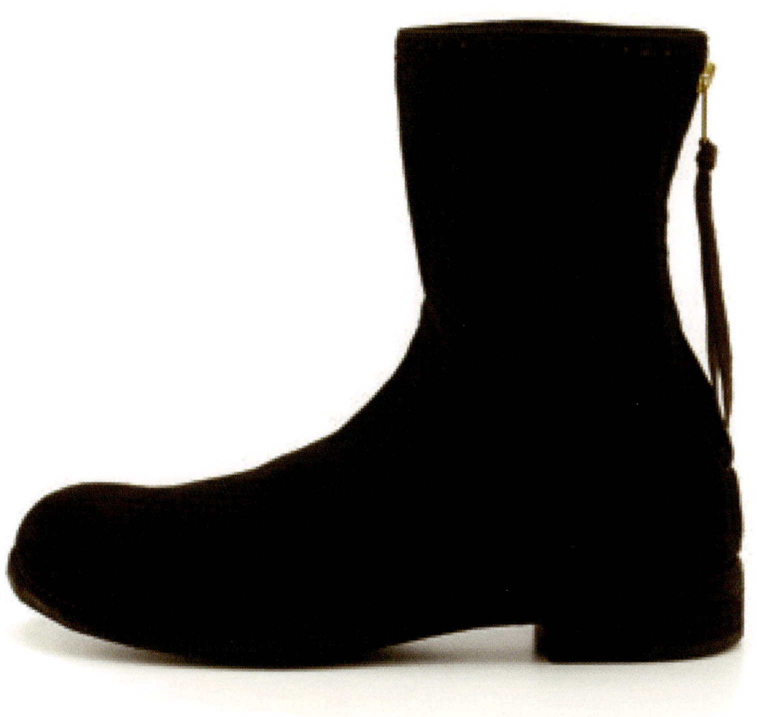

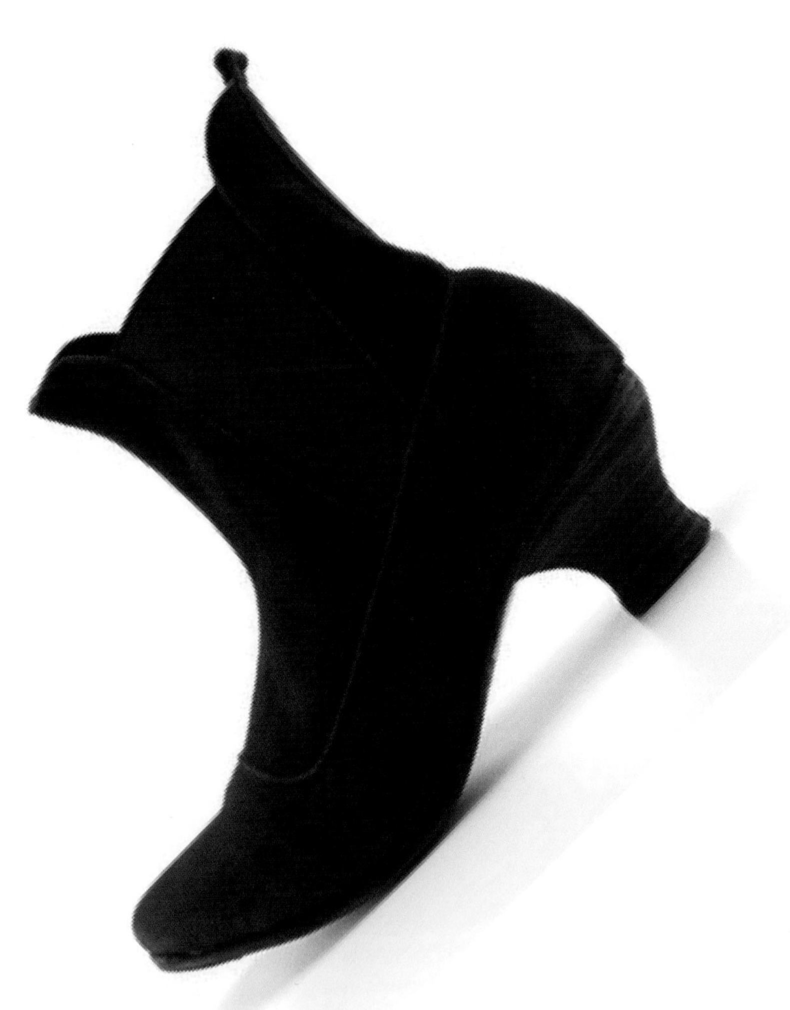

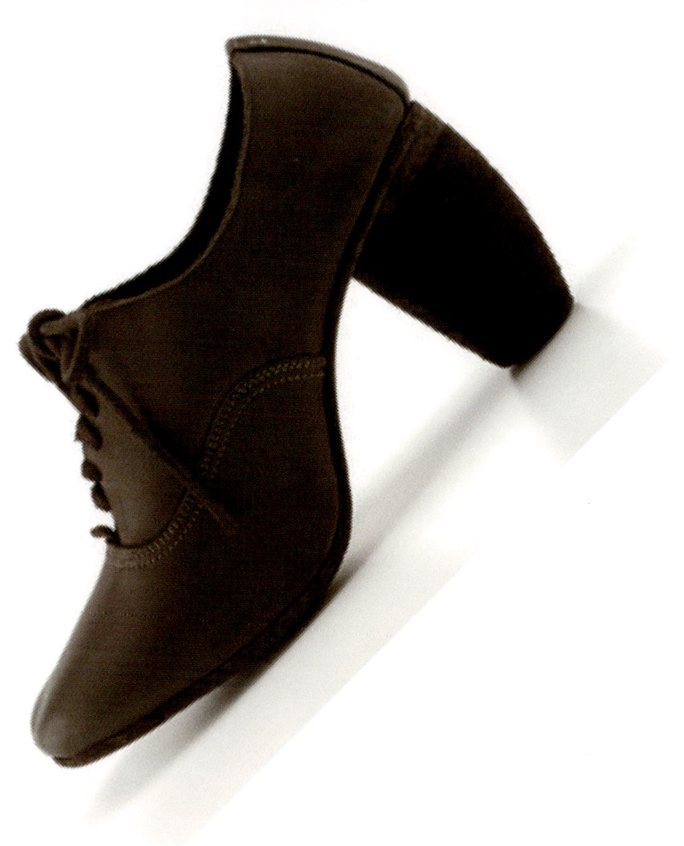

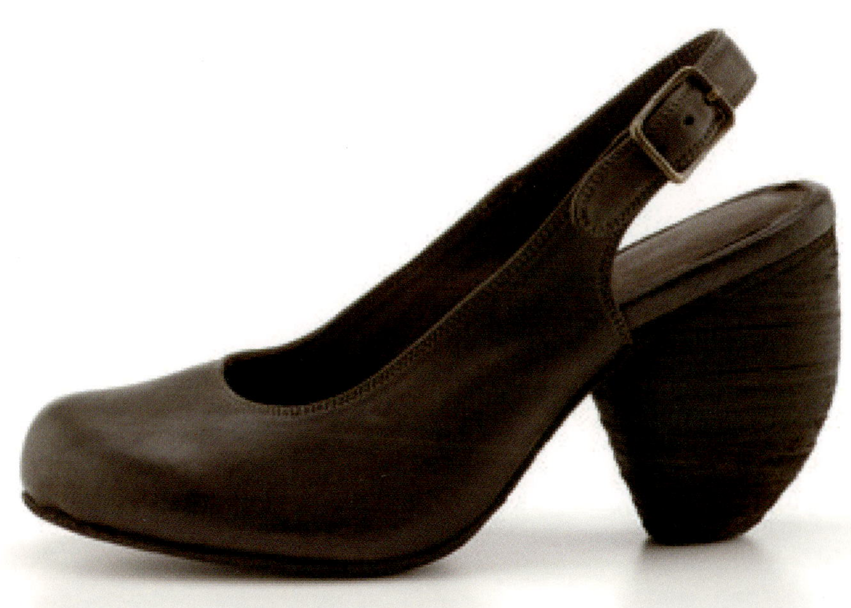

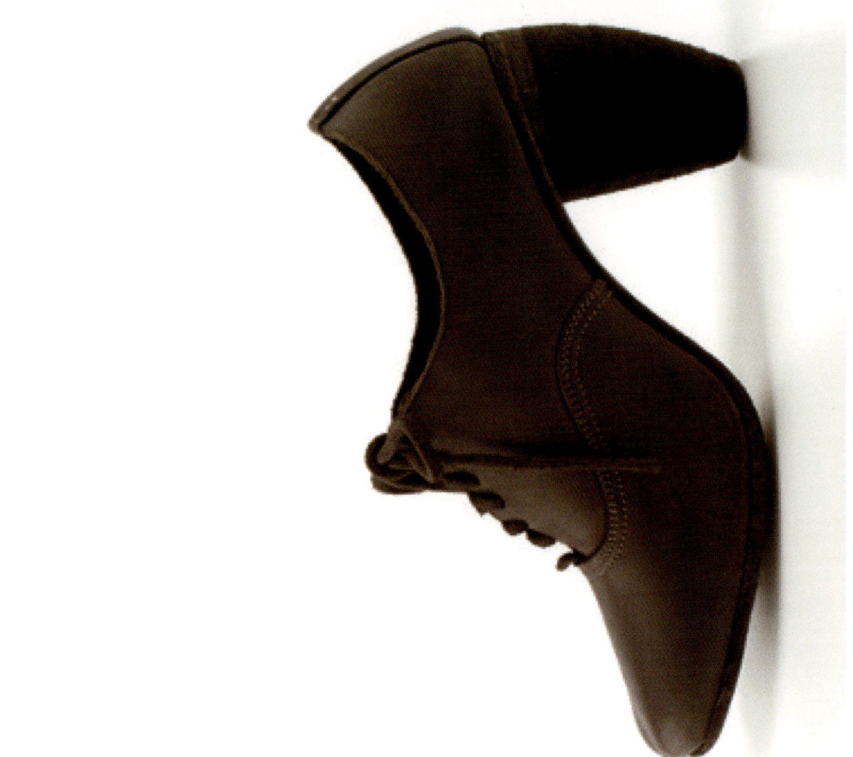

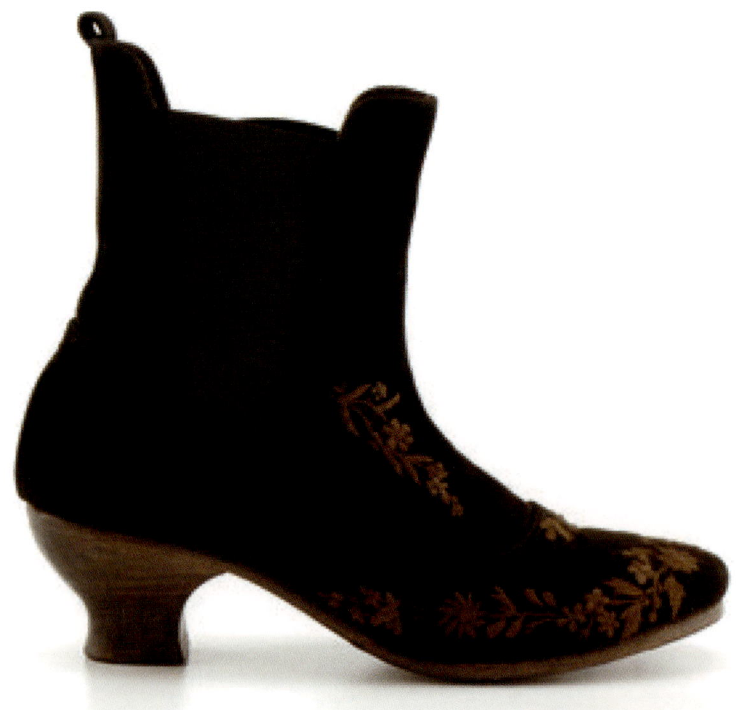

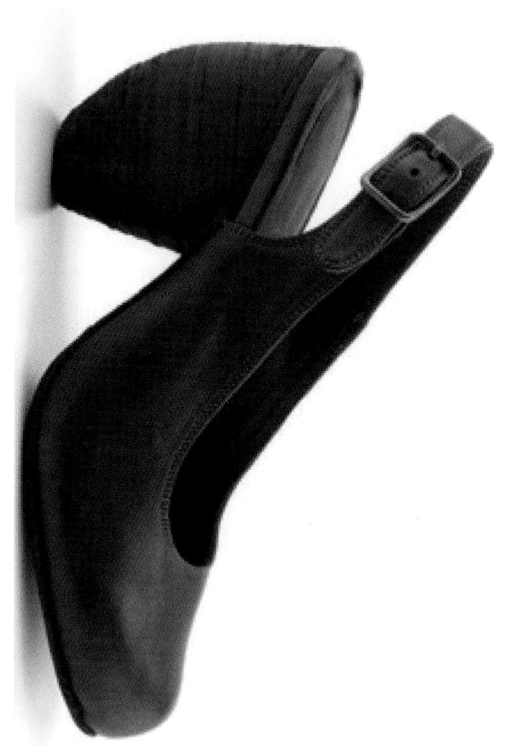

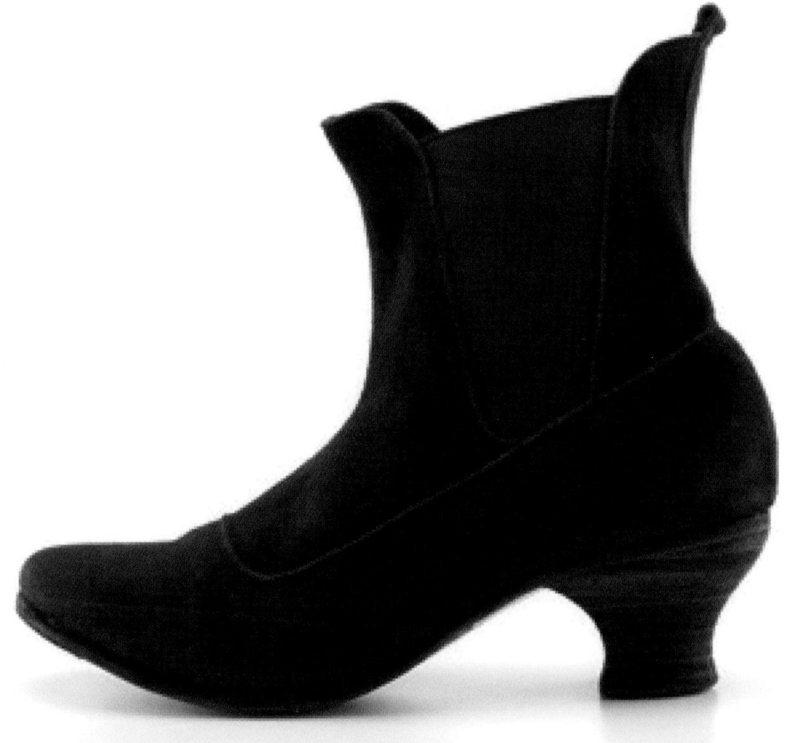

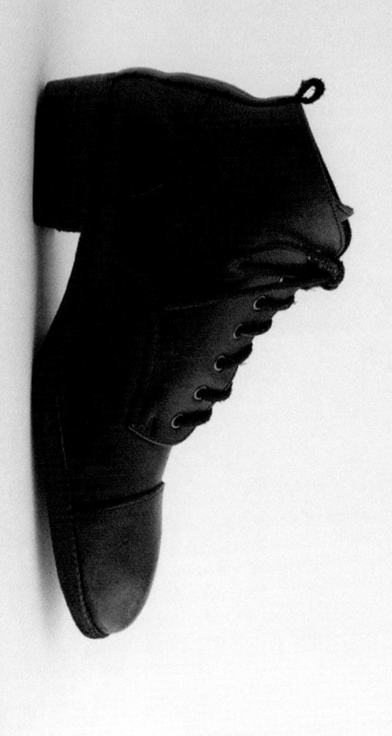
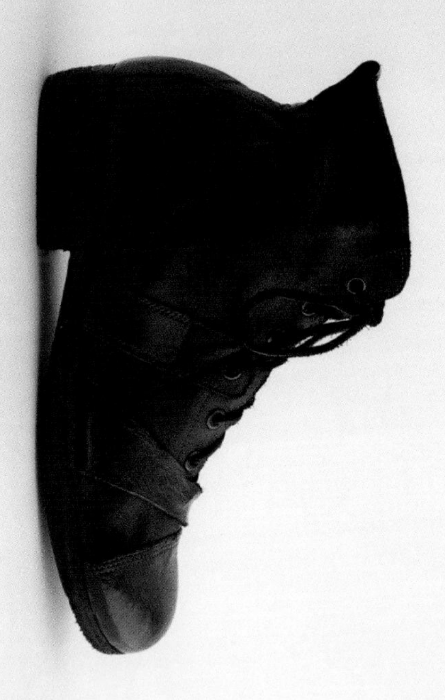

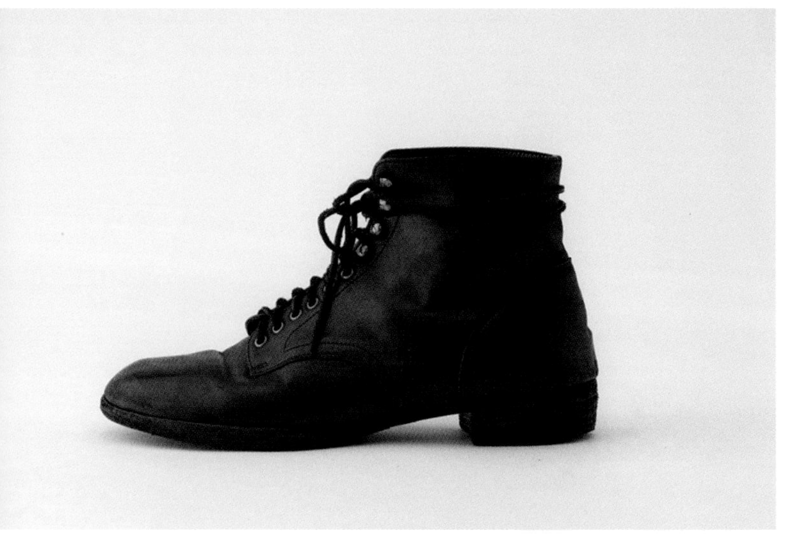

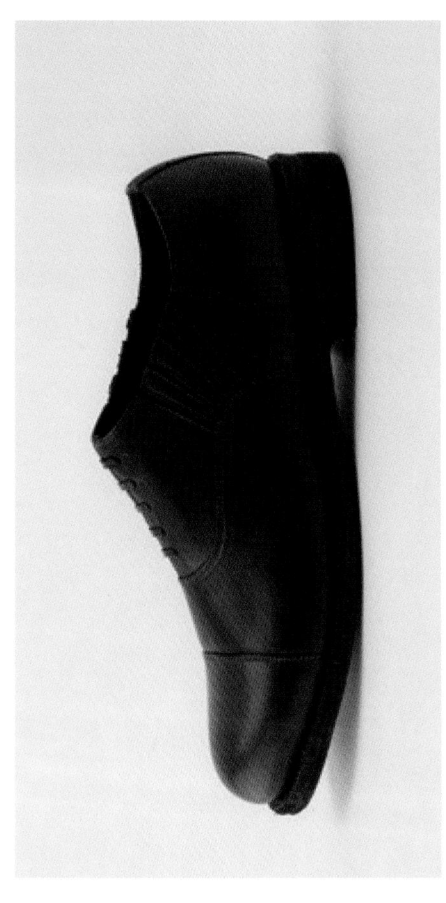

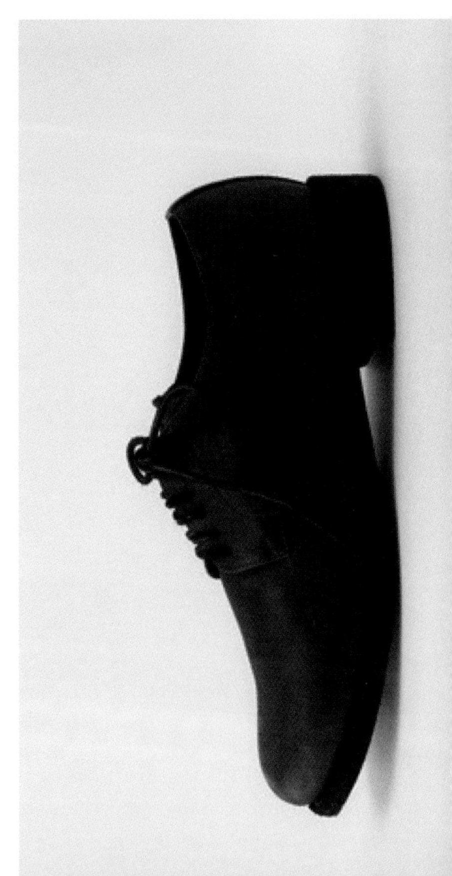

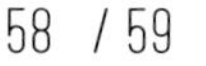

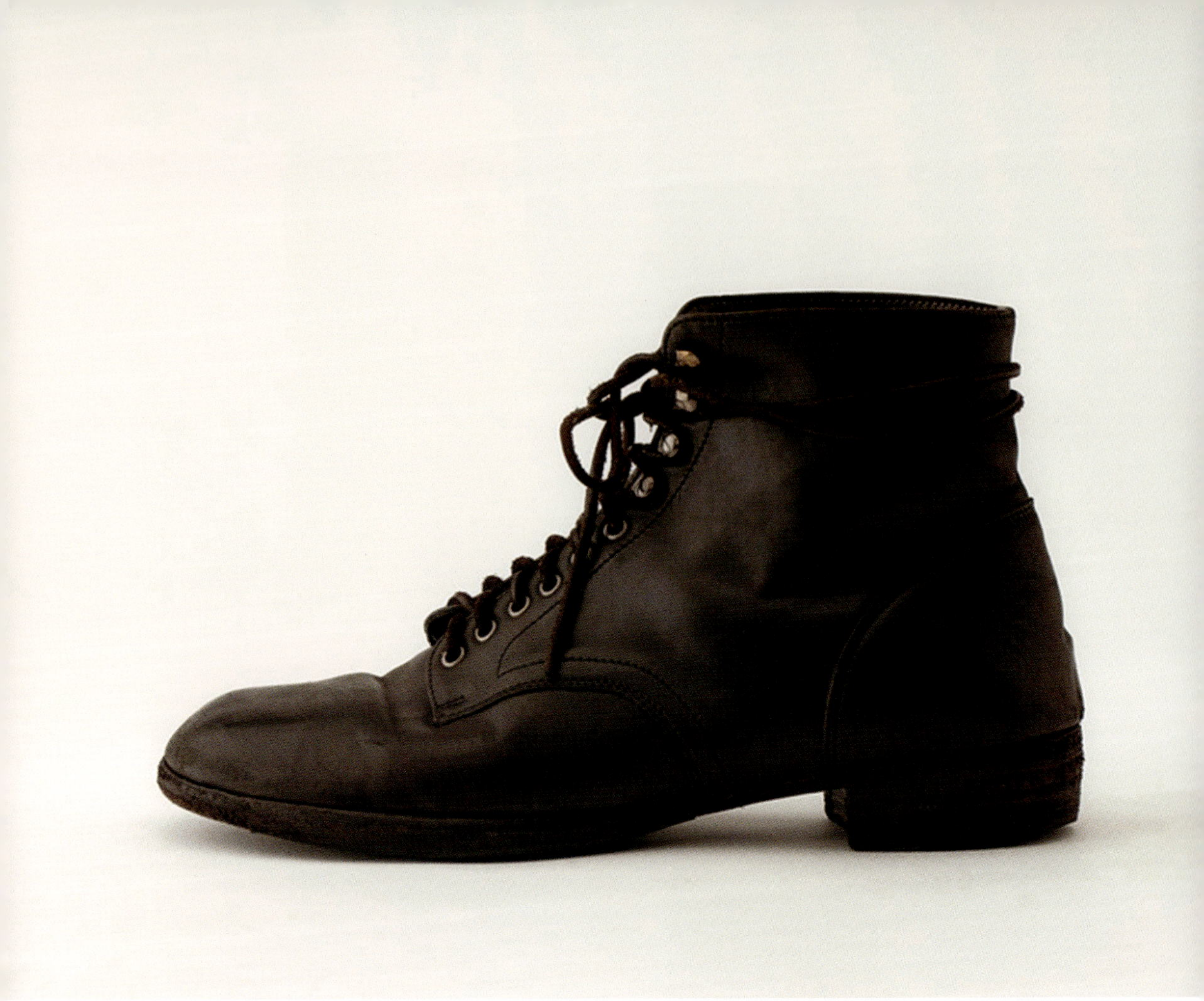

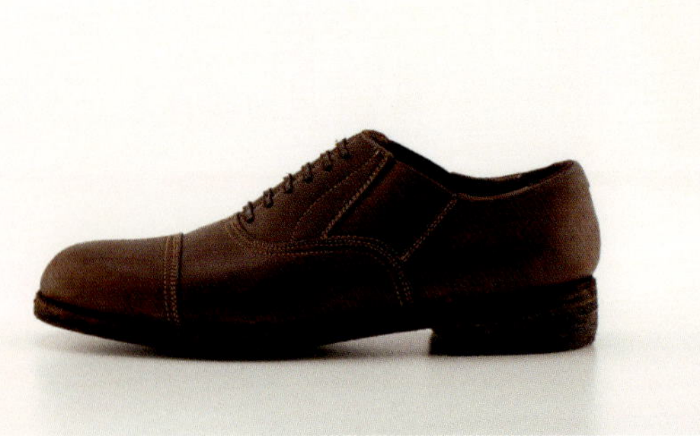

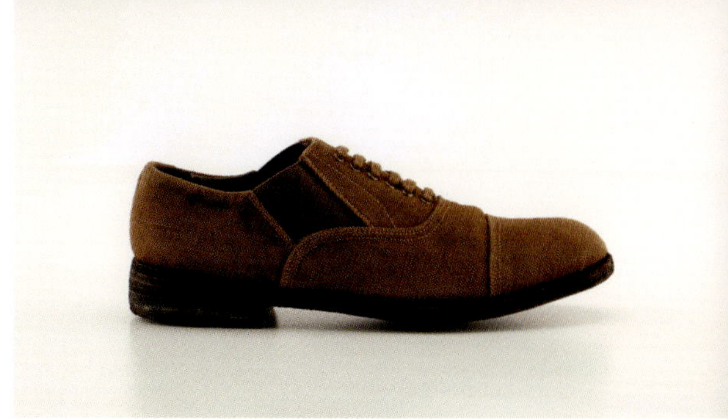

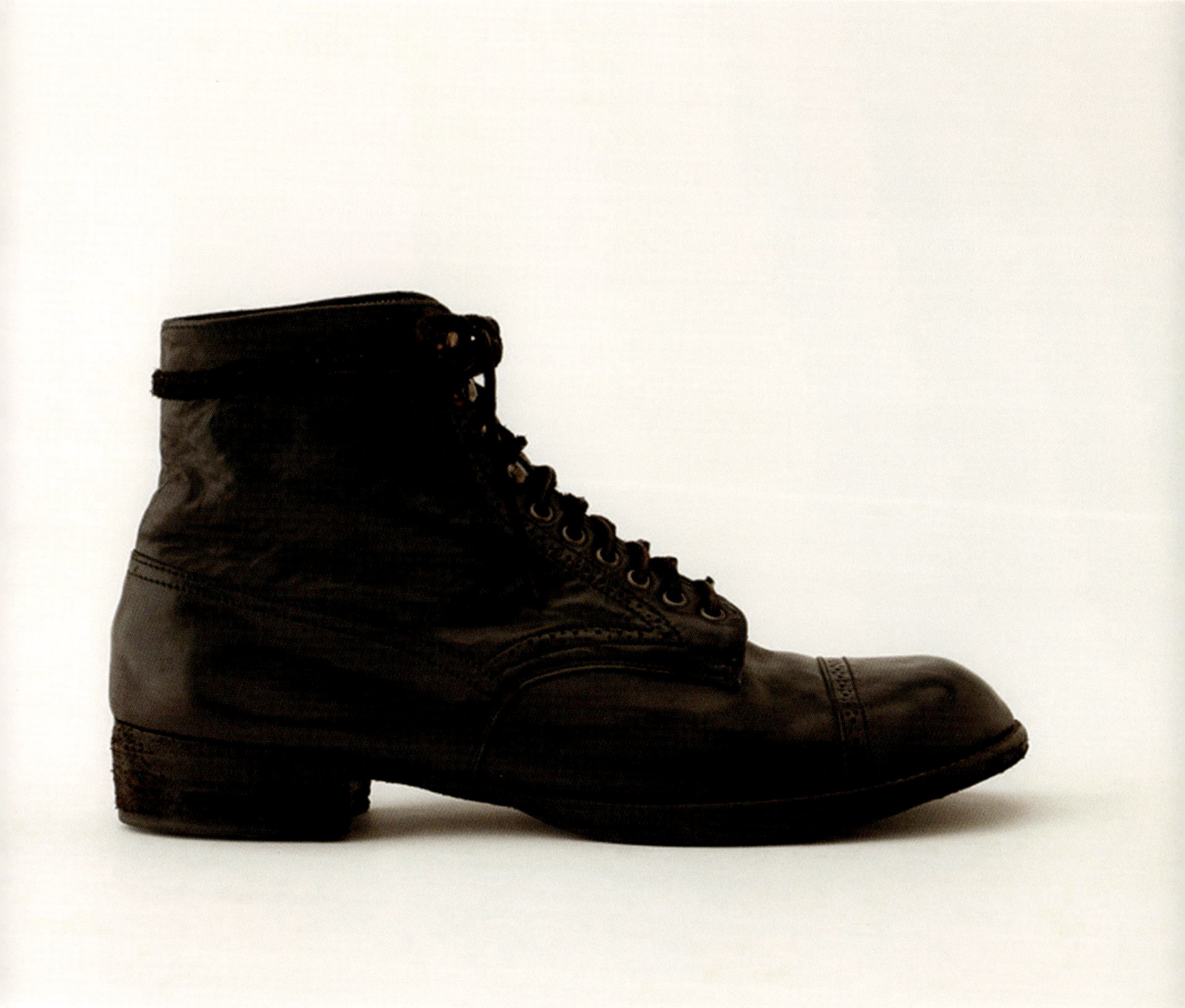

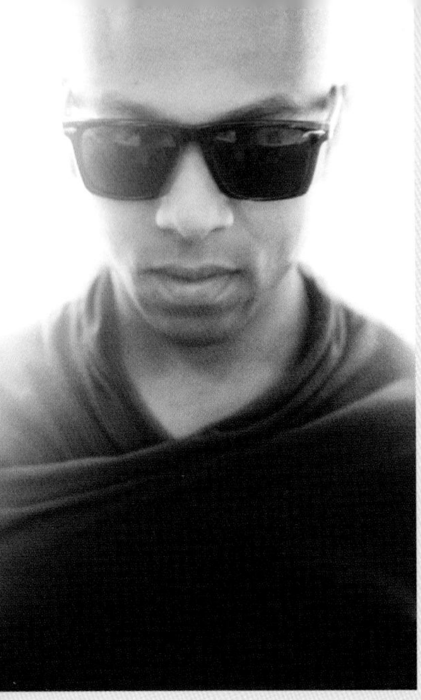

CIPHER

Cipher began in 2007 with the creative vision of its founder Collin Thompson. Inspired by cinema, the global economic shift and emerging internet and media technologies, Cipher was born out of a desire to create a modern, global, fashion and lifestyle brand that embraced the values of our emerging, social and connected world. What started as innovative designer shoes has now turned into a cultural statement for the global creative class, reaching like-minded professionals in design, fashion, art, music, architecture and film. **OUR CORE AIM IS TO FOSTER A VIBRANT AND DIVERSE GLOBAL CULTURE THROUGH INSPIRING HIGH CONCEPT EXPERIENCES AND CREATING INNOVATIVE DESIGNER PRODUCTS. WE BELIEVE THAT MUSIC IS THE UNIVERSAL SPIRIT OF CREATIVITY AND THAT ORGANISATIONS BUILT AROUND DESIGN AND CULTURE CAN MAKE A SIGNIFICANT CONTRIBUTION TO SOCIETY. INSPIRATION COMES FROM THE ICONIC NEW WAVE CINEMATIC STYLE OF JEAN LUC GODARD, ALAIN RESNAIS, CHRIS MARKER, WONG KAR WAI, THE ARCHITECTURE OF ZAHA HADID AND SANTIAGO CALATRAVA AND THE DESIGN PRINCIPLES OF DIETER RAMS.** With simple, resonant asymmetric graphic lines, black to white tonal palettes and streaks of metallic, our design aesthetic is about modern urban elegance. We combine eighties Neo Tokyo electropop colours with the chiaroscuro style of film noir and the Neo-Futuristic design of Blade Runner, creating products that echo the fluid lifestyles of creative professionals.

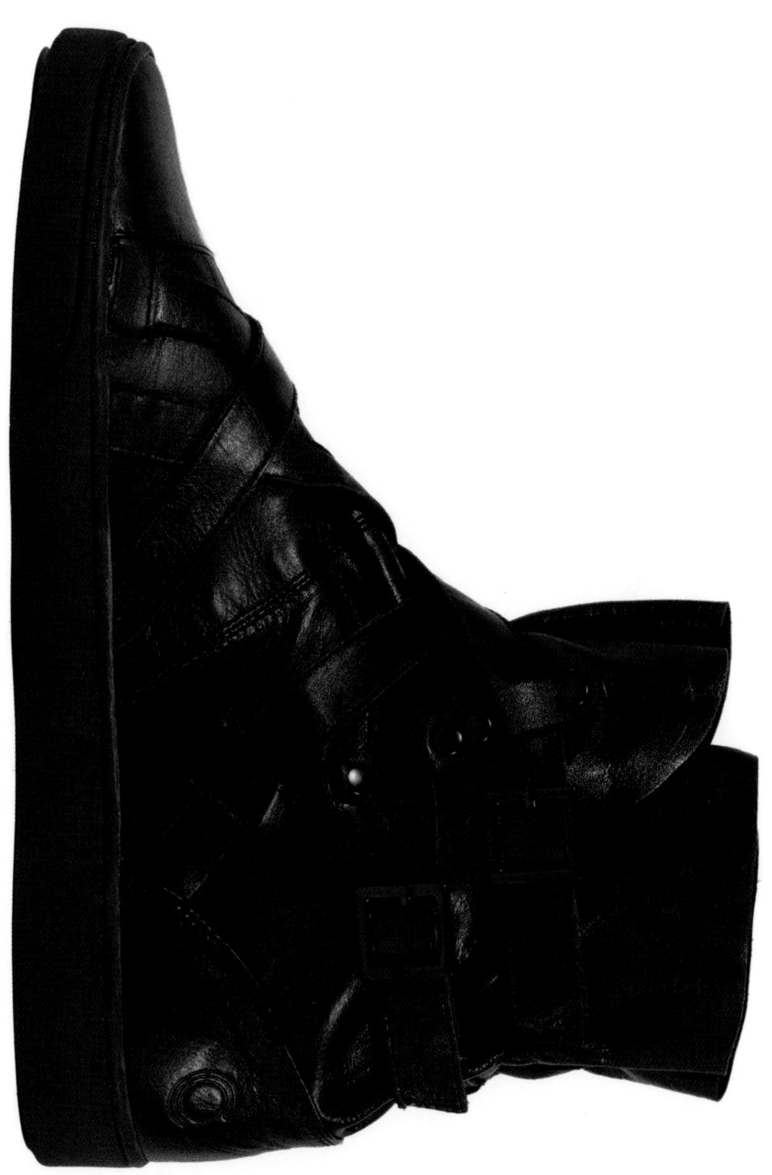

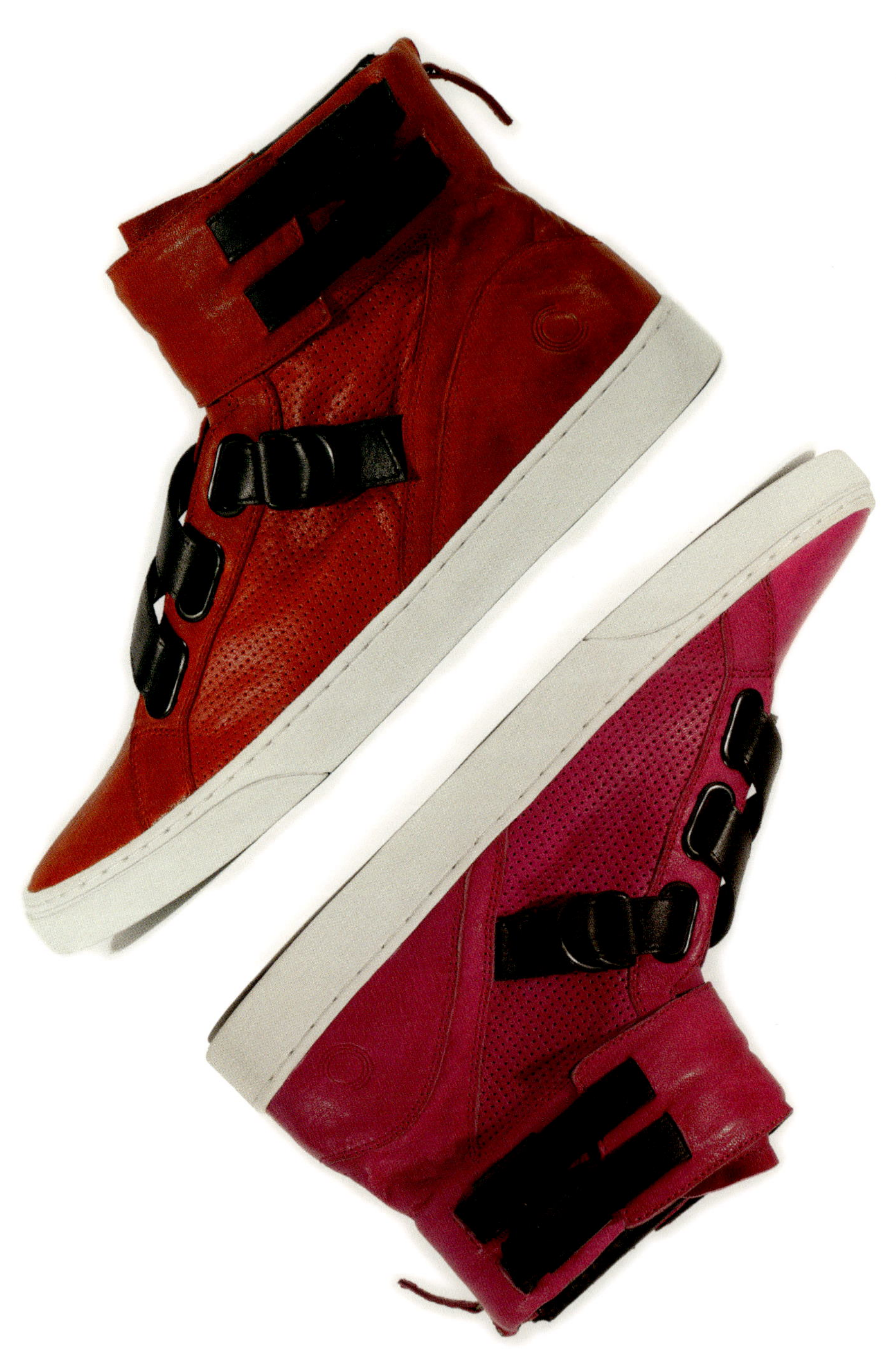

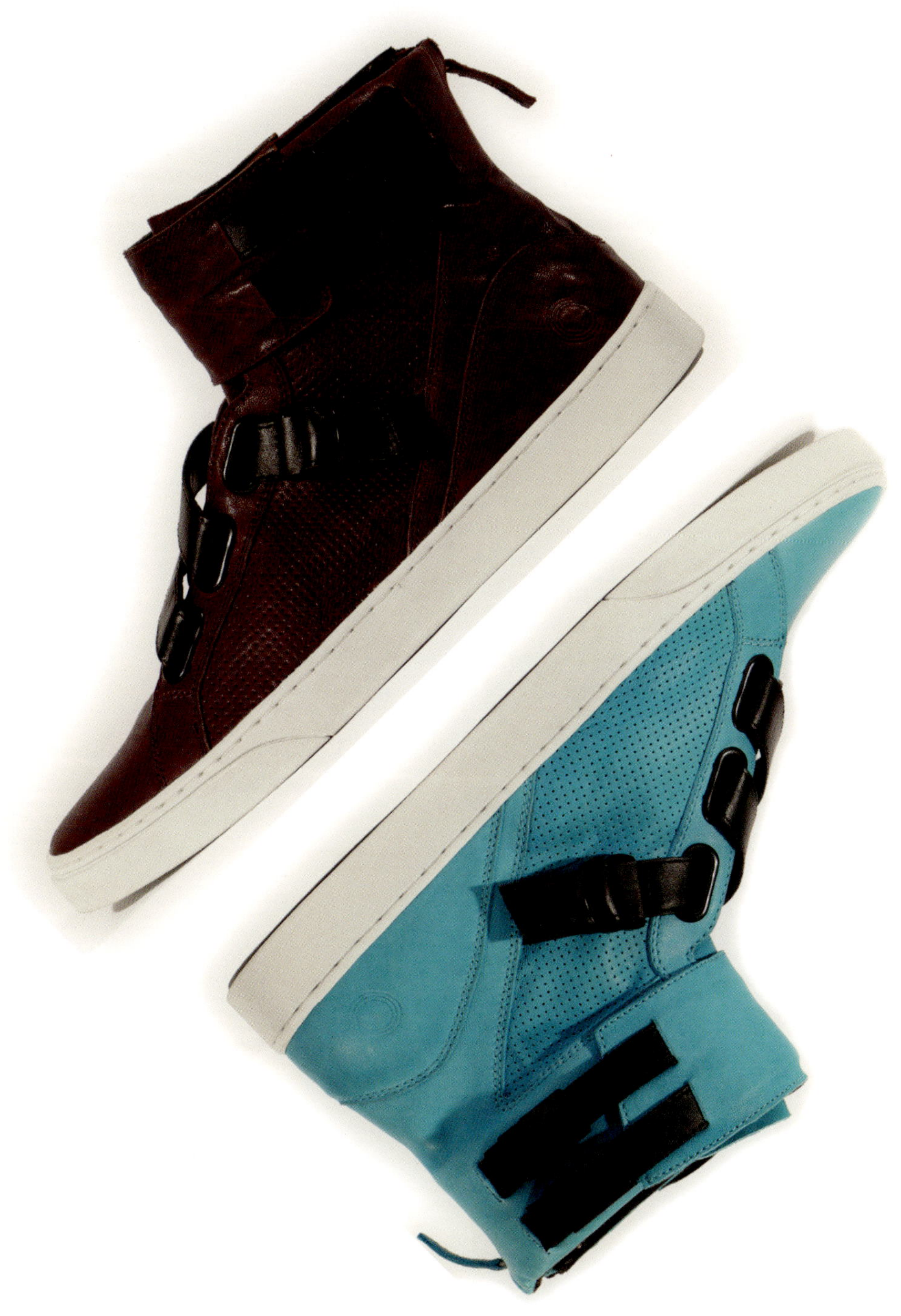

CIPHER

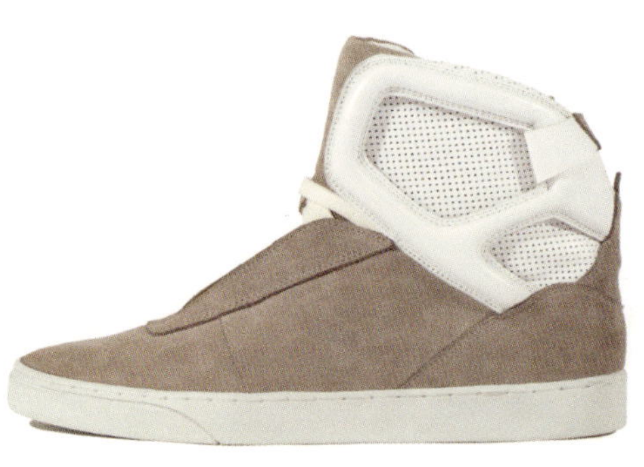
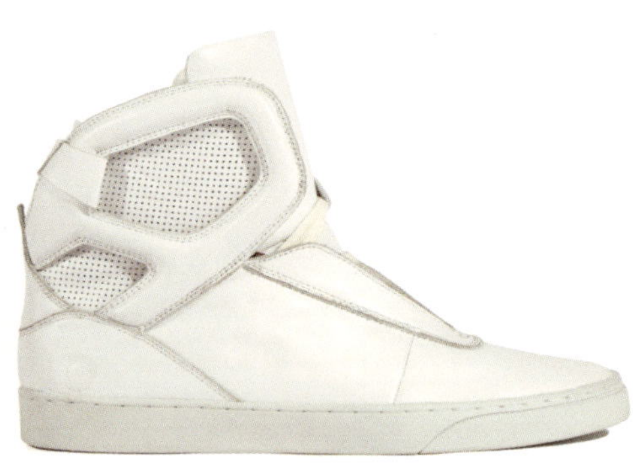
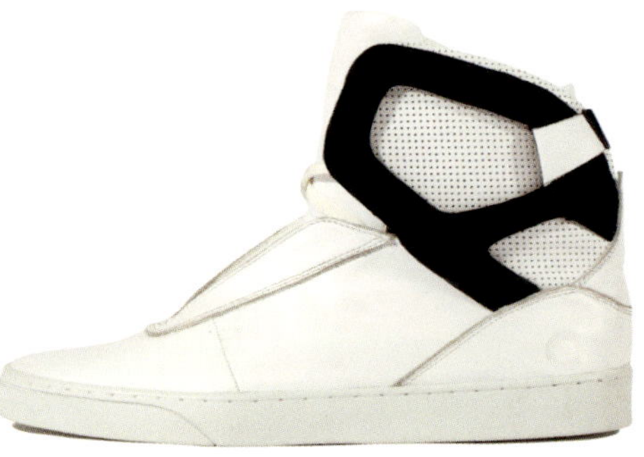
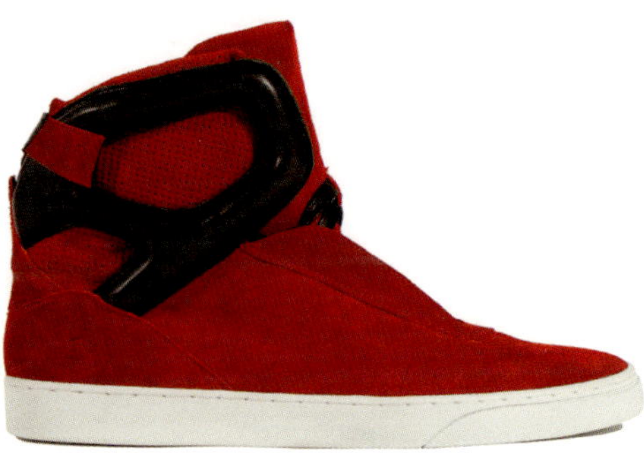
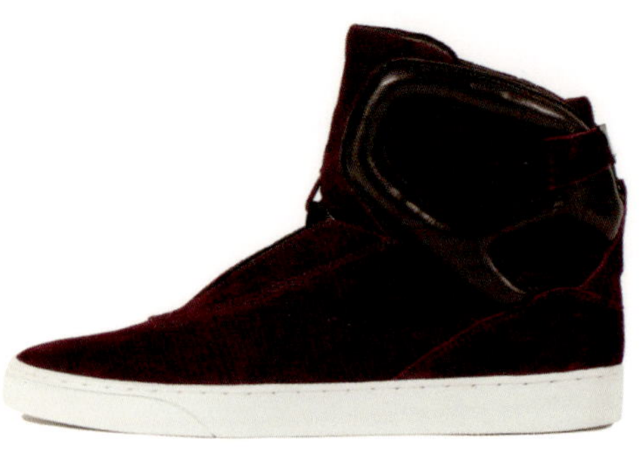
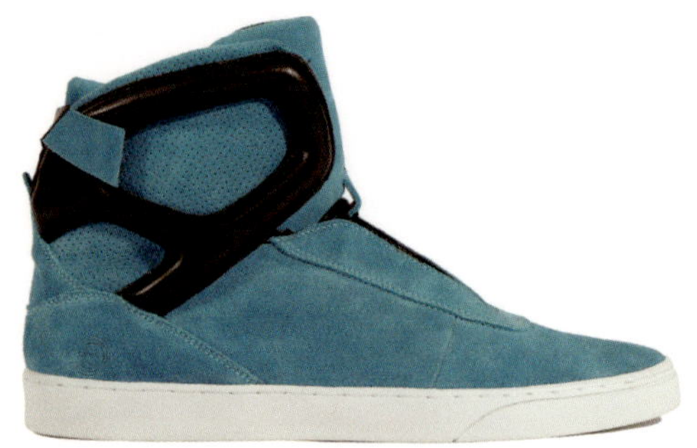

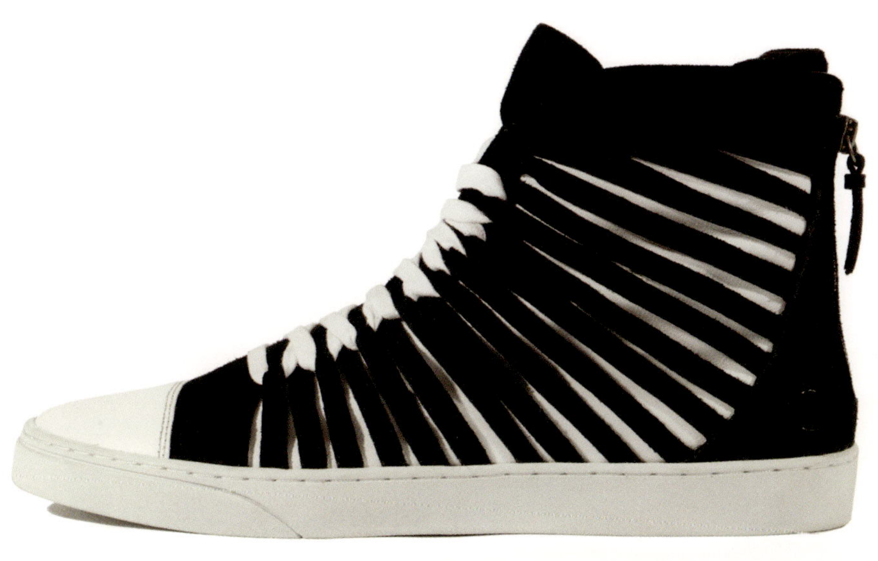

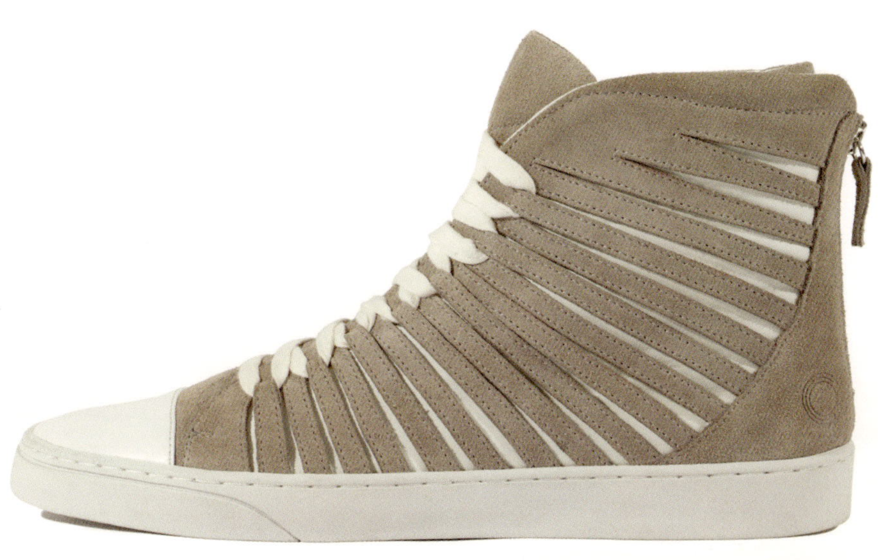

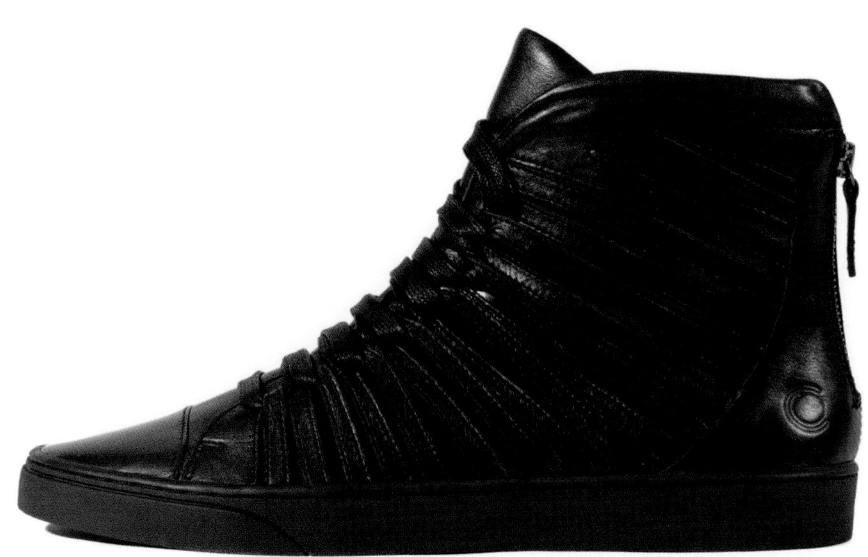

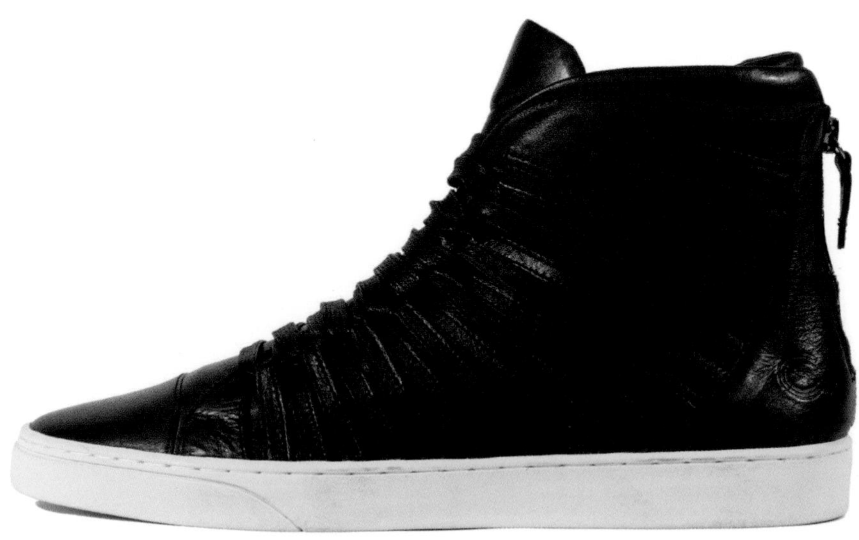

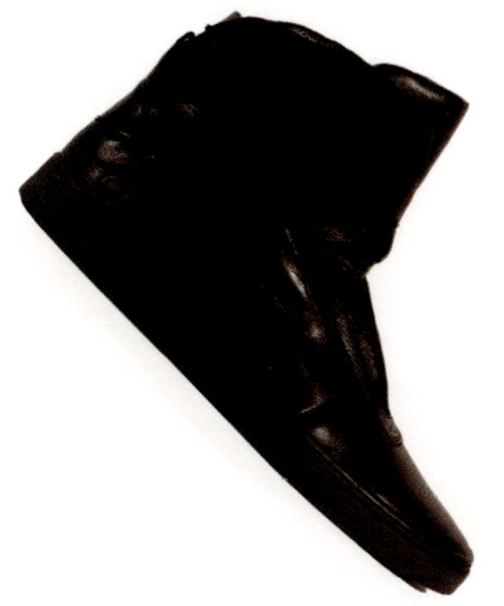

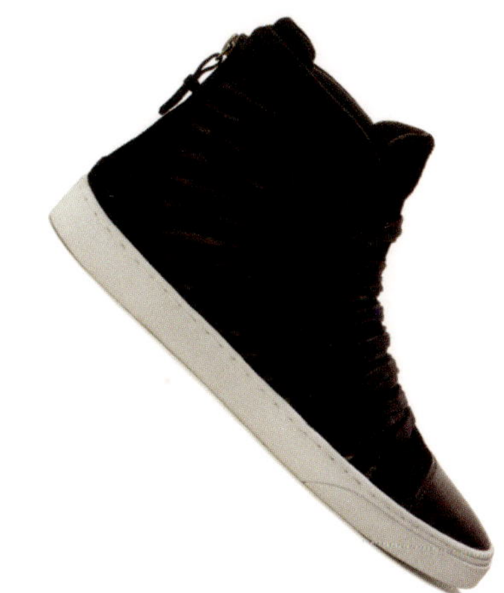

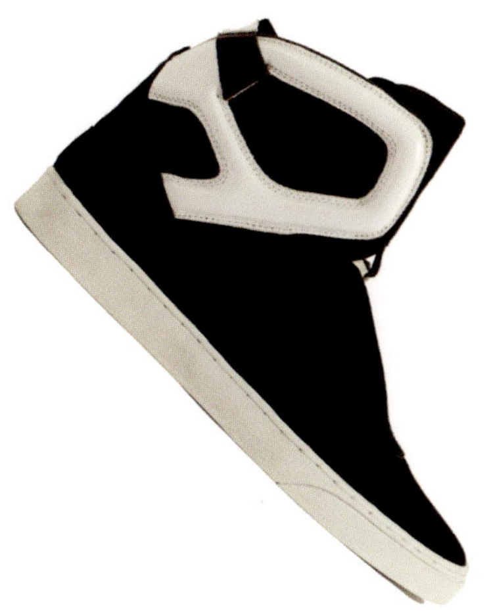

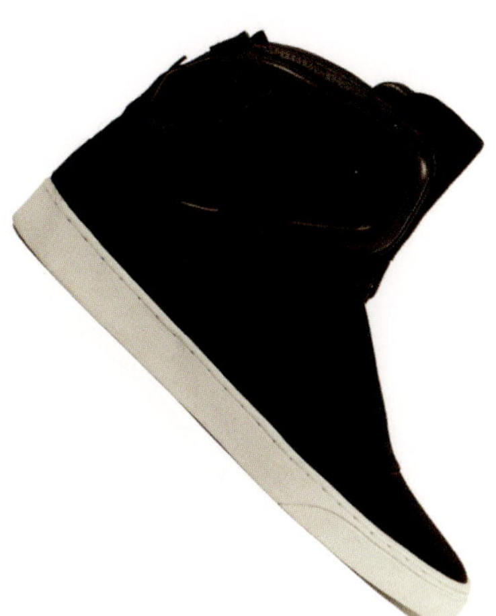

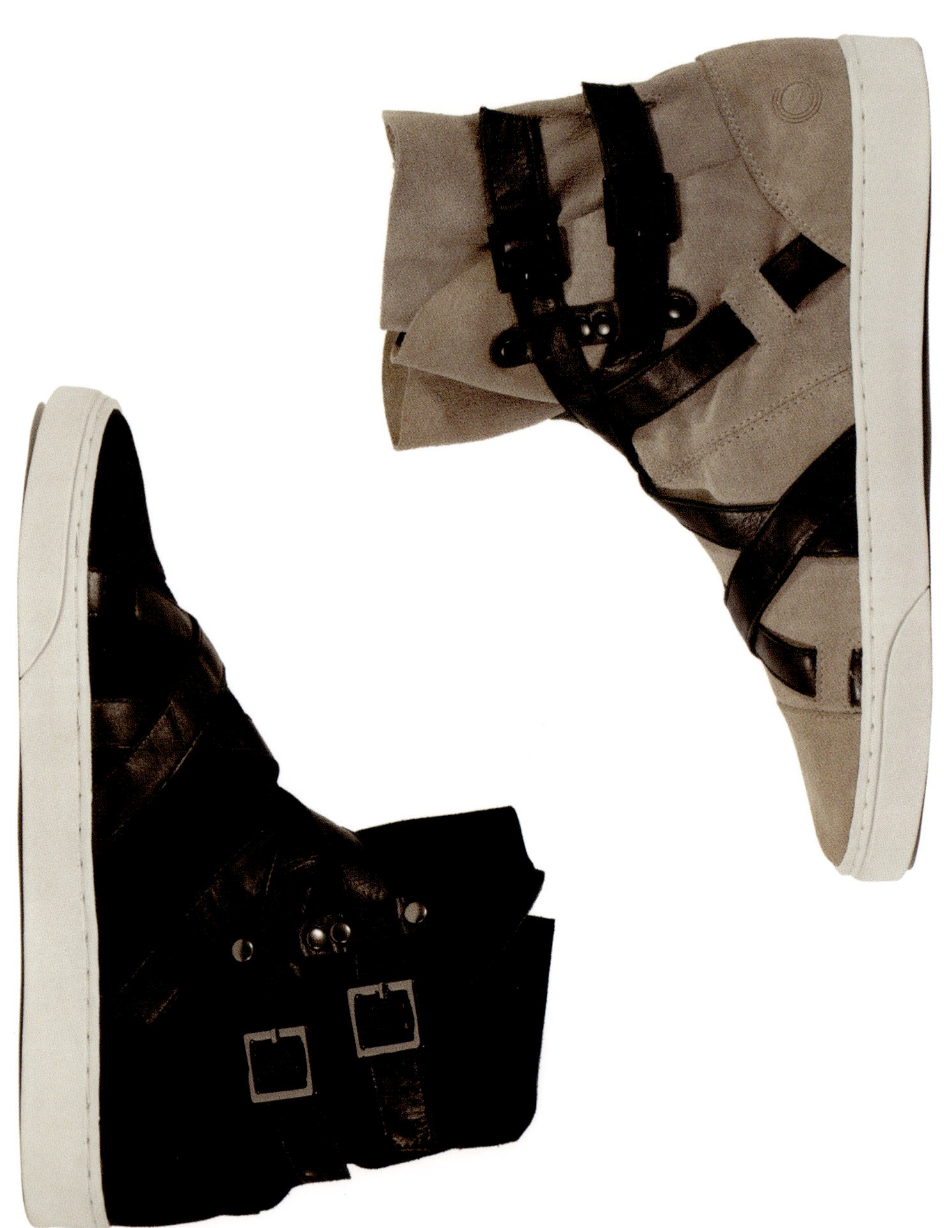

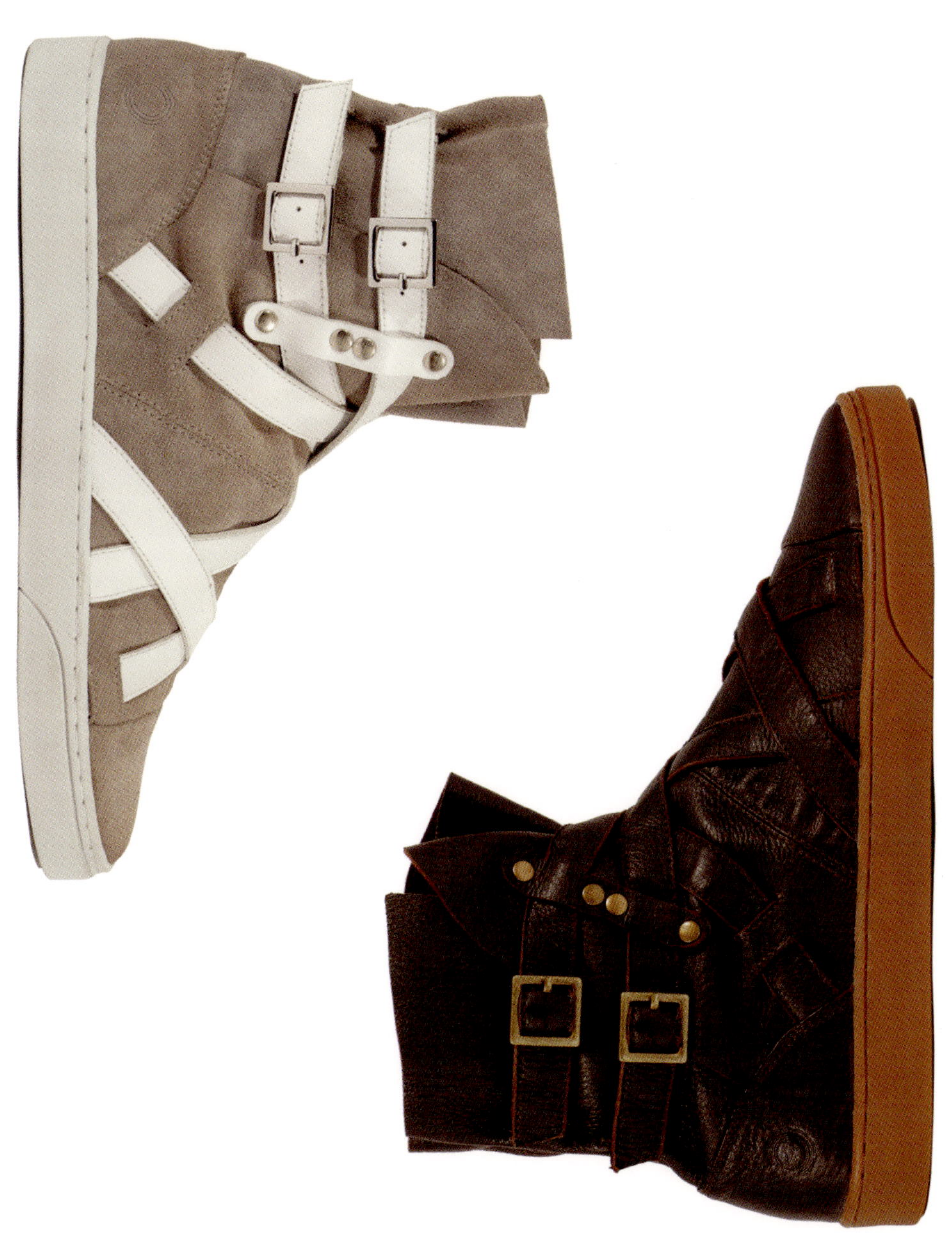

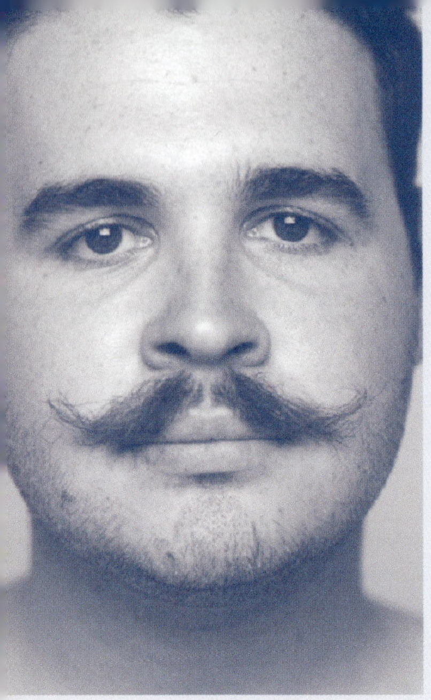

ELIA MAURIZI

How did you get started? **I AM A SHOEMAKER'S SON SO I FELL IN LOVE WITH SHOES FROM A YOUNG AGE** What do you consider your most innovative design so far? **THE FIRST FASHION SHOE I CREATED, THE PARROT SHOE** Tell us something about the design process. **FIRST I DO SOME COOL HUNTING WHICH I LOVE, THEN SOME BRAIN STORMING WITH THE STAFF BEFORE FINALLY DEVELOPING A PROTOTYPE. I THEN SHOW IT TO THE SALES TEAM TO FIND THE RIGHT WAY TO MARKET IT.** Who or what has played a part in your development as an artist? **MAYBE A DESIGNER WHO A LONG TIME AGO LIVED WITH MY FAMILY FOR A COUPLE OF YEARS.** If you had to choose one colour and one material for an important piece, what would they be? **YELLOW VEGETAL LEATHER.** Who or what inspires you? **IN GENERAL, I SEE MANY INTERESTING THINGS COMING FROM YOUNG DESIGNERS IN NORTHERN EUROPE** What do you consider vulgar and what elegant? **VULGAR IS ROBERTO CAVALLI, ELEGANT IS JIL SANDER** What is beauty? **A POINT OF VIEW**

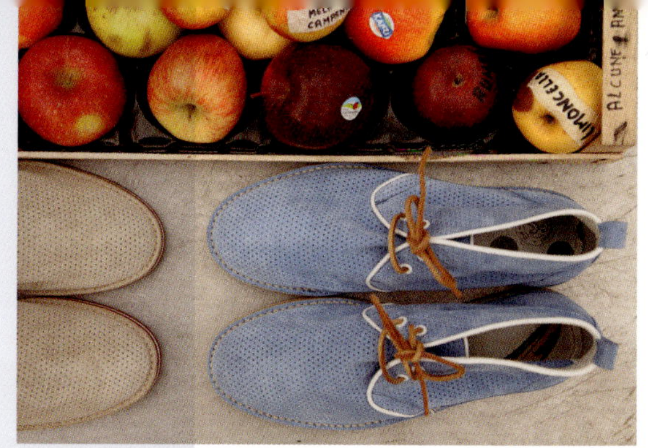

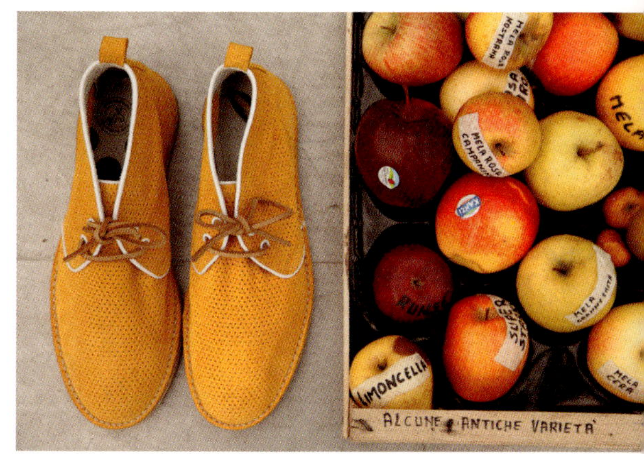
LIMONCELLA
ALCUNE ANTICHE VARIETA'

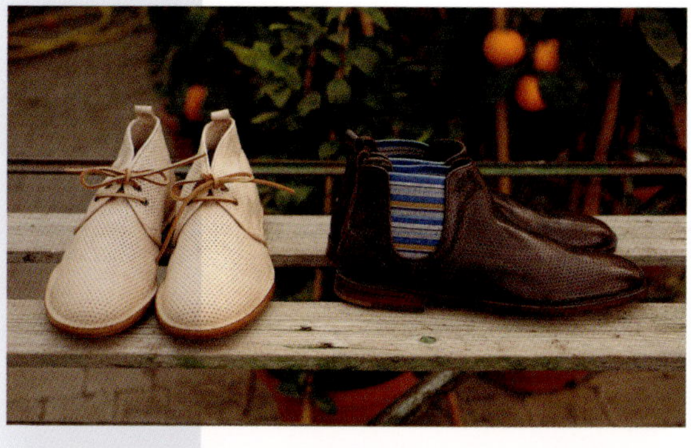

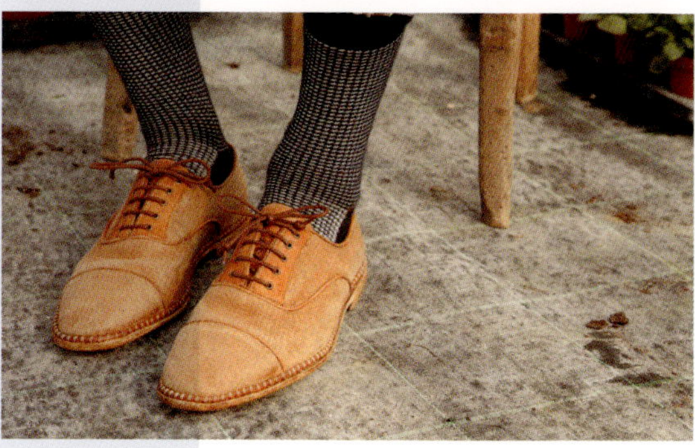

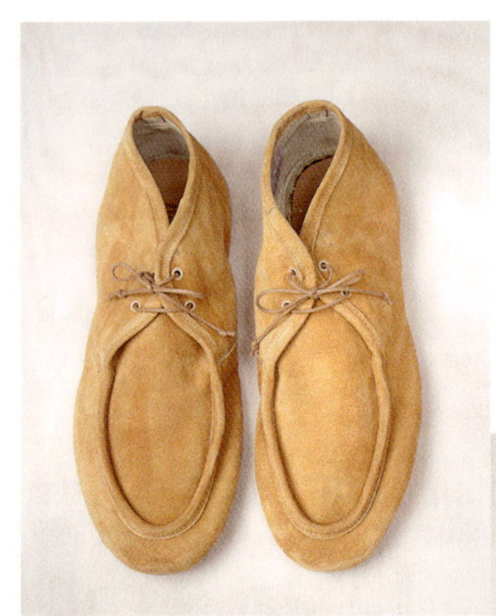
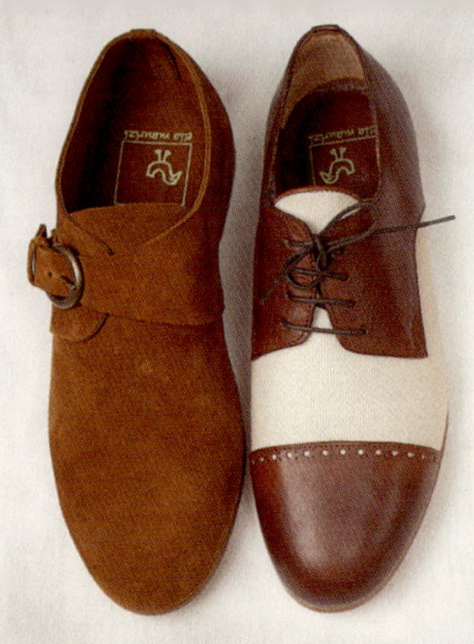
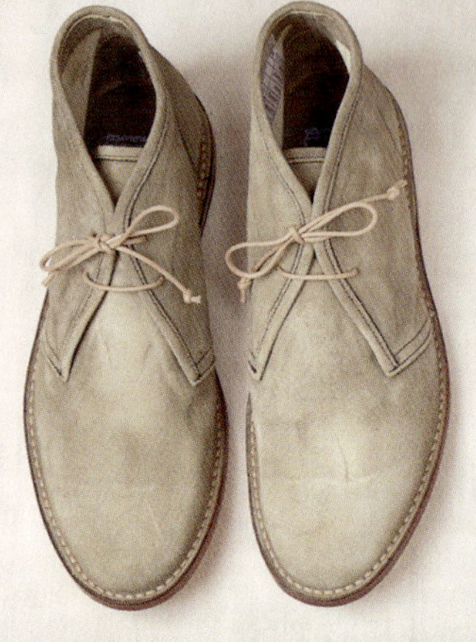
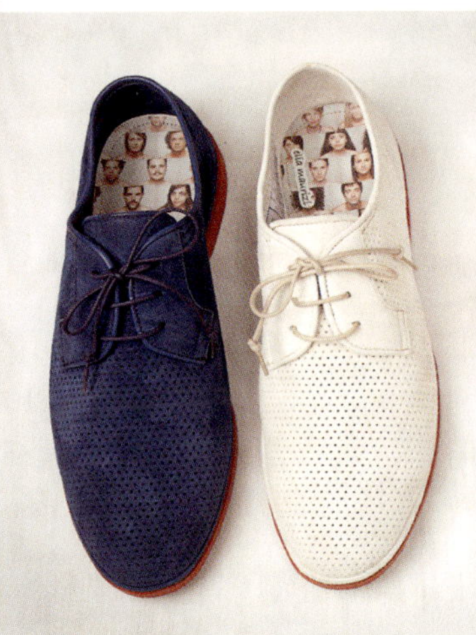
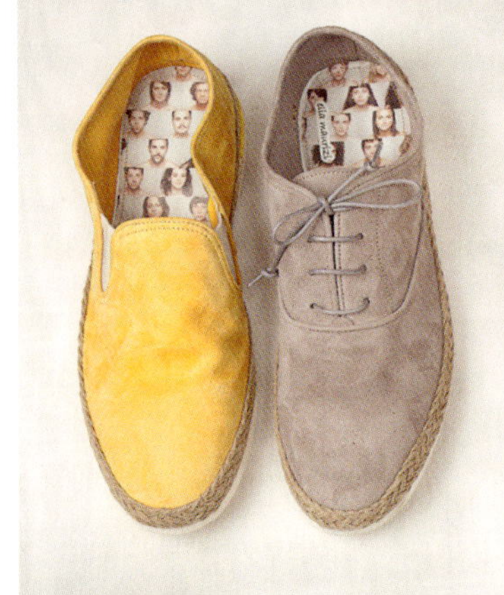
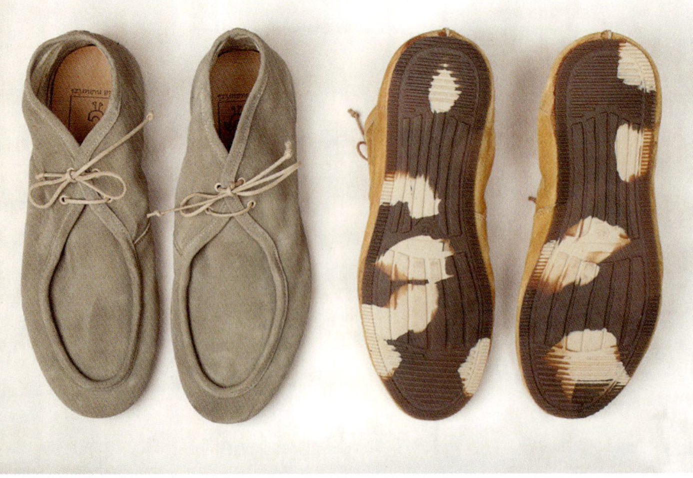

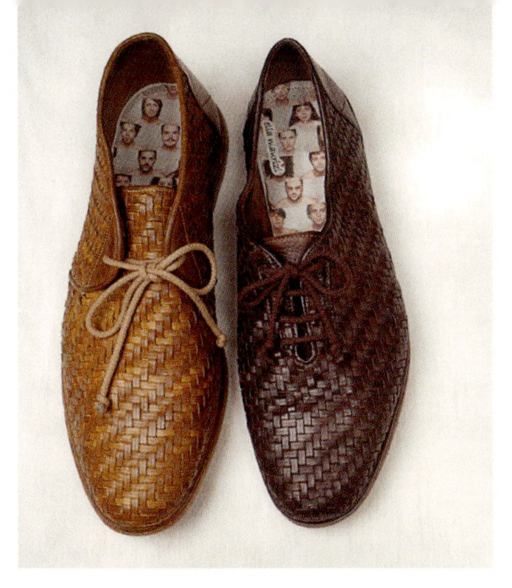

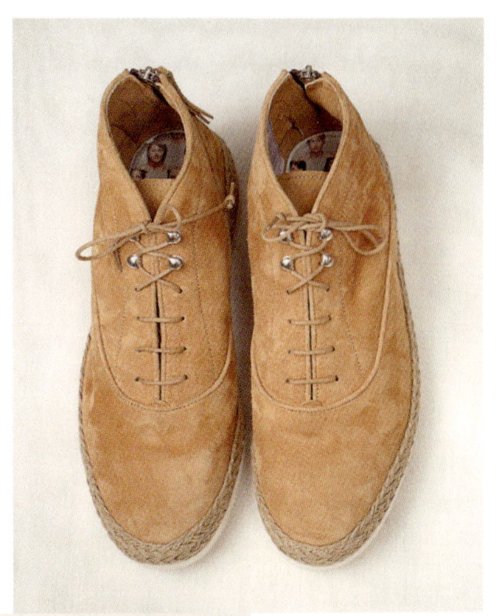

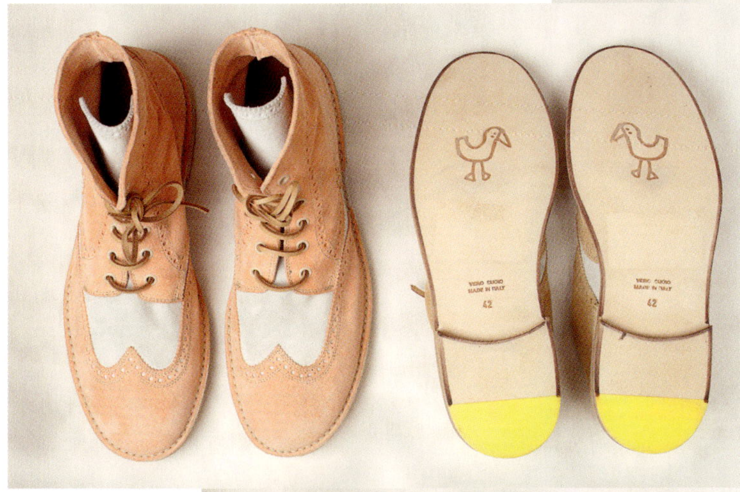

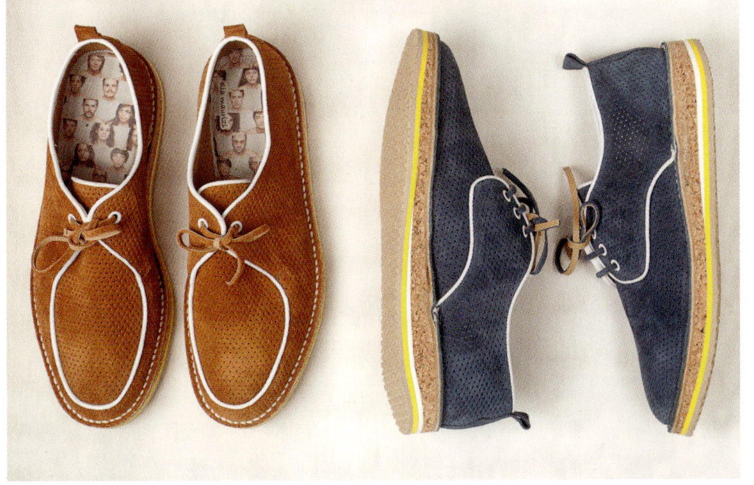

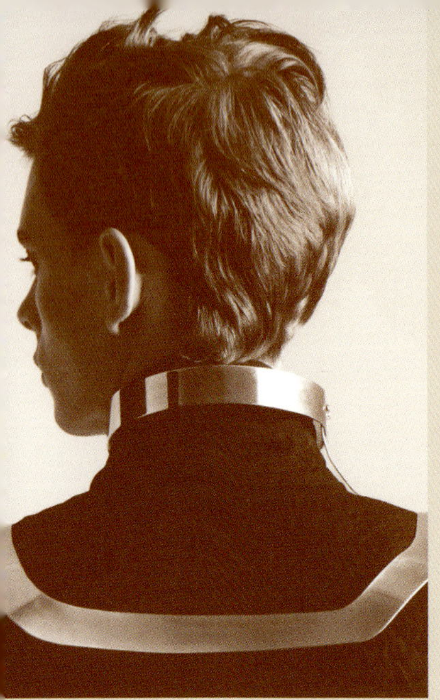

ERÏK BJERKESJÖ

I am a Swedish-born designer with an MA in Advanced Fashion Footwear Design from Polimoda Institute under the guidance of Patrick de Muynck and Linda Loppa. I initially worked in fashion design with a tailoring orientation but when I moved into footwear I immediately felt it was my destiny to make shoes. **MY WORK IS AN EVERYDAY ROMANCE. IT IS ABOUT MAKING THOUGHTFUL, INNOVATIVE AND ELEGANT DESIGN USING OLD TRADITIONS. I STRIVE TO CREATE WELL MADE PRODUCTS THAT STICK FOR MANY SEASONS. I ALSO CHOOSE NOT TO MAKE MY COLLECTION TOO BROAD. I WORK ON MY COLLECTIONS WITH AN OLDER GENERATION OF CRAFTSMEN IN TUSCANY, ITALY. TO LEARN THE TRADITIONS OF THE CRAFTSMEN AND SEE MY IDEAS BECOME SOMETHING THAT CAN BE WORN IS VERY SATISFYING.** The design process takes place in my atelier and in the workshop where fine leather is punctuated with delicate hammers. Construction begins in the clicking room, where the elements are cut out based on my design sketches, one at a time. The individual pieces then pass through the prep room where thread making takes place and they are hand-sewn together. From there, they head into the closing room where the completed segments of the upper are united. After some fine punching on the toe cap and rounded soles, the shoe is born. **ONE OF MY MOST INNOVATIVE DESIGNS IS THE SHOE TRANSMISSION, MADE OF EMBOSSED ORGANIC CALF LEATHER. THE NAME DERIVES FROM A SONG BY JOY DIVISION THAT I HAVE BEEN LISTENING TO SINCE MY TEENAGE YEARS. THE SHOE IS BASED ON MY FEELINGS TOWARDS THE SONG AND LYRICS, AS WELL AS CHILDHOOD MEMORIES OF MY GRANDFATHER. HE WAS ALWAYS DRESSED IN A BLACK SUIT WITH PERFECTLY POLISHED BLACK SHOES.** I was a quite politically active when I was growing up. I often took part in demonstrations and used to listen to the Swedish band Refused. I believed that the expectations society had of teenagers were hopeless and that we lived in a mass produced, fast forward atmosphere. When I started my journey as a designer I felt that I could at least make some difference in the making process. I never wanted to go into mass production to make something fast for a fast society. **OVER-COMMERCIALISATION MAKES PEOPLE BLIND. I ALSO THINK THE 'HANDMADE' STAMP HAS TURNED INTO A COMMERCIAL BRANDING STRATEGY WITH MANY BIG BRANDS TRYING TO LOOK LIKE THEY ARE MAKING SOMETHING HANDCRAFTED. AS A DESIGNER YOU HAVE RESPONSIBILITIES AND I BELIEVE TRUE TALENT AND WELL MADE DESIGN WILL ALWAYS PREVAIL.**

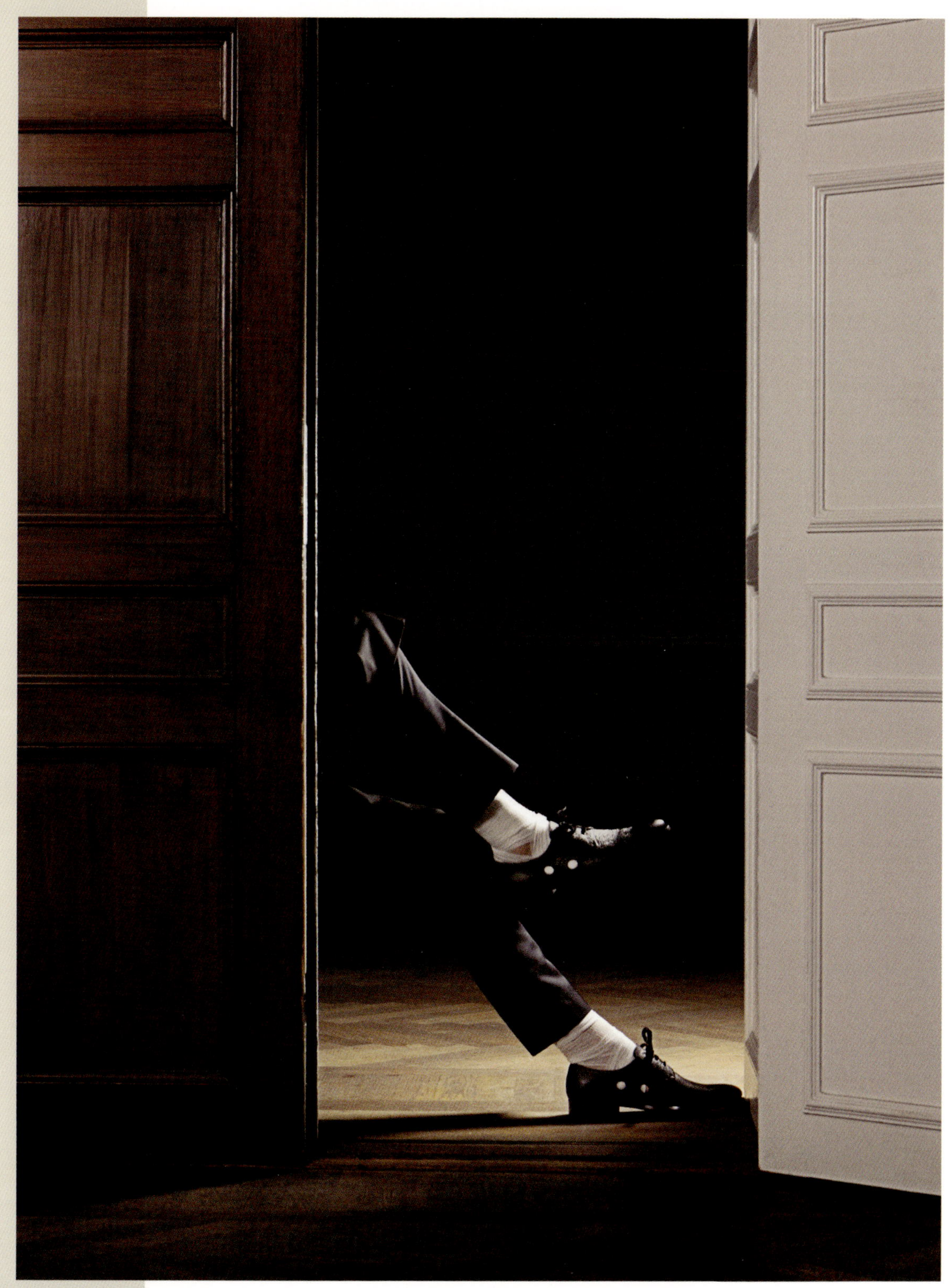

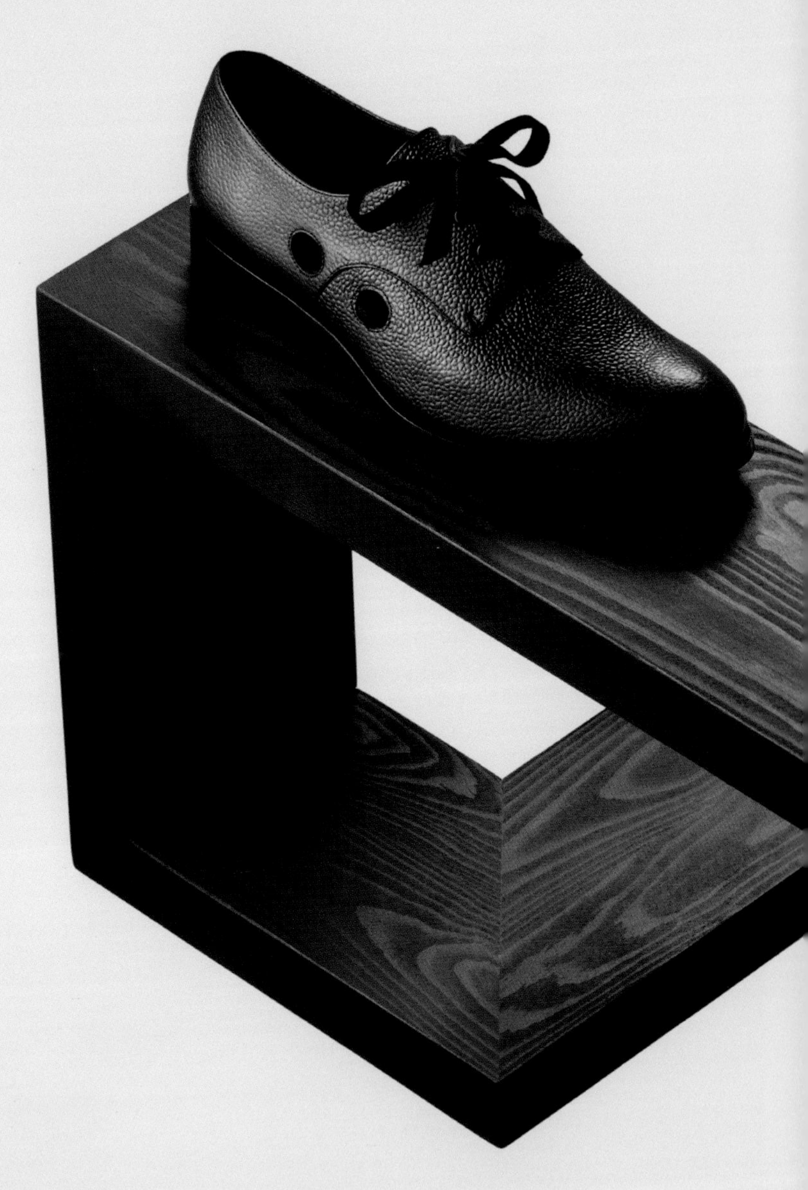

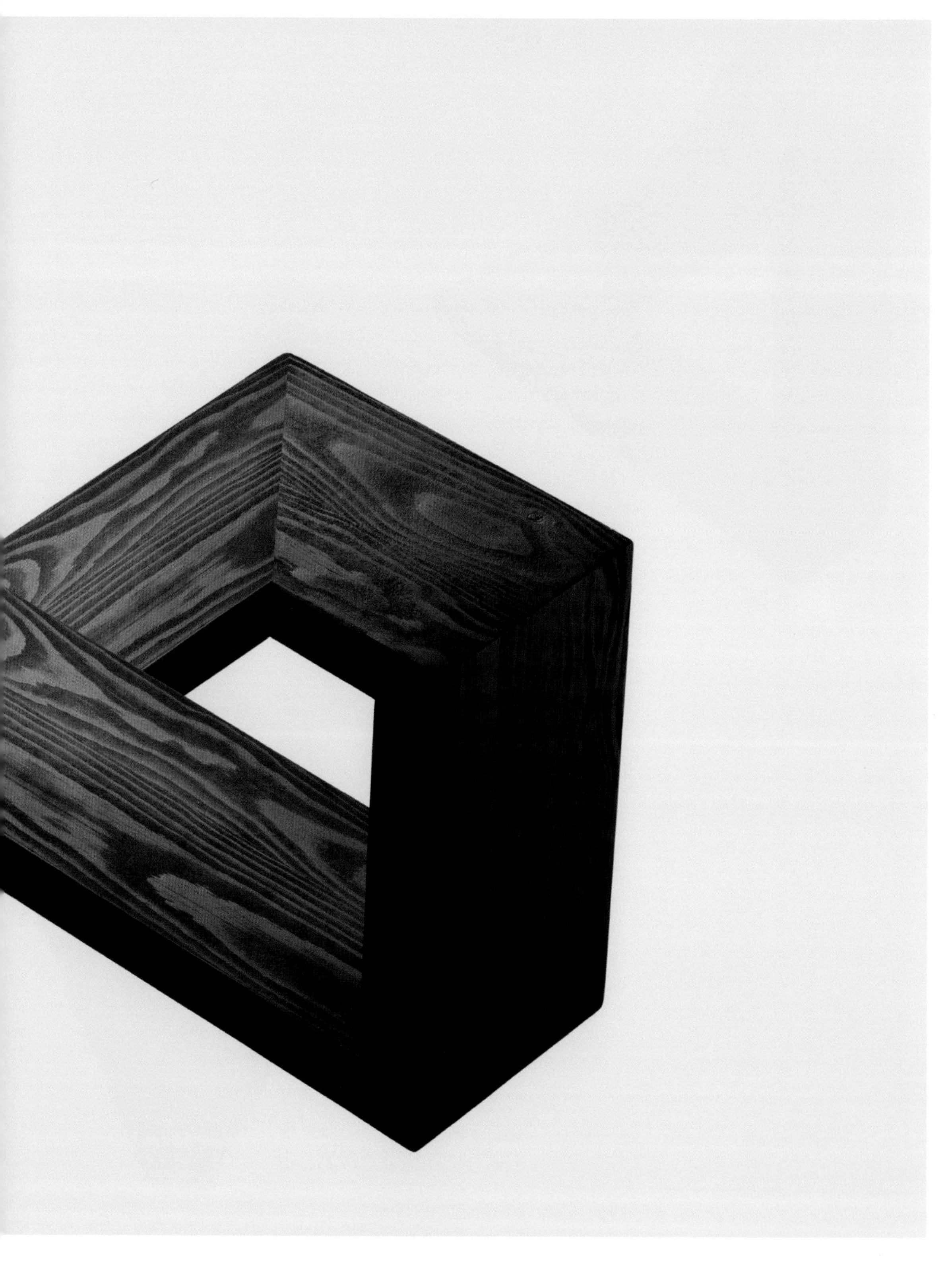

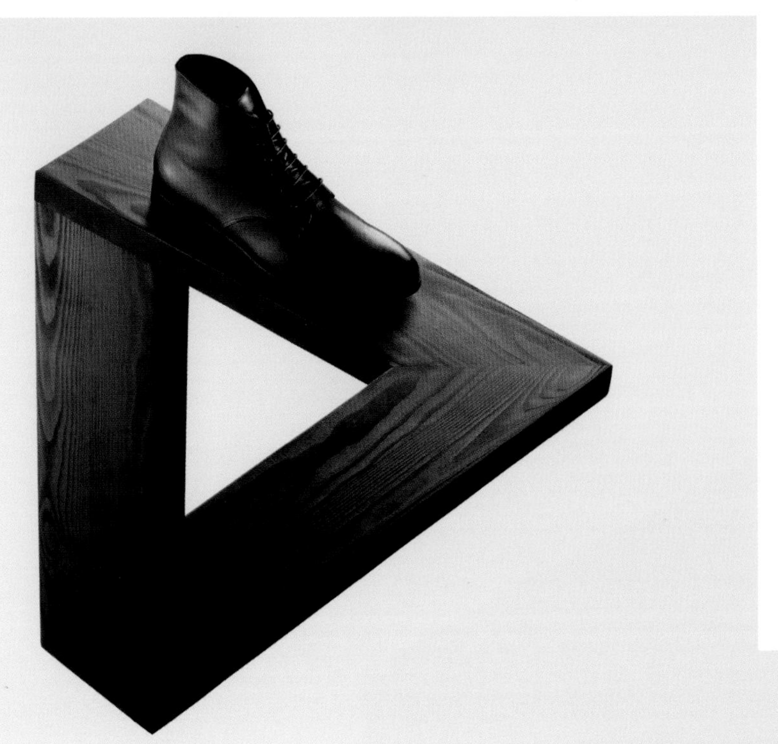

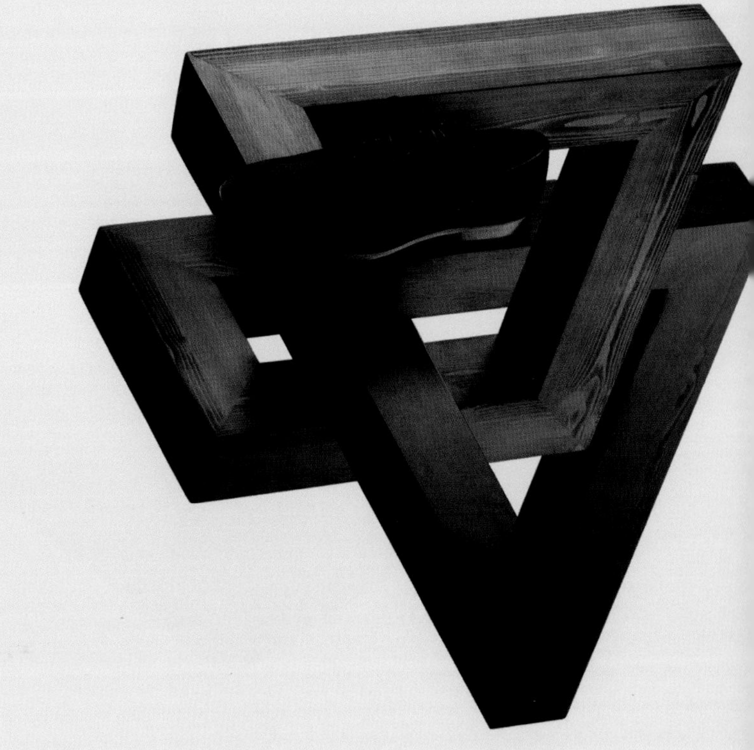

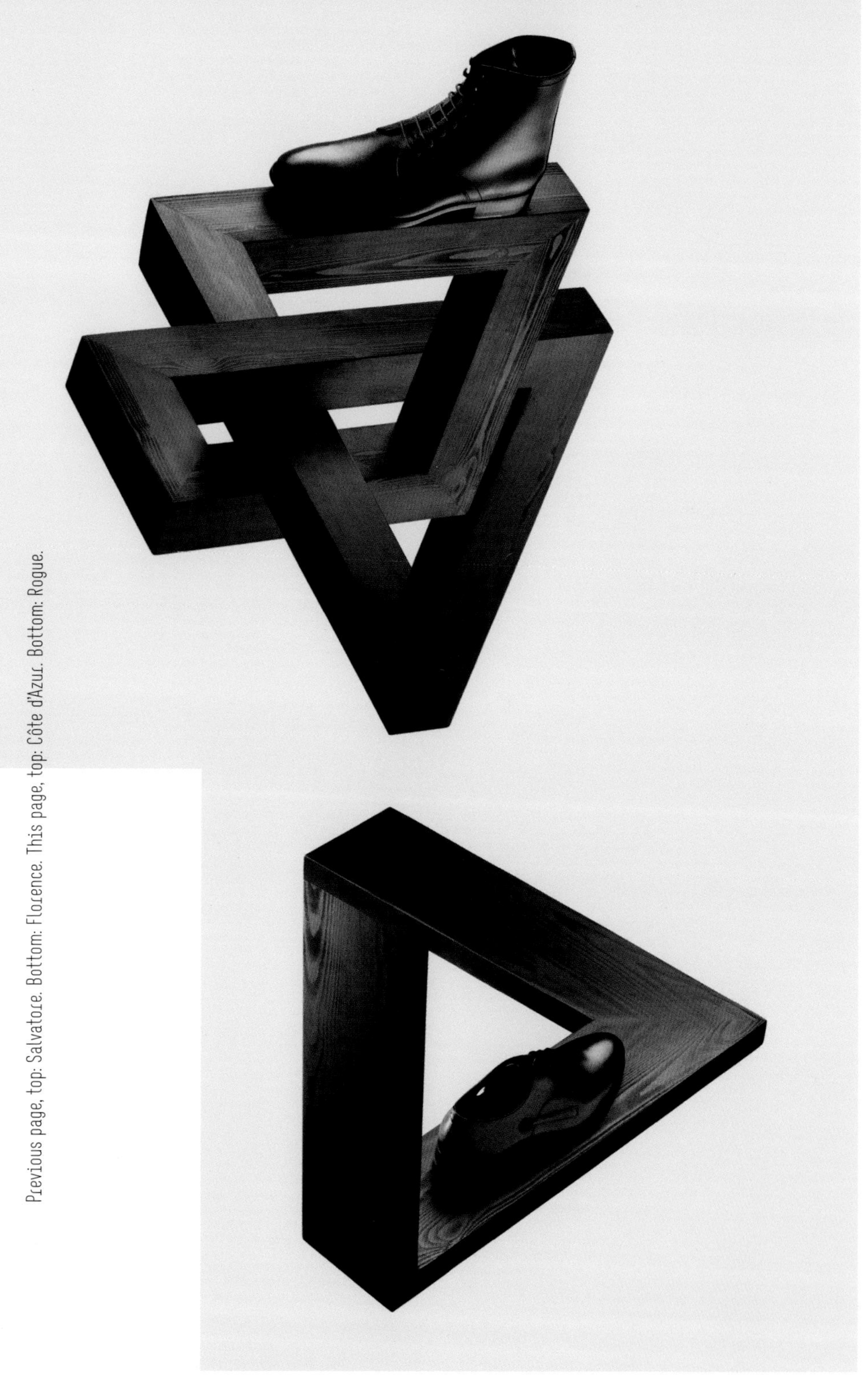

Previous page, top: Salvatore. Bottom: Florence. This page, top: Côte d'Azur. Bottom: Rogue.

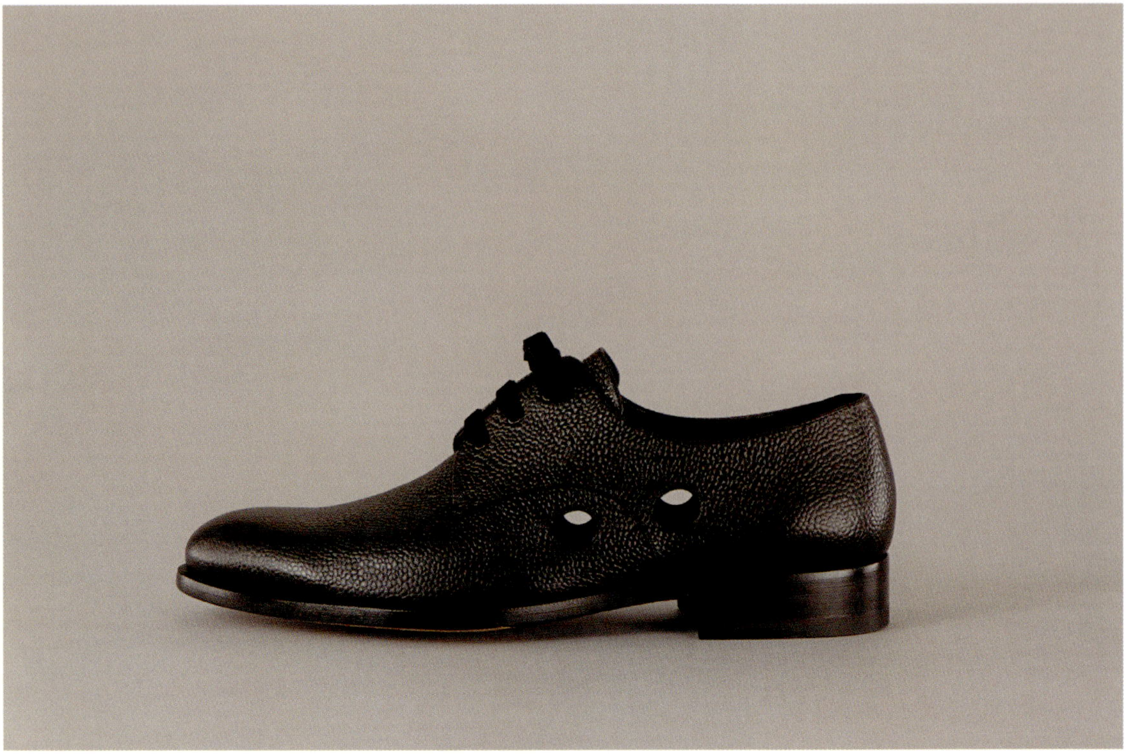

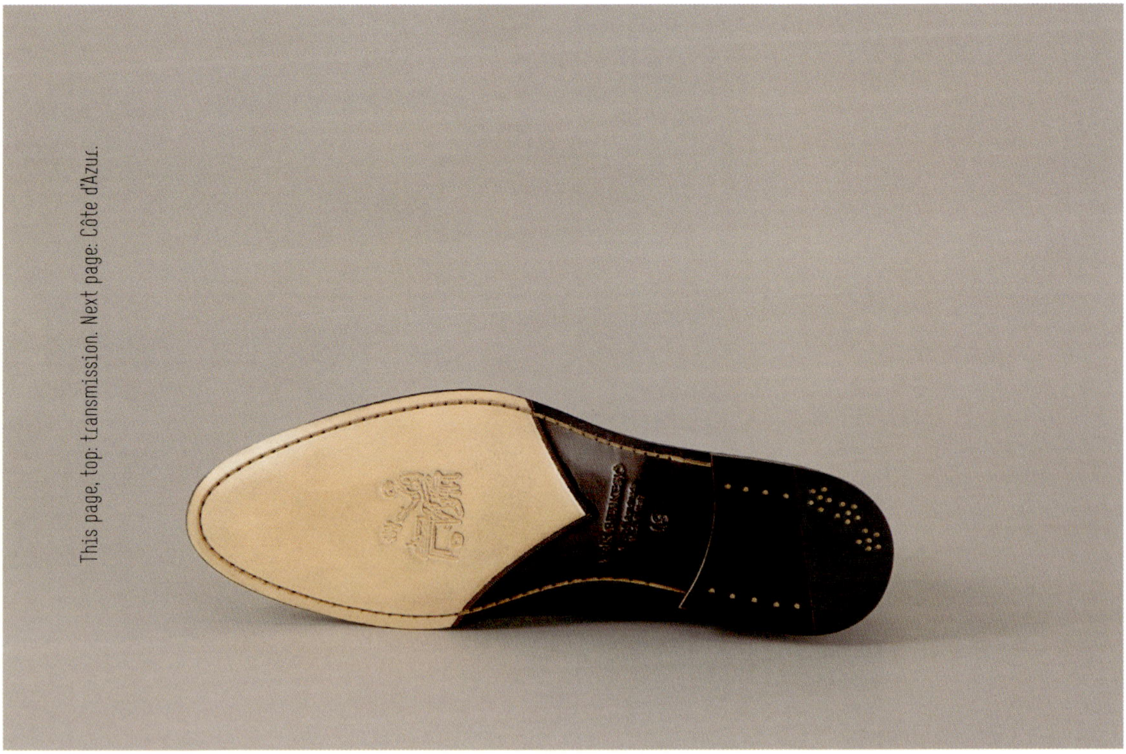

This page, top: transmission. Next page: Côte d'Azur.

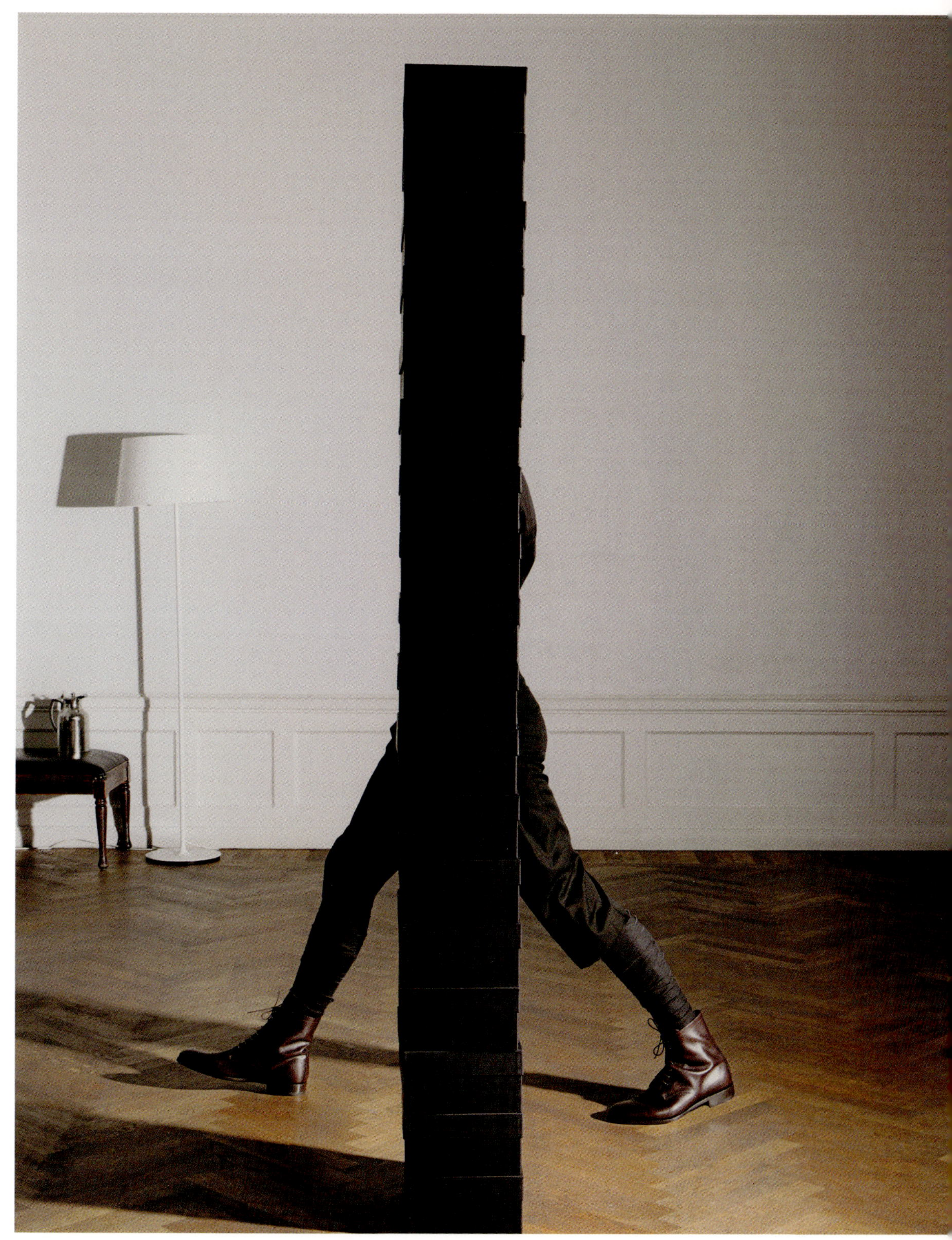

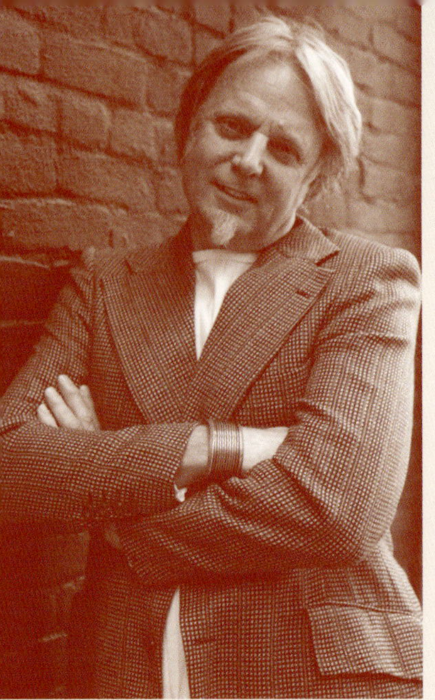

FLUEVOG

Please introduce yourself **I AM A MAN WHO HAS THOUGHT ABOUT SHOES FOR A LONG TIME.** What is your work about? **GIVING PEOPLE GOOD 'SOLE' AND PERSONAL IDENTITY WITH SMART, UNIQUE DESIGNS.** Is there a specific reason why you chose shoe design? **IT FOUND ME. I FITTED INTO THE PATH THAT OPENED. SHOE DESIGN IS UNIQUE IN THAT IT'S HARD TO GET STARTED AND HARD TO KEEP IT GOING, ESPECIALLY IN WESTERN CANADA.** What makes your work different from others? **I AM TOTALLY ON MY OWN — NO ONE TO ANSWER TO EXCEPT MYSELF AND MY CUSTOMERS.** Which of your designs do you favour the most? **LIKE A GOOD PARENT I LIKE THEM ALL BUT I DO LIKE THE UNUSUAL ONES. THEY ARE GENERALLY NOT THE ONES THAT SELL WELL.** Tell us something about the design process. **IDEAS POP IN TO MY BRAIN AT RANDOM TIMES, WHEN I'M DRIVING, BIKING, SLEEPING. I PANIC TO WRITE THEM DOWN.** What stage of the creative process do you find most gratifying? **THE VERY BEGINNING. THE IDEA, THE SOLE, THE LAST, THE FOUNDATION. ONCE THAT'S DONE, THE PATTERNS AND EVEN THE COLOURS DON'T MATTER AS MUCH.** Who or what has played a part in your development as an artist? **PETER FOX AND ART DECO** What colours would you choose to make an important piece? **TEAL BLUE AND GREY** What are your thoughts on the culture of quick consumption and over-commercialisation? **I REALLY DISLIKE MASS-MARKETED TRENDS. I LOVE IT WHEN I MAKE PIECES THAT GO AGAINST THE TRENDS AND THEN SEE THEM SELL.** How do you see the current state of your profession in general? **IT'S AN AWESOME TIME. A SMALL INDEPENDENT CAN HAVE AN INFLUENCE ON DESIGN, THOUGHT AND SPIRITUAL VALUES.** What do you consider vulgar and what elegant? **VULGAR IS BORING, OUT OF DATE, MAINSTREAM FASHION.** What does beauty mean to you? **BEAUTY IS CREATION. IT IS ORIGINAL, DELICATE, SIMPLE, STRANGE, BOLD, HUGE, FLOWING, SHARP, DEEP, HIGH, CRAZY, COLOURFUL, MOVING, HERE TODAY, GONE TOMORROW, ETERNAL. IT'S LAYERED AND NOT ALWAYS EASY TO SEE AT FIRST. IT'S THE UNIQUE EXPRESSION OF WHO WE ARE. THERE HAS NEVER BEEN ANOTHER PERSON LIKE US AND THAT'S BEAUTIFUL.**

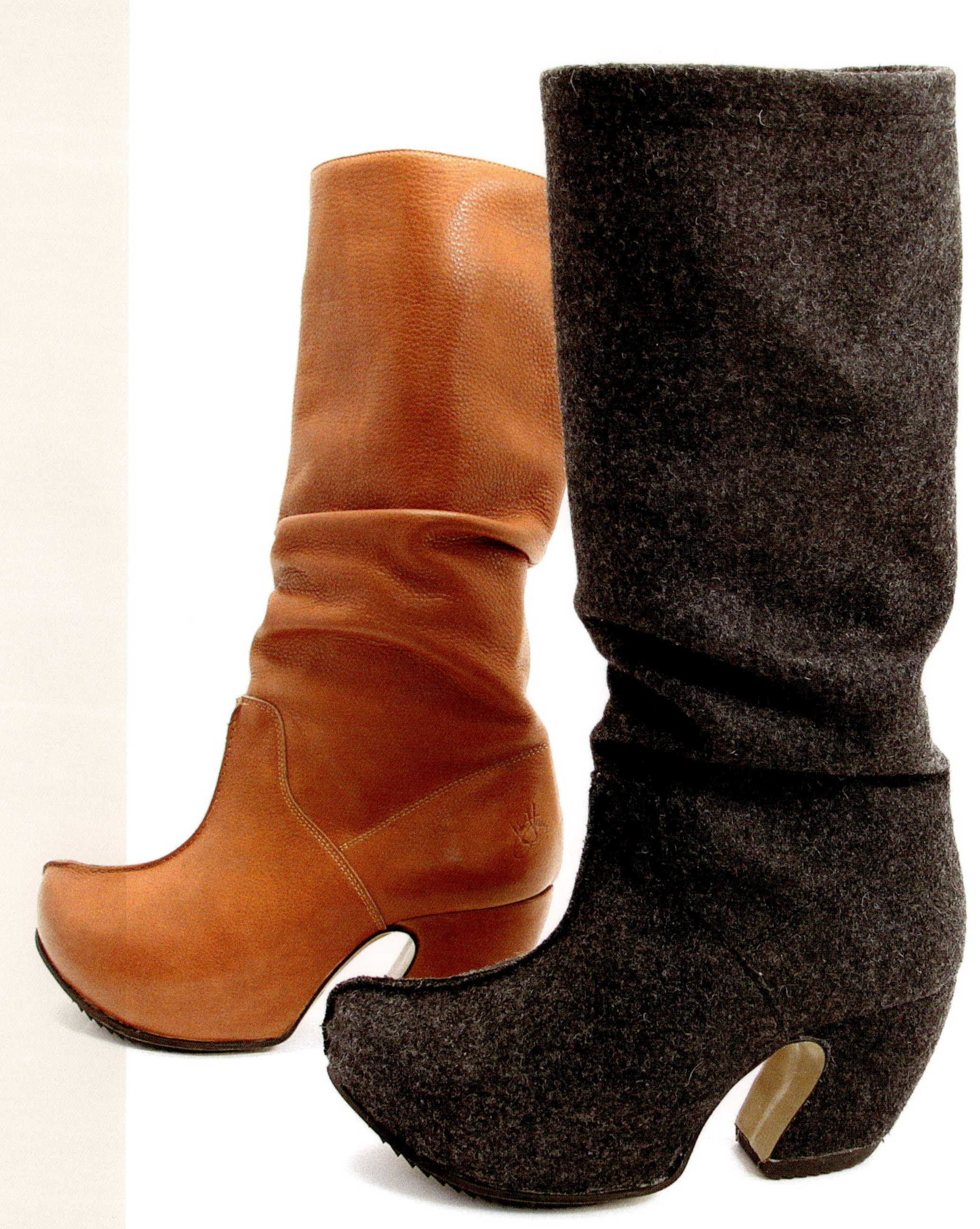

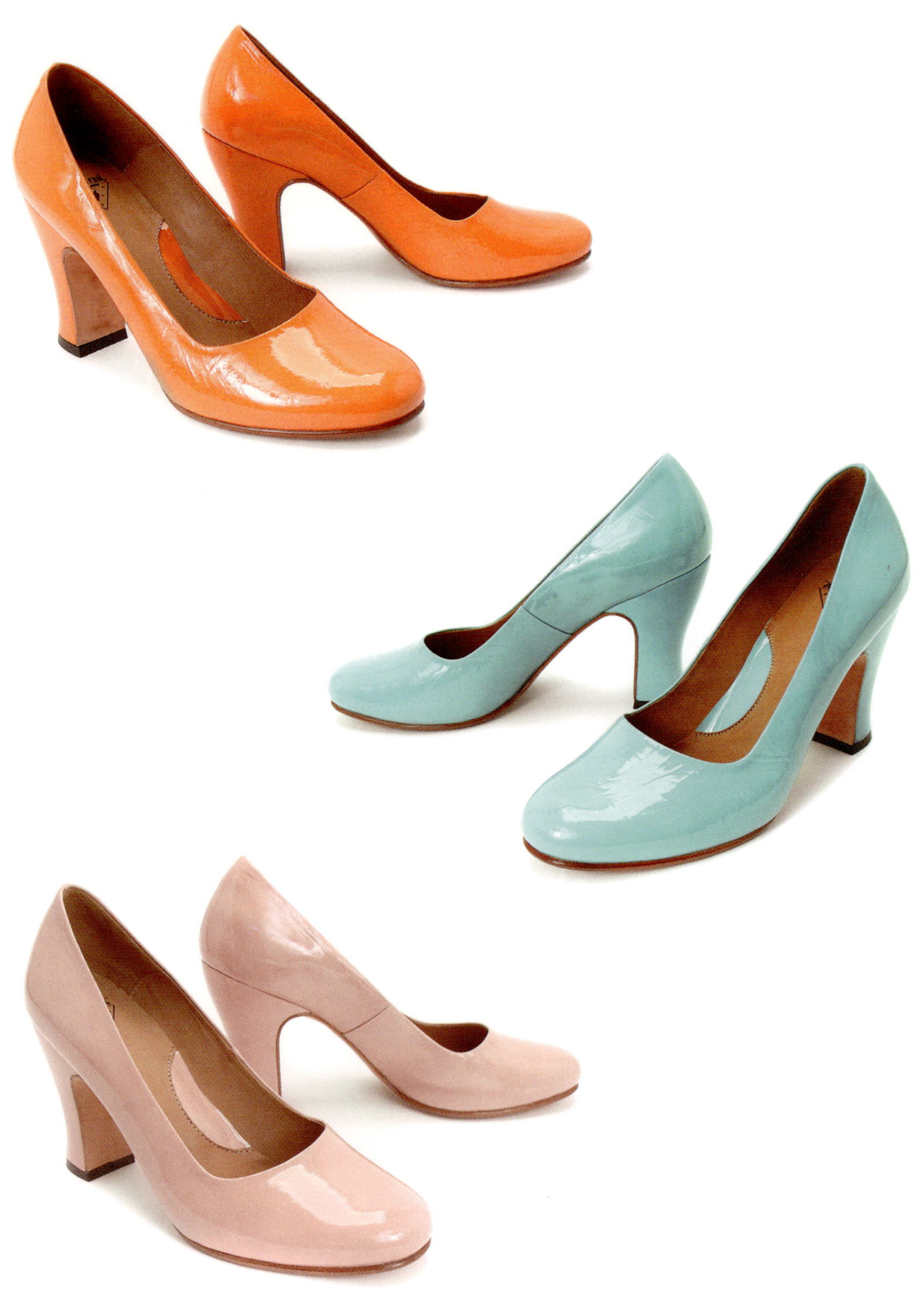

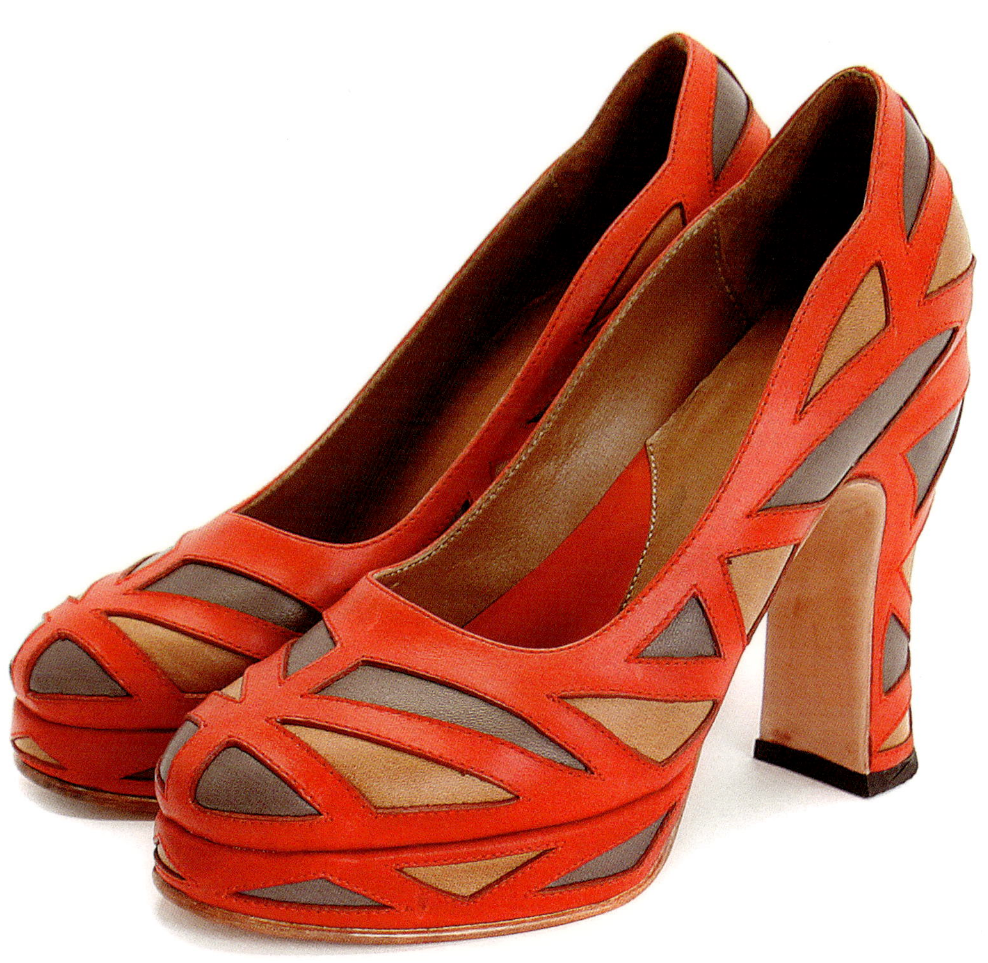

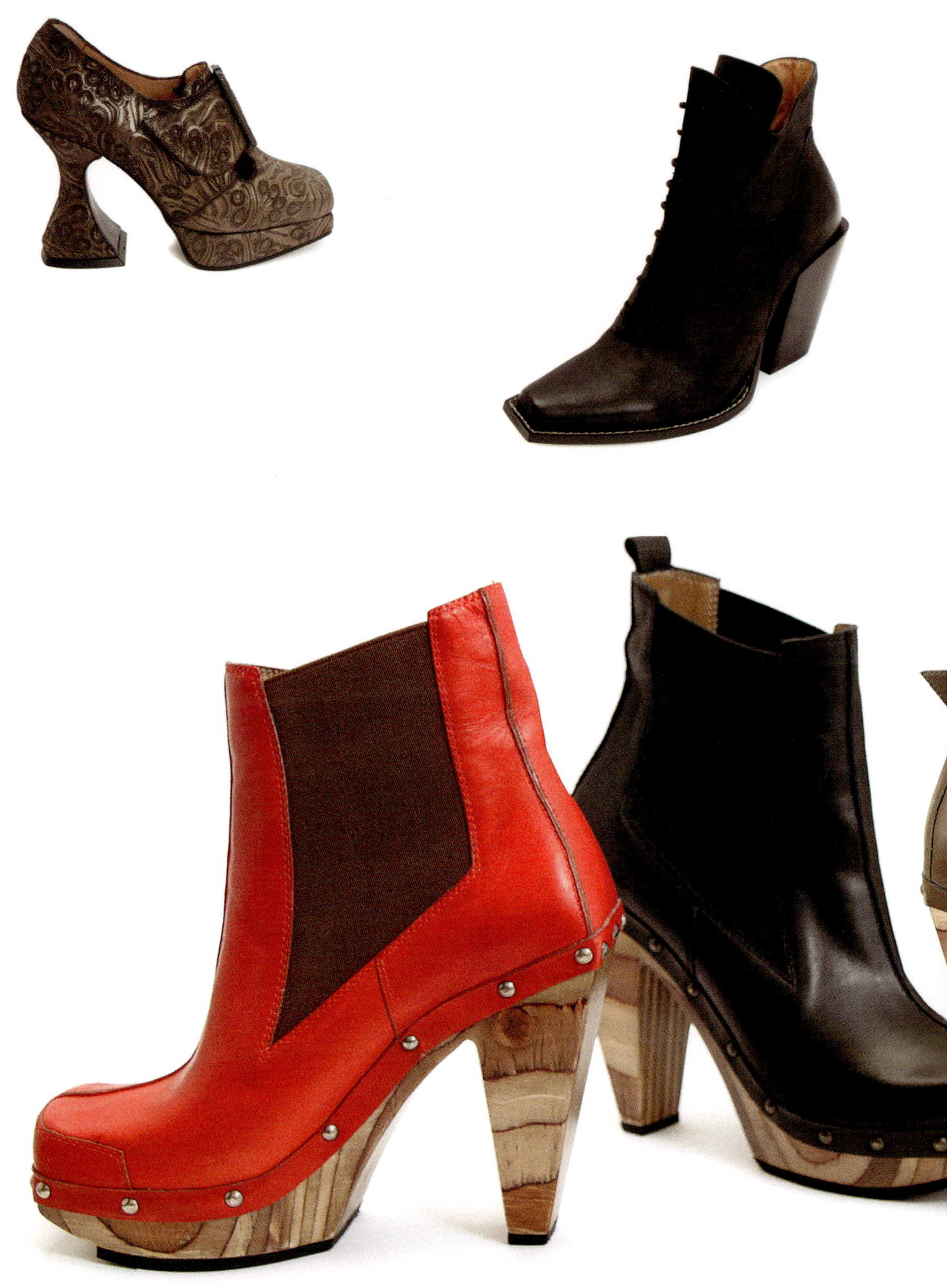

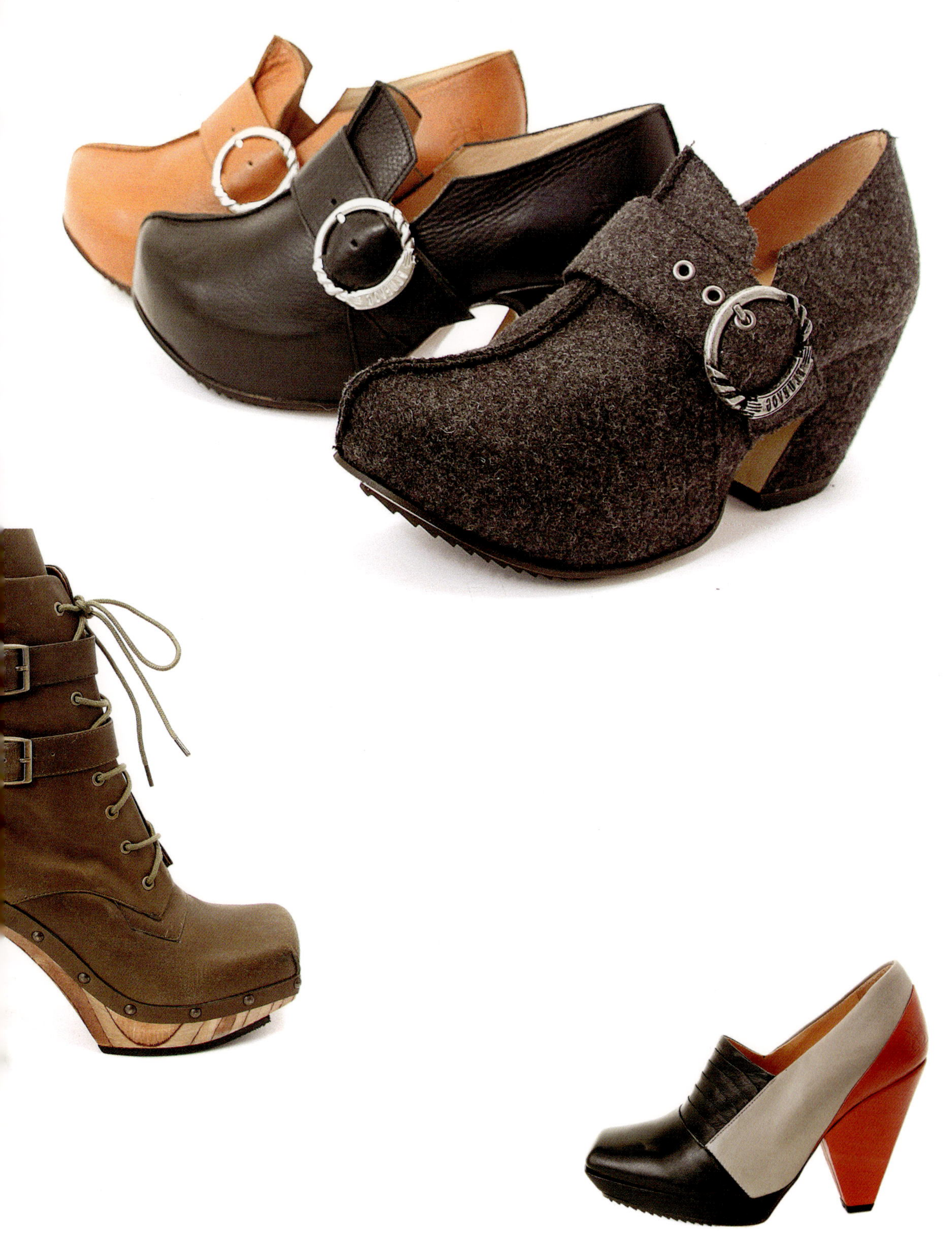

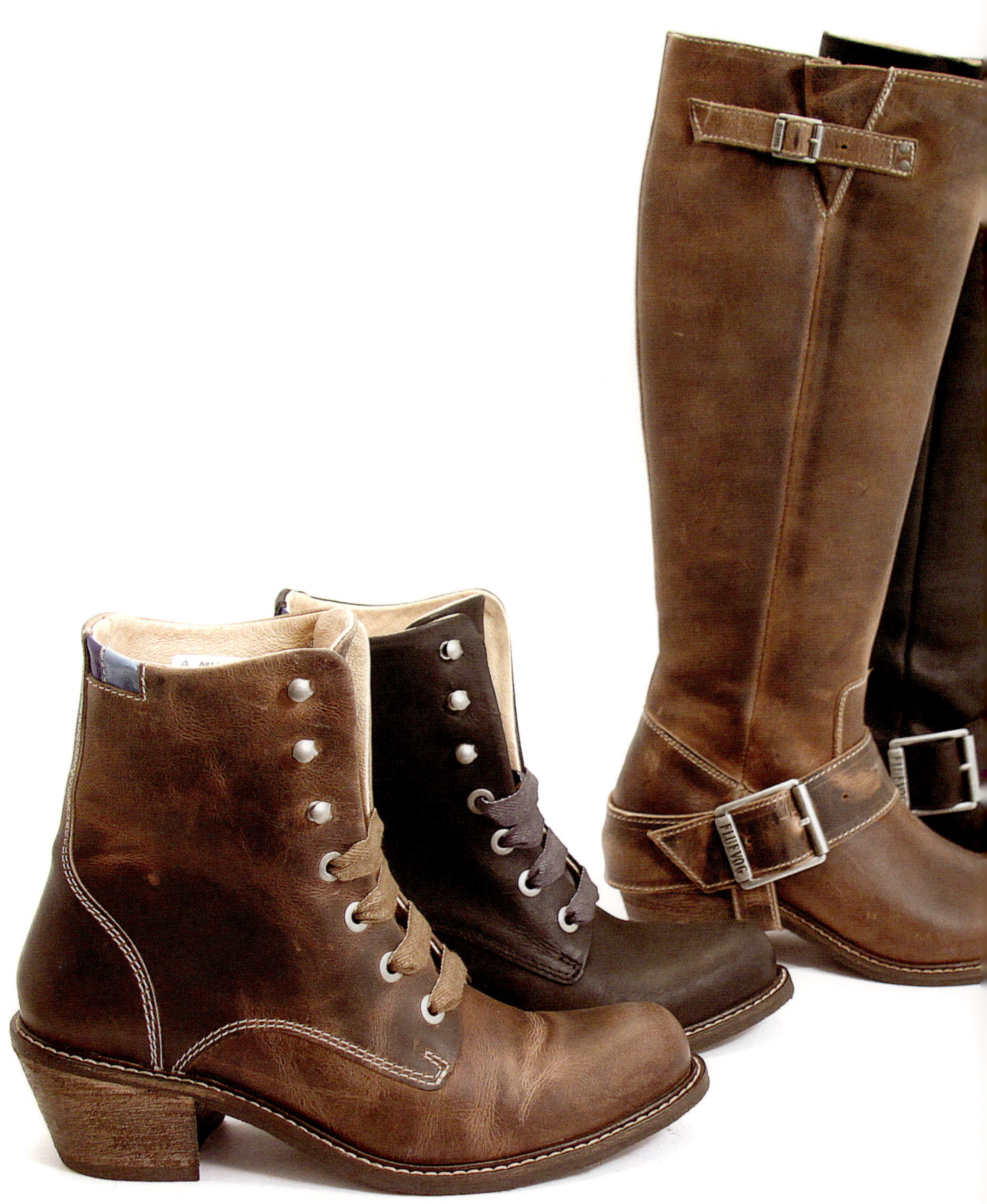
FLUEVOG

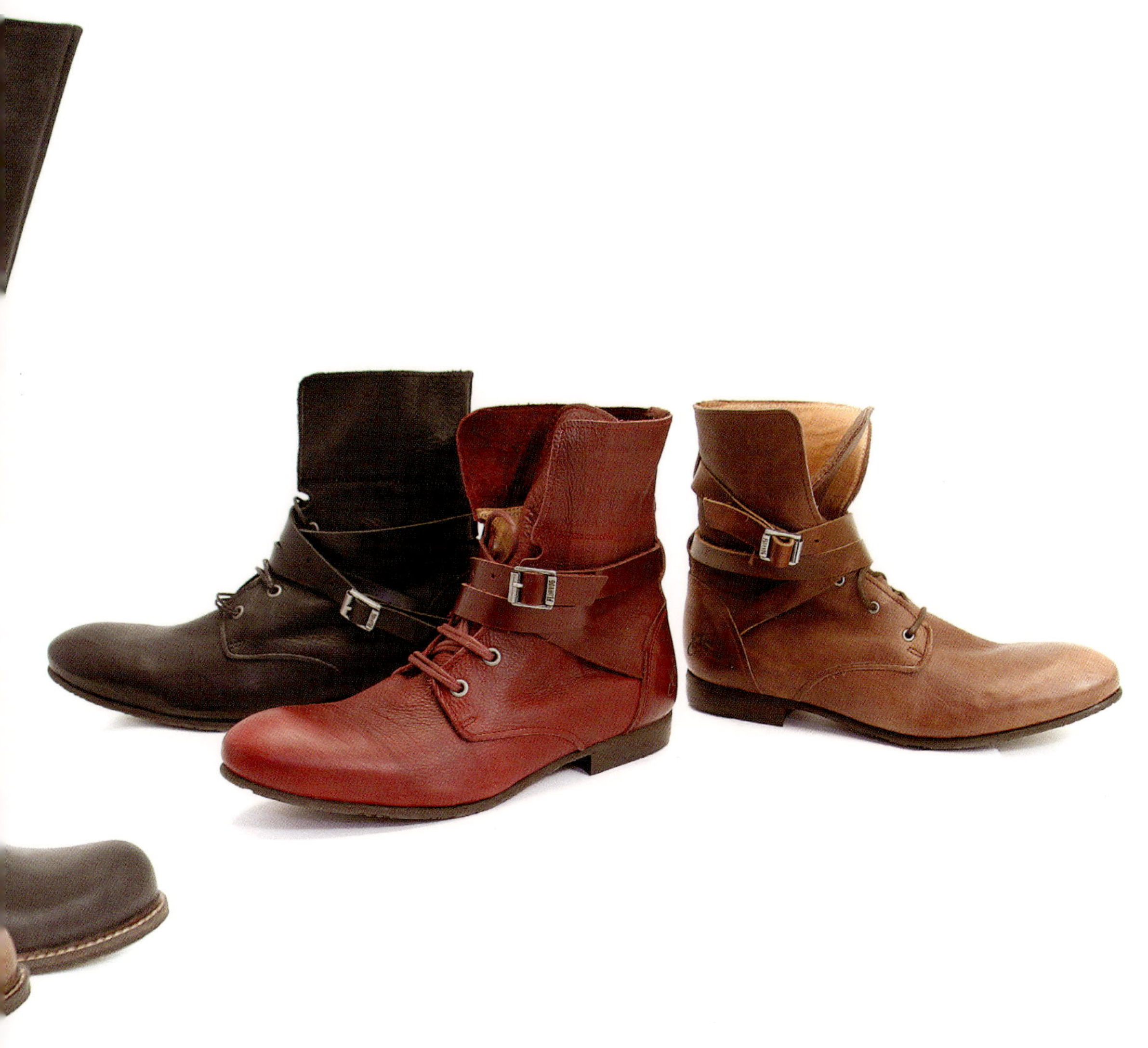

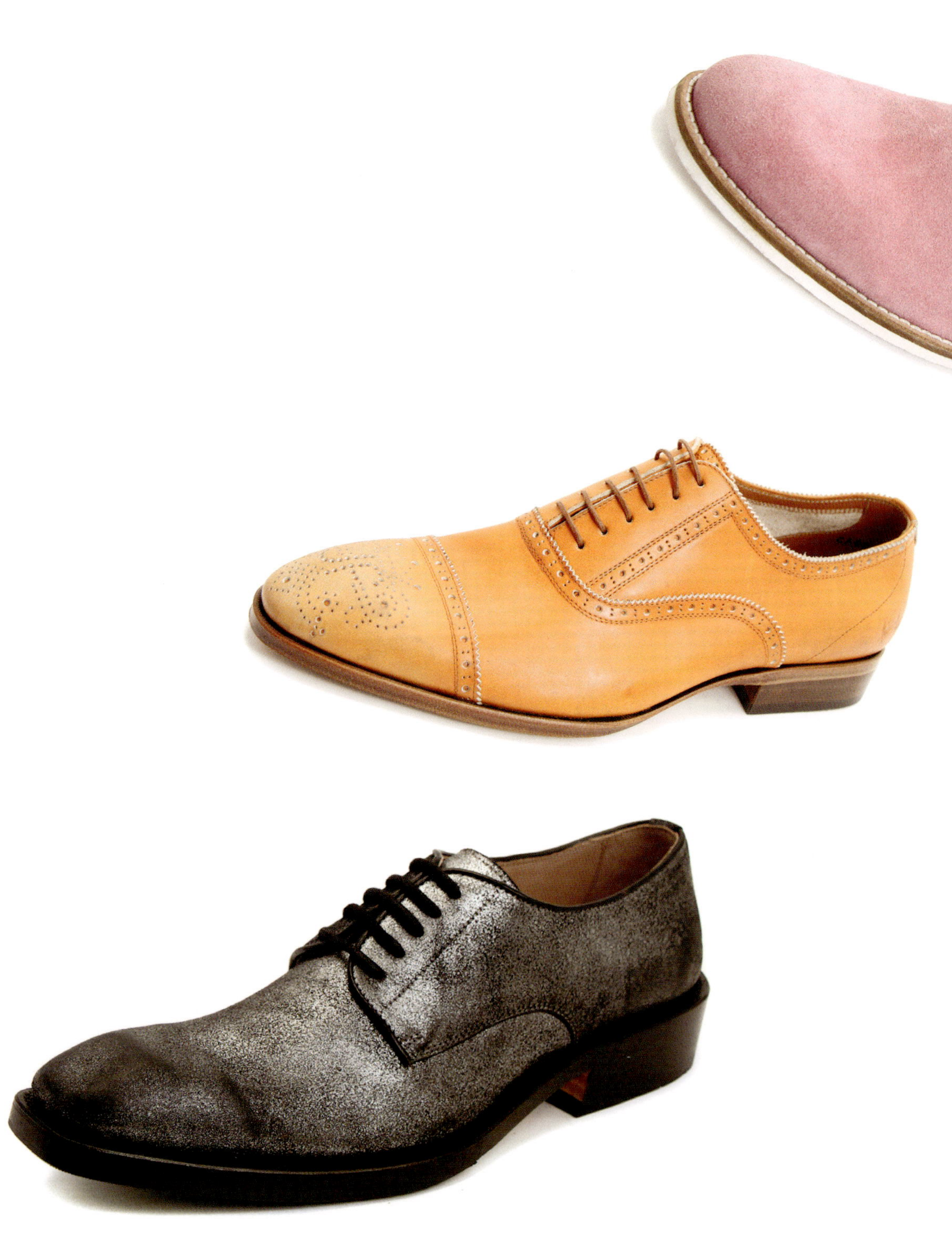

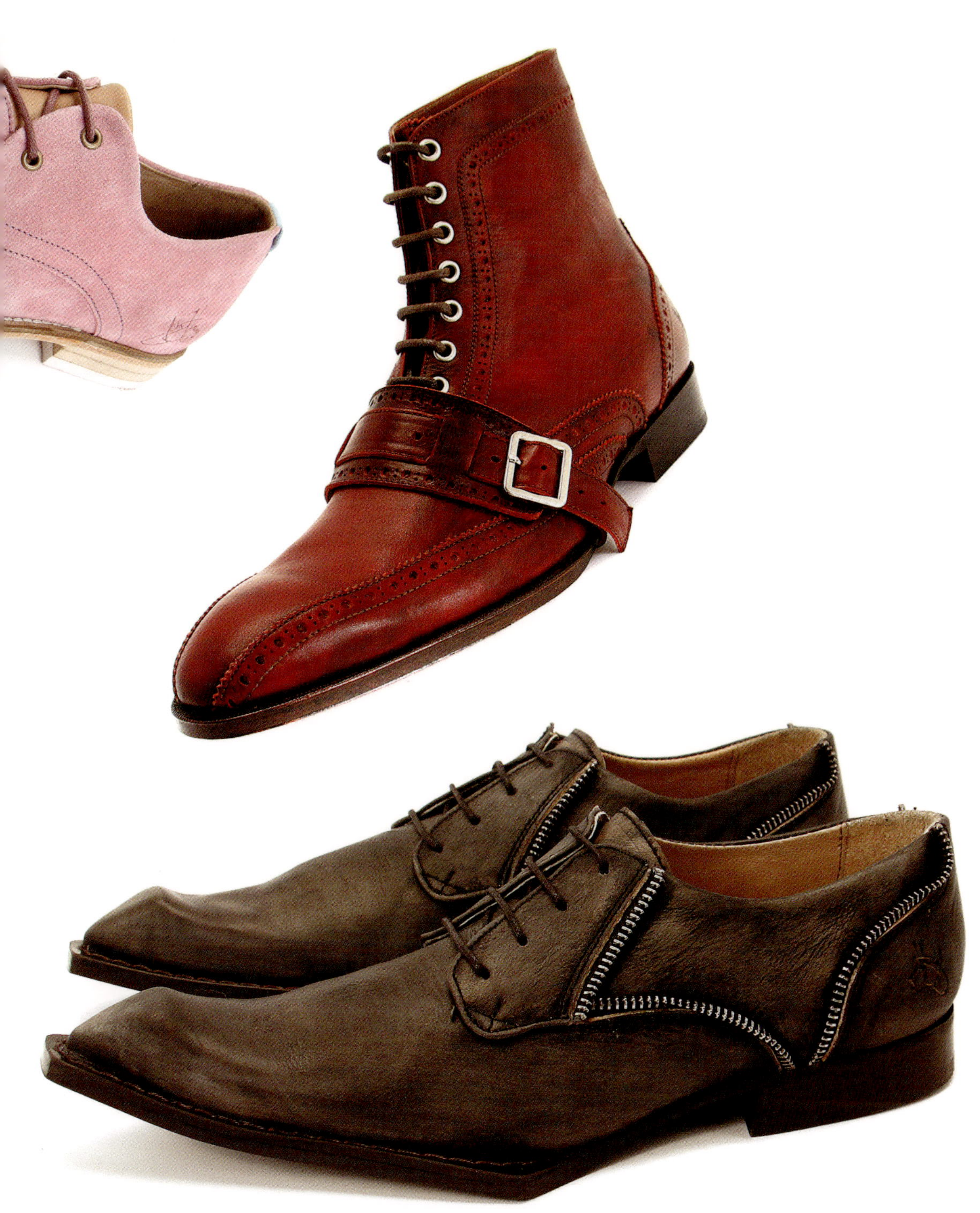

GEORGIA TURRI, GEORGIA TURRI/GETU

My name is Georgia Roehe Turri and I am shoe designer for the Italian brands Georgia Turri and GETU. My dreams came true when I launched my own collection in 2007 after winning a competition organised and supported by the Italian Fashion Chamber. My work is about femininity and harmony between dream and reality. **PASSION GIVES ME THE ENTHUSIASM AND DETERMINATION TO DO WHAT I DO. I GREW UP AMONG MULTICOLOURED PIECES OF FRESH TANNED LEATHERS AT MY FAMILY TANNERY IN NOVO HAMBURGO, THE CENTRE OF THE RENOWNED BRAZILIAN SHOE DISTRICT. MY SHOE DESIGNS ARE A RESULT OF A LONG PROCESS OF STUDYING AND GAINING EXPERIENCE OVER THE LAST TEN YEARS, AFTER I MOVED TO ITALY IN 2000.** Every day I try to innovate, designing harmonious shapes whilst seeking out unexpected and beautiful materials. I also focus my research on models that can become an icon of my style. I do not look to create shocking styles but rather those that reflect the essence of feminine shoes: seductive shapes, physical and psychological comfort, elegant colours and sophisticated materials. I am always looking for something special and pleasant. Details make the difference, the no-noisy heel tip for example. **DESIGN IS A LEARNING PROCESS. IT STARTS SLOWLY AND CULMINATES IN A RIVER OF VIBRATING IDEAS AND FEELINGS. MATCHING COLOURS IS THE MOST SATISFYING PART. I LOVE THE CHALLENGE OF FINDING UNEXPECTED HARMONIES. MY TWO MOST INNOVATIVE DESIGNS ARE THE HIGH HEEL SANDALS AND FLAT BALLERINAS, BOTH HANDMADE IN ITALY, WITH A SPECIAL FIVE-FOLDED RIBBON, CREATED AND DEVELOPED OUT OF MY LOVE FOR PLISSÉ.** This creative profession is constantly evolving, with competition getting harder and people's desires getting more complex. I have an inner will to detach from the mainstream, always seeking unreachable perfection yet in harmony with the here and now.

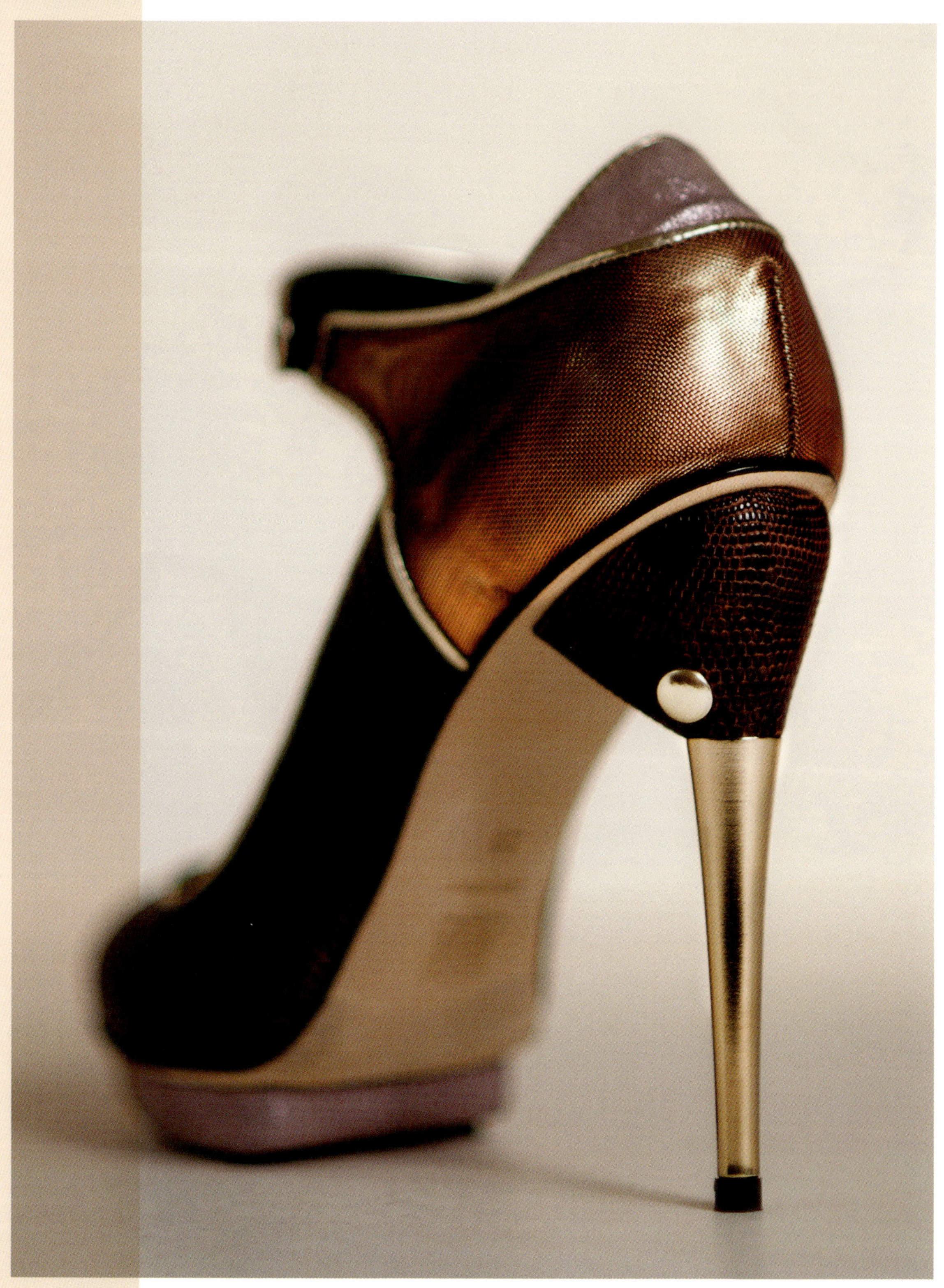

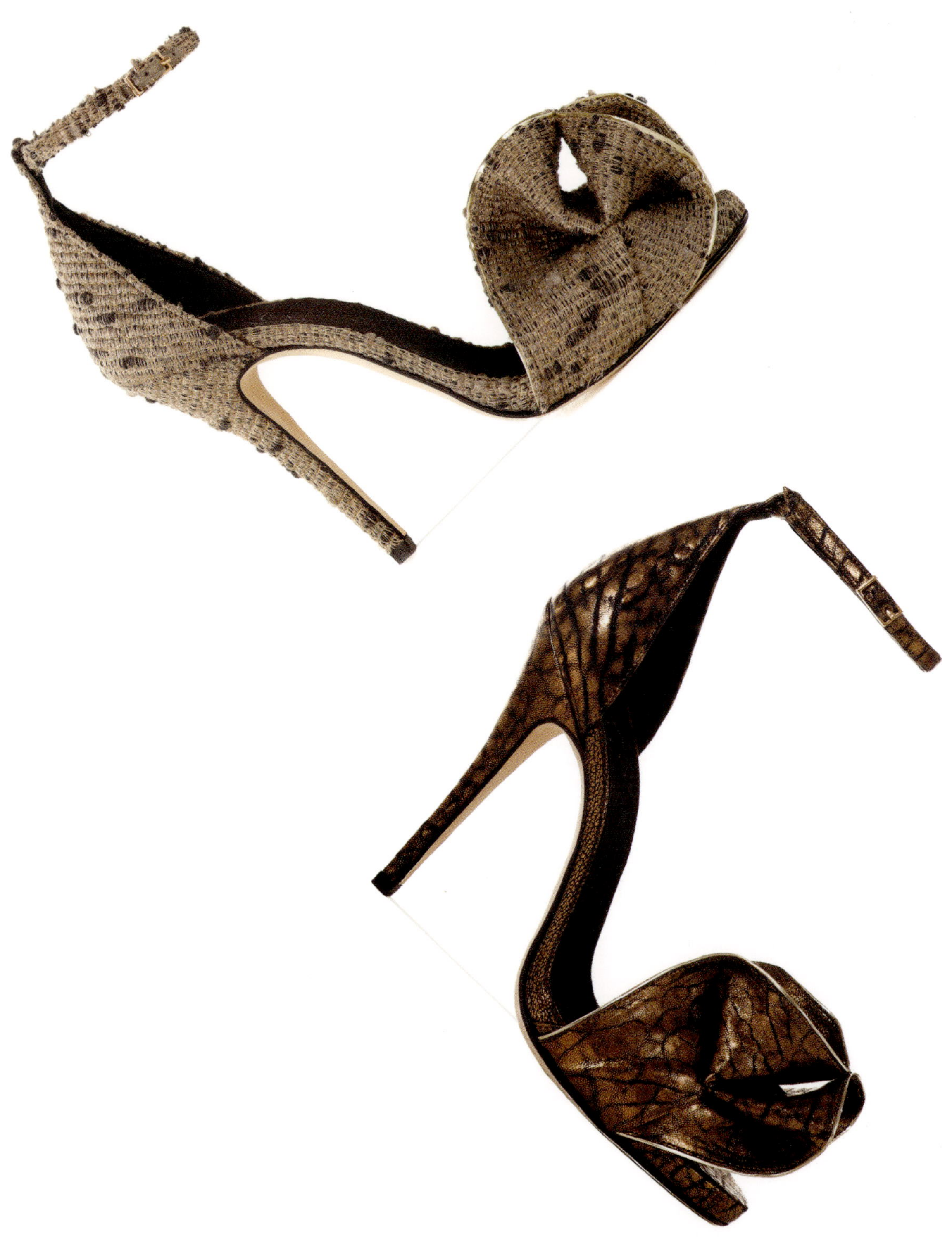

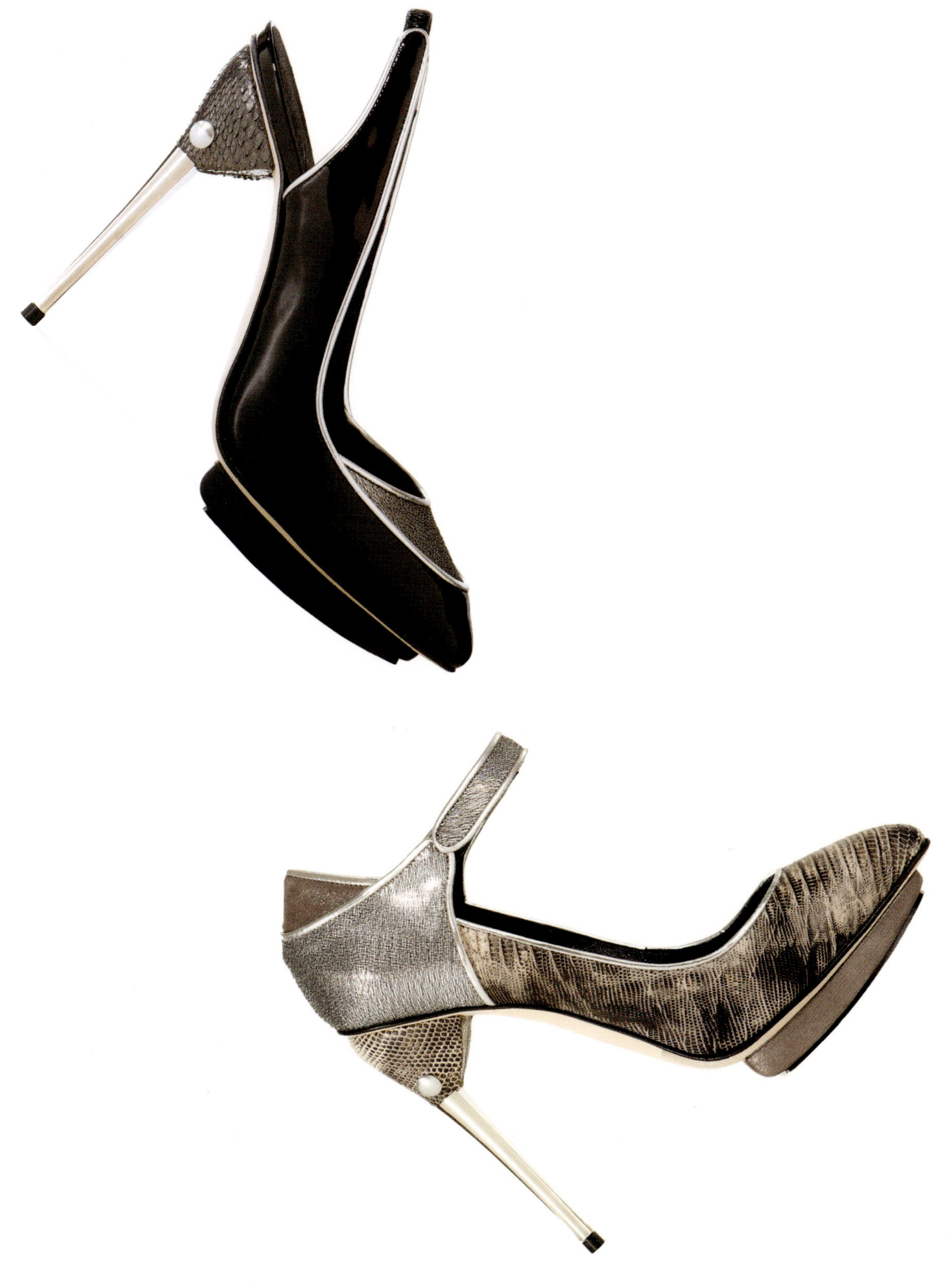

 GEORGIA TURRI/GETU

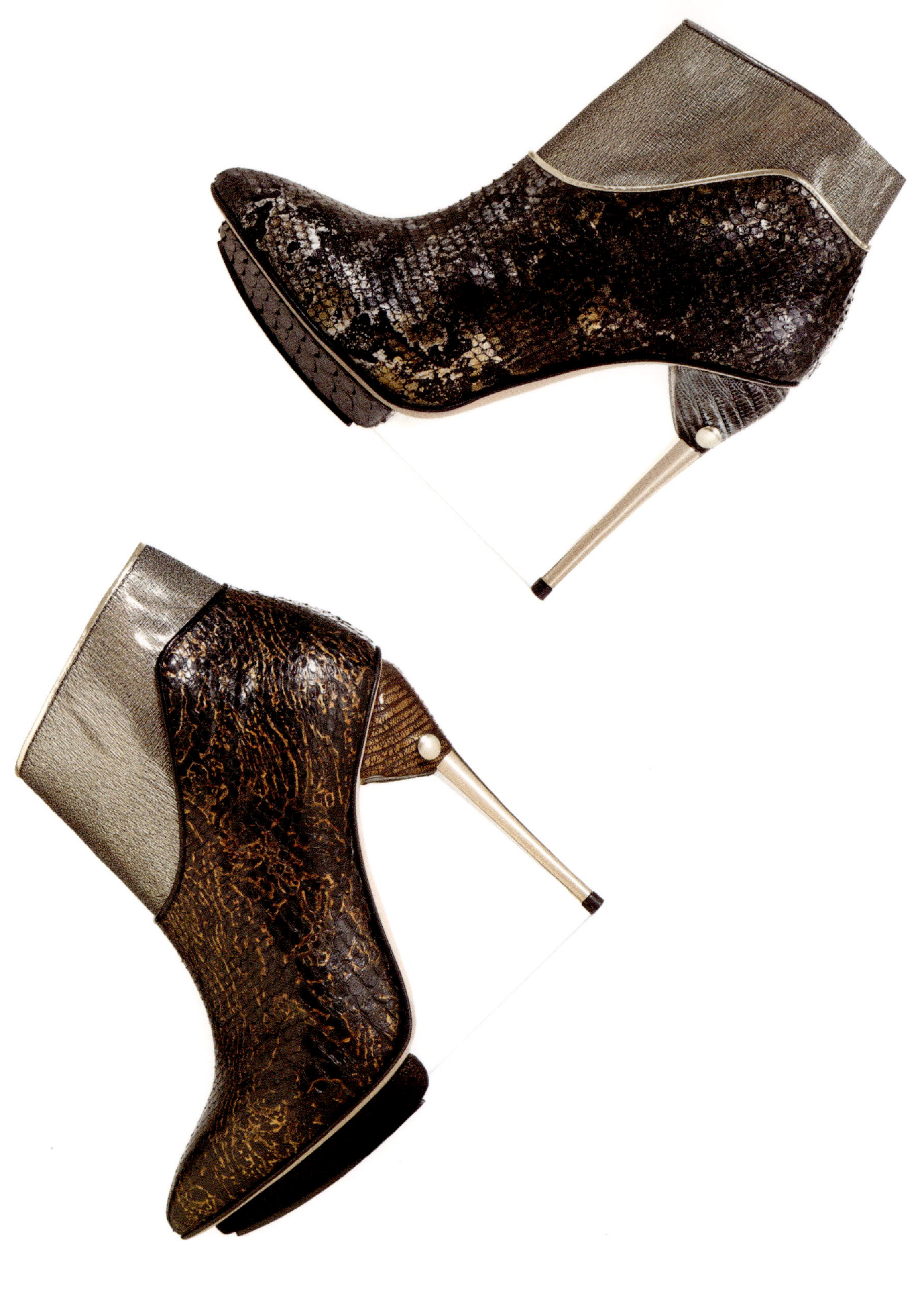

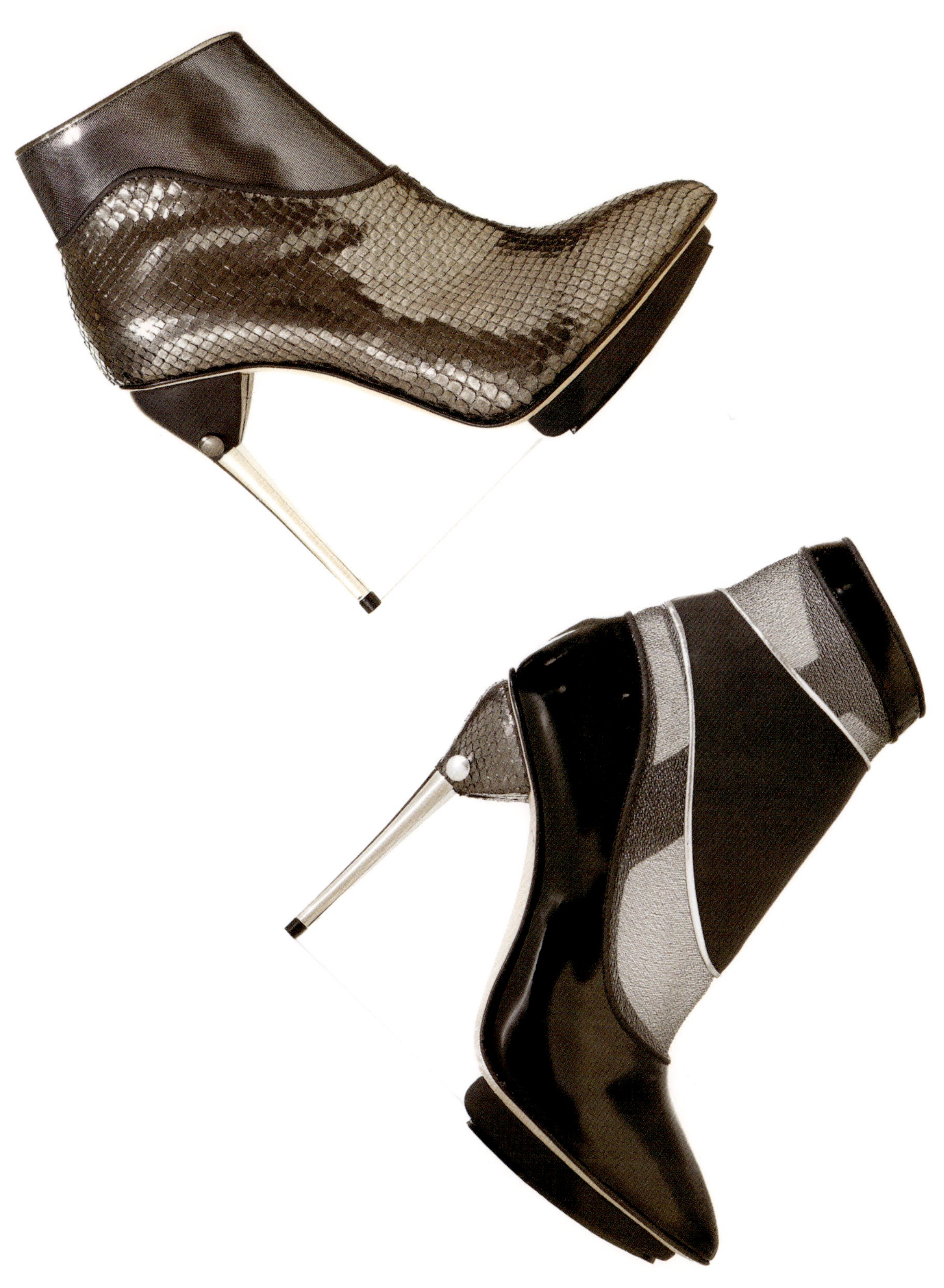

 GEORGIA TURRI/GETU

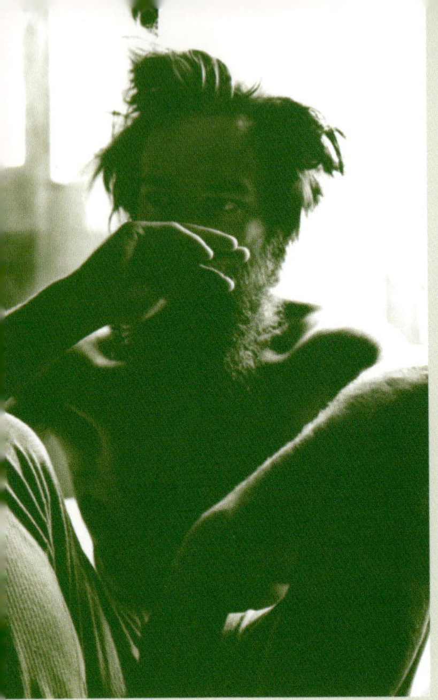

GIENCHI

Please introduce yourself **I'M GIENCHI. I'M 21-YEARS-OLD AND I LOVE THE DARK.** How did you get started? **I STARTED BECAUSE I HATED ALL THE SHOES THAT EXISTED.** What is your work about? **DRAWING.** What do you consider the most innovative piece of your designs so far? **ALL WHITE SHOES.** Who or what inspires you? **THE TATE MODERN AND BLACK.** Tell us something about the design process. **THERE ARE NO RITUALS. I DESIGN FROM ANYWHERE.** If you had to choose one colour and one material to make an important piece, what would they be? **BLACK AND DIRTY METAL.** What is the most gratifying part of the creative process? **WHEN I SEE THE PENCIL USED.** What role does work play in your life? **IT KEEPS ME OFF ALCOHOL.** What do you consider elegant? **MY BLACK CAT.** What does beauty mean for you? **LONELINESS.**

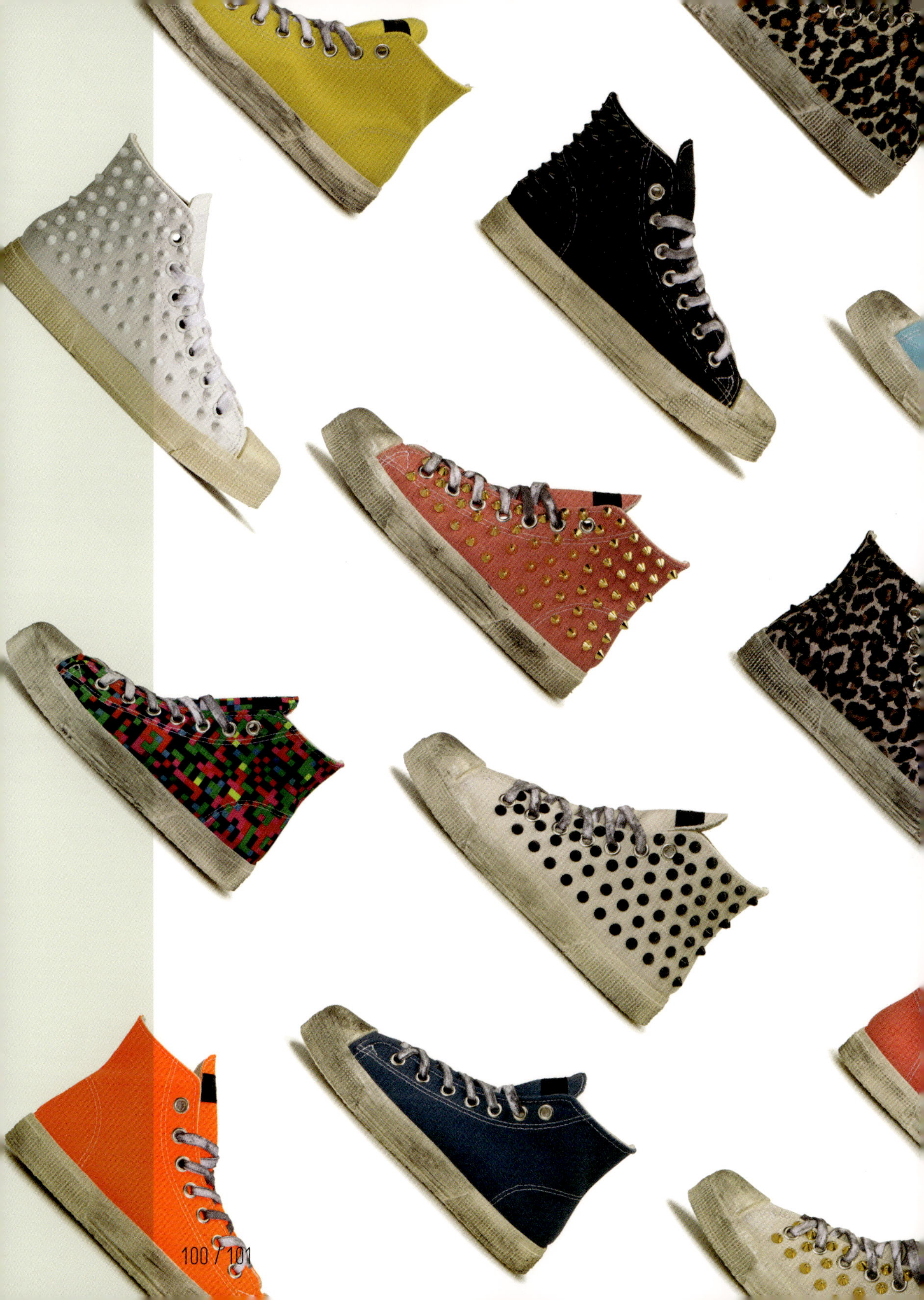

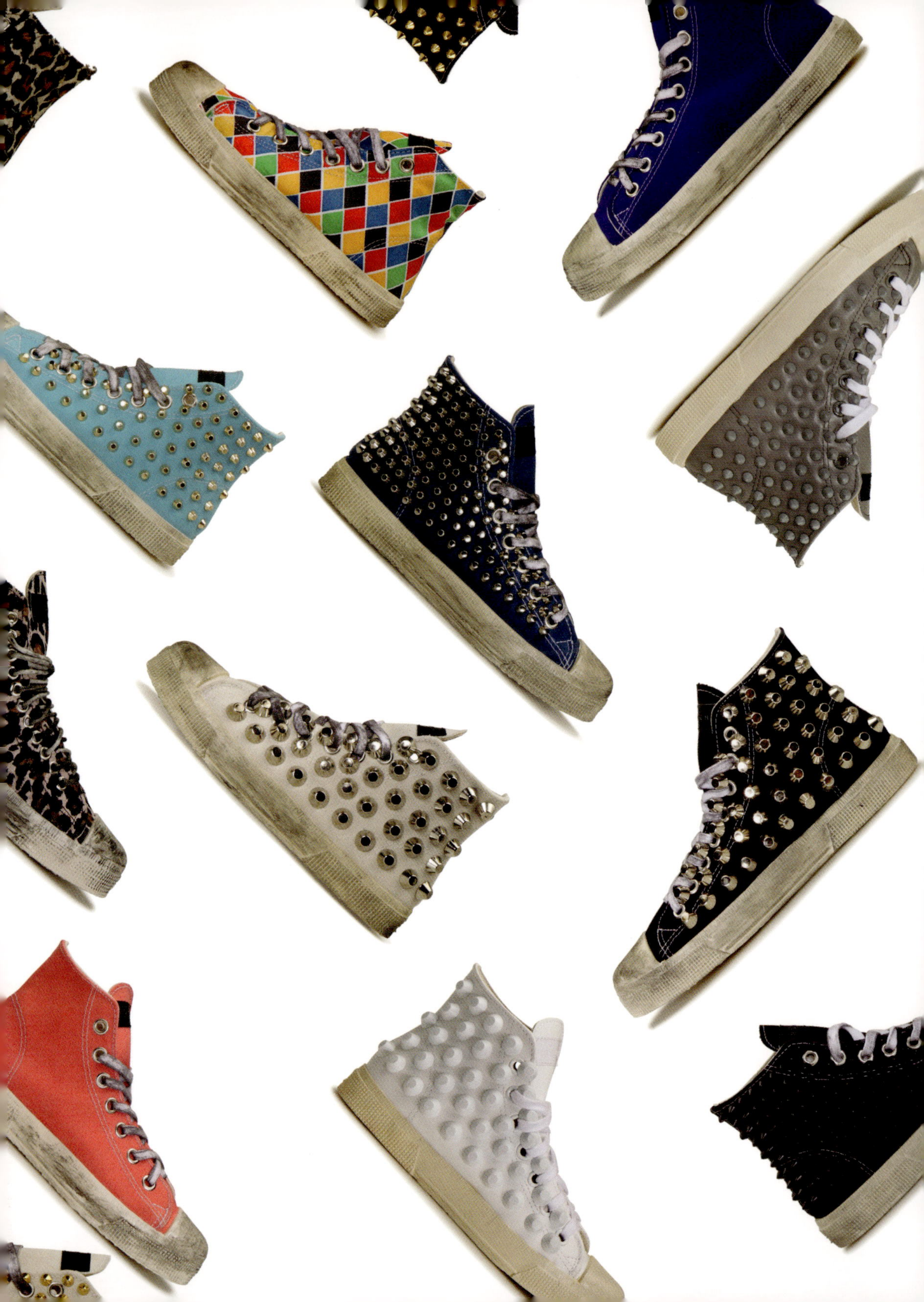

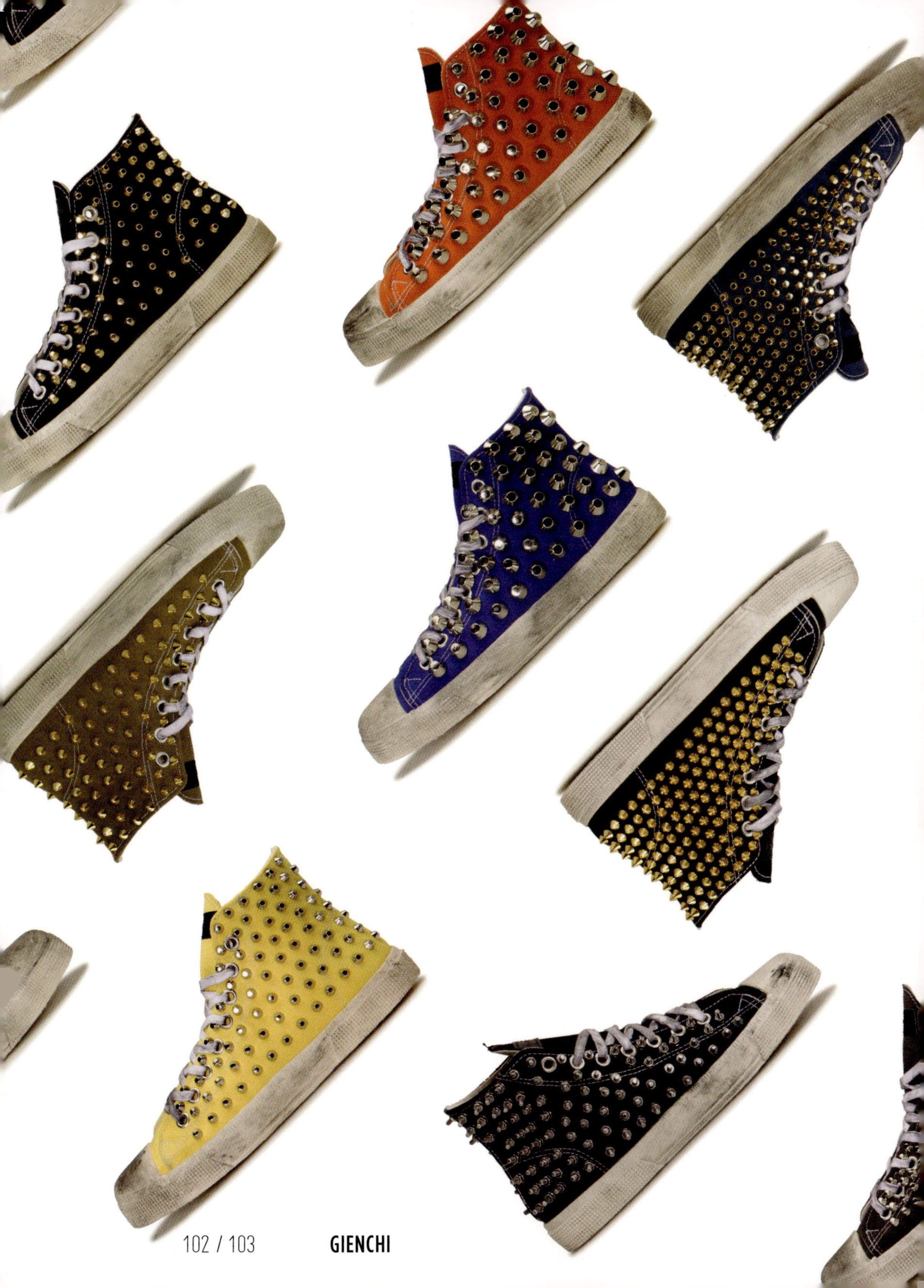

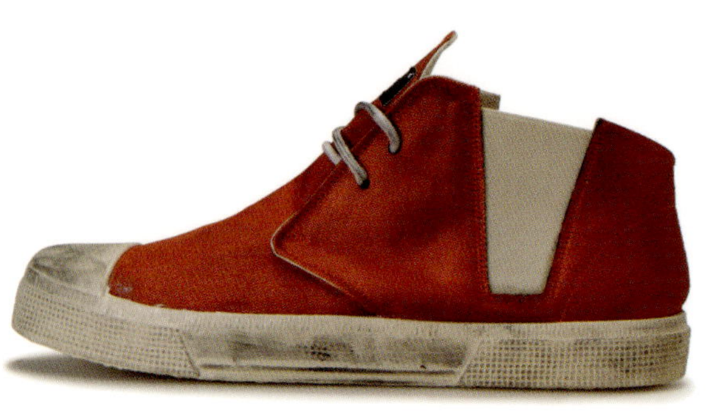

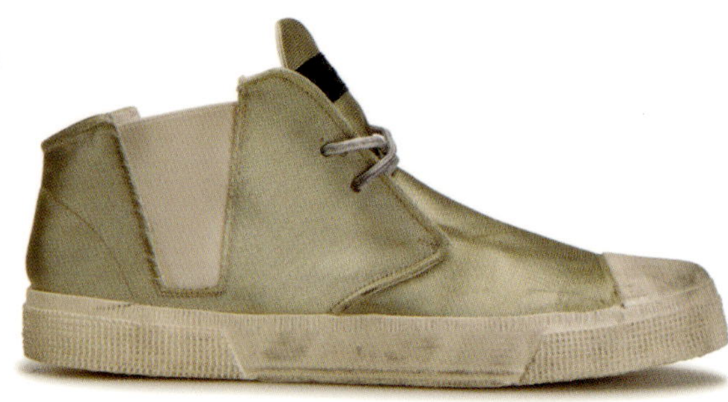

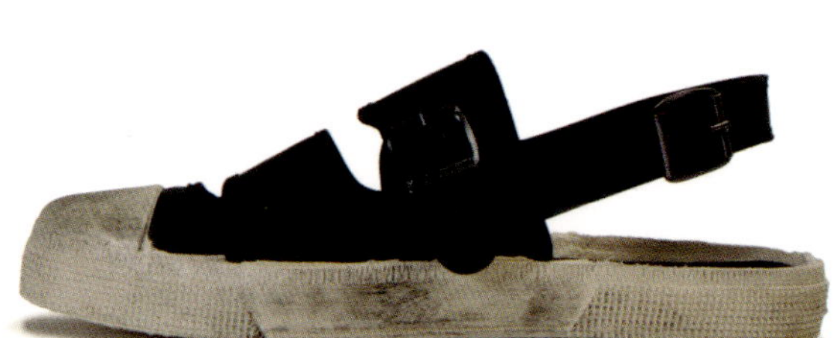

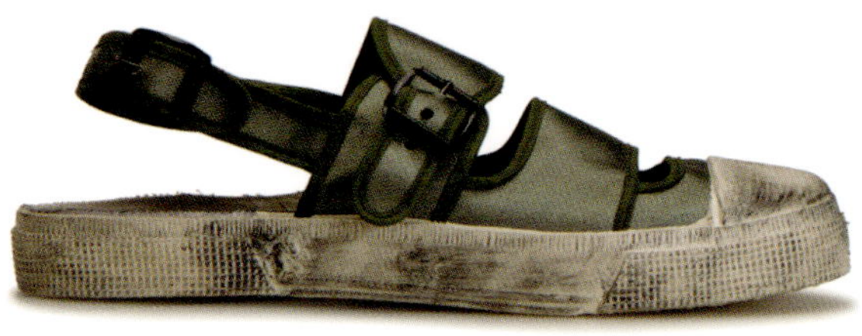

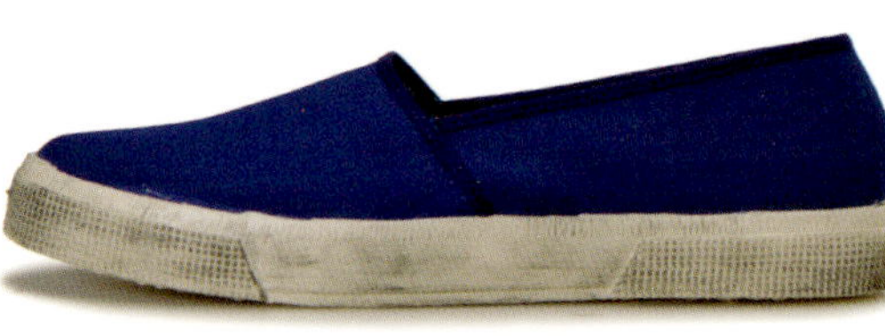

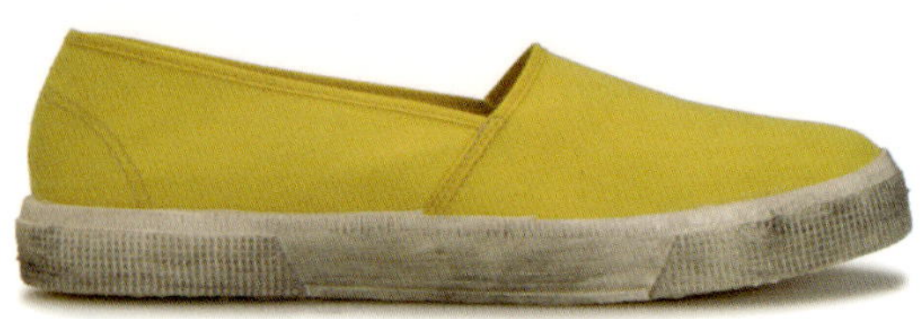

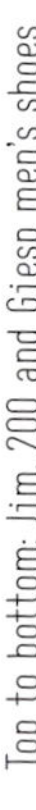

Top to bottom: Jim, 200 and Giesp men's shoes.

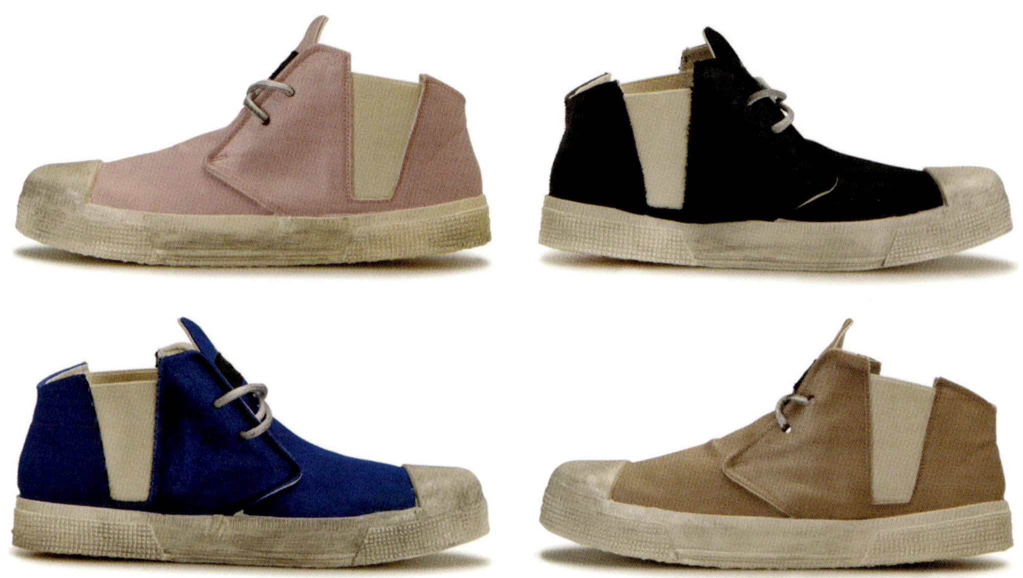

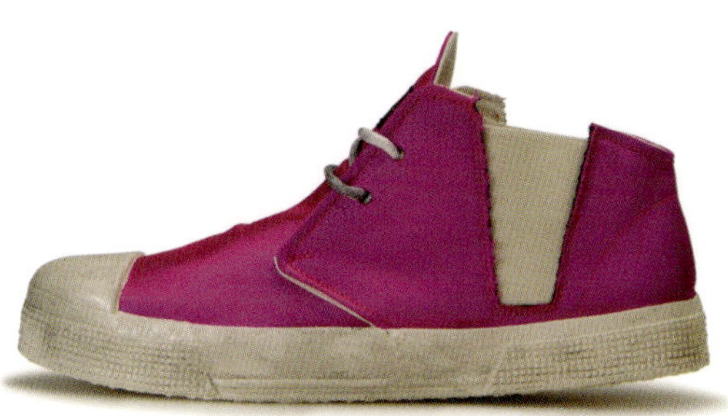

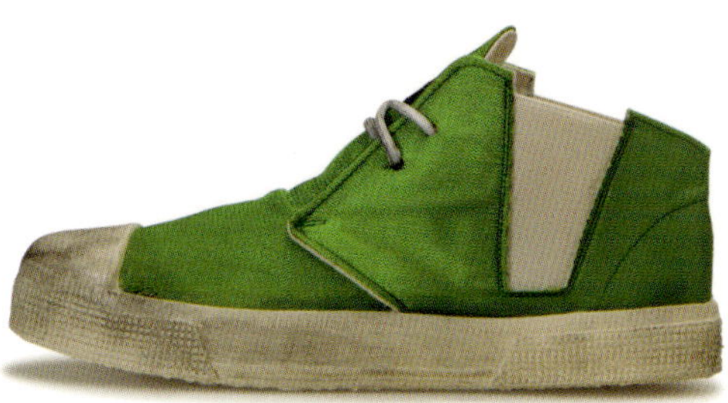

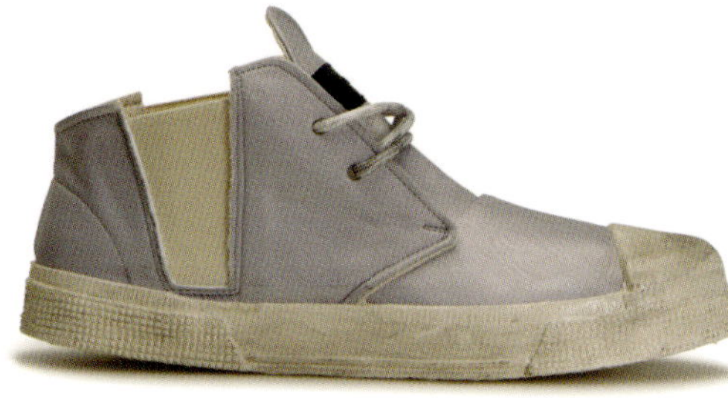

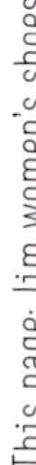

This page: Jim women's shoes.

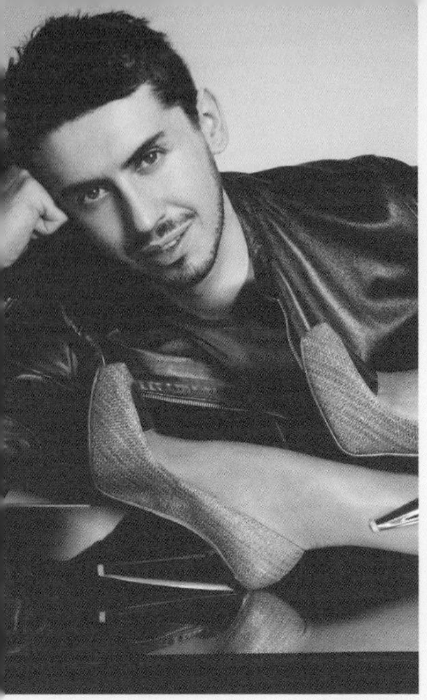

GIO METODIEV, GIO DIEV

I moved to New York when I was 19. My dream was to work in television and my heroes were Charlie Rose and Larry King. I became immersed in NYC nightlife and was exposed to the endless creativity that made the clubs so special during that time. I often went to a club called SPA and everyone was so theatrically dressed. As I didn't have any money to buy designer clothes I started creating my own one-of-a-kind pieces from the East Village thrift stores. Many people took notice and kept telling me that I should go into fashion. **DESIGNING SHOES HAS BEEN A PASSION OF MINE FOR A LONG TIME. I ALWAYS USED TO SKETCH SHOES DURING MY FREE TIME, INITIALLY JUST FOR FUN. ONE DAY I LOOKED AT ALL THE DRAWINGS AND REALIZED IT WAS TIME TO MAKE SOMETHING OF THEM. MY NEXT STEP WAS TO MOVE TO ITALY AND LEARN ABOUT THE CRAFT FROM THE SHOE ARTISANS THEMSELVES. SPENDING MONTHS AT A TIME AT THE ARTISANS' STUDIO, CUTTING LEATHERS, DEVELOPING HEELS AND LEARNING ABOUT MAKING LASTS GAVE ME THE BEST SKILL SET AND PREPARED ME TO SUCCESSFULLY LAUNCH MY OWN COLLECTION.** I have an innate appreciation and obsession with shoes. A beautifully made shoe is an art object its own right. I also adore women and find that shoes are one of the few objects that can perfectly capture their own style of femininity and the many aspects of their personality. Beauty is about being original. There is not one standard for beauty and there never should be. Each of my designs is extremely personal and each derives from a distinct story or path of inspiration e.g. Joan of Arc's armour or Marlene Deitrich's veil in Shanghai Express. **A SIGNATURE HEEL FOR THE COLLECTION IS THE SILVER SWORD HEEL. FOR SPRING 2012 WE HAVE INTRODUCED THE SAMURAI HEEL AND ISLAND PLATFORM IN BLACK AND SCARLET RED LACQUER. MOST OF ALL I ENJOY DESIGNING BOOTS AND THE WATERLOO SILVER BOOT HOLDS A SPECIAL PLACE FOR ME. I AM ALSO FOND OF THE MILO SANDALS FROM SPRING 2012 AND THE SYDNEY SHOE, WHICH WAS INSPIRED BY THE SYDNEY OPERA HOUSE IN AUSTRALIA.** I spend a lot of time at photo libraries, watching old movies and going to galleries. When you're a creative person you never stop working. Whenever I'm walking on the street, watching a movie or having dinner at a restaurant, I'm constantly registering all that's around me, adding colours, shapes and all kinds of images to my visual memory. I recently designed a boot based on a YouTube video about the human body. It's very important to be open-minded and try to see things with a new set of eyes. I find swimming very helpful. Somehow it helps me to think clearer.

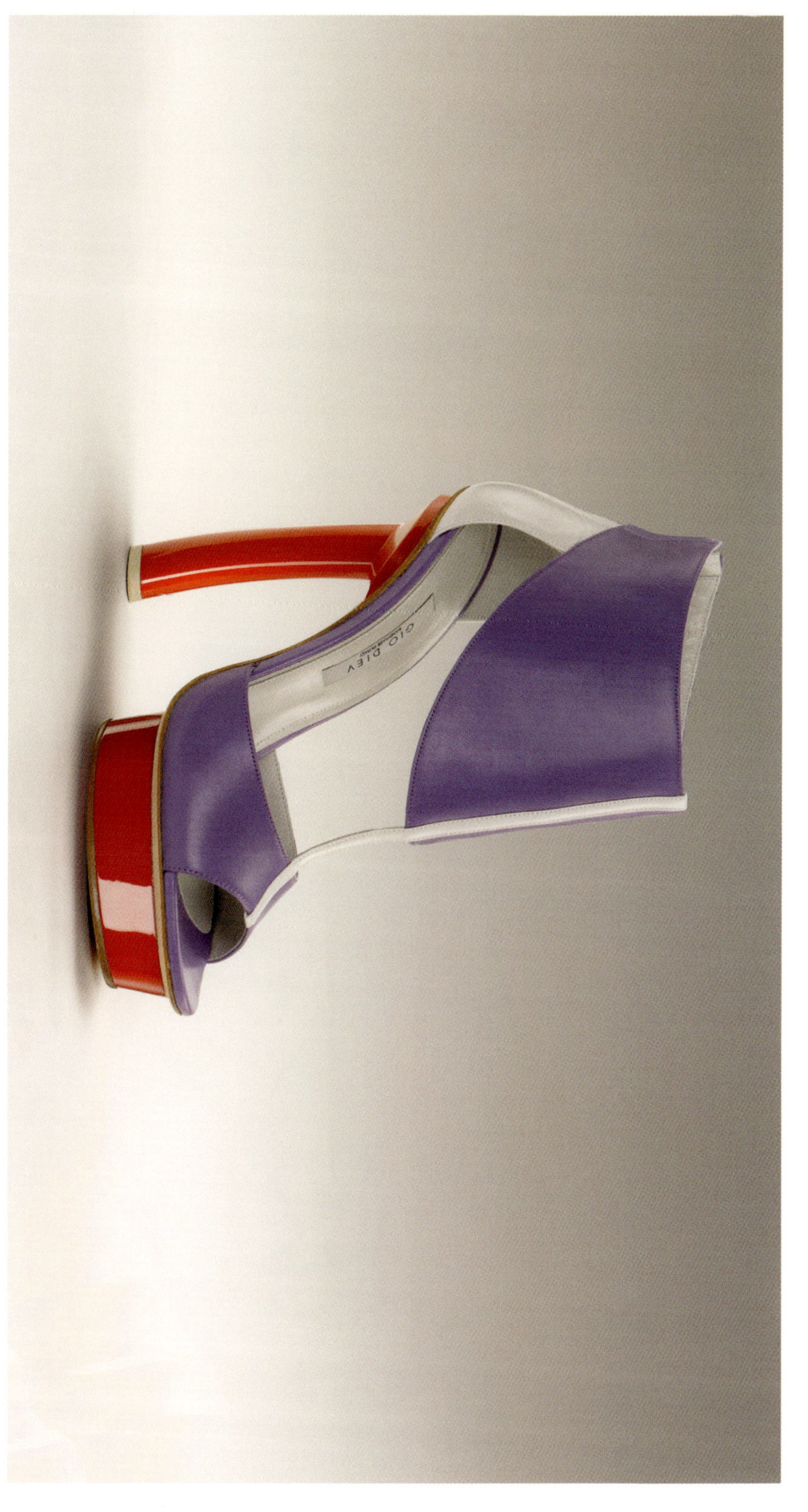

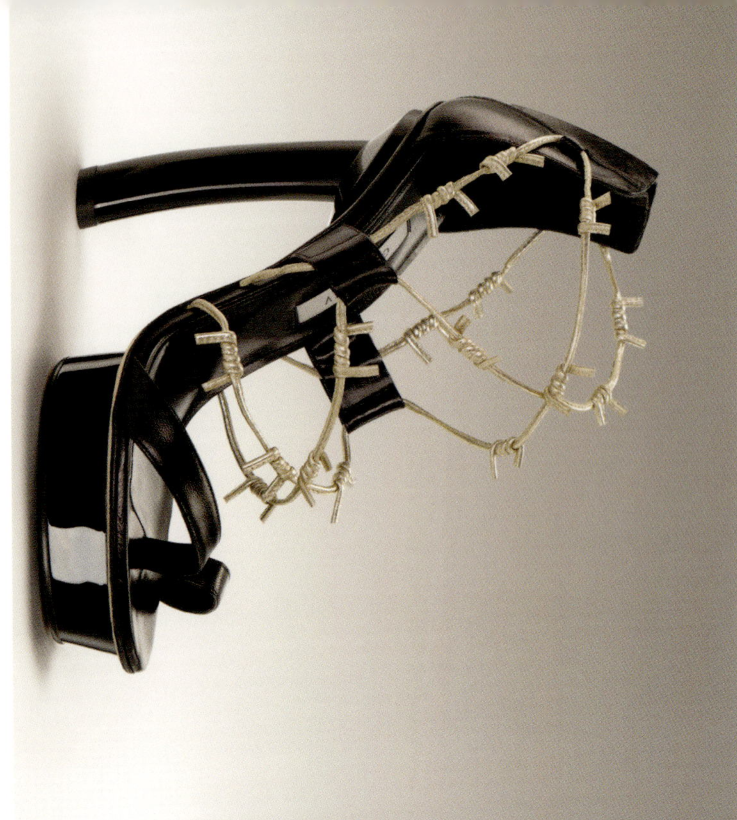

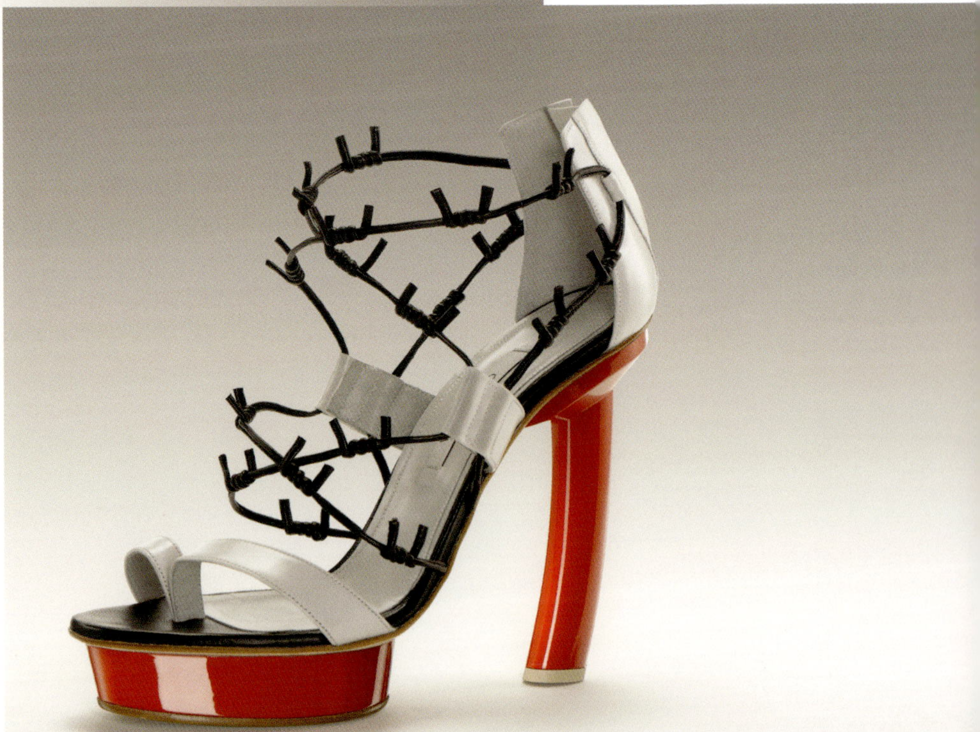

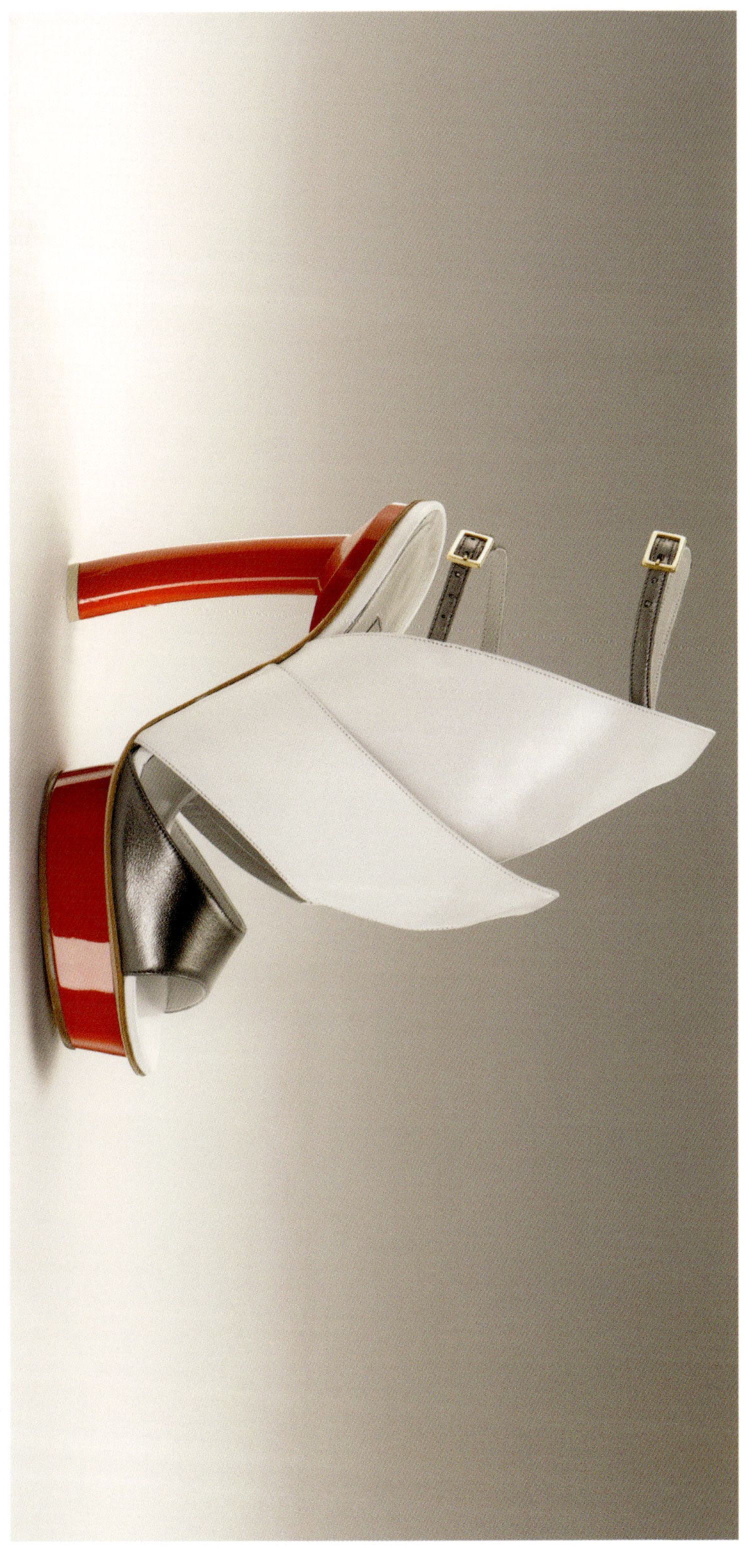

 GIO DIEV

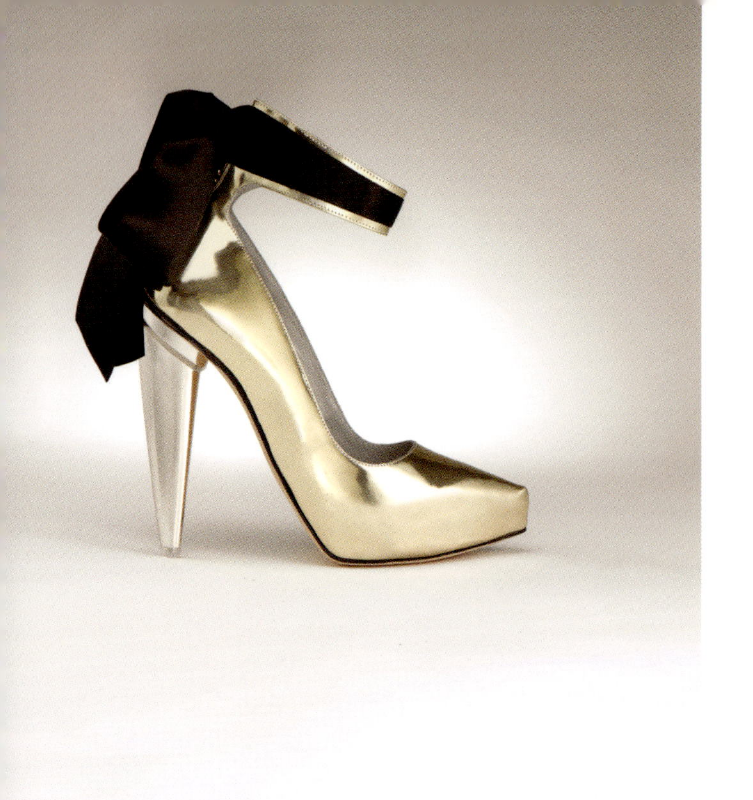

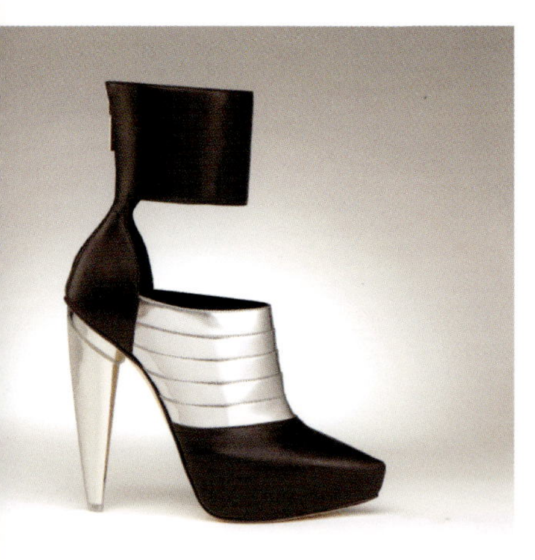

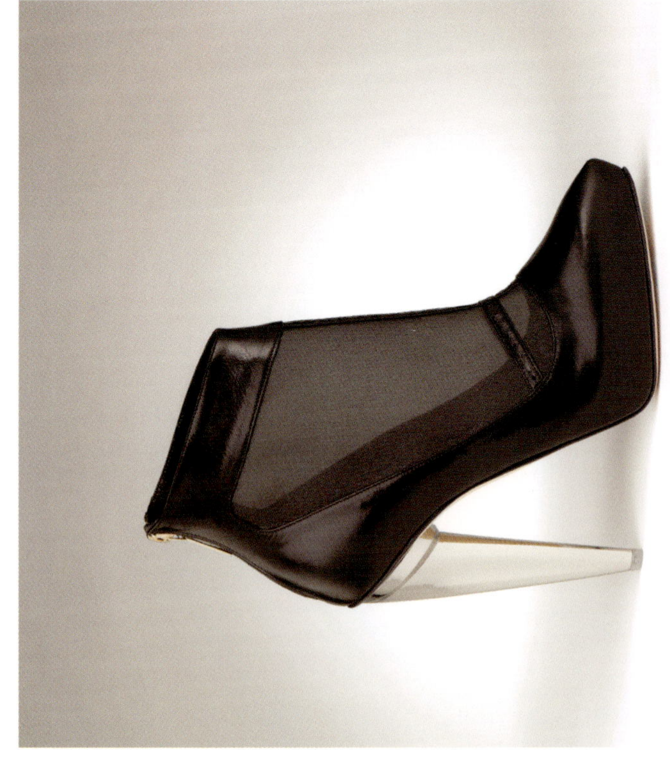

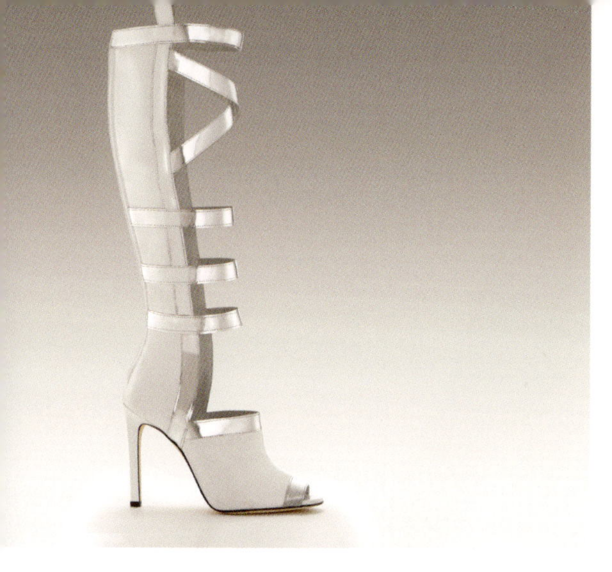

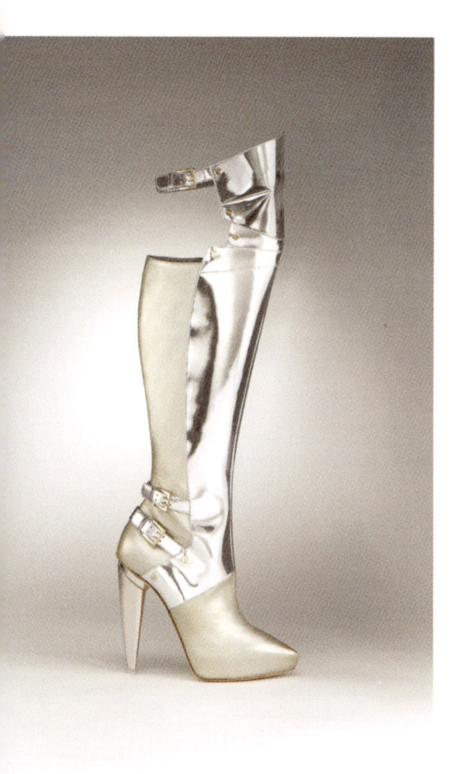

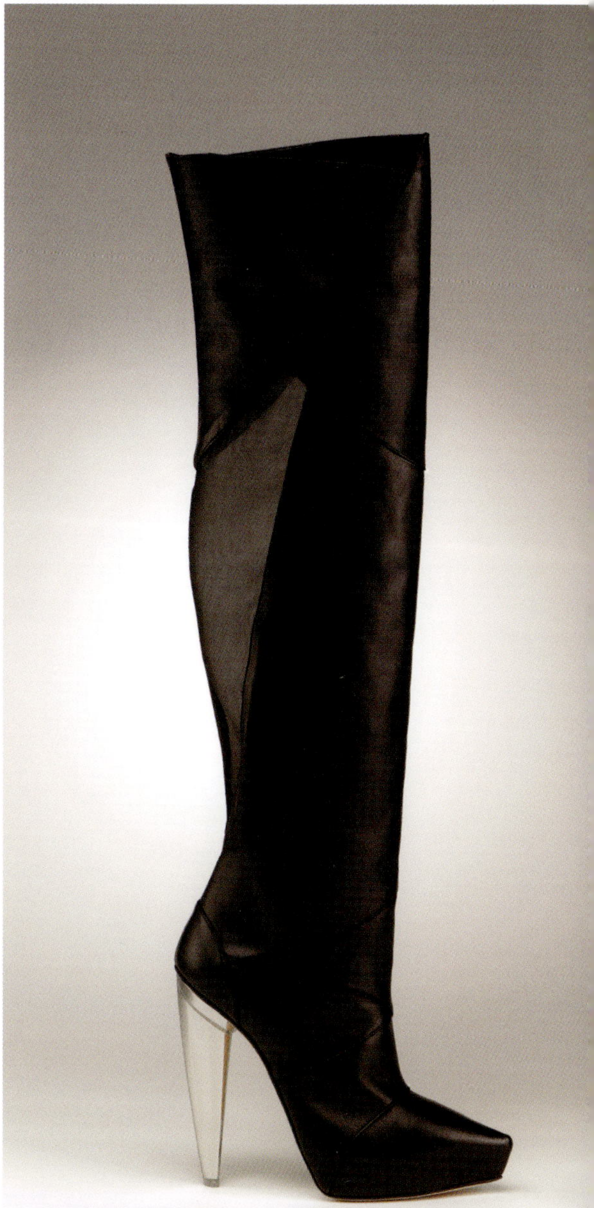

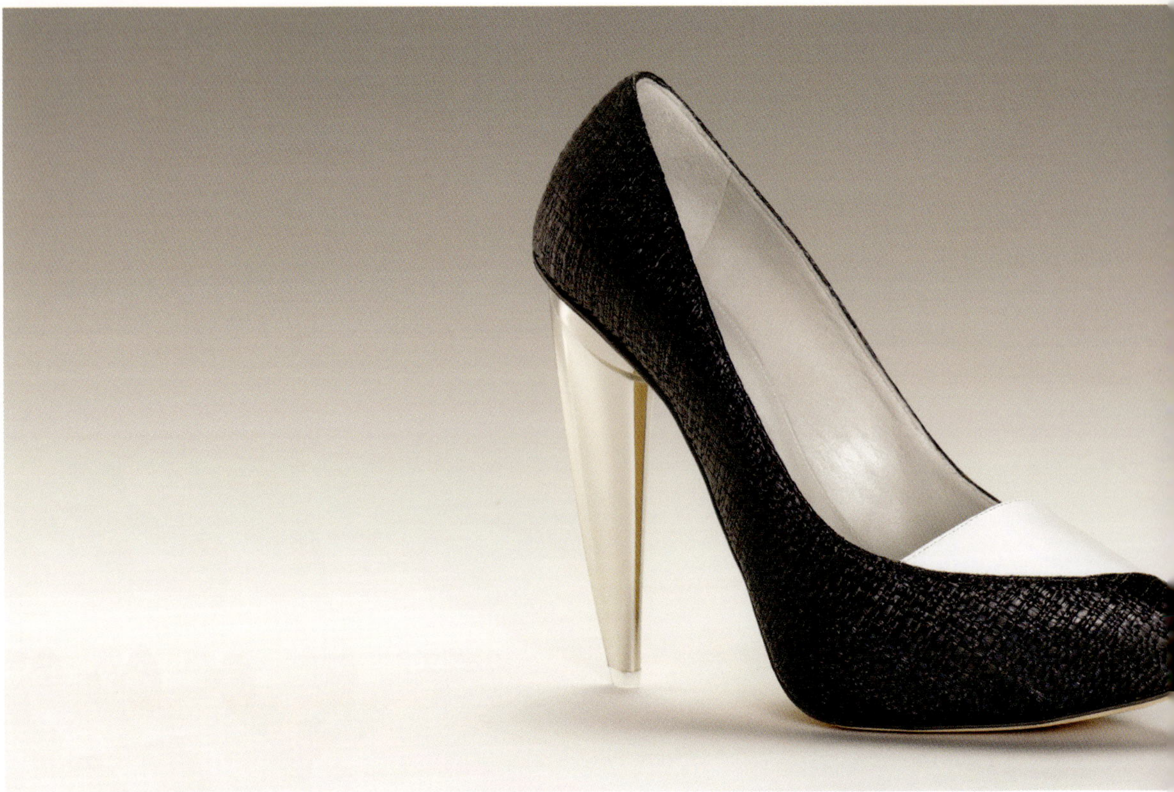

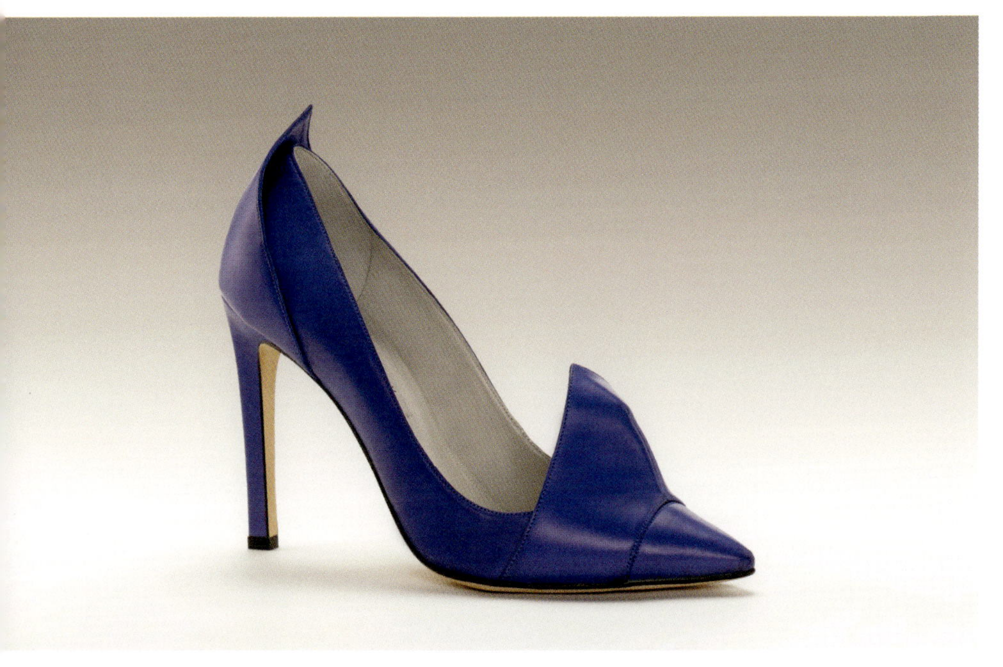

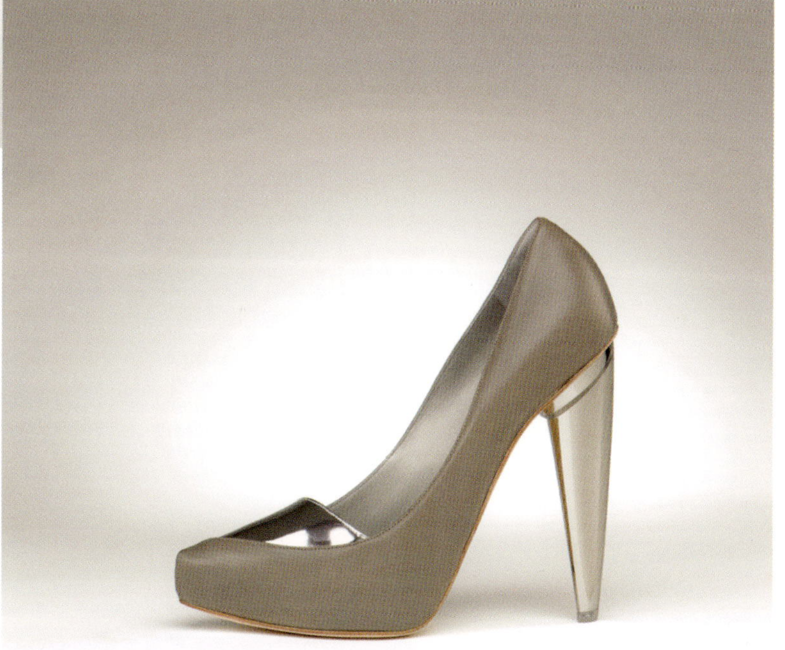

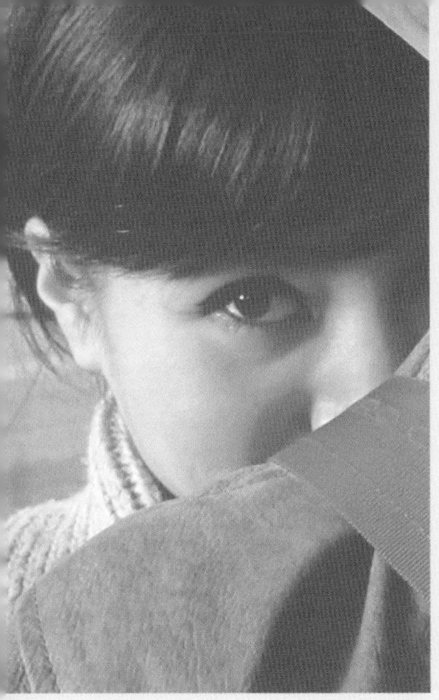

MICHELLE WU, HEAVY MACHINE

Please introduce yourself **I AM THE YOUNGEST AT HOME, BUT I HAVE THE LOUDEST VOICE.** What is your work about? **IT IS A REFLECTION AND EXTENSION OF MYSELF WITH AN AIM TO MAKE LIFE MORE INTERESTING AND FUN.** Is there a specific reason why you chose shoe design? **I CHOSE IT FOR FUN AND I COULDN'T FIND THE SHOES I WANTED SO I THOUGHT WHY NOT MAKE MY DREAM SHOES MYSELF.** Can you tell us something about the design process? **I COLLECT PICTURES AND WORDS THAT INSPIRE ME AND WITH THAT INSPIRATION, START DRAWING.** Which stage of the creative process do you find the most gratifying? **THE MOST GRATIFYING STAGE IS WHEN I DRAW SOMETHING OUT OF NOWHERE THAT SURPRISES ME. SOMETIMES IT FEELS AS IF IT WASN'T ME WHO CREATED IT.** If you had to choose one colour and one material to make an important piece, what would they be? **GOLD AND GOLD, BECAUSE GOLD SHIMMERS WITH LIGHT AND MOVEMENT. MOVEMENT IS LIFE.** What role does work play in your life? **IT'S A JOURNEY OF EXPERIMENTS THAT MOTIVATES ME TO KEEP ON FINDING NEW INGREDIENTS THAT MAKE LIFE MORE JOYFUL** What do you consider vulgar and what elegant? **SOMETIMES VULGARITY IS JUST TRYING TOO HARD TO CHALLENGE SOMETHING TO THE EXTREME, BE IT SOCIAL EXPECTATION OR PERSONAL TASTE. HOWEVER, SOMETIMES VULGARITY IS THE CHAOTIC ELEMENT OF A STORY THAT MAKES IT INTERESTING. ELEGANCE IS SOMETHING FROM THE HEART THAT'S NOT FALSE, SOMETHING REVEALED FROM A GESTURE OR MENTALITY.** What does beauty means for you? **I THINK BEAUTY IS SOMETHING THAT FASCINATES AND TOUCHES ME FOR A LONG TIME. IT DOESN'T NECESSARILY HAVE TO BE AN OBJECT, BUT A THOUGHT, A MOMENT OR AN ILLUSION.**

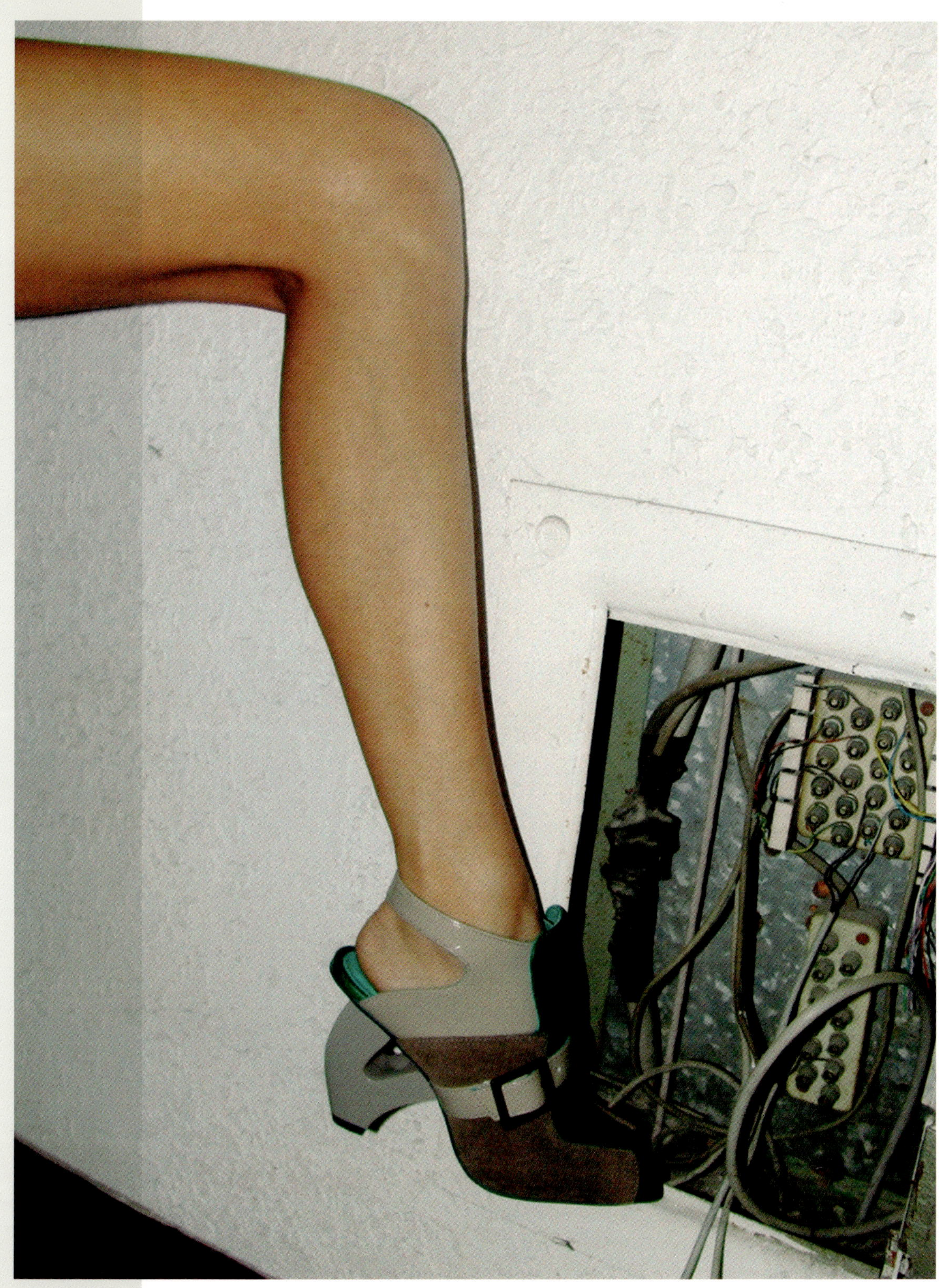

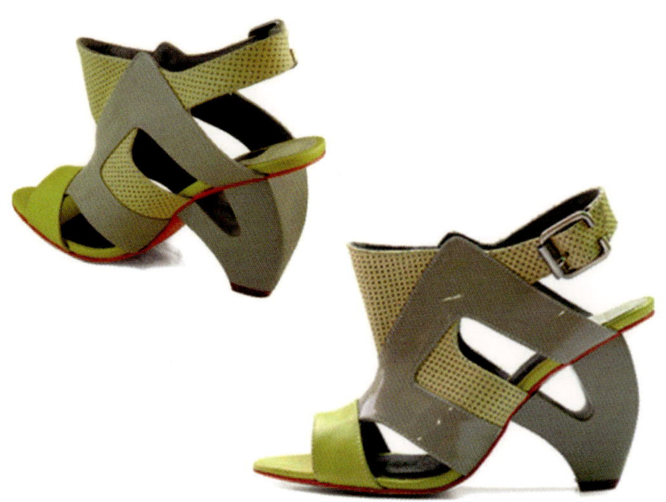

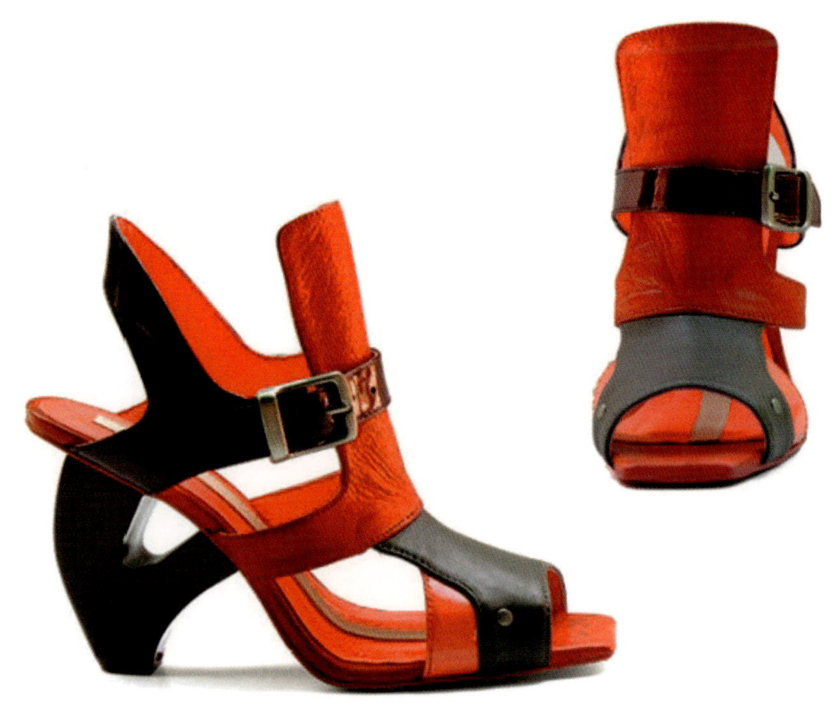

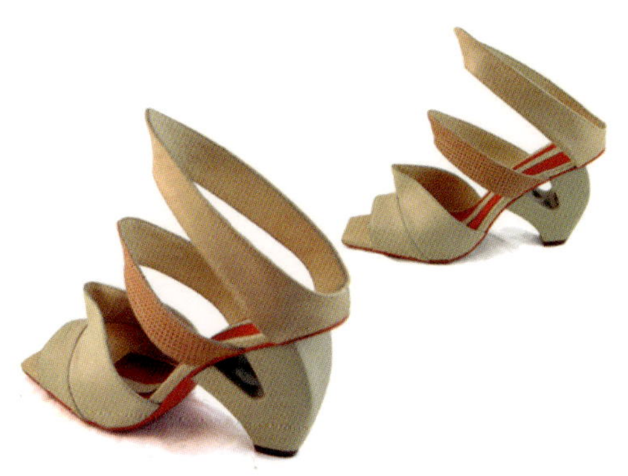

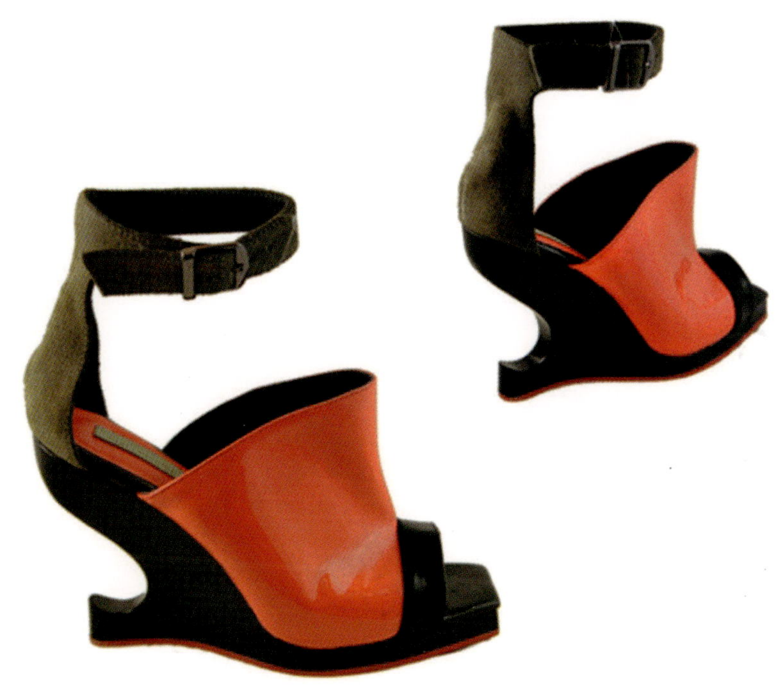

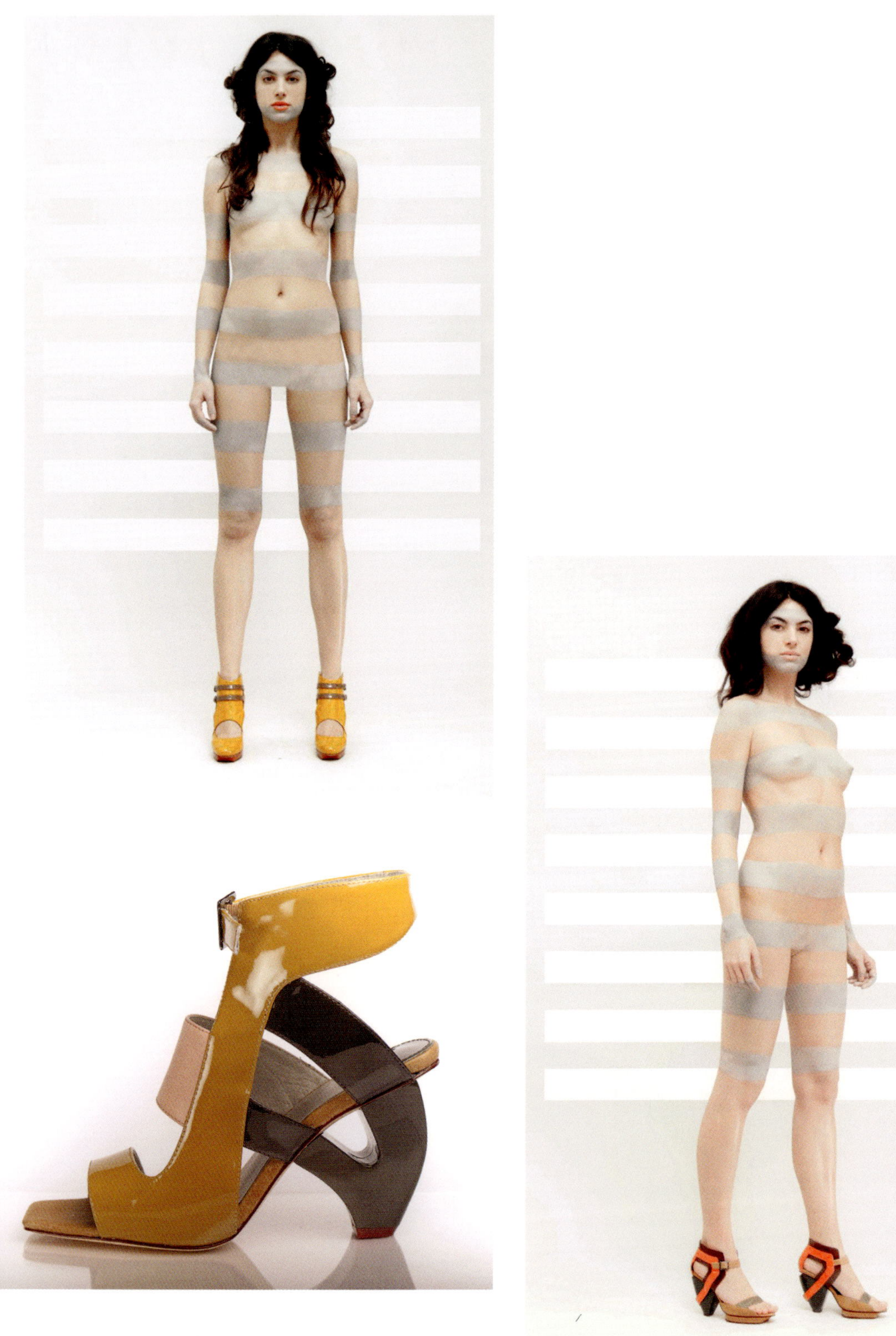

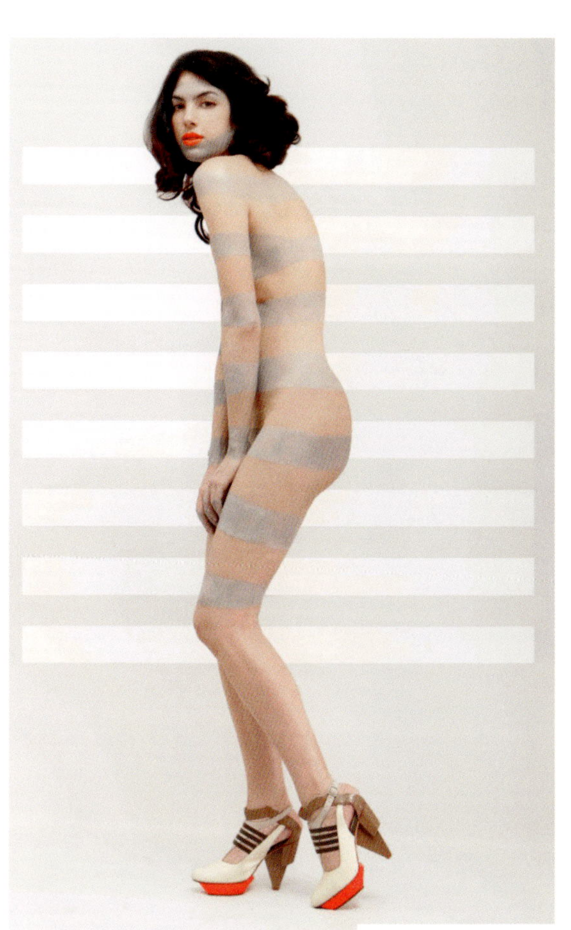

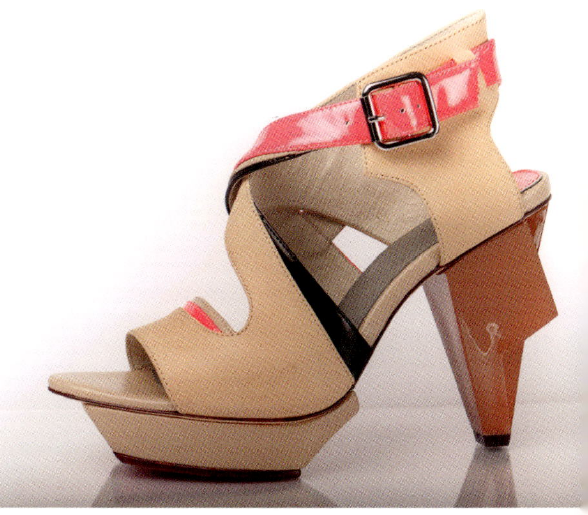

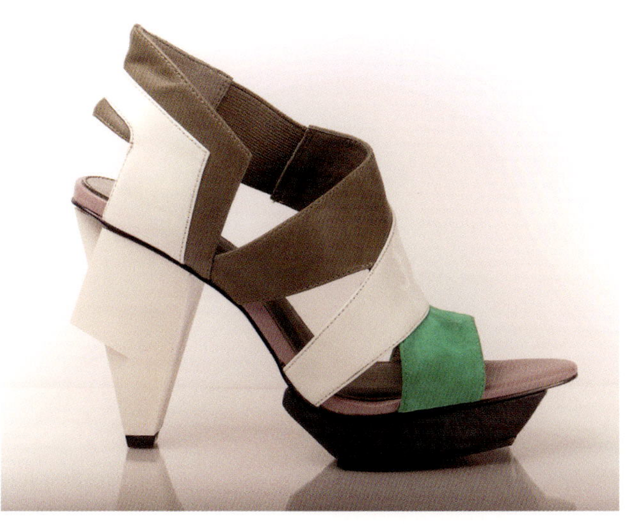

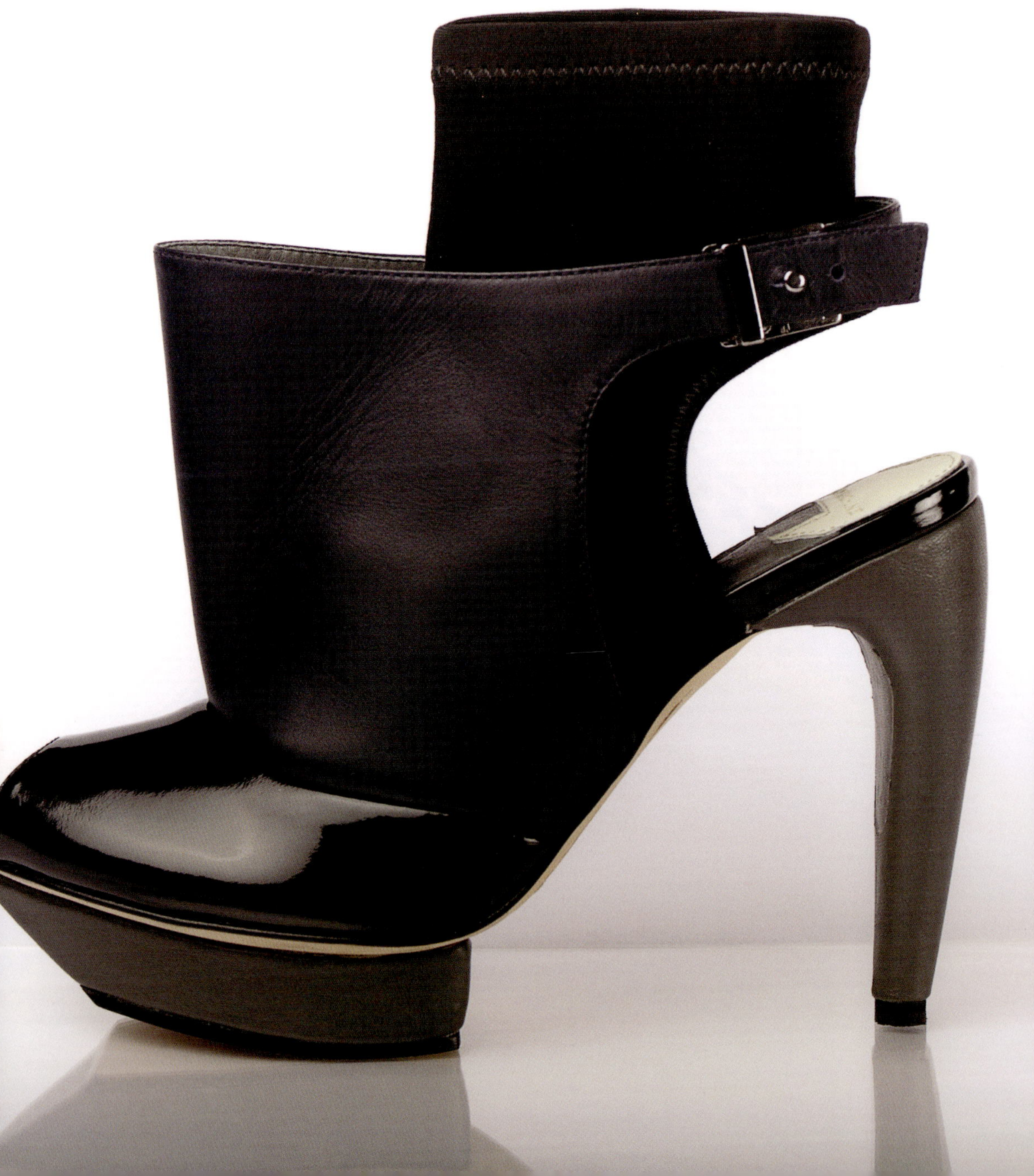

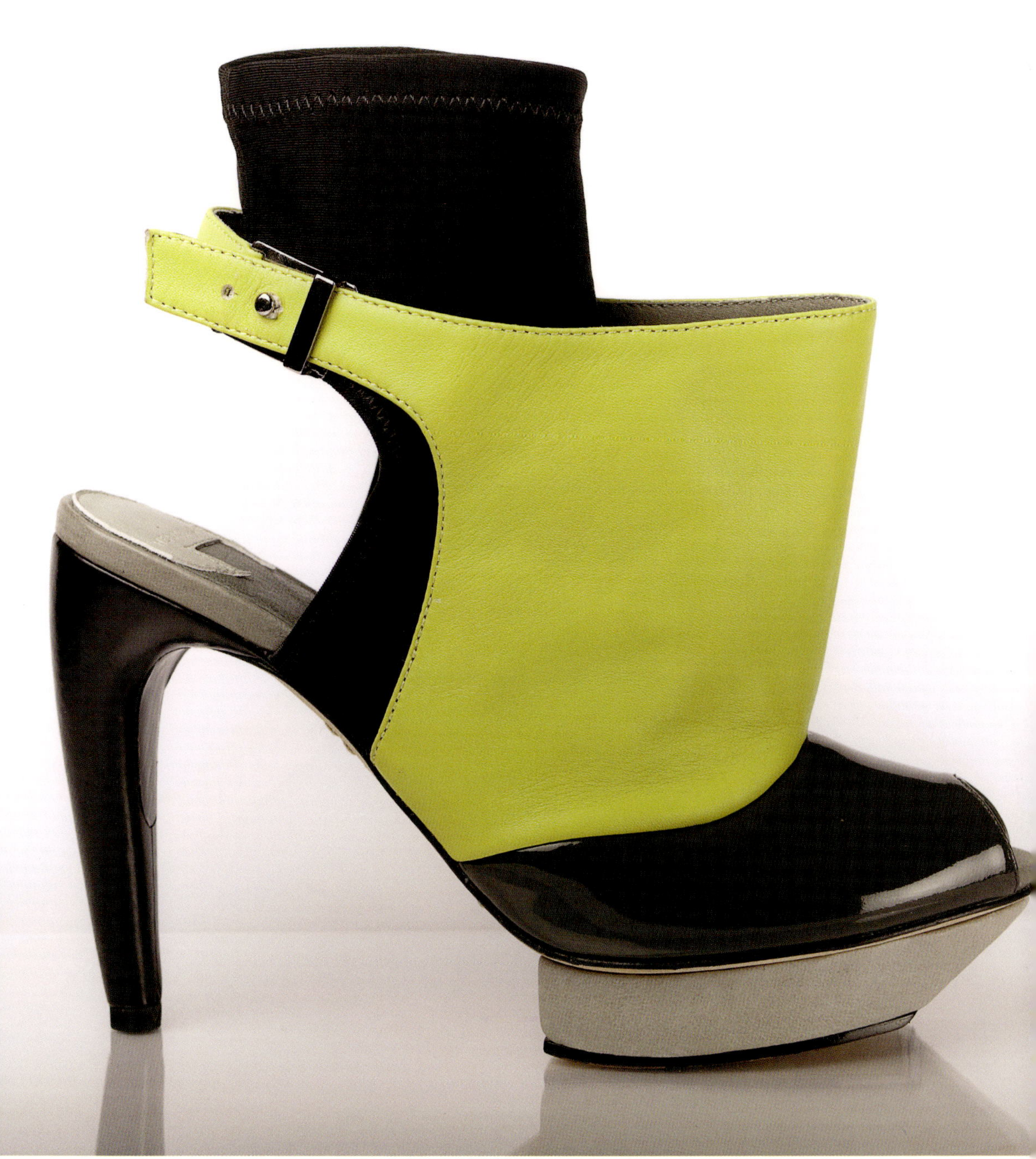

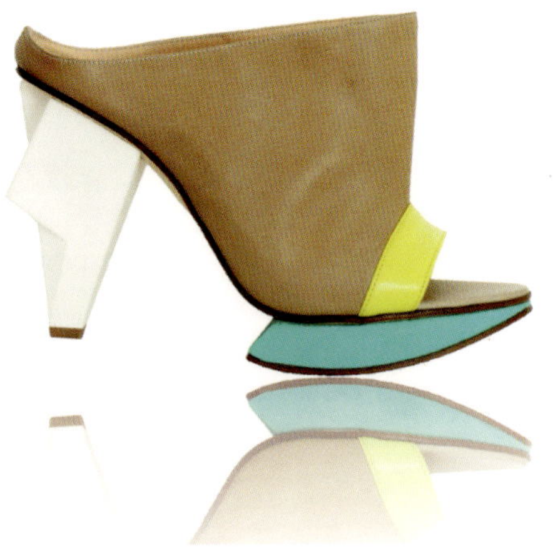

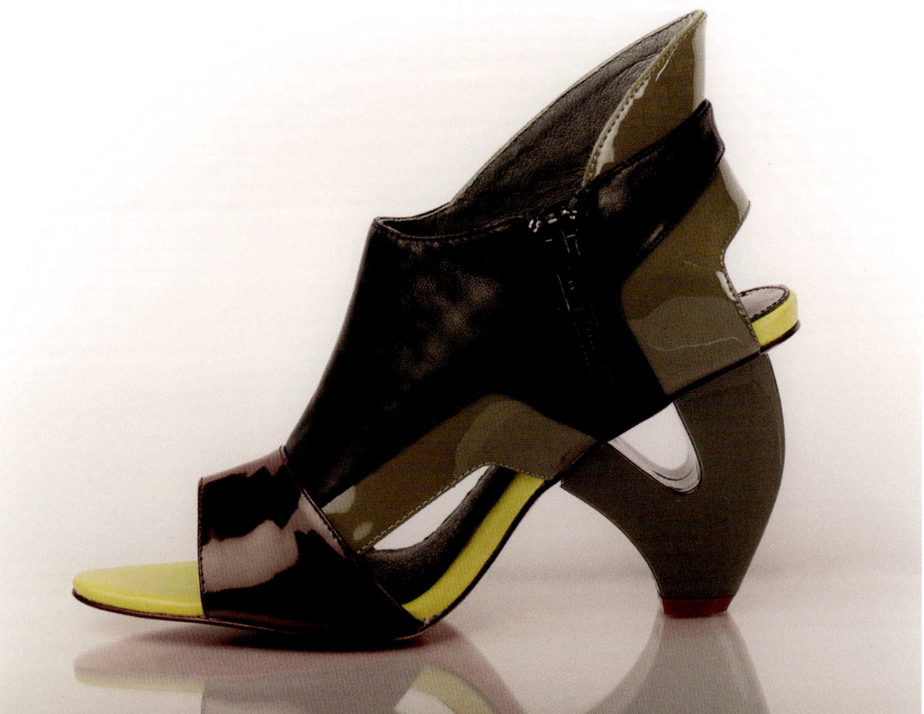

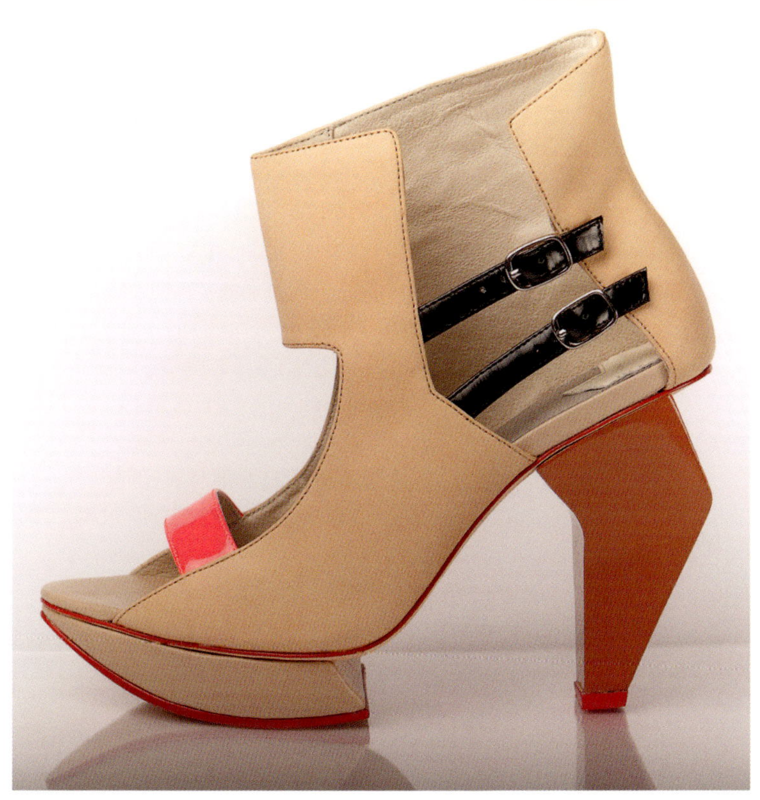

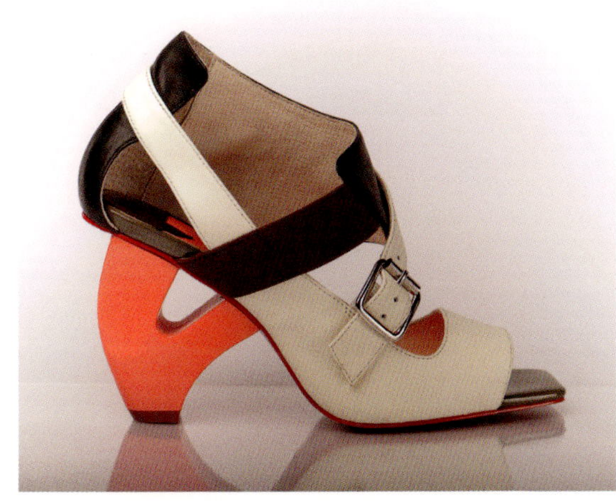

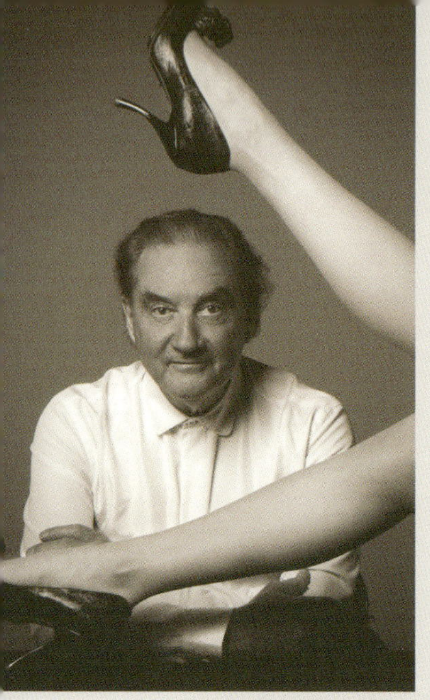

JAN JANSEN

How did you get started? **I HAVE BEEN DESIGNING SHOES FROM THE AGE OF 6. AT 20-YEARS-OLD I LEARNED HOW TO MAKE SHOES BY HAND IN THE ATELIERS OF FOLLIE AND ALBANESE IN ROME WHERE SOPHIA LOREN'S SHOES WERE MADE.** Why shoes? **I CHOSE SHOES BECAUSE THEY ARE THREE-DIMENSIONAL. I LIKE THE FACT THAT A SHOE CAN STAND ON ITS OWN LIKE A SCULPTURE. CLOTHING ONLY TAKES SHAPE WHEN YOU PUT A BODY INTO IT.** What makes your work different to others? **MOST DESIGNERS MAKE PATTERNS ON A LAST. I FLATTER MYSELF WITH THE IDEA THAT I CAN FEEL HOW A WOMAN FEELS WHEN SHE PUTS HER FEET IN MY SHOES.** What do you consider your most innovative design? **THE BAMBOO SHOE I DESIGNED IN 1973. I MADE A REMAKE OF IT IN 2006. ANOTHER SHOE WAS THE TUTTI PIEDI, A FLAT SHOE MADE OUT OF ONE PIECE OF LEATHER, PULLED TOGETHER WITH LACE.** Tell us something about the design process. **MY WORK IS NOT INSPIRED BY SPECIFIC PAINTINGS OR SCULPTURES OR MUSEUMS. WHEN I CLOSE MY EYES I SEE IMAGES AND I MAKE THE SHAPES THAT I SEE. THESE BECOME THE FOUNDATION OF THE SHOE: THE LAST, THE HEEL, THE PLATFORM, THE SILHOUETTE. ONCE THE BODY IS THERE, I THEN DRAPE THE DRESS (THE UPPER) OVER IT.** Which parts of the creative process do you find the most gratifying? **THE MOST GRATIFYING IS WHEN I'VE PLACED A PROTOTYPE ON TOP OF THE TELEVISION SET AND HAVE LOOKED AT IT FOR MANY EVENINGS TOGETHER WITH MY WIFE TONNY AND I SAY TO MYSELF, AFTER MY WIFE'S APPROVAL, THIS IS PERFECT. I DON'T HAVE TO MOVE THE HEEL 3MM BACKWARDS OR FORWARDS — IT'S PERFECT.** Who or what has played a part in your development as an artist? **ROGER VIVIER, SALVATORE FERRAGAMO, SALVADORE DALI, HENRY MOORE, KARL LAGERFELD , JOHN GALLIANO, ALEXANDER MCQUEEN, BALLET DANCERS AND MANY ARTISTS. MOVEMENTS HAVE NEVER INFLUENCED ME. I WAS USUALLY WAY AHEAD OF THEM. I MADE SHOES WITH STEEL CAPS IN 1977, LONG BEFORE PUNK.** What would be your colour of choice for an important piece? **IT WOULD DEFINITELY BE RED.** What are your thoughts on quick consumption culture and over-commercialisation? **I HATE IT. IT IS VERY DIFFICULT TO FIND TRULY INTERESTING AND ORIGINAL WORK WITH ARTISTIC INTEGRITY. THIS IS WHAT I HAVE TRIED TO ACHIEVE ALL MY LIFE. A GOOD DESIGN SURVIVES DECADES. I TRY TO CREATE THINGS THAT NOBODY HAS DONE BEFORE AND THAT INSPIRES OTHERS TO DO THE SAME. THAT IS WHAT MAKES THE WORLD GO ROUND.** How do you view the current state of your profession? **THE WORLD IS RUN BY STYLISTS, TREND WATCHERS AND PR PEOPLE. THERE ARE VERY FEW ORIGINAL DESIGNERS. MY PROFESSION IS TO FEED STYLISTS, TREND WATCHERS AND TRENDSETTERS. WITHOUT ORIGINAL DESIGNERS THEY HAVE NO WORK. WE ARE TEMPORARILY ON A FINANCIAL DIET NOW. I HOPE THIS PASSES SOON.** What do you consider vulgar and what elegant? **VULGAR IS TO SQUEEZE POOR MANUFACTURERS TO ENRICH YOURSELF. ELEGANT IS TO LIVE AND LET LIVE.** What does beauty mean to you? **BEAUTY IS TO LOVE YOURSELF AND TO MAKE OTHERS HAPPY.**

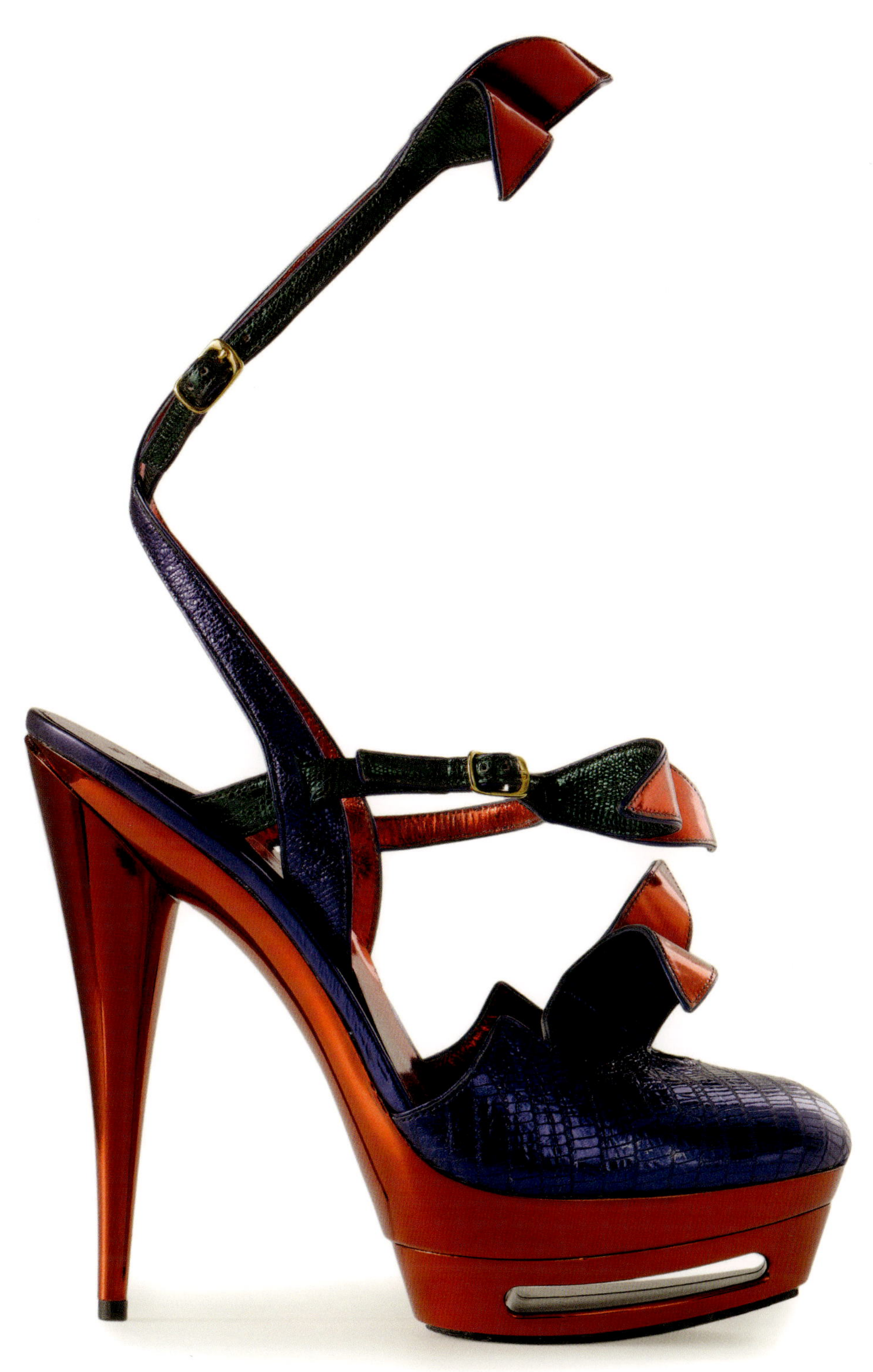

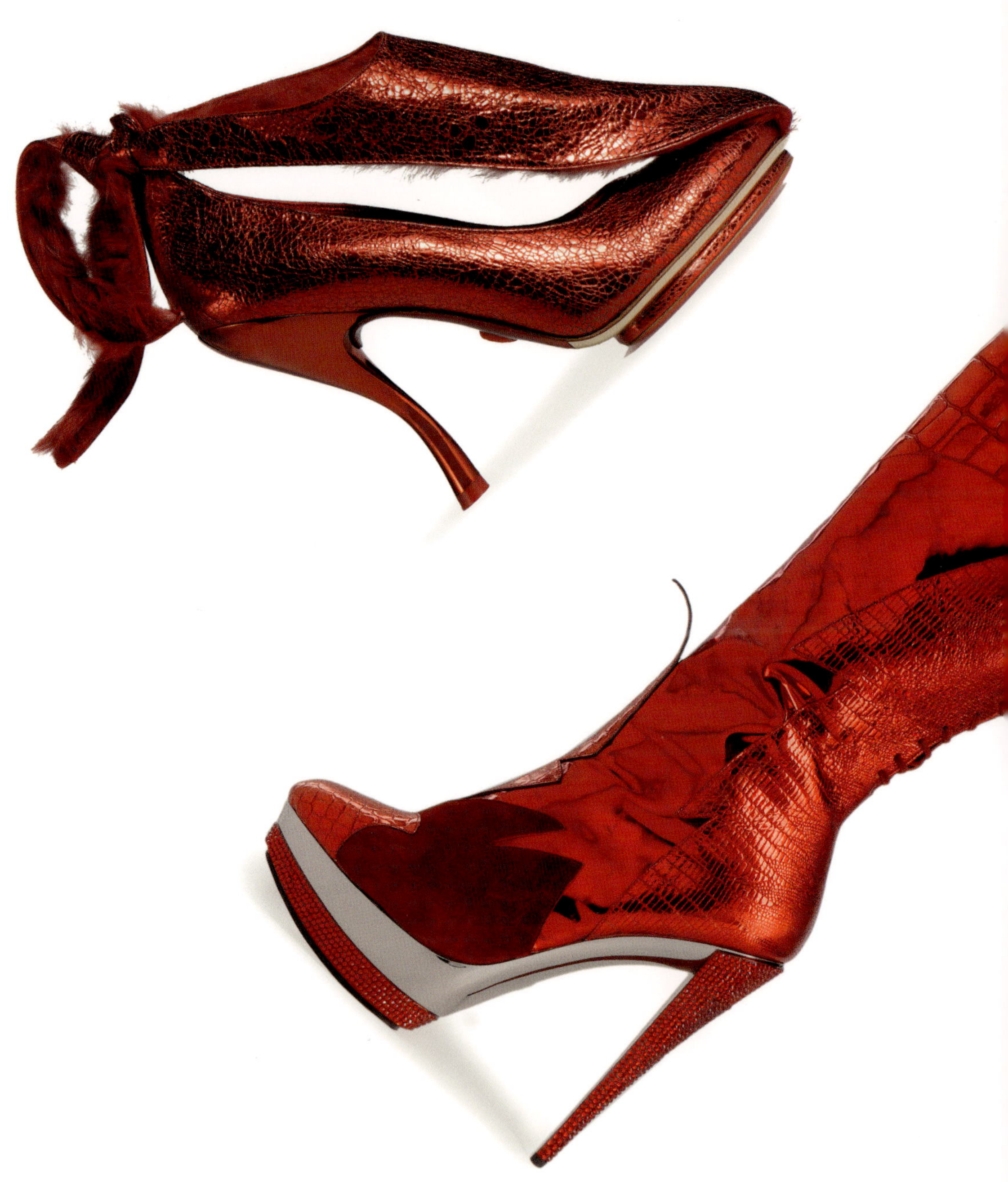

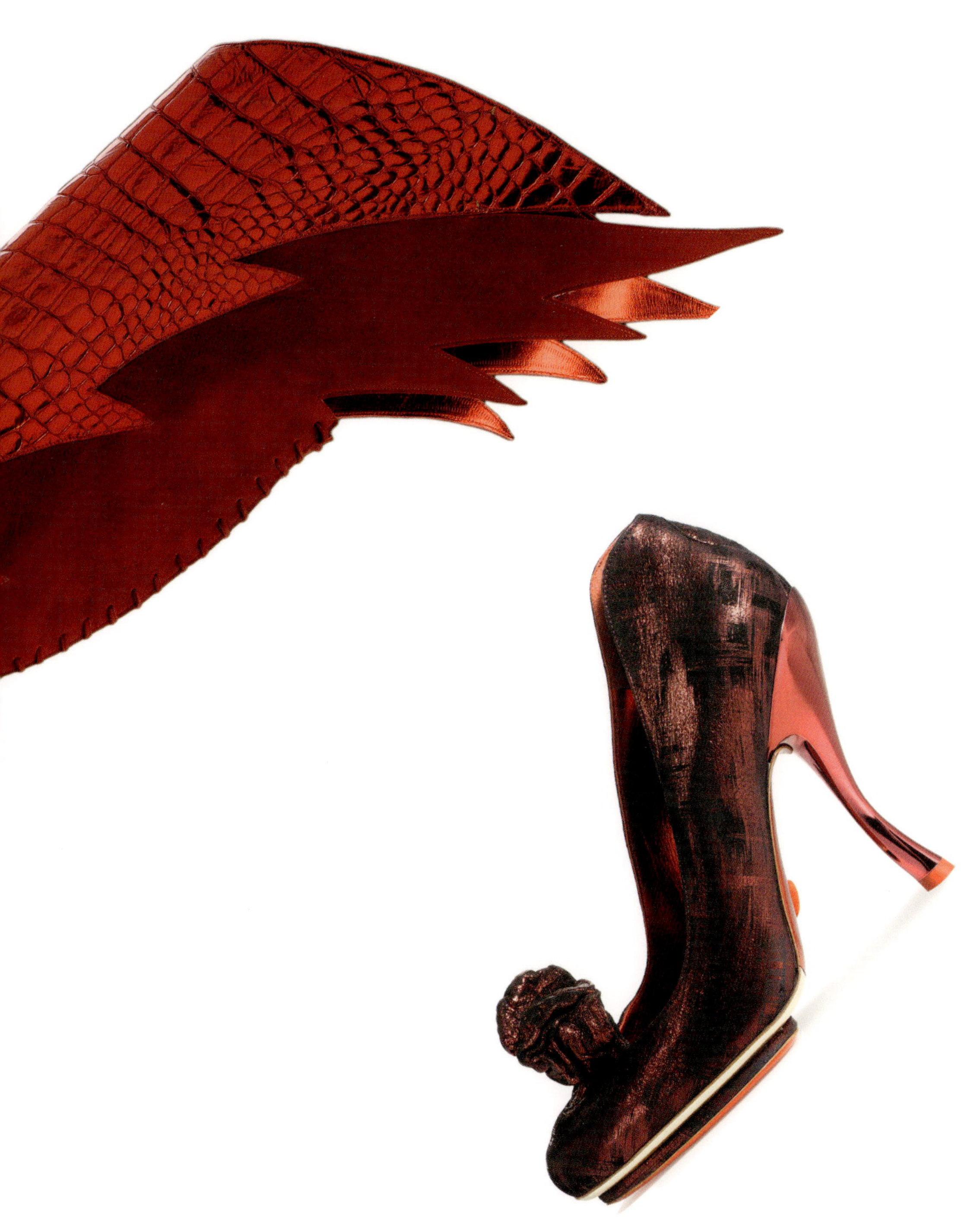

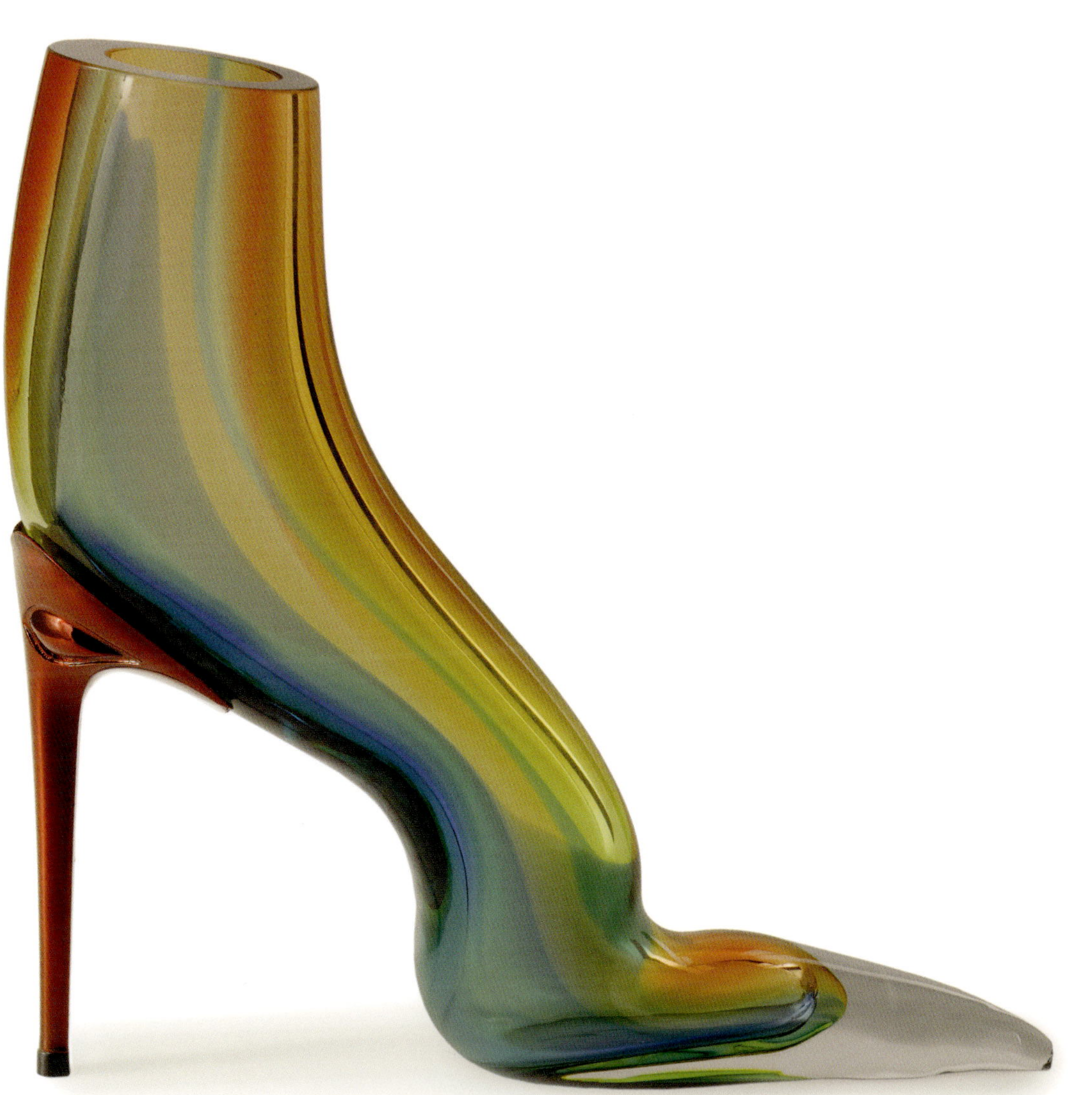

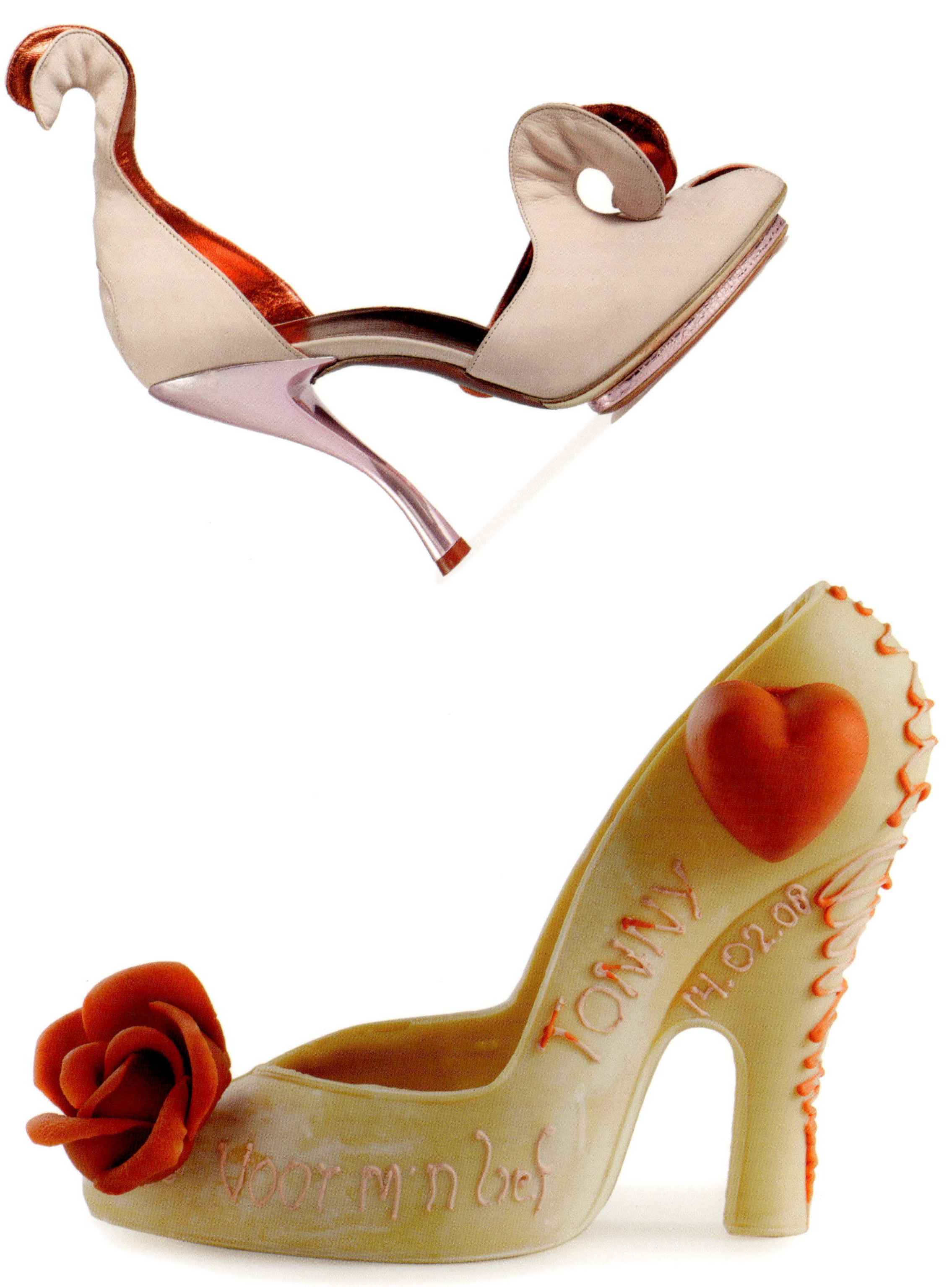
TONNY
14.02.08
voor m'n lief

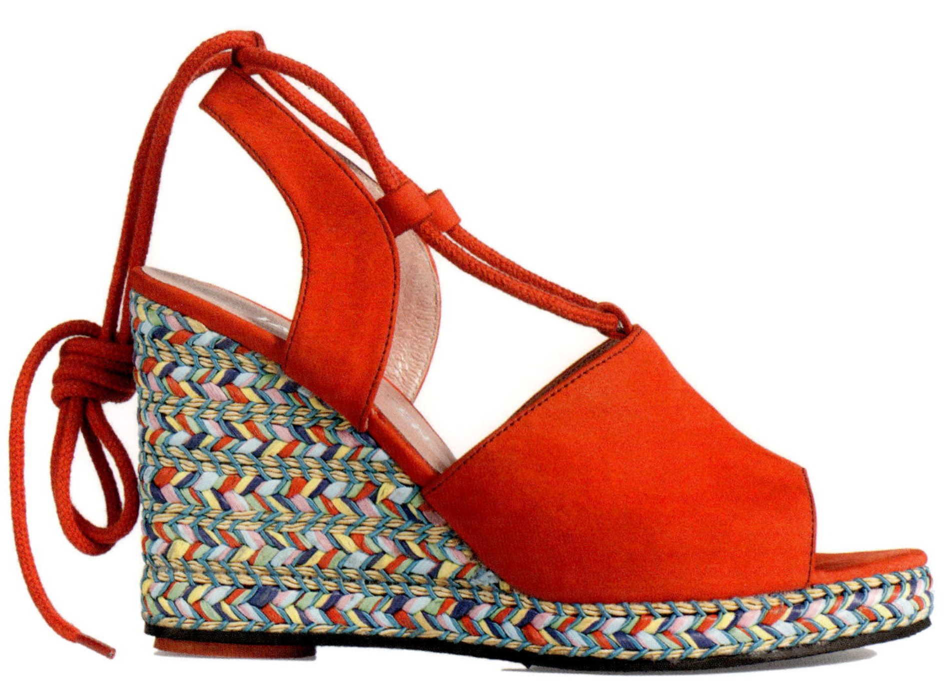

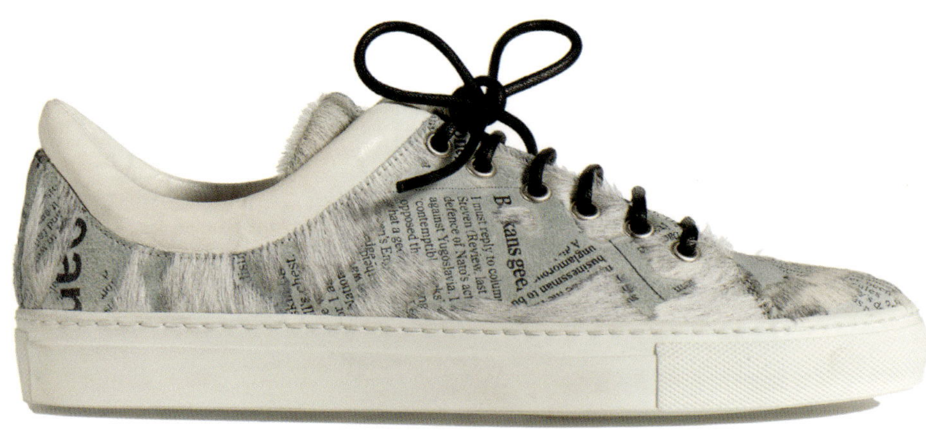

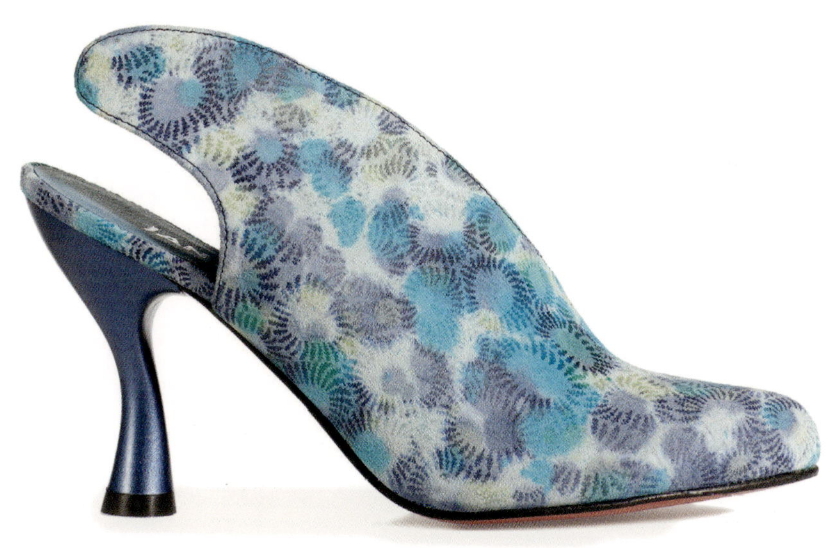

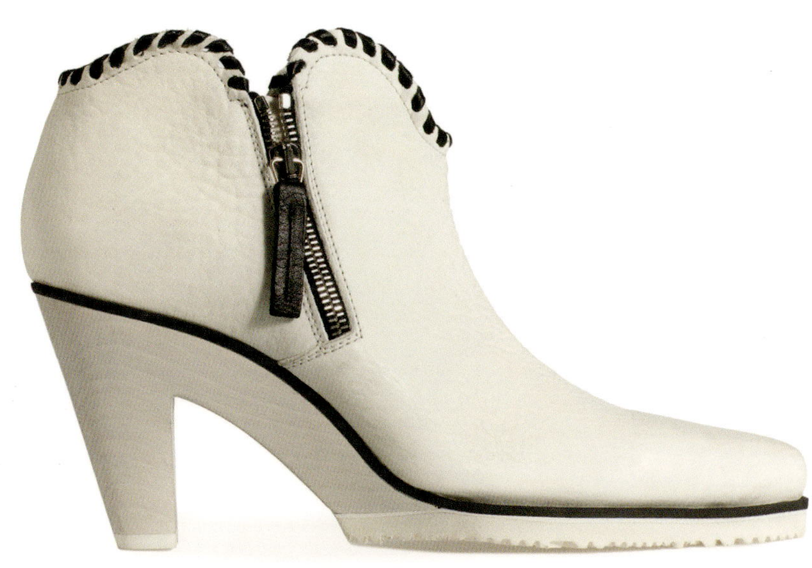

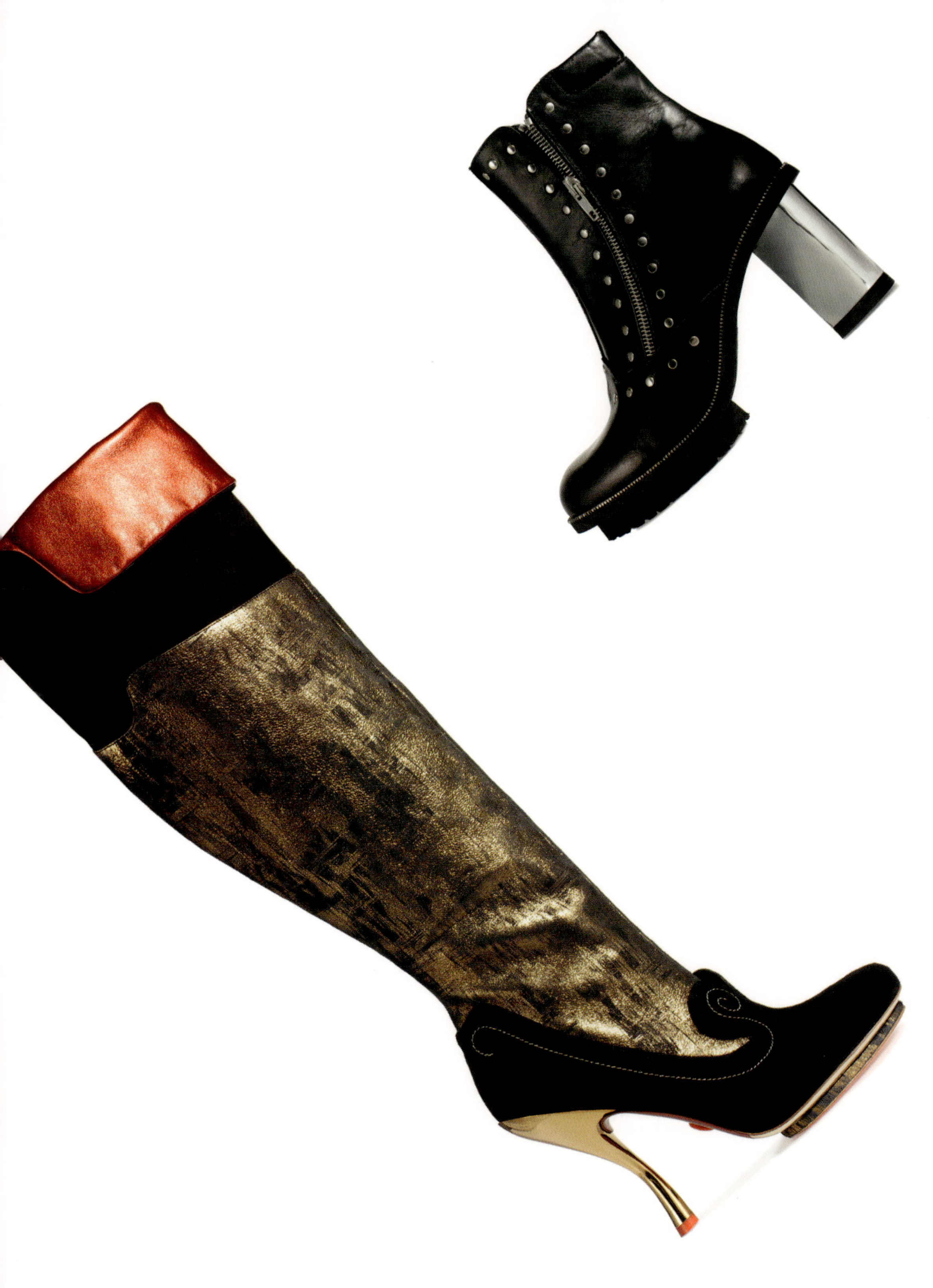

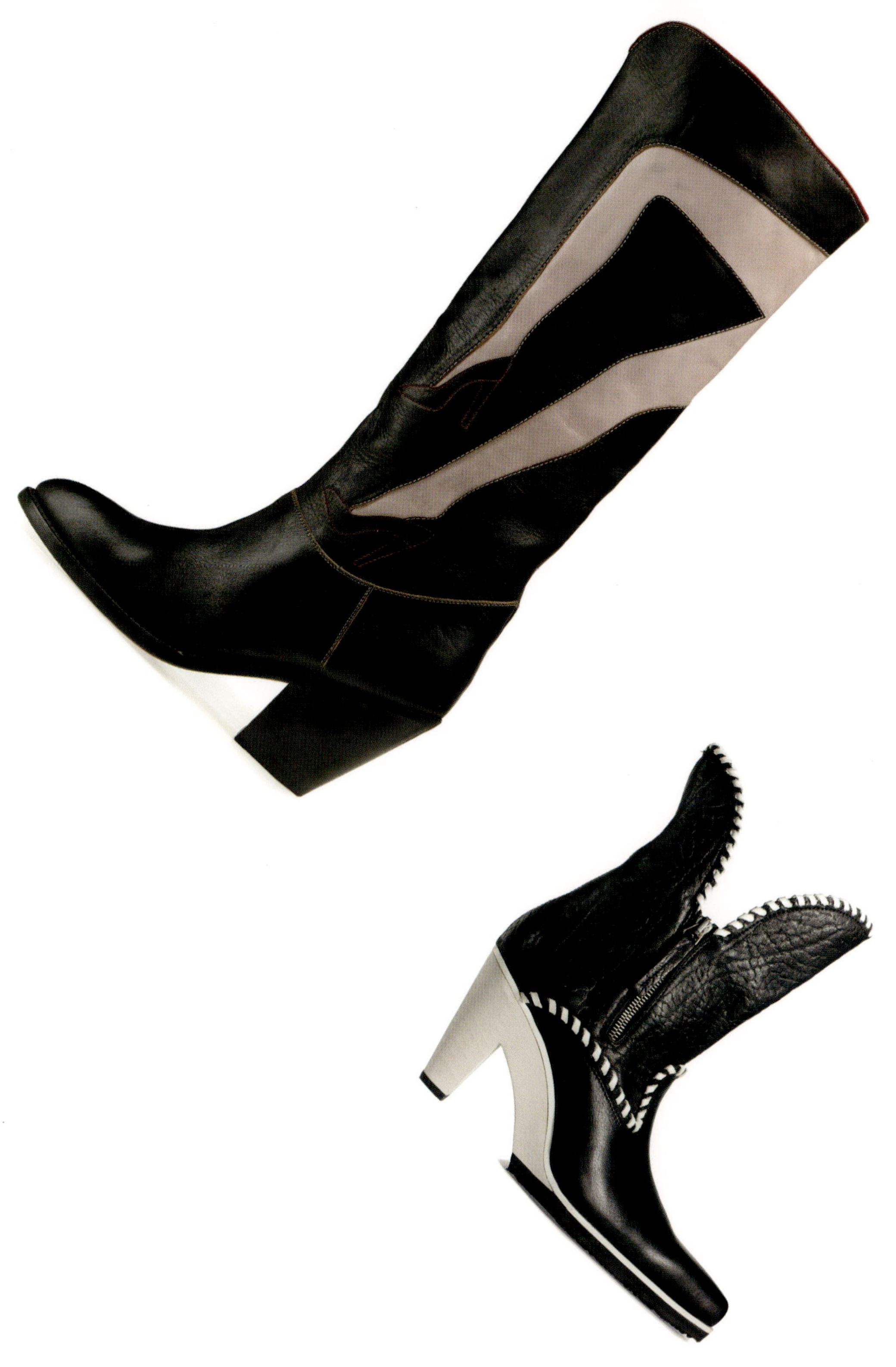

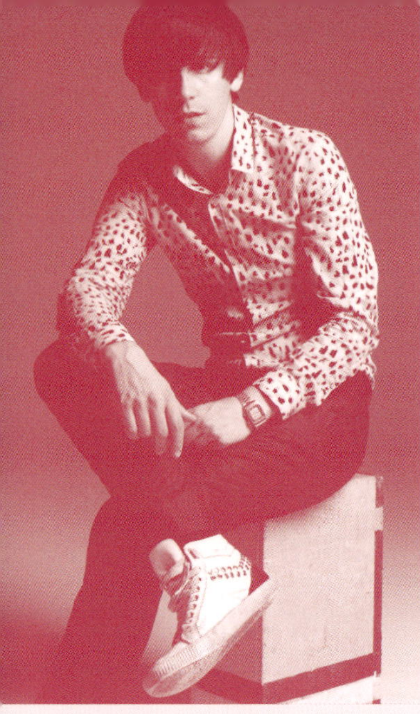

JEROME C. ROUSSEAU

I was born in Quebec, Canada but I spent ten years in London initially to study shoe design at Cordwainers College. I then worked with designers such as Matthew Williamson, John Richmond and John Rocha before relocating to Los Angeles and launching my label with the Autumn 2008 collection. **MY INTEREST IN FOOTWEAR DESIGN STARTED IN A RATHER UNUSUAL WAY. AS A YOUNG TEENAGER, THERE WAS A BAND ON MTV CALLED DEEE-LITE, WITH THEIR HIT "GROOVE IS IN THE HEART". THE VIDEO CLIP COMPLETELY BLEW ME AWAY, MAINLY BECAUSE OF THE TALL PLATFORM SHOES THEY WERE WEARING. I STARTED DRAWING THOSE SHOES IN ART CLASSES IN HIGH SCHOOL AND RESEARCHING THE HISTORY OF FOOTWEAR. MY PASSION GREW FROM THERE.** My shoes are designed to look perfect on a woman's foot. The lines elongate the leg and the heels are sensual but they also have an edge. I like the fine line between edge and elegance and I think my shoes walk that line beautifully. **LAST YEAR, DISNEY APPROACHED ME TO SEE IF I WOULD BE INTERESTED IN COLLABORATING WITH THEM ON THEIR NEW TRON RELEASE. I AM A HUGE FAN OF THE ORIGINAL TRON SO I WAS VERY EXCITED ABOUT THIS. I DIDN'T WANT TO CREATE A GIMMICKY SHOE WITH REFLECTIVE LIGHT STRIPS AS THAT WAS TOO OBVIOUS AND NOT IN LINE WITH THE DNA OF MY LABEL. I DECIDED TO CREATE A SANDAL INSPIRED BY THE LINES OF THE ARCHITECTURE IN BOTH THE ORIGINAL AND NEW TRON MOVIES. THIS SANDAL HELPED ESTABLISH A STRONG FOLLOWING FOR MY LABEL. THE DESIGN IS VERY DISTINCTIVE WITH A STRONG FUTURISTIC FEEL THAT'S ALSO FEMININE AND ELEGANT. ANOTHER FAVOURITE IS FROM MY SPRING 2012 COLLECTION. THE KIO LOOPS HAS FUN LITTLE LOOPS AT THE BACK OF THE SHOE. IT'S SIMPLE YET SOMEWHAT PLAYFUL.** Inspiration for a new collection comes from different things I have fallen in love with over the preceding months. It could be music, cinema, someone I met, nature, nightlife or a book that I've borrowed. Sketching ideas is my favourite stage of a project. I completely clean my desk and tidy everything before starting. It somehow helps me turn the page on the previous collection and get ready for the next one. **THE MOST DIFFICULT PART OF THE PROCESS IS PERHAPS SELECTING THE DESIGNS THAT WILL MAKE IT INTO THE COLLECTION. IT IS DIFFICULT TO DROP A STRONG DESIGN PURELY BECAUSE IT CONFUSES THE MESSAGE I'M TRYING TO CREATE RATHER THAN BECAUSE IT'S NOT GOOD.** As a designer and a small business owner it's a very interesting challenge to juggle artistic integrity with keeping a business alive. I've always had great respect for artists who are able to do this effortlessly. I think of myself as a designer and a product person as opposed to a fashion person, but fashion is the industry that keeps my work alive and allows me to share it. The seasonal calendar of fashion is something I have to work with if I want to grow my label. I do think it's possible to meet in the middle and not compromise artistic integrity.

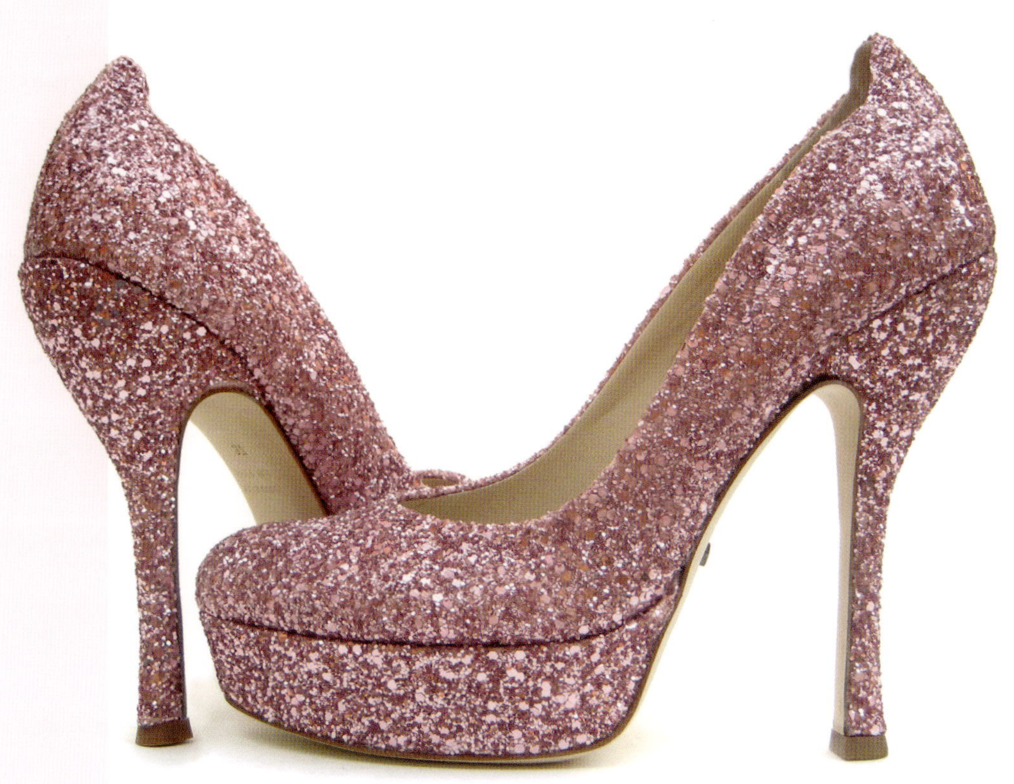

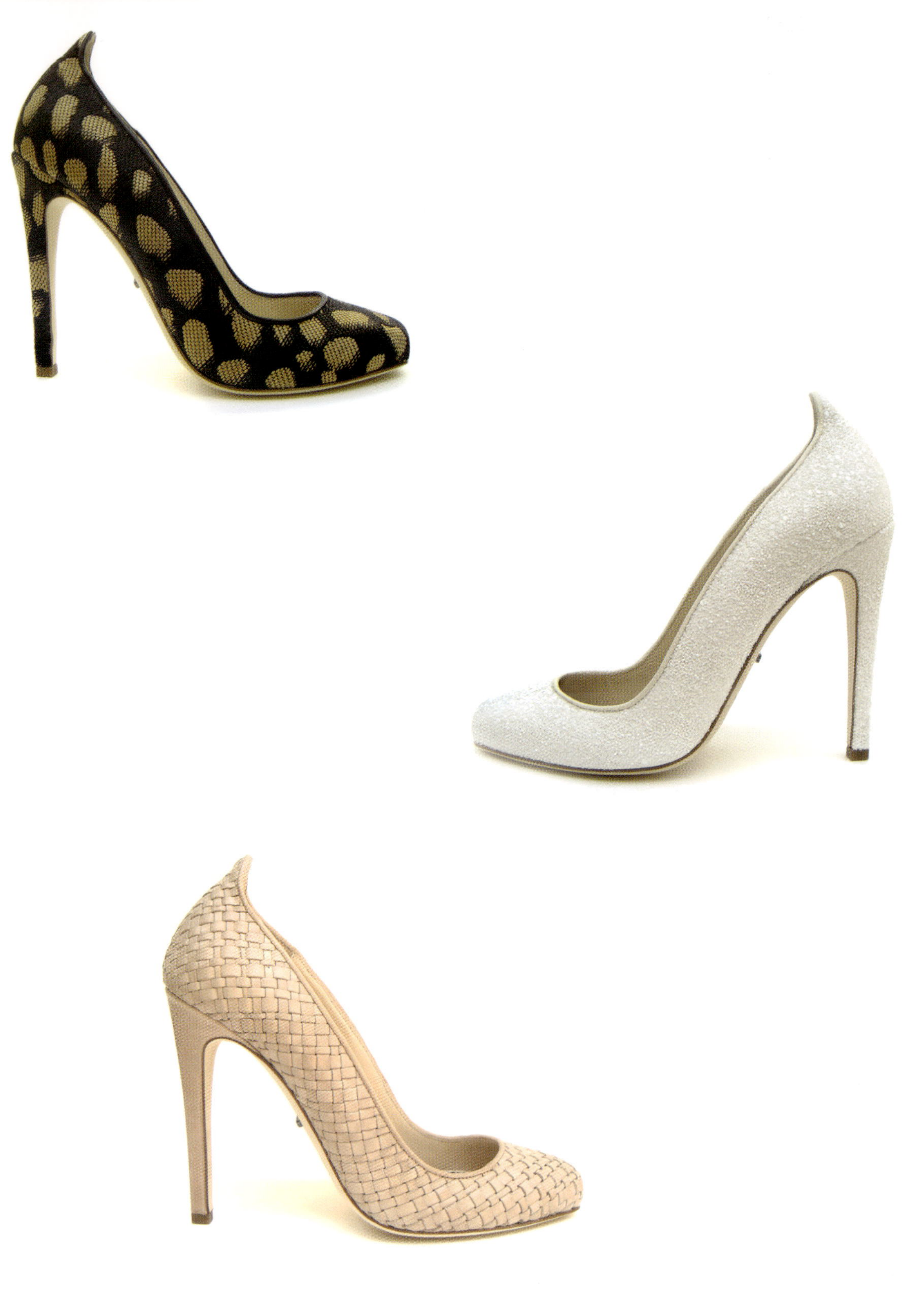

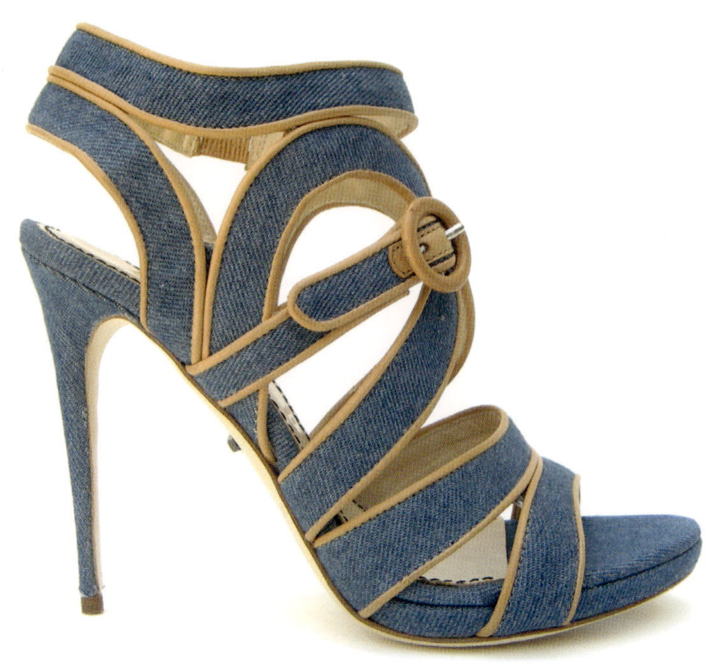

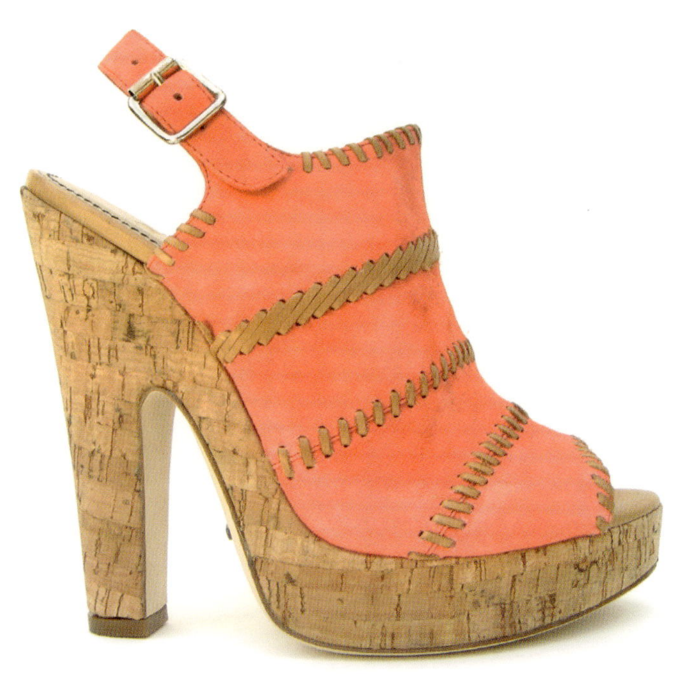

 JEROME C. ROUSSEAU

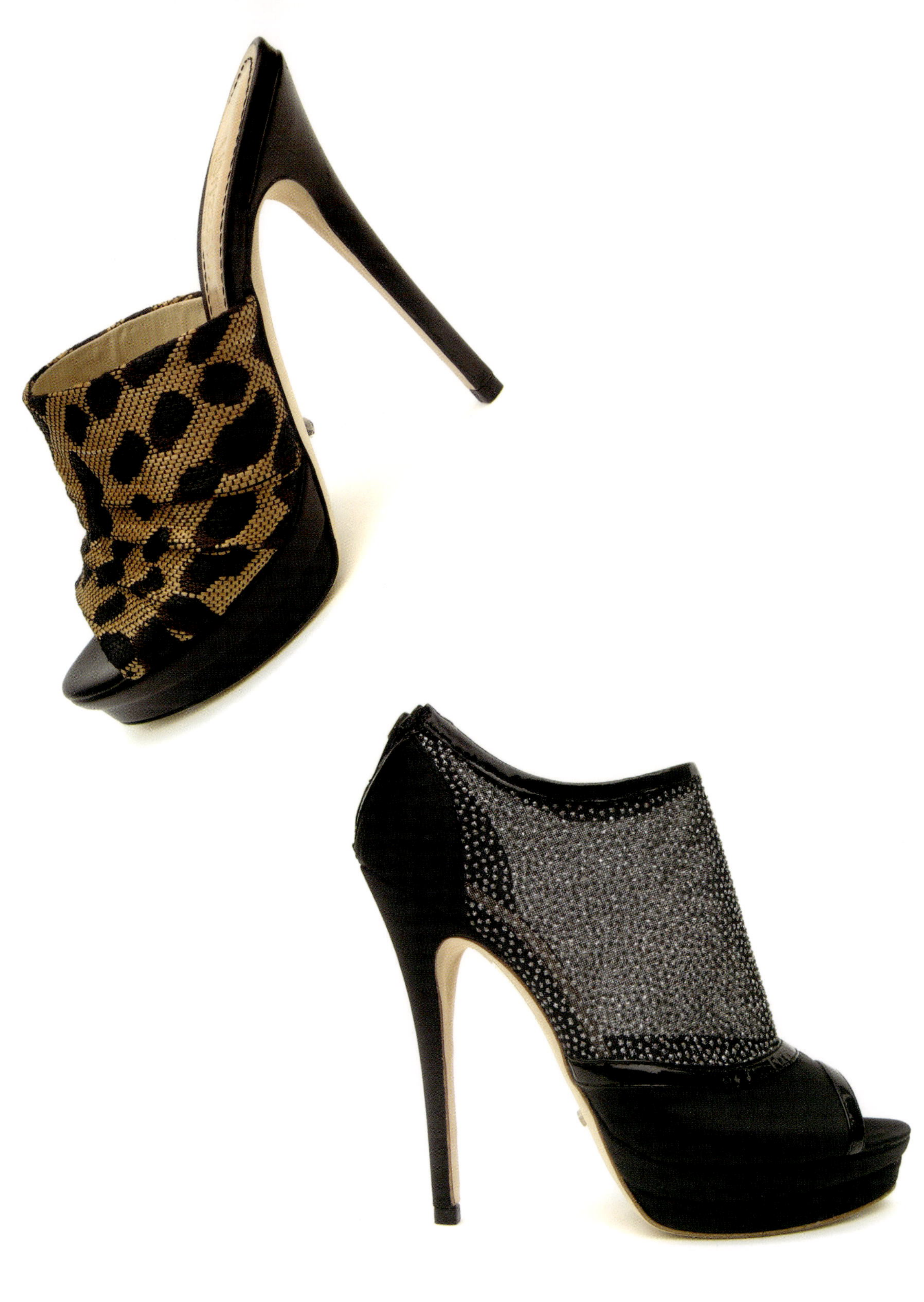

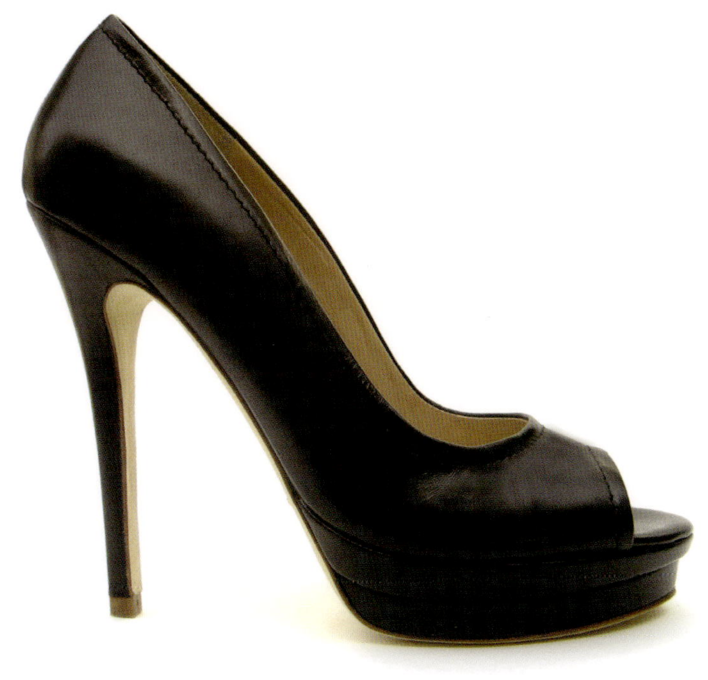

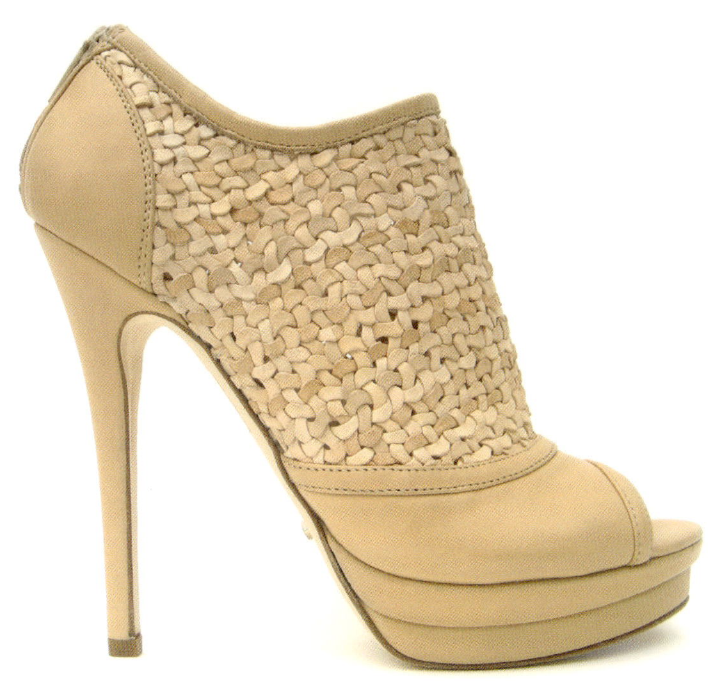

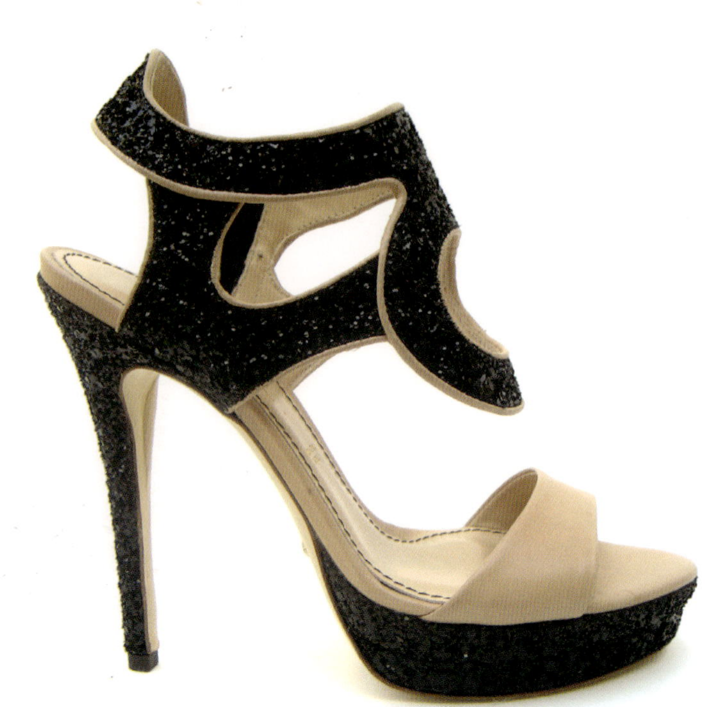

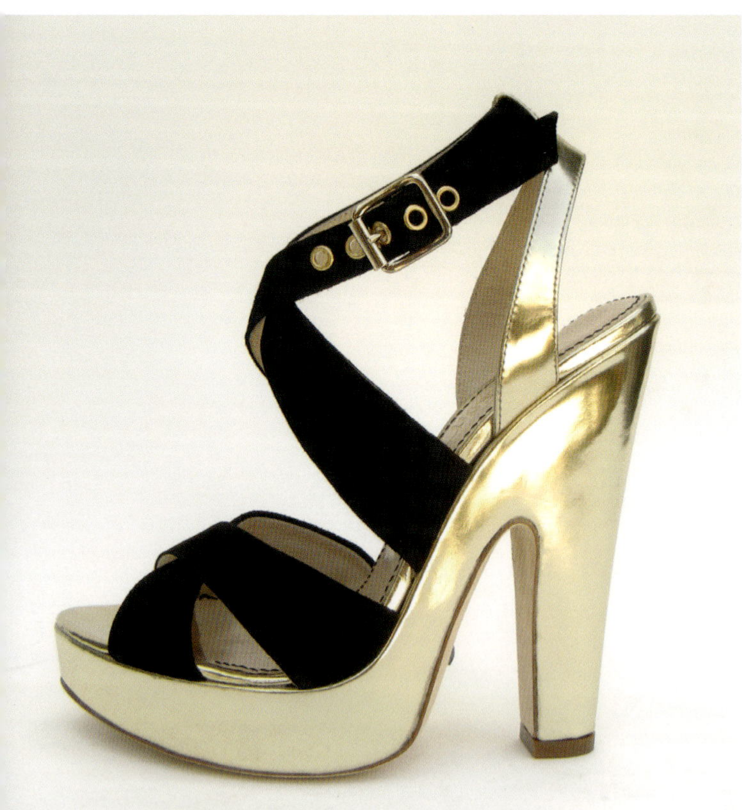

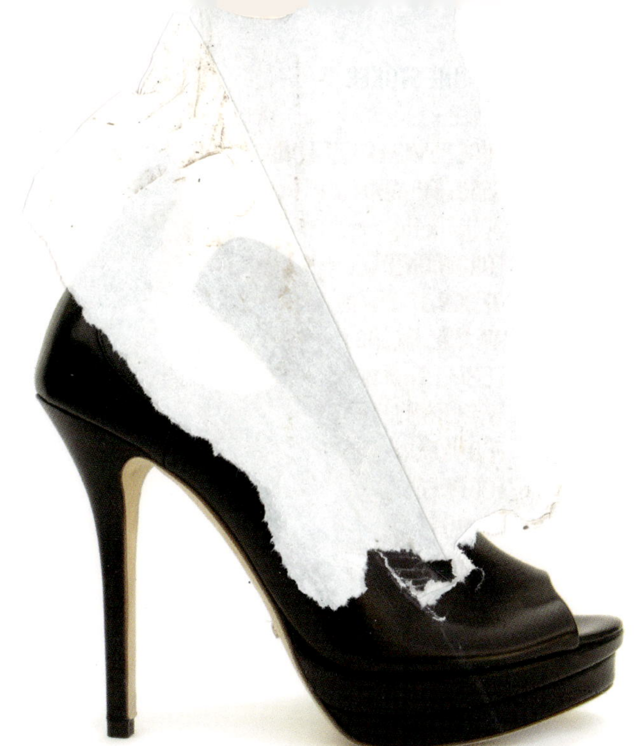

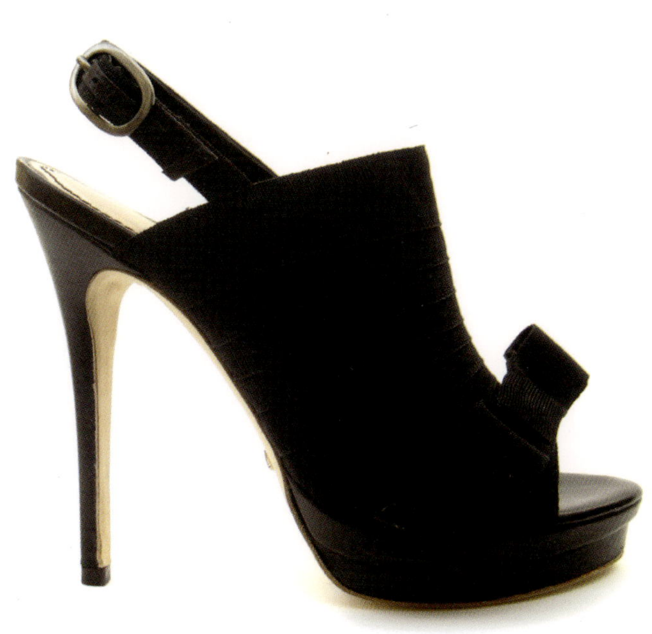

JEROME C. ROUSSEAU

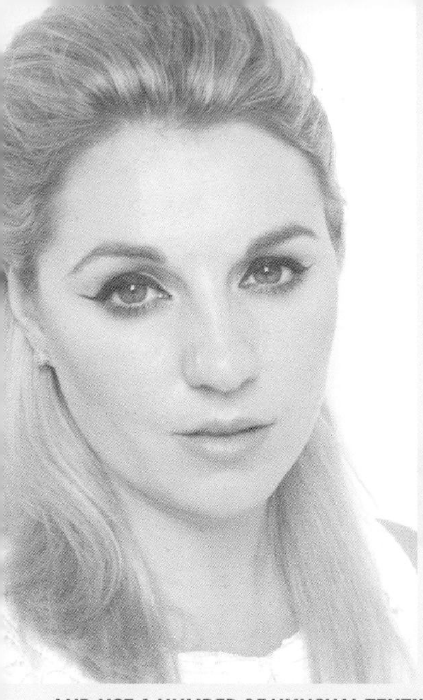

JOANNE STOKER

Please introduce yourself **I AM A LONDON BASED LUXURY SHOE DESIGNER WITH ONLY ONE THING IN MIND — TO CREATE BEAUTIFUL AND CONCEPTUAL SHOES THAT ASTOUND AND DELIGHT.** How did you get started? **I GRADUATED FROM CORDWAINERS COLLEGE IN 2009 WITH AN MA IN FOOTWEAR DESIGN. I HAVE BEEN FORTUNATE ENOUGH TO WIN MANY AWARDS INCLUDING THE INTERNATIONAL TALENT SUPPORT COMPETITION HOSTED IN ITALY, THE FIRST INTO FASHION AWARD WITH JIMMY CHOO AND MELANIE RICKEY AS WELL AS THE FOOTWEAR FRIENDS AWARD SPONSORED BY THE BRITISH FOOTWEAR ASSOCIATION. I THEN WENT ON TO COMPLETE A MENTORSHIP WITH JIMMY CHOO BEFORE ESTABLISHING MY OWN LUXURY LABEL LAST YEAR.** How would you describe your style? **ARCHITECTURAL INNOVATION MEETS FUTURISTIC GLAMOUR. I TAKE A LOT OF INSPIRATION FROM ARCHITECTURE AND USE A NUMBER OF UNUSUAL TEXTILES EACH SEASON TO CREATE SCULPTURAL COUTURE PIECES.** Tell us something about the design process. **I SPEND A LOT OF TIME RESEARCHING, PULLING TOGETHER MOOD BOARDS, SKETCHING SILHOUETTES AND PRODUCING 3D MODELS OF SHOES. I PERFECT EACH LINE AND SHAPE UNTIL I NARROW IT DOWN TO THE FINAL TEN DESIGNS FOR THE SEASON. I BELIEVE THAT MY SHOES SHOULD BE ORNAMENTAL PIECES AND REFLECT THE QUALITY OF TRADITIONAL ITALIAN CRAFTSMANSHIP. MATERIAL AND LEATHER IS SELECTED FROM THE FINEST ITALIAN MAKERS AND EACH EXQUISITE COMPONENT CAREFULLY CONSTRUCTED.** What do you consider your most innovative design so far? **MY LED LIGHT HEELS. THEY ARE USB CHARGEABLE AND COME IN A RANGE OF COLOURS INCLUDING RED, BLUE, GREEN, ORANGE, WHITE AND YELLOW. THEY ARE SUCH GOOD FUN TO WEAR.** What is the least gratifying part of the job? **WHEN I DESIGN SOMETHING I HAVE DREAMT ABOUT FOR WEEKS AND IT DOESN'T COME TOGETHER HOW I IMAGINED. LUCKILY THAT DOESN'T HAPPEN OFTEN.** Who or what inspires you? **I REALLY ADMIRE MIUCCIA PRADA. HER DESIGNS AND CREATIONS ARE SO FANTASTIC EACH SEASON, ESPECIALLY THE SHOES AND ACCESSORIES.** What are your thoughts on the culture of quick consumption and over-commercialisation? **I THINK IN RECENT YEARS THE QUICK CONSUMPTION CULTURE HAS BECOME OUT OF CONTROL. THE MOST WORRYING PART IS THE AMOUNT OF WASTE IT PRODUCES. WHEN I DESIGN I WANT PEOPLE TO LOOK AT MY SHOES AS KEEPSAKE ITEMS, SOMETHING THEY WILL LOVE FOREVER AS OPPOSED TO SOMETHING THEY WILL WEAR FOR SIX MONTHS. QUALITY AND WEARABILITY IS KEY, ALONG WITH UNIQUE STYLE THAT IS ALMOST IMPOSSIBLE TO MAKE COMMERCIAL WITHOUT COMPROMISING THE DESIGN.** What do you consider vulgar and what elegant? **VULGAR IS PEOPLE WHO DON'T RESPECT THEMSELVES. ELEGANT IS EXHIBITING A REFINED GRACE AND DIGNITY.** What does beauty mean to you? **BEAUTY FOR ME IS TRAVEL — DIFFERENT CULTURES, DIFFERENT FOODS, ARCHITECTURE AND ENVIRONMENTS.**

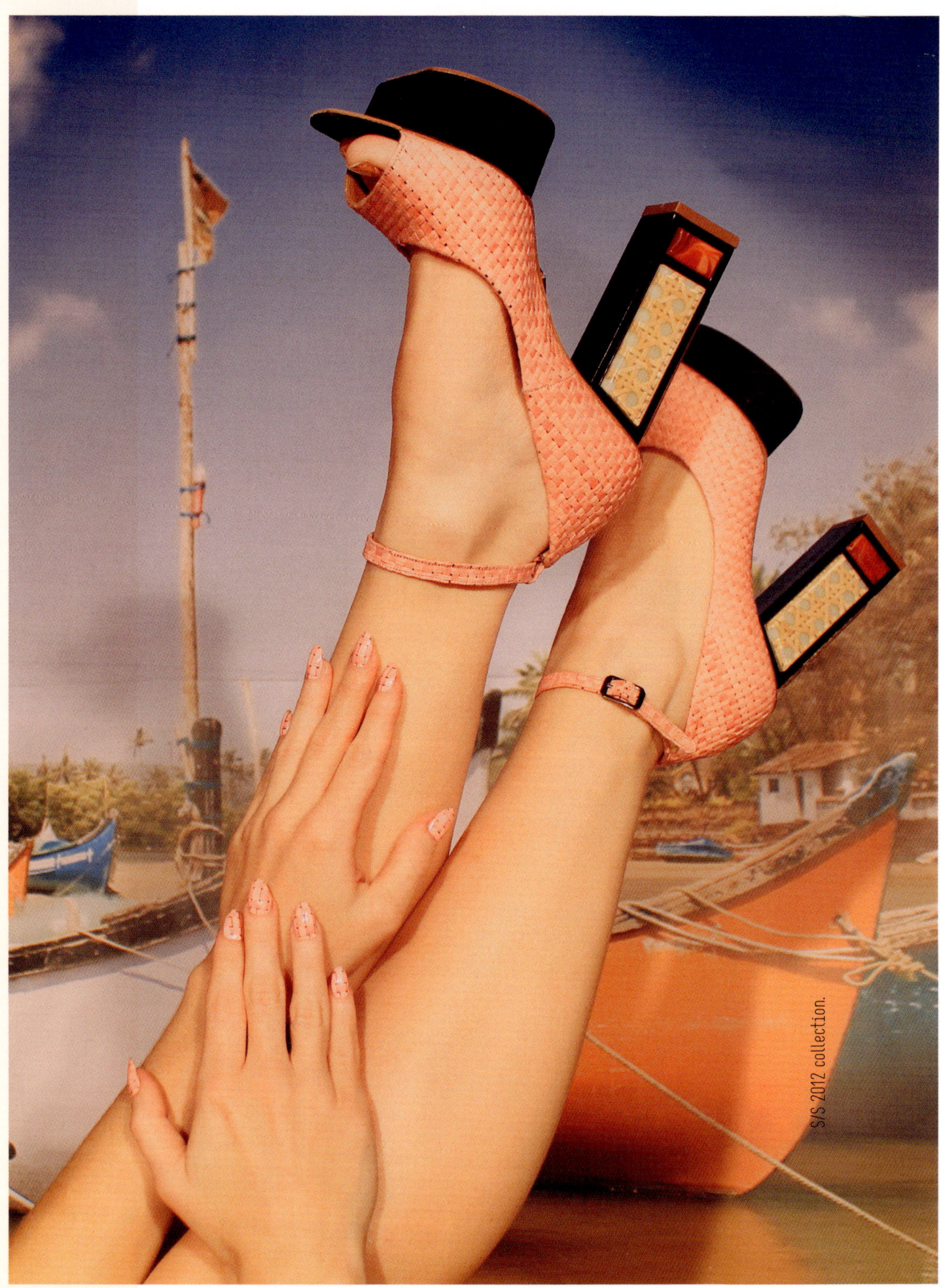

S/S 2012 collection.

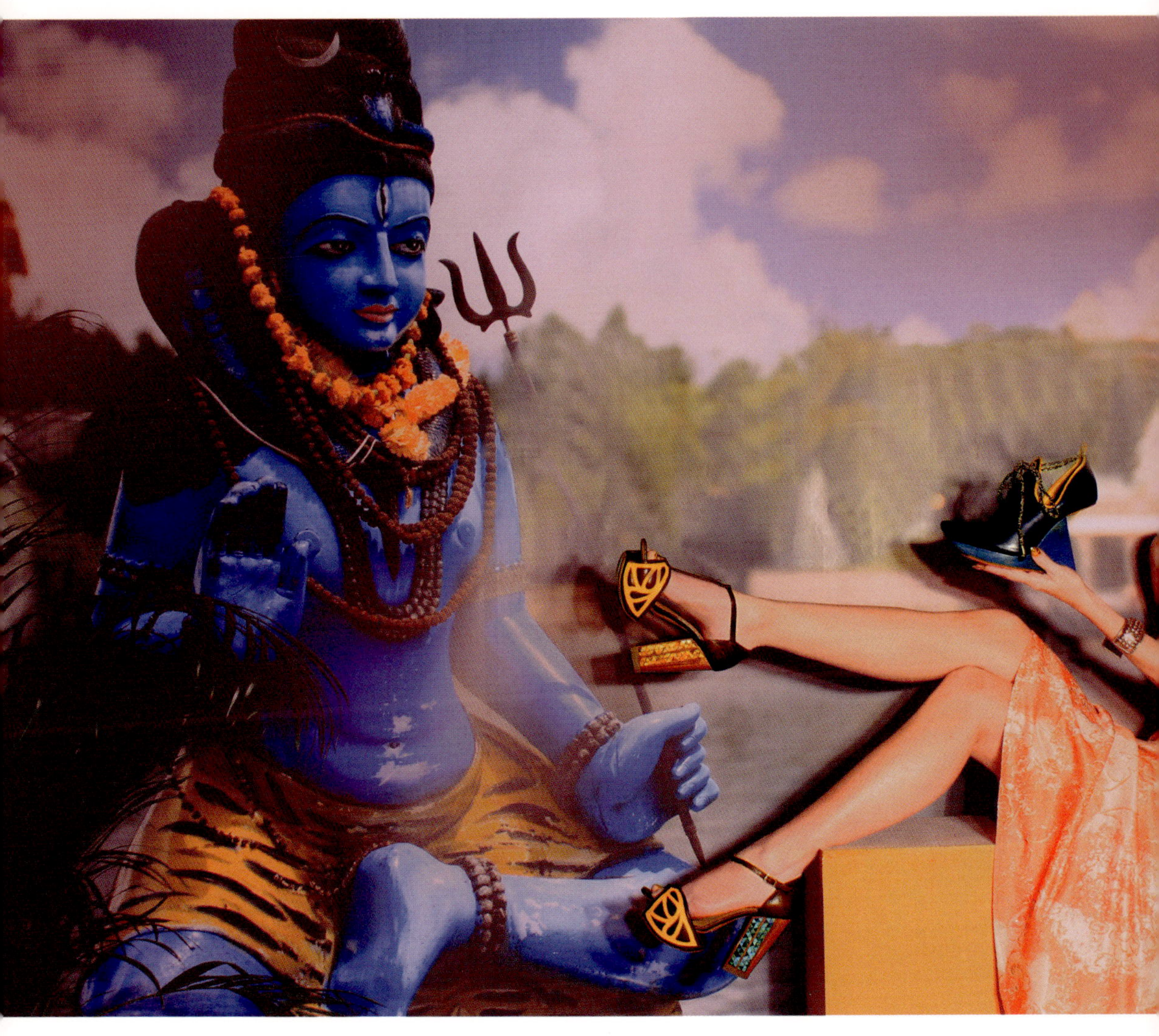

S/S 2012 collection.

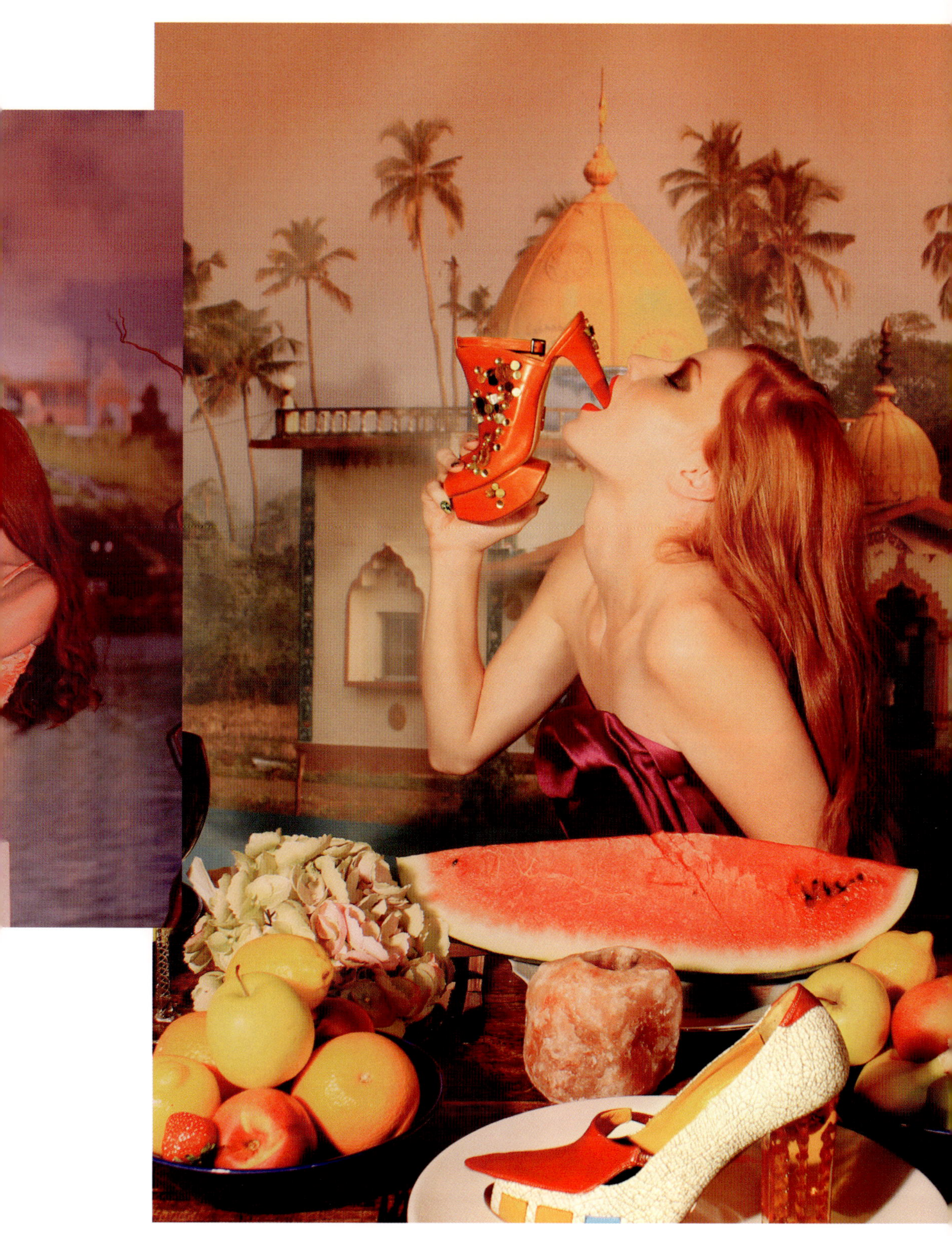

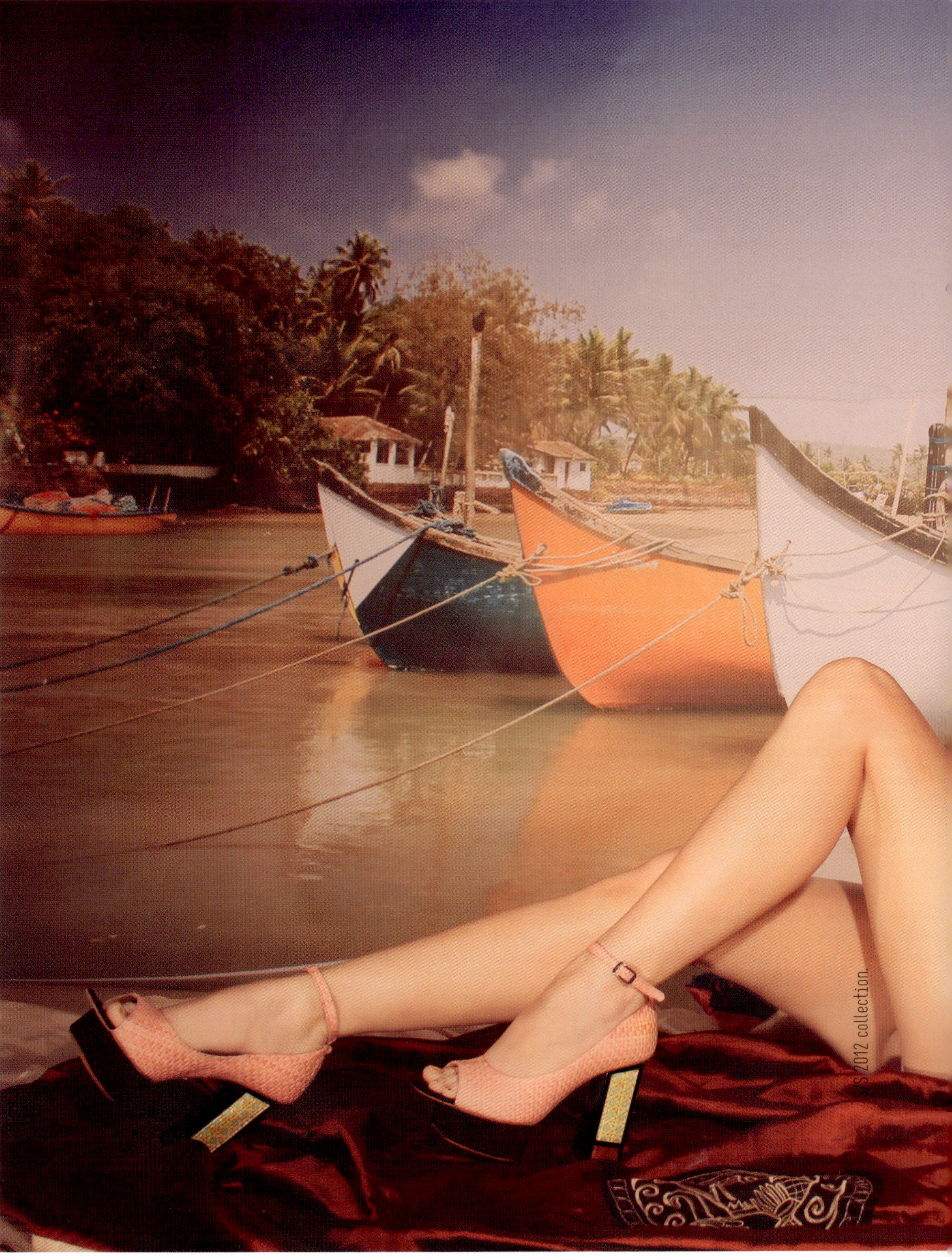

S/S 2012 collection.

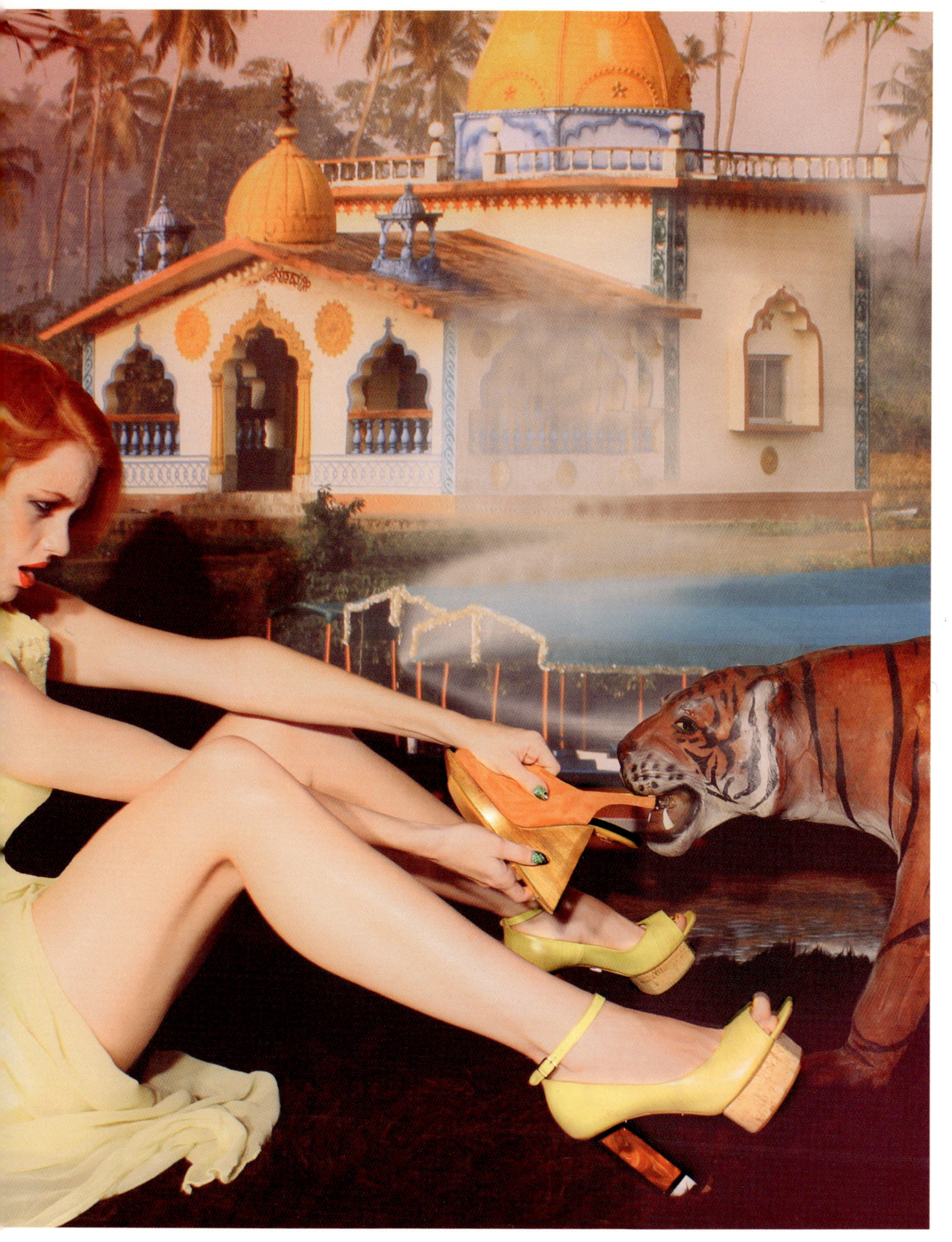

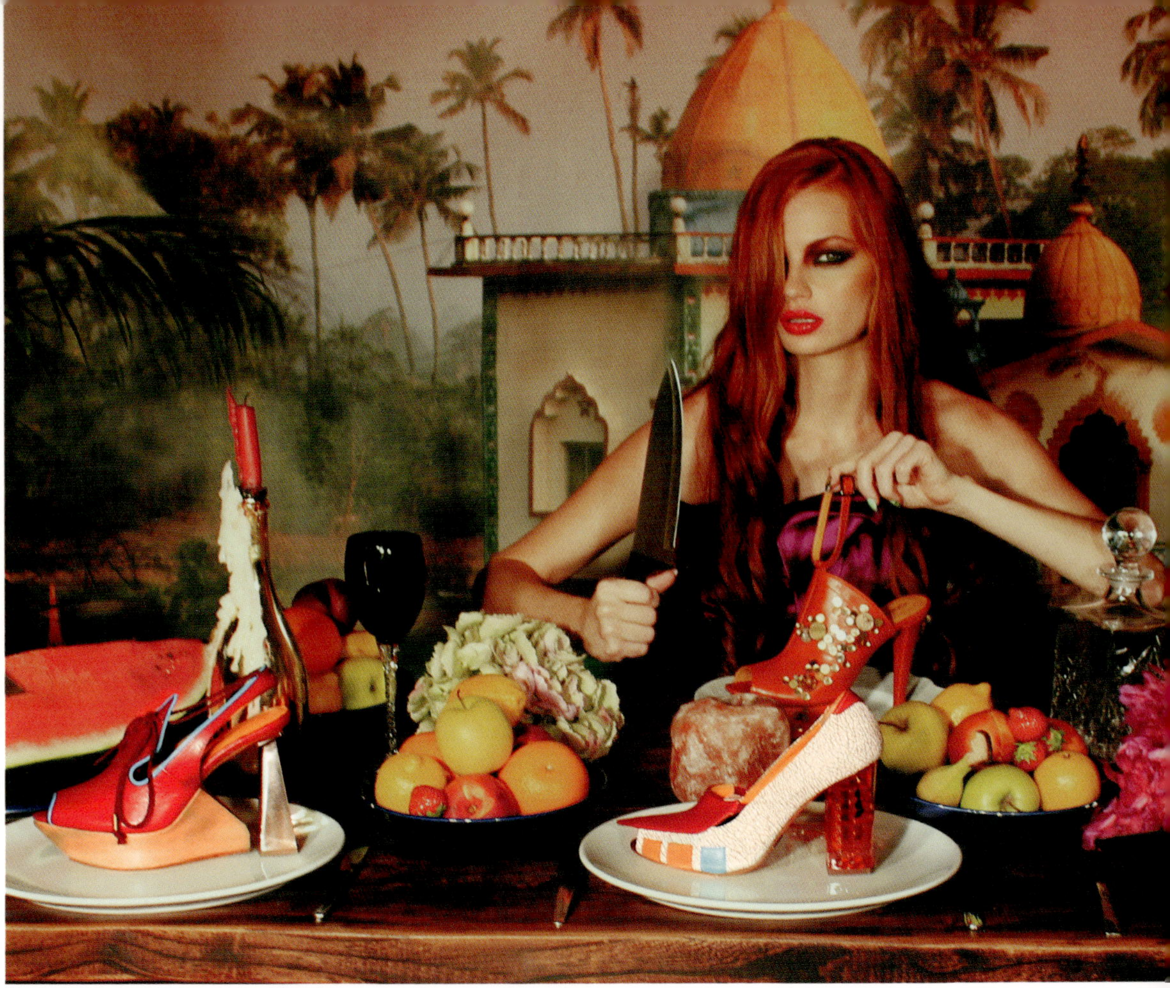

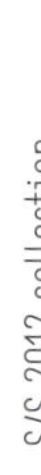

S/S 2012 collection.

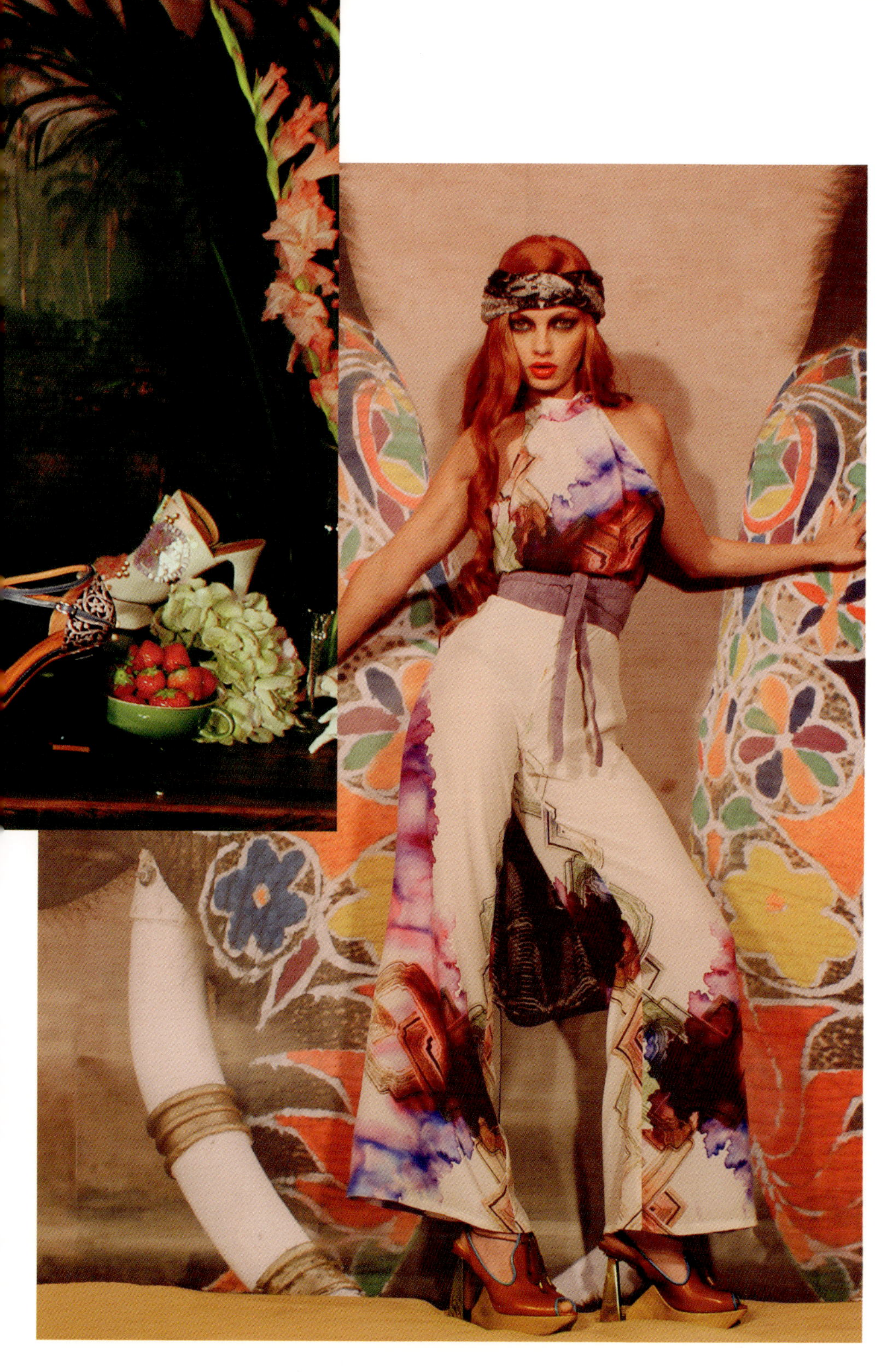

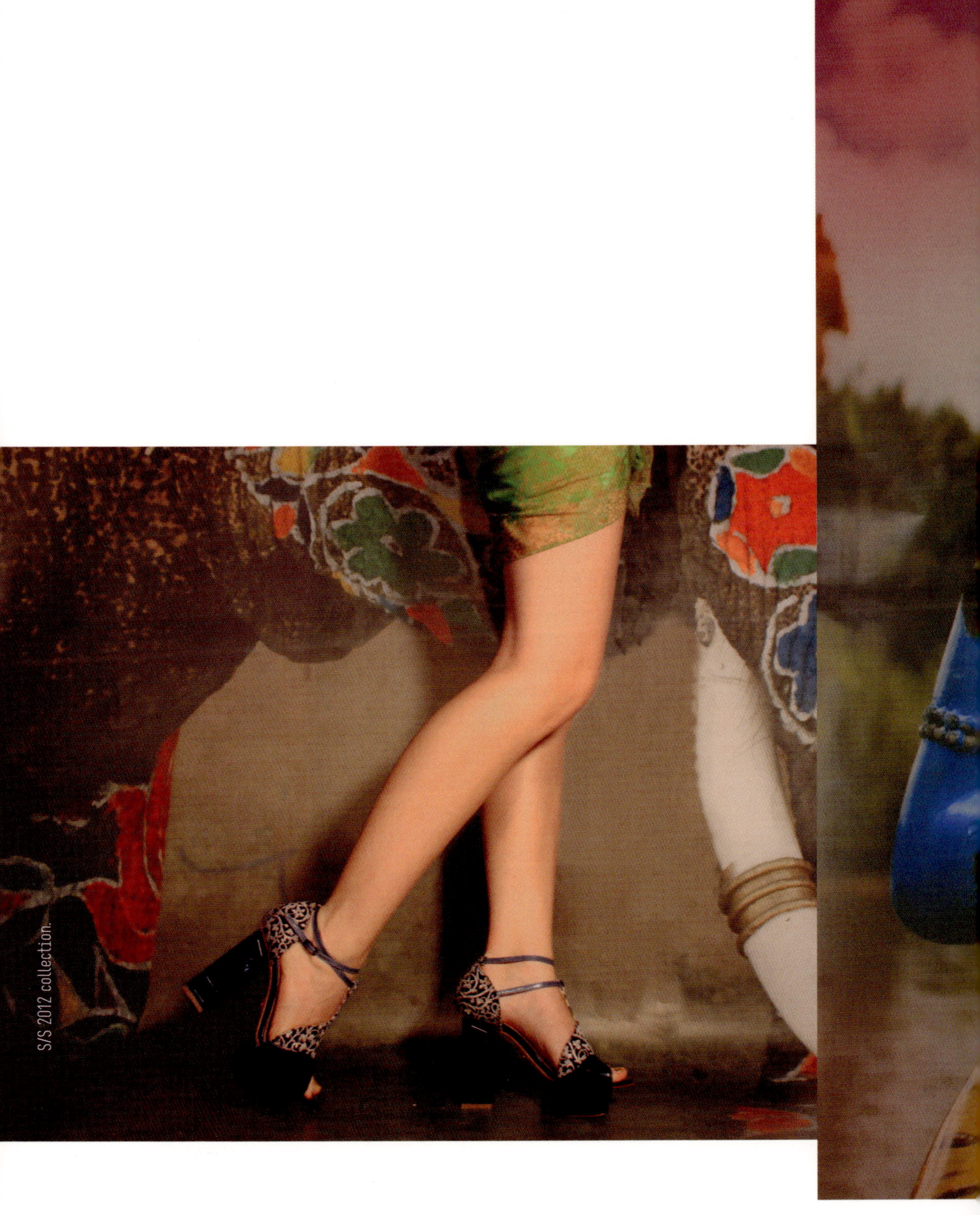

S/S 2012 collection.

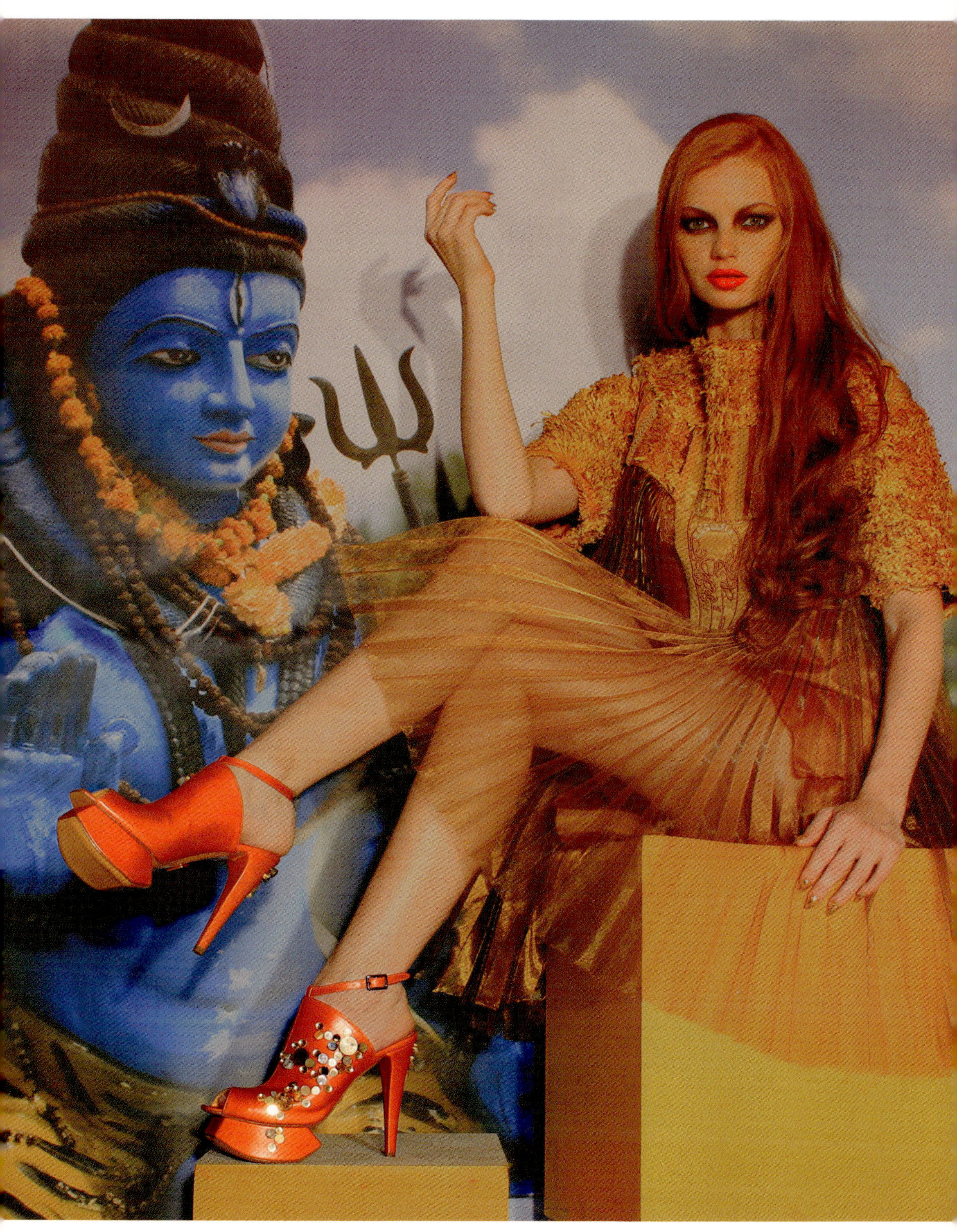

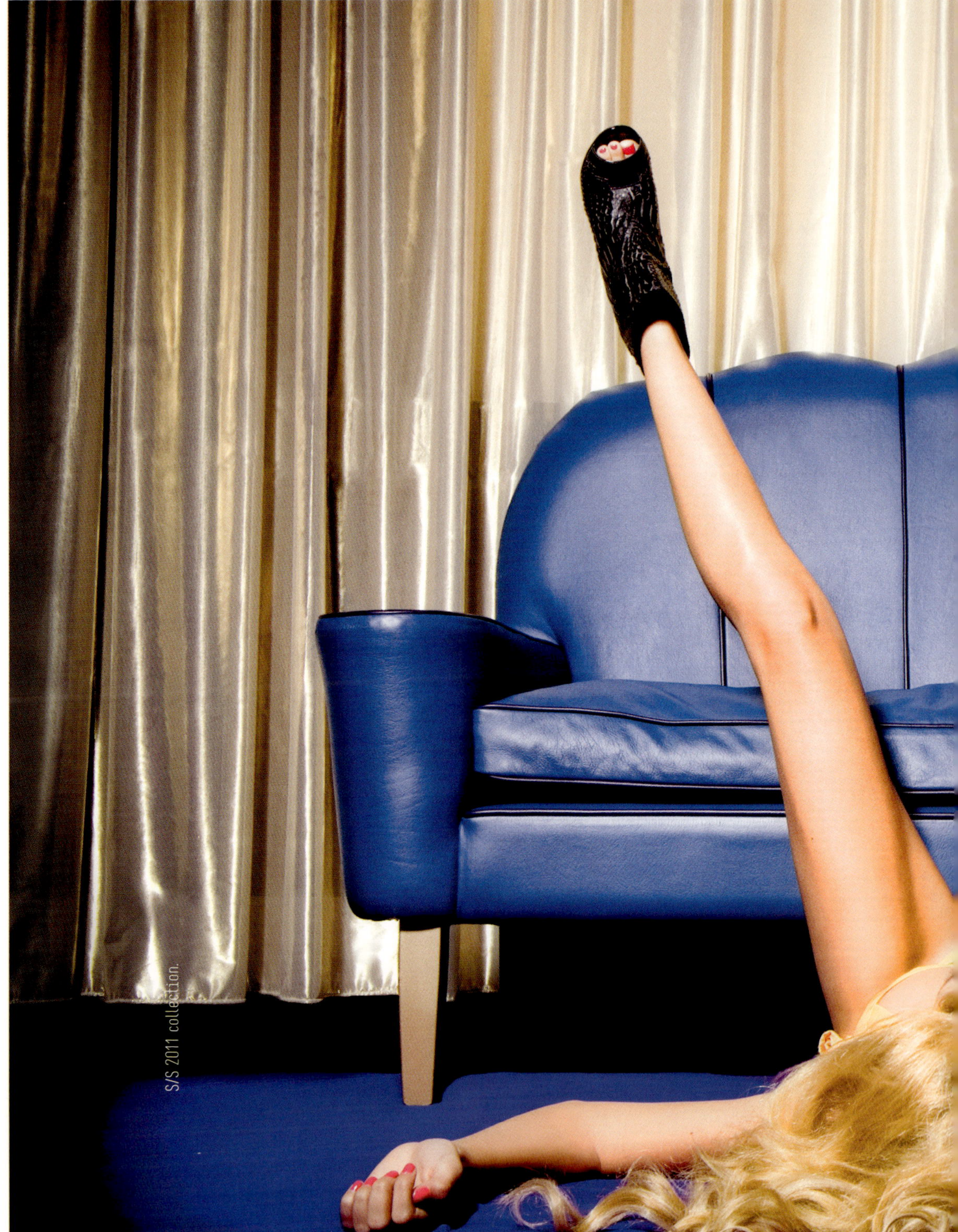
S/S 2011 collection.

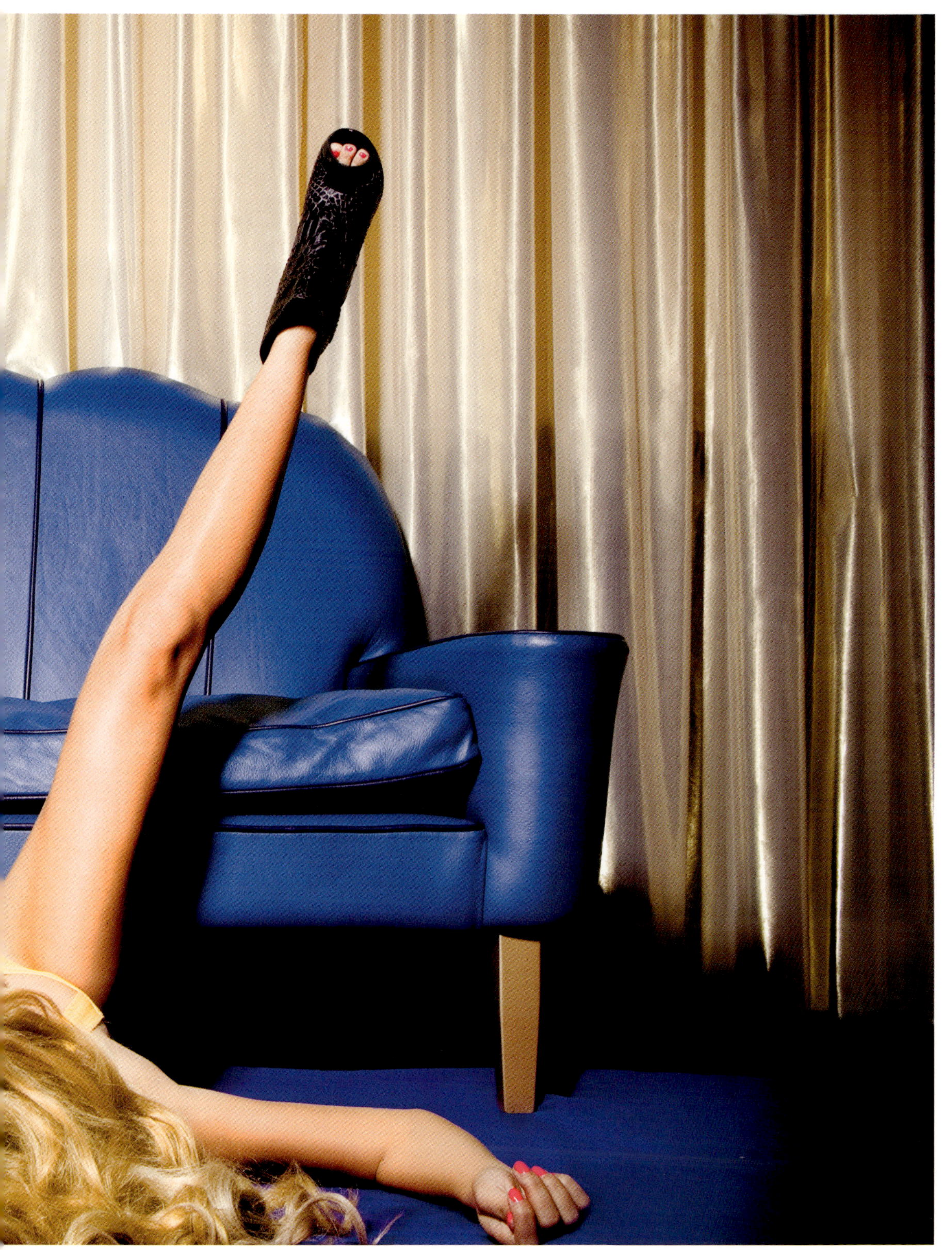

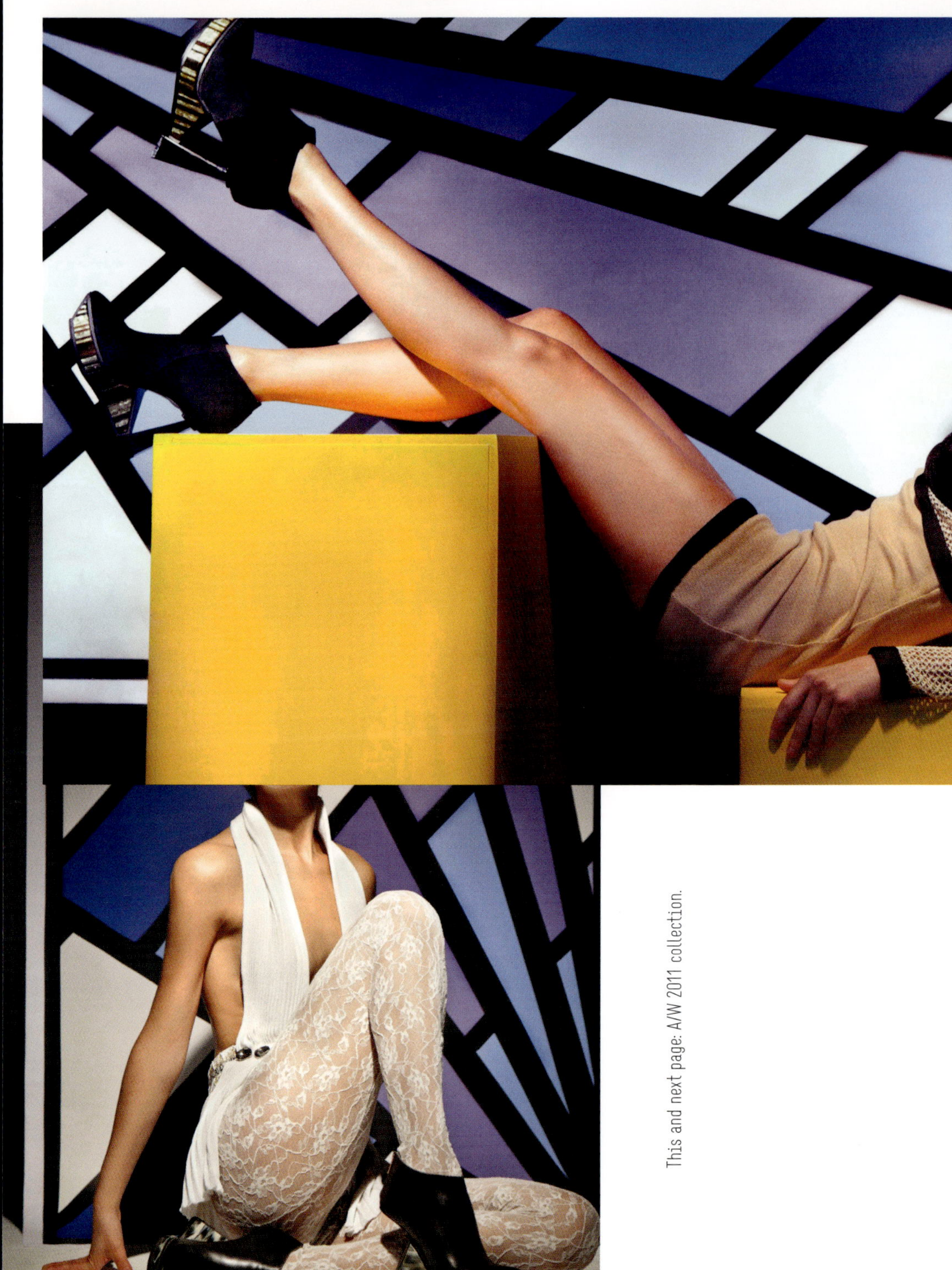

This and next page: A/W 2011 collection.

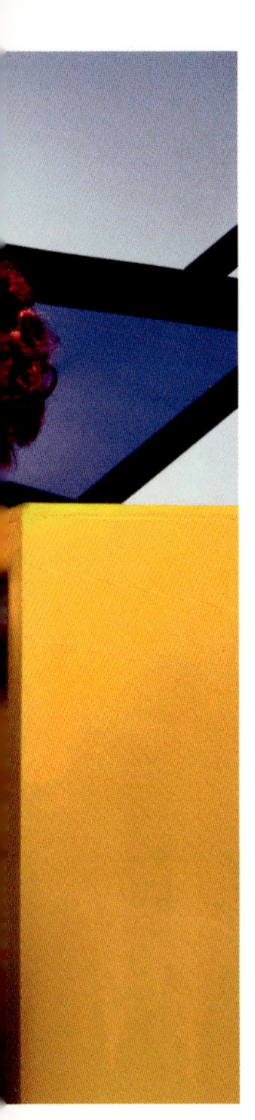

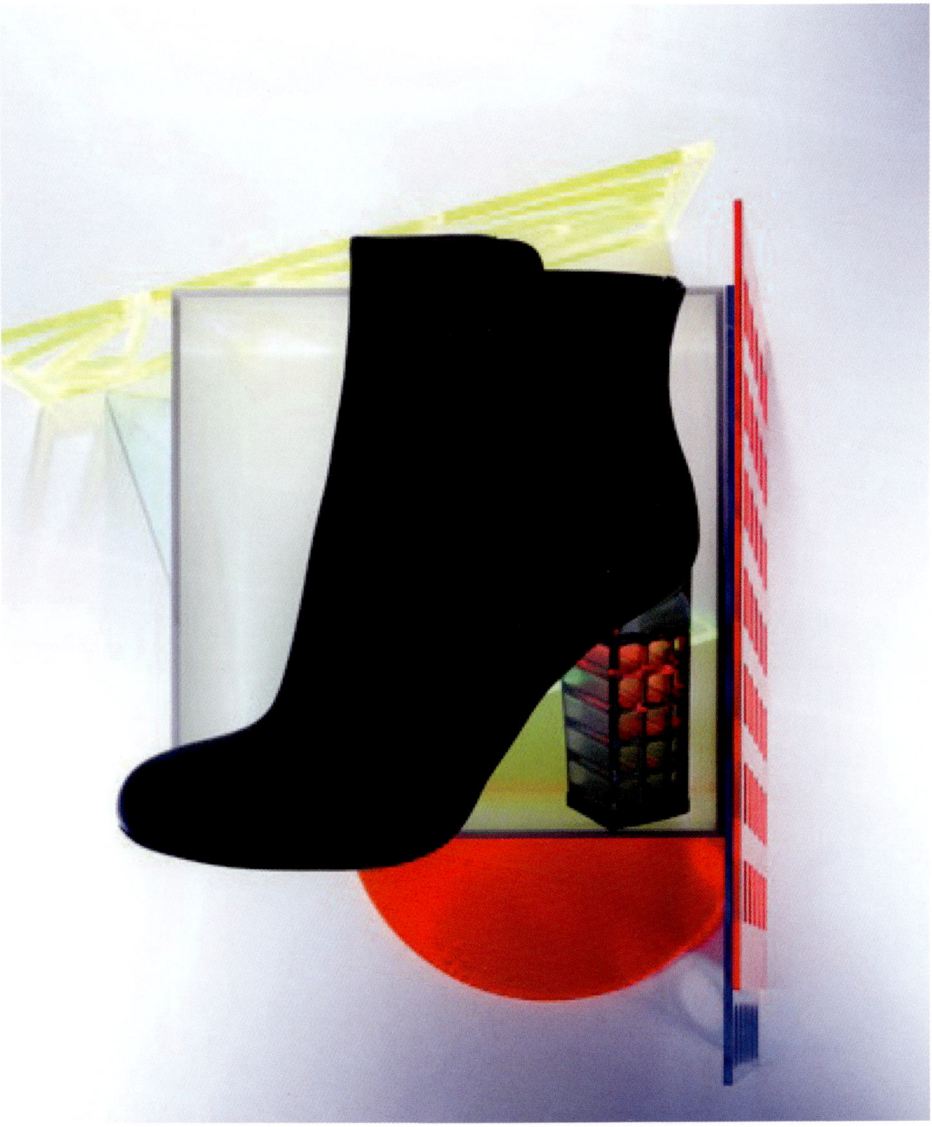

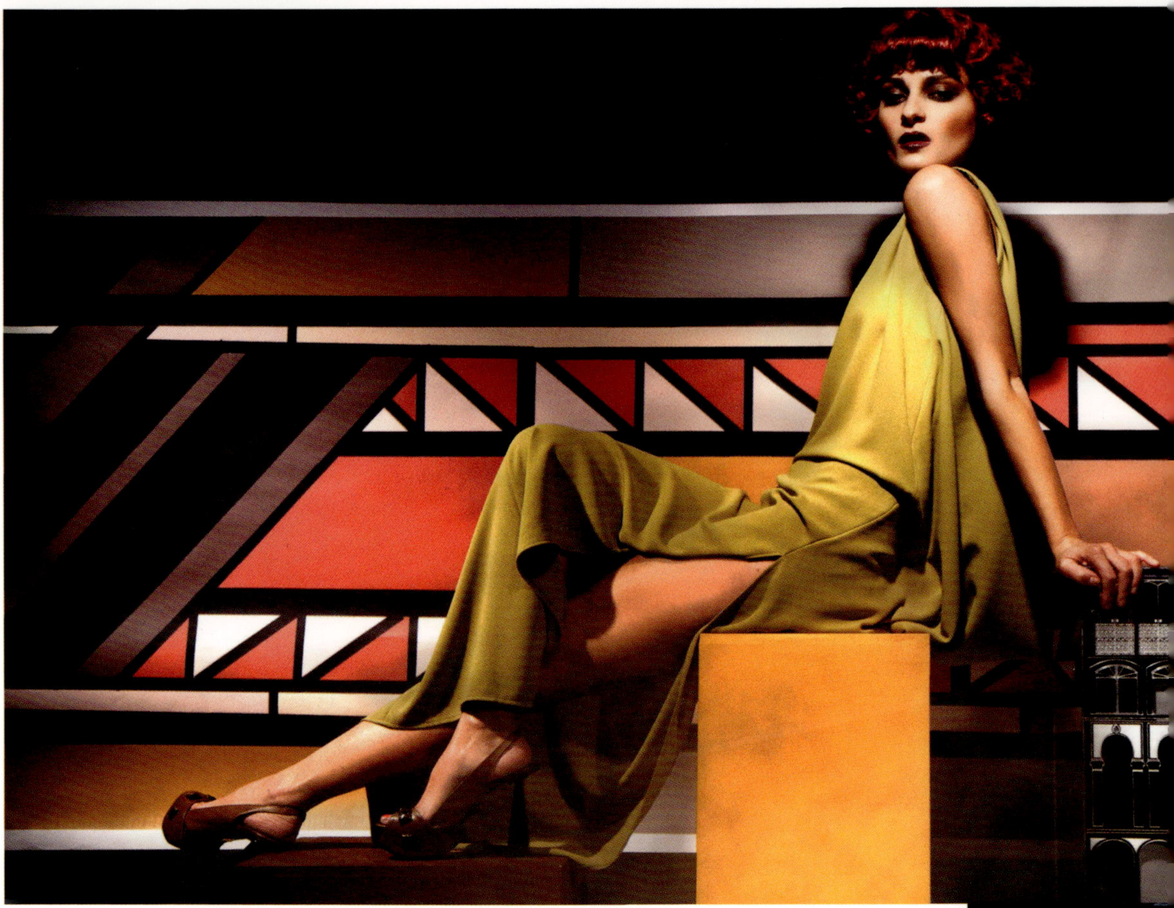

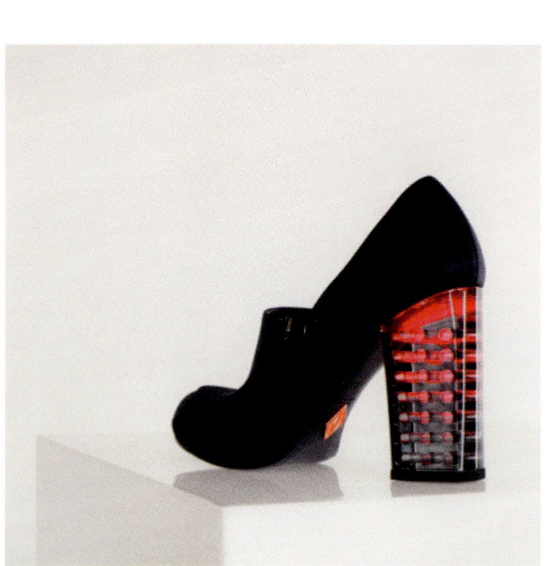

This and next page: A/W 2011 collection.

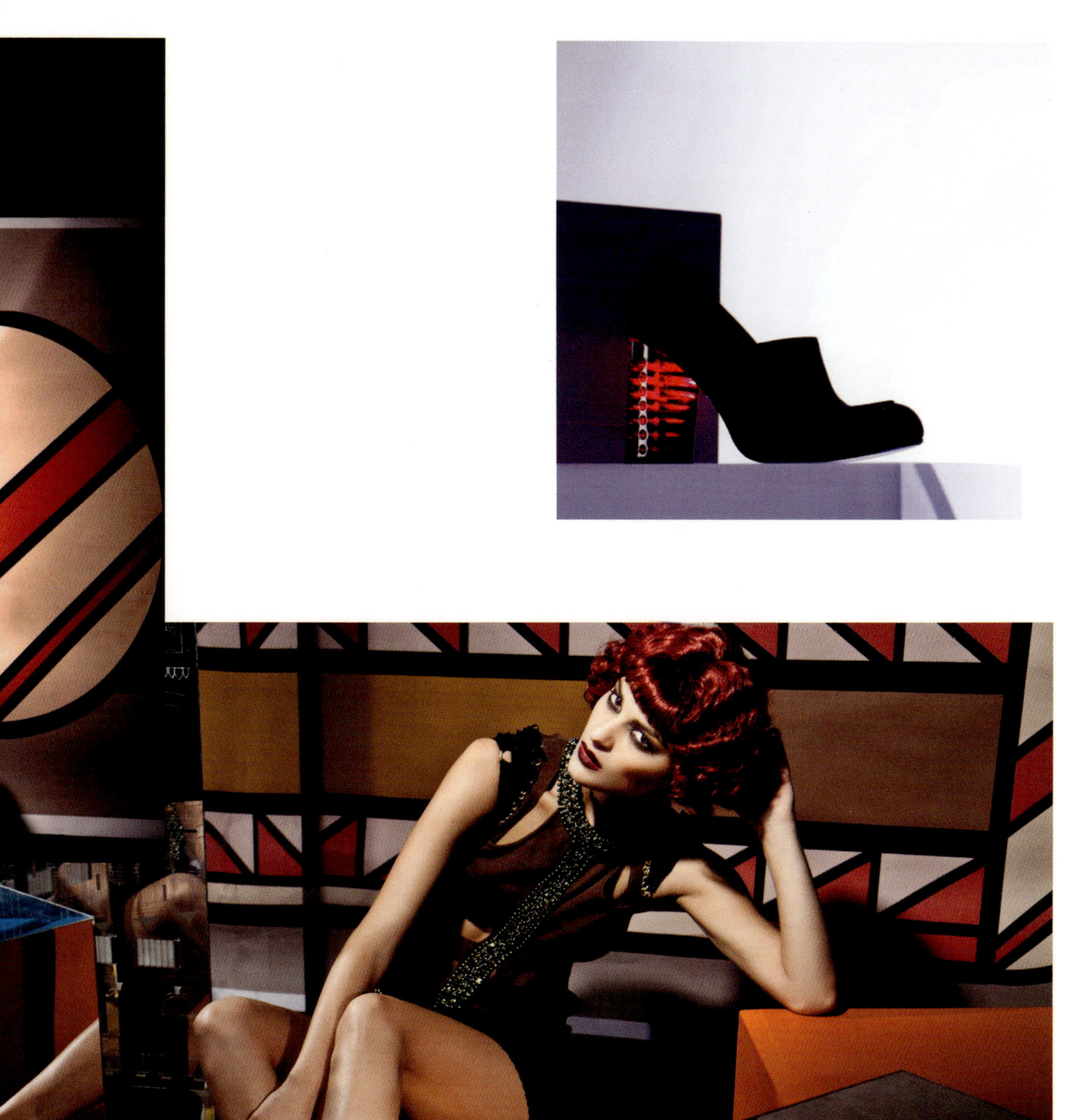

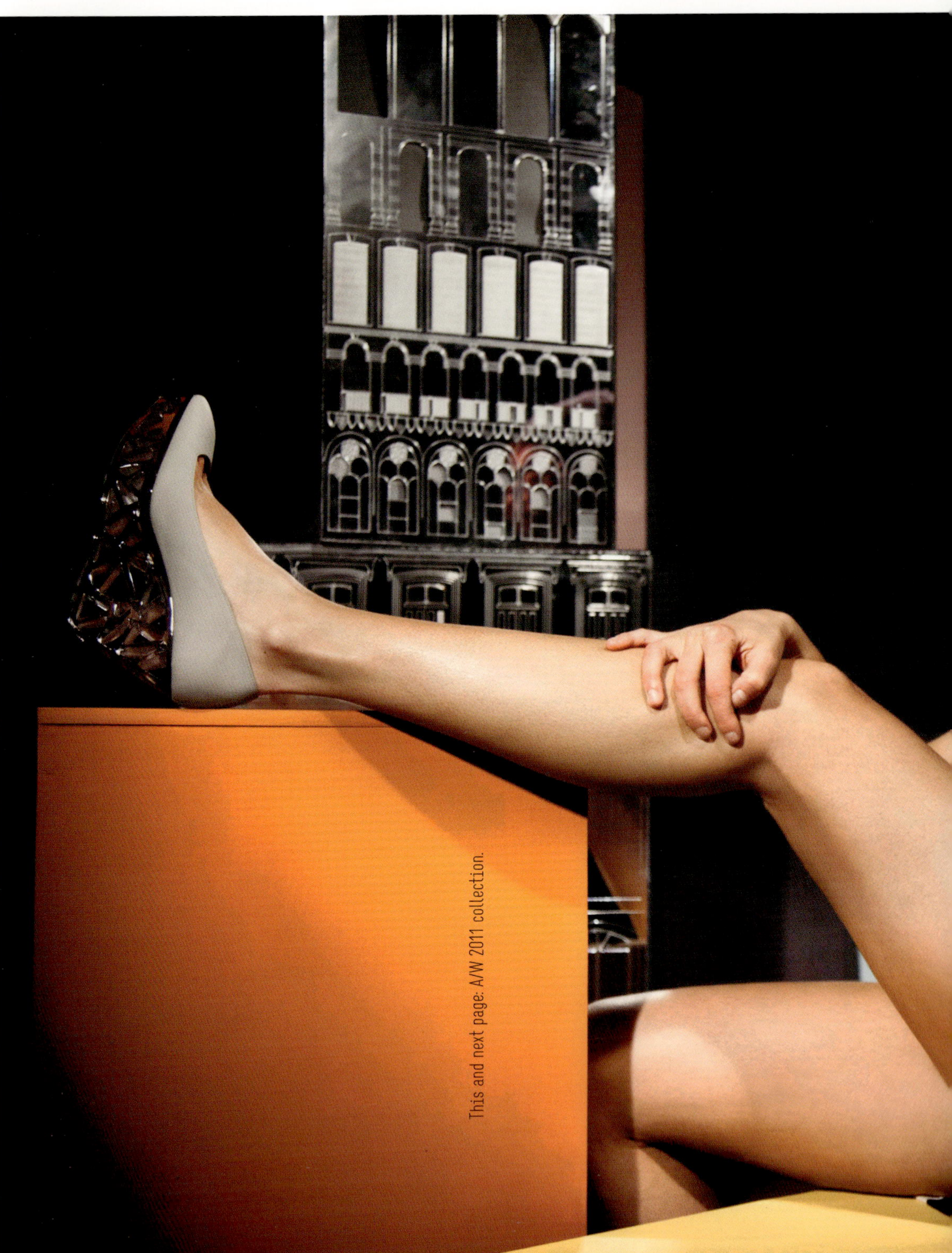

This and next page: A/W 2011 collection.

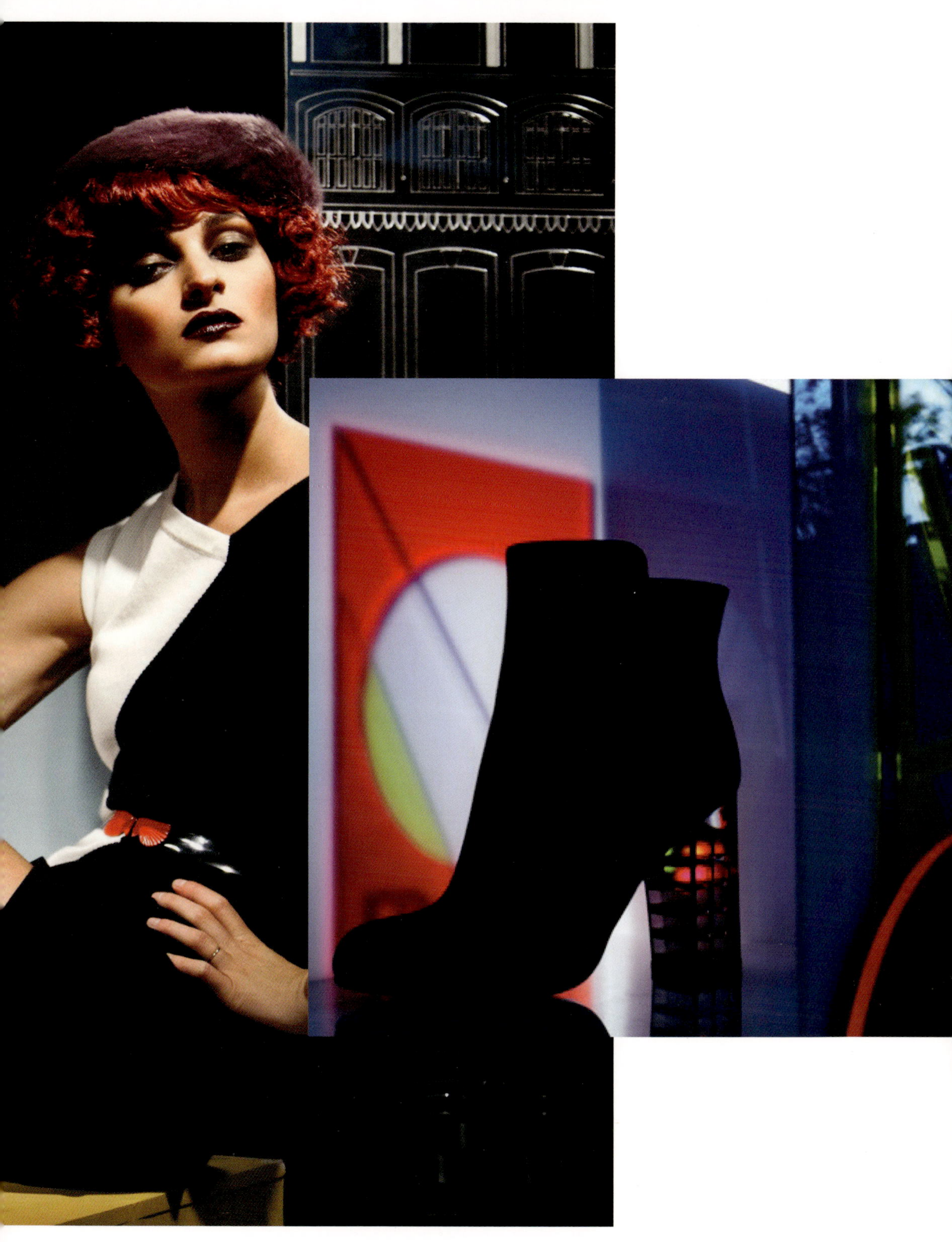

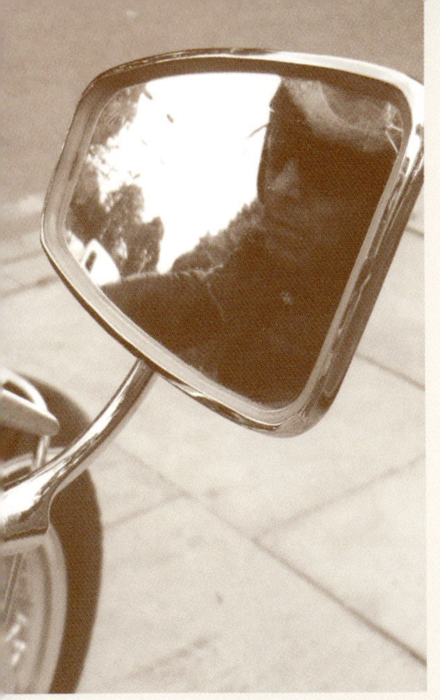

KEI KAGAMI

Please introduce yourself **I AM KEI KAGAMI, A FASHION DESIGNER BASED IN LONDON.** What is your work about? **IT IS ABOUT EXPRESSION THROUGH SPACE AND STRUCTURE.** Is there a specific reason why you chose shoe design? **I DID NOT CHOOSE SHOE DESIGN AS I AM BASICALLY A FASHION DESIGNER AND IT FEEDS ME. I AM NOT AN ARTIST EITHER BUT I THINK I AM A CREATOR AT LEAST.** How do you differentiate your work from others? **THERE ISN'T ANYTHING SPECIFIC AS I CONCENTRATE ON TRYING TO EXPRESS WHAT I WANT, AS SINCERELY AS POSSIBLE.** What do you consider your most innovative design so far? **THE FLYING U-BOAT WHICH I DID FOR THE SOME/THINGS MAGAZINE GALLERY IN PARIS THIS YEAR.** Can you tell us something about the design process? **I FIRST DECIDE WHAT I WOULD LIKE TO EXPRESS. TO DO SO, I ALWAYS ANALYSE MYSELF FIRST. I LOOK AT WHAT I AM CURRENTLY INTERESTED IN, WHAT ATTRACTS ME, WHAT I SEE BEAUTY IN, WHAT I HAVE ANGER AGAINST AND SO ON. I WOULD THEN CHOOSE THE STRONGEST OF THE SUBJECTS AND THIS BECOMES THE MAIN THEME OF THE COLLECTION. I THEN LOOK AT MATERIALS AND DO THE TECHNICAL RESEARCH. ONCE I'VE DECIDED THE THEME, MATERIALS AND TECHNIQUES, I TRY TO TRANSFER THE IMAGE IN MY HEAD INTO A PHYSICAL OBJECT.** Which stages of the design process do you find the most and least gratifying? **THE MOMENT I REALISE SOMETHING INTO THE SHAPE I'M LOOKING FOR IS VERY GRATIFYING. WHEN IT GOES WRONG, IT DEPRESSES ME INDEED BUT ULTIMATELY I AM HAPPY JUST TO BE MAKING SOMETHING WITH MY HANDS.** Could you name people you admire or who have played a part in your development as an artist? **ALBERT EINSTEIN'S IMAGINATION AND FRIEDRICH NIETZSCHE'S PHILOSOPHY HAVE ALWAYS ENCOURAGED ME TO KEEP GOING ON AS I LIKE.** If you had to choose one colour and one material to make an important piece, what would they be? **I WOULD SAY A COUTURE DRESS MADE OF SUPER 150S WOOL GABARDINE IN BLACK.** How is your work affected by the culture of quick consumption and over-commercialisation? **I THINK MANY THINGS ARE TOO COMMERCIALISED IN ALL FIELDS INCLUDING FASHION, MUSIC AND EVEN THE ART BUSINESS. OFTEN MONEY HAS THE POWER TO TAKE AWAY IDENTITY, PERSONALITY AND SYMBOLISM FROM PEOPLE AND THINGS. THIS MEANS THERE ARE NO MORE CULTURAL AND EDUCATIONAL VALUES LEFT. THIS SITUATION AFFECTS MY BUSINESS AS MY WORK MAY BE NOT COMMERCIAL ENOUGH. THIS ISSUE NEEDS TO BE ADDRESSED BEFORE CULTURE AND CIVILIZATION STOPS DEVELOPING COMPLETELY.** How do you see the current state of your profession in general? **GENERALLY THIS TIME IS NOT VERY GOOD IN MANY WAYS, ECONOMICALLY, POLITICALLY AND CULTURALLY. HOWEVER, I AM STILL HAPPY AND LUCKY ENOUGH TO KEEP DOING WHAT I LOVE TO DO, SO I SHOULD NOT BE COMPLAINING.** What is vulgar to you and what elegant? **FASHION VICTIMS ARE VULGAR. ELEGANCE IS A SENSE OF CLASS.** What does beauty mean for you? **BEAUTY IS SOMETHING WHICH CAN PURIFY THE MIND.**

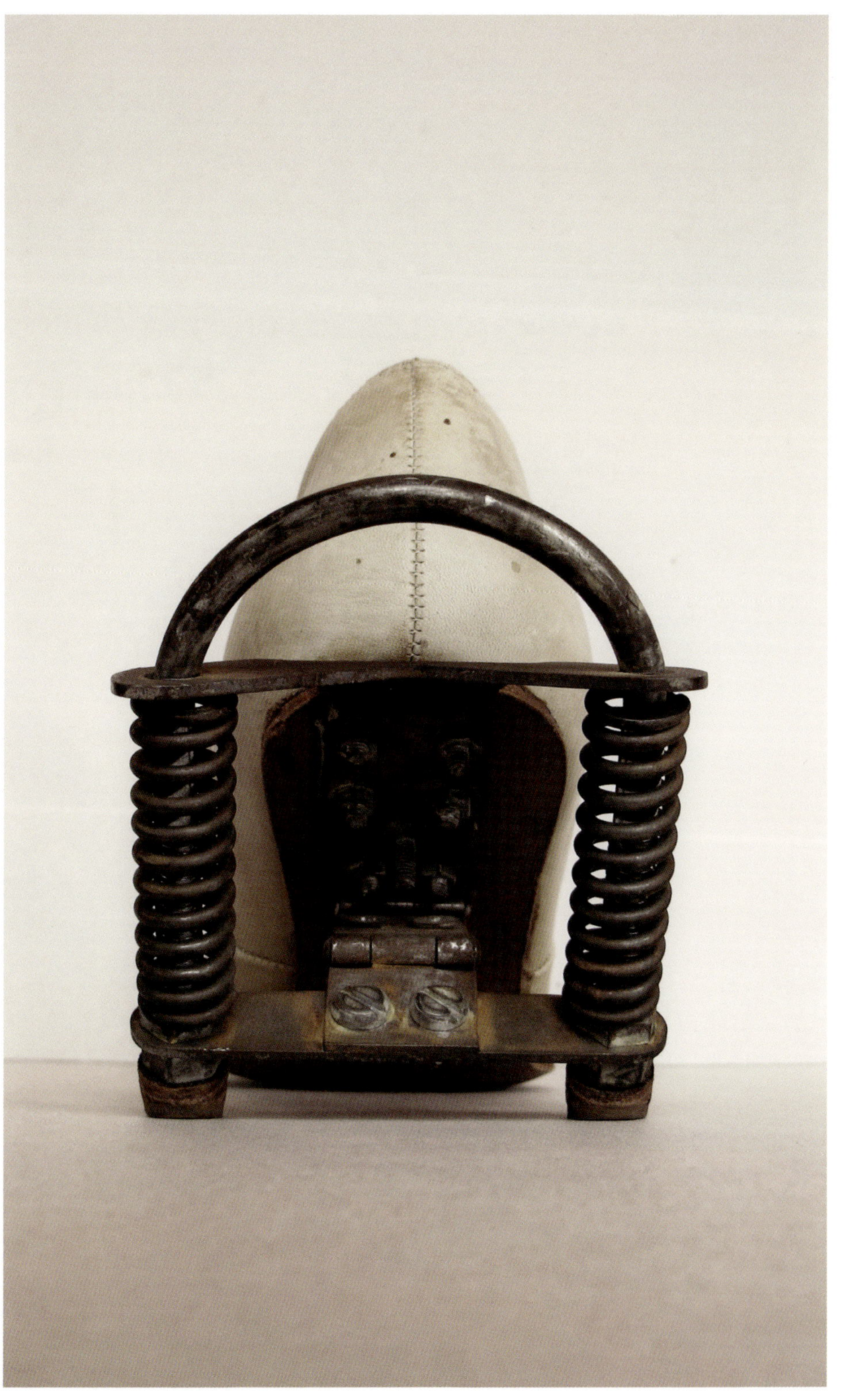

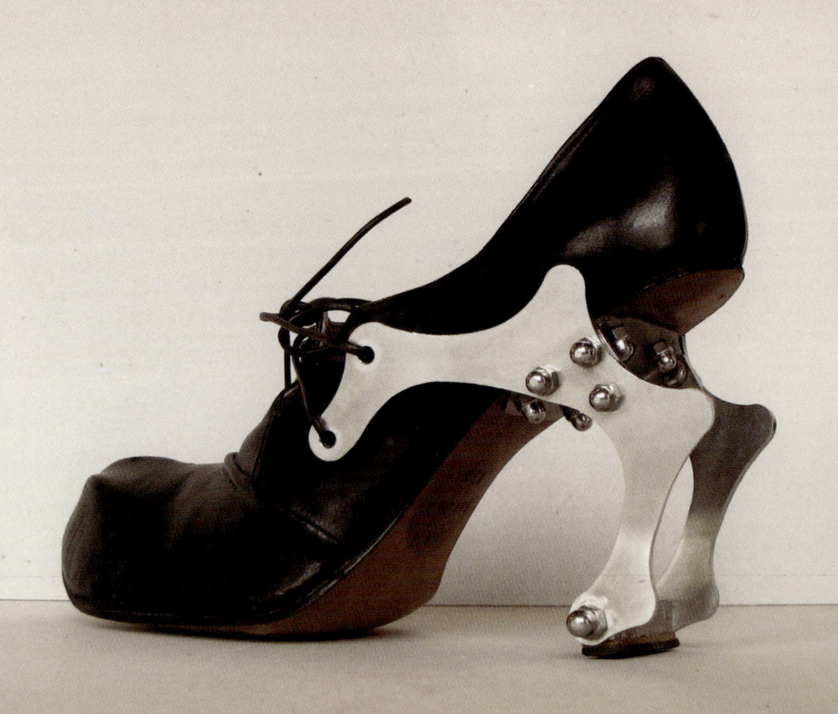

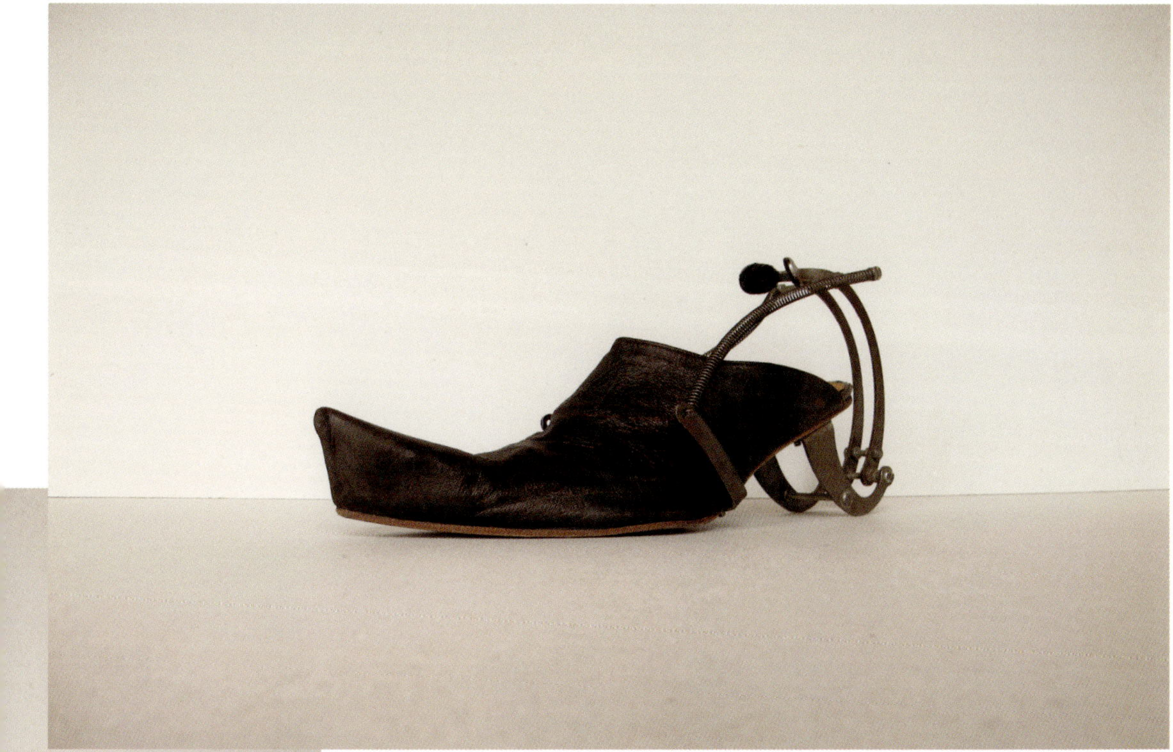

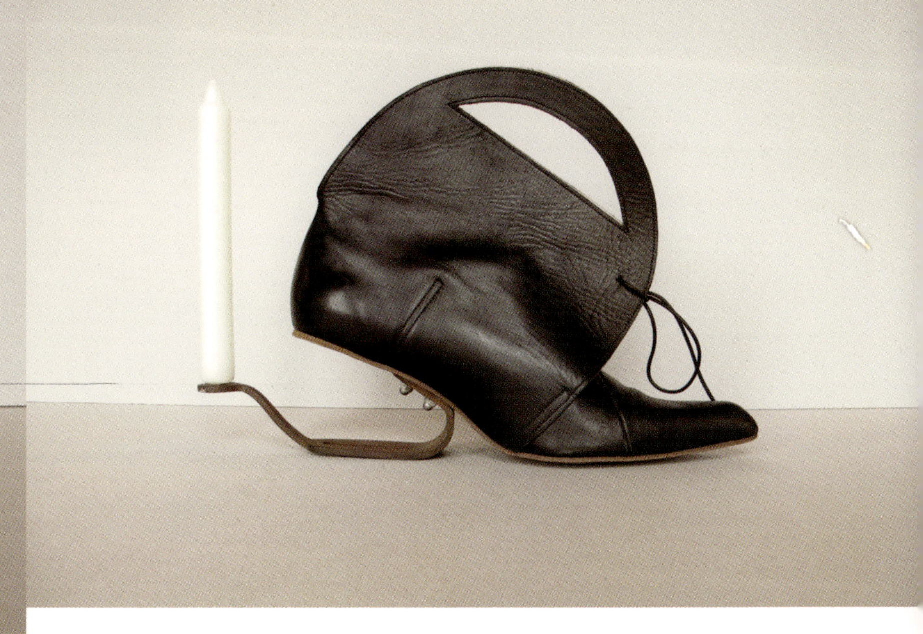

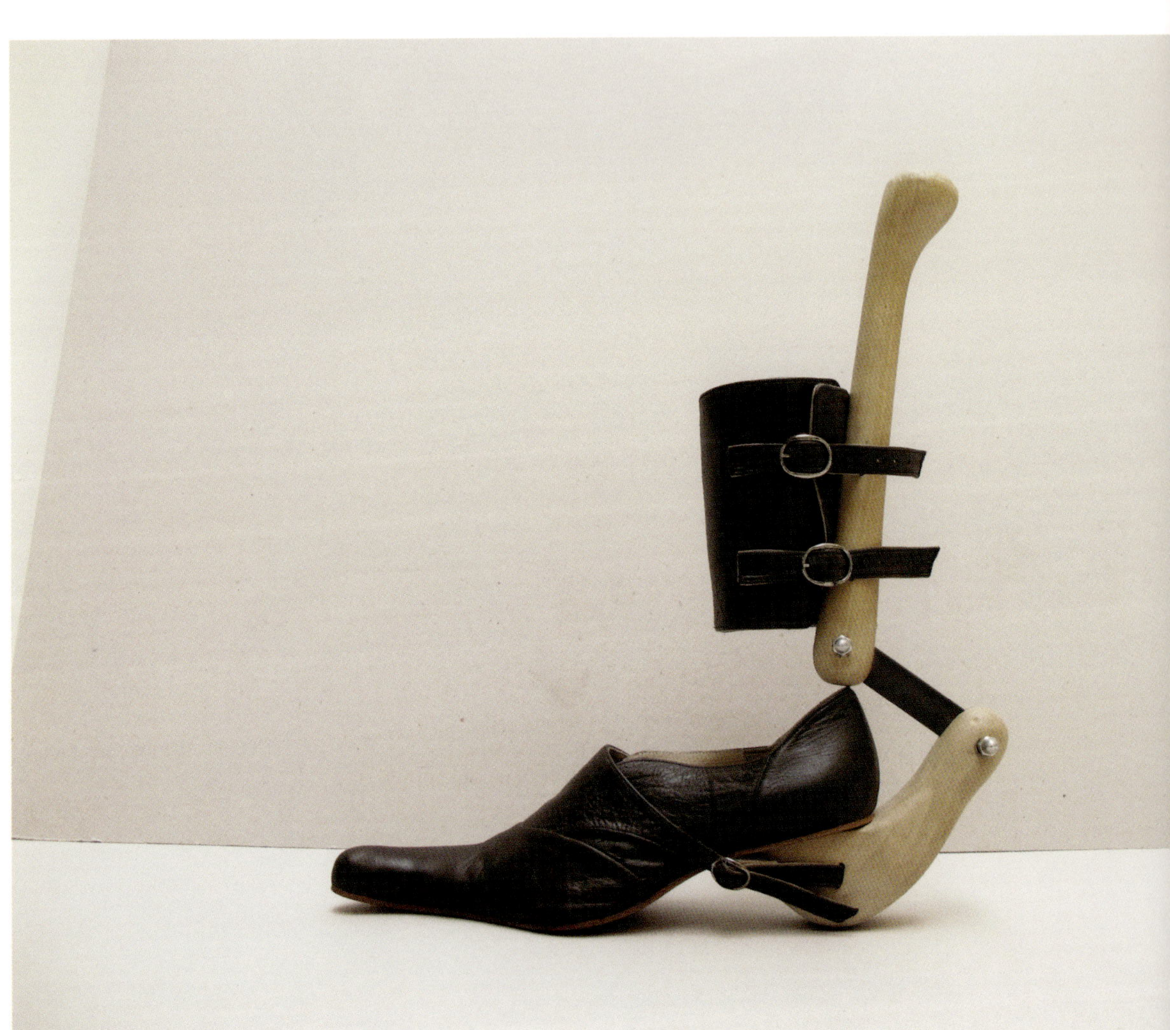

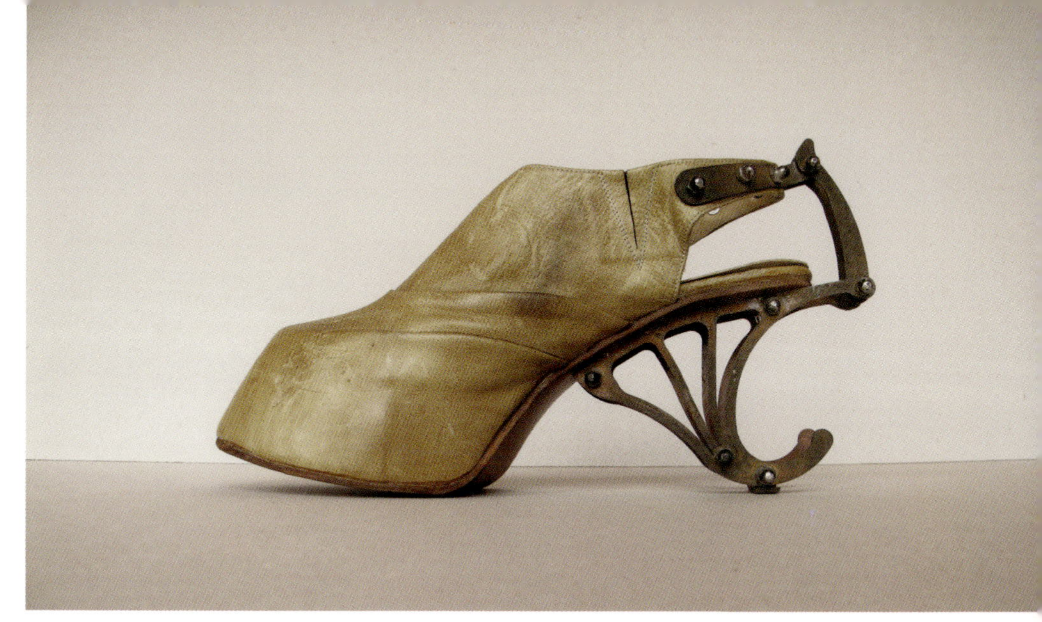

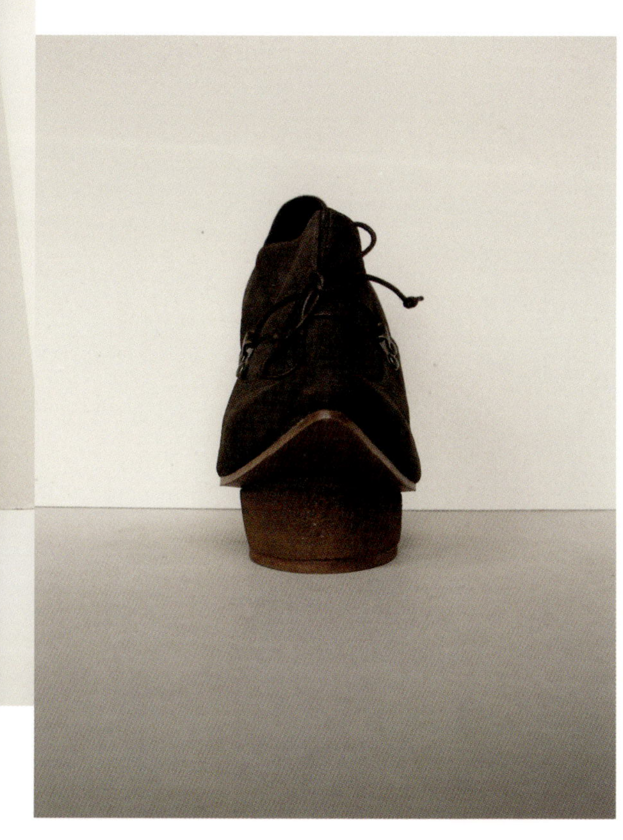

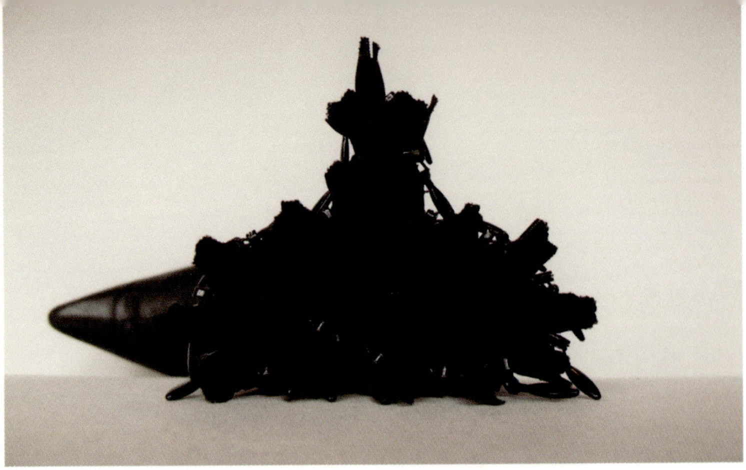

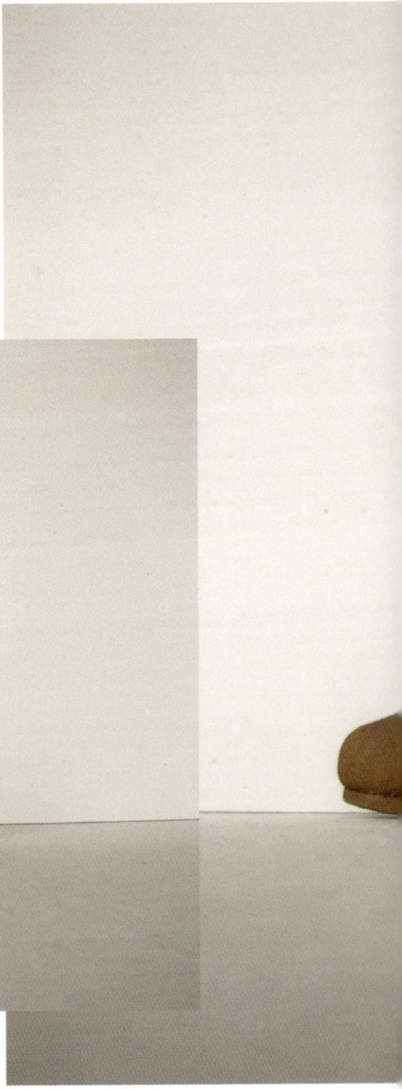

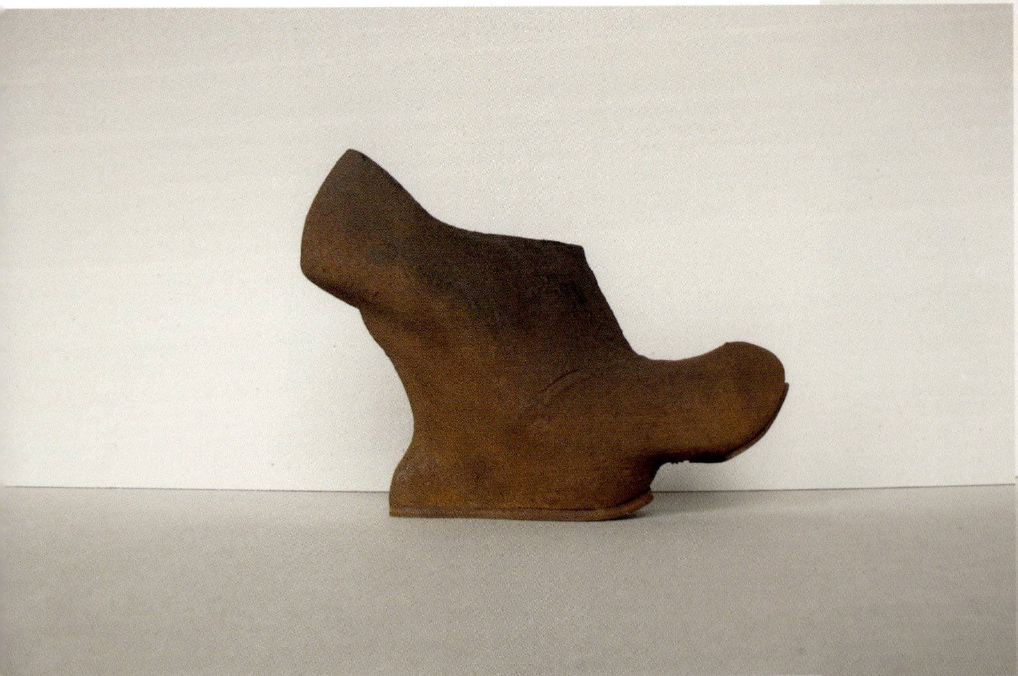

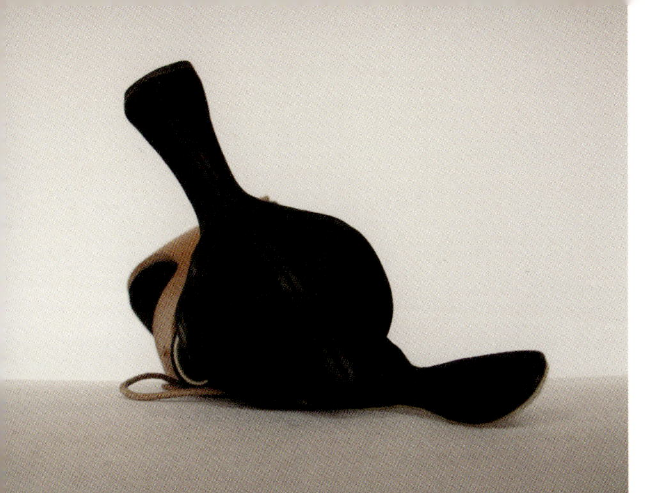

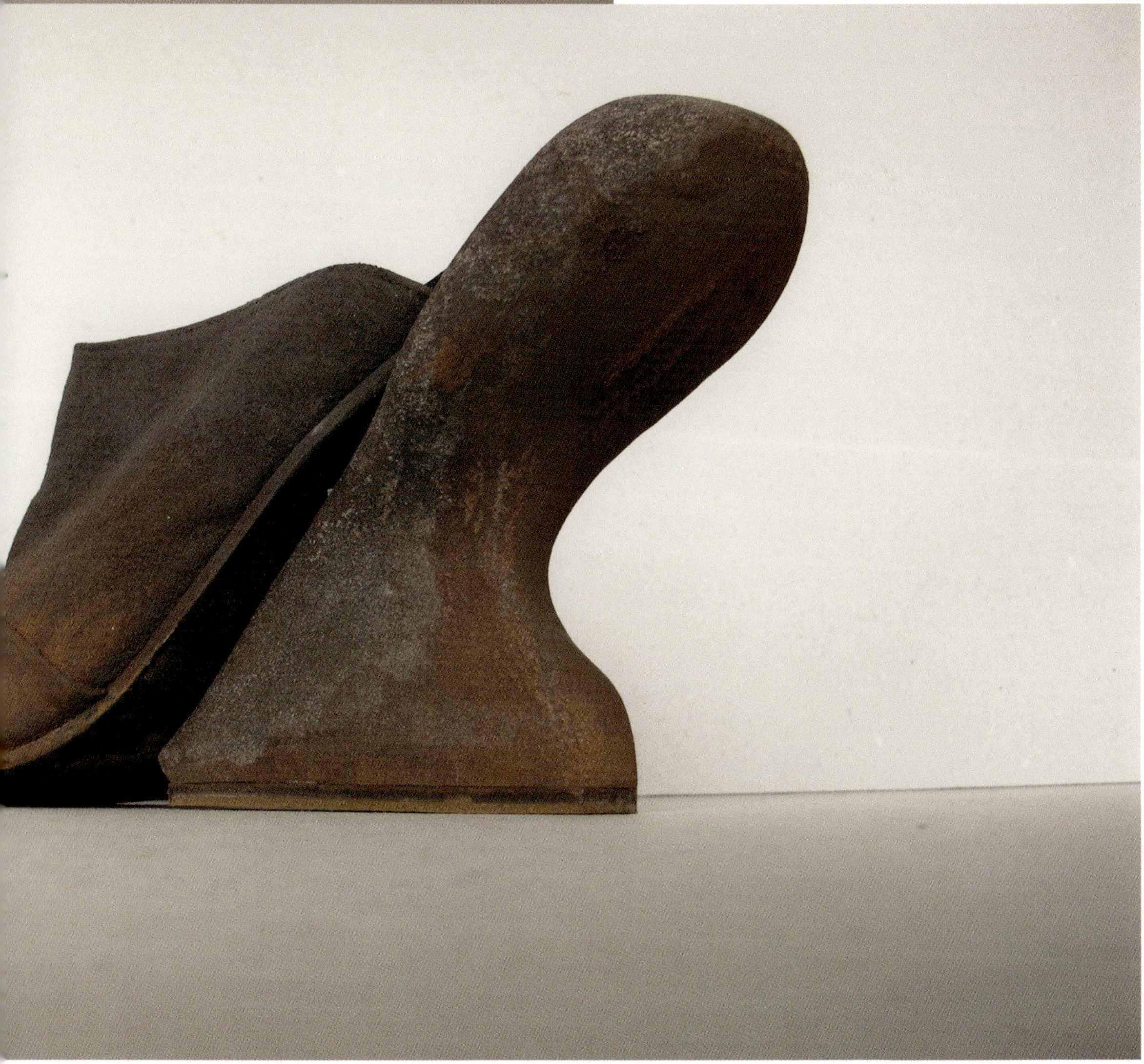

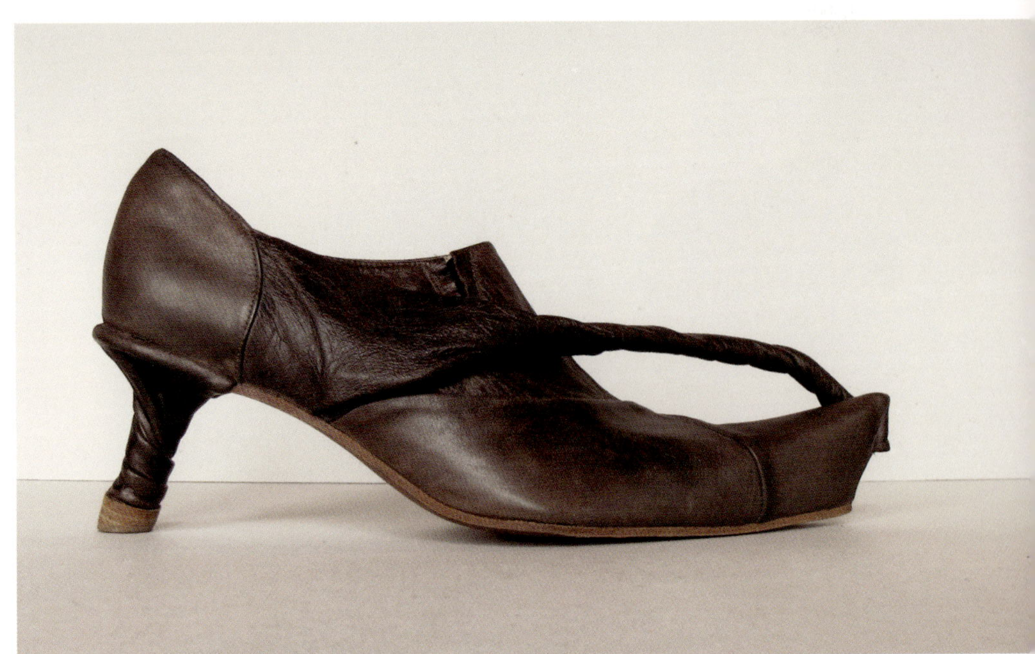

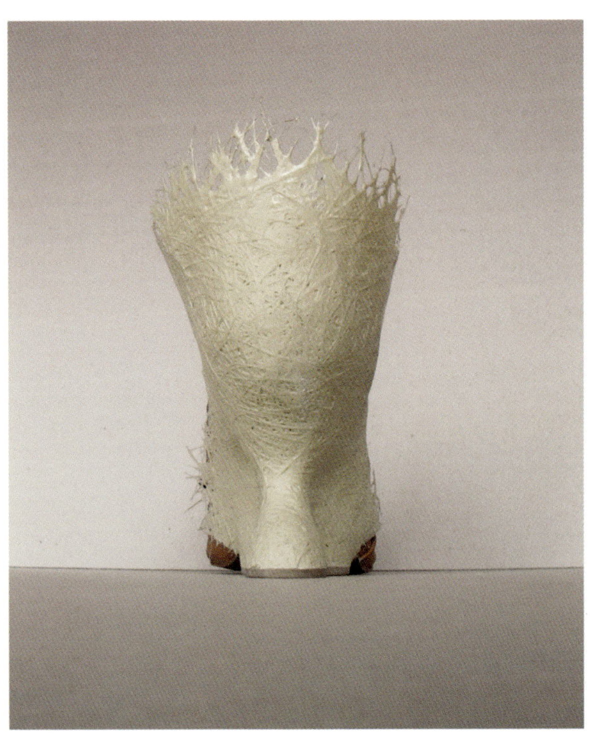

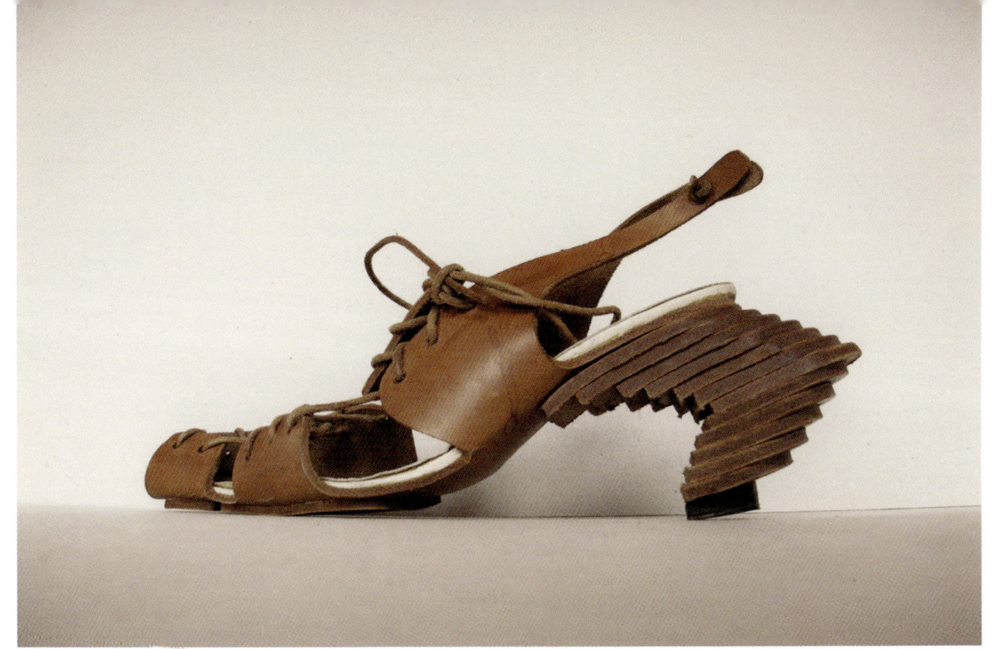

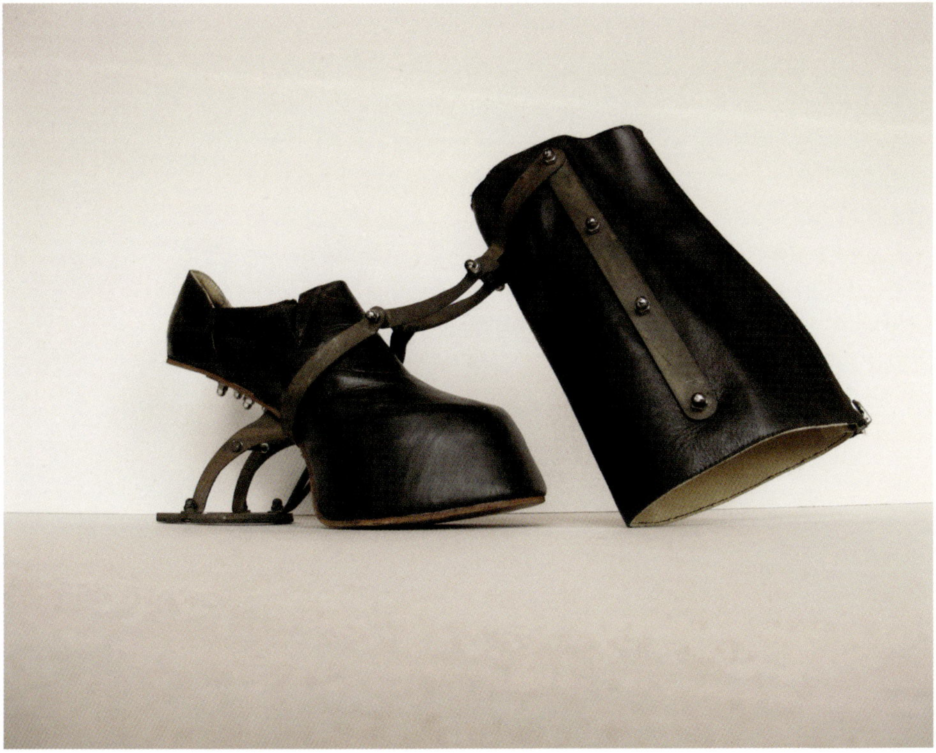

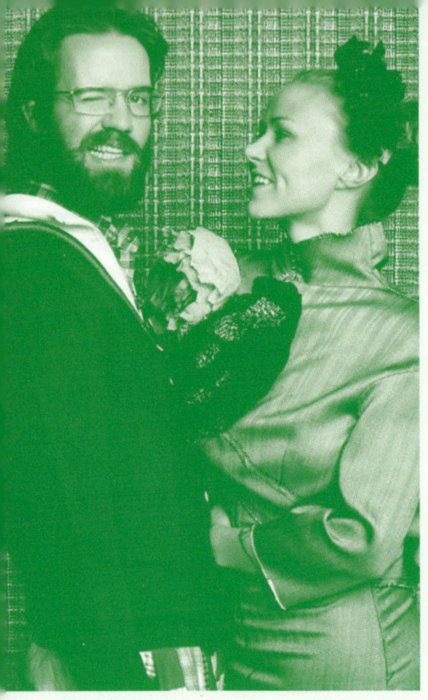

KRON BY KRONKRON

We went on a blind date eleven years ago, Hugrún moved in the day after and three months later we opened our shoe store Kron. This was the year 2000. Today we have our stores Kron and Kronkron and our shoe and clothing brand Kron by Kronkron. Hugrún studied fashion design at Studio Bercot in Paris and Magni is a hair designer. Our different backgrounds seem to be a good mix. **THE OPENING OF OUR SHOE STORE KRON WAS OUR FIRST STEP INTO THE SHOE WORLD AND FOR US IT WAS LIKE JUMPING IN TO CANDY LAND. IN 2004 WE OPENED OUR CLOTHING STORE KRONKRON WHERE WE DEVELOPED A NOSE FOR FASHION. THIS PREPARED US FOR THE NEXT BIG STEP, LAUNCHING KRON BY KRONKRON IN 2008.** Details are our signature. Timeless is the main objective. We want each style to stand on its own without being identified by time or place. Every shade of colour or pleat can make a huge difference and that's the magic that keeps us satisfied. **WHEN DESIGNING WE TRY TO CLEAR OUR MINDS SO THAT WE CAN BE TRUE TO OURSELVES INSTEAD OF FOLLOWING TRENDS. THE STAGES OF THE CREATIVE PROCESS CAN BE COMPARED TO THE DIFFERENT SEASONS. SOMETIMES IT'S SUNNY, OTHER TIMES IT CAN BE RAINING, FREEZING OR JUST FULL OF COLOUR, BUT WE LOVE THEM ALL.** When it comes to fashion we feel that in the past shoes have always been in the background without getting the attention they deserve. Now they are coming out of the shadows. Shoes tell you so much about the personality of the person wearing them. People may be a little more daring when it comes to clothing but it gives them greater pleasure when they find a pair of shoes that pleases them. It seems that people have a more intimate relationship with their shoes than with clothing. **WHAT IS MOST PLEASING TO US IS WHEN OUR EFFORTS GET THE ATTENTION OF SO MANY DIFFERENT CUSTOMERS, ESPECIALLY THOSE WHO WOULD NOT NORMALLY THINK ABOUT WHAT LIES BEHIND EACH PRODUCT. THE FACT WE HAVE MANAGED TO OPEN THEIR EYES MAKES OUR WORK VERY VALUABLE AND REWARDING.**

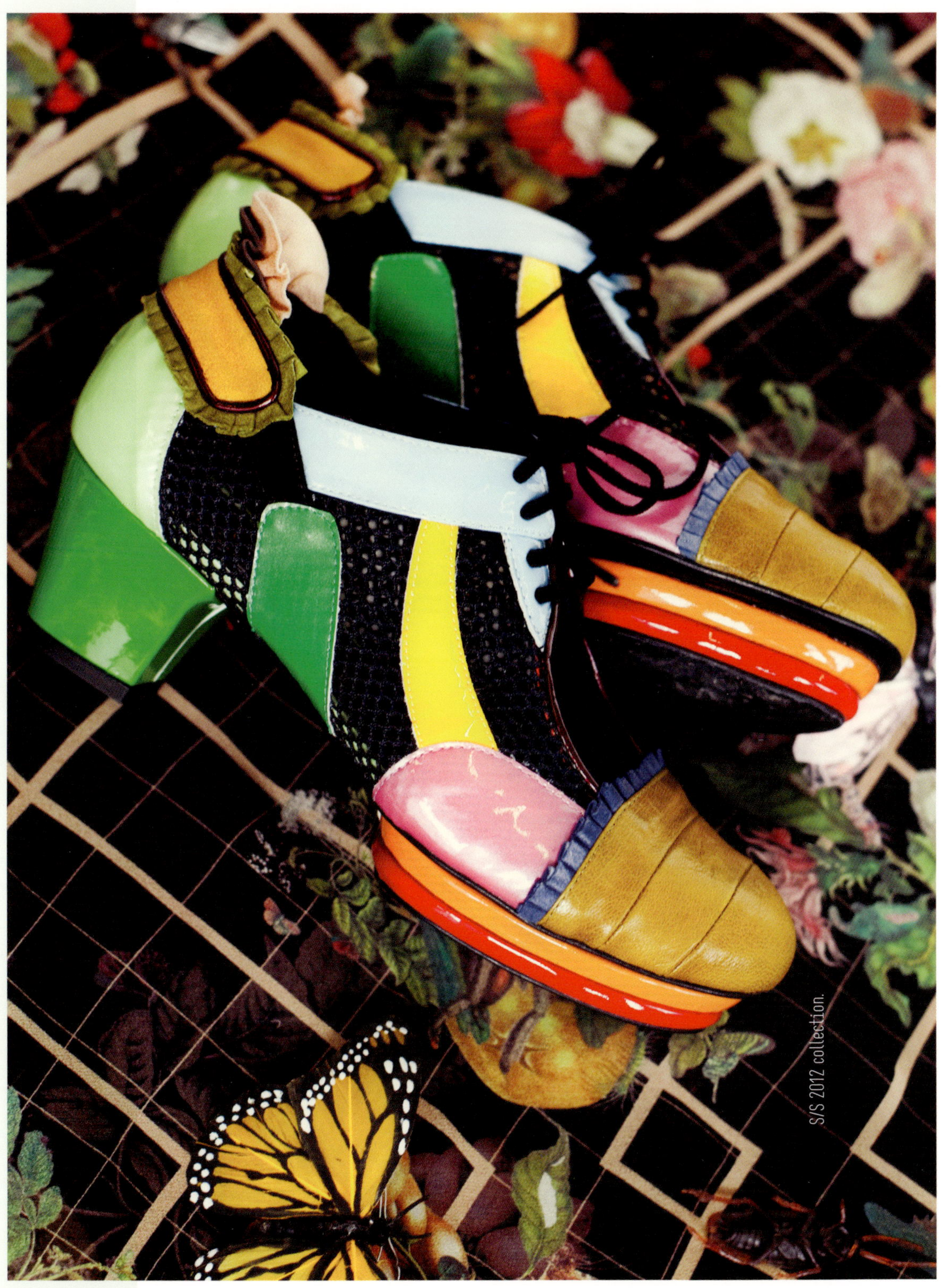

S/S 2012 collection.

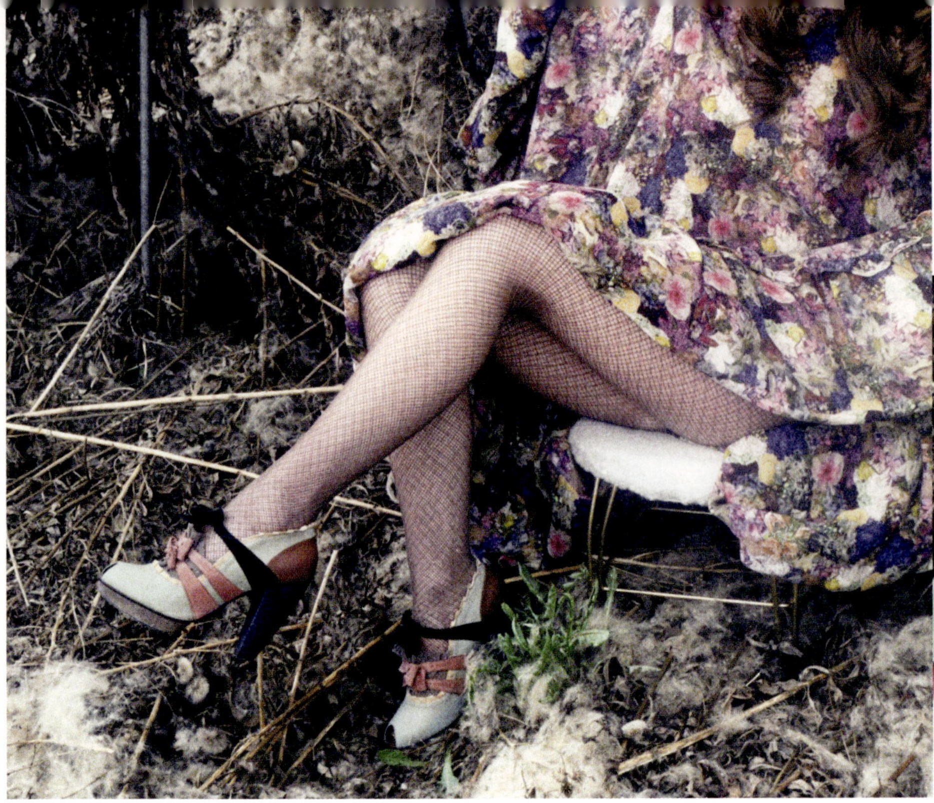

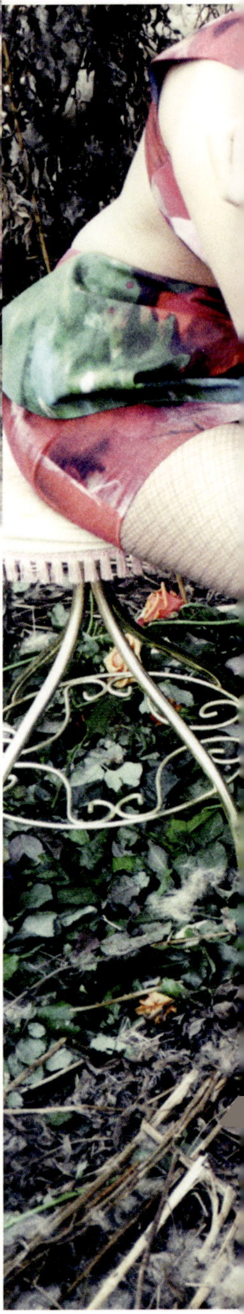

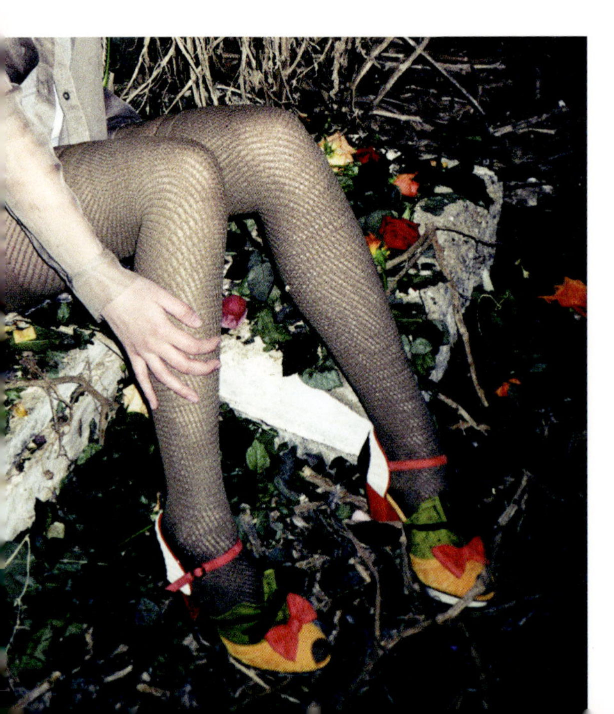

S/S 2010 collection.

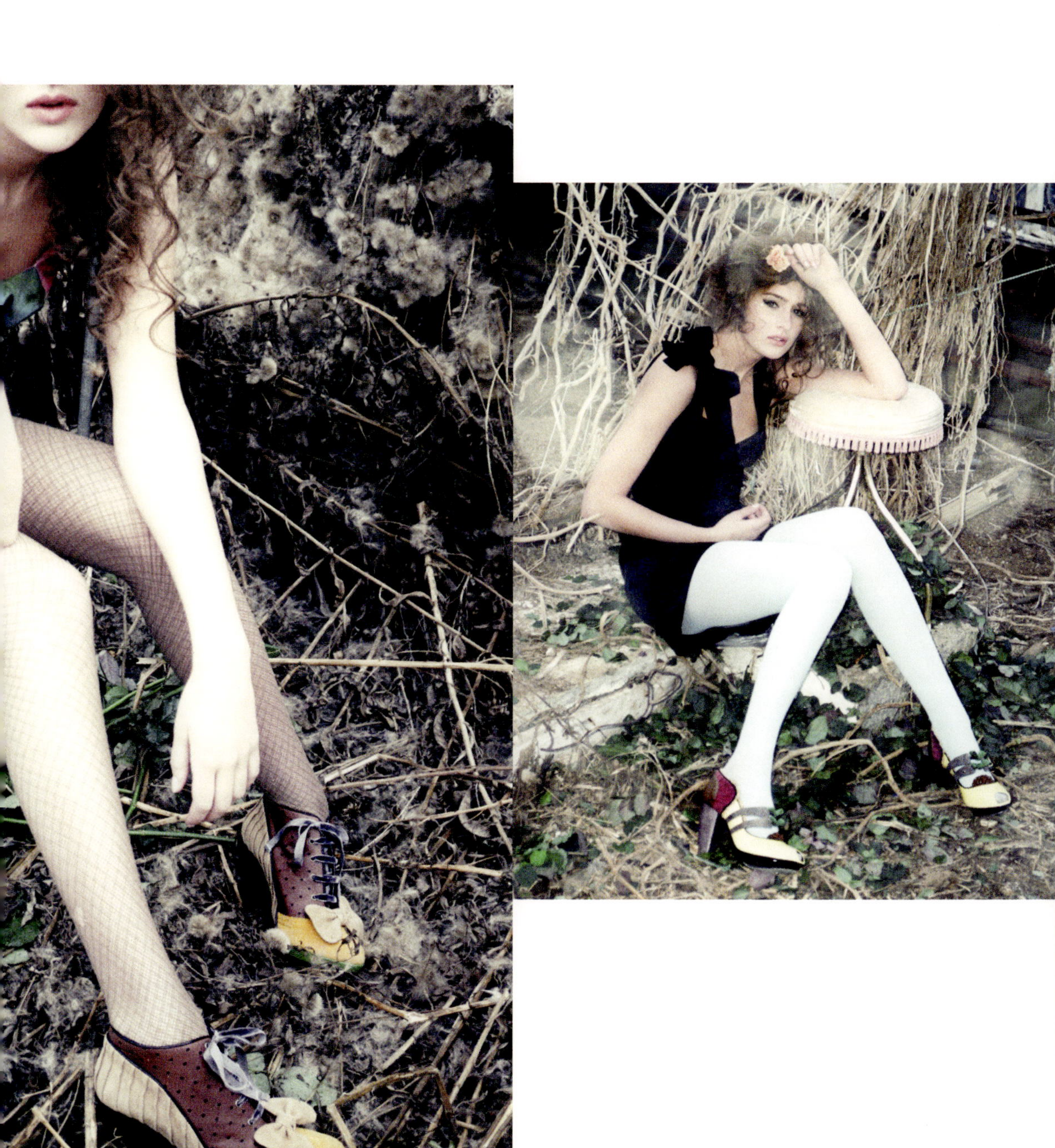

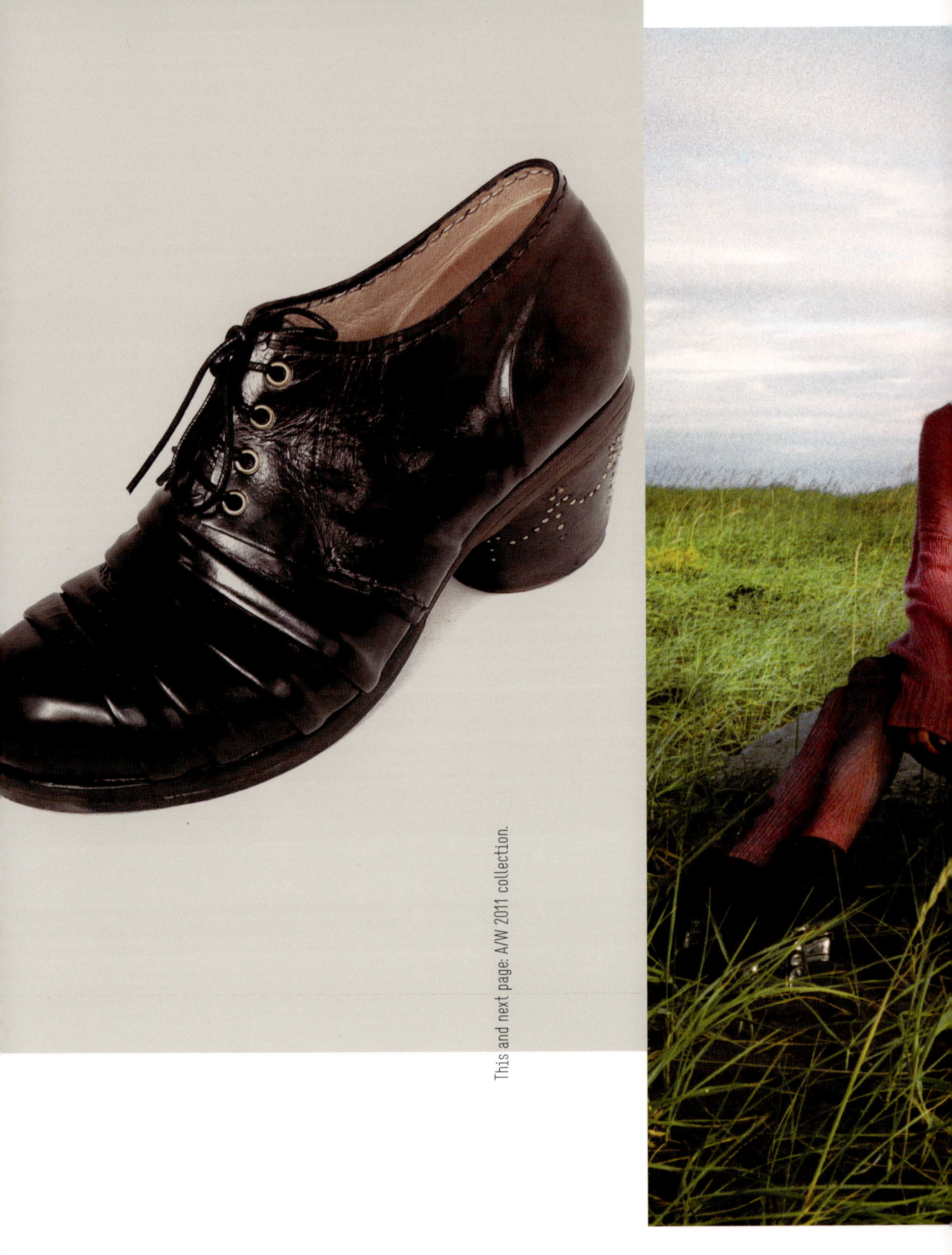

This and next page: A/W 2011 collection.

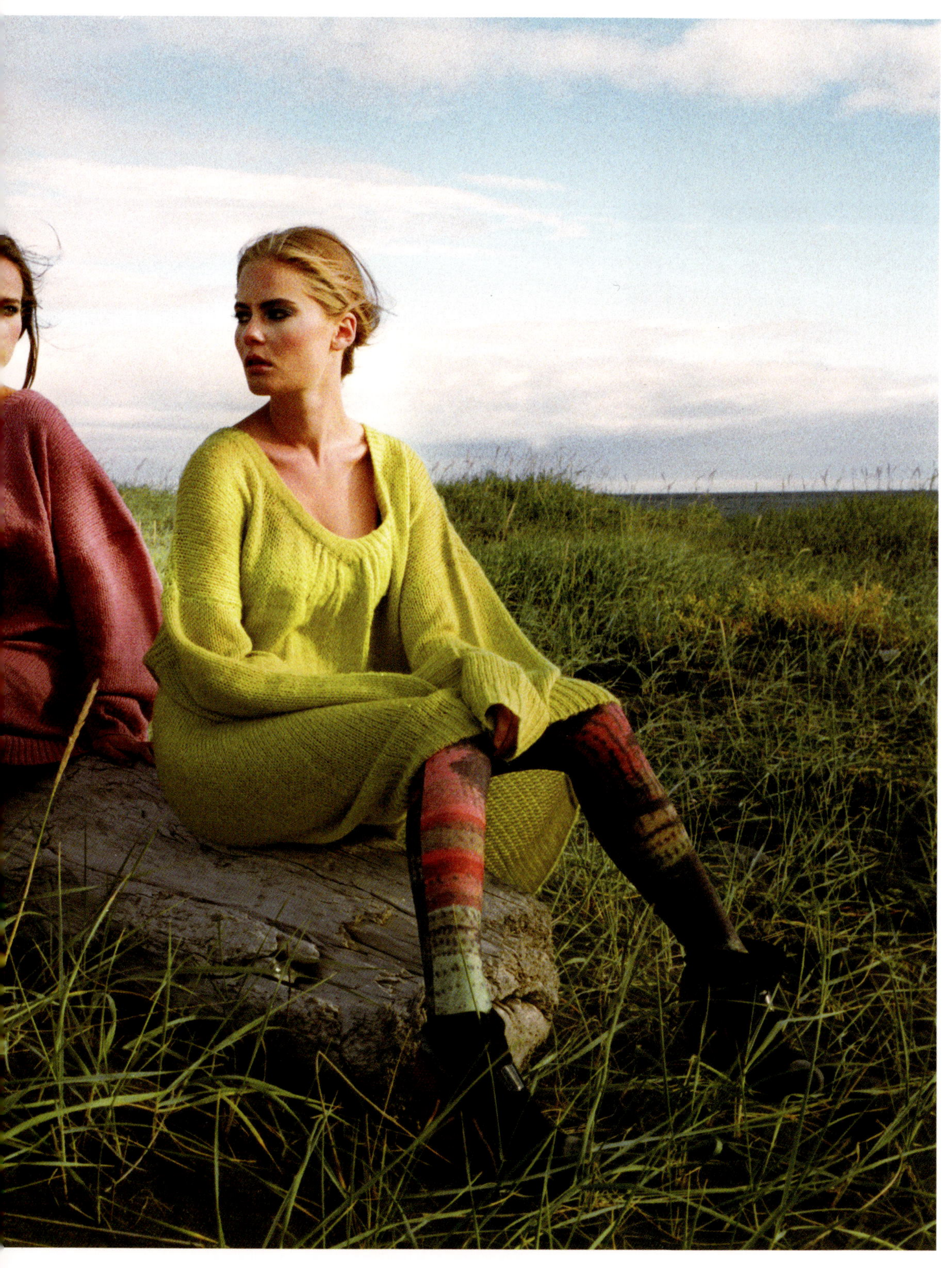

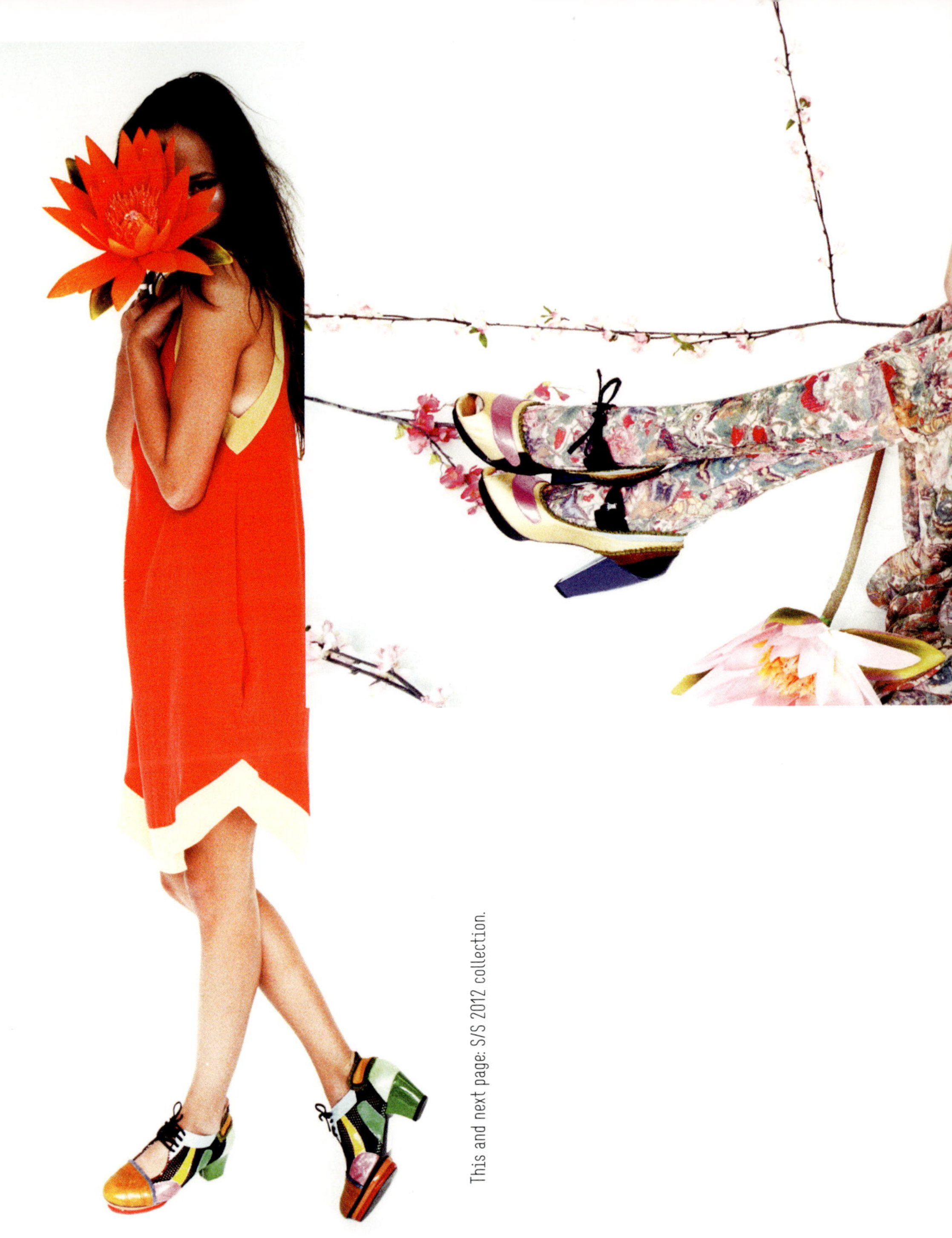

This and next page: S/S 2012 collection.

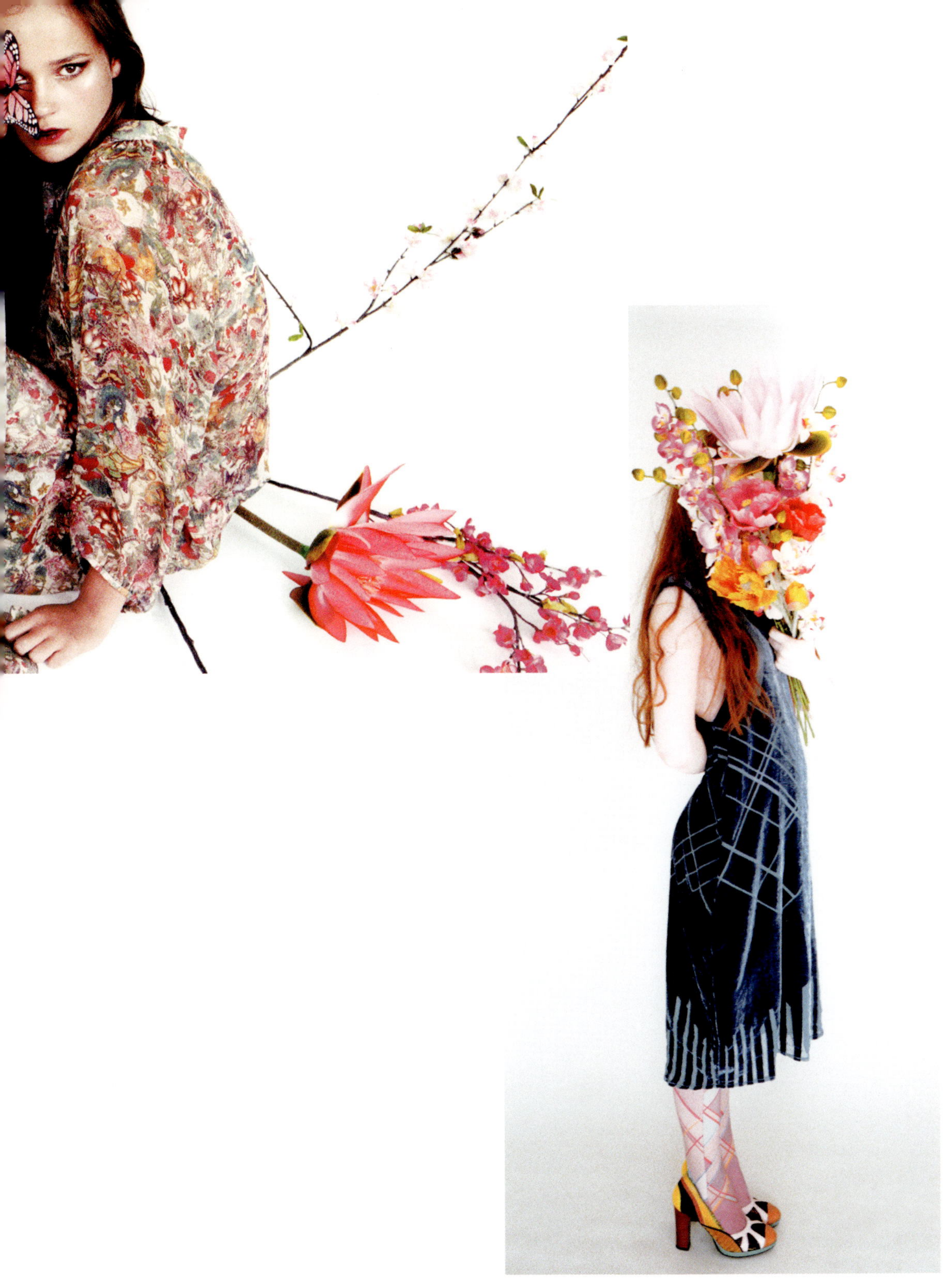

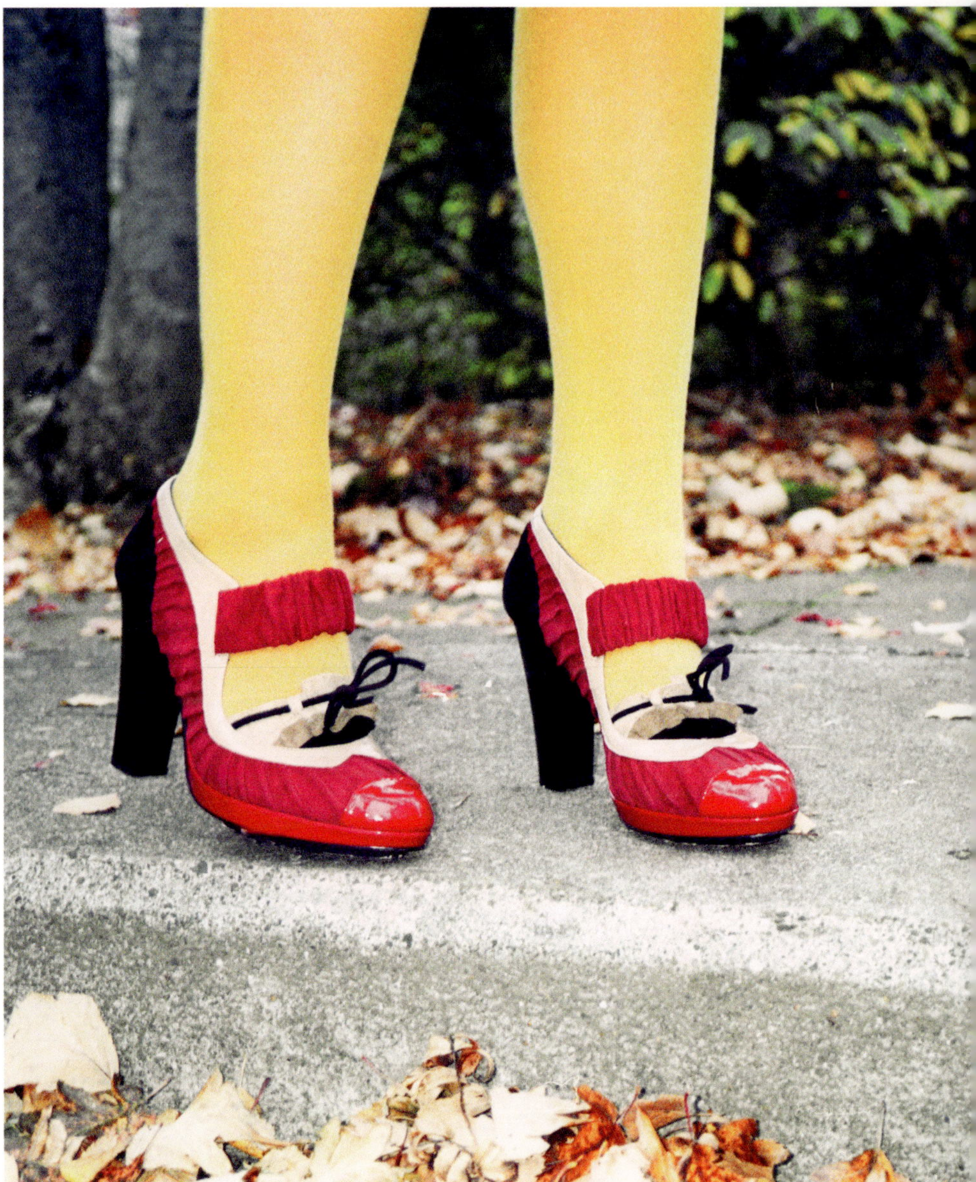

This and next page: A/W 2010 collection.

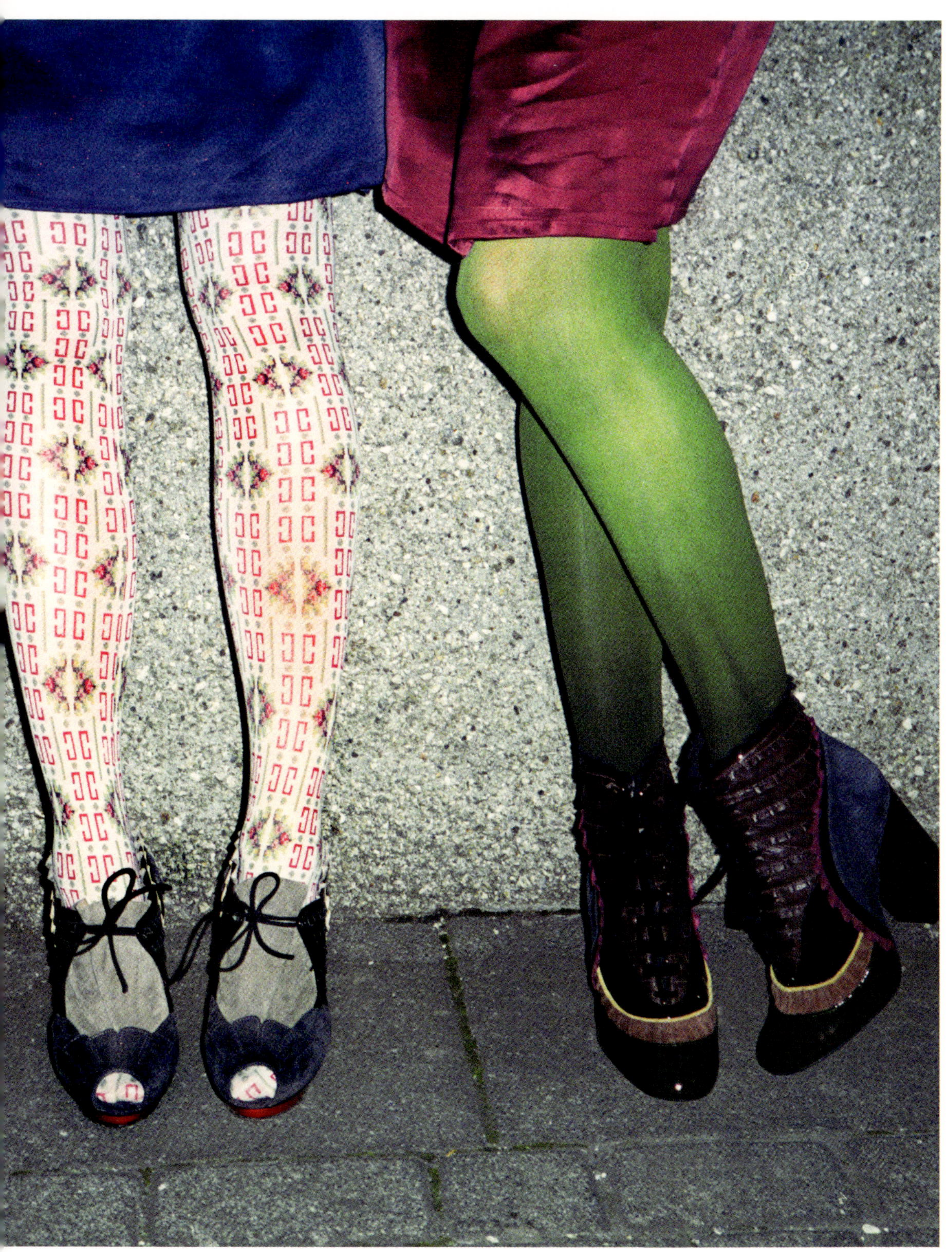

LIAM FAHY

Shoes have been a passion since I was a child. I grew up in Africa where shoes carry cultural value and significance. I studied footwear design and worked with many multinational brands before winning the first Fashion Fringe Accessory award judged by Manolo Blahnik. As a result I became the protégé to British Accessory Designer of the Year Rupert Sanderson and moved to Italy to learn how luxury shoes are made. **MY WORK IS ABOUT ELEGANCE AND LUXURY. OUR SHOES ARE THE MOST EXPENSIVE SHOES IN THE LUXURY MARKET AND POSSESS A MUCH MORE HANDCRAFTED ELEMENT THAN MOST DESIGNER LABELS. EACH SOLE IS HANDCRAFTED WITH AN EIGHT CHARACTER NICKEL TYPOGRAPHY THAT ESSENTIALLY TAKES MORE TIME TO CONSTRUCT THAN MOST SHOE UPPERS. IT'S OUR SIGNATURE.** Footwear design is a medium for expressing and exploring my passions: design philosophy, athletics, science and psychology. Every detail, stitch, colour and proportion will play a specific part and all these aspects will be based on some principle of one of my passions, whether visual or conceptual. **RESEARCH IS THE MOST CAPTIVATING PART OF A PROJECT. IT IS A CONTINUAL PROCESS OF LEARNING AND EXPANDING ONES UNDERSTANDING. DESIGN IS THE EVOLUTION OF THE PRODUCT AND THEREFORE THE LEAST GRATIFYING PART IS SEEING THE PROCESS OF NATURAL SELECTION. WHETHER IT'S DOWN TO THE BUYERS, CONSTRUCTION LIMITATIONS OR FINANCIAL RESTRICTIONS, I HAVE TO DILUTE MY DESIGNS INTO SOMETHING THAT ULTIMATELY MUST SELL OR NEVER BE PRODUCED.** I would probably consider the Wassail shoe my most innovative so far. It is constructed, assembled and designed unlike any other shoe. It's upgradable, replaceable and uses a metal chassis with leather stretched over the frame to create a suspended foot bed. Black would always be my preferred colour of choice. Black is to fashion as carbon is to chemistry. Carbon is the most abundant element and the most compatible with any other element in much the same way that black is. **COMMERCIALISATION IS THE NATURAL SELECTION OF DESIGN AND IT RESTRICTS CREATIVITY. MOST PEOPLE CONSUME WHAT IS APPLICABLE TO THEM, ESPECIALLY IN FASHION. I THINK MY WORK ILLUSTRATES THE STATUS QUO OF THIS. I HAVE WON AWARDS FOR ECCENTRICALLY AND CONCEPTUALLY INNOVATIVE PRODUCTS HOWEVER THEY ARE HARDER TO MAKE A REALITY. ONE OF MY FAVOURITE QUOTES IS BY HERMAN MELVILLE, "IT IS BETTER TO FAIL IN ORIGINALITY THAN SUCCEED IN IMITATION." IT'S A DESIGNERS PURPOSE TO CONSTANTLY PUSH THE PARAMETERS OF INNOVATION, HOWEVER IT TAKES AN UNDERSTANDING OF MASS THINKING TO MAKE IT HAPPEN.** The footwear industry constantly changes depending on the weather of the global financial climate. Ultimately, when a middle class reaches a certain populous, their cost of manufacture rises and the global field changes again. Ten years ago a €2000 pair of shoes would have been inconceivable, now it is a reality. Fifteen years ago there were not a tenth of the luxury shoe labels that exist now in the world. I suspect the natural selection of shoe designers will happen through the global financial crisis and innovation will be a designers' strongest card to fight it.

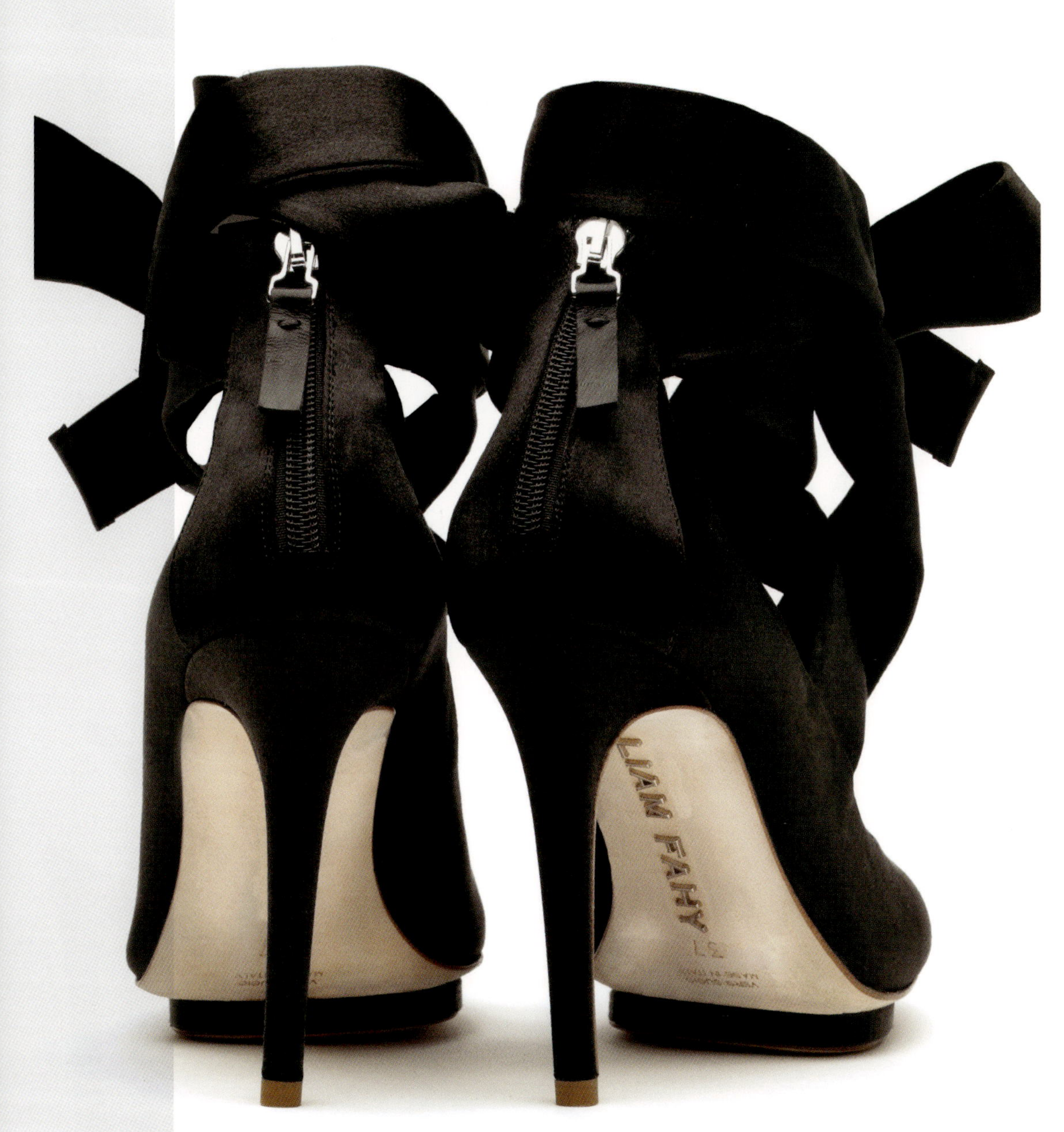
LIAM FAHY

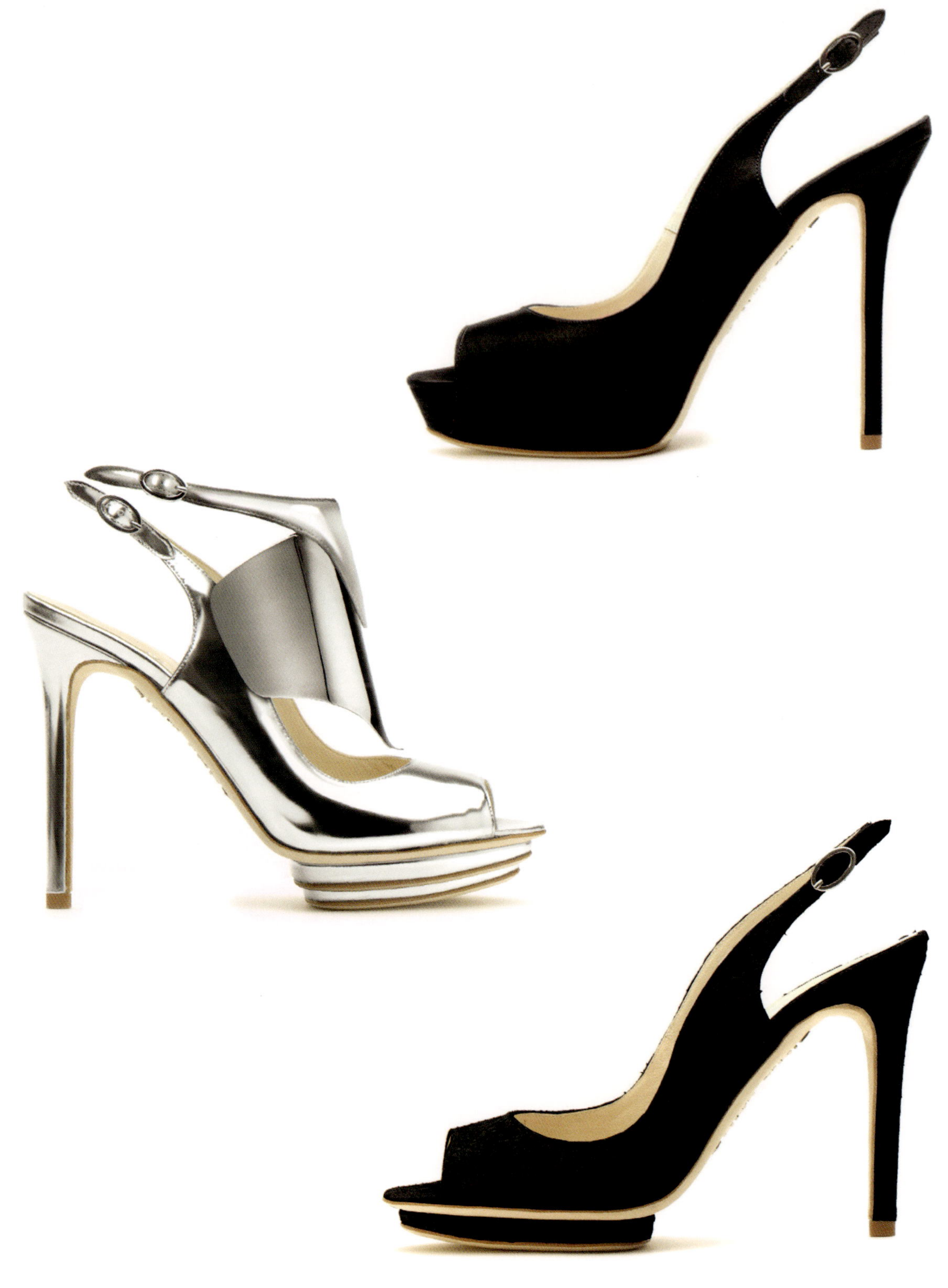

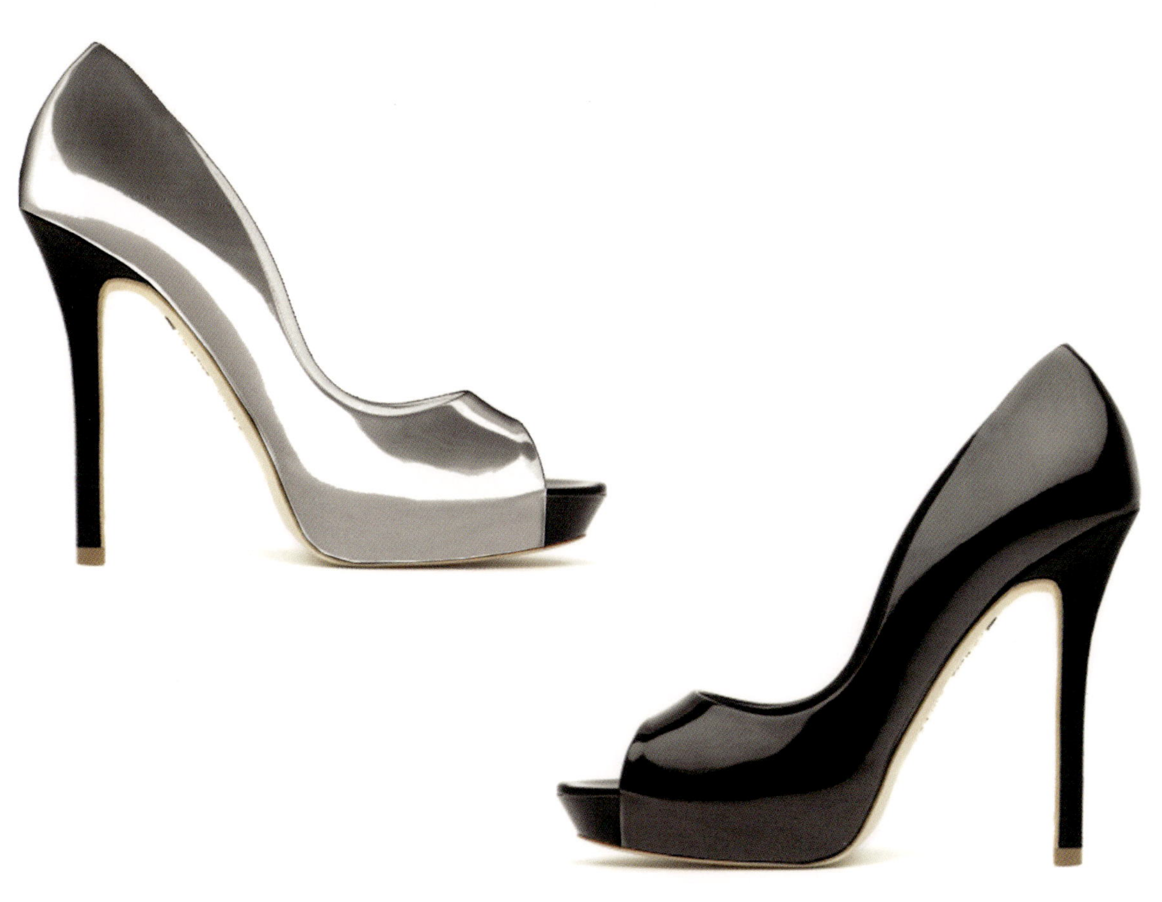

LIAM FAHY

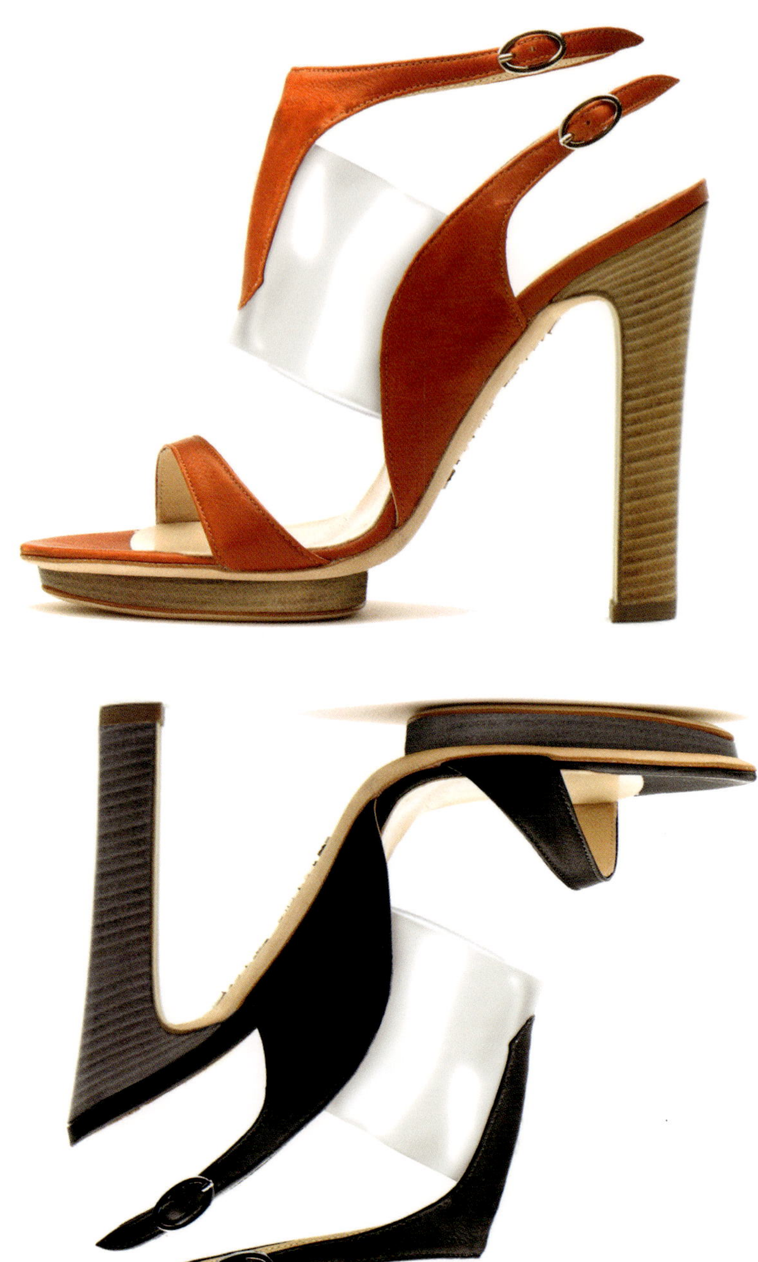

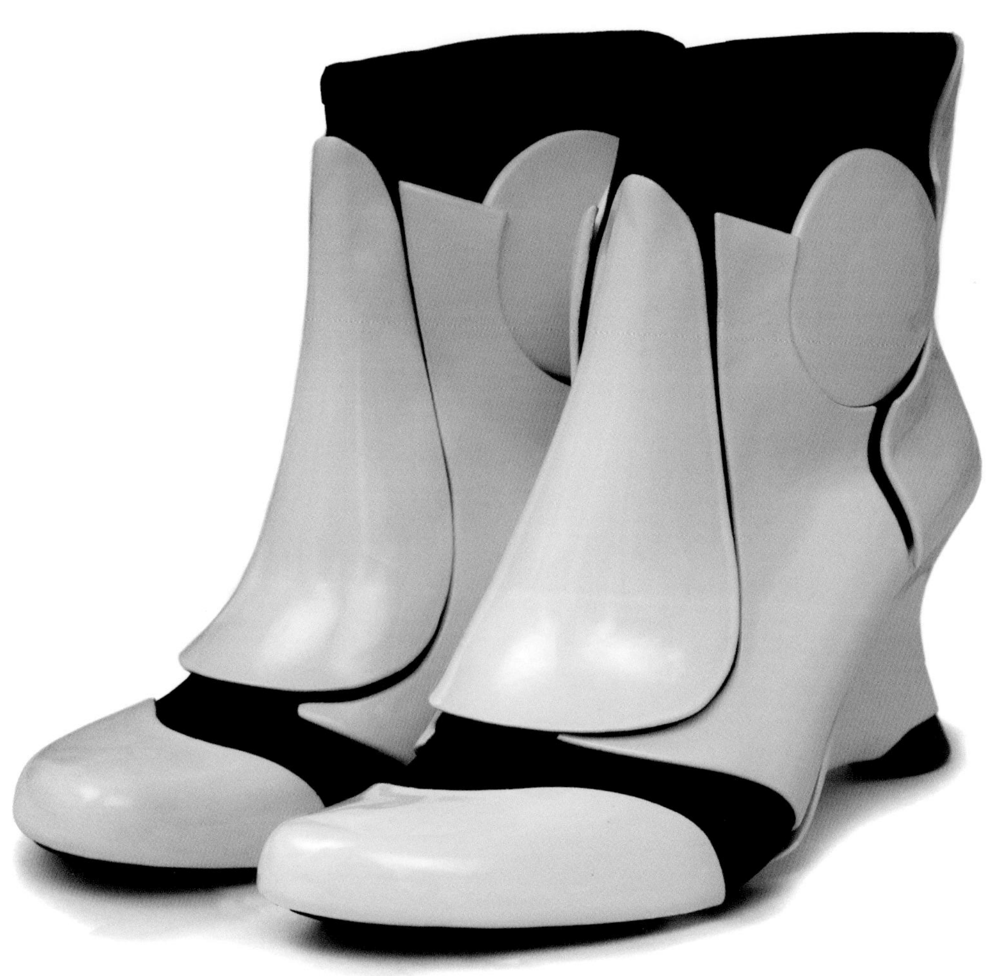

 LIAM FAHY

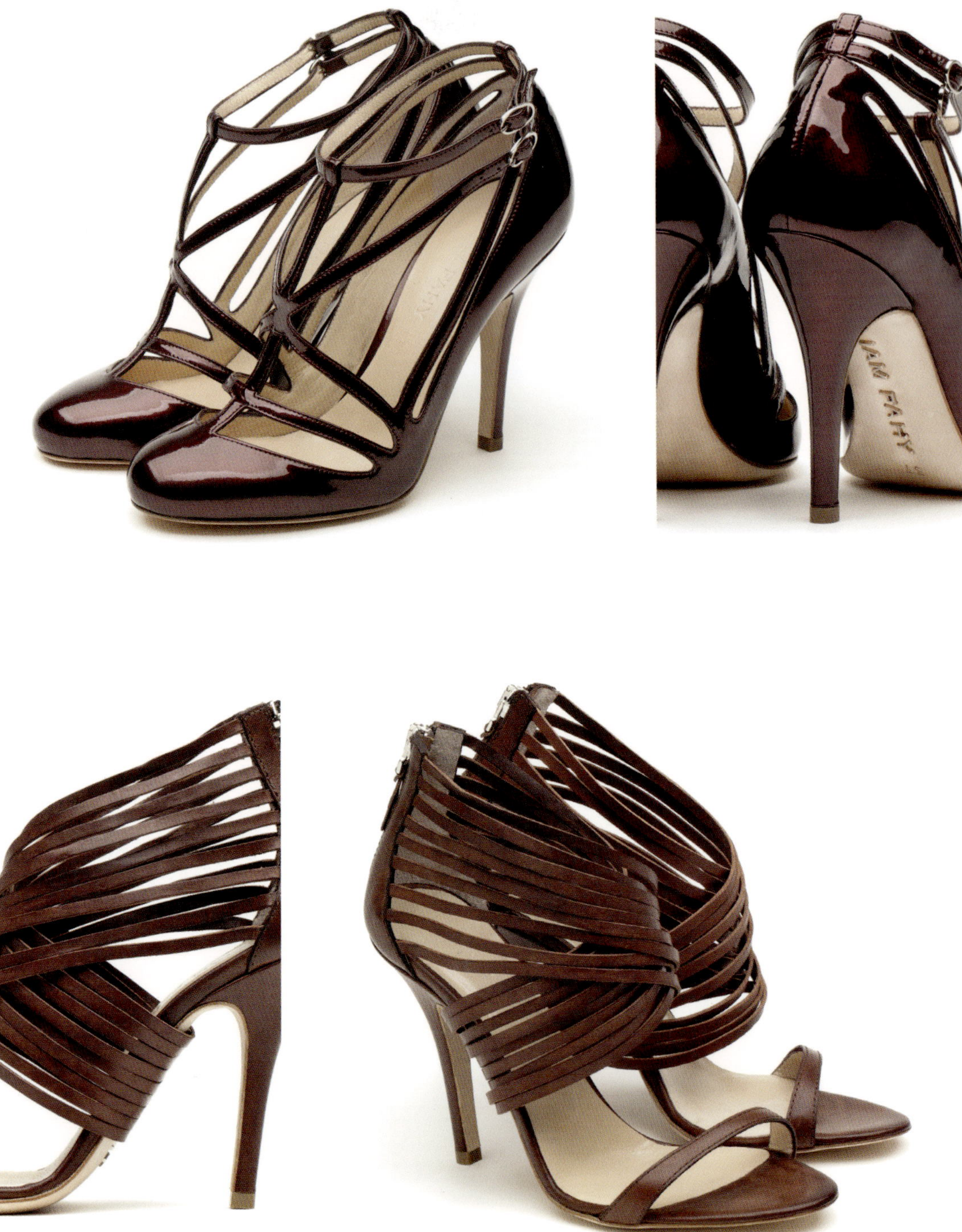
IAN FAHY

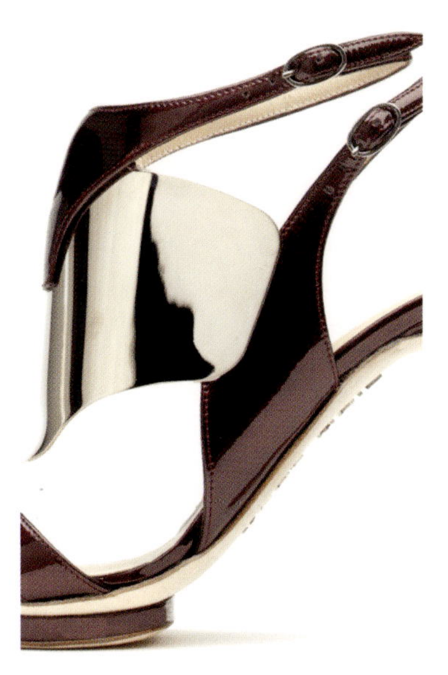

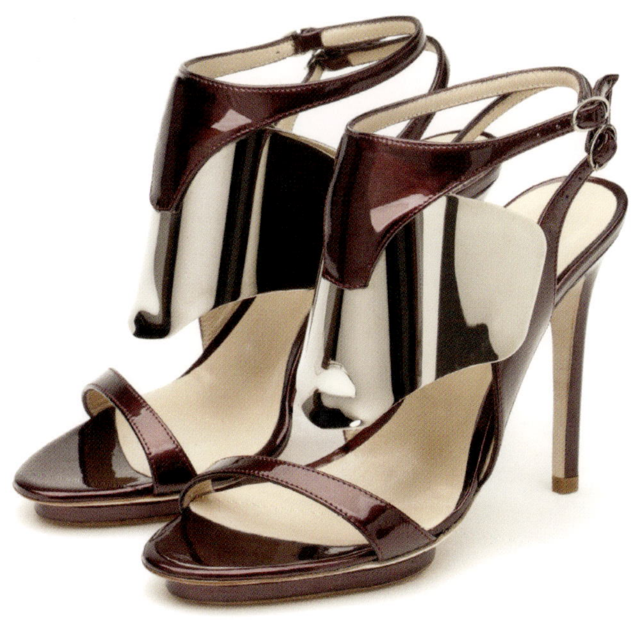

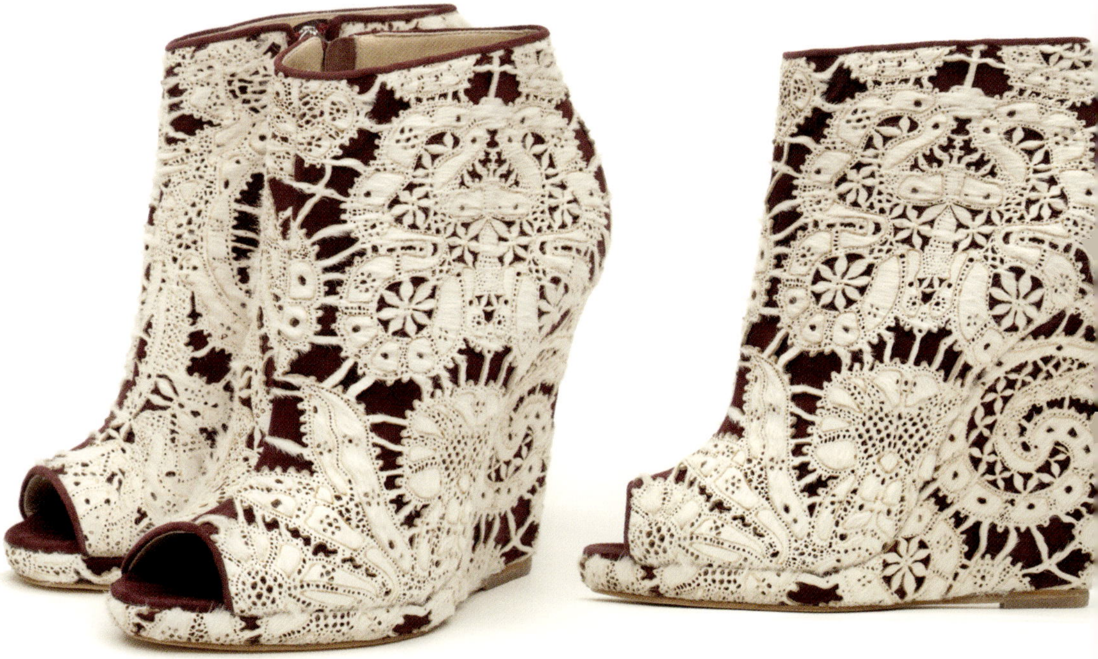

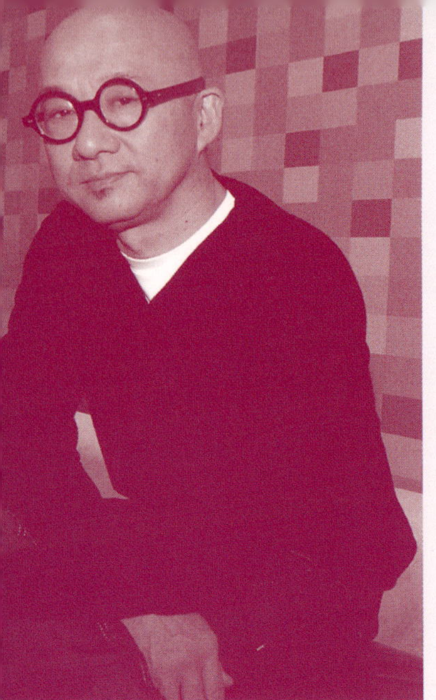

EDSON MATSUO, MELISSA

Please introduce yourself **I AM A PERSON WITH EXTREME CURIOSITY WHO FEELS PRIVILEGED TO LEARN FROM EXPERIENCES.** What was your first introduction to design? **I REMEMBER THAT I ASSEMBLED AND DISASSEMBLED WATCHES WHEN I WAS 5-YEARS-OLD AND THERE WERE ALWAYS A FEW PIECES LEFT OVER AT THE END. IT WAS A LEARNING EXPERIENCE TO SEE HOW THE CLOCKS WORKED.** What is your work about? **CREATIVE EXPERIMENTS WITH PLASTIC MATERIALS.** What excites you about shoes? **IT'S THE WAY IN WHICH THE SHOE INTERACTS WITH THE BODY LANGUAGE AND MOVEMENT OF THE PERSON, LIKE A CHOREOGRAPHED DANCE.** What makes your work different from others? **WE ARE ALL NATURALLY DIFFERENT.** What do you consider your most innovative design so far? **MELISSA ULTRA GIRL.** Can you tell us something about the design process? **EACH DESIGN HAS ITS OWN DESIGN PROCESS BASED ON THE SCENARIO AND THE PERSON CHOSEN. THERE IS DESIGN OF THE DESIGN PROCESS.** Which stage do you find the most gratifying? **SEEING THE WHOLE TEAM, CO-CREATING FOR A CAUSE TO CHANGE THE WORLD. ALSO THE END, CELEBRATING THE COMPLETION OF THE PROJECT.** Can you name a person or movement that has influenced you as a designer? **THOMAS EDISON.** If you had to choose one colour and one material to make an important piece, what would they be? **TRANSPARENT PLASTIC.** What role does your work play in your life? **THE KEY IS TO TRY NOT SEPARATE WORK FROM VACATION AND SEE IT ALL AS LIFE.** What is vulgar to you and what elegant? **VULGARITY AND ELEGANCE ARE RELATIVE CONCEPTS.** What does beauty mean for you? **BE SIMPLE.**

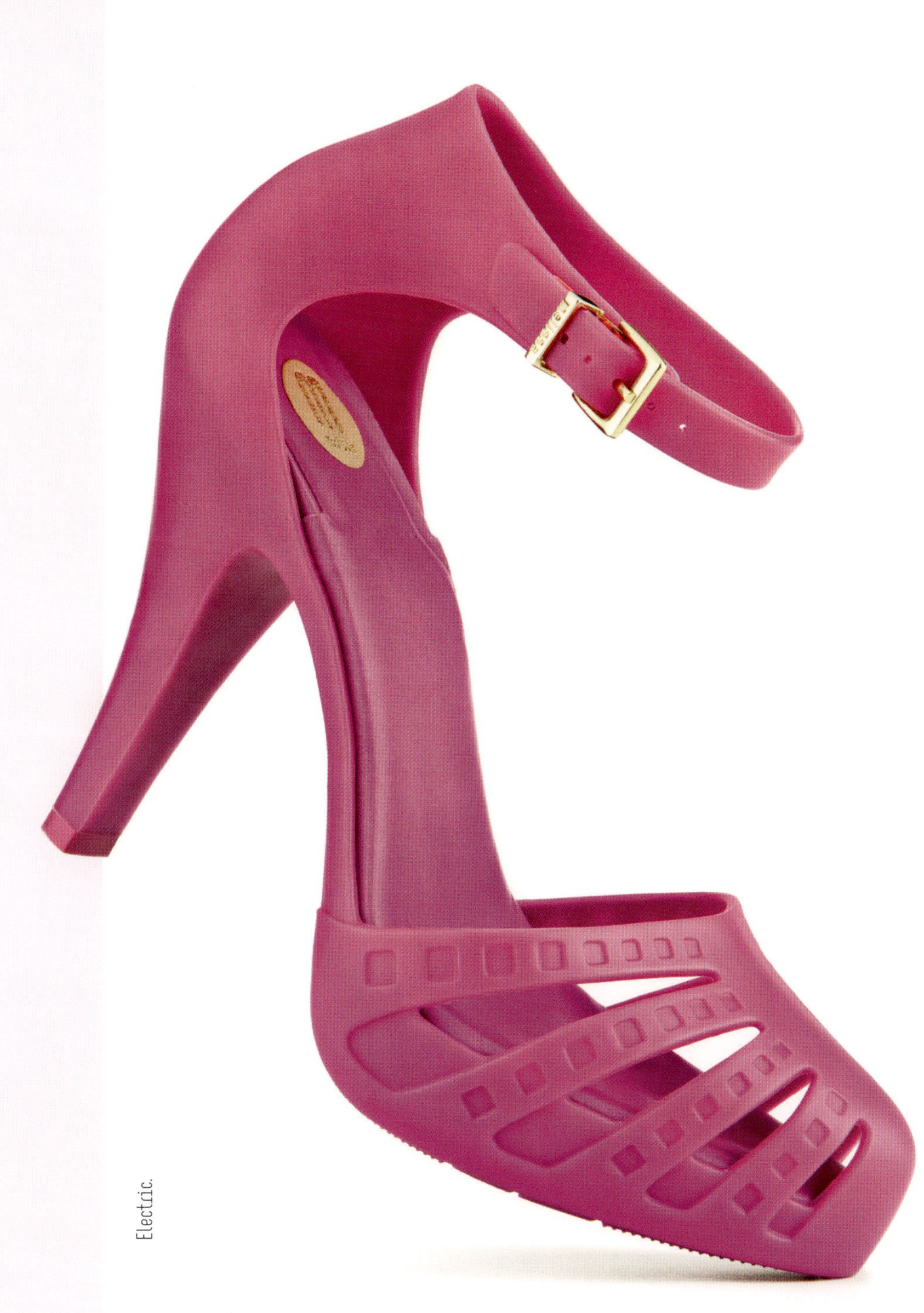

Electric.

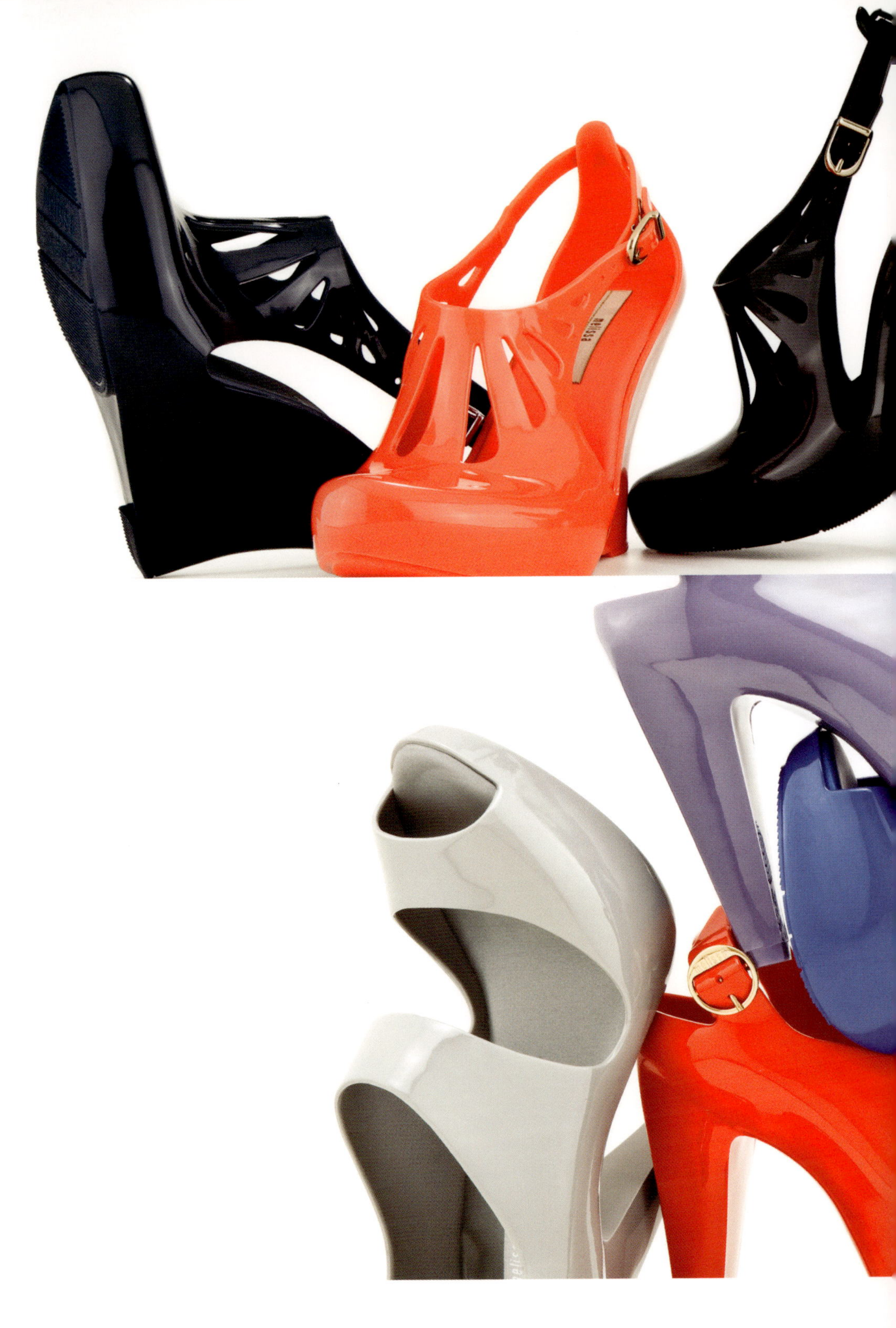

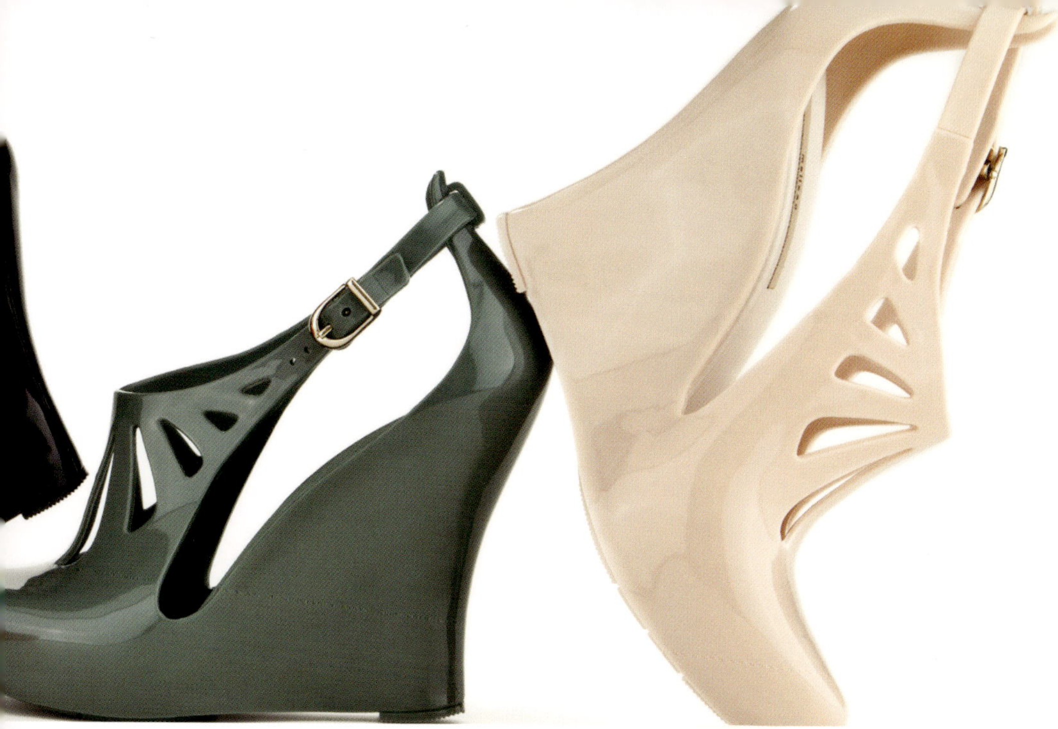

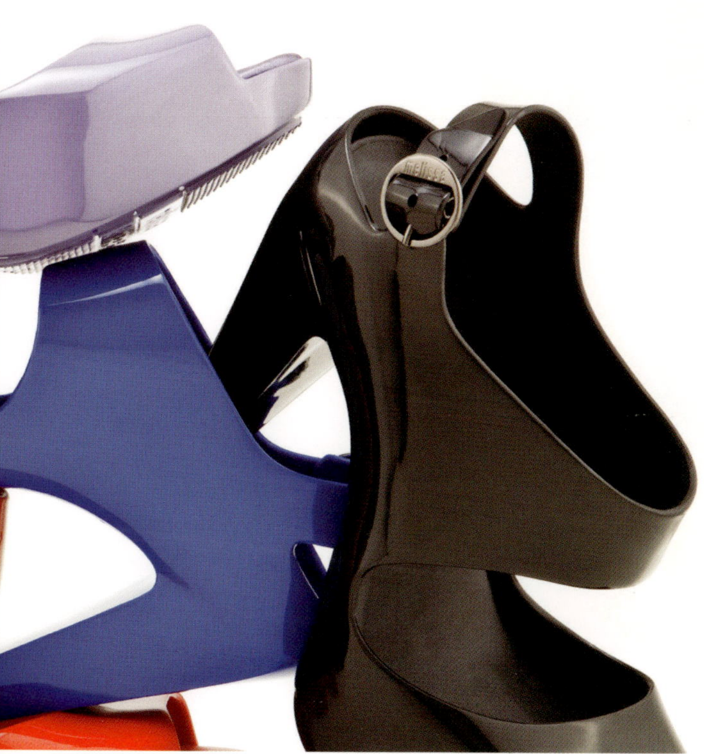

Top: Cristal. Bottom: Amazonas.

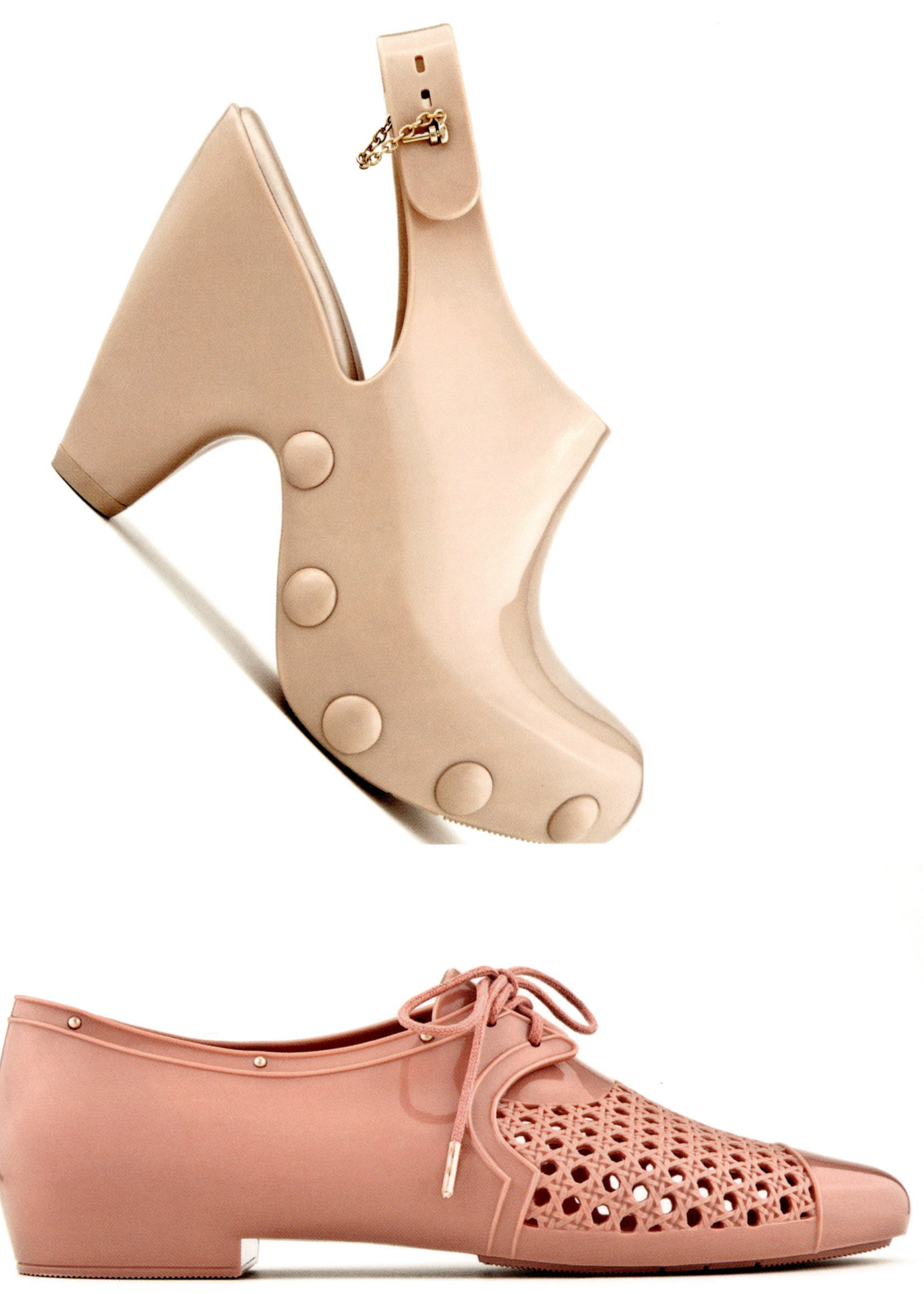

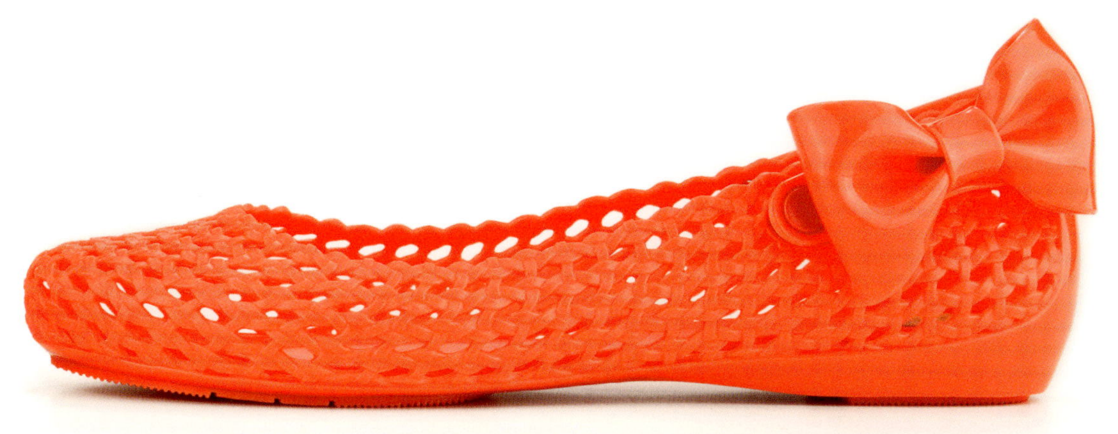

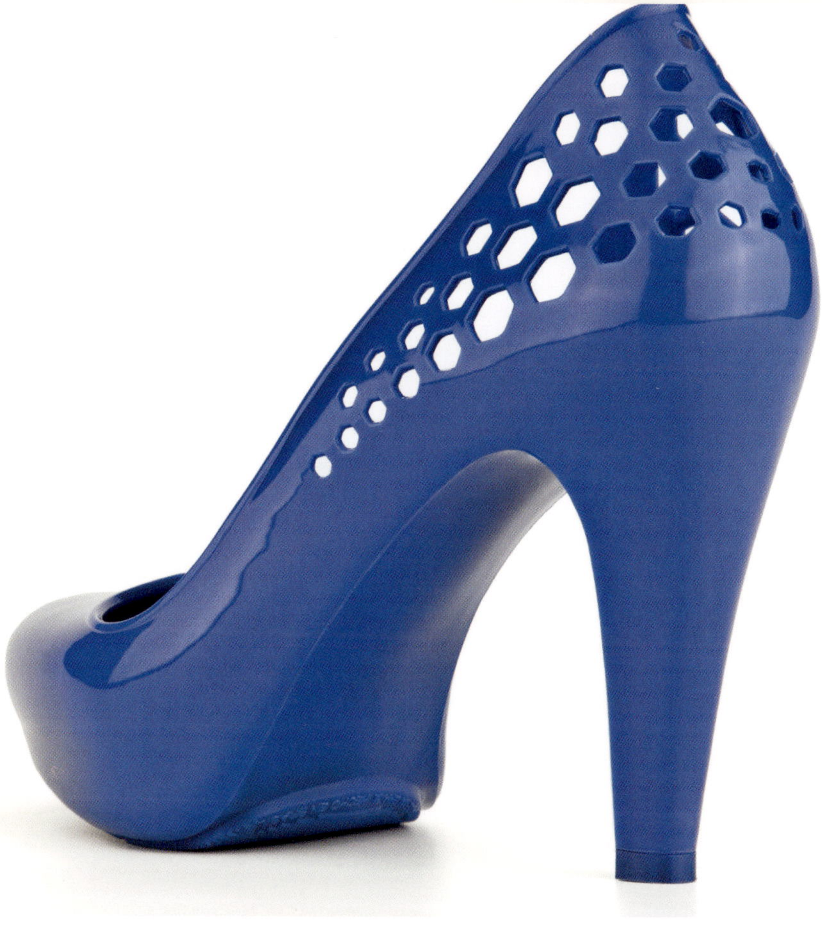

Previous page top: Loving. Bottom: Enjoying. This page top: Galactic. Bottom: Eagle.

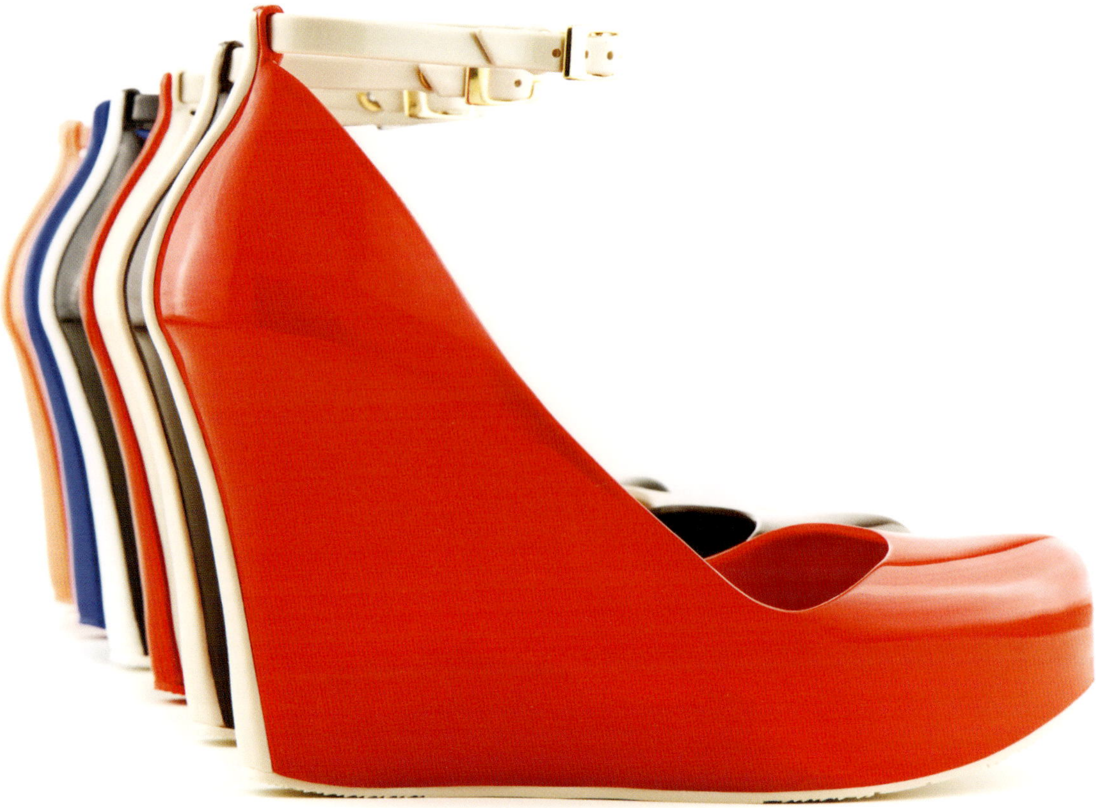

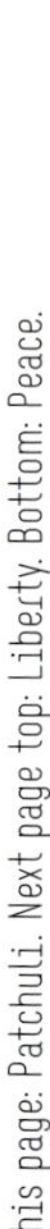

This page: Patchuli. Next page top: Liberty. Bottom: Peace.

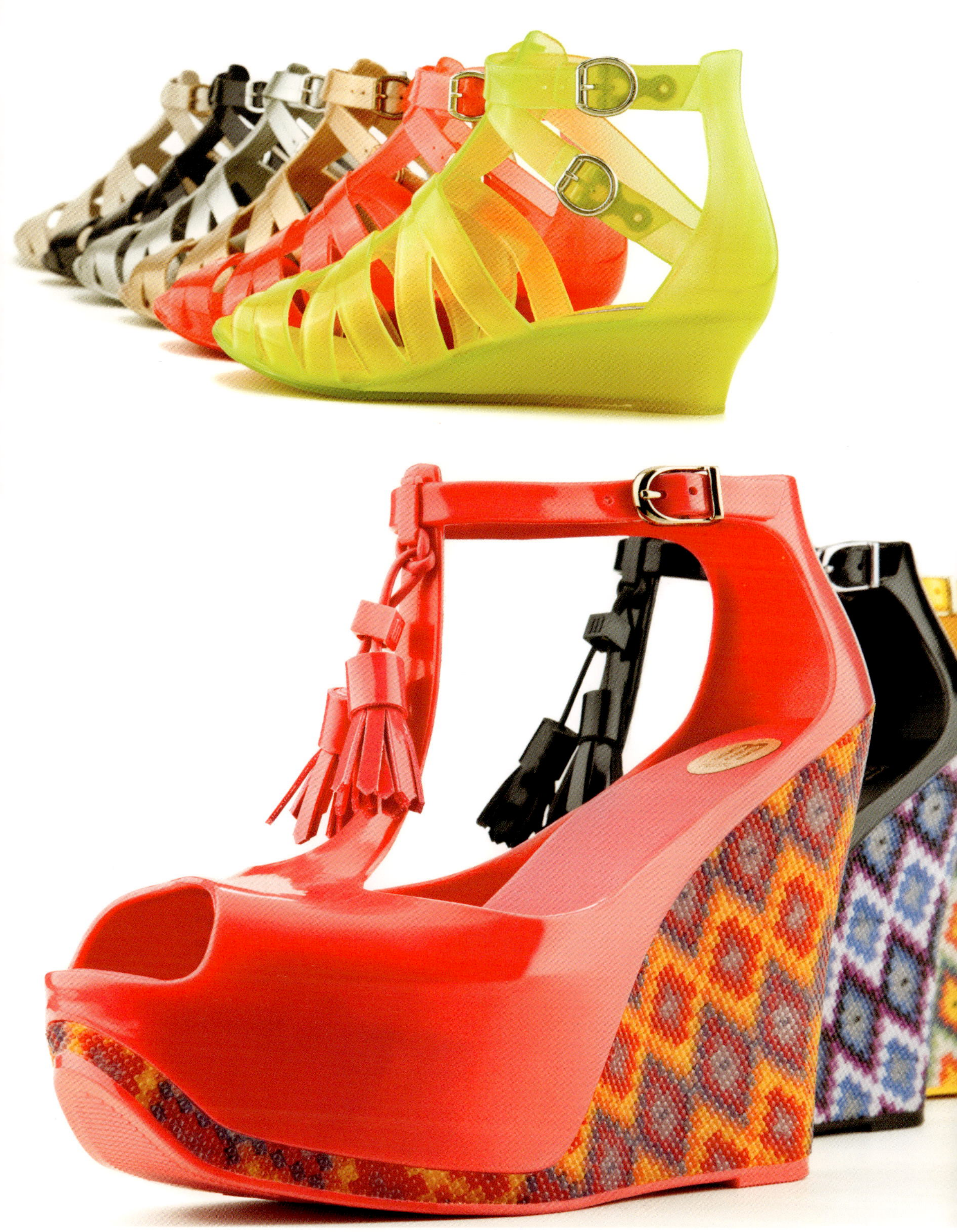

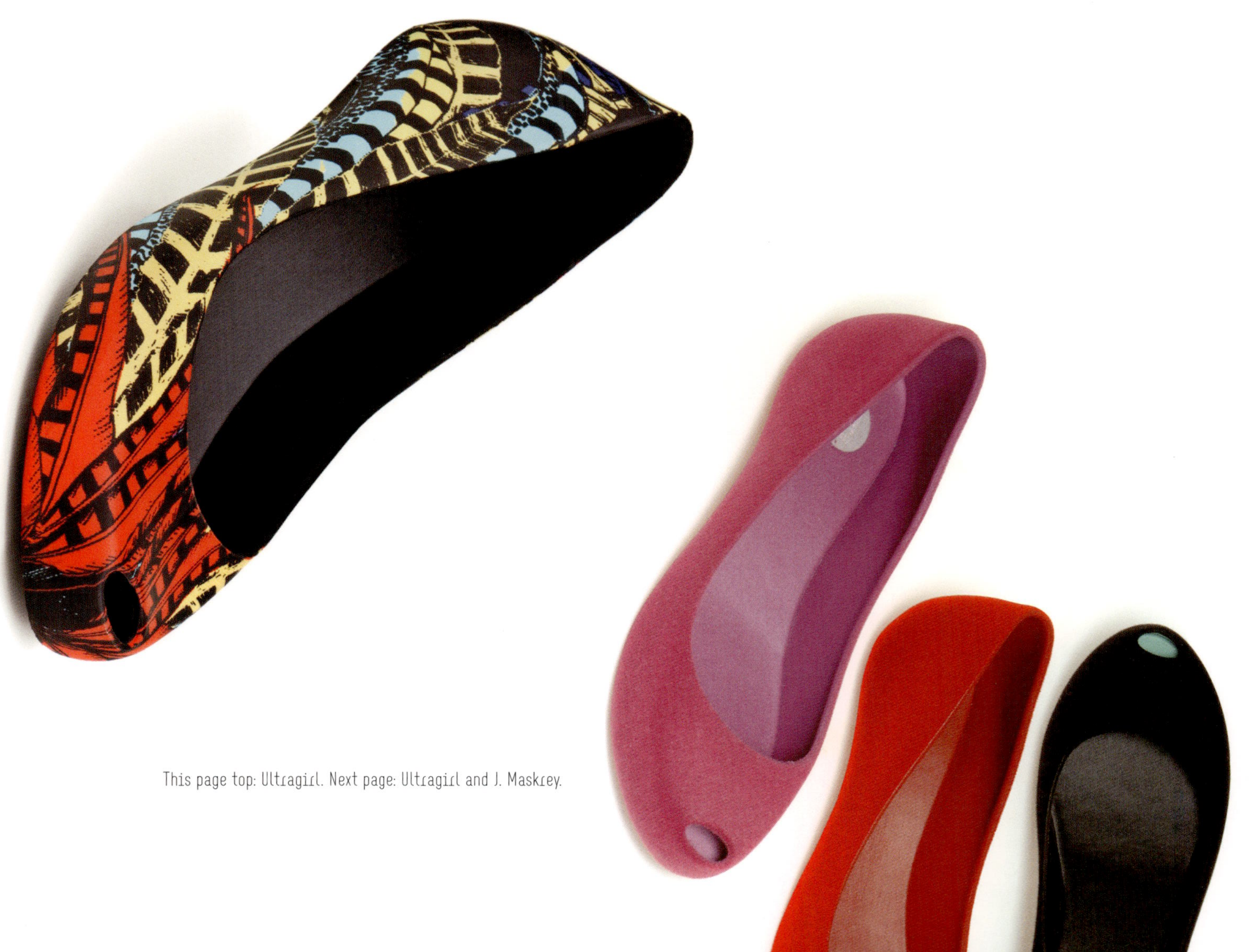

This page top: Ultragirl. Next page: Ultragirl and J. Maskrey.

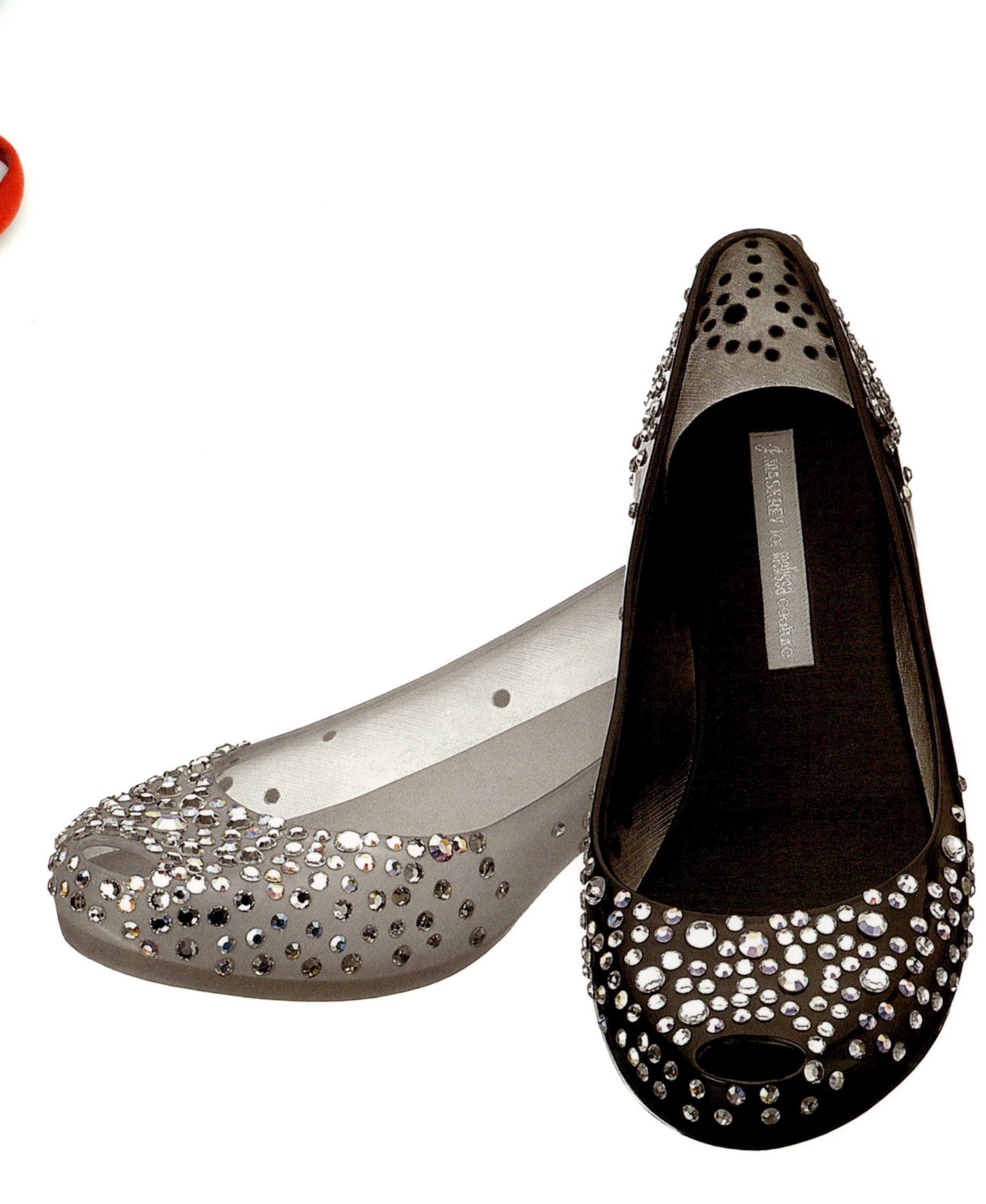

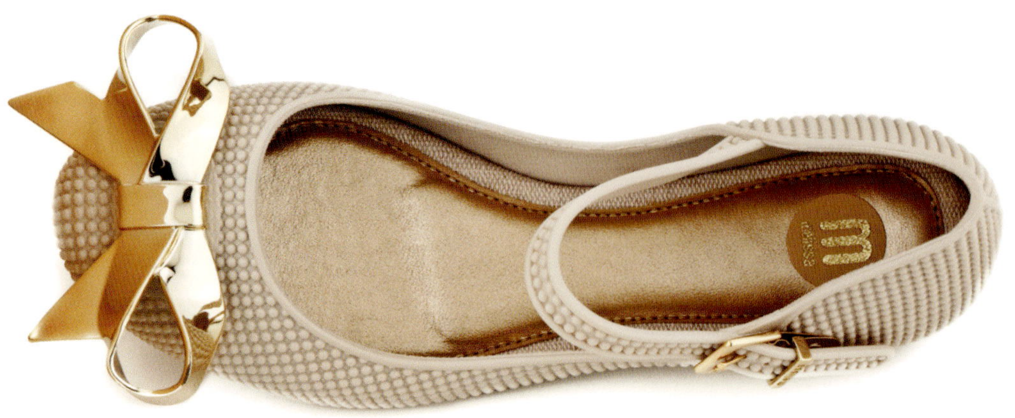

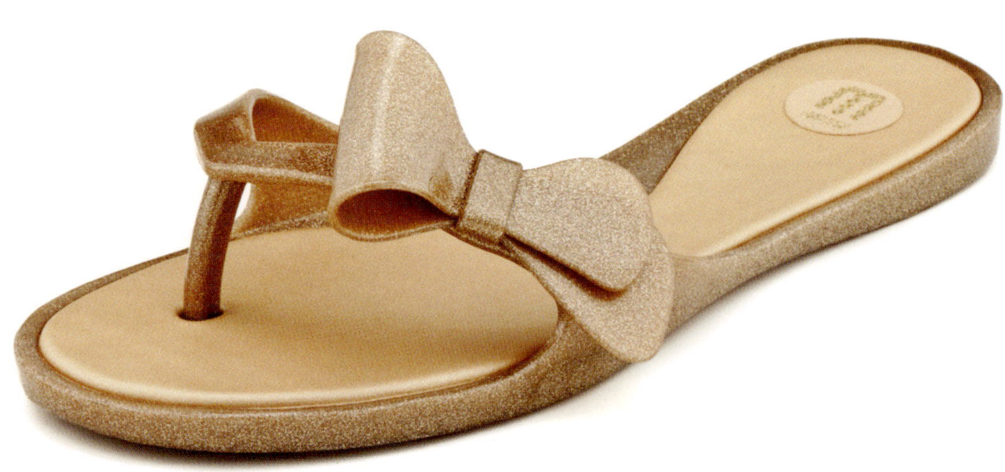

Previous page top: Hoop. Bottom: Juta. This page: Wind.

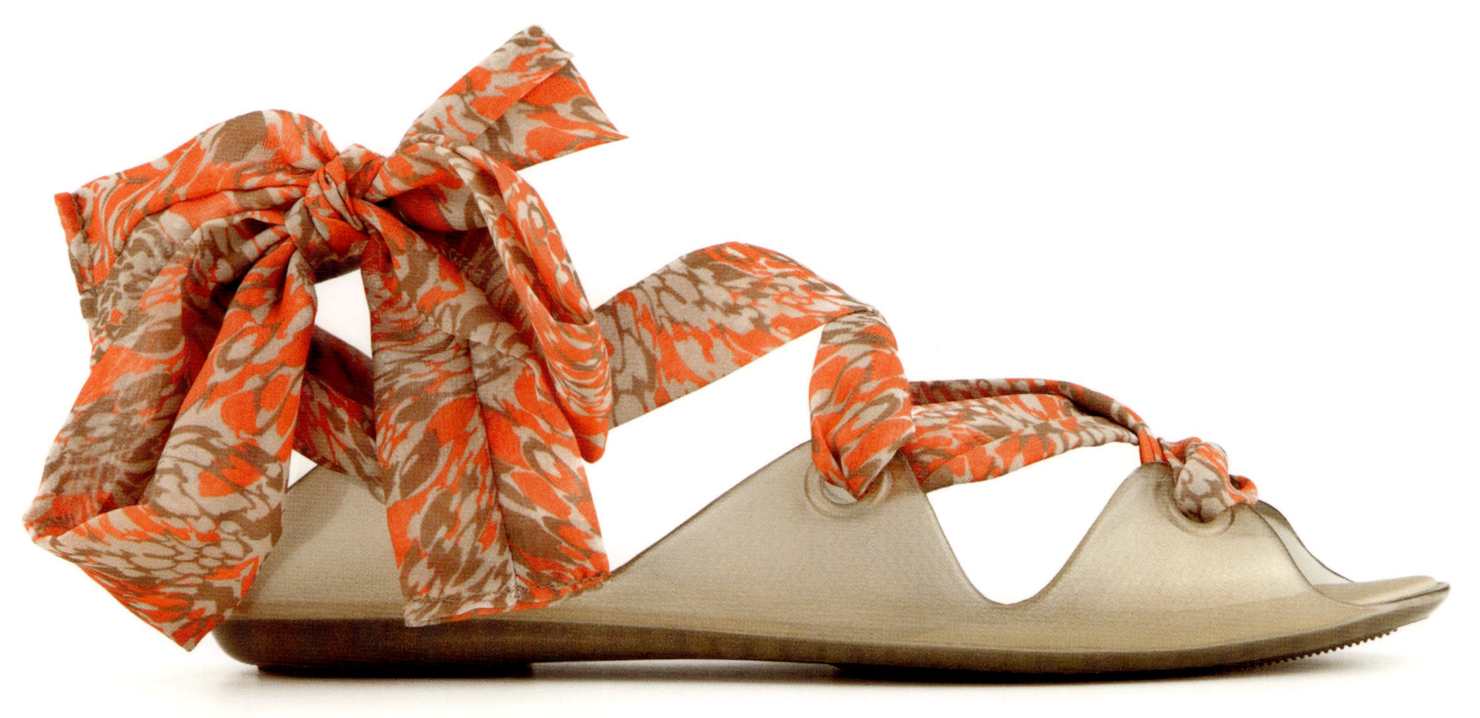

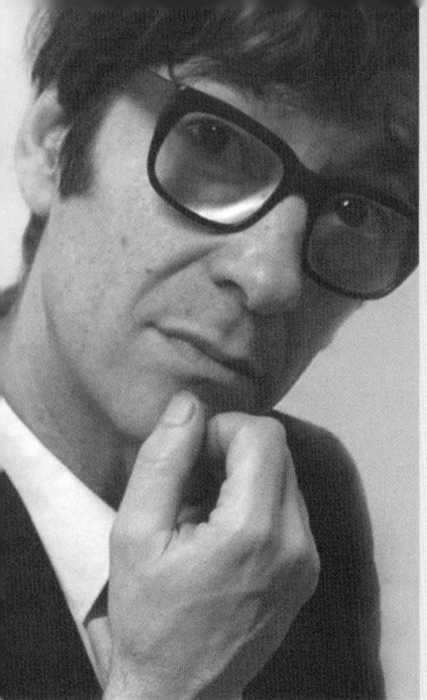

MIGUEL MUÑOZ WILSON, MUNOZ VRANDECIC

Please introduce yourself **I'M MIGUEL MUÑOZ WILSON. I WAS BORN IN CHILE AND AM NOW BASED IN BARCELONA.** How did you get started? **AFTER STUDYING IN CHILE, I MOVED TO MADRID TO CONTINUE STUDYING FINE ART, MAJORING IN SCULPTURE. I WORKED AS A SCULPTOR FOR MANY YEARS AND HAVE ALWAYS SEEN THE WORLD IN 3D. HOWEVER WITH SCULPTURE I FELT I WASN'T ABLE TO MEET MY OWN EXPECTATIONS SO I VENTURED INTO FASHION WHERE I FOUND A WAY TO EXPRESS THINGS THREE DIMENSIONALLY THROUGH MY SHOES, JEWELLERY AND CLOTHES. MY PIECES HAVE A SCULPTURAL CHARACTER.** What is your work about? **MY BRAND IS AN INDEPENDENT ONE. EACH PIECE IS HAND CRAFTED AND HANDLED WITH SENSIBILITY. I HAVE A SMALL NUMBER OF STAFF WORKING WITH ME. I LIKE TEACHING THEM WHAT I'VE LEARNED. IT IS A LONG SPIRITUAL PROCESS. WE WORK VERY LONG HOURS AND YOU REALLY HAVE TO LOVE IT IN ORDER TO DO IT.** What do you consider your most innovative design so far? **IN 2004 WHEN I GOT STARTED WITH MY COMPANY MUÑOZ VRANDECIC, I SHOWED MY FIRST COLLECTION AT L'ECLAIREUR STORE IN PARIS. THE COLLECTION WAS TOTALLY COUTURE, USING NATURAL TANNED LEATHER, SCULPTED WOOD HEELS AND CHISELLED METALS. NO ONE HAD MADE THESE SHOES BEFORE. IT WAS MY LITTLE INNOVATION.** Can you tell us something about the design process? **EACH COLLECTION IS LIKE A LITTLE POEM. I MAKE OBJECTS THAT LAST FOREVER, MADE BY PEOPLE RATHER THAN MACHINES. I DIG INTO ABANDONED PLACES — THE ANTHROPOLOGY OF FASHION.** Which stage of the creative process do you find the most gratifying? **THE MOST GRATIFYING IS WHEN I FINISH A CREATION AND THE LEAST GRATIFYING IS WHEN THIS CREATION LEAVES. THIS PROCESS IS A BIT EPHEMERAL. FORTUNATELY THERE IS ALWAYS THE BEGINNING OF THE NEXT CYCLE.** Who or what has influenced your development as an artist? **THE NINETEENTH CENTURY TRANSITION BETWEEN THE MAN AND THE MACHINE. ISAMU NOGUCHI HAS INSPIRED ME ARTISTICALLY. I ADMIRE FERRAGAMO'S WORK.** If you had to choose one colour and one material to make an important piece, what would they be? **BLACK AND GOLD** What do you consider vulgar and what elegant? **FOR ME VULGAR IS LACK OF LOVE AND WHAT COMES OUT OF THIS. ELEGANT IS A BALENCIAGA DRESS.** What does beauty mean for you? **FOR ME BEAUTY IS MY DAUGHTER JUANA WITH HER TEN MONTHS OF LIFE.**

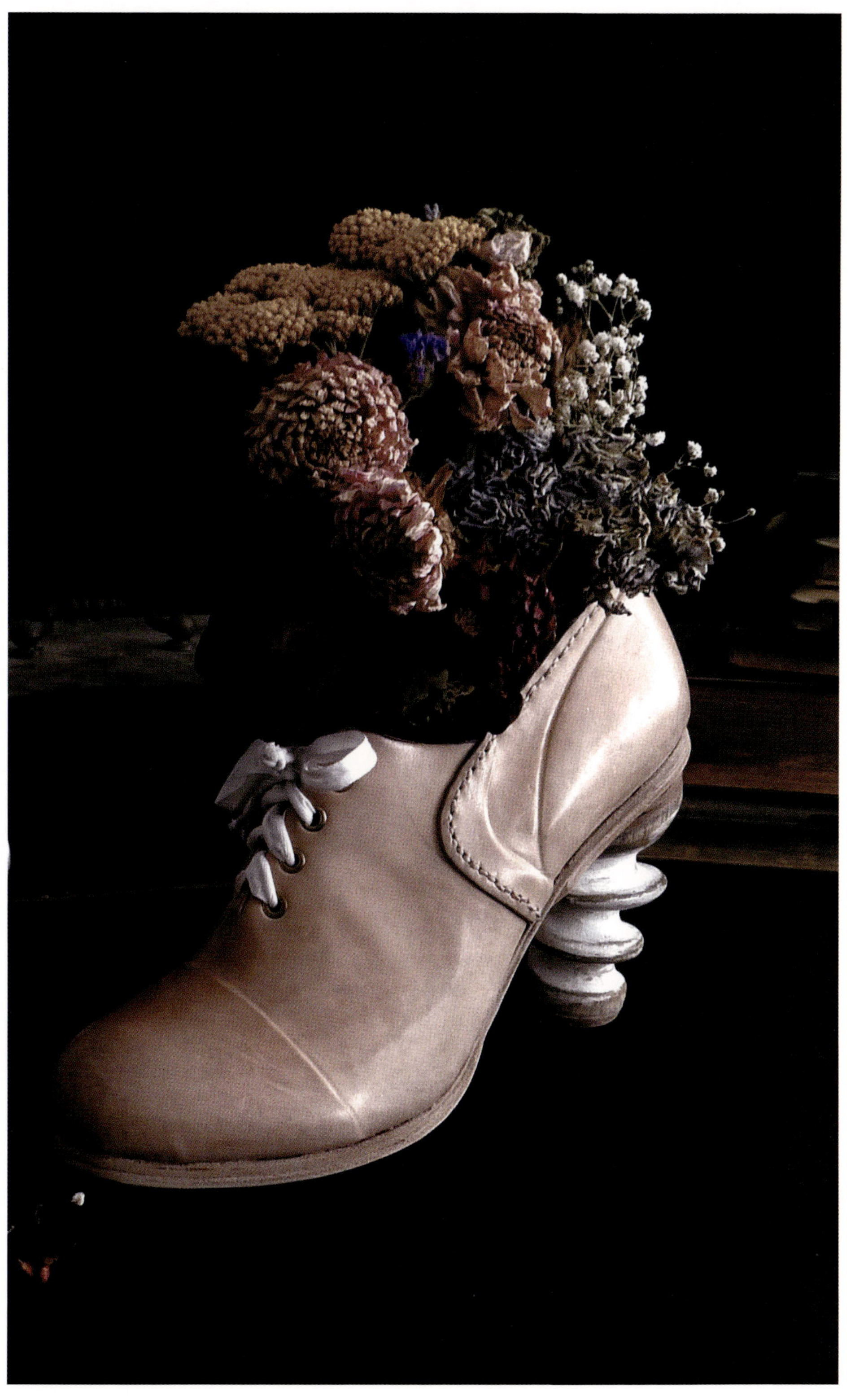

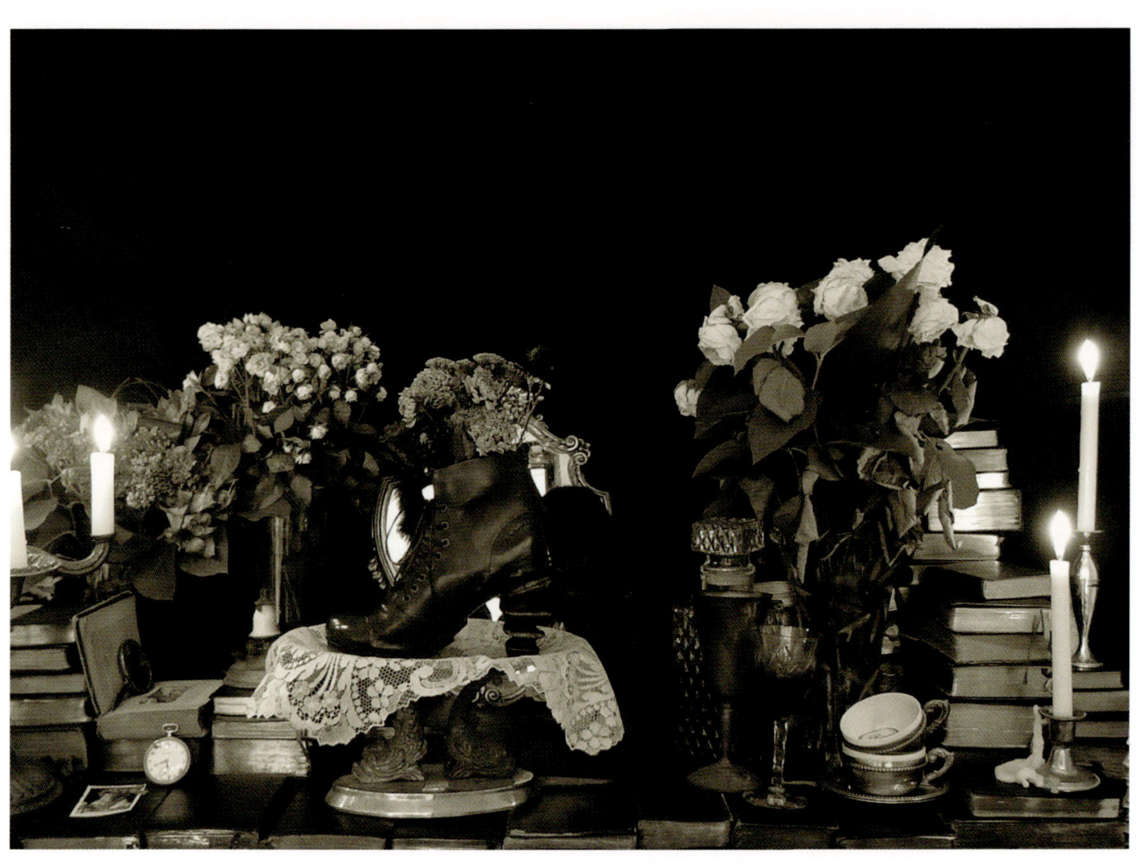

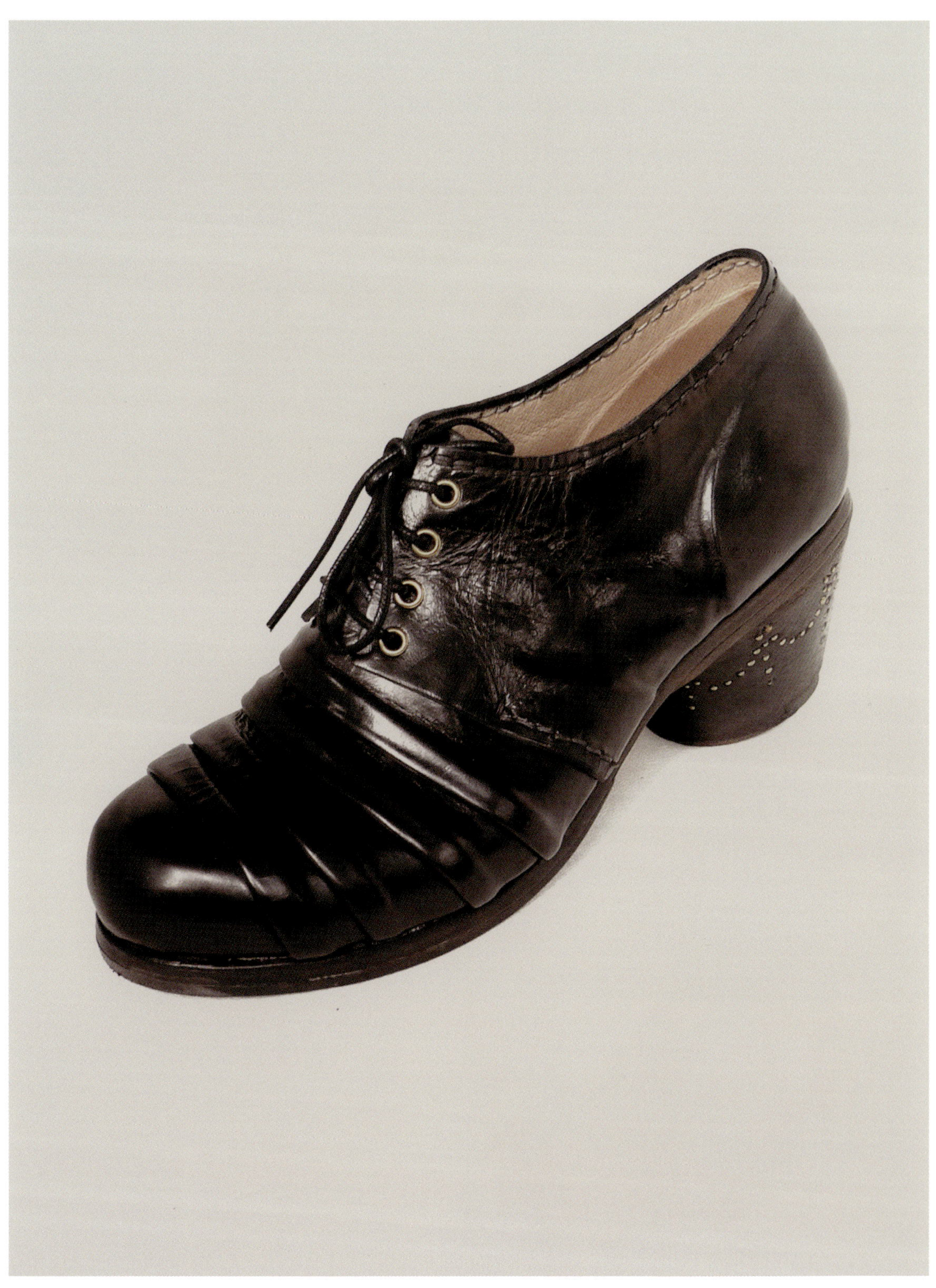

 MUNOZ VRANDECIC

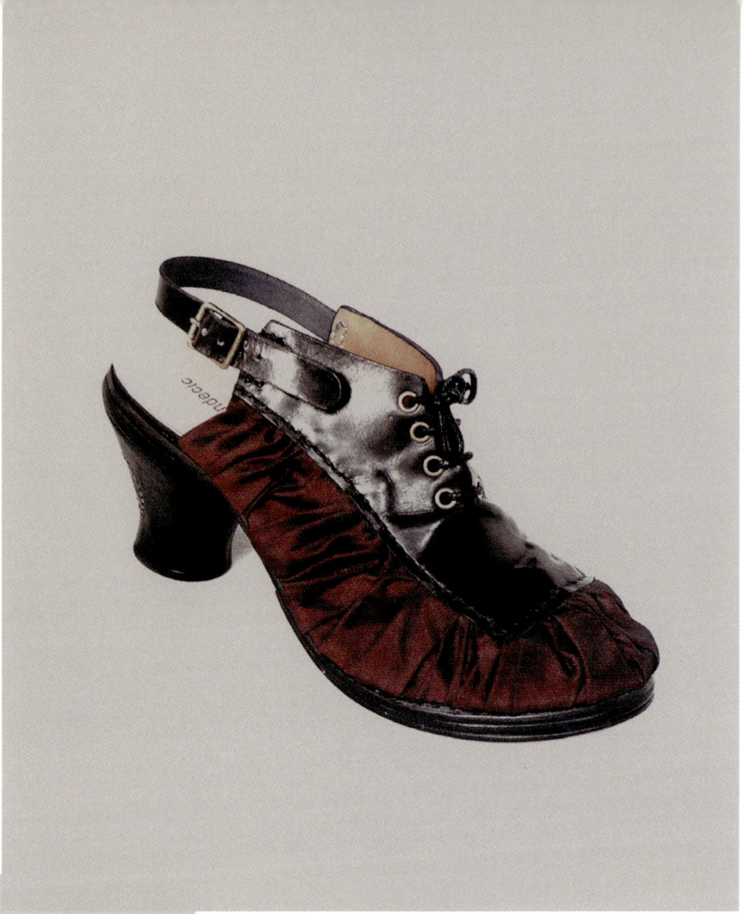

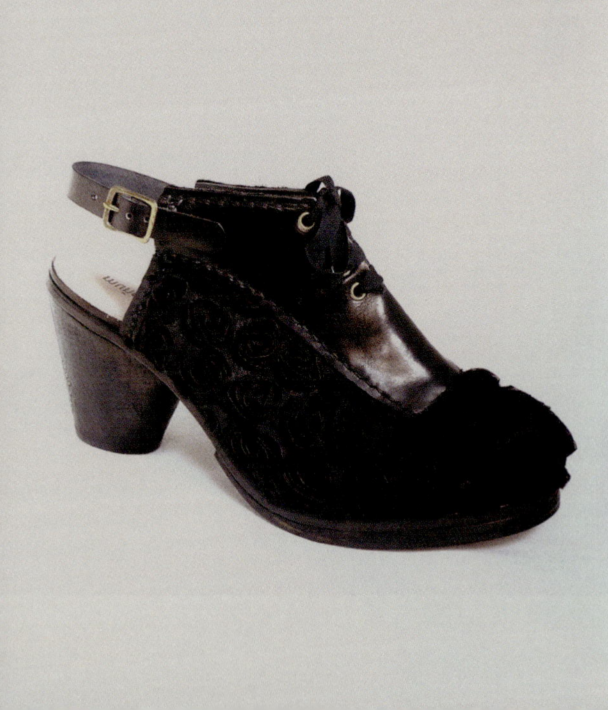

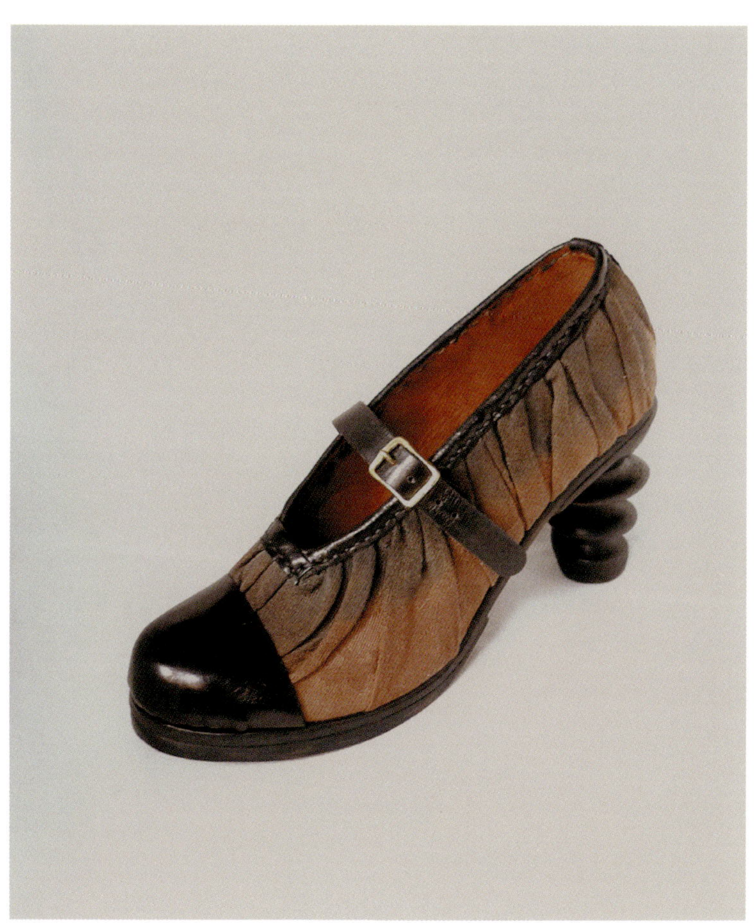

MUNOZ VRANDECIC

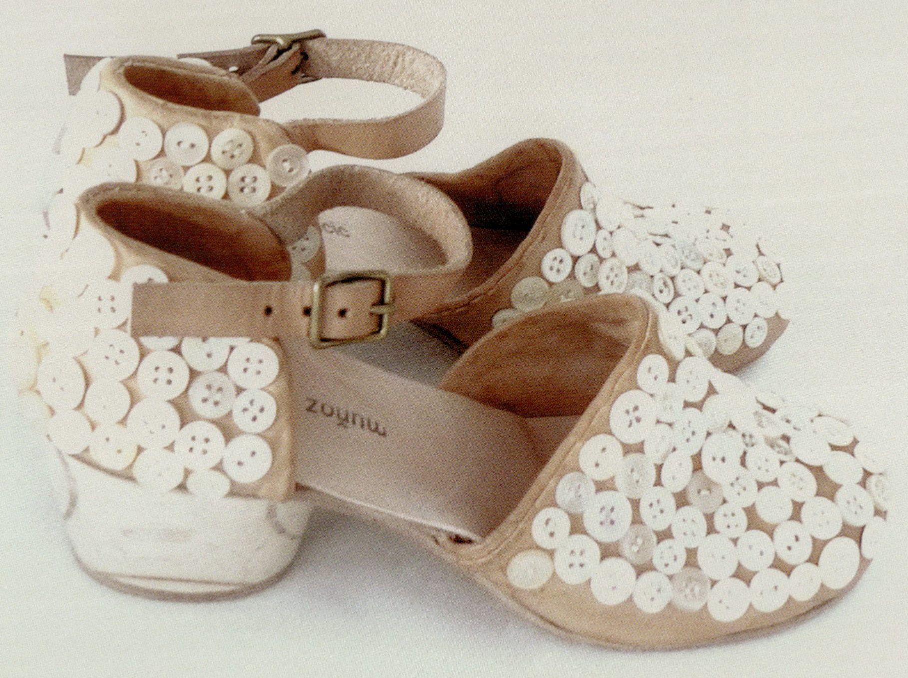
muñoz

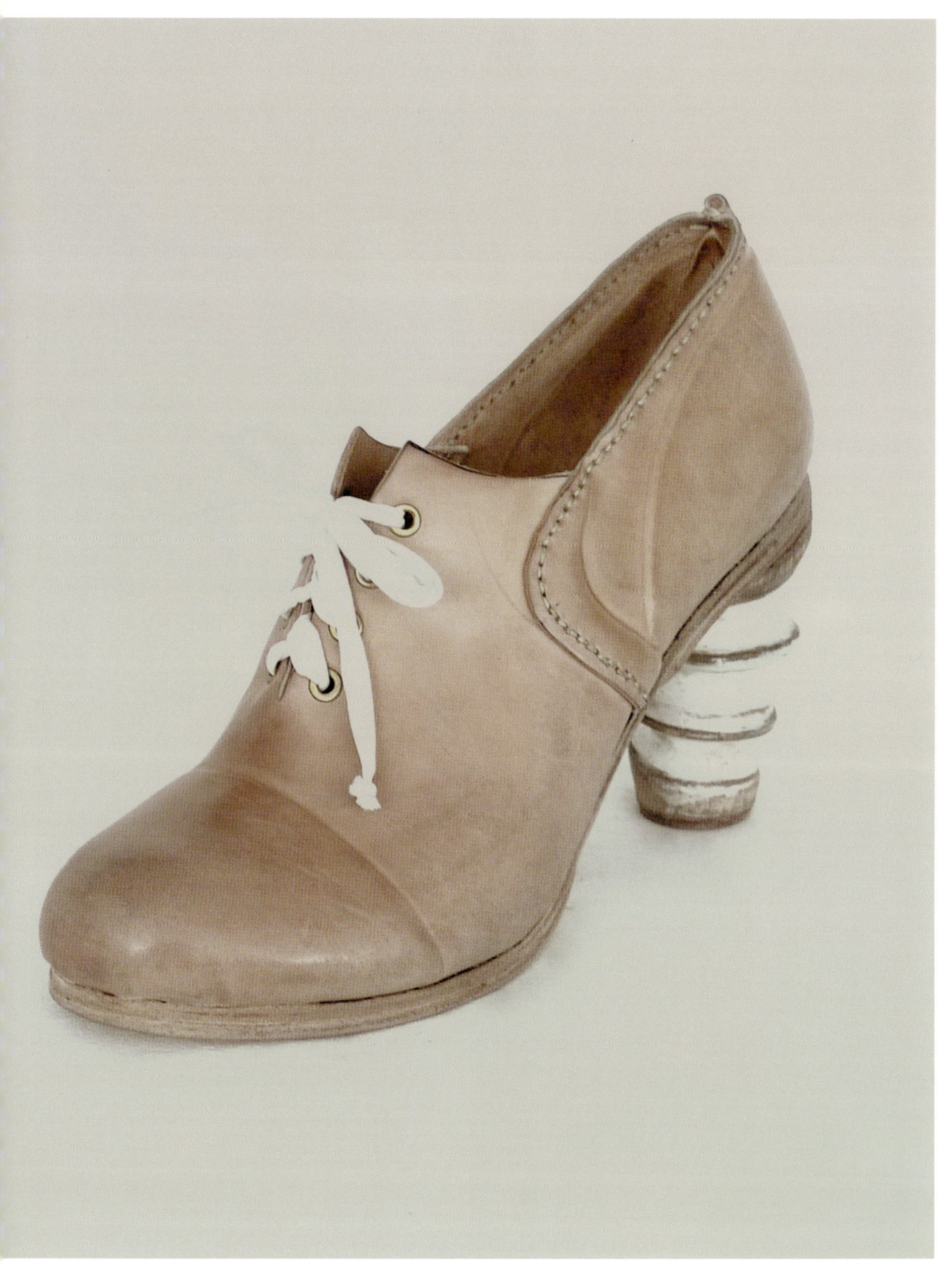

 MUNOZ VRANDECIC

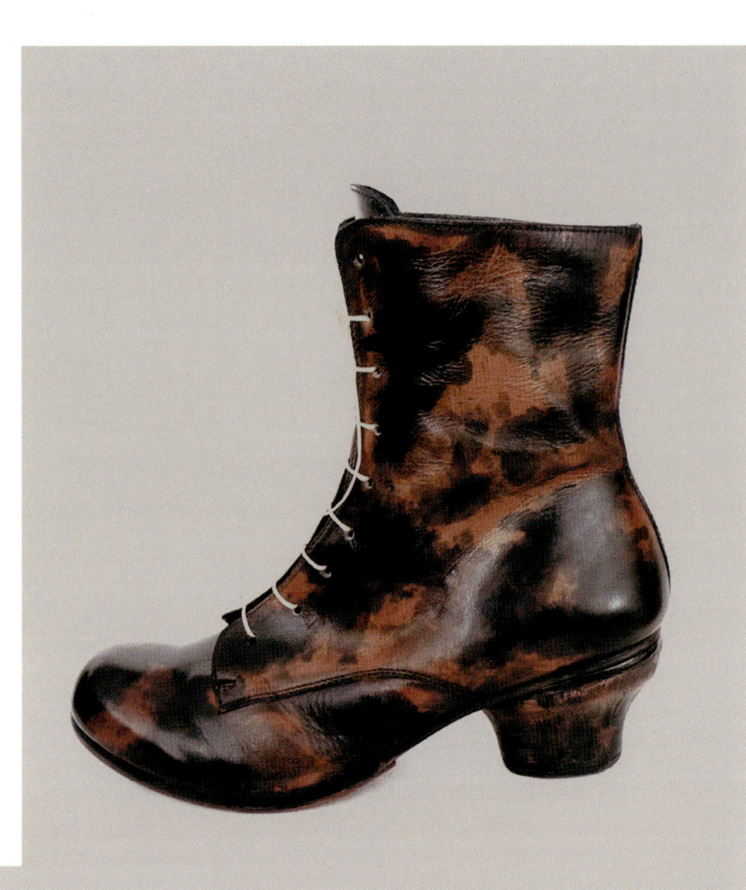

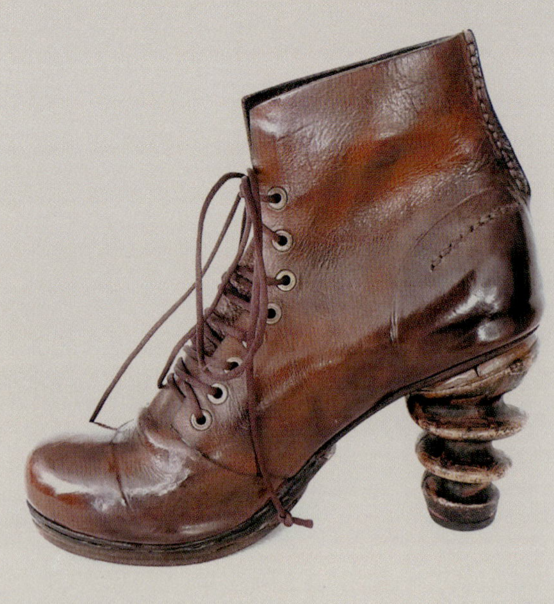

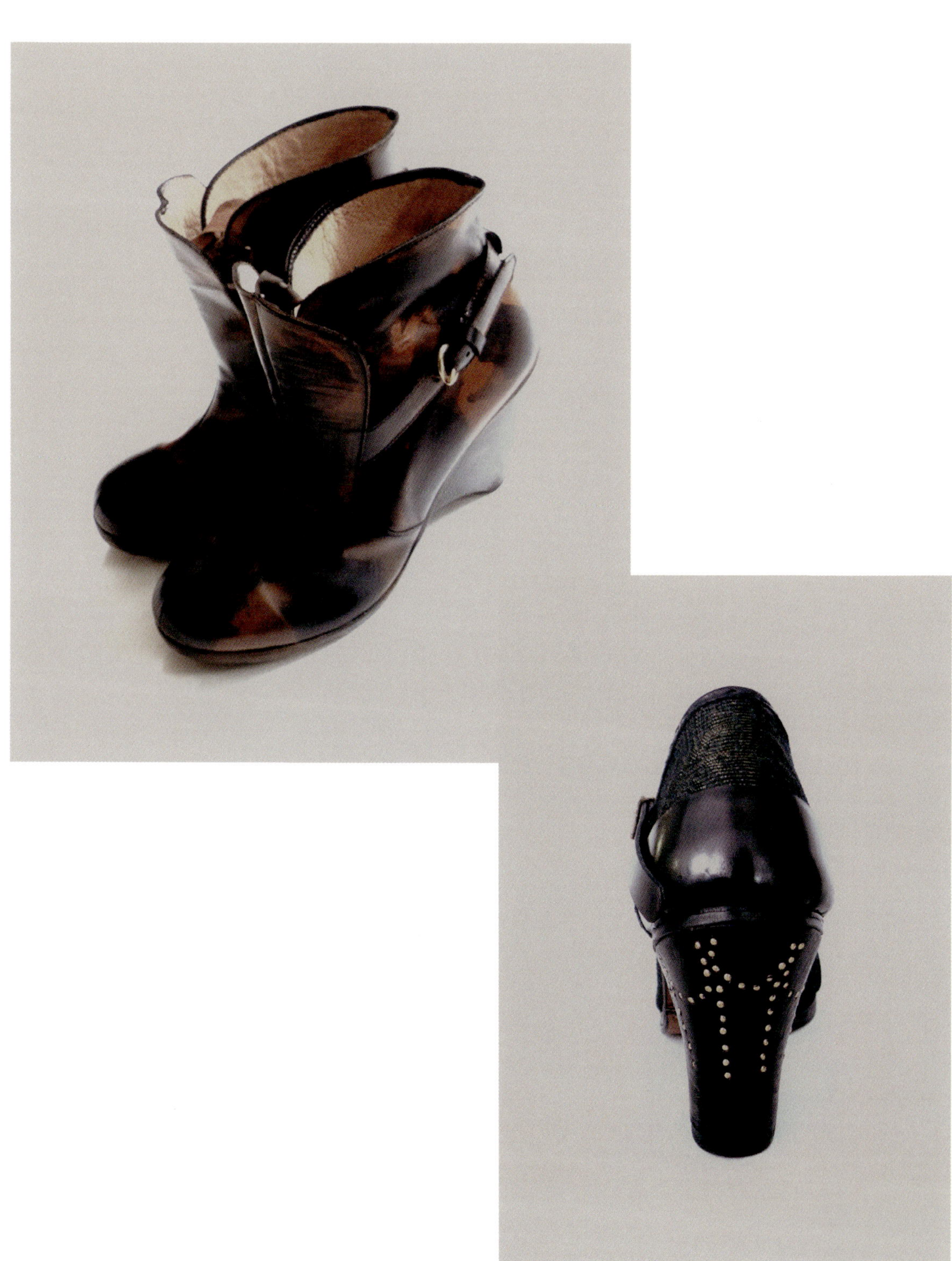

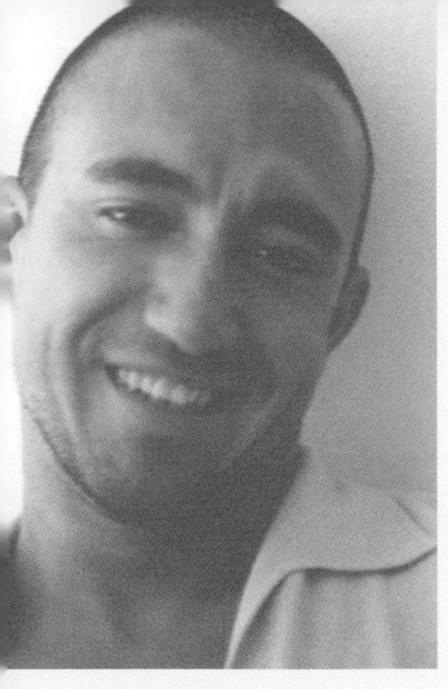

ENRIQUE CORBI, N.D.C. MADE BY HAND

How did you get started? **I WAS BORN AND RAISED IN SOUTH-EASTERN SPAIN WHICH IS FAMOUS FOR ITS SHOEMAKING TRADITION. AS A TEENAGER I WORKED AFTER SCHOOL AND IN MY SUMMER HOLIDAYS AT LOCAL SHOE FACTORIES, NOT ONLY TO EARN A FEW EXTRA DOLLARS BUT BECAUSE I FOUND THE WHOLE PROCESS OF SHOE MAKING FASCINATING. IN MY EARLY TWENTIES I WAS OFFERED A GREAT JOB WORKING FOR A MAJOR SHOE CORPORATION WHICH MOVED ME TO LONDON. IT WAS THERE THAT I STUDIED FASHION ACCESSORIES DESIGN AND FASHION AND TEXTILES AT THE ROYAL COLLEGE OF ART. THIS WAS ALSO WHERE I MET MY FUTURE N.D.C. BUSINESS PARTNER ARNAUD ZANNIER.** What is your work about? **SIMPLICITY, ORIGINALITY, TRADITION AND KNOW HOW. I MAKE SHOES THAT MYSELF, MY FRIENDS AND FAMILY WOULD LIKE TO WEAR.** What do you consider your most innovative design so far? **THIS WOULD HAVE TO BE THE ALITHIA BOOT WHICH WAS CREATED BACK IN 2002 AND HAS BEEN TALKED ABOUT AND ENDLESSLY COPIED EVER SINCE. WHEN DESIGNING THE ALITHIA, OUR OBJECTIVE WAS TO RETHINK THE BOAT SHOE AND IMPROVE ITS FUNCTION WITHOUT MAKING IT TOO COMPLICATED OR OVER DESIGNED. THE RESULT WAS A UNIQUE BOAT SHOE WITH A MOCCASIN/SANDWICH CONSTRUCTION NEVER SEEN BEFORE ON THE MARKET. IT HAD THE LOOK OF A BOAT SHOE WITH THE COMFORT OF A SLIPPER.** Tell us something about the design process. **ONCE I HAVE AN IDEA FOR A FAMILY OF SHOES, I START DOING SOME QUICK SKETCHES BY HAND THEN DRAW IT ON THE COMPUTER. SOMETIMES THE DESIGN IS READY TO GO TO THE PATTERN MAKER THE SAME DAY, SOMETIMES I LIKE TO HANG THE DRAWING ON THE WALL BESIDE MY COMPUTER AND LET IT SETTLE FOR A WHILE. I THEN COME BACK TO IT TO PERFECT IT.** What is the most gratifying part of your job? **TO SEE SOMETHING THAT WAS PREVIOUSLY A TWO DIMENSIONAL DRAWING BECOME SOMETHING WITH A LIFE OF ITS OWN IS A GREAT THING. IT IS ALSO EXTREMELY GRATIFYING TO SEE PEOPLE WEARING YOUR SHOES AND HUMBLING TO KNOW THAT THEY APPRECIATED THE IDEA ENOUGH TO BUY THEM.** Who or what has played a part in your development as an artist? **JOAN MANUEL SERRAT, GUSTAVO ADOLFO BÉCQUER, HENRY MOORE AND FRANK LLOYD WRIGHT. HOWEVER, IT IS THE PEOPLE I COME ACROSS IN EVERYDAY LIFE WHO HAVE INFLUENCED ME THE MOST.** What are your thoughts on the culture of quick consumption and over-commercialisation? **A GOOD SHOE IS A WORK OF ART AND NOT SIMPLY A COMMODITY TO GENERATE PROFITS FROM. OUR SHOES ARE MADE BY GOOD PEOPLE WHO ARE PASSIONATE ABOUT WHAT THEY DO DESPITE PROFIT. A GOOD SHOE WILL LIVE WITH YOU, PROTECT YOU AND HELP PROJECT A MAGNIFIED IMAGE OF THE REAL YOU.** How do you view the current state of your profession in general? **IT IS BOTH INTERESTING AND CHALLENGING WORKING IN THE DIFFICULT TIMES OF A FINANCIAL CRISIS. BUYERS ARE PURCHASING VERY CAREFULLY. WE HAVE STAYED TRUE TO OURSELVES INSTEAD OF TRYING TO SOURCE CHEAPER MATERIALS AND LABOUR LIKE MANY OTHER BRANDS.**

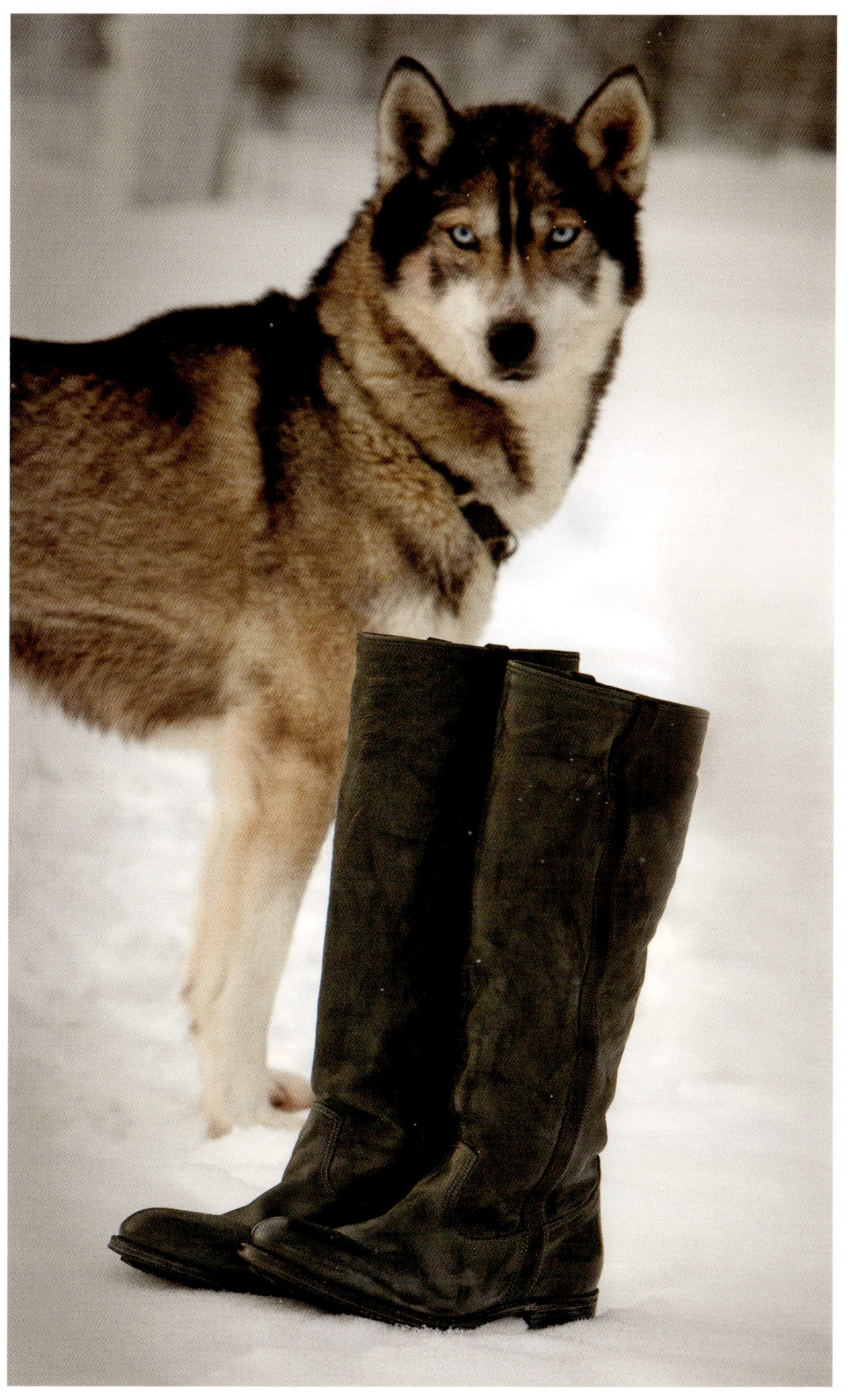

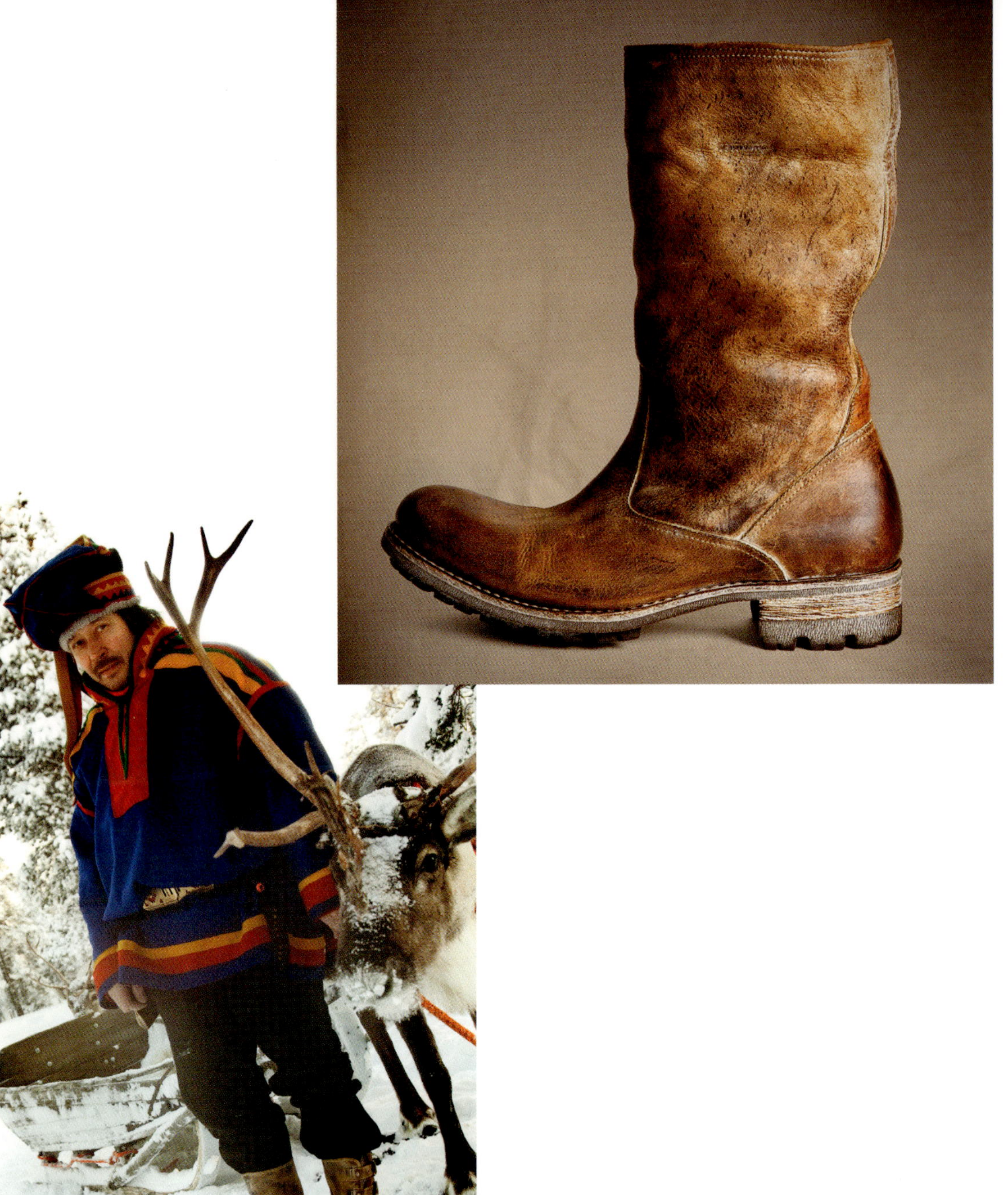

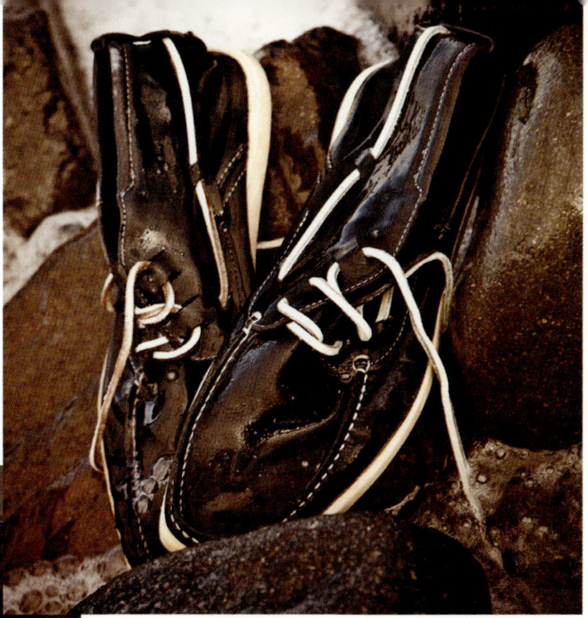

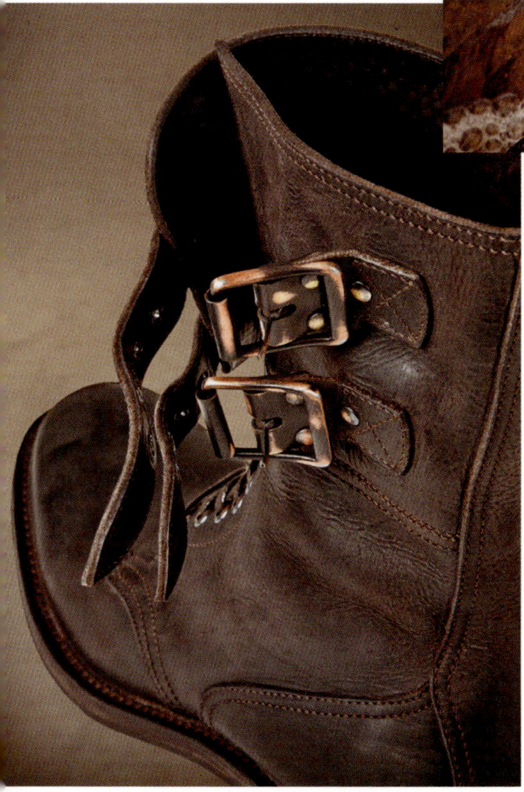

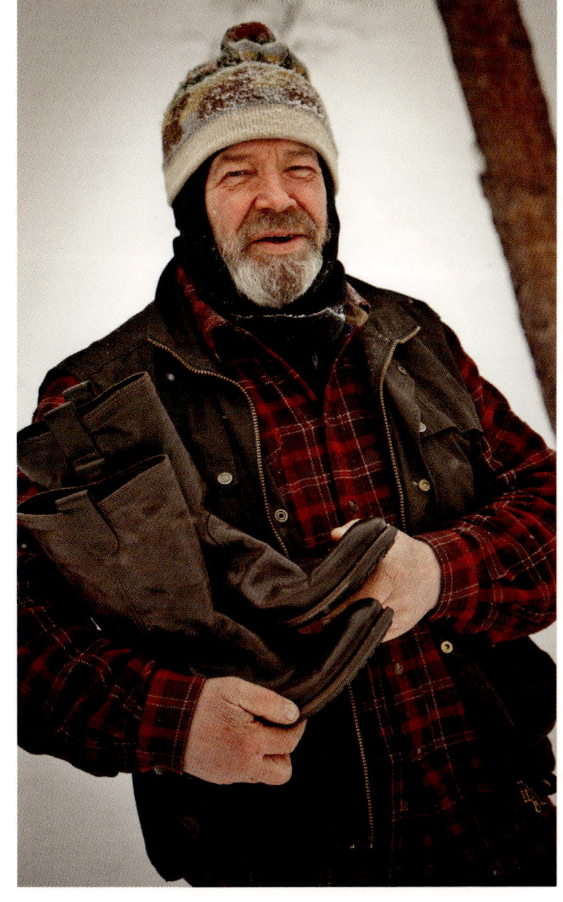

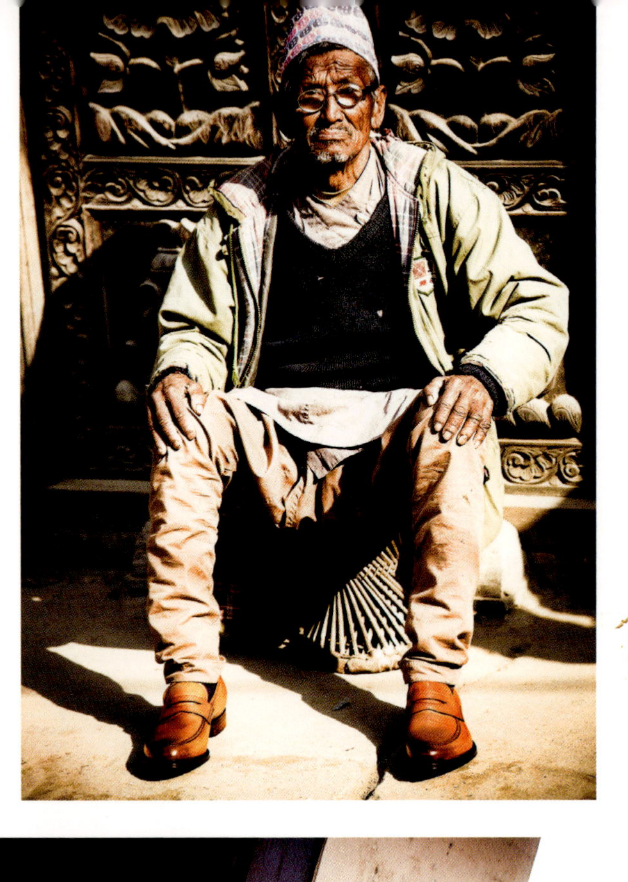

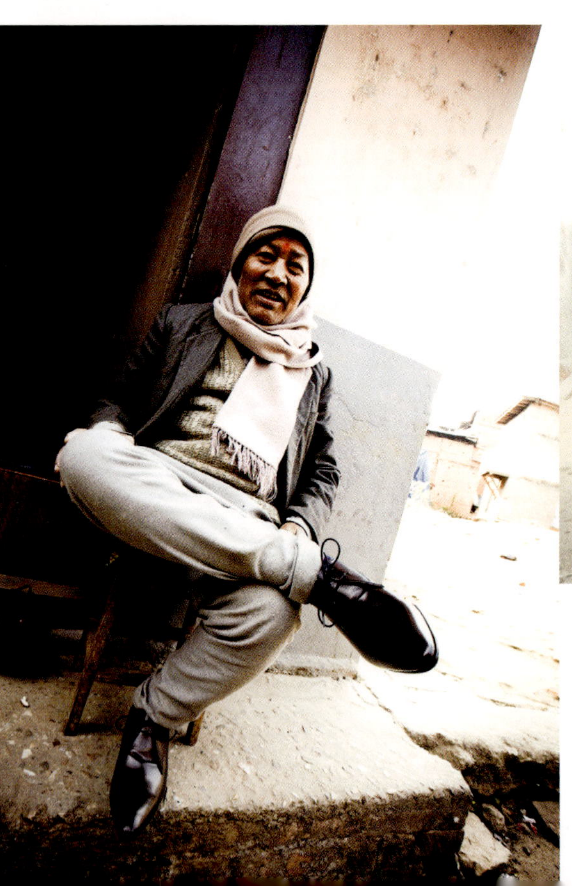

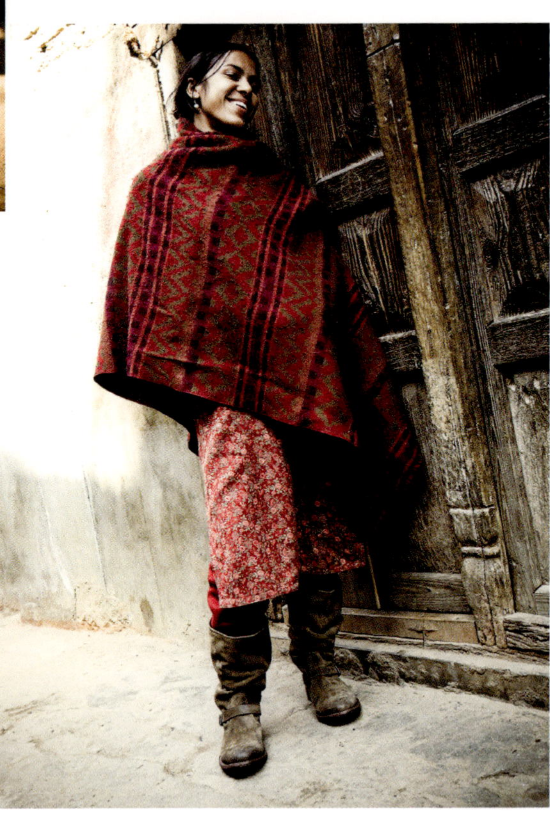

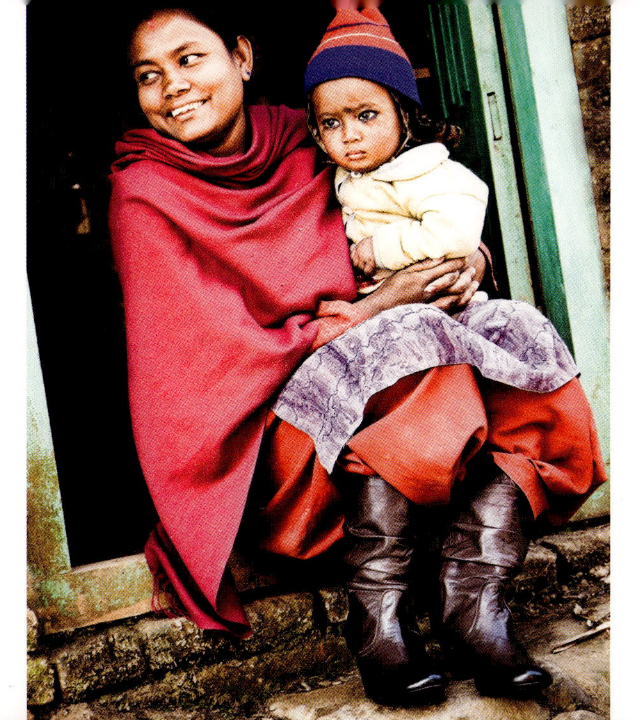

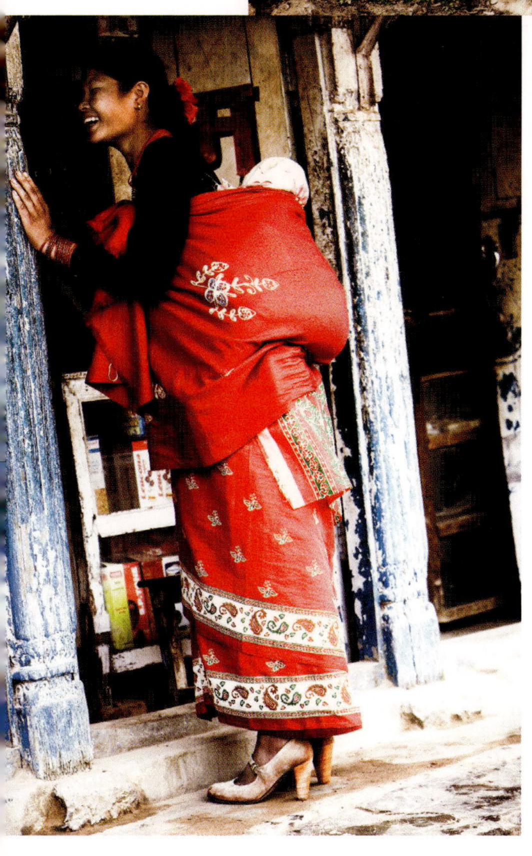

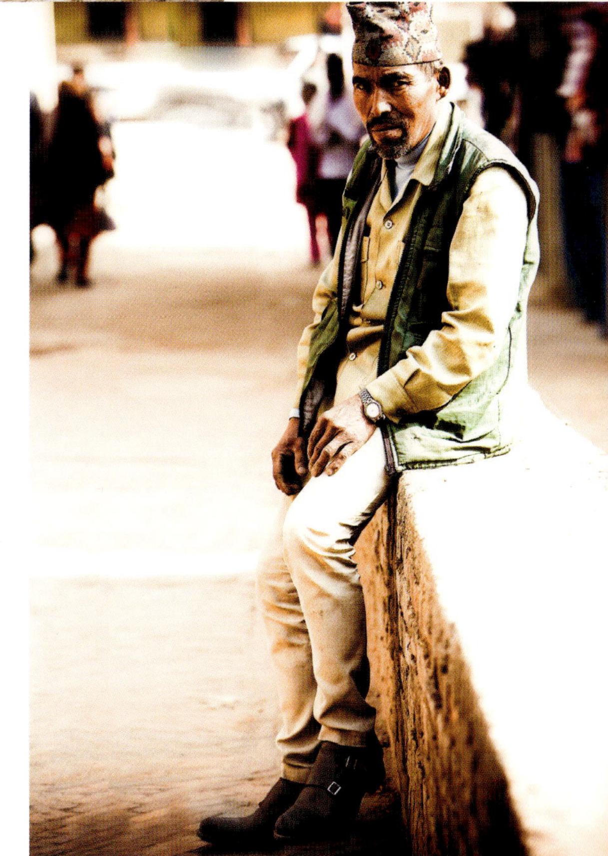

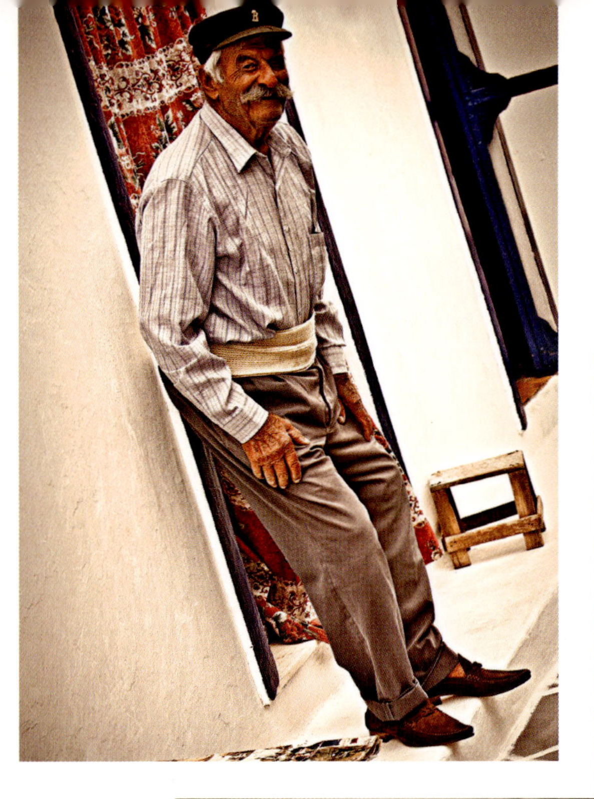

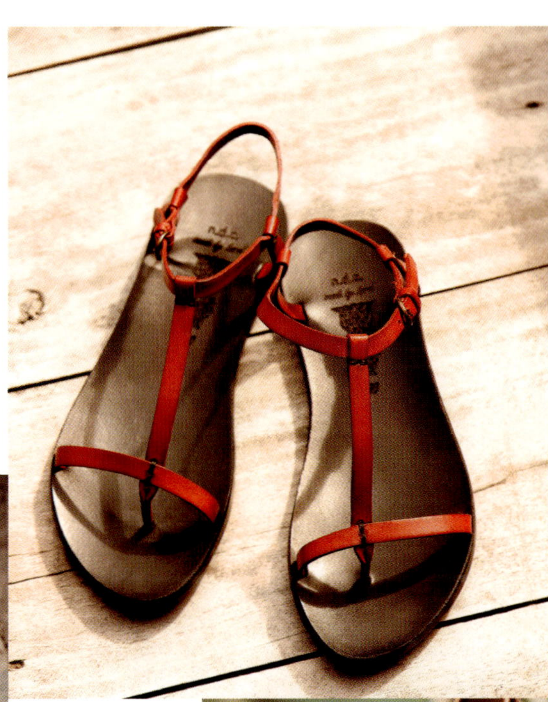

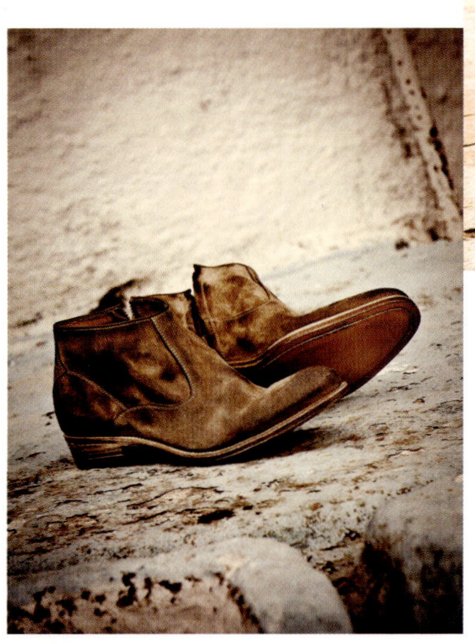

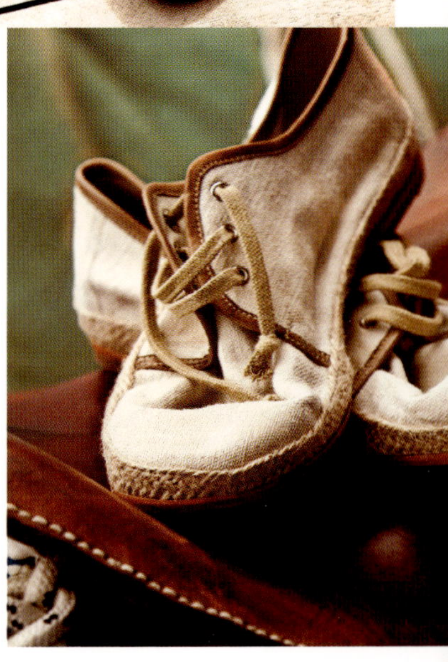

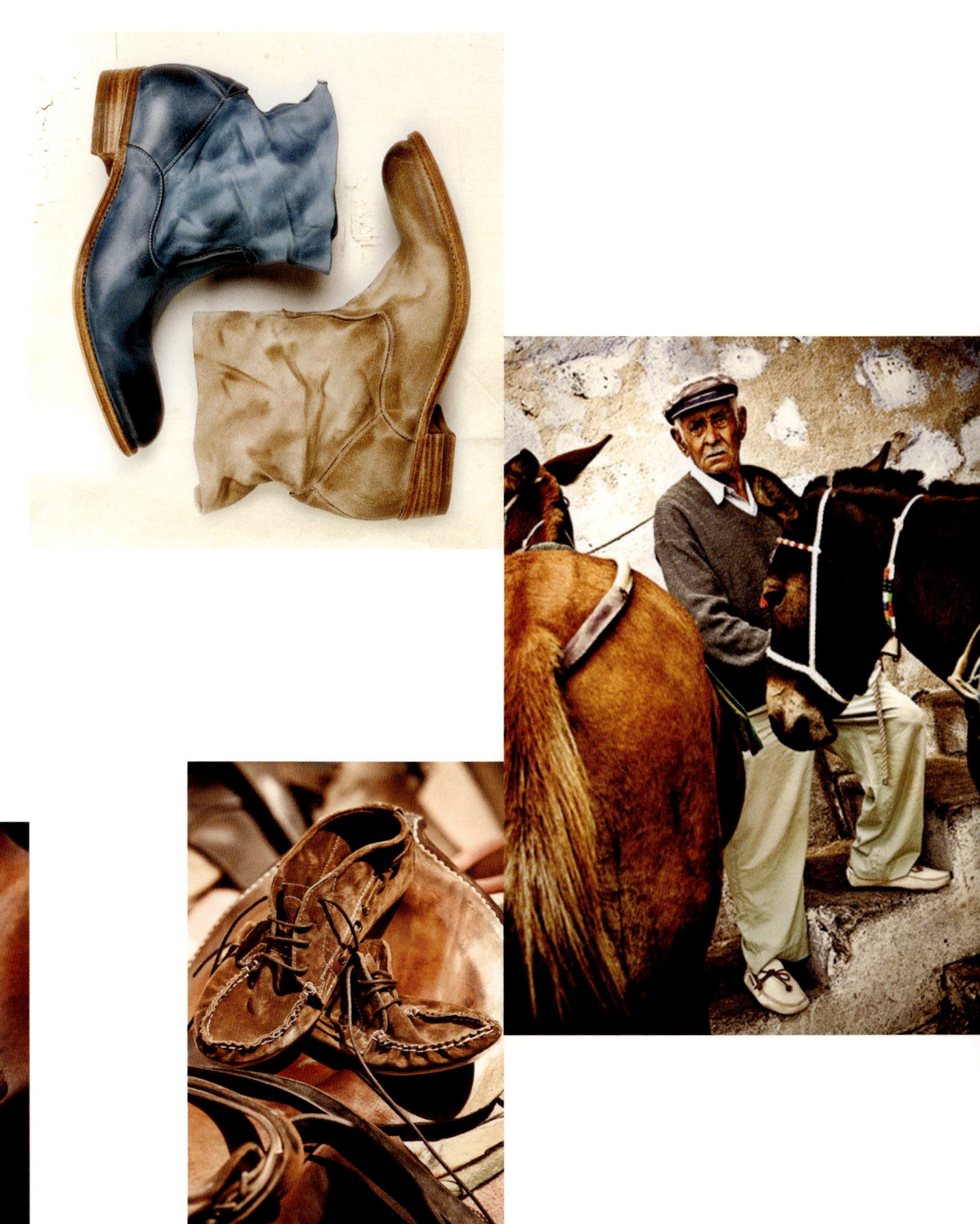

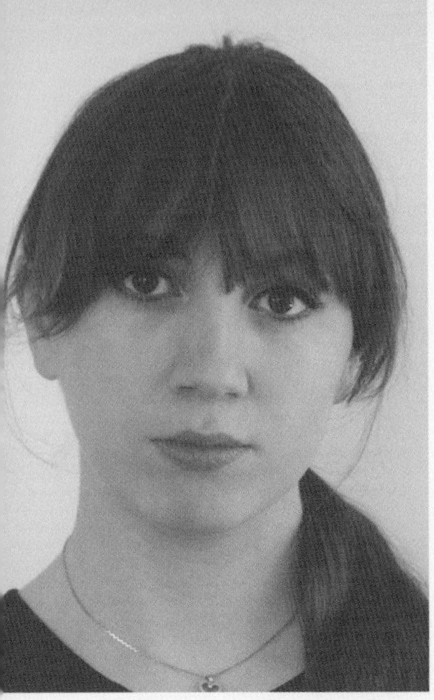

NINA HJORTH

How did you get started? **WITH MY FINAL COLLECTION FROM MY MA AT THE ROYAL COLLEGE OF ART.** What is your work about? **SIMPLICITY.** Is there a specific reason why you chose shoe design? **IT WAS AN AREA WHERE I FELT I HAD SOMETHING NEW TO CONTRIBUTE.** What makes your work different to others? **MY APPROACH TO COLOUR.** Which part of the creative process do you find the most gratifying? **RESEARCH, SKETCHING, DEVELOPING THE LAST AND HEEL, CHOOSING COLOURS AND MATERIALS.** Who or what do you admire? **I ESPECIALLY ADMIRE THE ART FORM OF PAINTING.** If you had to choose one colour and one material to make an important piece, what would they be? **IT WOULD DEPEND ON THE SEASON. MY WORK IS VERY DEPENDENT ON THE COMBINATION OF COLOURS SO I COULD NOT CHOOSE JUST ONE.** What are your thoughts on quick-consumption culture and over-commercialisation? **I THINK WE ALL CONSUME TOO MUCH WITHOUT QUESTION. I DON'T NECESSARILY BELIEVE THERE IS TOO MUCH ON OFFER BUT I DO BELIEVE THAT THE ACT OF SHOPPING SHOULD BE A MINOR PART OF ONE'S LIFE.** What role does work play in your life? **IT IS MY HOBBY AND I AM VERY FORTUNATE TO BE ABLE TO WORK AS A FOOTWEAR DESIGNER.** What do you consider vulgar and what elegant? **EXCESS IN ORDER TO SHOW YOU HAVE MONEY IS VULGAR, ALSO 'IN YOUR FACE' BRANDING. SOMEONE WHO IS KIND AND WHO HAS GREAT INDIVIDUAL STYLE IS ELEGANT.** What does beauty mean for you? **BEAUTY IS IN THE EYE OF THE BEHOLDER. IN THE CONTEXT OF SHOES OR FASHION, BEAUTY IS CRAFTSMANSHIP COMBINED WITH GREAT DESIGN.**

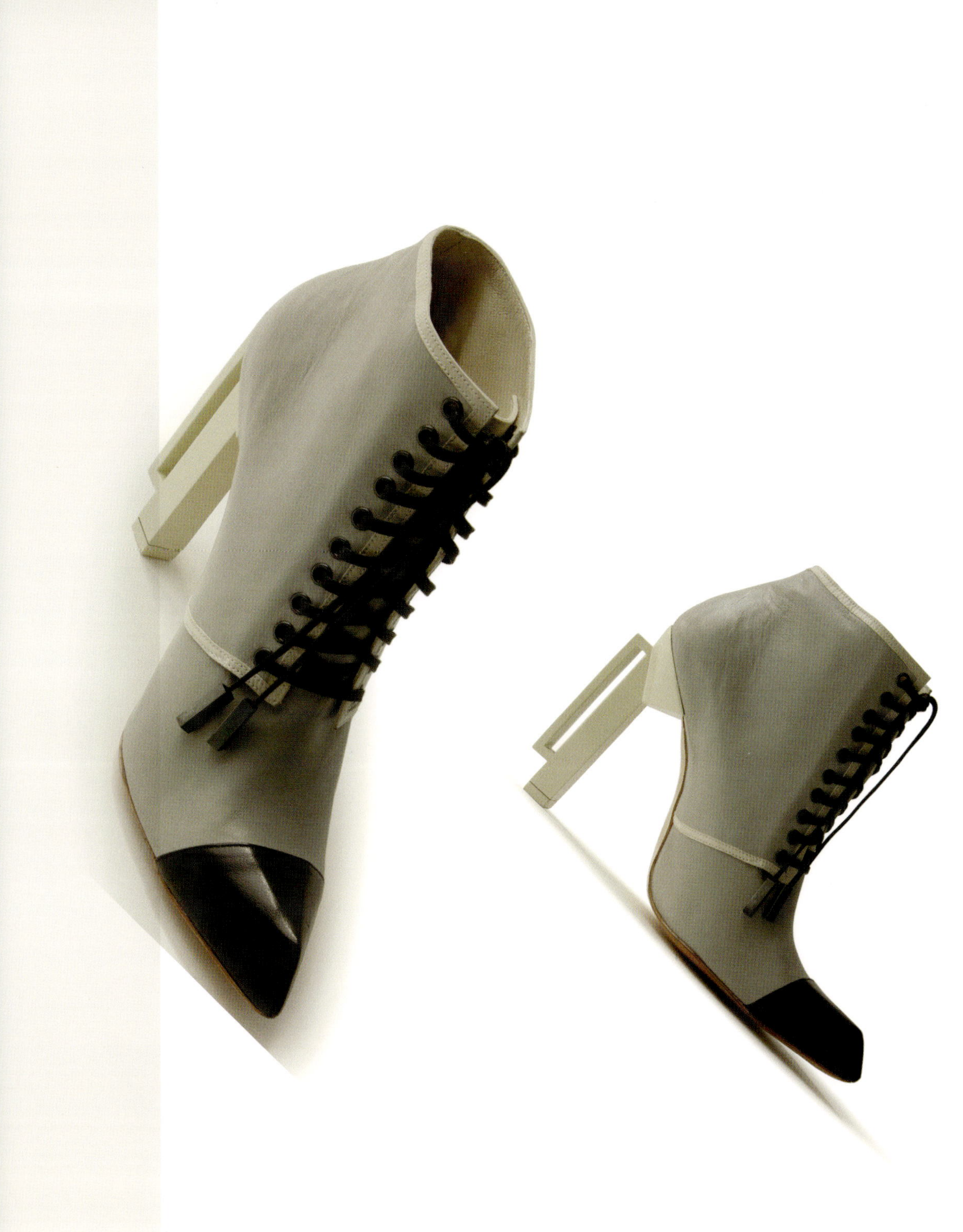

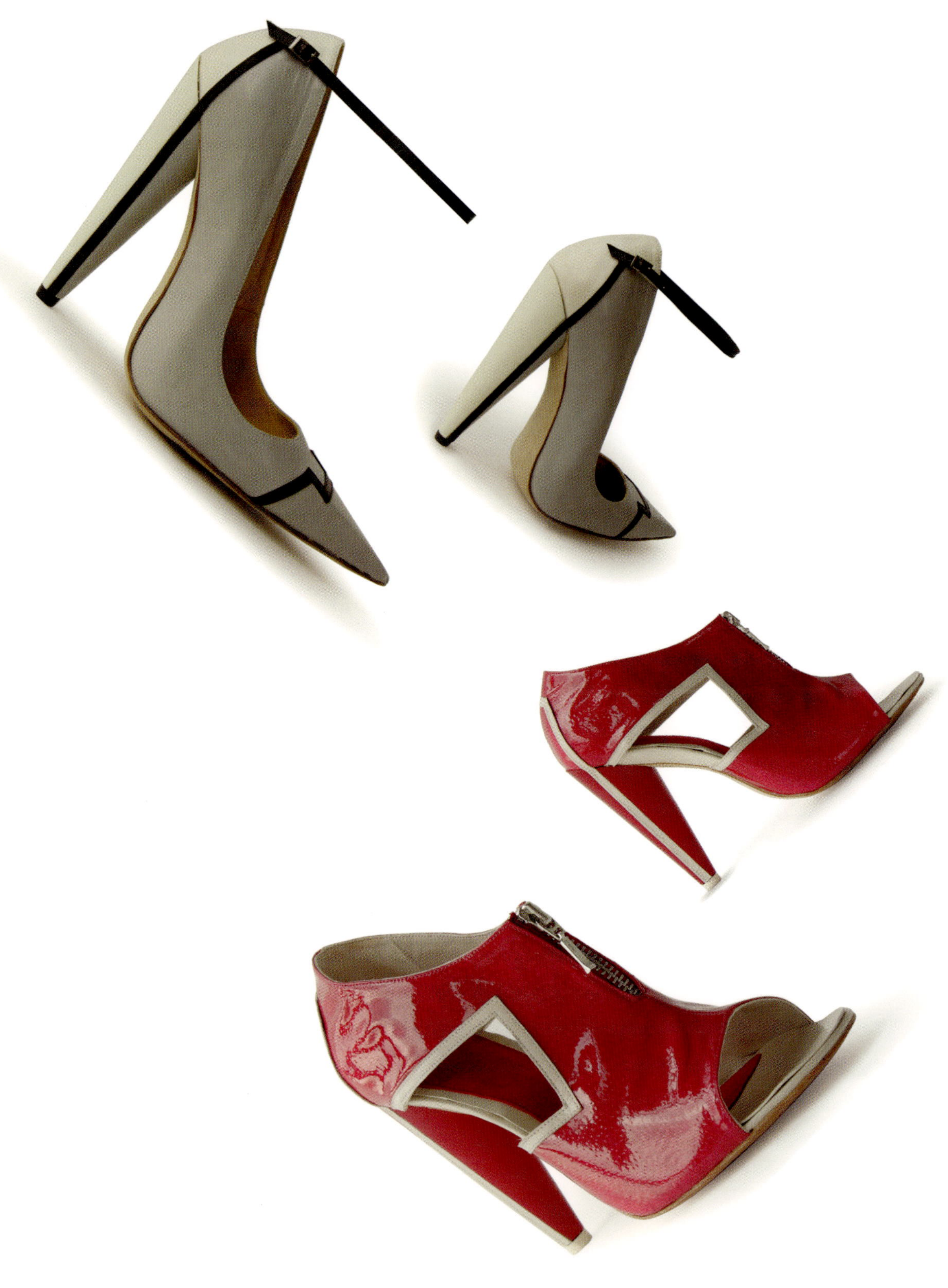

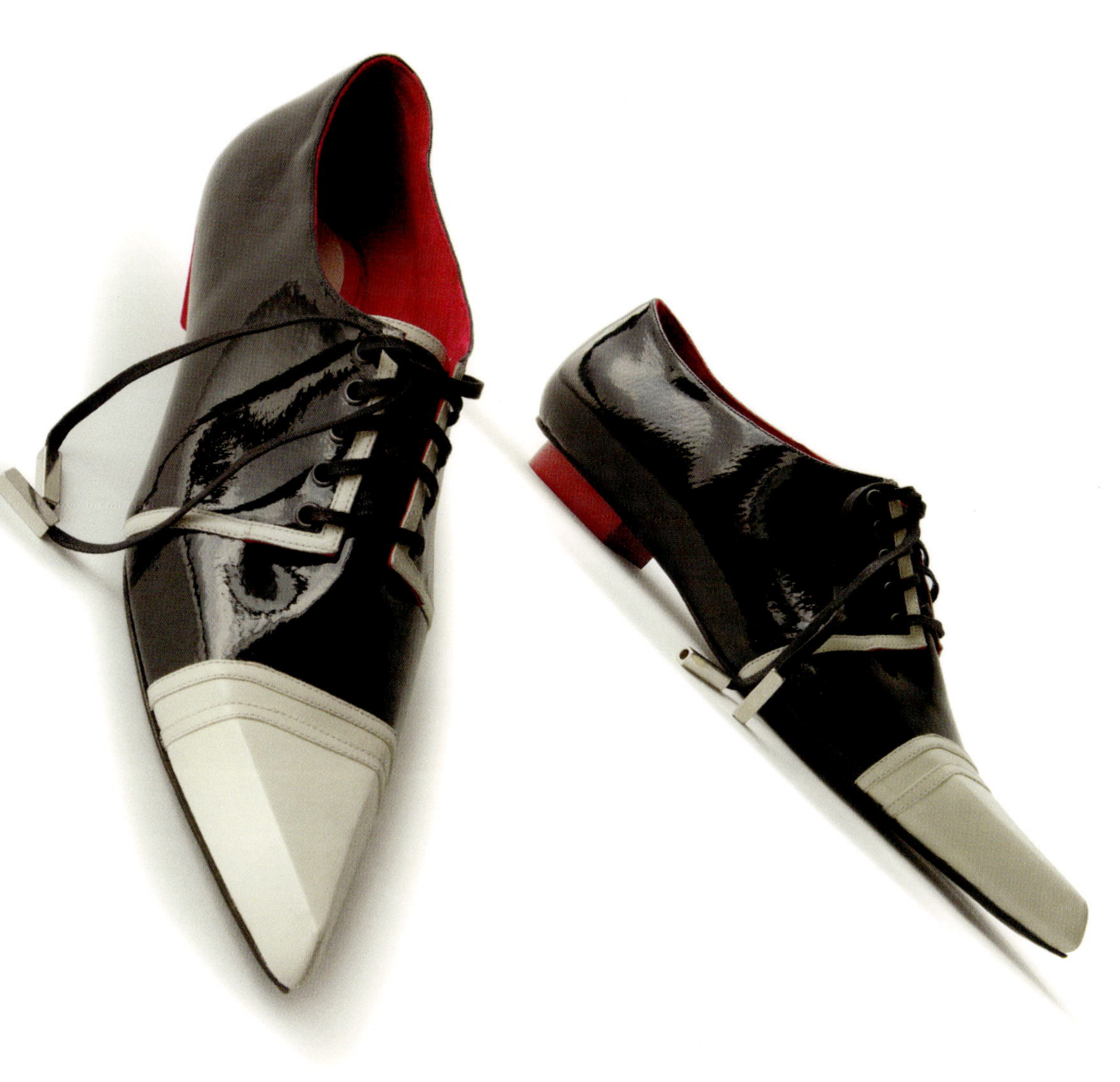

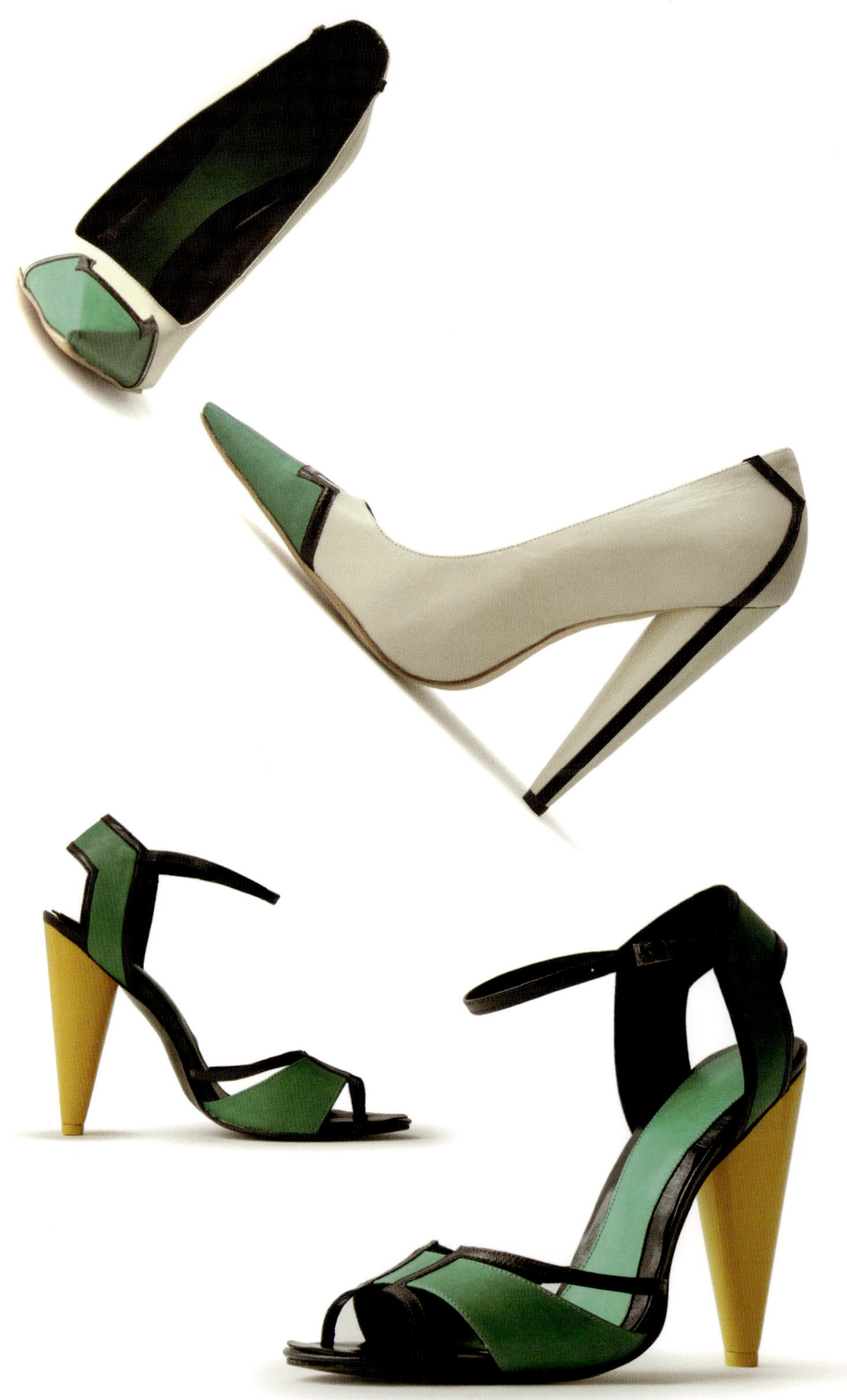

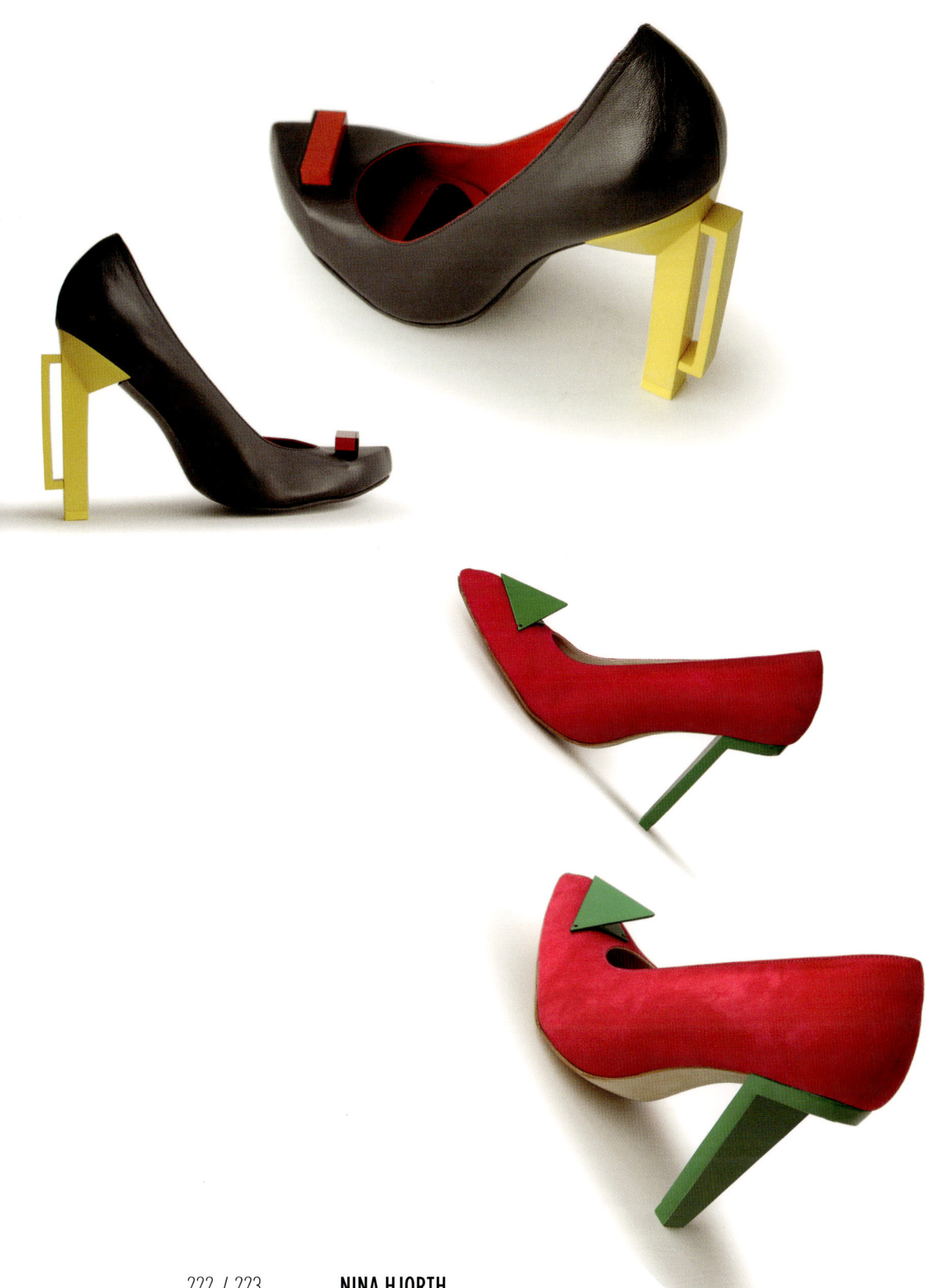

DOMINIKA NOWAK, NUNC

Please introduce yourself **NUNC IS A SIMPLE CONCEPT CREATED BY MYSELF, DOMINIKA NOWAK. I AM A POLISH BORN FASHION DESIGNER LIVING BETWEEN PARIS, ITALY AND POLAND. SHOES ARE MANUFACTURED IN THE BEST POLISH AND ITALIAN FACTORIES, HAND CUT AND HAND LASTED USING THE HIGHEST QUALITY LEATHER.** How did you get started? **BY ACCIDENT. I ALWAYS WANTED TO MAKE CLOTHES, NEVER SHOES. I MADE ONE PAIR OF BOOTS FOR MYSELF USING MY MOTHER'S OLD HAIRY CARPET. STARTING WITH HAIRY LEATHER I USED EACH SKIN AS A UNIQUE CHALLENGE. I WAS CHANGING THE DIRECTIONS AND PLAYING WITH THE NATURAL PATTERNS ON THE SKIN. AS WITH FINGER PRINTS, EACH PAIR OF SHOES WAS UNIQUE.** Is there anything that you feel makes your work different from others? **NO, I DON'T FEEL SPECIAL OR DIFFERENT. I AM FOLLOWING MY OWN PATH RATHER THAN LOOKING AT OTHERS.**

What do you consider your most innovative design so far? **THE NEW CONCEPT INFINI. THIS IS SOMETHING VERY NEW IN SHOE DESIGN. IT'S NOT THE DESIGNER WHO CREATES THE FINAL OBJECT BUT THE CUSTOMER.** Who or what has played a part in your development as an artist? Are there any art movements that have influenced you? **AS A SHOE DESIGNER I VERY MUCH ADMIRE PIERRE HARDY. AS I STUDIED HISTORY OF ART I HAVE A STRONG INCLINATION TO LOOK INTO THE PAST AND AM FASCINATED BY OLD ÉPOQUES. THE LAST TWO SEASONS HAVE BEEN INFLUENCED MOSTLY BY TWENTIES AND THIRTIES MODERNISM AND ART DECO.** What are your thoughts on quick-consumption culture and over-commercialisation? **I TRY NOT TO FOLLOW THE TRENDS AND FOCUS ON MY OWN STORY BUT THIS IS NOT VERY EASY IF YOU WANT TO SURVIVE ON THE MARKET. IN THE PAST, PEOPLE WOULD HAVE ONLY A FEW PAIRS OF SHOES FOR LIFE. I WOULD LIKE TO GO BACK TO FASHION THAT IS DESIGNED FOR MORE THAN ONE SEASON AND CREATE HIGH QUALITY SHOES THAT YOU CAN OWN FOR MANY YEARS BECAUSE THEY ARE DIFFERENT TO THE MAINSTREAM. I WOULD ALSO LIKE TO MAKE SHOES ACCESSIBLE AND LESS EXPENSIVE UNLIKE THE HIGH END FASHION GARMENTS WHICH ARE ONLY FOR RICH PEOPLE. IT IS VERY DIFFICULT TO RECONCILE AFFORDABLE PRICE WITH GOOD QUALITY.**

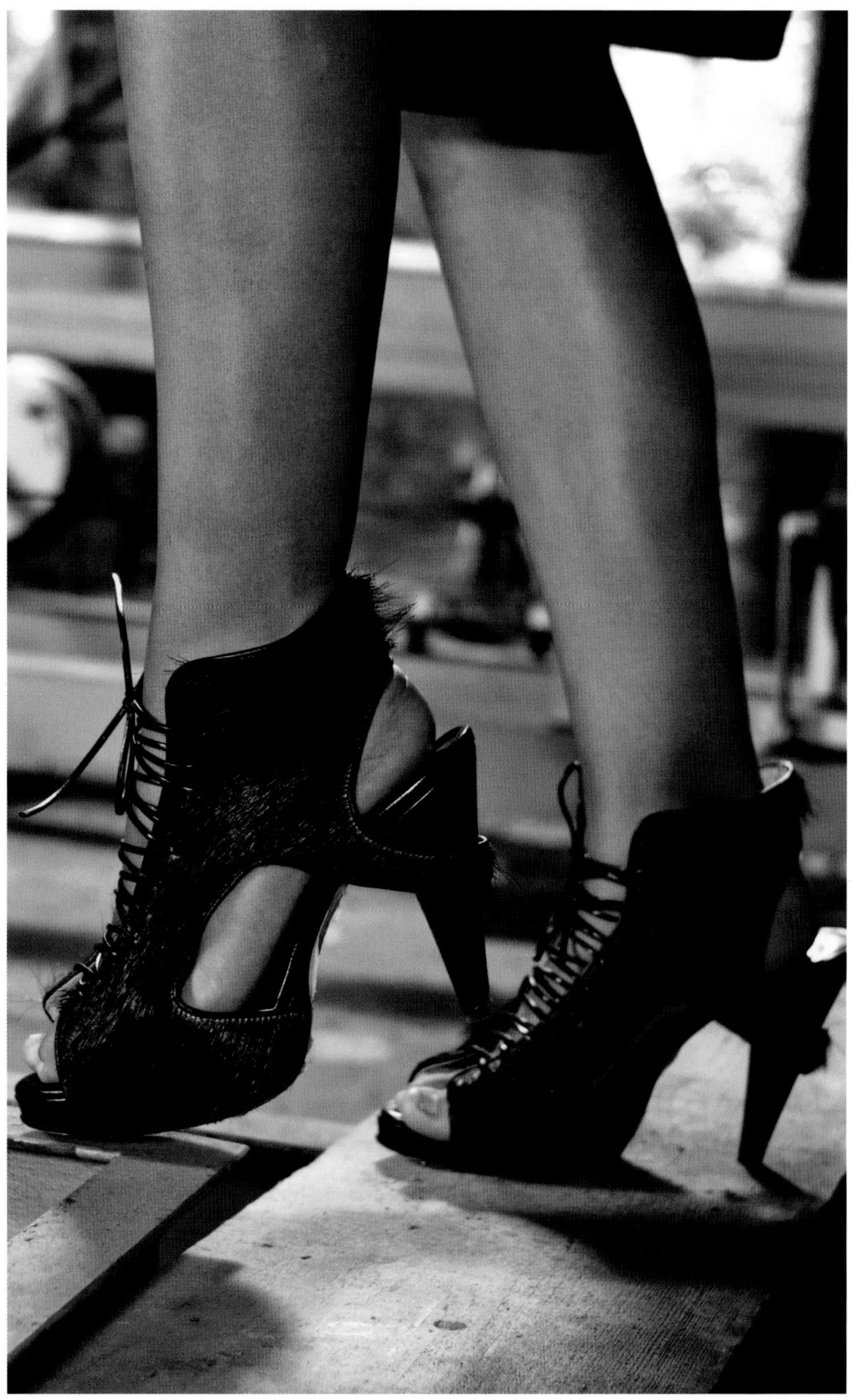

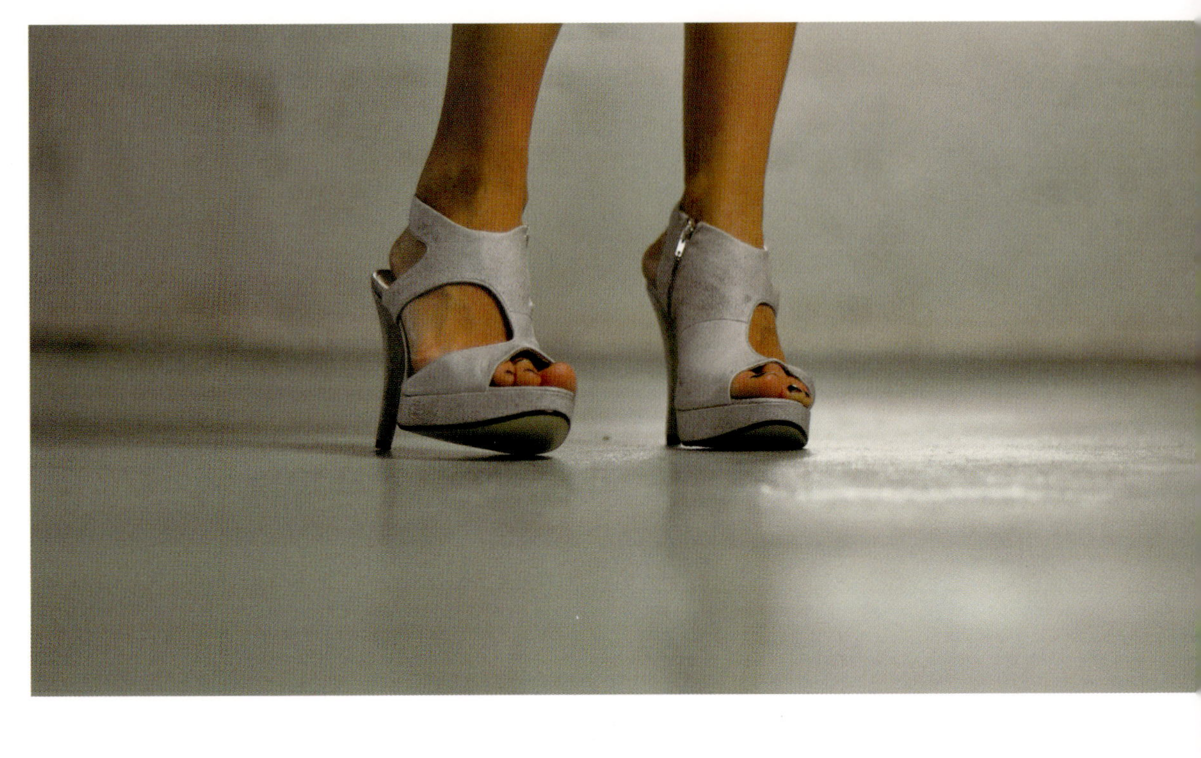

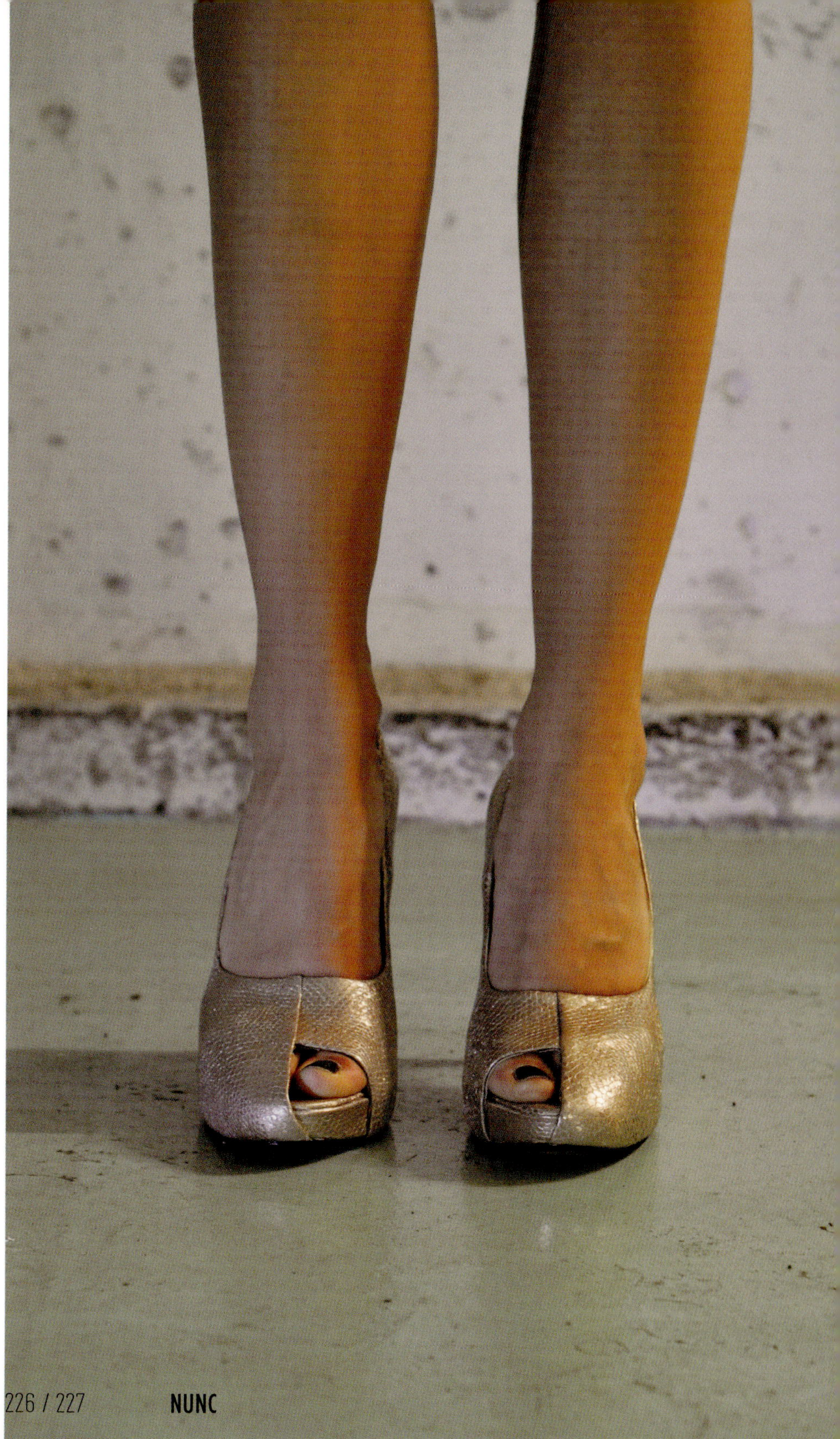

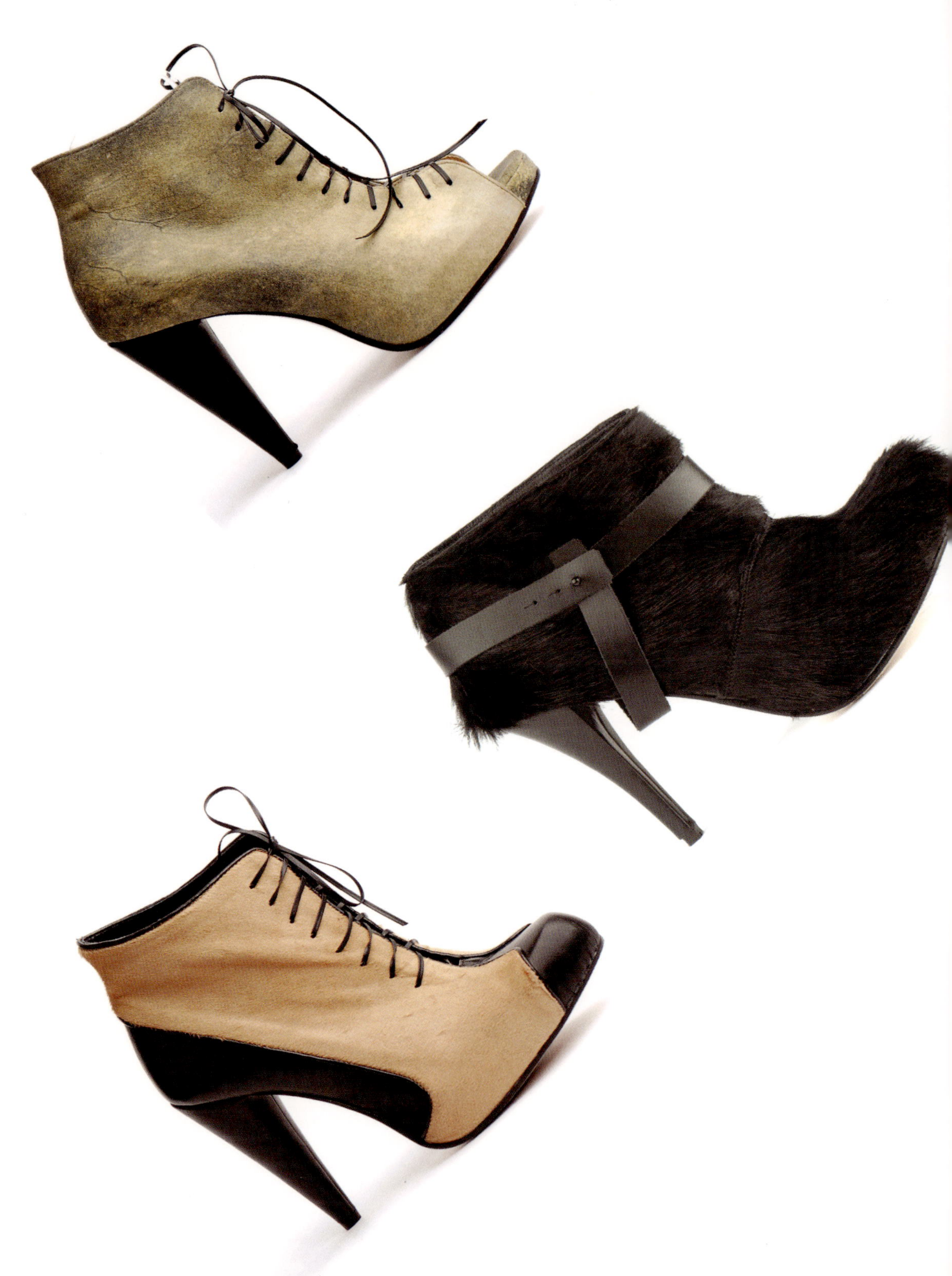

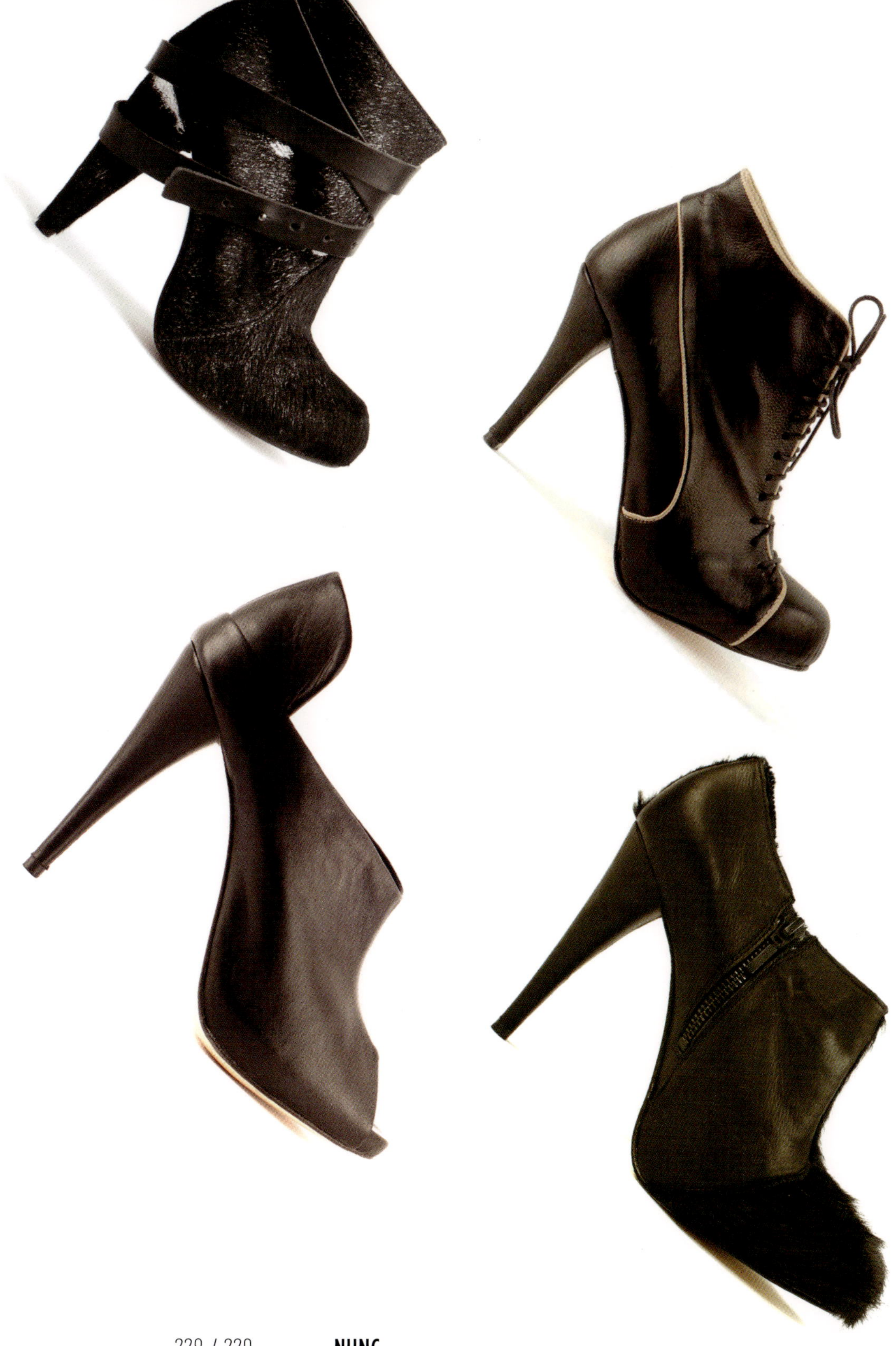

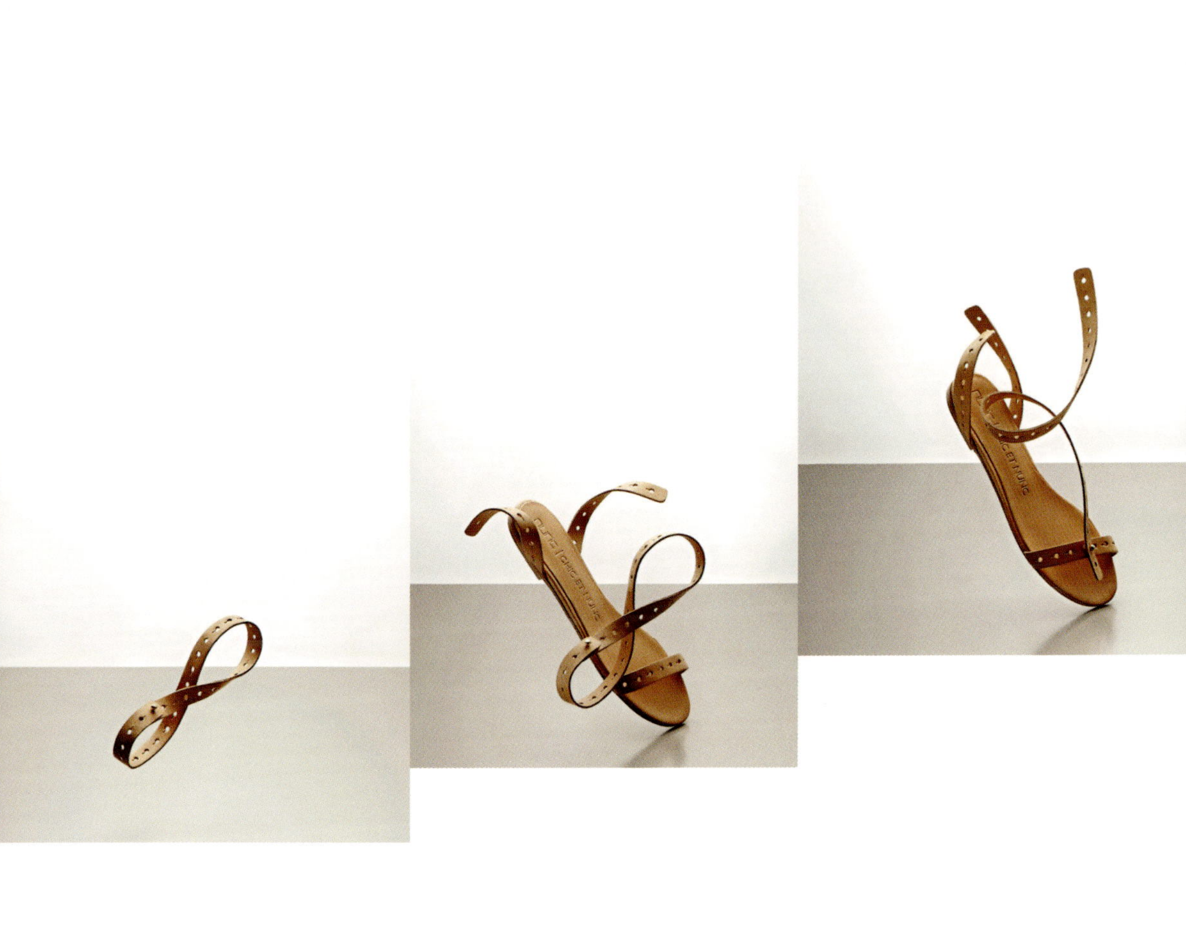

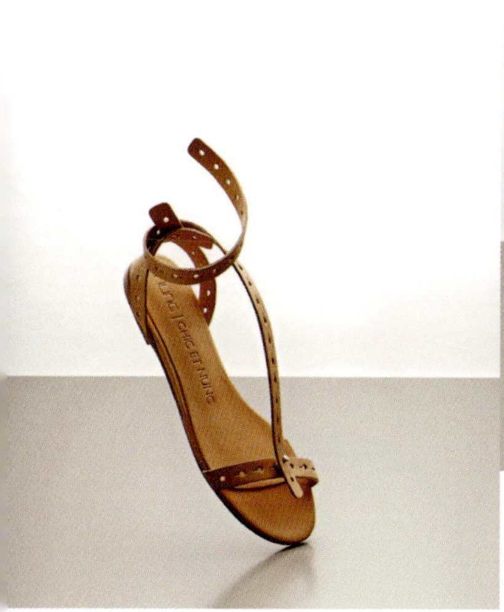

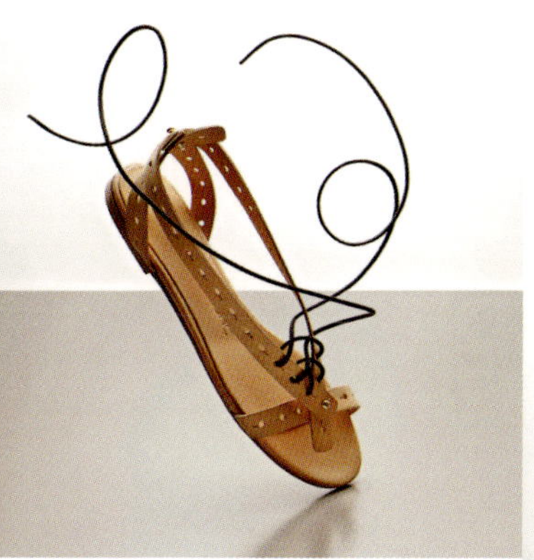

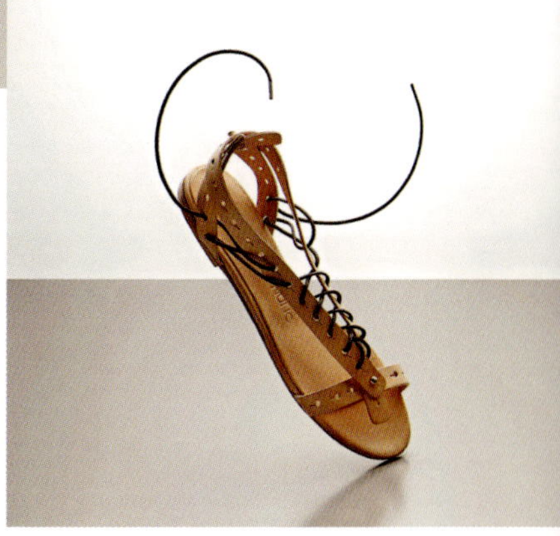

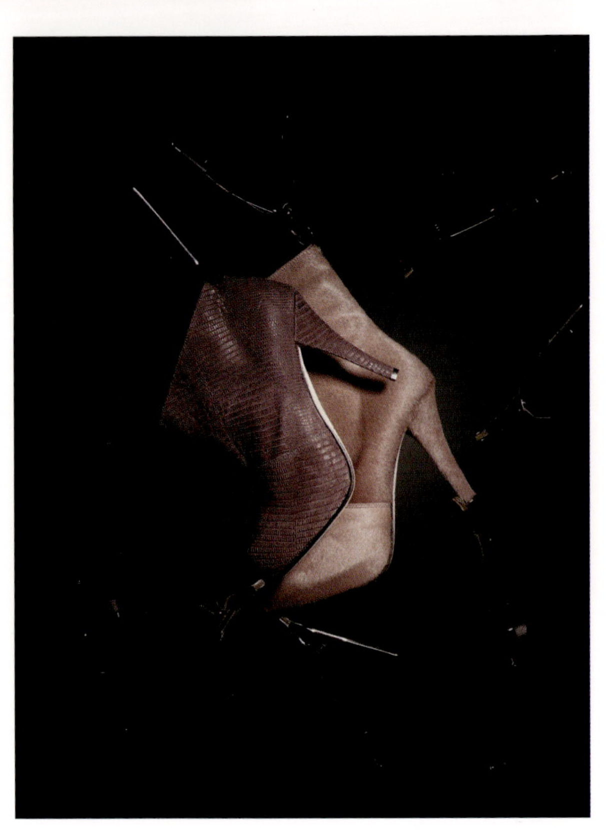

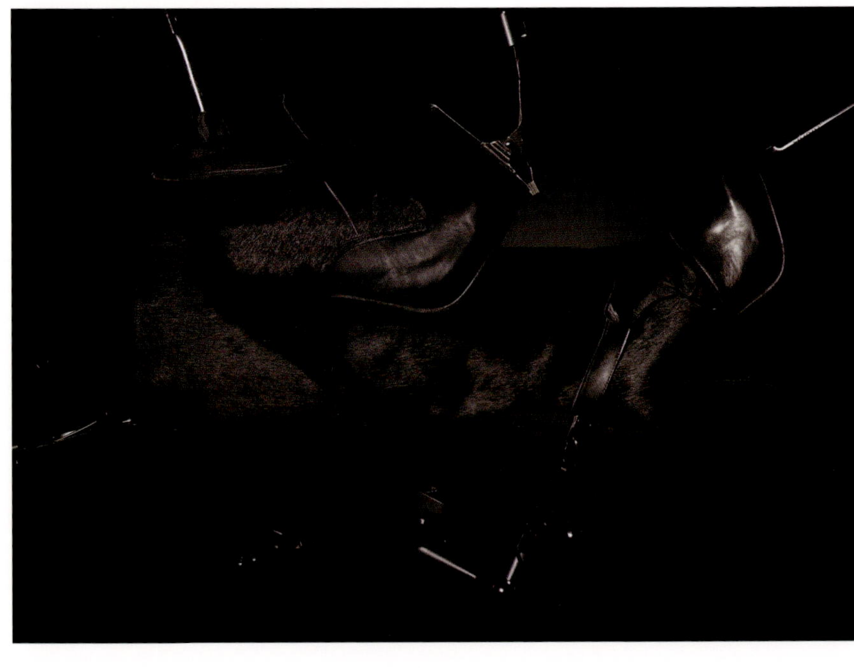

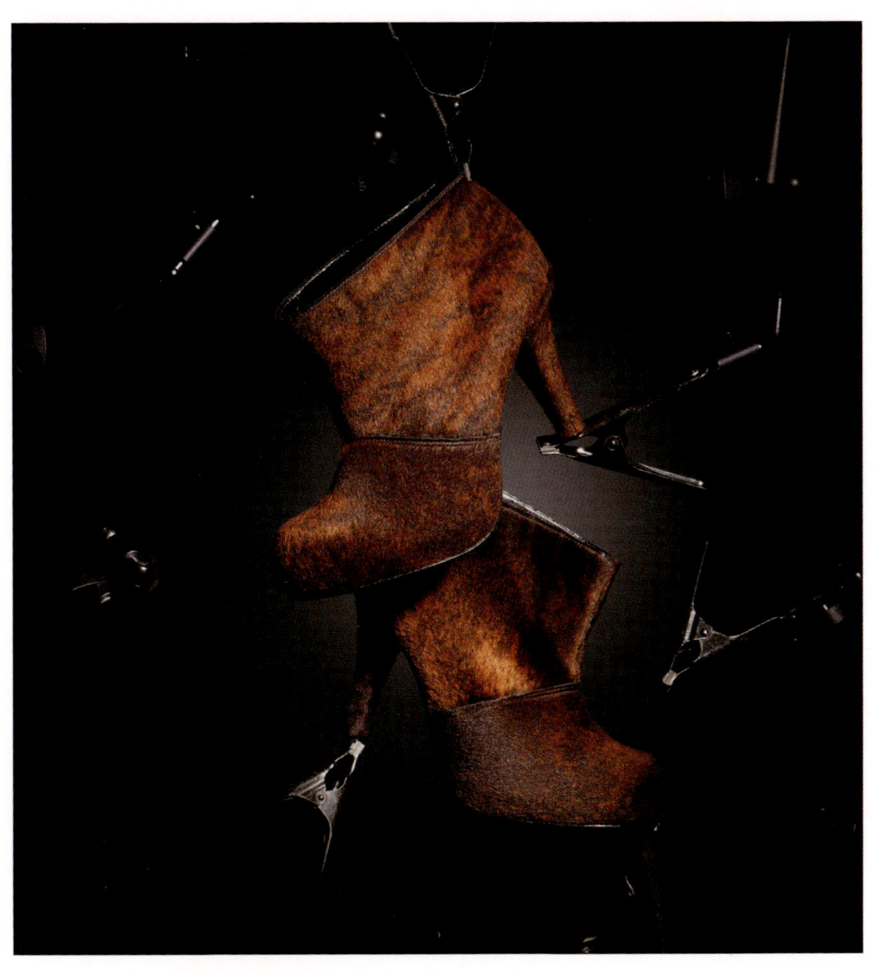

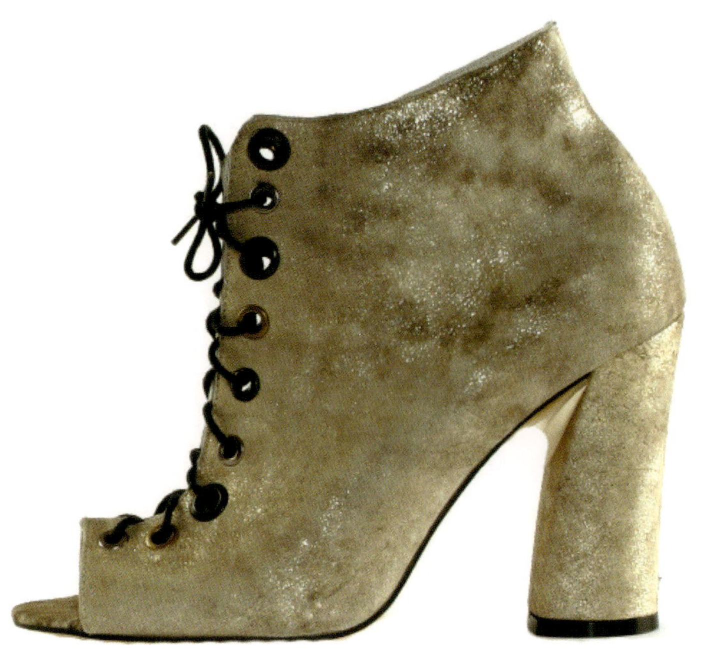

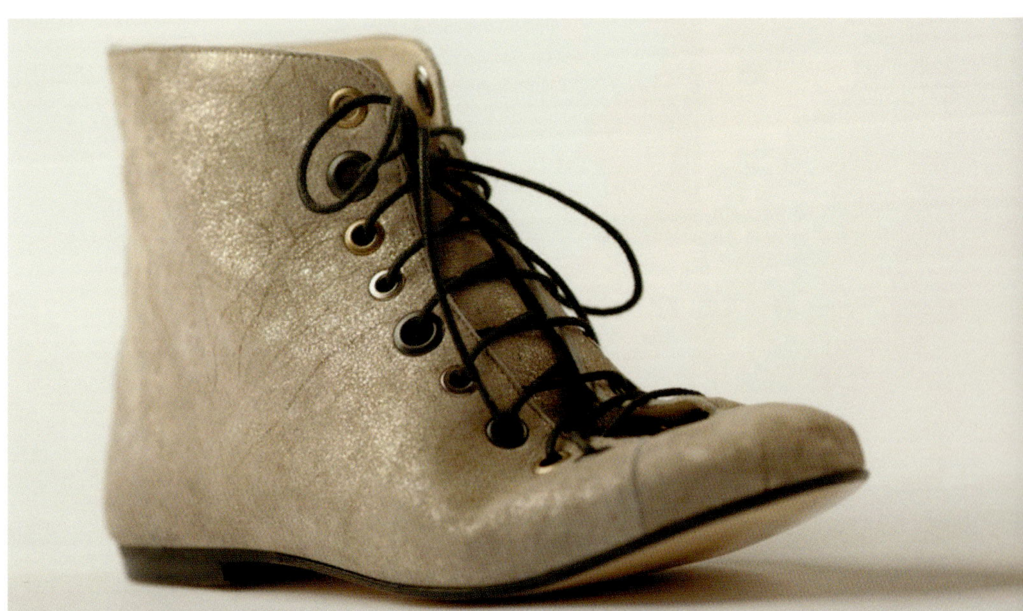

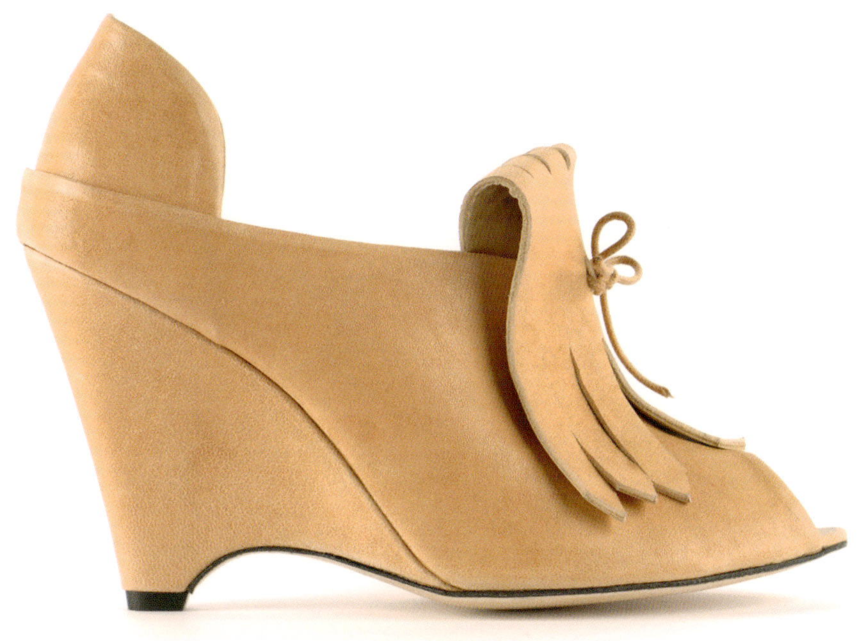

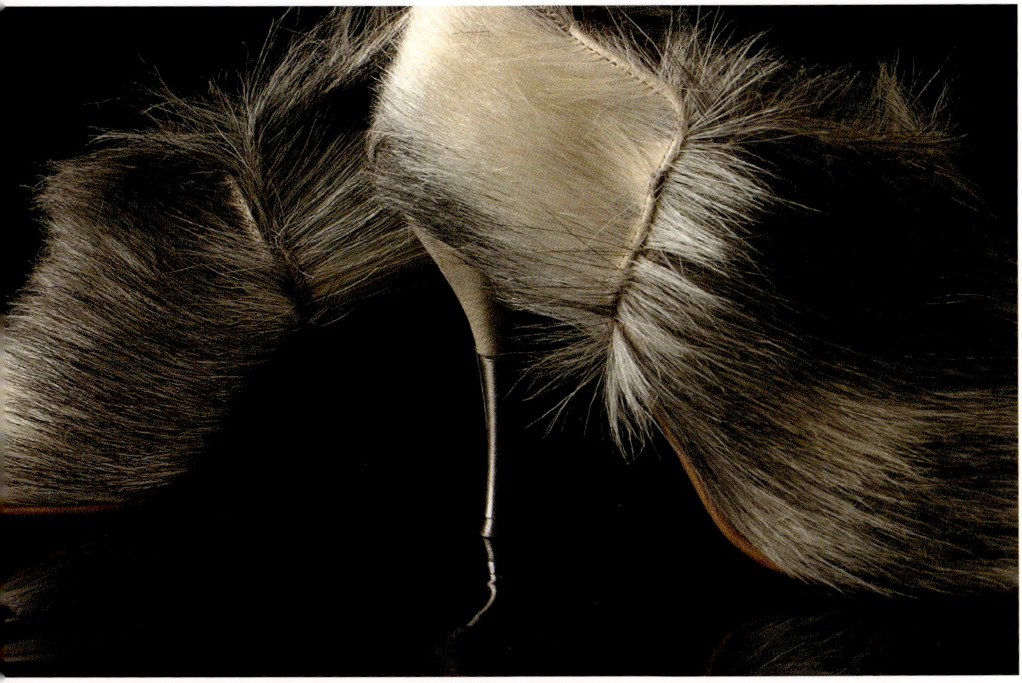

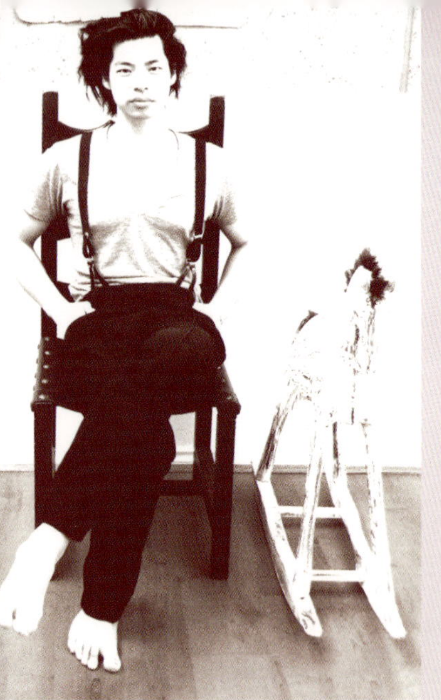

PHONG CHI LAI

The idea of making shoes began when I lived in Paris, but was never acted upon. When I returned to Australia I decided to study the art of hand making shoes. It was a means to fulfil a desire to create functional objets d'art but it was also with the intention of making shoes for myself that I embarked on this journey. **THE INDULGENCE LED ME DOWN THE PATH OF FOOTWEAR AS A PROFESSION. AFTER STUDYING I MOVED FROM ADELAIDE TO MELBOURNE WHERE I WORKED AT A SMALL DESIGN COMPANY IN FOOTWEAR PRODUCTION FOR A SHORT TIME. THROUGH THIS EXPERIENCE, I DECIDED TO LAUNCH MY OWN LABEL.** The integration of form, function and detail presides over my work. Initial design sketches are sketched for weeks. One design will feed into another until I have to tell myself to stop. I will sketch whatever comes into my head with the intention that it doesn't matter if it is feasible or not. From there, details will emerge which bind the collection. **EVEN WHEN THE SKETCHES SEEM CONCRETE, THE ORGANIC PROCESS OF TRIAL AND ERROR COMES INTO PLAY. SAMPLES ARE MADE FROM LEATHER TO TEST FOR FIT, FORM AND AESTHETIC APPEAL. SOMETIMES, THE END RESULT MAY LOOK NOTHING LIKE WHAT WAS INTENDED. ONCE I HAVE FINALISED ALL THE DESIGNS, I START TO SOURCE LEATHERS AND TRIMS. I WOULD HAVE TO SAY I AM MOST HAPPY WITH MY LATEST COLLECTION AW12 SOUTHERN HEMISPHERE.** With so many financial factors influencing consumers' decisions on spending and the deregulation of import taxes into Australia on footwear, I do worry that my area of expertise is a very niche market. The Australian footwear market is inundated with commercially driven and derivative products. Having said this, I hope that what I do highlights a craft that is fast becoming forgotten. Much of the time it is about creating shoes that I would wear myself rather than limiting myself to societal boundaries. **QUICK-CONSUMPTION CULTURE AND OVER-COMMERCIALISATION IS UNFORTUNATELY NOW A FACT OF LIFE. I THINK IT IS SOMETHING THAT AFFECTS EVERY YOUNG DESIGNER OR ARTIST. IT IS VERY HARD TO RETAIN INTEGRITY AND STILL BE FINANCIAL VIABLE. SOMETIMES IT COMES TO A POINT WHEN YOU DECIDE YOU WANT ONE OR THE OTHER. I KNOW I NEED MONEY, BUT I AM A STUBBORN PURIST. I PERSIST WITH WHAT I AM DOING BECAUSE IT IS A REPRESENTATION OF ME BUT MAYBE I WILL CHANGE MY MIND IN THE NEXT COUPLE OF YEARS, WHO KNOWS?**

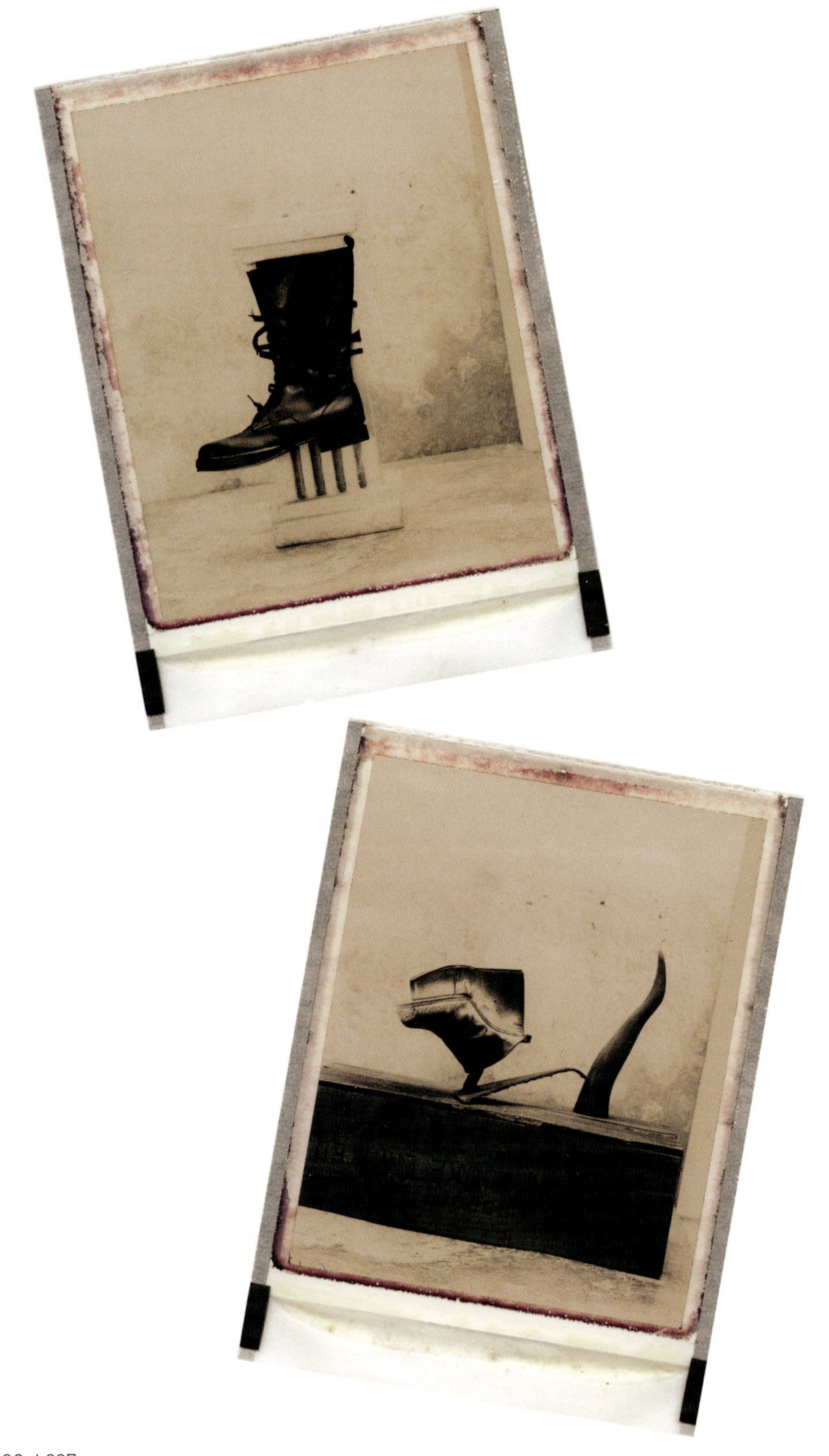

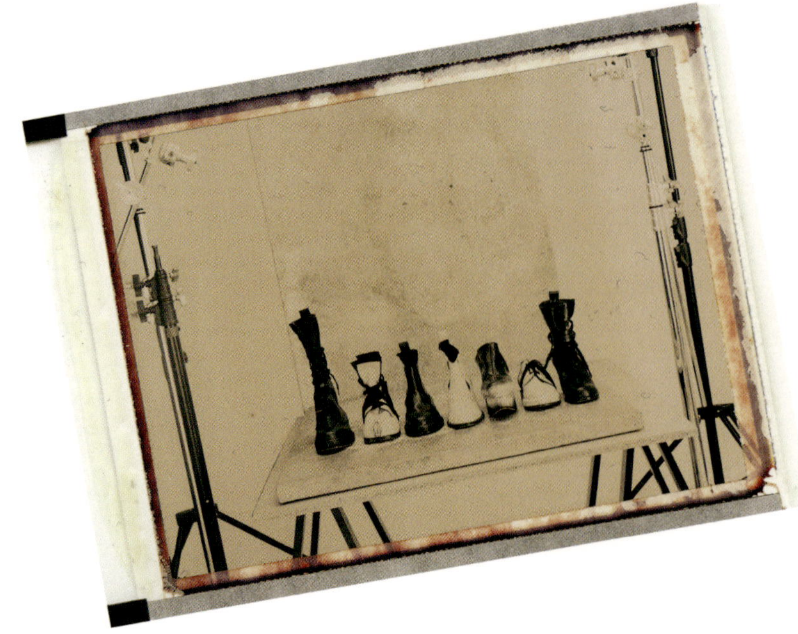
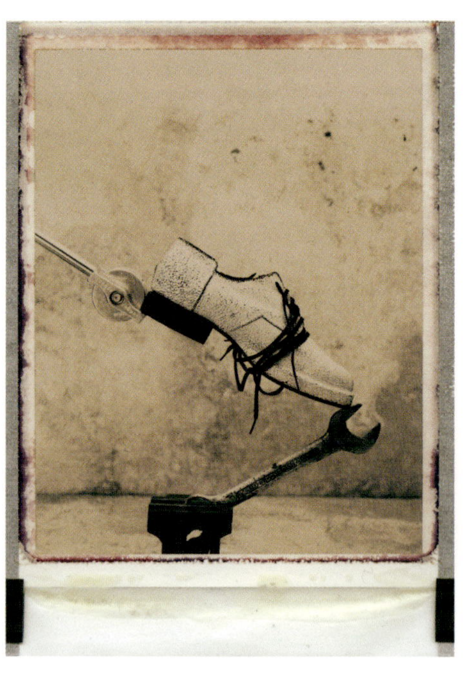
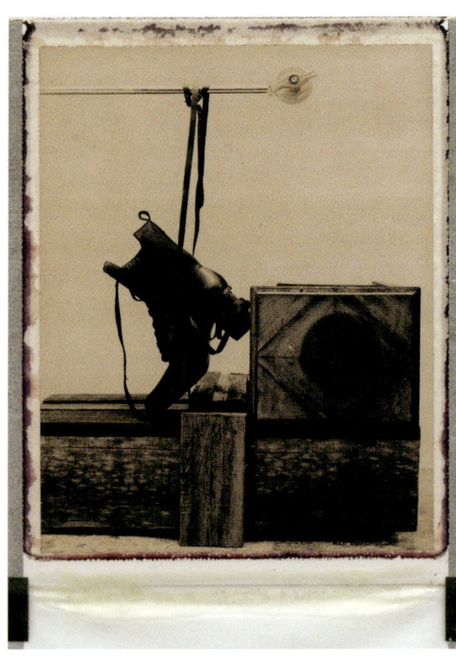

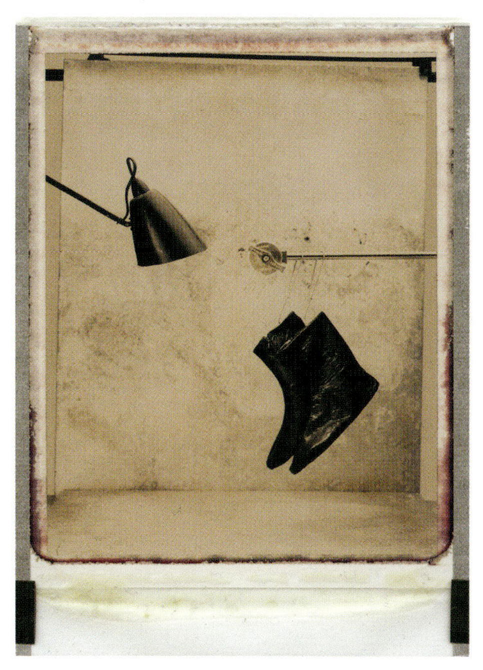

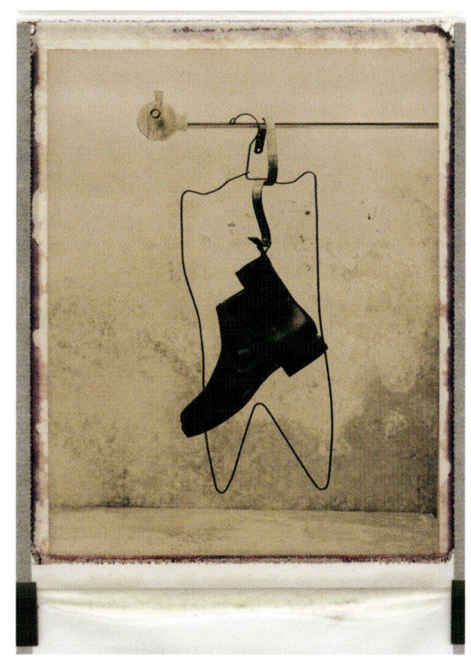

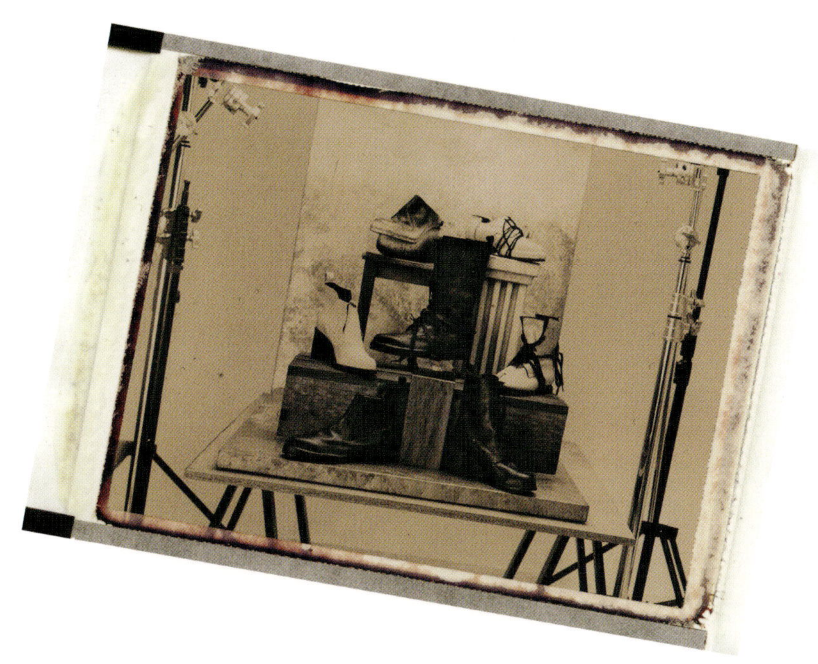

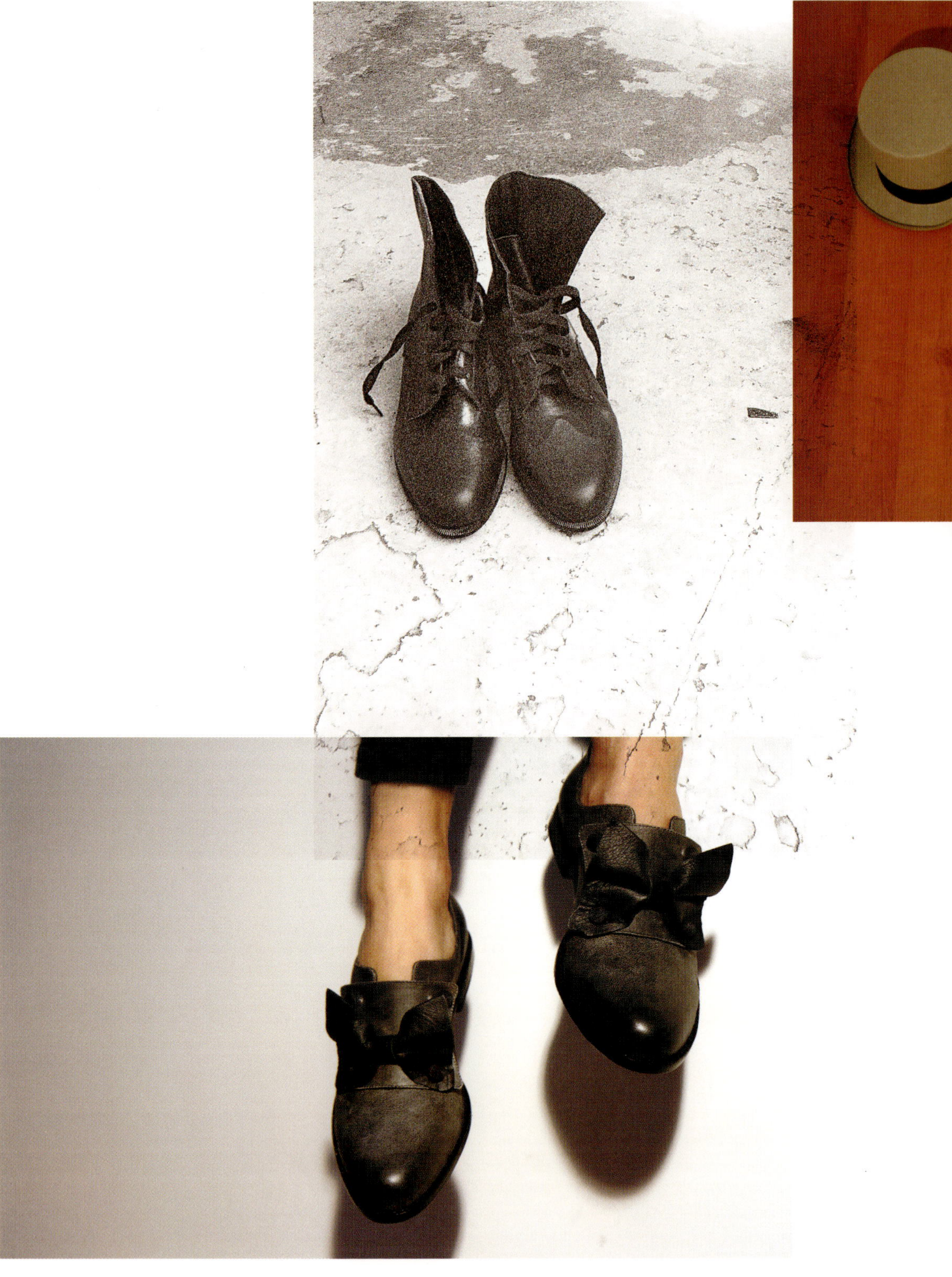

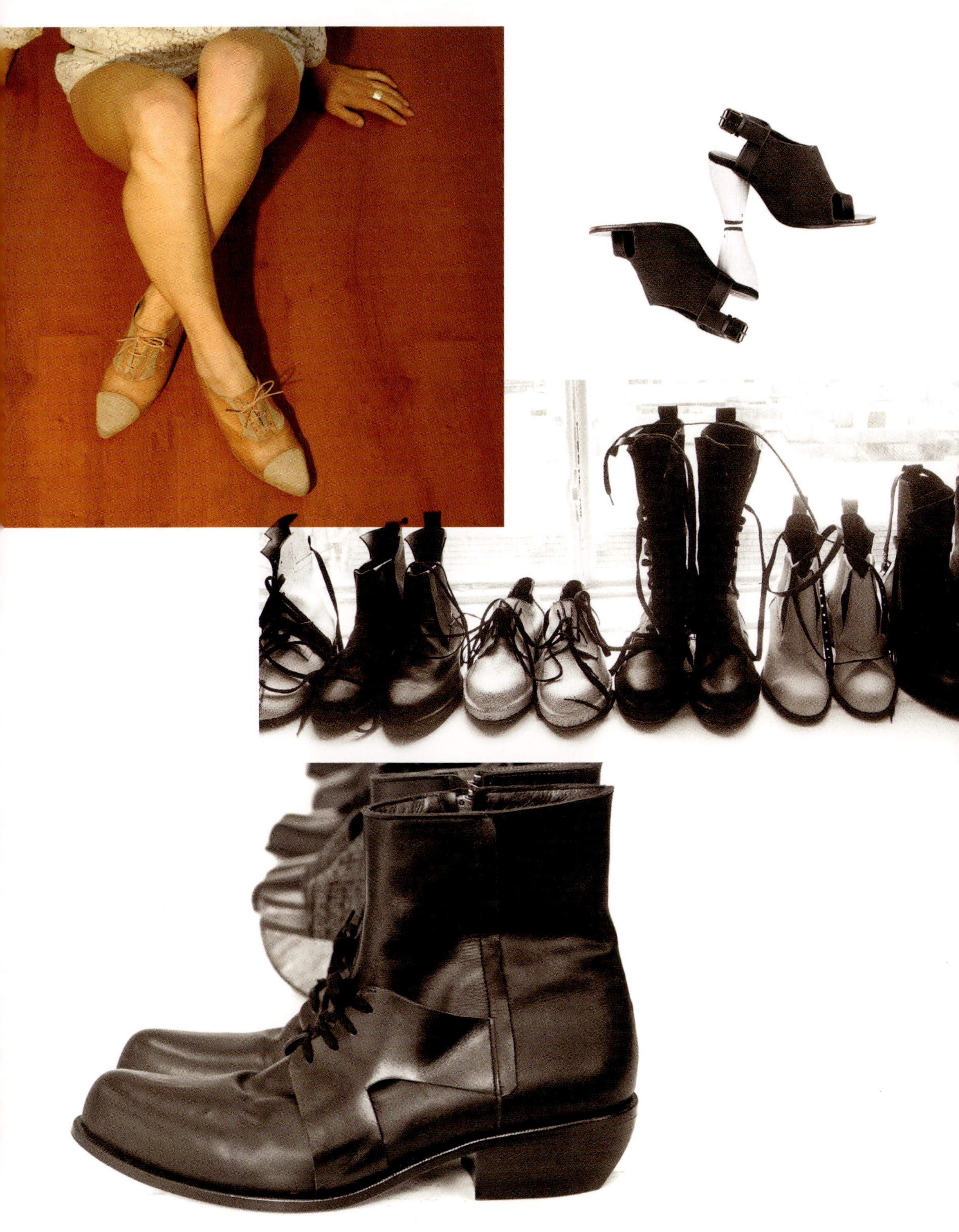

PHONG CHI LAI

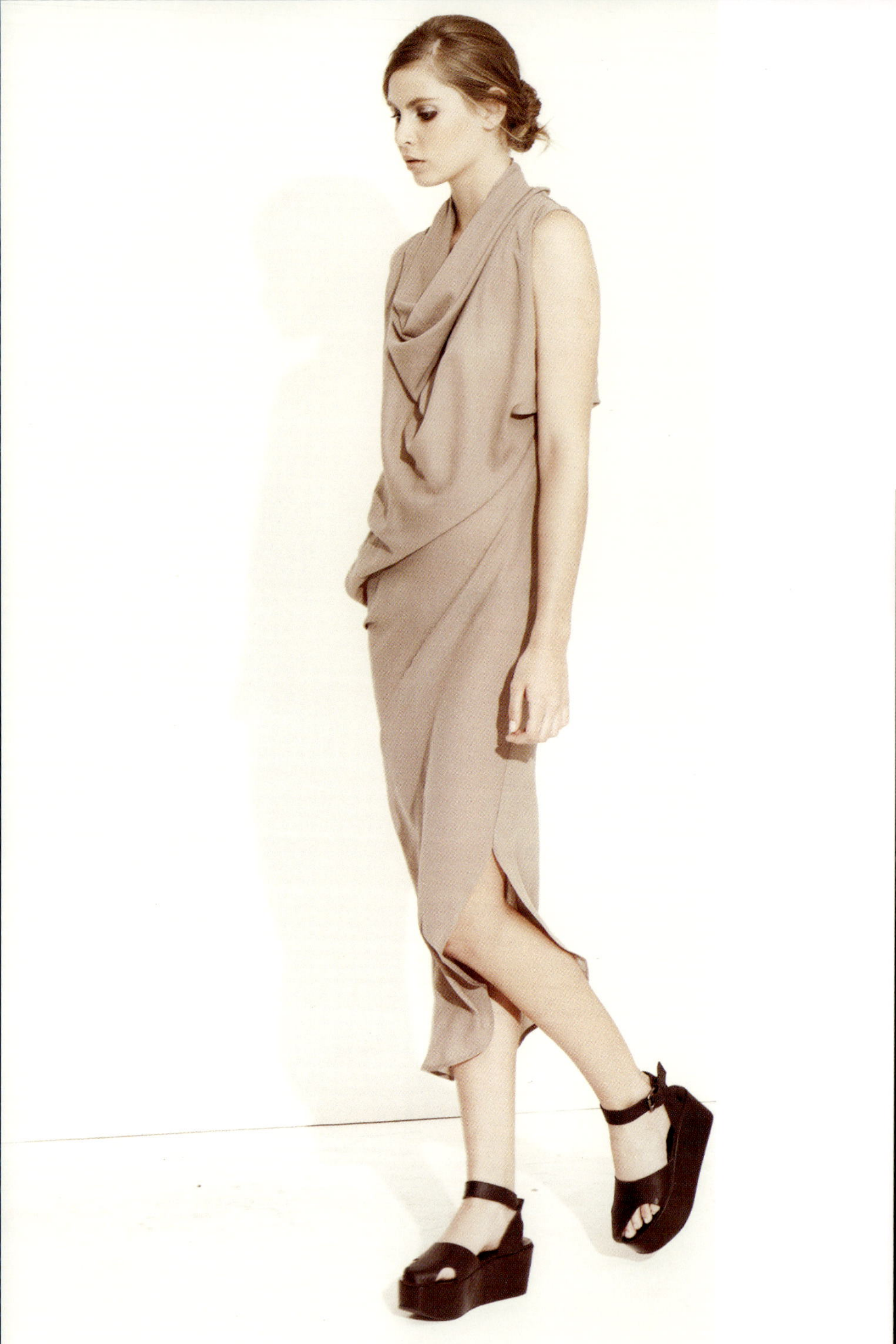

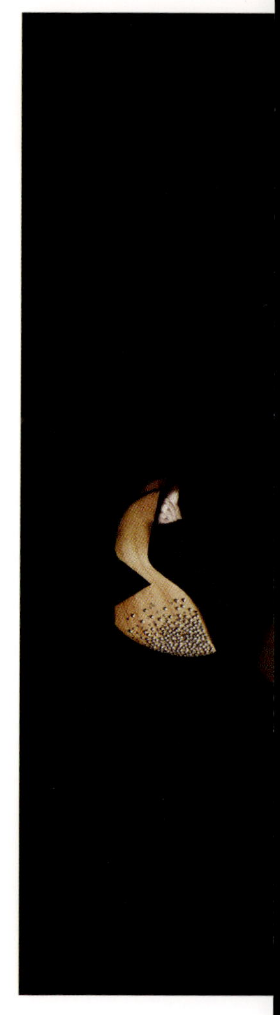

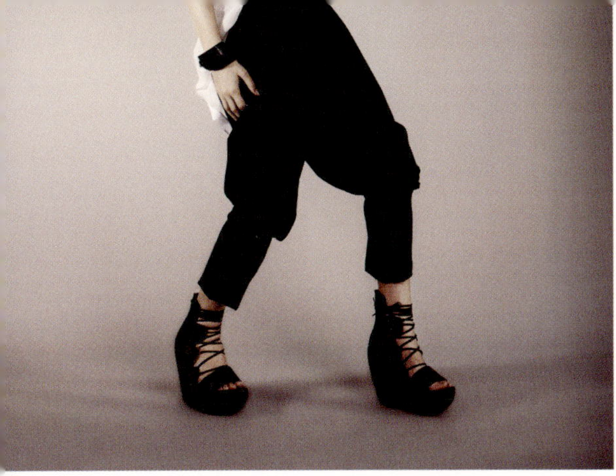

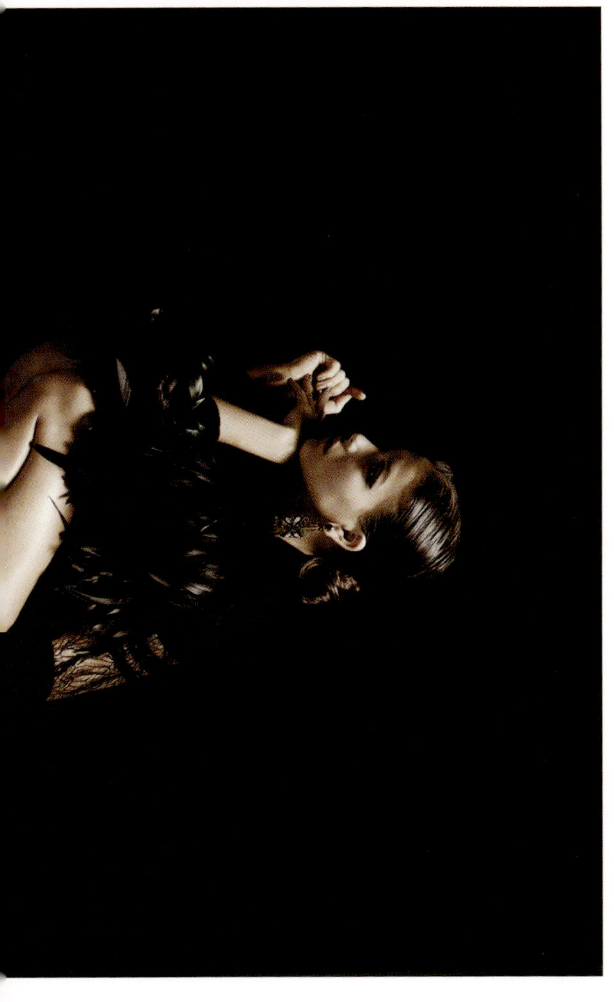

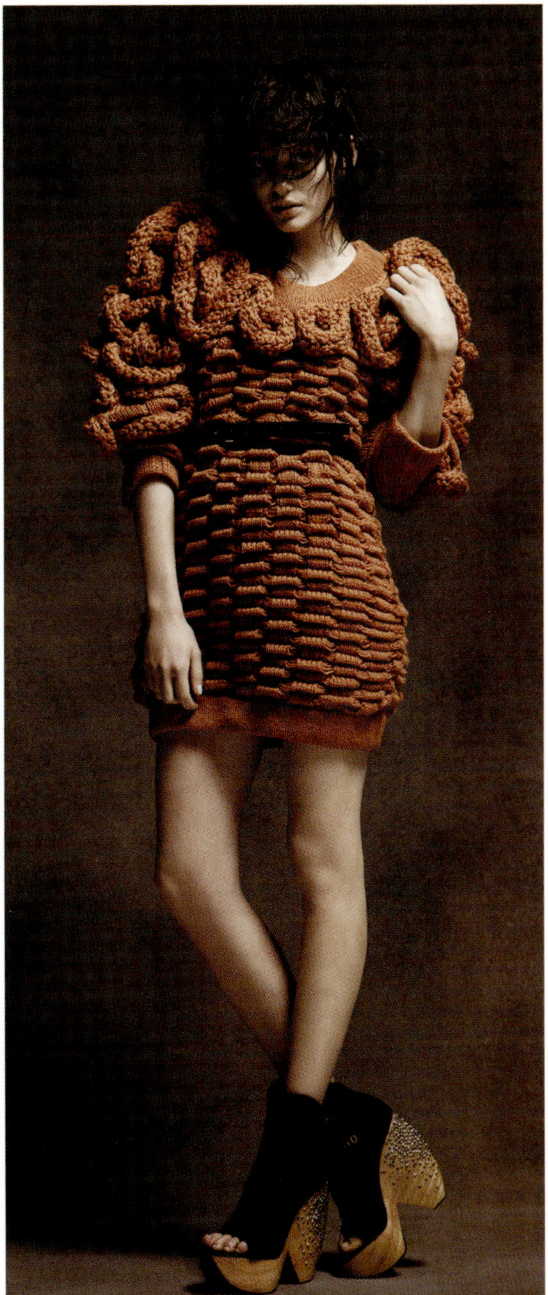

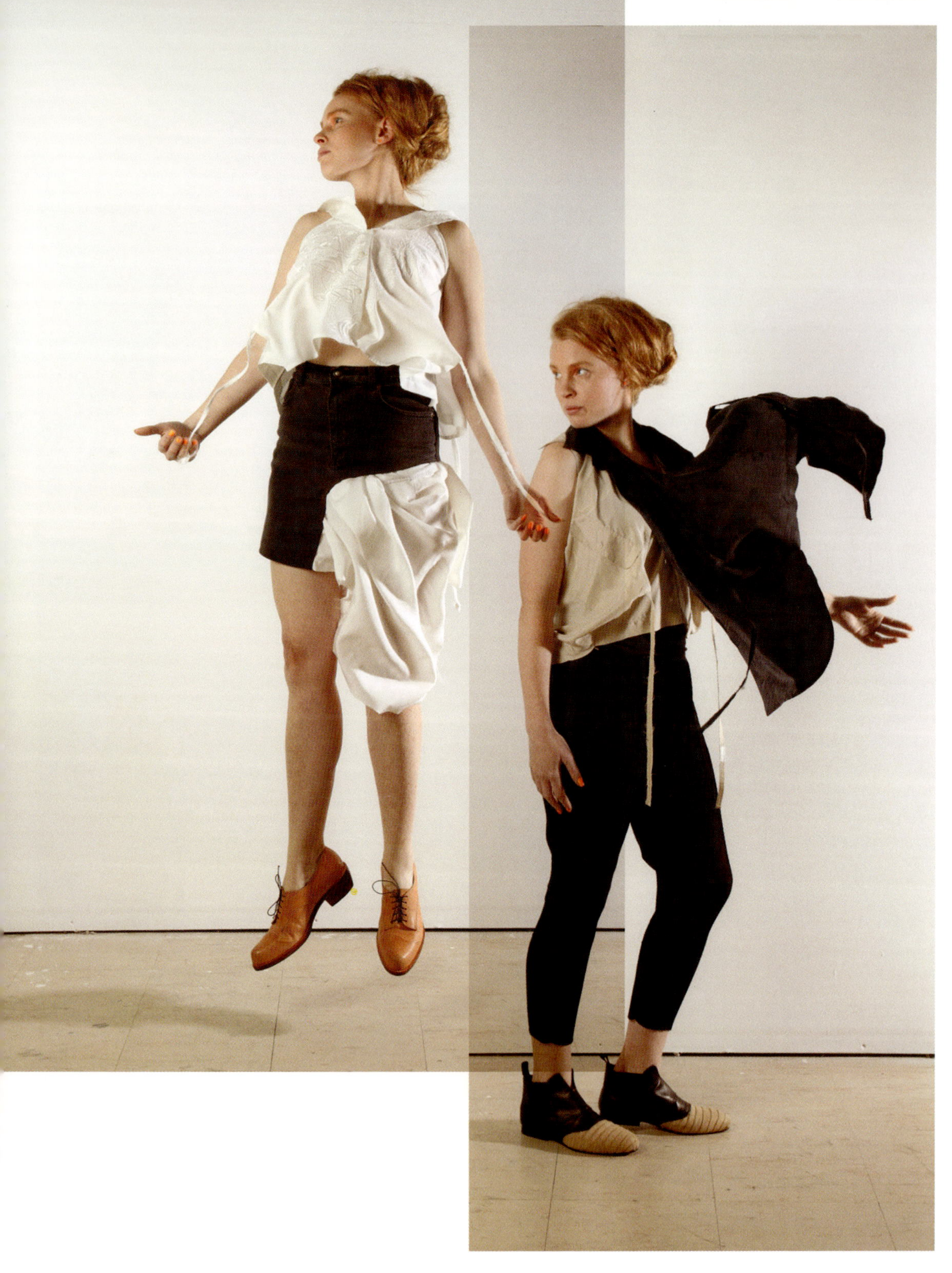

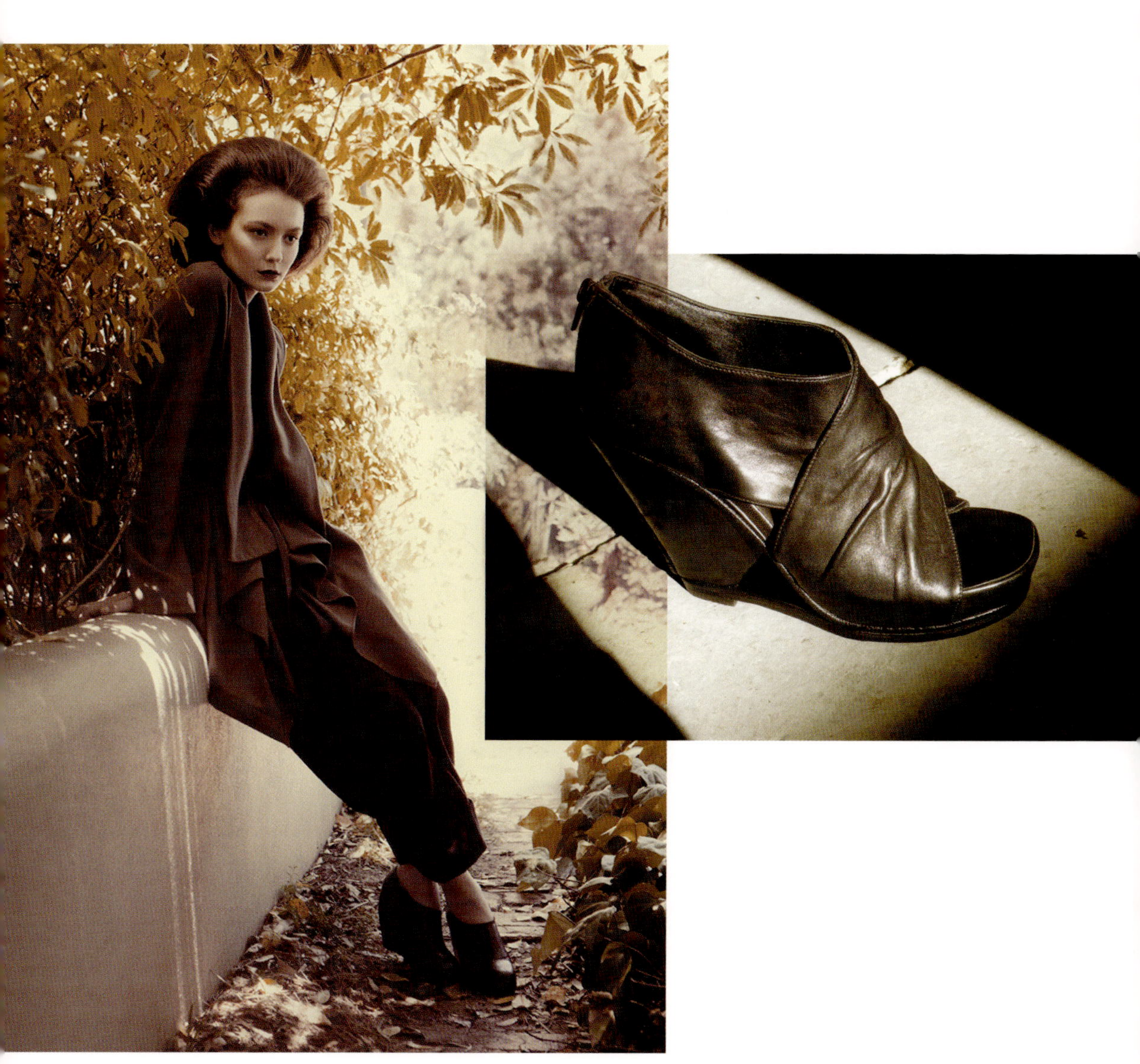

DAITA KIMURA, THE OLD CURIOSITY SHOP

How did you get started? **I STARTED WORKING WITH A SHOE DESIGNER IN LONDON.** What is your work about? **MY WORK IS UNIQUE, ORIGINAL AND WEARABLE.** Is there a specific reason why you chose shoe design? **I HAVE ALWAYS BEEN A 3D PERSON.** What differentiates your work from others? **THE SHAPES OF THE SHOES.** What do you consider the most innovative piece of your designs so far? **BIG FOOT FOR SMELLY FEET** Which stages of the creative process do you find the most and least gratifying? **THE MOST AND LEAST GRATIFYING STAGE IS WHEN THE FIRST SAMPLE ARRIVES.** Who do you admire? **JOHN MOORE** What are your thoughts on quick-consumption culture and over-commercialisation? **THERE WILL ALWAYS BE PEOPLE WHO APPRECIATE ORIGINAL DESIGN.** What does beauty mean for you? **BEAUTY AGES WELL.**

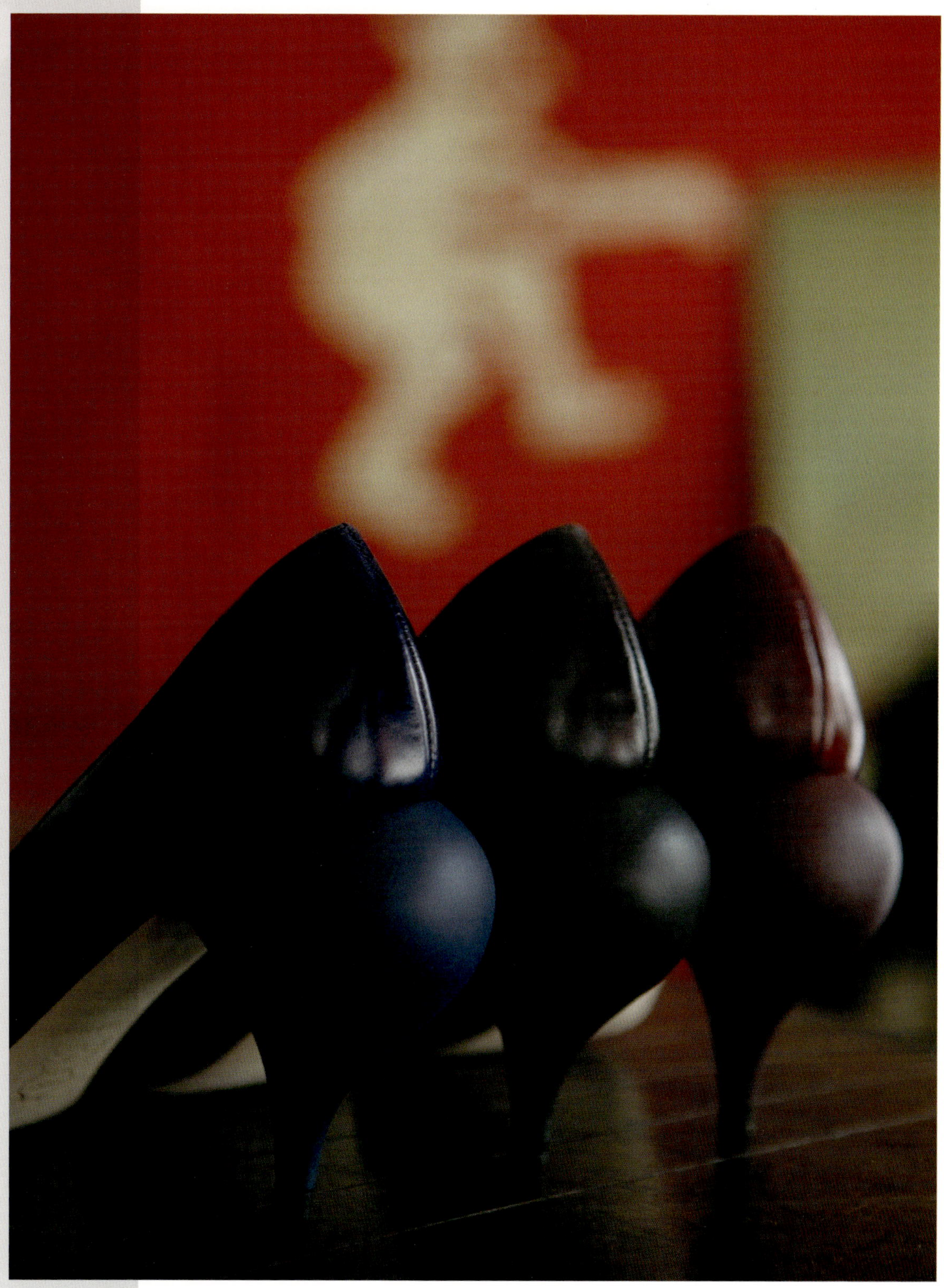

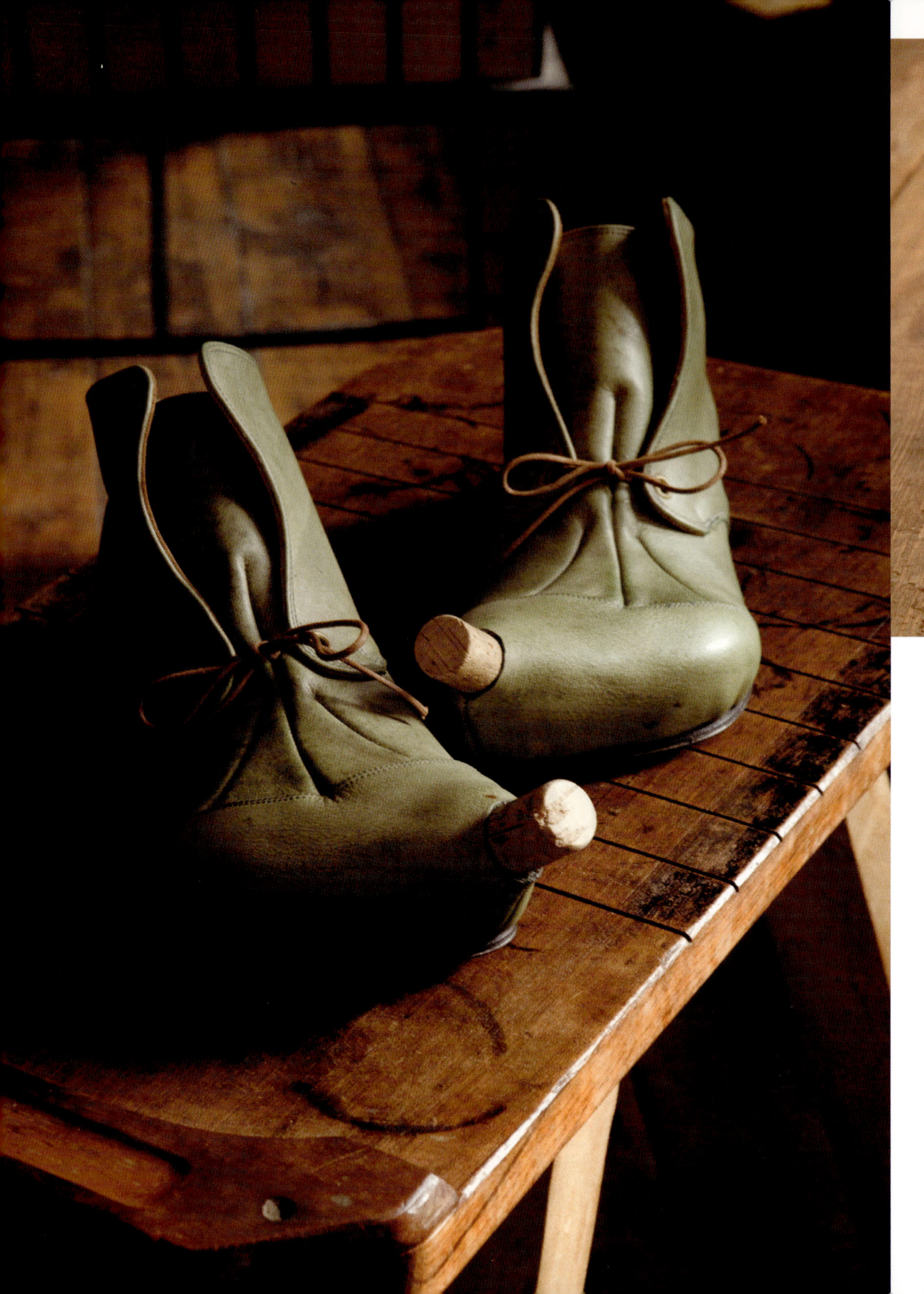

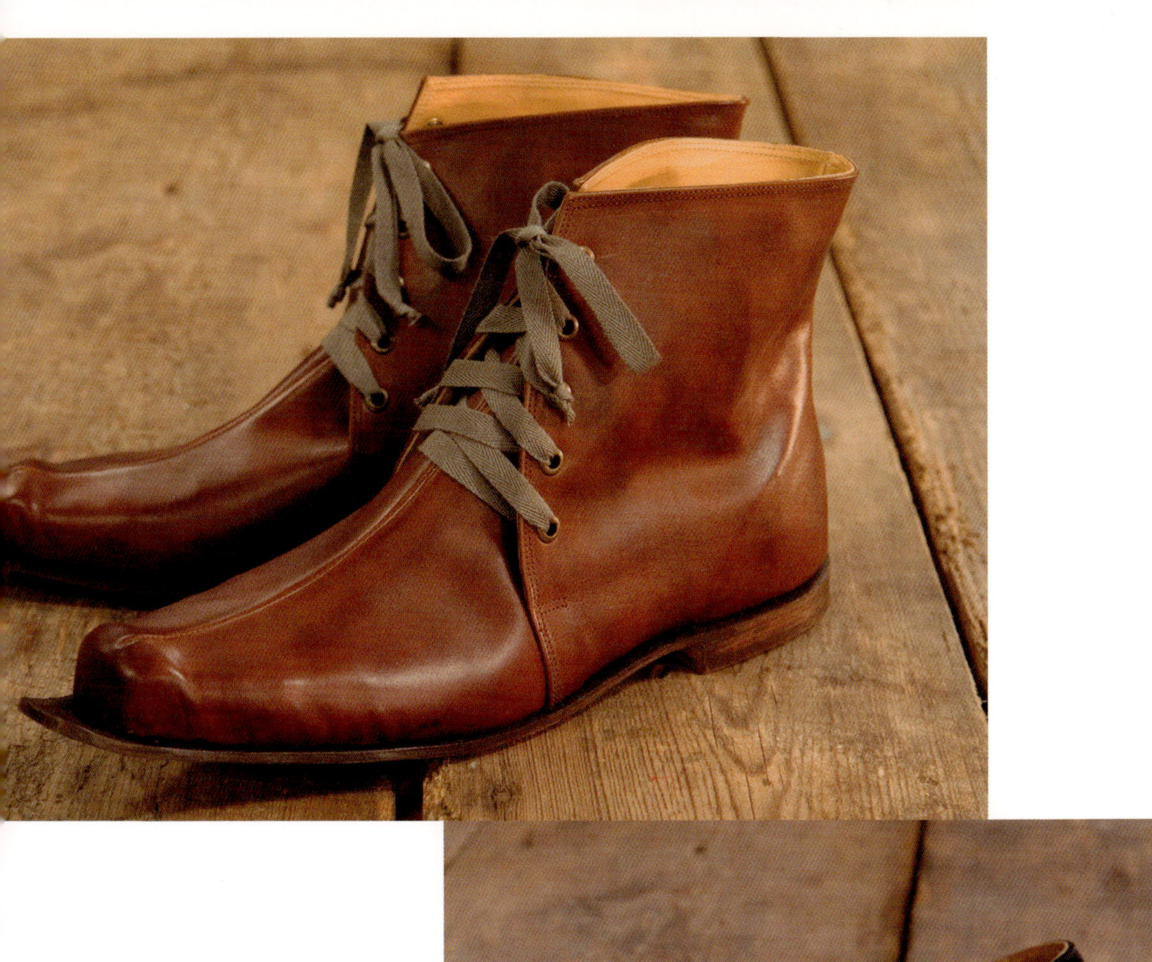

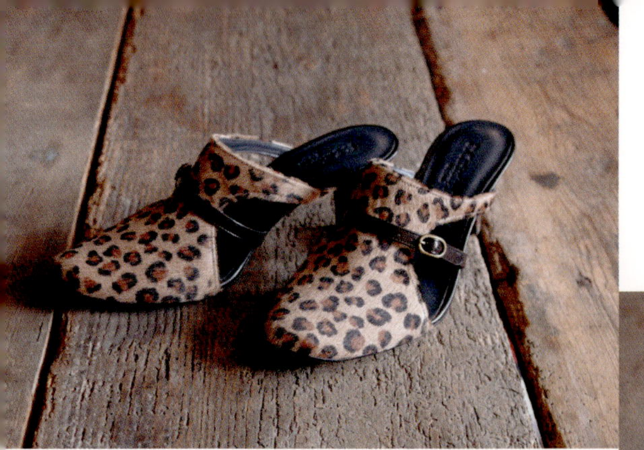

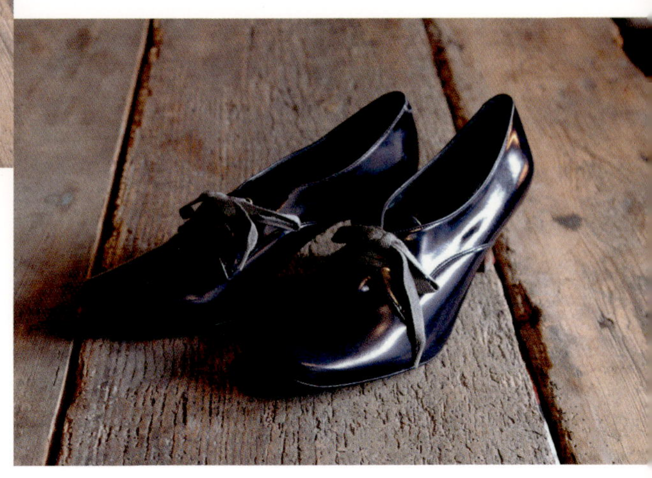

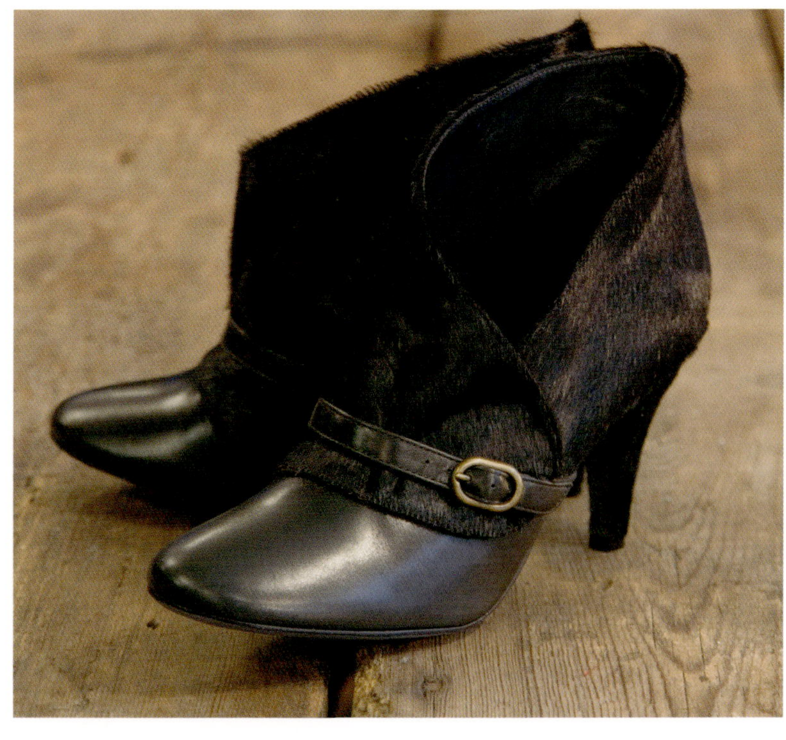

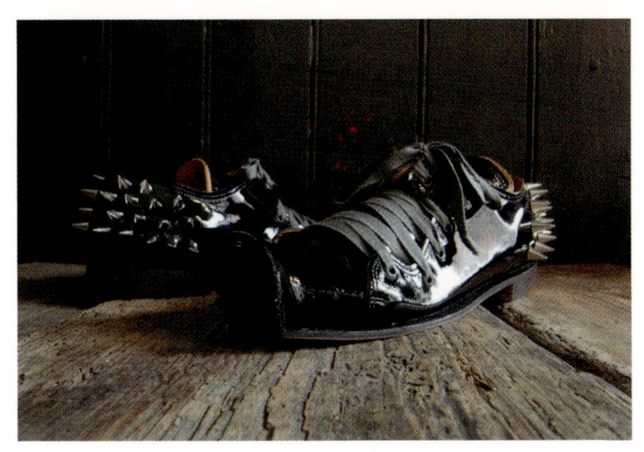

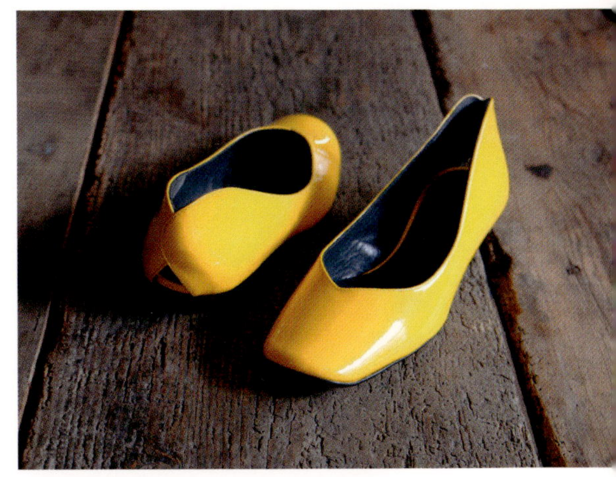

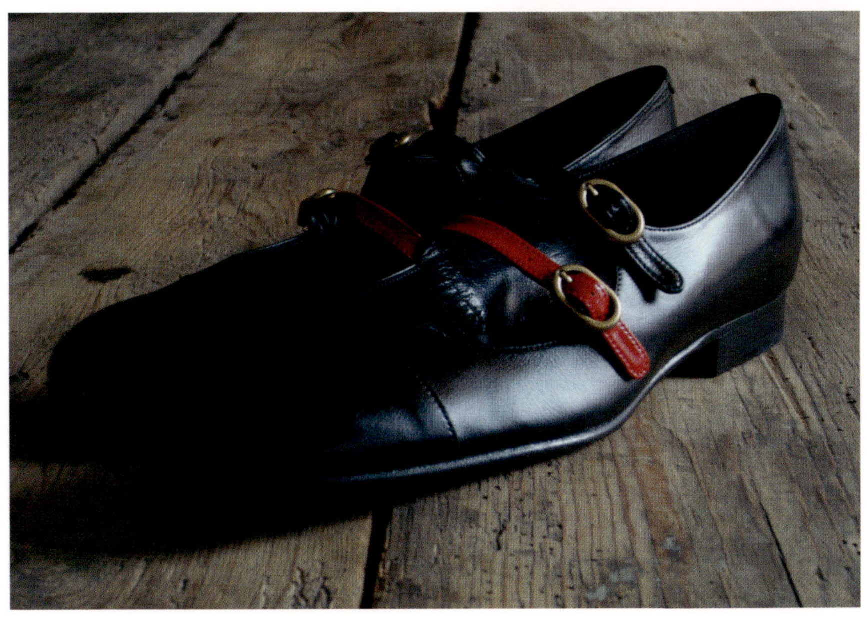

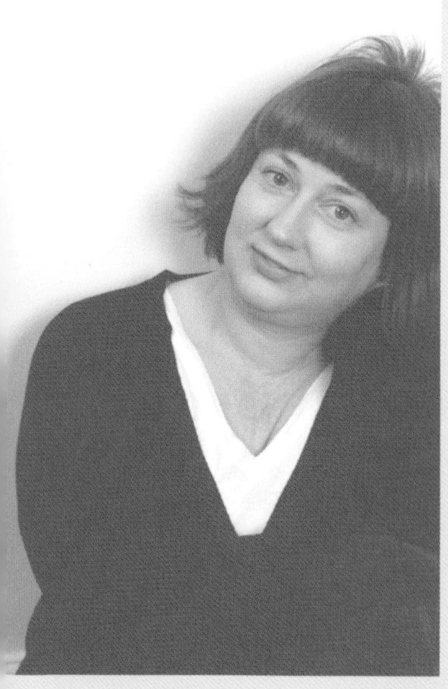

TRACEY NEULS

How did you discover your passion for shoe design? **WHEN I WAS A CHILD I USED TO MAKE SHOES WITH TOILET ROLLS FOR HEELS. I WOULD LITERALLY WALK AROUND TOWN WITH THEM. I FEEL QUITE GRATEFUL THAT MY CAREER PATH WAS PREDETERMINED!** How did you get started? **DURING MY STUDIES, MY FINAL SHOW WAS PICKED UP BY A CLOTHING FASHION DESIGNER CALLED TRACY MULLIGAN. I STARTED DOING HER CATWALK SHOES WHICH TURNED OUT TO BE A HIT AND WENT INTO PRODUCTION. WE FIRST PRODUCED IN THE UK AND THEN IN ITALY TO PRODUCE ON A LARGER SCALE. THE HUGE AMOUNT OF WORK ON TOP OF TRYING TO LEARN ANOTHER LANGUAGE WAS OVERWHELMING. FOR THE SMALL AMOUNT OF PAY, I THOUGHT I WOULD HAVE NOTHING TO LOSE THAN TO WORK FOR MYSELF.** How would you describe your style? **MY WORK IS VERY SCULPTURAL. I AM OBSESSED WITH THE SHADOW LIKE QUALITIES OF SHOES. IN SOME WAYS MY SHOES ARE MORE AKIN TO FURNITURE THAN FASHION. THEY TEND TO BE MINIMALIST WITH A TWIST. 'LESS IS MORE' IS DIFFICULT TO ACHIEVE, BUT WHEN YOU GET IT RIGHT, IT IS VERY SATISFYING. PULLING THE LEATHER OVER THE HEEL FROM THE UPPER IN ONE PIECE WAS SOMETHING I STARTED DOING IN 1998 AT COLLEGE AND HAVE CARRIED THIS THROUGH TO EACH AND EVERY COLLECTION. THIS SUBTLE DEVELOPMENT IN SHOE MAKING IS NOW REPRODUCED IN CHINA AND BRAZIL AND HAS BECOME MORE OR LESS THE NORM. I WANT MY FOOTWEAR TO BE TIMELESS SO I DON'T FOLLOW TRENDS. I BELIEVE FOOTWEAR SHOULD BE ORIGINAL AND NOT WHAT FASHION DICTATES. WITH SO MANY PEOPLE IN THE WORLD, IT IS IMPORTANT TO BE INDIVIDUAL. YOU WILL NEVER HEAR SOMEONE SAY 'THAT IS SO LAST SEASON' TO ANY OF MY DESIGNS.** Tell us something about the design process. **MY CREATIVE PROCESS IS VERY INSULAR. I TRY TO CAPTURE THAT CHILD LIKE IMAGINATION AND INNOCENCE OF YOUTH WHERE YOU ARE NOT INFLUENCED BY THE WORLD AROUND YOU. MY STARTING POINT IS OFTEN MY FINGER TIPS. WHEN IT COMES TO SCULPTING A NEW SHAPE, I USE PLASTICENE AS I DID WHEN I WAS A KID. JUST THE SMELL OF PLASTICENE IS ENOUGH TO GET THE CREATIVE JUICES FLOWING. I LOVE THE HAND SCULPTING STAGE.** What are your thoughts on the culture of quick consumption and over-commercialisation? **THE OTHER DAY A CUSTOMER BROUGHT IN A PAIR OF SHOES THAT WE MADE BACK IN 2000 WITH A SMALL FAMILY RUN FACTORY IN VICTORIA PARK. SHE NEEDED THE HEEL SORTING. THE FACT THAT THE SHOES WERE STILL UP THERE AS ONE OF HER FAVOURITES, AS WEARABLE TODAY AS THE DAY SHE BOUGHT THEM IS THE PERFECT SCENARIO FOR ME. IT CONCERNS ME THAT THE NEXT GENERATION OF CONSUMERS HAVE GROWN UP WITH HIGH STREET VIEWS OF WHAT FOOTWEAR HAS TO OFFER. IN GENERAL, HIGH STREET RETAIL PRICES DON'T EVEN COVER THE COST OF THE LEATHERS WE USE. WHAT SORT OF LONGEVITY OR COMFORT CAN THESE SHOES DELIVER? IF YOU KNOW YOUR SHOES ARE TEMPORARY, WHAT SORT OF RELATIONSHIP CAN BE MADE WITH THEM? I HOPE THAT ONE DAY AN APPRECIATION OF QUALITY AND TIMELESSNESS ALONG WITH RESPECT FOR ONE'S INDIVIDUALITY WILL REAPPEAR IN OUR SOCIETY.**

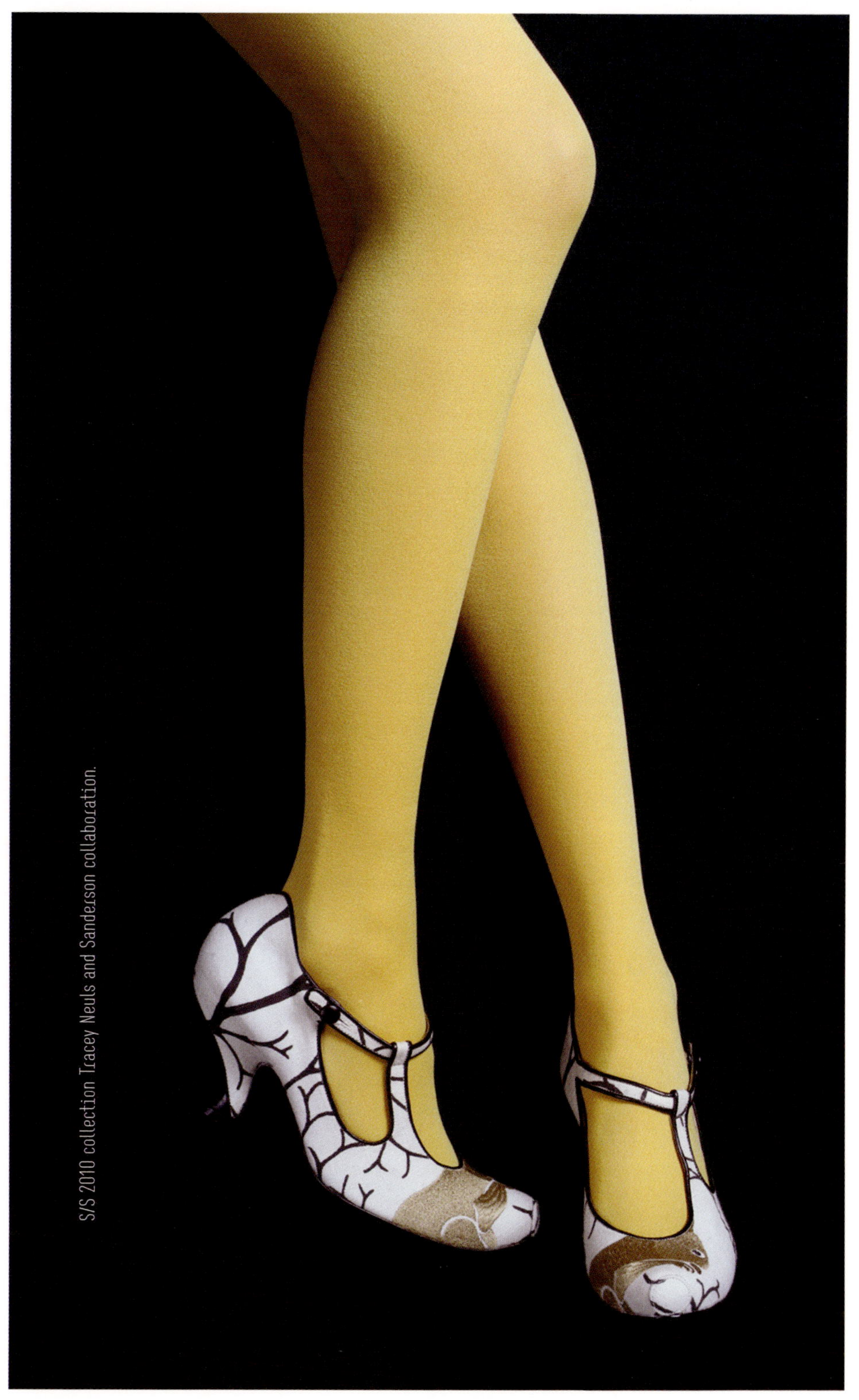

S/S 2010 collection Tracey Neuls and Sanderson collaboration.

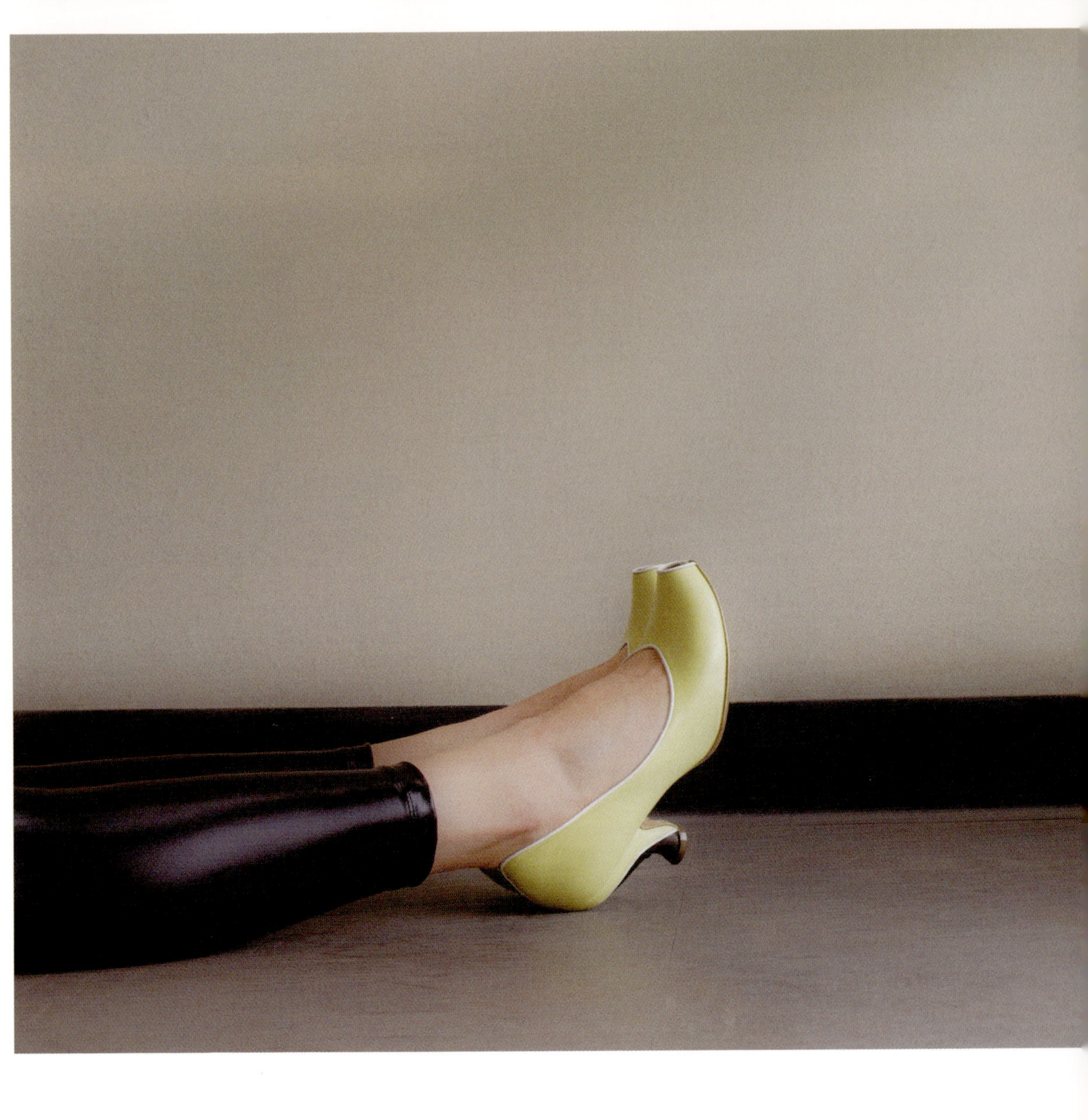

Previous page: S/S 2010 collection. This page: S/S 2010 Tracey Neuls and Moroso collaboration.

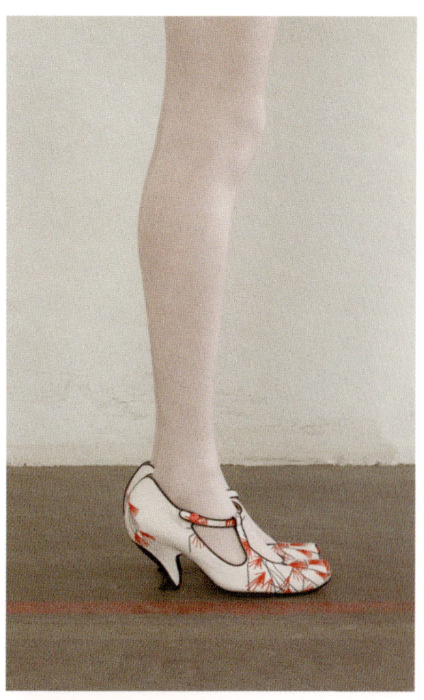

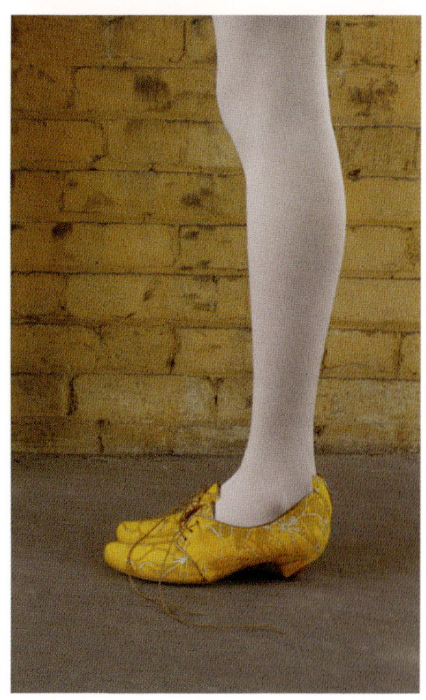

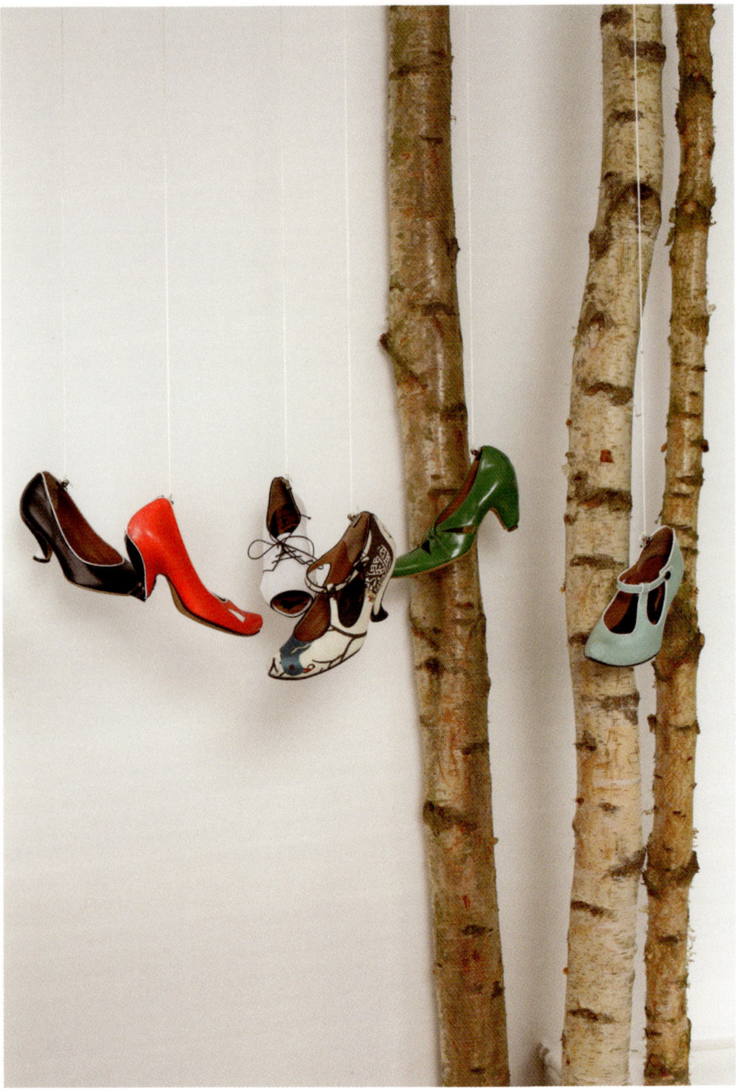

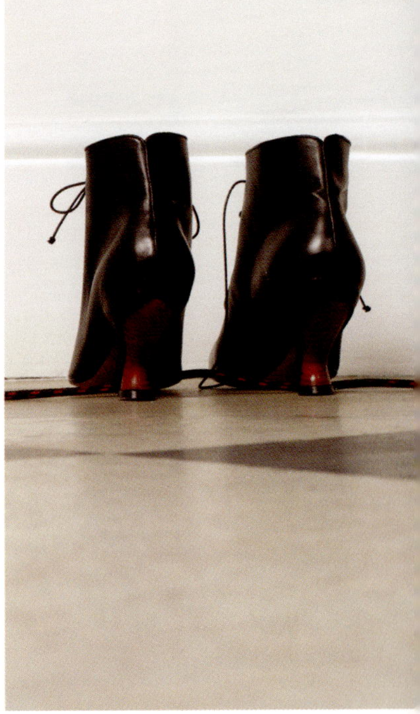

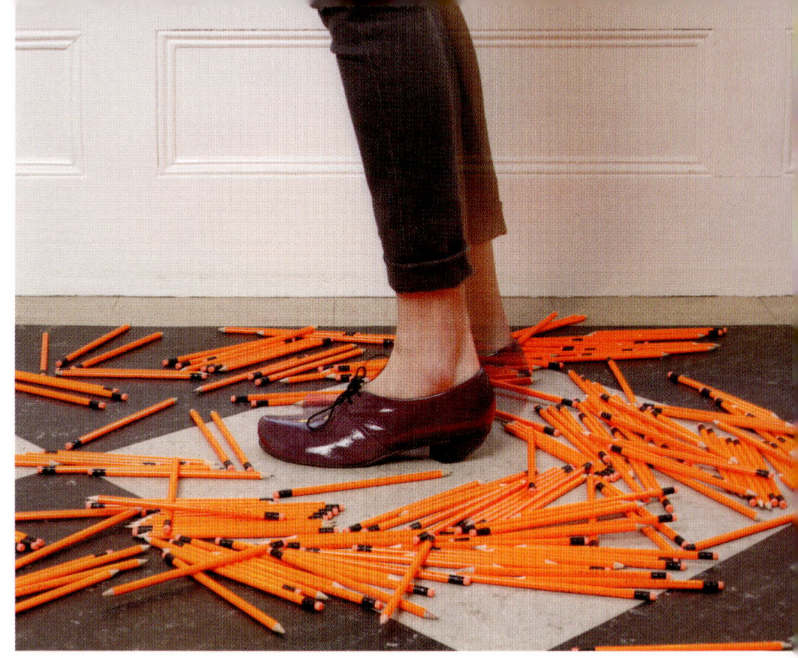

Previous and this page: S/S 2010 collection. This page top: A/W 2010 TN29 collection.

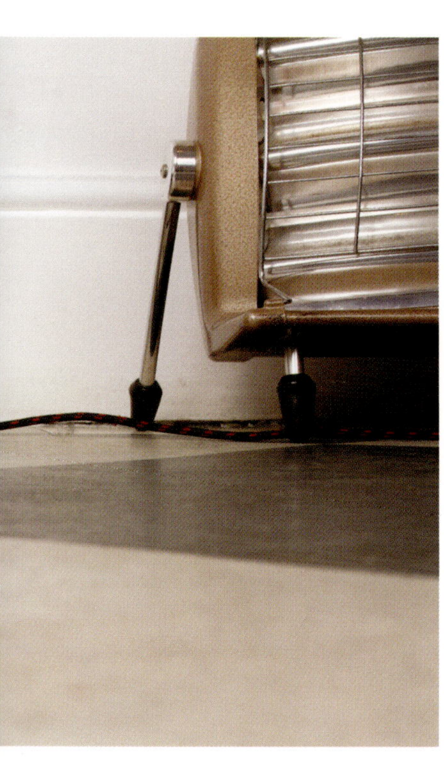

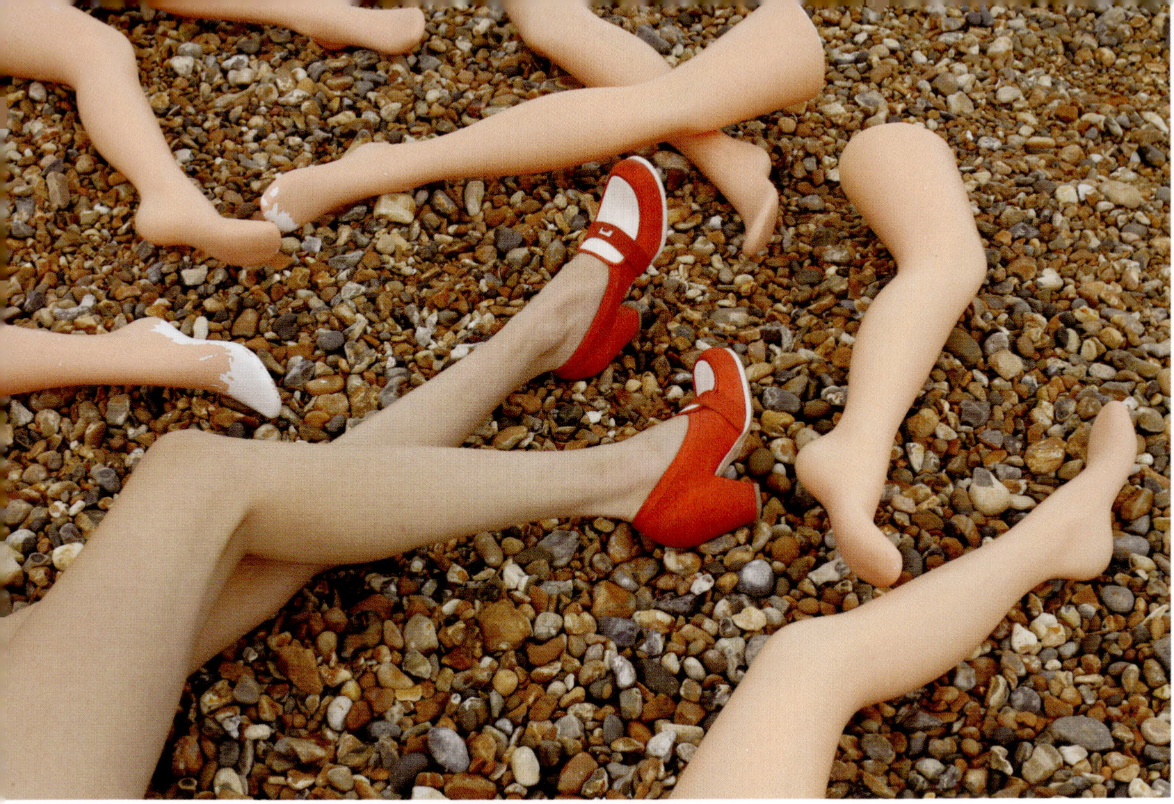

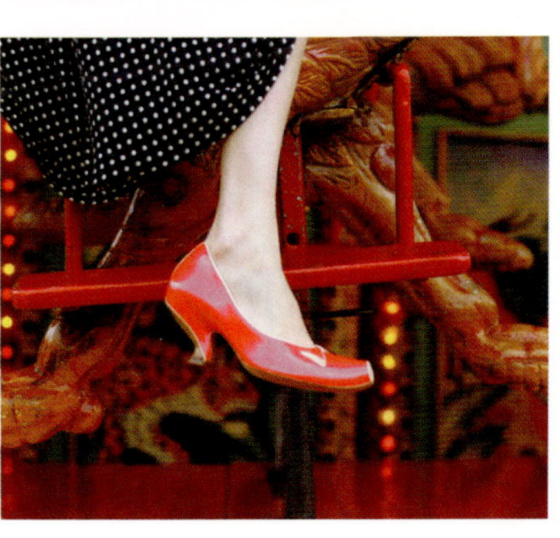

This page top: S/S 2011 TN29 collection. Bottom: S/S 2011 collection.
Next page top: A/W 2011 collection. Bottom: A/W 2011 TN29 collection.

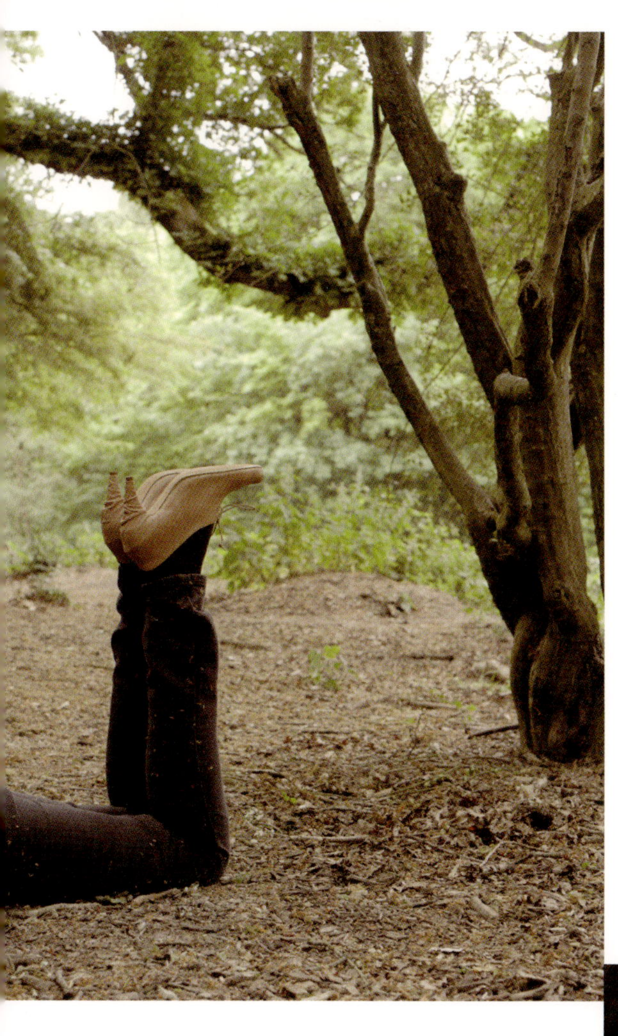

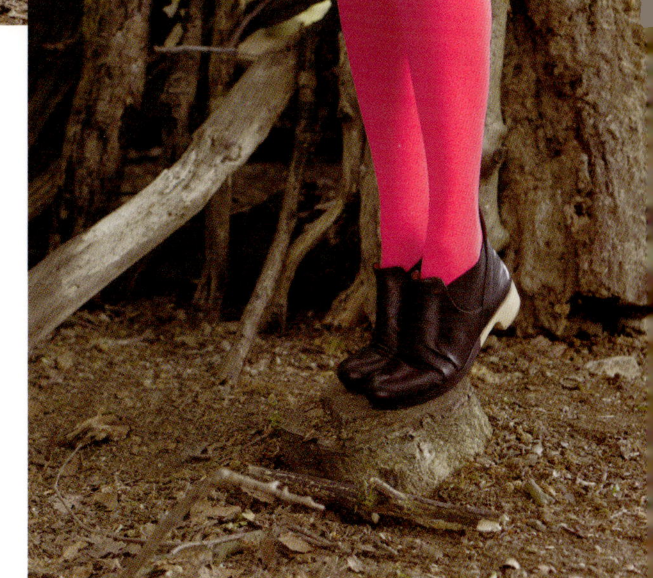

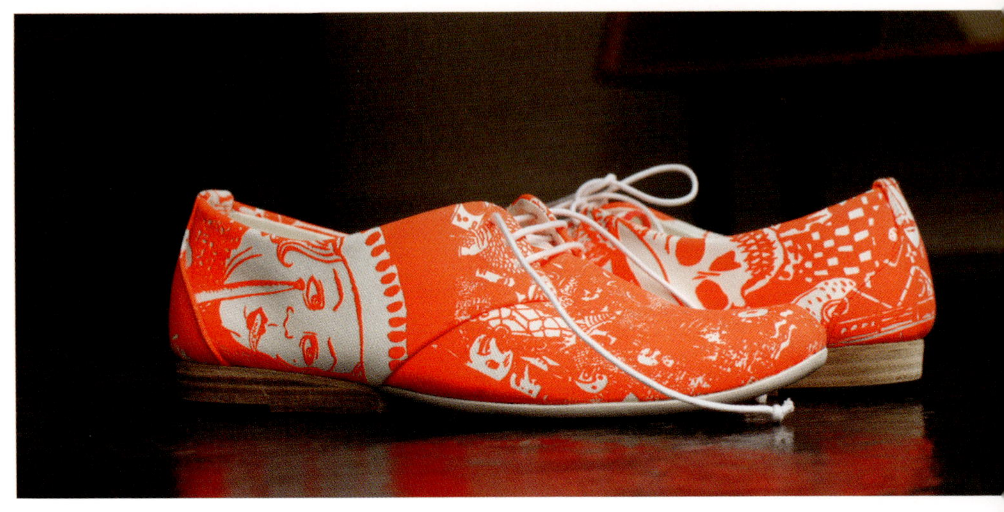

This page: S/S 2012 Tracey Neuls and Le Gun collaboration.
Next page: A/W 2011 collection.

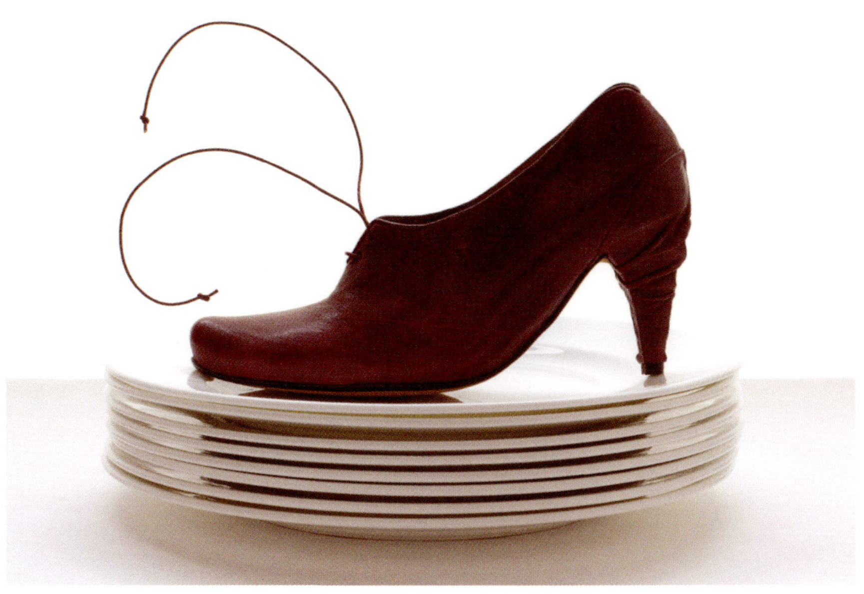

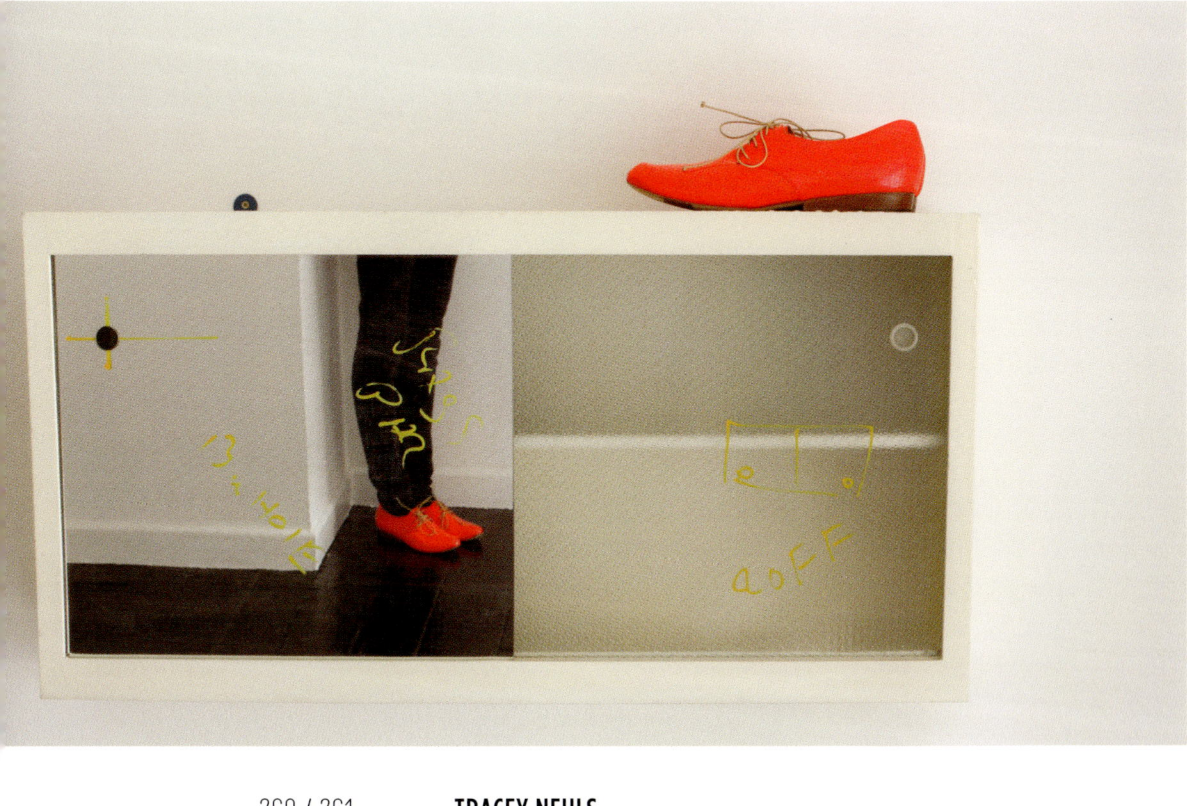

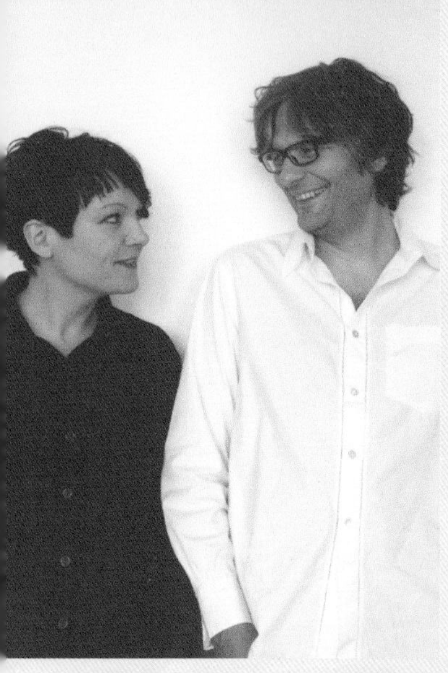

ANGELA SPIETH AND MICHAEL OEHLER, TRIPPEN

Please introduce yourself **ANGELA: I MOVED TO WEST BERLIN IN THE MID-EIGHTIES AND STUDIED FASHION DESIGN AT THE UNIVERSITY OF THE ARTS. AFTER LEAVING UNIVERSITY IN 1987, I JOINED A GERMAN SHOE MANUFACTURER FOR AN INTERNSHIP AND STAYED ON FOR THREE YEARS. IN THE SUBSEQUENT YEARS I WORKED AS A FREELANCE FOOTWEAR DESIGNER IN MANY COUNTRIES AROUND THE WORLD, FIRST IN EUROPE, THEN THE US AND LATER IN ASIA. IN ALL THESE YEARS I GAINED DEEP INSIGHTS INTO THE INDUSTRY AND IT BECAME CLEAR TO ME THAT I HAD TO ESCAPE THE LOGIC OF THE MASS MARKET: INNOVATION, IMITATION, MASS PRODUCTION, TRASH AND A SENSELESS DESTRUCTION OF RESOURCES.MICHAEL: I GREW UP IN LINDAU AT LAKE CONSTANCE AND MOVED TO WEST BERLIN IN THE EARLY EIGHTIES WHERE I SIGNED UP WITH A SHOEMAKER TO LEARN THE TRADE FROM START TO FINISH. LATER I SET UP MY OWN WORKSHOP IN KREUZBERG. THERE I BUILT CUSTOM MADE SHOES FOR THEATRE AND FILM AS WELL AS FOR INDIVIDUAL CLIENTS, PROVIDING HIGH QUALITY AND ECOLOGICALLY SENSIBLE PRODUCTS.** How did you get started? **WE FIRST MET IN THE DESIGNTRANSFER GALLERY IN BERLIN AT AN EXHIBITION OF ANGELA'S THEN EMPLOYER. IN THE EARLY NINETIES WE VISITED AN OLD SHOE LAST FACTORY IN THE HARZ MOUNTAINS WHERE WE FOUND UNUSED WOODEN SOLES FROM THE SEVENTIES. IN FOUR INTENSIVE WEEKS EXPERIMENTING IN MICHAEL'S WORKSHOP IN KREUZBERG, WE DEVELOPED OUR FIRST SERIES OF SHOES WHICH WE EXHIBITED AT THE GALERIE FÜR KUNSTHANDWERK IN BERLIN. THE EXHIBITION WAS A TREMENDOUS SUCCESS AND BECAME THE STARTING POINT FOR OUR LABEL TRIPPEN.** What is your work about? **OUR WORK IS ABOUT DESIGNING INTELLIGENT FOOTWEAR THAT BALANCES PRACTICAL AND ECOLOGICAL ASPECTS WITH FASHION APPEAL. OUR DESIGNS TAKE FASHION TRENDS ON BOARD, BUT NOT THEIR THROWAWAY NATURE. ENVIRONMENTAL AND ECOLOGICAL PRODUCTION METHODS ARE NOT ONLY TAKEN INTO CONSIDERATION, BUT HAVE DIRECT INFLUENCE ON OUR DESIGNS. AT THE SAME TIME OUR APPROACH TO PATTERN TECHNIQUE IS OFTEN EXPERIMENTAL AND RATHER SIMILAR TO COUTURE.** What makes your work different from others? **WE MADE THE CONSCIOUS DECISION TO TAKE RESPONSIBILITY WITH PRODUCTION, SETTING UP OUR OWN FACTORY JUST OUTSIDE BERLIN. THIS MEANS CLOSE INVOLVEMENT AND HIGHER WAGE COSTS, BUT ALSO A FLEXIBILITY THAT ALLOWS ATTENTION TO BE PAID TO CUSTOMER REQUESTS AND PROVIDES US WITH THE FACILITY TO PRODUCE SMALL QUANTITIES OR EVEN SINGLE PAIRS.** What do you consider the most innovative piece of your designs so far? **THE CLOSED COLLECTION WITH ITS RECESSED, MECHANICALLY ATTACHED AND EASILY REPLACEABLE SOLE.** Are there any artists or art movements that have influenced you? **THE BAUHAUS WITH ITS HOLISTIC APPROACH TO DESIGN. LOUIS SULLIVAN AND HIS PRINCIPLE OF 'FORM FOLLOWS FUNCTION'.** If you had to choose one material to make an important piece, what would it be? **IT WOULD BE PUB, A VEGETABLE-TANNED BUFFALO LEATHER TREATED WITH OIL AND WAX. SCRATCHES AND IRREGULARITIES ARE CHARACTERISTIC OF THIS NATURAL MATERIAL.** Tell us something about the current state of your profession in general. **WE ARE QUITE SUCCESSFUL IN CHINA AT THE MOMENT. NOW THE QUESTION IS HOW TO CONVINCE OUR PARTNERS OF A SUSTAINABLE GROWTH.**

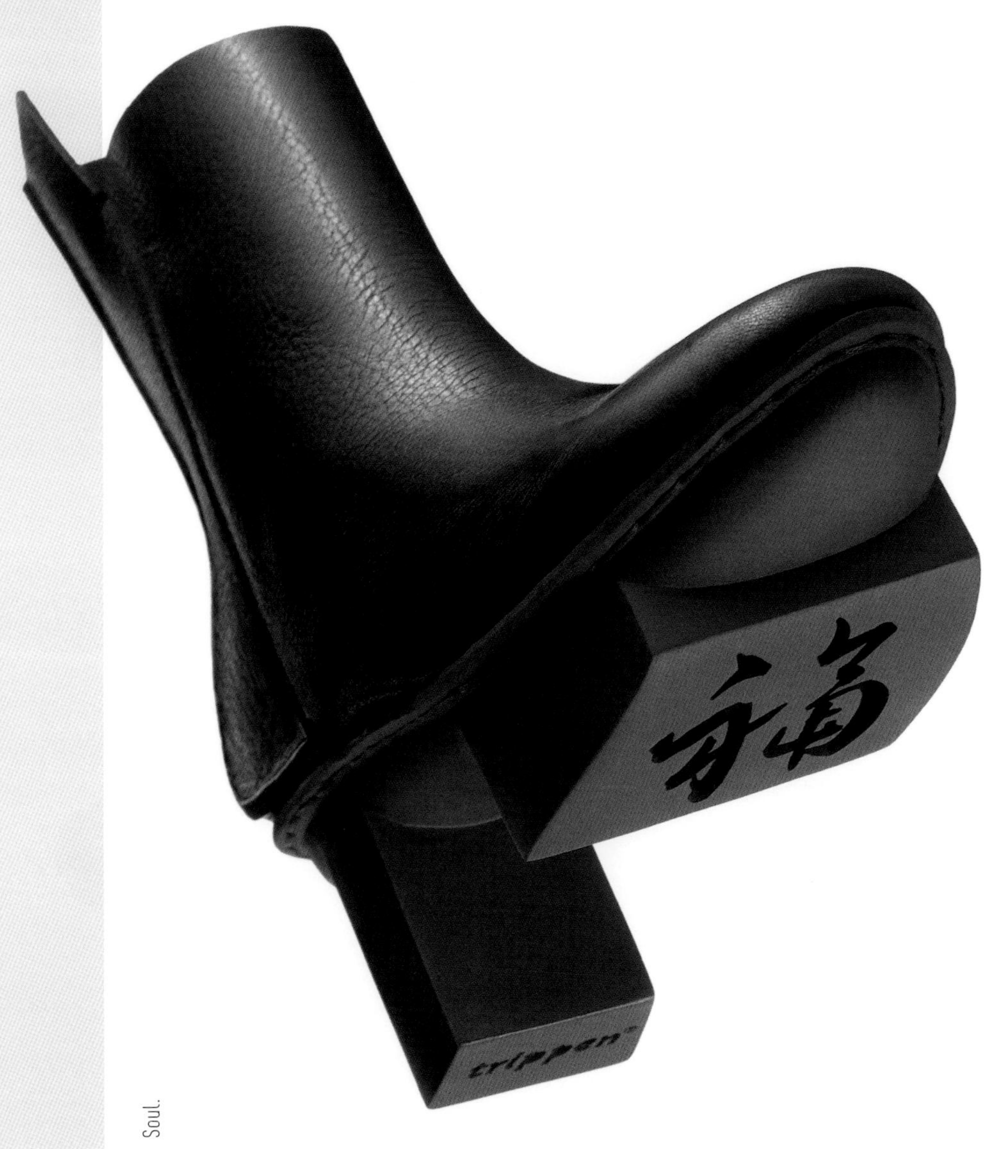

Soul.

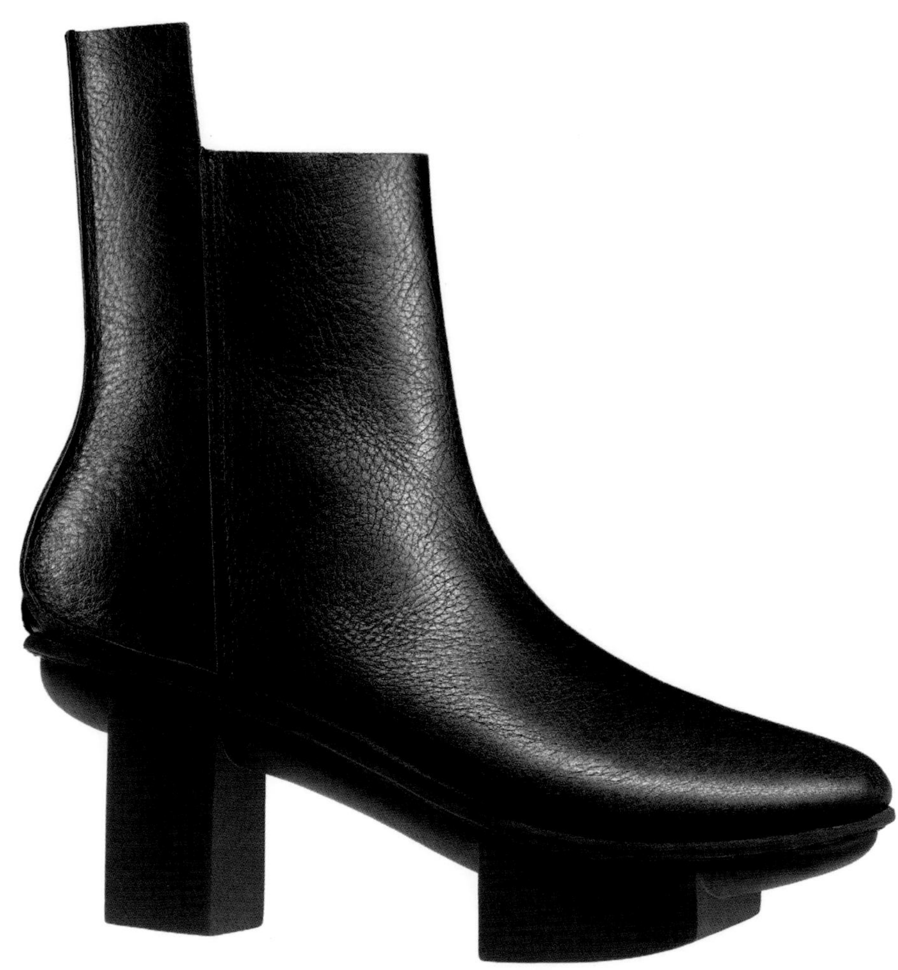

This page: Soul. Next page: Dream.

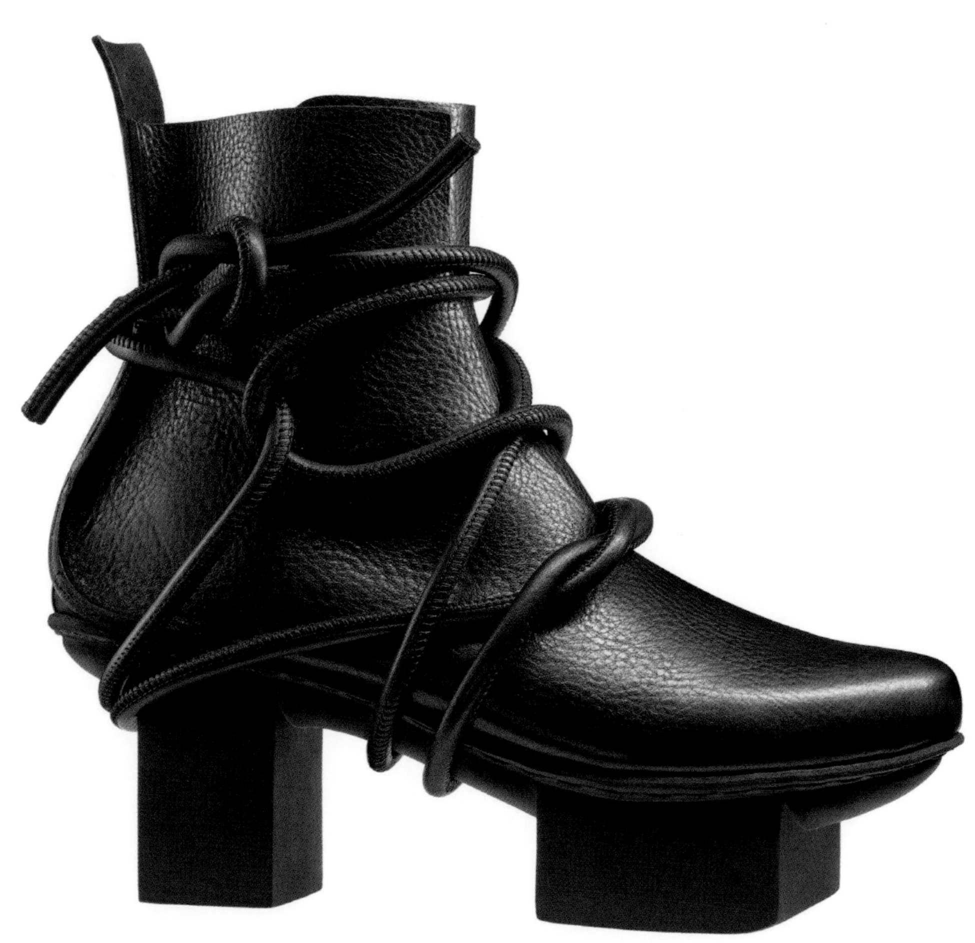

Left: Rectangle. Right: Volume.

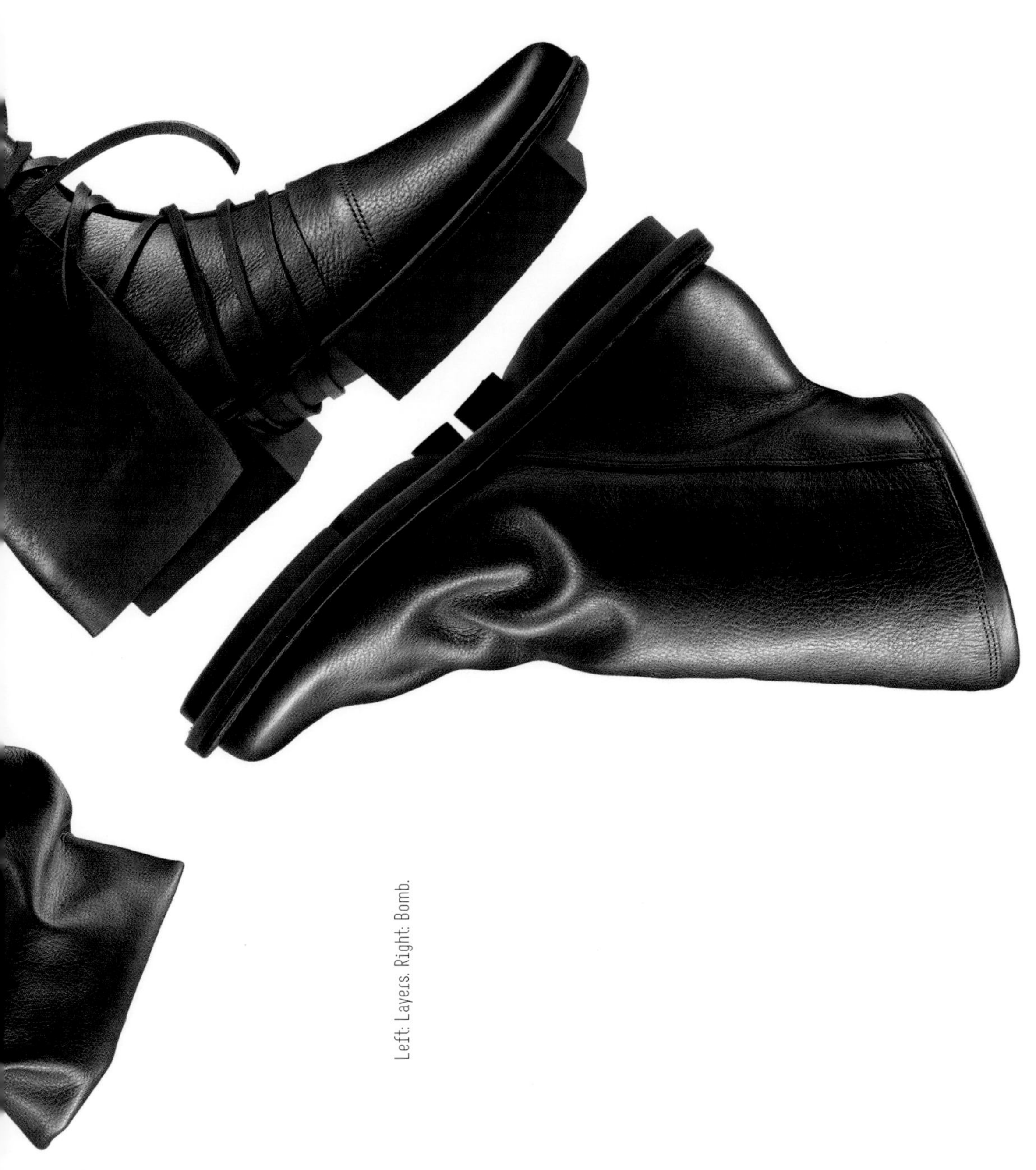

Left: Layers. Right: Bomb.

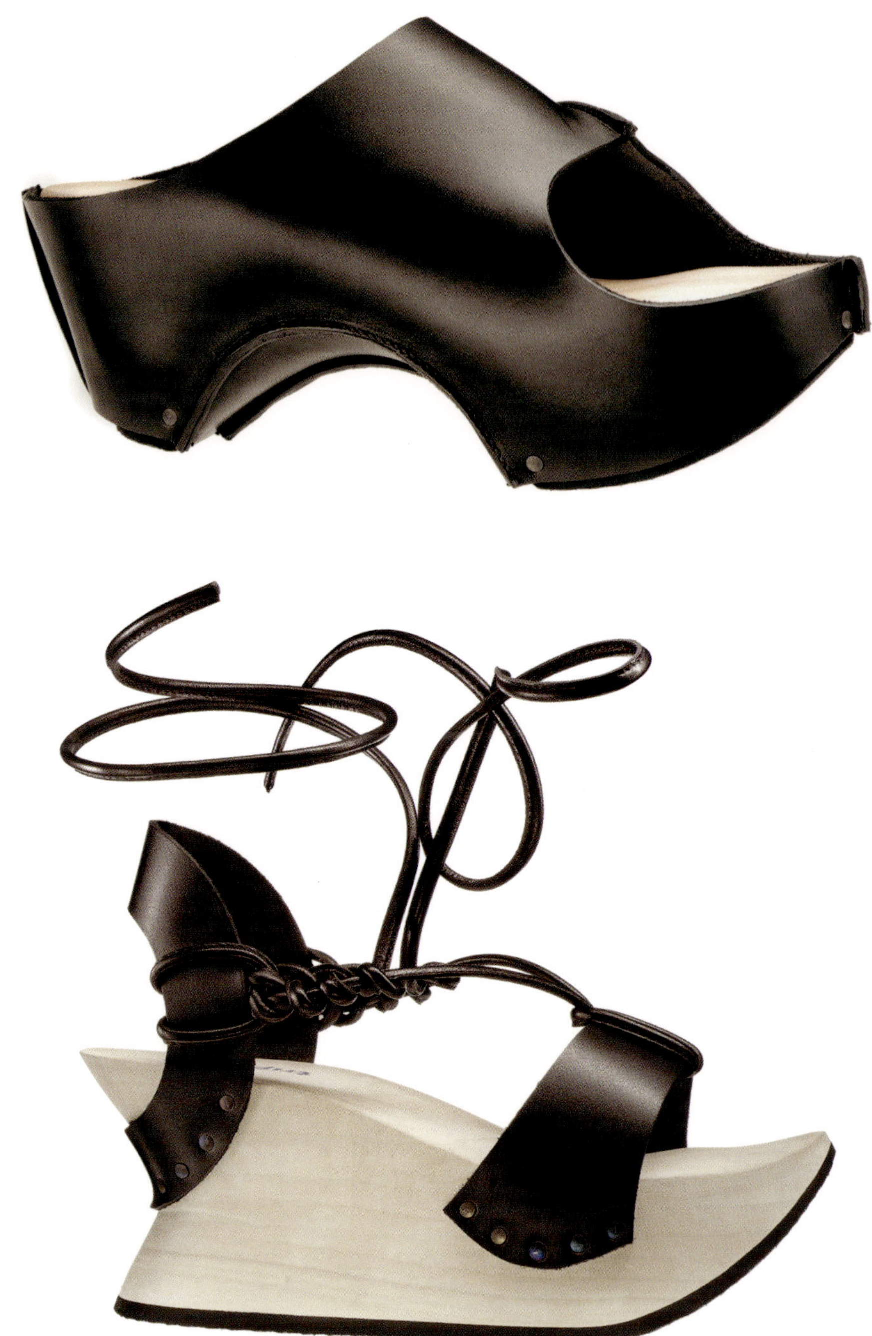

Top: Hutu. Bottom: Sailor. Next page top: Rivet. Bottom: Cape.

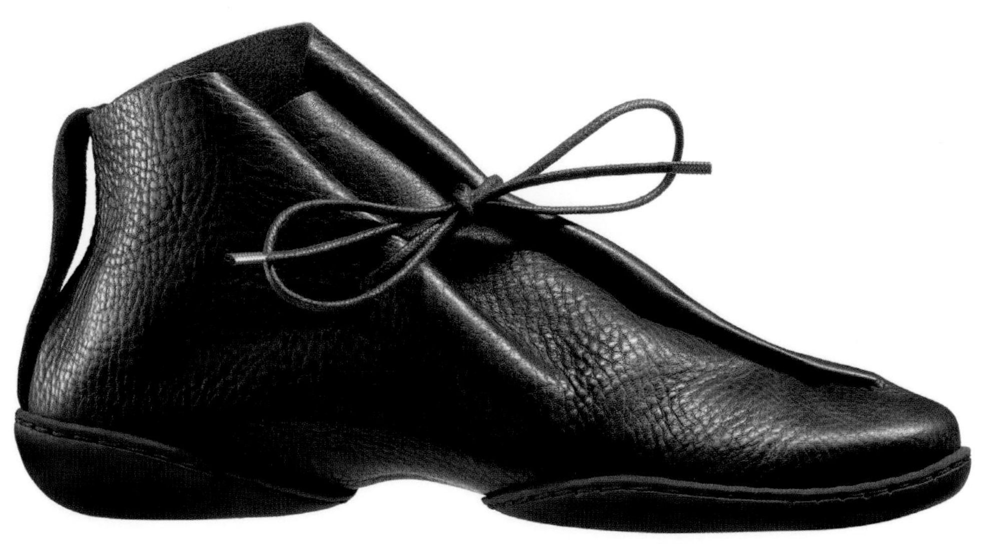

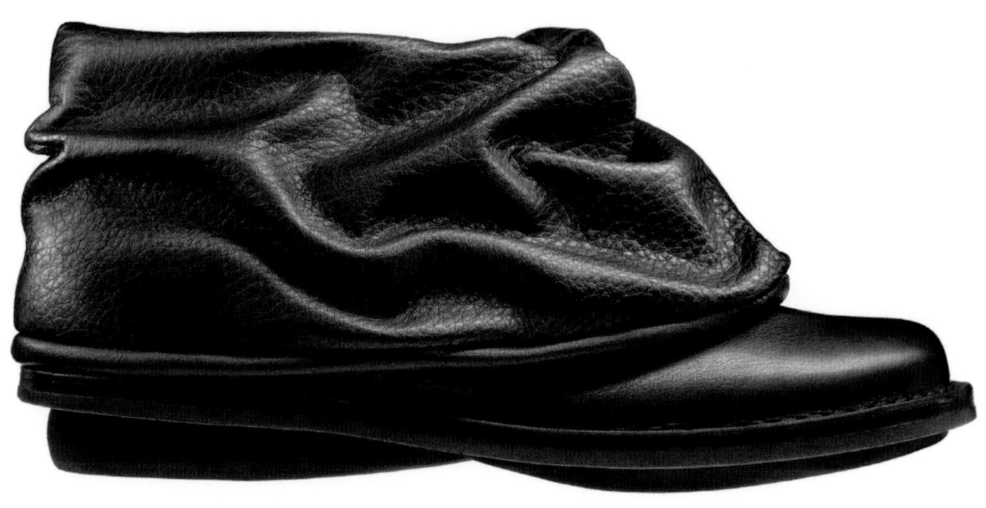

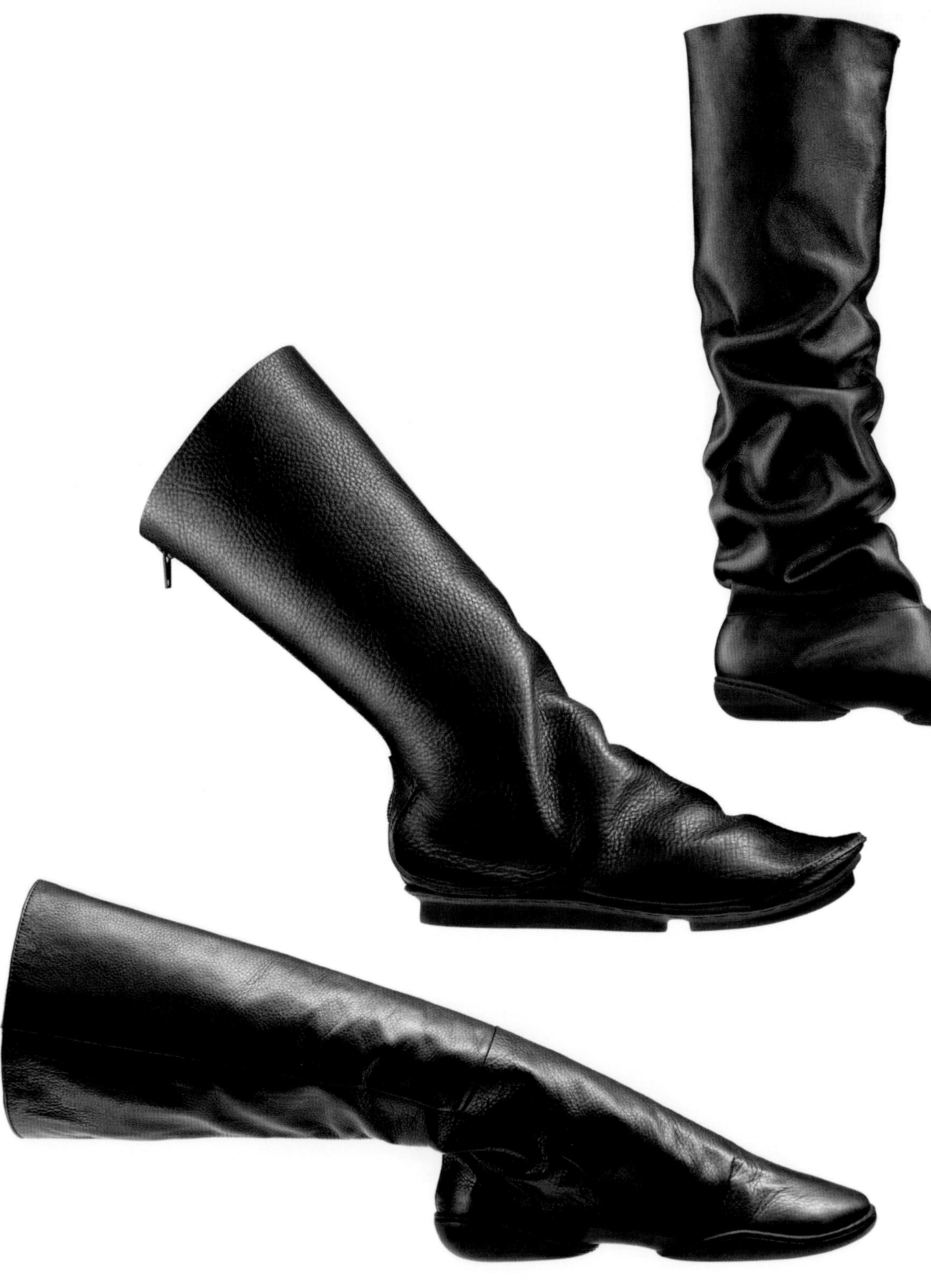

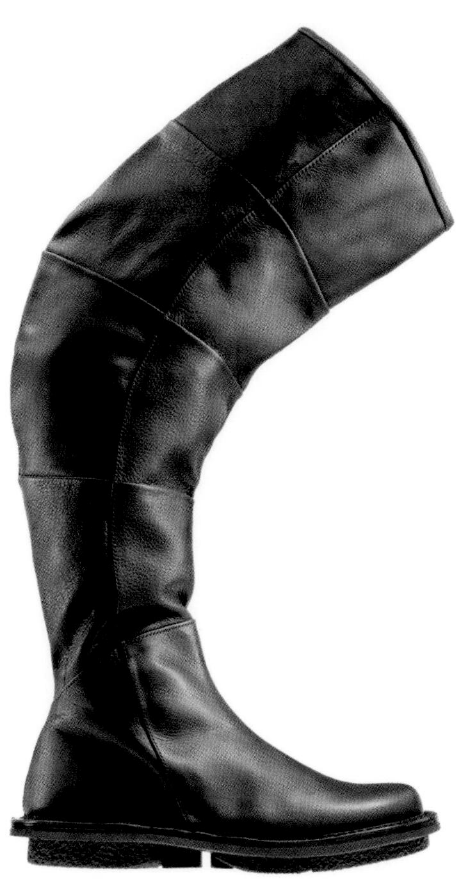

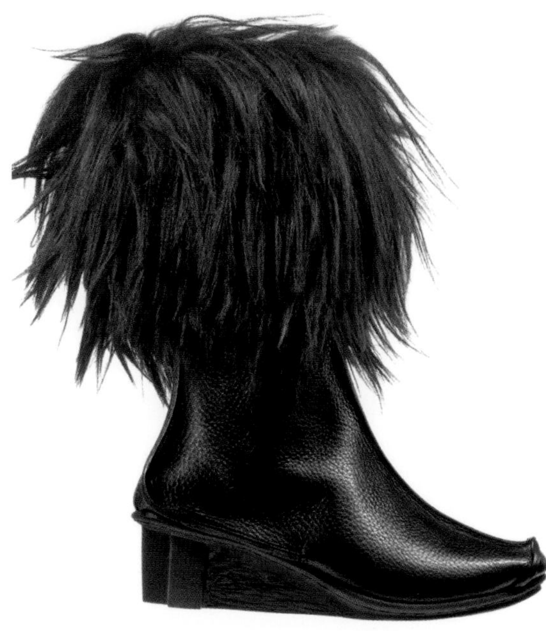

Left to right: Lotus, Napoleon, Nox, Parachute and Beast.

REM D. KOOLHAAS AND GALAHAD CLARK, UNITED NUDE

Rem D. Koolhaas is a Dutch architect trained at the Technical University of Delft in Holland. He is also creative director and founder of United Nude. In 2000 he produced and edited a documentary film entitled Moving Manhattan with Neville Mars along with an accompanying book called Shadow Book. **GALAHAD CLARK IS ALSO FOUNDER OF UNITED NUDE AND A SEVENTH GENERATION SHOEMAKER FROM SOMERSET, ENGLAND. HE LEARNED THE FAMILY TRADE WORKING SUMMERS ON PRODUCTION LINES FOR CLARK'S SHOES IN NORTHAMPTON AND ITALY. AS A MOREHEAD SCHOLAR HE STUDIED CHINESE AND ANTHROPOLOGY AT THE UNIVERSITY OF NORTH CAROLINA. GALAHAD FOUNDED STUDENTS 4 STUDENTS INTERNATIONAL, A HUMANITARIAN ORGANIZATION PROJECT TO BENEFIT STUDENTS IN AFRICA. IN 2002 HE TOOK OVER THE TERRA PLANA SHOE BRAND WHICH HE HAS RUN EVER SINCE.** The United Nude story begins with a broken heart. Rem's attempt to get the girl back was made by downsizing architecture to the scale of a woman's foot. Through the inspiration of romance, the Möbius shoe was born and in 2003 Rem was nominated for the Rotterdam Design Award. When Galahad saw the Möbius design he was immediately convinced that a new brand had to be formed. Together Rem and Galahad created United Nude, the name deriving from the fact that products evolve from international teams in an open way with direct recognition. **SINCE UNITED NUDE LAUNCHED IN 2003 WITH MÖBIUS SHOE, IT HAS ESTABLISHED ITSELF AS AN ICONIC BRAND WITH ARTISTIC STRUCTURAL FOOTWEAR COLLECTIONS FOR MEN AND WOMEN. THEIR PRODUCTS ARE ABOUT CLEAR CONCEPTS, ELEGANCE AND INNOVATION. TODAY, THE UNITED NUDE IS SOLD IN OVER FORTY COUNTRIES WORLDWIDE WITH STORES IN NEW YORK, LONDON, VIENNA, SHANGHAI, TIANJIN, GUANGZHOU AND MANY MORE.**

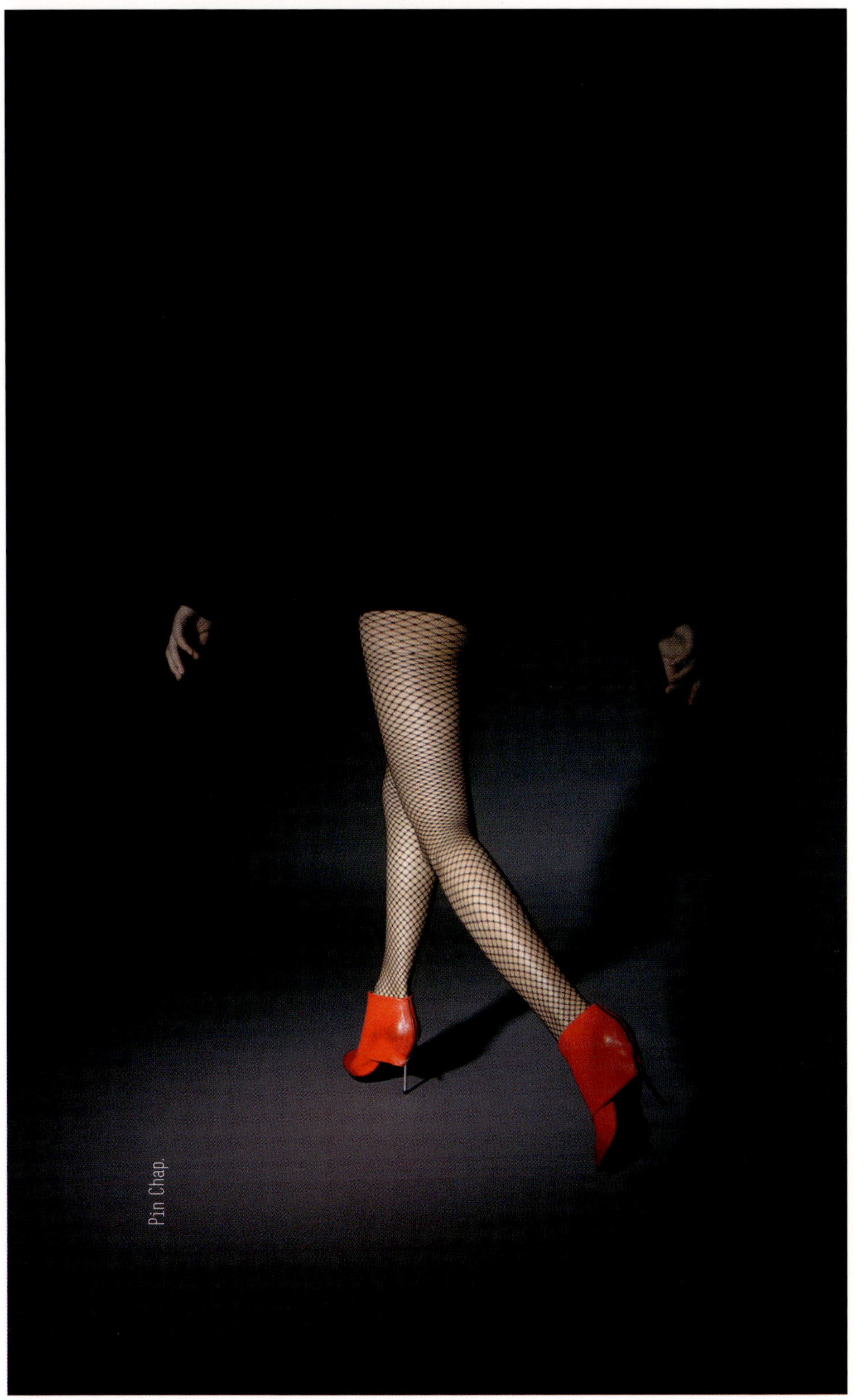
Pin Chap.

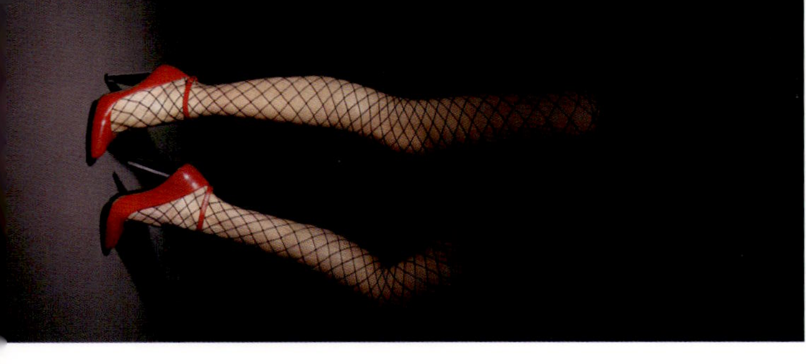

Top to bottom, left to right: Hollow Bootie, Helix Mens, Fold Mens, Cross Ankle Strap, Fold Hi and Eamz Pump.

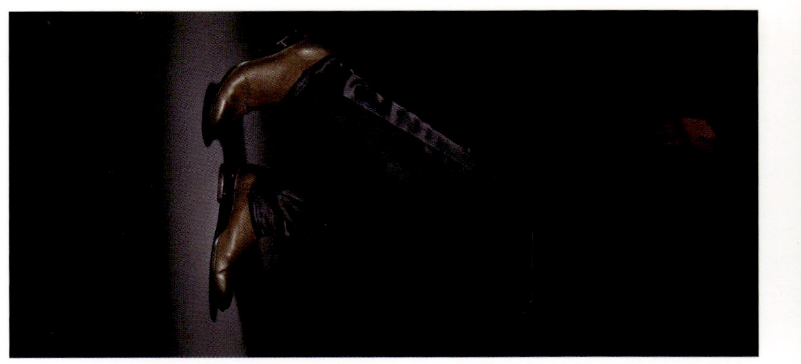

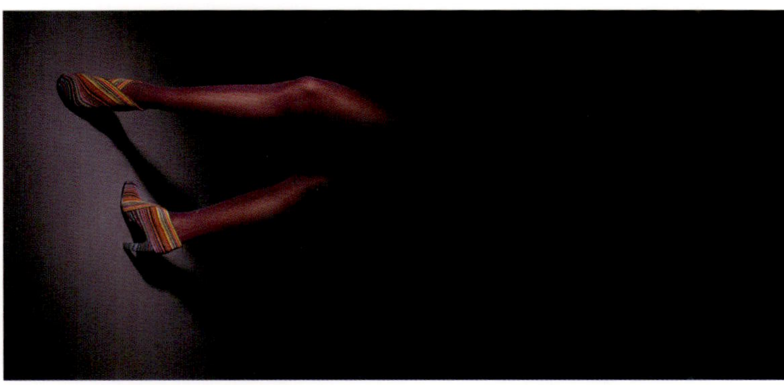

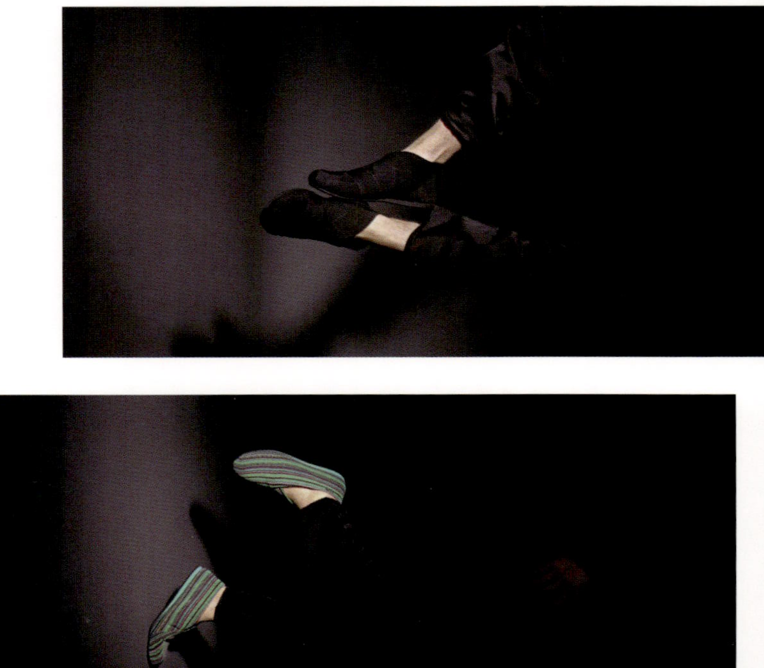

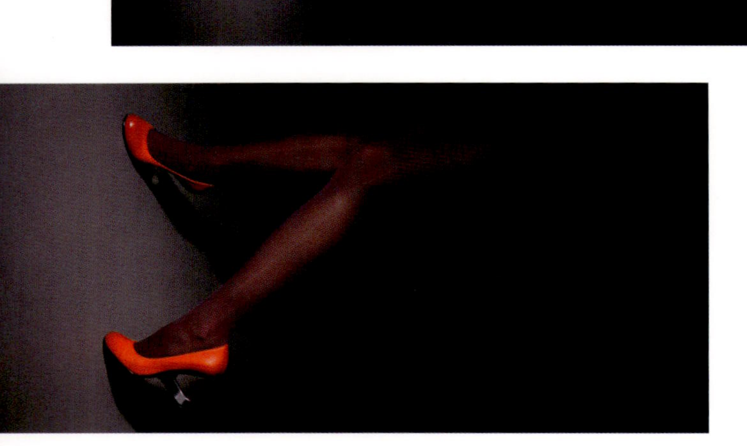

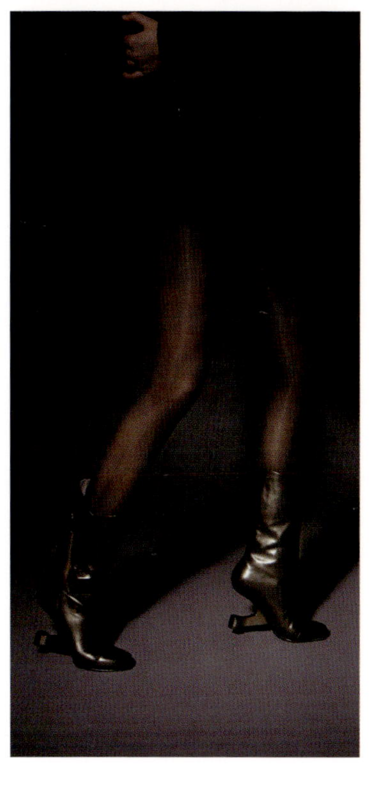

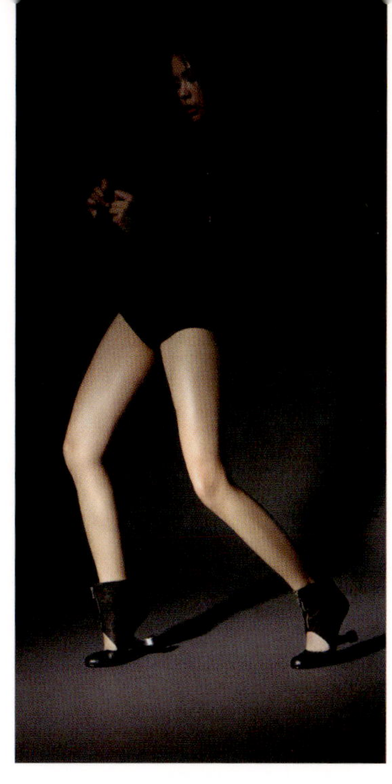

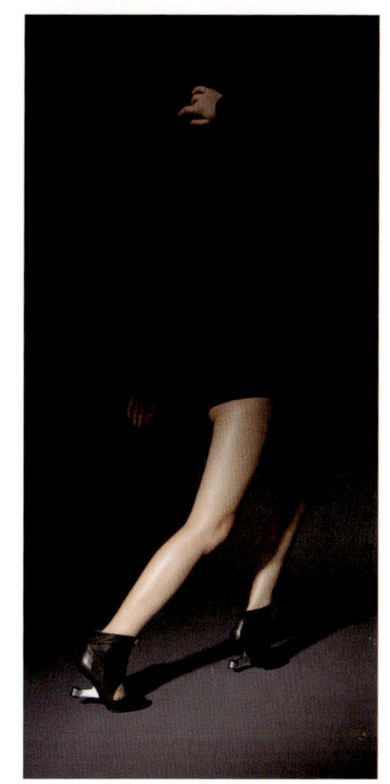

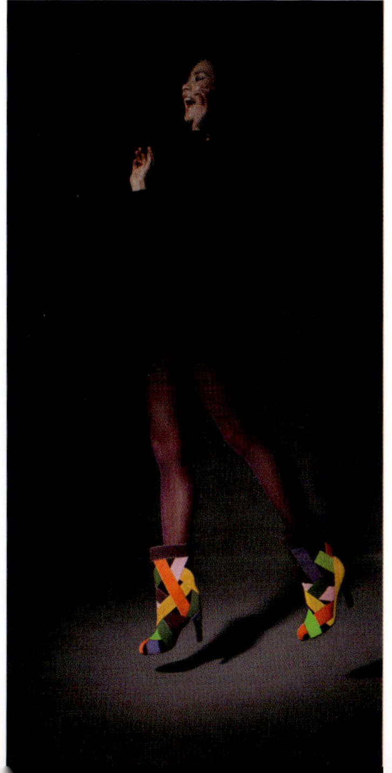

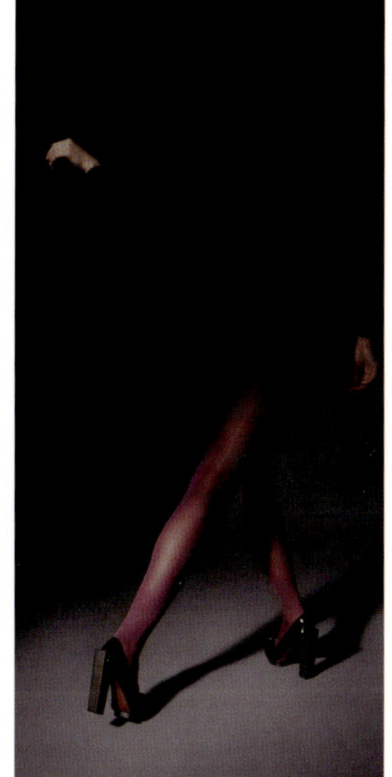

Top to bottom, left to right: Eamz Zip Boot, Eamz Parka, Helix Boot Hi, Block Loafer Hi and Abstract Pump.

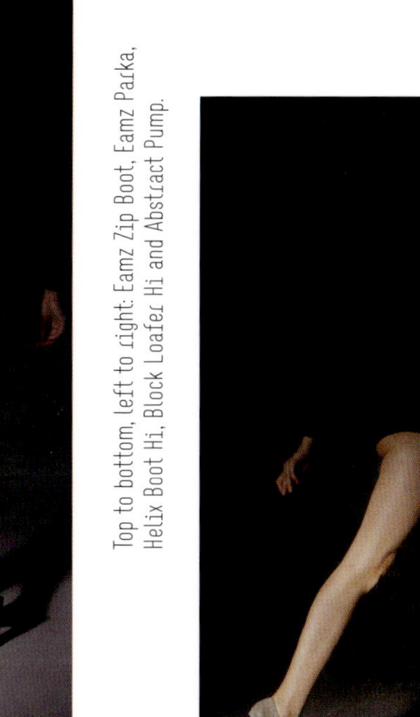

UNITED NUDE

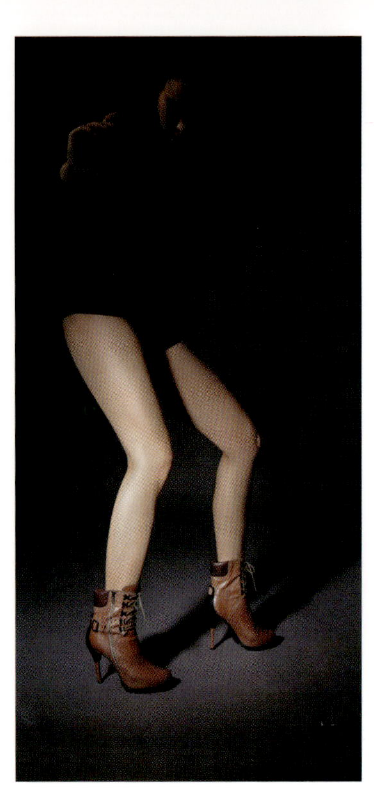

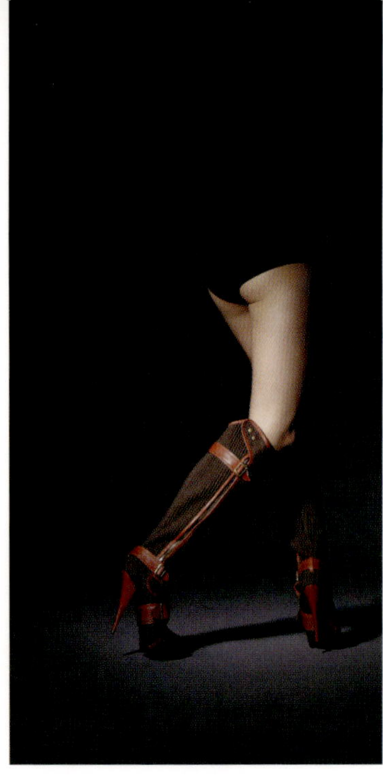

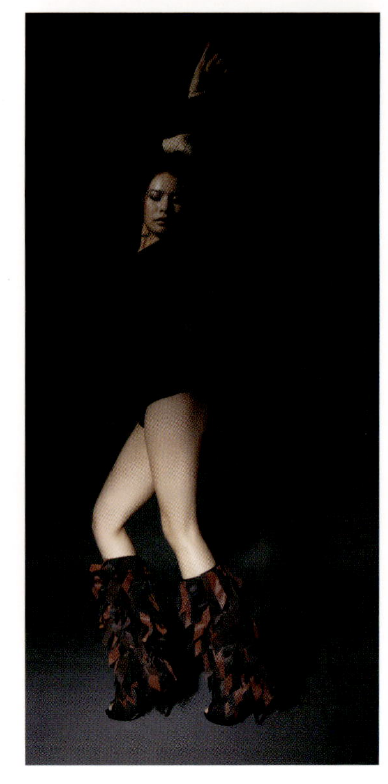

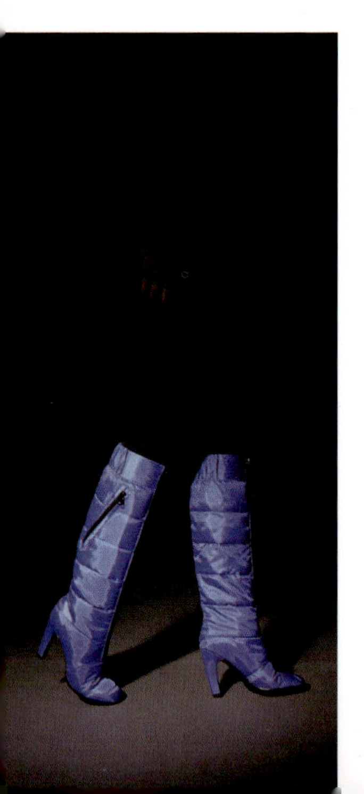

Top to bottom, left to right: Cup Kelly Boot, Spat Boot, Falcon, Bubble Zip Hi, Scuba and Step Mobius Velcro Boot Hi.

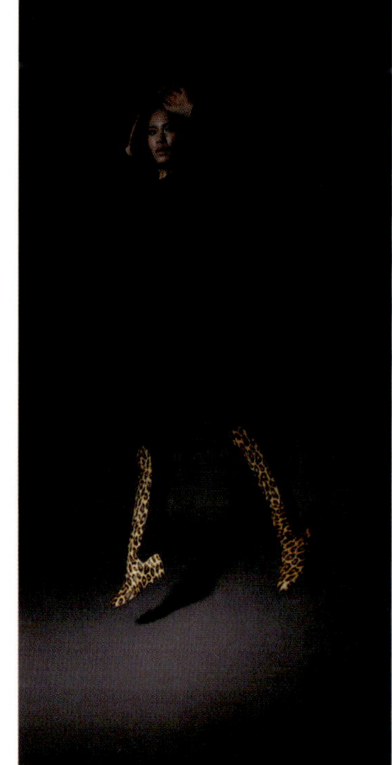

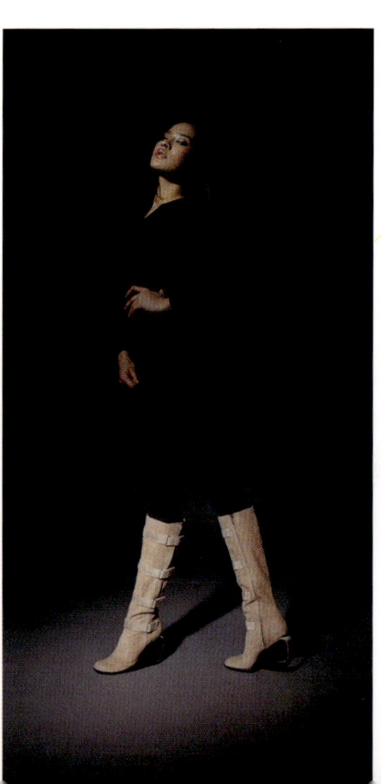

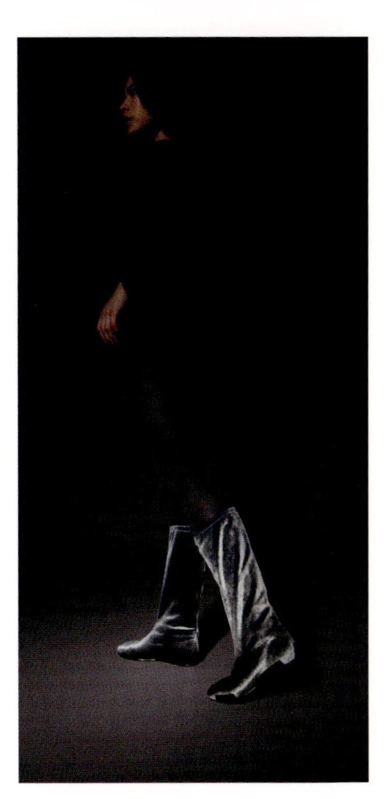

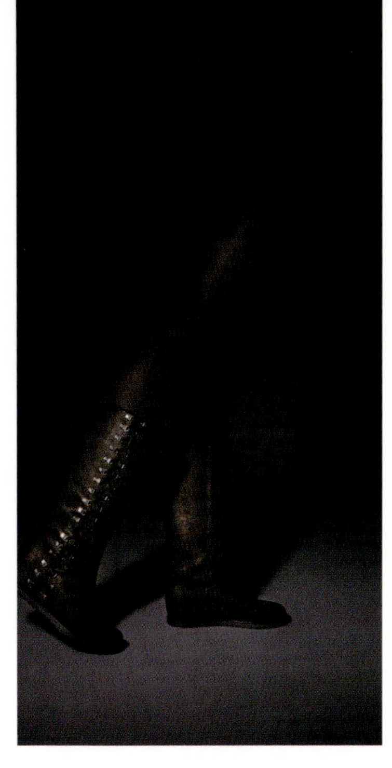

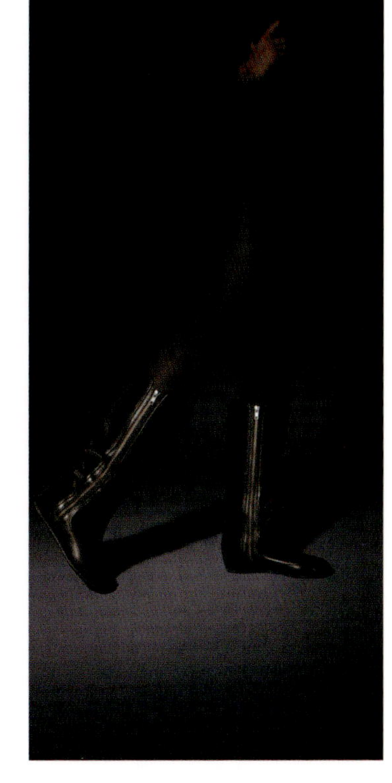

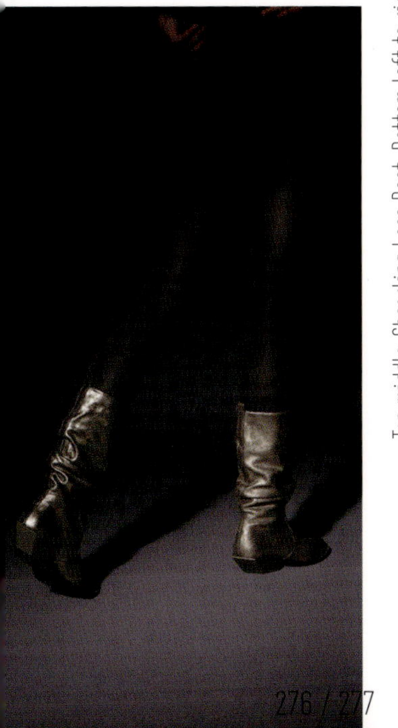

Top middle: Shearling Lace Boot. Bottom left to right: Cowboy Boot, Fold Deluxe and Block Ballet Square Toe.

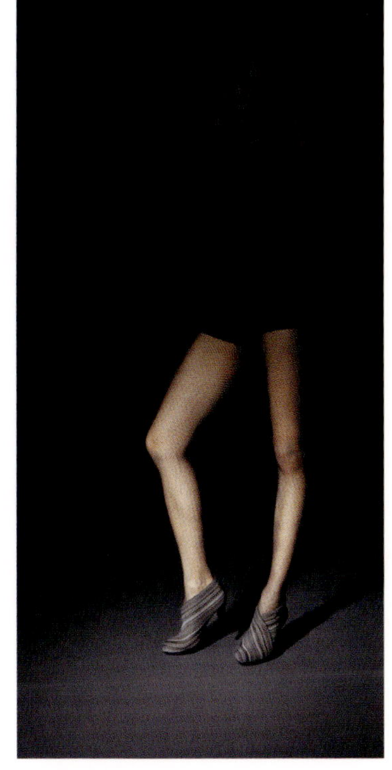

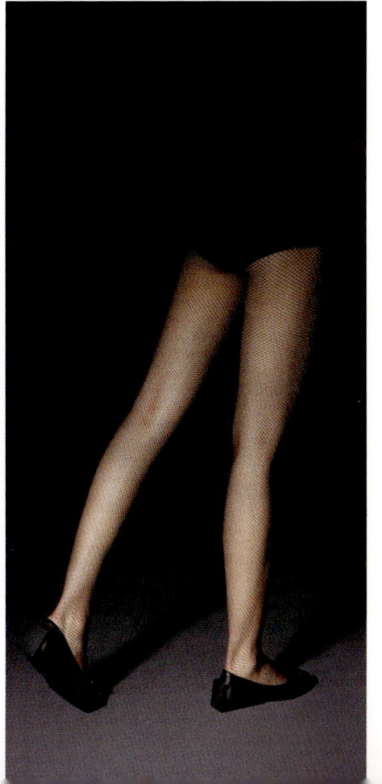

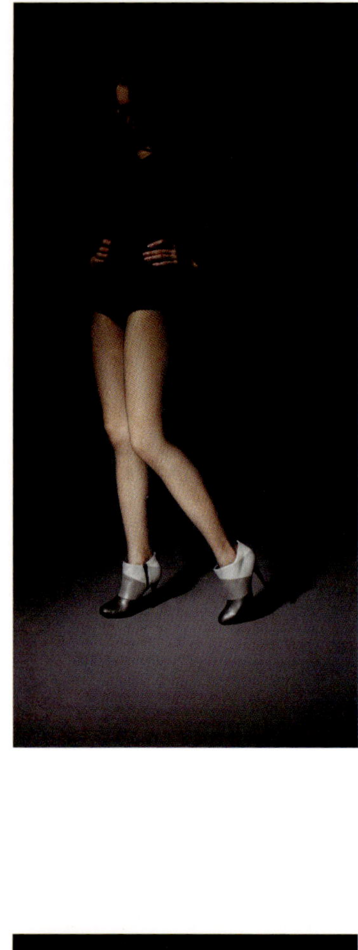

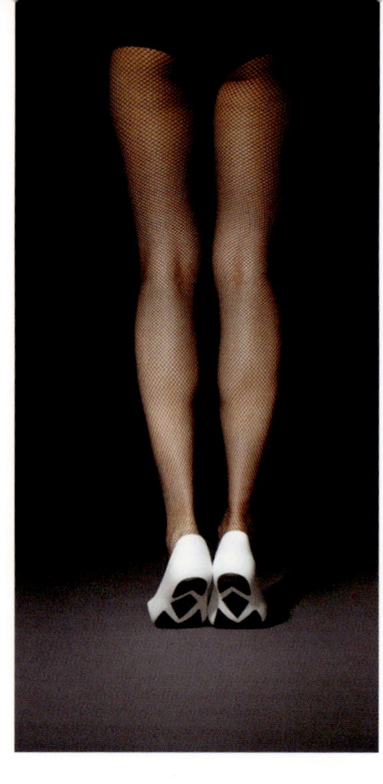

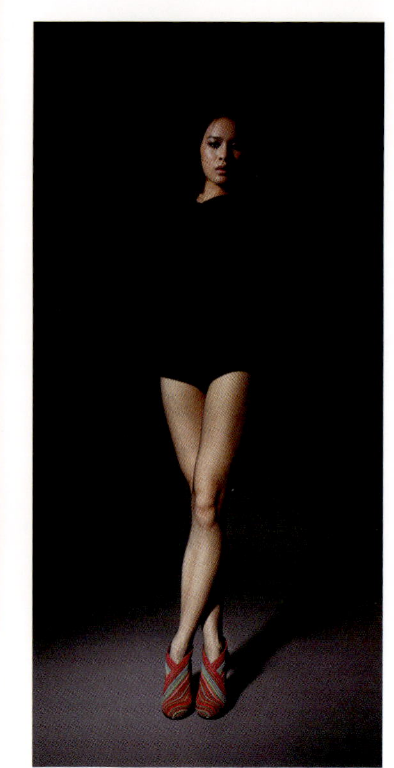

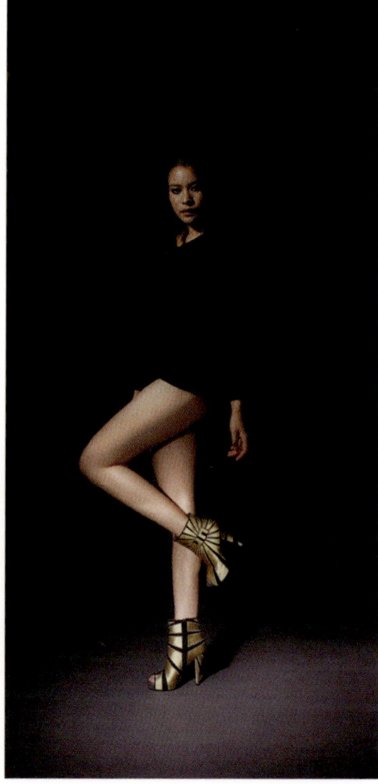

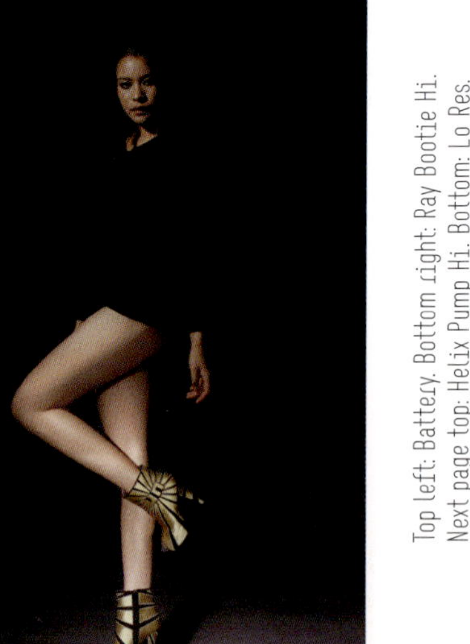

Top left: Battery. Bottom right: Ray Bootie Hi.
Next page top: Helix Pump Hi. Bottom: Lo Res.

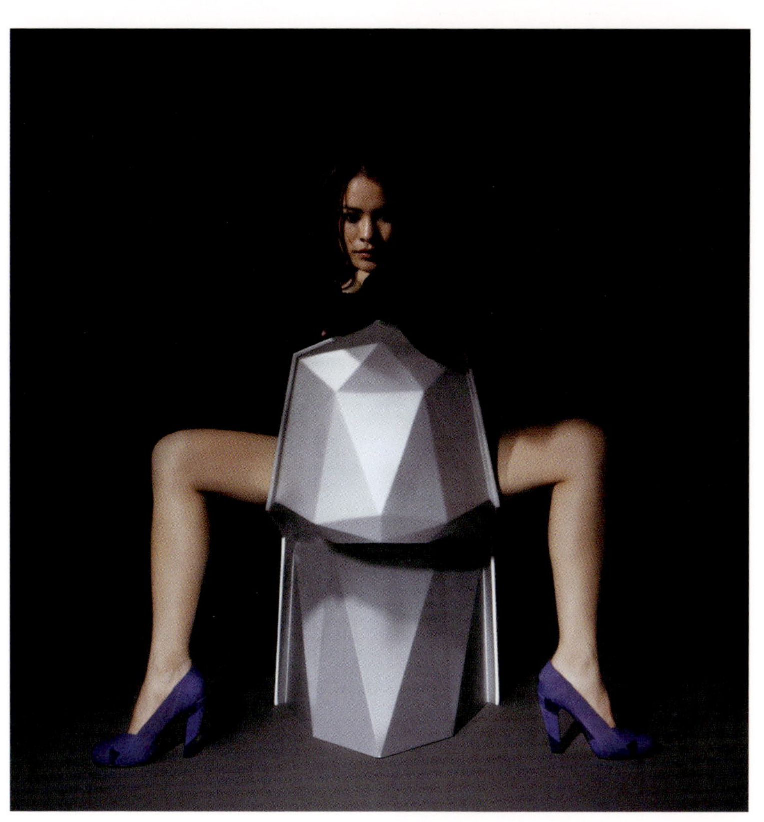

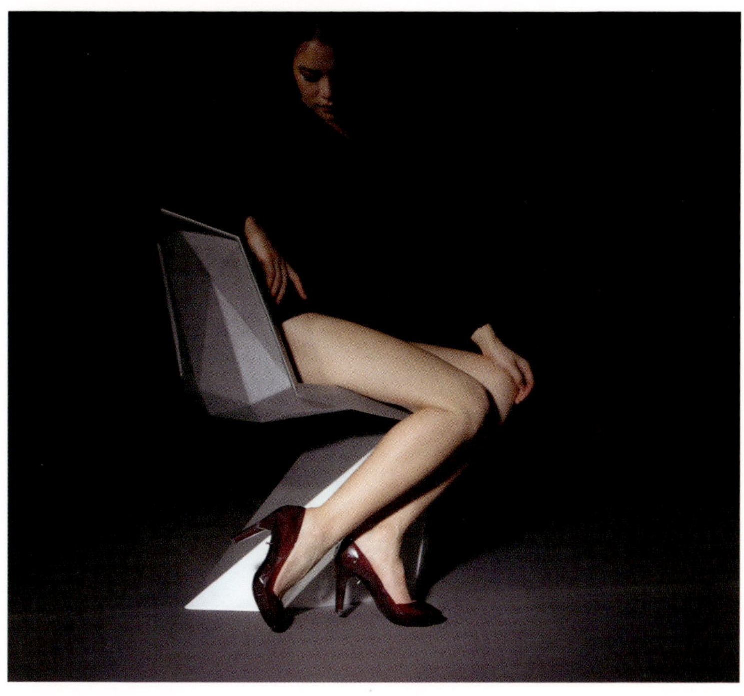

ZJEF VAN BEZOUW, ZJEF WORKS

I am a multimedia artist from Amsterdam and San Francisco. I graduated from art school in 1991 with an MA in Theatre and then trained to be a shoemaker. **I CHOSE SHOEMAKING TO HONOUR MY FATHER WHO WAS THE SHOEMAKER IN OUR SMALL HOME TOWN. WE HAD A SHOP IN THE BACK OF OUR HOUSE SO I GREW UP AROUND THE SMELL OF LEATHER AND GLUE. MY FATHER ALWAYS FELT IT WAS JUST A JOB BUT FOR ME IT BECAME AN INSPIRATIONAL FIELD TO EXPLORE AND RESEARCH WHILE I WAS STUDYING COSTUME DESIGN AS PART OF MY THEATRE STUDIES.** My work is a means of exploring my curiosity and allows me to communicate with people. I like to create images and designs that burn onto the retina, leaving an unforgettable impression. It is very much about expressing personal and intimate statements.

My designs are often fetish related, for example. **I AM INSPIRED BY CONTEMPORARY ARTISTS SUCH AS ANISH KAPOOR, BILL VIOLA, LEIGH BOWERY AND MATTHEW BARNEY. I SOAK UP THE WORLD AROUND ME IN ALL ITS DIVERSITY. IN TERMS OF DESIGN IDEAS, SOMETIMES MY THOUGHTS ARE FASTER THAN I AM ABLE TO CATCH THEM. OTHER TIMES SOMETHING TRIGGERS ME TO IMAGINE AN IDEA THEN I START TO DRAW OR COLLECT MATERIALS AROUND IT. THINGS SLOWLY FALL INTO PLACE UNTIL SOMETHING CLEAR AND VIVID MATERIALISES.** My most innovative design is the 100% Polyurethane Boot which is cast from my favourite worn boots. In a three stage mould, inside and outside, I was finally able to create an exact replica of my leather boot in polyurethane, which is completely wearable. I also got my breakthrough with my Penis Shoe which expresses how a man needs nothing more than shoes to be properly dressed. The presentation of this design became a performance and was much talked about in the press. It actually feels good to wear as well. **MY WORK IS DEFINITELY LESS 'FASHION' THAN MOST DESIGNERS. I AM MORE INTERESTED IN MAKING ARTISTIC STATEMENTS WITH MY SHOES USING PERFORMANCES AND INSTALLATIONS. IT'S LIKE CREATING MY OWN LITTLE THEATRE WITHOUT BEING IN ONE.**

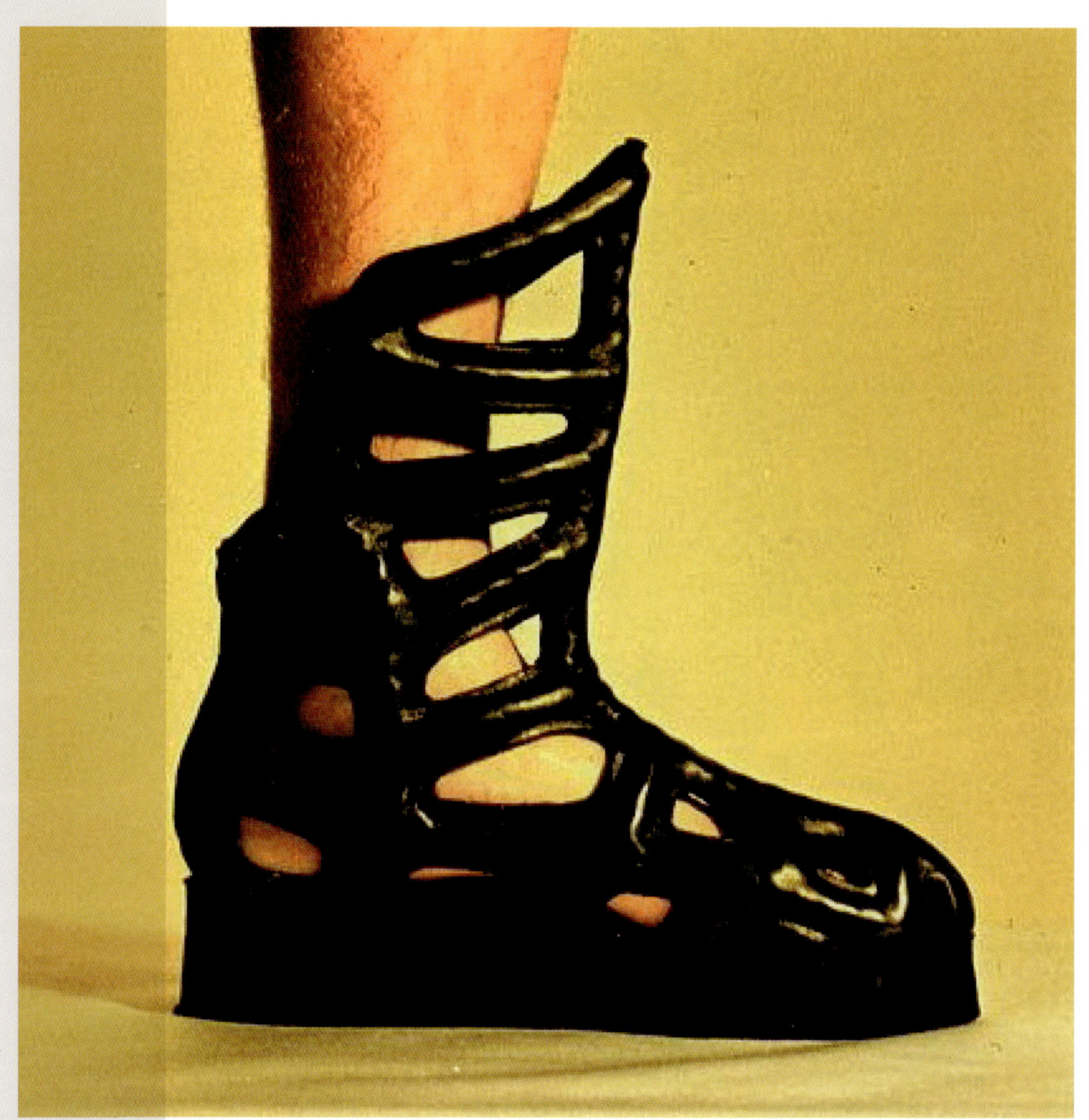

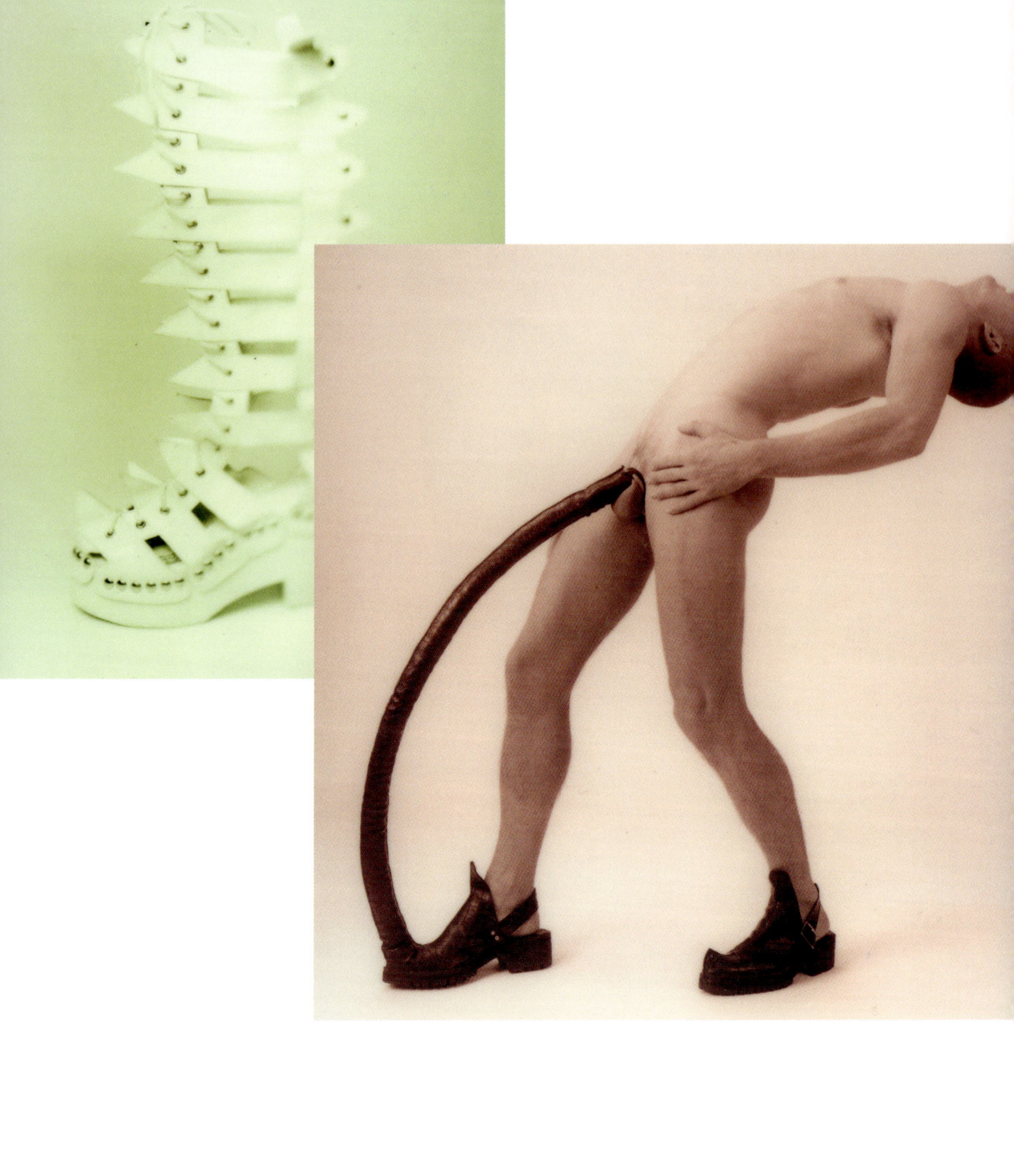

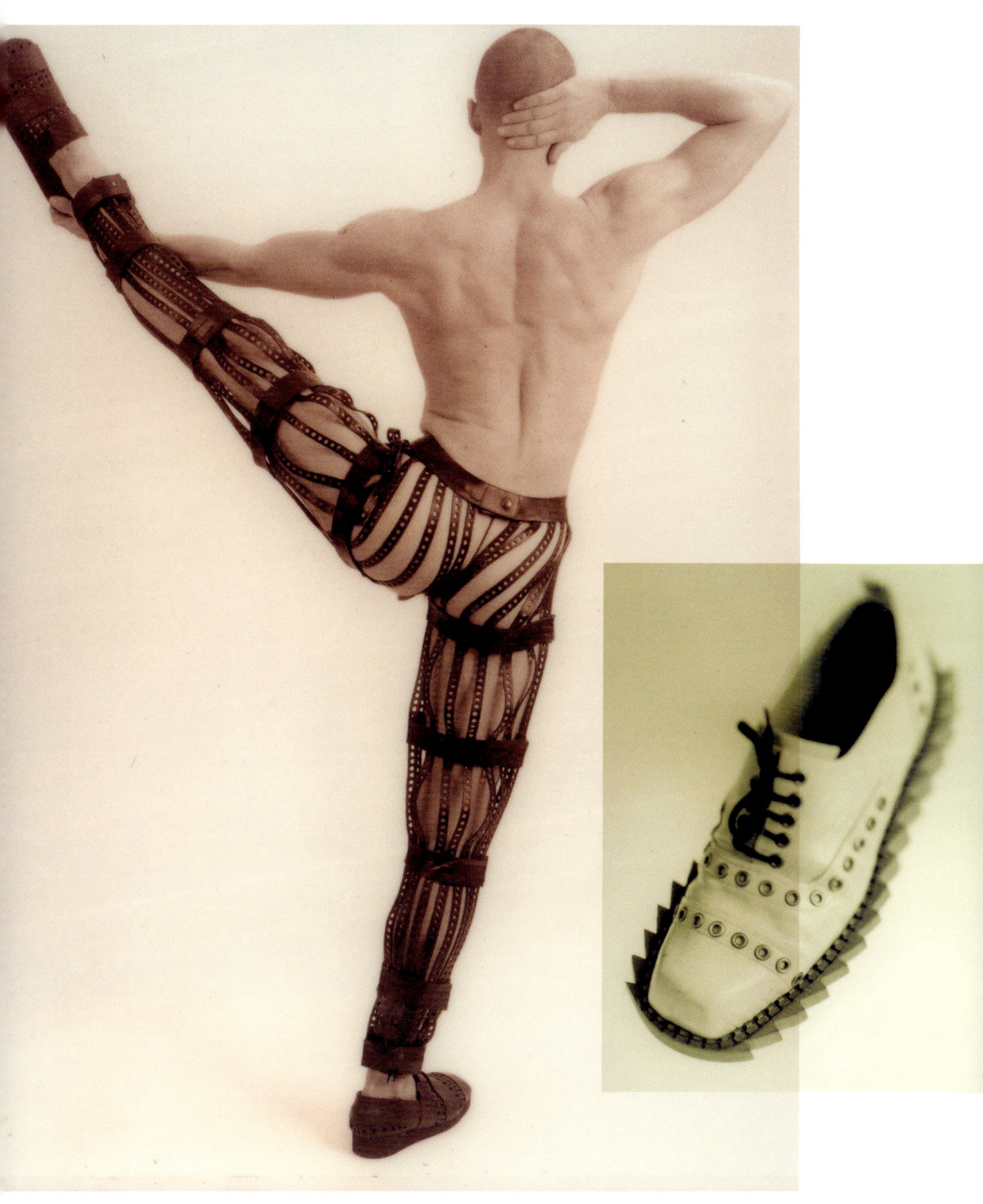

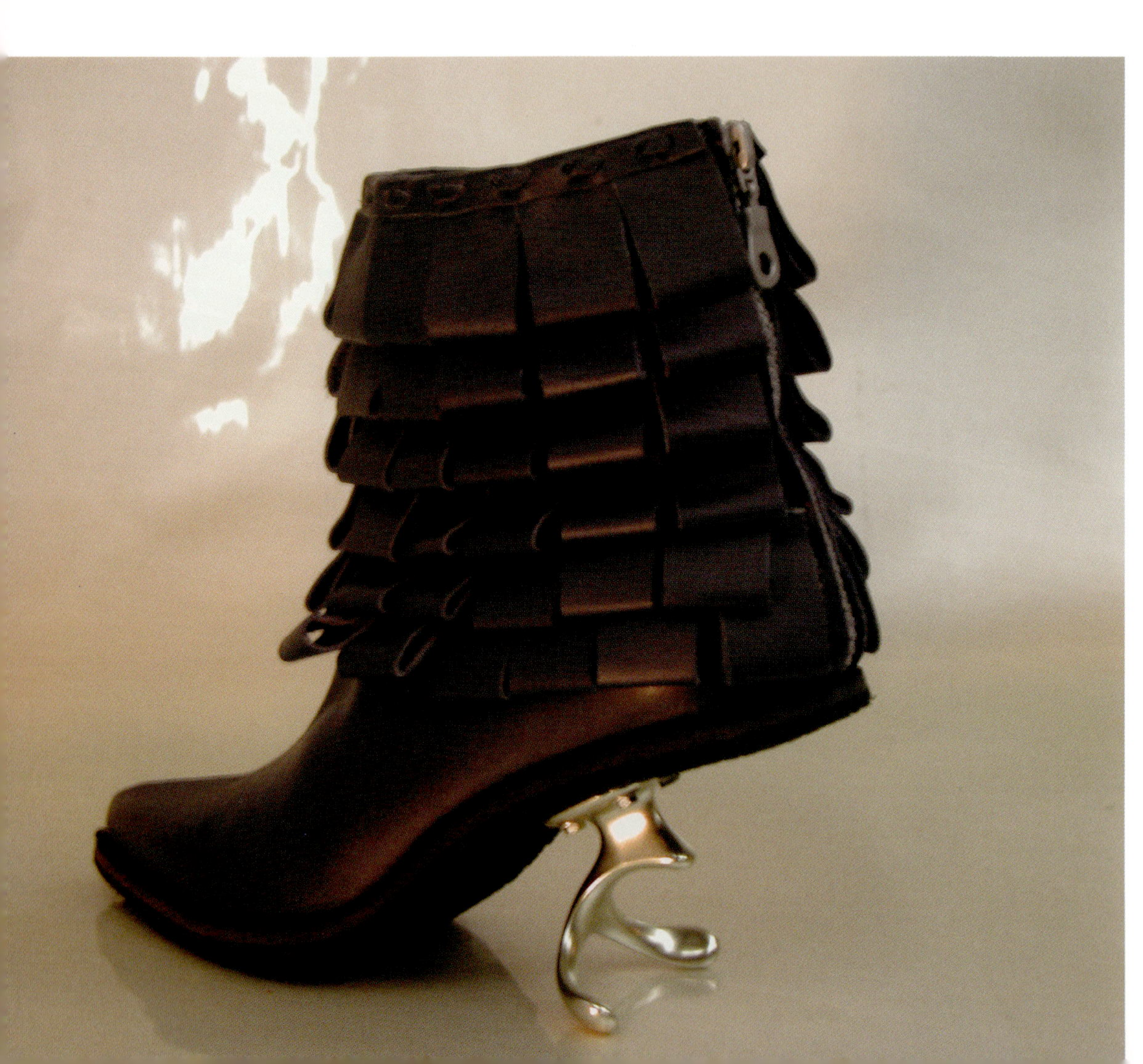

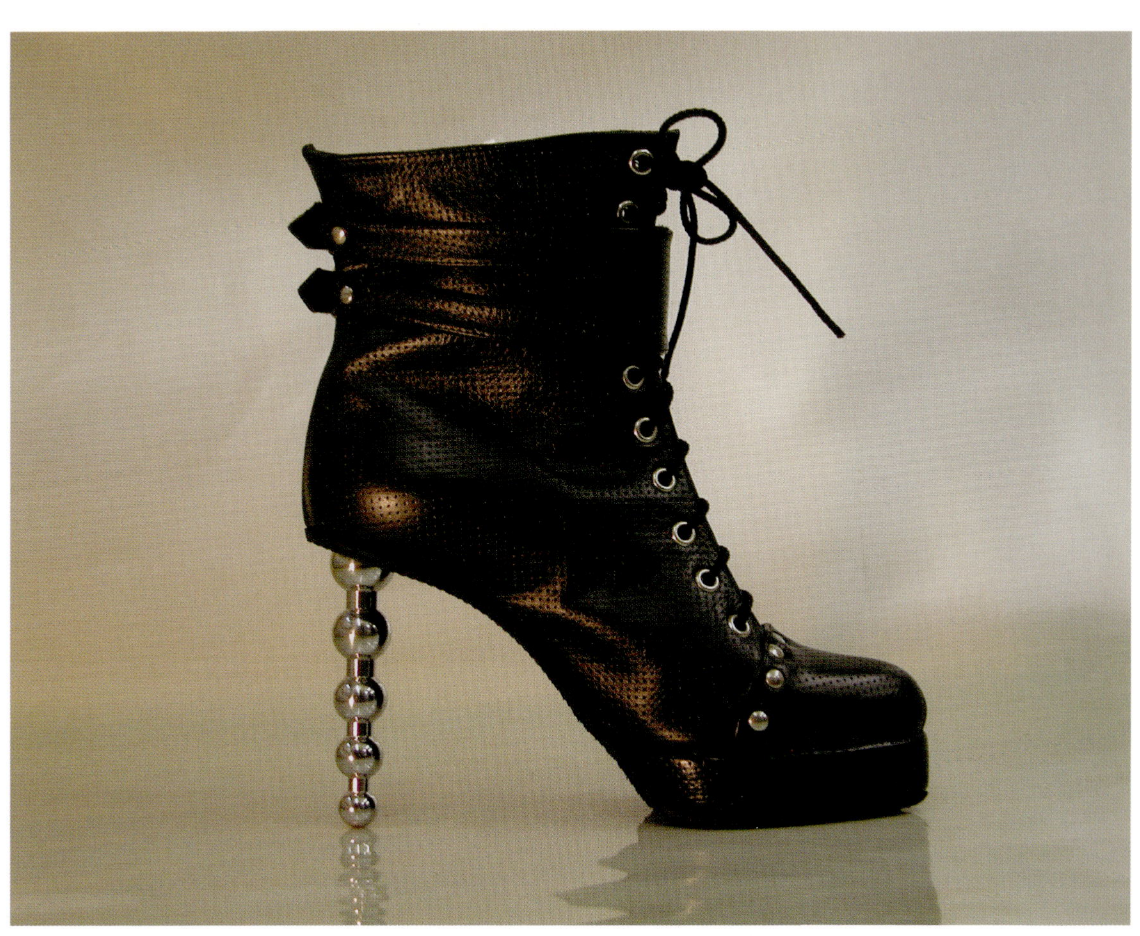

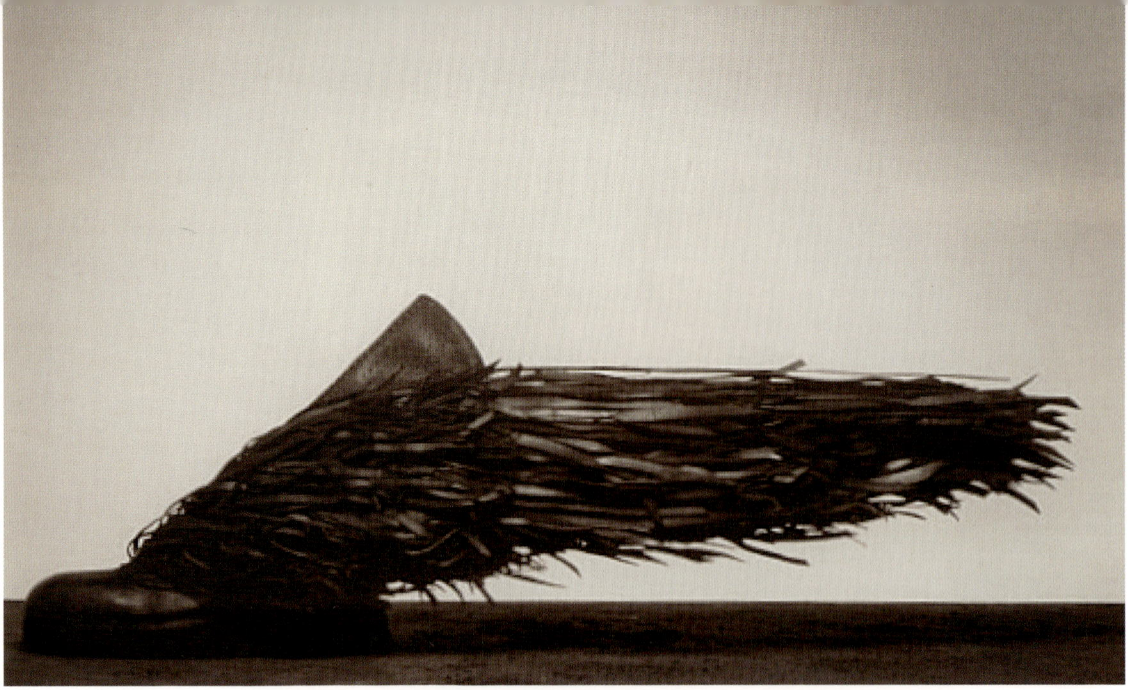

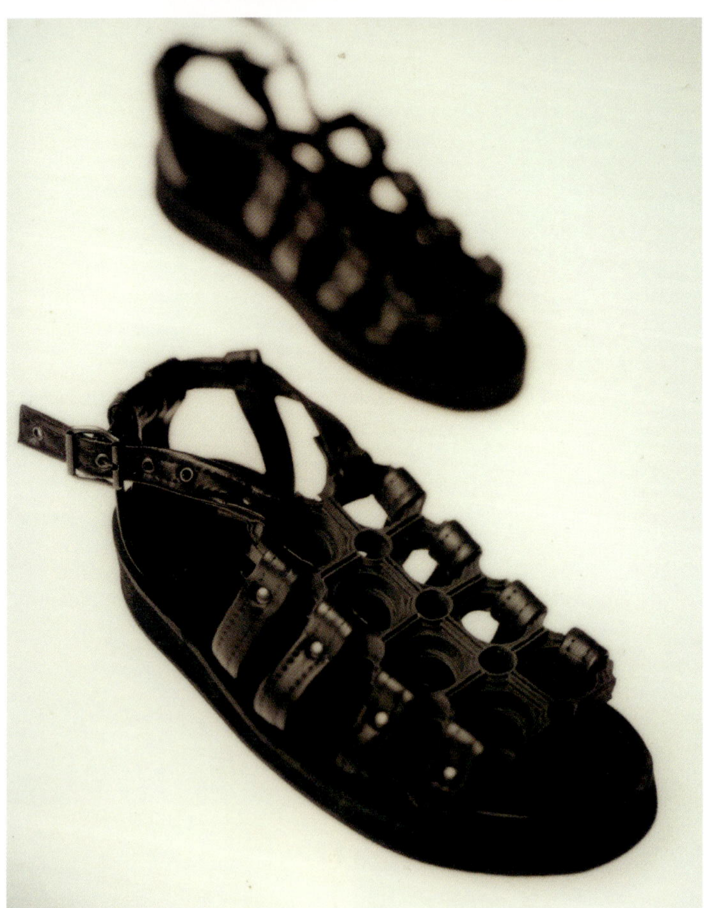

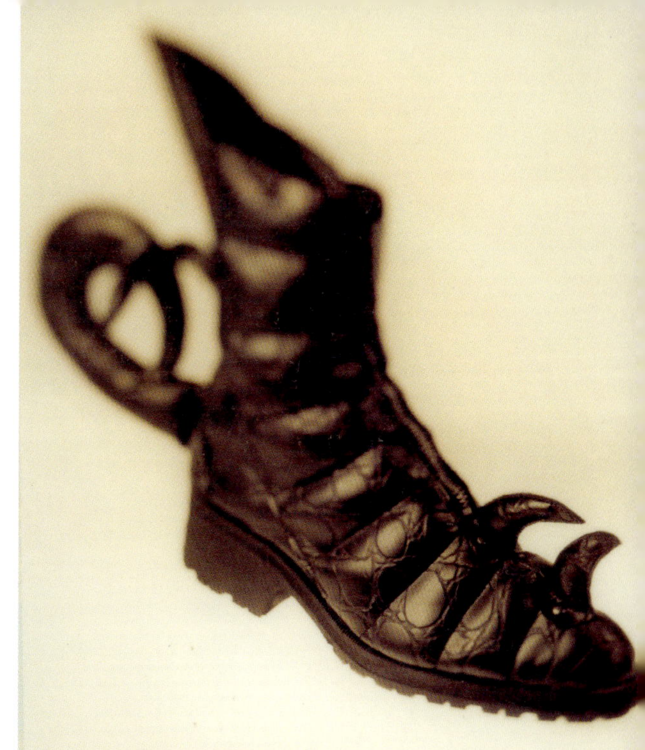

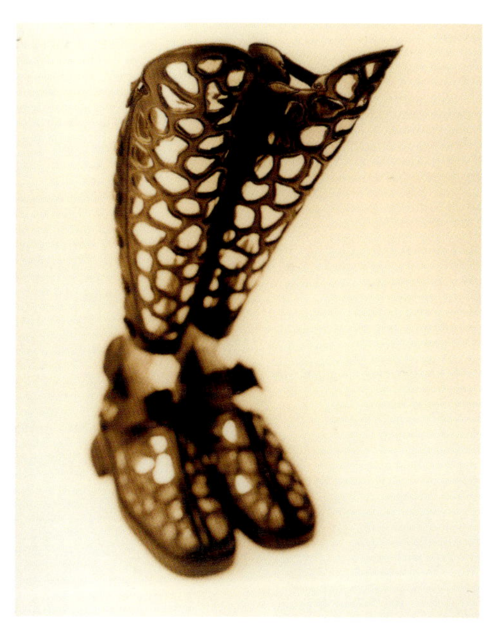

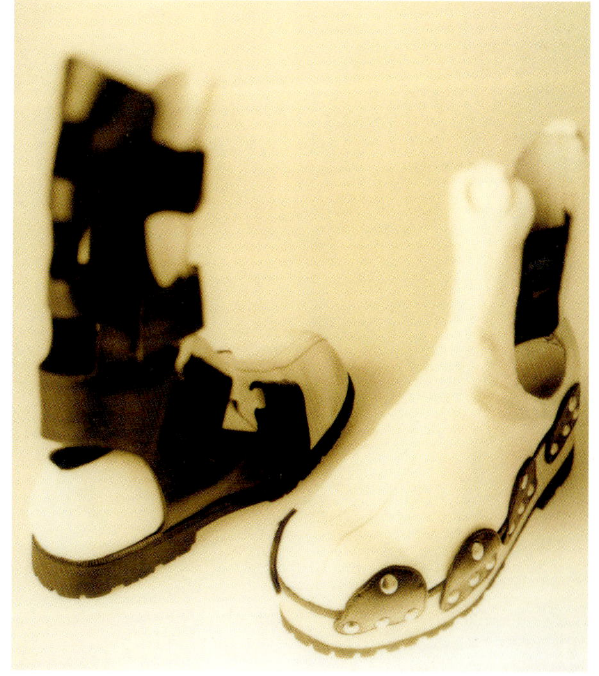

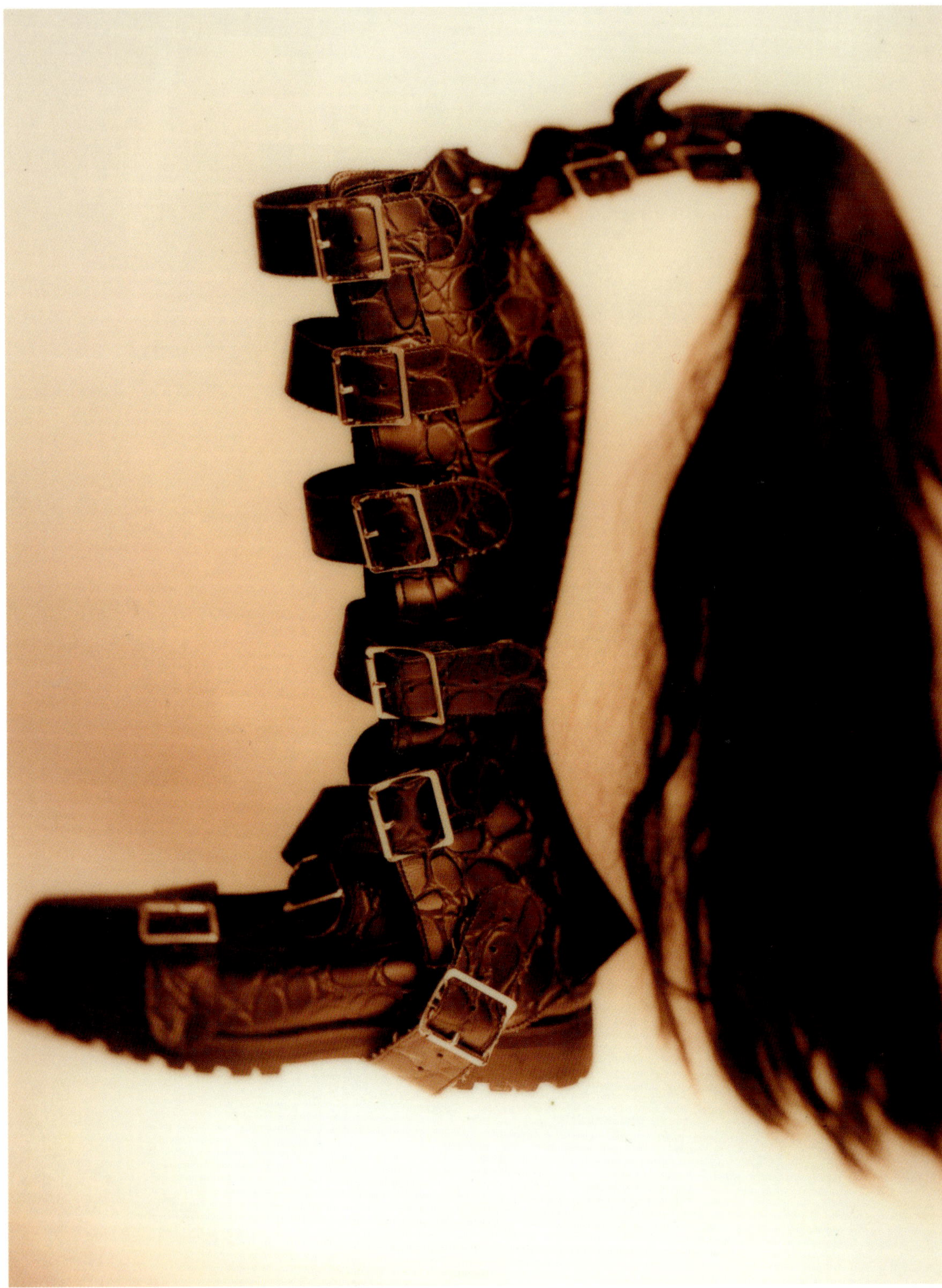

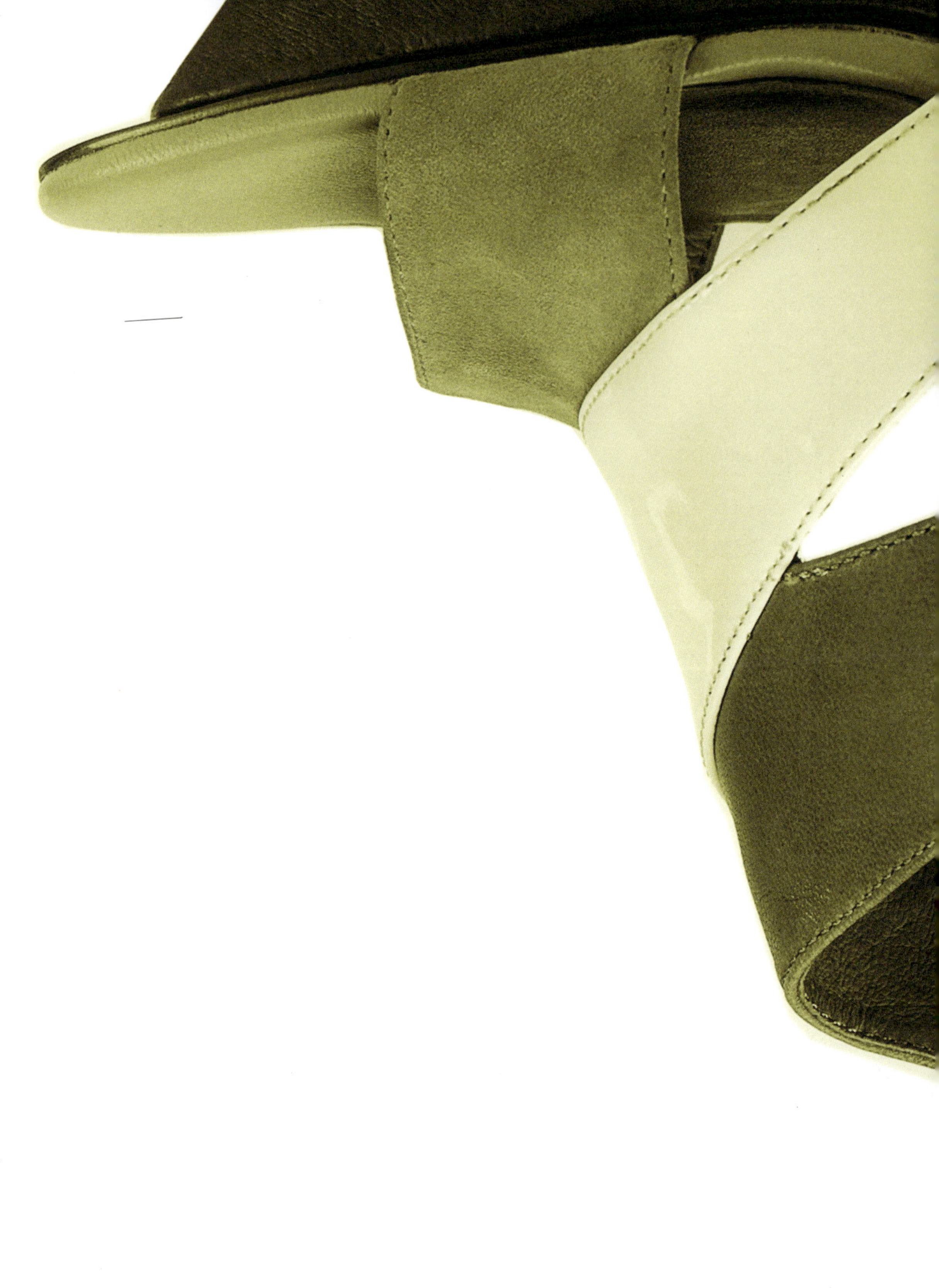